Social Problems

Joseph Julian

California State College at Bakersfield

third edition

Social Problems

PRENTICE-HALL, INC., Englewood Cliffs, New Jersey

Library of Congress Cataloging in Publication Data

Julian, Joseph.
   Social problems.

   Includes bibliographies and indexes.
    1. Sociology. 2. Social problems. 3. United
States—Social conditions. I. Title.
HM51.J84 1980   309.1'73   79-19564
ISBN 0-13-816777-X

Printed in the United States of America

10 9 8 7 6 5 4 3 2

Credits.
Art Director: Florence Silverman; Cover photo: Marc Anderson.
Left to right—pp. ii–iii: UPI, UPI, UPI; pp. xx–1: UPI, UPI, UPI; pp.
22–23: UPI, UPI, Bill Stanton/Magnum Photo, Inc.; pp. 68–69: UPI, UPI,
UPI; pp. 118–119: Jim Anderson/Woodfin Camp & Assoc., UPI, Gerry
Cranham/Photo Researchers, Inc.; pp. 160–161: UPI, UPI, UPI; pp.
208–209: UPI, Library of Congress, Rene Burri/Magnum Photos, Inc.; pp.
238–239: UPI, UPI, UPI; pp. 278–279: UPI, UPI, UPI; pp. 316–317: UPI,
UPI, UPI; pp. 352–353: UPI, UPI, Bill Stanton/Magnum Photos, Inc.; pp.
390–391: United States Department of Agriculture, Christa Armstrong/
Photo Researchers, Inc., Russ Kinne/Photo Researchers, Inc.; pp. 420–421:
UPI, UPI, UPI; pp. 442–443: UPI, UPI, UPI; pp. 472–473: UPI, UPI, UPI;
pp. 500–501: UPI, UPI, UPI; pp. 526–527: UPI, UPI, UPI.

Prentice-Hall International, Inc., *London*
Prentice-Hall of Australia, Pty. Ltd., *Sydney*
Prentice-Hall of Canada, Ltd., *Toronto*
Prentice-Hall of India Private Limited, *New Delhi*
Prentice-Hall of Japan, Inc., *Tokyo*
Prentice-Hall of Southeast Asia (Pte.) Ltd., *Singapore*
Whitehall Books Limited, *Wellington, New Zealand*

Contents

The Sociological Approach to Social Problems 1

Physical and Mental Health 23

Variations in
Human Sexuality 69

3

Problems of
Chemical Dependency 115

4

Affluence and Poverty 239

7

Prejudice and Discrimination 279

8

Sex Roles and Inequality 317

9

Aging 353

10

Family Stress 391

11

Corporate Power 421

12

Work 443

13

Urban Problems 473

14

The Population Crisis 501

15

The Environmental Crisis 527

16

Preface

This book seeks to present a progressive, comprehensive, and engaging approach to contemporary social problems. Its goal is to provide the student with a conceptual framework, a way of looking at social problems. It systematically discusses the sociological perspective on social problems and tries to convey the information generated by the research of outstanding sociologists and others who work in that particular field. The approach is eclectic, exploring different points of view among sociologists, but emphasizing the most current thinking on each of these problems.

The chapter sequence reflects a broad approach to social problems, following a logical micro to macro (individual to global) pattern that reflects the interrelation of most social problems and the possibility of approaching them from several points of view. The chapters are sufficiently self-contained, so that they may be used in a variety of sequences, although, of course, some chapters are more closely related than others.

Early chapters focus on relatively individual behaviors, such as drug use or crime. Of course, the social institutions and other environmental factors affecting these behaviors are noted and described. The middle chapters focus on inequality and discrimination in discussions of such topics as poverty, prejudice, sexism, and ageism. Every attempt has been made to indicate the effects of large-scale discrimination on individuals as well as to deal with the concept of institutionalized inequalities—institutional racism, institutional sexism, and ageism. Later chapters discuss problems common to many societies, such as those relating to family, sexuality and work. The final chapters, those on the problems of life in the cities, of overpopulation, and of environmental pollution, focus on matters of global significance. It seemed best to discuss each subject in a separate chapter in order to deal with it comprehensively and in depth. An attempt has been made throughout the book, however, to indicate how different problems overlap and are interrelated.

While there is a flexible organization for the book as a whole, within each chapter a clear and consistent structure is utilized as much as possible in order to maintain a logical flow to the material. First, the nature of the problem and the various explanations for its causes are explored. From there, the discussion shifts first to social control and social action—that is, how the problem might be dealt with or eliminated—and finally, to the prospects for dealing wth the problem within the immediate future.

The latter two sections, on social control and on future prospects, are particularly important. We are all aware of the many problems that face us and of their constantly changing nature. It is important for students to understand that these problems are complex, but this book has been written in the strong belief that it is equally important for students to think in terms of what can be done about social problems. More than other social problems texts, this book examines the possibilities for social action (or social control) and the prospects of each problem in the near future.

Pedagogical Devices

Social Problems has been designed to be as helpful as possible to both students and teachers. Each problem is discussed in what I believe is a well organized and readable manner. As much as possible, sociological terminology has been avoided. The treatment of each problem is analytical as well as descriptive, and includes the most up-to-date findings available. The illustrative material—photographs, tables, and graphs—were chosen primarily to clarify points which are difficult to make verbally.

At the end of each chapter, there is a concise chapter summary which distills and reviews the important concepts of the chapter. There is also a bibliography of both important classical works and the most up-to-date books in the field which may be used as a suggested reading list.

Supplemental Aids

The text is accompanied by a Study Guide and Workbook, an Instructor's Manual, and a Test Item File. The Workbook is designed to help students review and understand the key concepts of each chapter and how they are interrelated. Each chapter in the Workbook features a detailed review outline, a series of self-test review questions, and an "Applications" section that helps students apply their knowledge to real-life situations. Each of the self-test review questions is keyed to a specific page in the text, so that students will find it convenient to review unfamiliar material.

The Instructor's Manual provides chapter outlines, additional material for classroom discussion, suggested topics for papers and research projects, a series of essay questions based on the material in the text, and an annotated list of popular and educational films. The separate Test Item File contains short-answer questions keyed to specific pages in the text.

Changes in the Third Edition

The reception given to the previous editions of *Social Problems* by both colleagues and students has been encouraging. Many of their suggestions and criticisms have, I believe, been put to good use. This third edition represents a continuing effort to present a contemporary social problems text. To this end, the text has been thoroughly revised and updated, and the chapter sequence changed. Two new chapters have been added, and the focus of the remaining chapters has been shifted whenever we considered such changes to be necessary. A thorough and consistent cross-referencing has been maintained to make it easier for students to grasp the interrelatedness of social problems.

"Corporate Power" and "Urban Problems" are entirely new. "Corporate Power" makes the student aware of the problems individual Americans face in a society dominated by large, impersonal bureaucracies. "Urban Problems" reflects the basic demographic fact that most Americans live in or around big cities and their problems are largely urban related.

Each of the remaining chapters was updated and underwent some revision. Seven chapters were significantly changed. Chapter Two ("Physical and Mental Health") now discusses the problems of the handicapped and includes a broader treatment of the social consequences of ill health. Chapter Three ("Variations in Human Sexuality") stresses sexual differences as variant, not deviant, behavior and has an expanded section on prostitution. Chapter Four ("Problems of Chemical Dependency") has been made more relevant to contemporary concerns with new material on cocaine and alcohol-drug interaction and cross-addiction. Chapter Six ("Violence") contains a new section on terrorism and increased coverage of rape. Chapter Nine ("Sex Roles and Inequality") has undergone a major revision and now includes an expanded discussion of women as workers and heads of families as well as new material on abortion and on how sexism affects men. Chapter Eleven ("Family Stress") has also been revised to include important new sections on domestic violence and on the stress produced in families by the rising divorce rate and the number of working mothers.

Acknowledgments

Putting together a quality, comprehensive social problems textbook and then keeping it up to date through subsequent editions is a formidable task. Social Problems is a far ranging field with a myriad of findings and concepts that accumulate rapidly and are often changed.

This edition has benefited from the reviews and comments of many sociologists. Most importantly, I want to thank William Kornblum, who read virtually the entire manuscript and contributed useful criticism and suggestions throughout. Other specialists read specific portions of the manuscript: Charles Nanry, Vern L. Bengston, Linda Burzotta Nilson, Joyce McCarl Nielsen, Robert M. Emerson, Gary L. Albrecht, H. Roy Kaplan, Michael Useem, Jeffrey S. Victor, Timothy H. Brubaker, Richard M. Levinson, André Cedras, John Scanzoni, David Ermann, Jon E. Simpson, Russell A. Ward, David H. Blake, Harold J. Abramson, Jeffrey K. Hadden, Michael P. Soroka, Jon Hendricks, Margaret E. Hartford, Charles Hirschman, William Cockerhan, Robert Wilson, Joe R. Feagin, Paul Tschetter, Miriam M. Johnson, Michael P. Farrell, Joane Nagel, Janet G. Hunt, Ivar Berg, Graham B. Spanier, Robert F. Meier, Anthony Orum, William T. Clute, Hallowell Pope, Sally Bould, Samuel H. Preston, Pauline Ragan and Paul Wehr. I thank all of them for their valuable suggestions.

This book has, of course, required the hard work and special talents of many people over the years. Virginia Hoitsma and Sheldon Czapnik worked with me on the first two editions. Gerald Lombardi is my present collaborator and this third edition owes much to his considerable efforts and abilities.

This edition has also had the benefit of a team of other publishing specialists: researcher Martin Levine, whose untiring work provided much of the raw material on which this revision is based; Mary Byrnes, Kevin Mulligan and Sue Waggoner, who contributed drafts which were then rewritten and refined into the final prose; Ellen Sacks, who shepherded the book through the production process; and Florence Silverman who ably supervised the book's art and design. I also want to thank Anita Duncan, Edward Glynn, Irene Fraga, Edward Stanford, and Cecil Yarbrough.

Finally, I want to express my appreciation to my support system—Lynn Julian, Jeff Julian, and Jay Julian—for their continued sustenance in this and other endeavors of mine.

Social Problems

1

The Sociological
Approach to Social
Problems

• An old woman sits in a home for the aged, staring at the TV set all day long. Two or three times a month her married son stops in to visit her. Last Christmas she spent the day with her daughter's family. She is not sick, but she cannot live alone. Neither of her children seems to want her to live with them. They attempt to supplement her Social Security which enables her to stay at a private old-age home. She feels lonely and isolated from the rest of the world.

• In the interest of equal educational opportunity the City of San Francisco decides to bus students from ethnically segregated districts to integrated schools. The Chinese minority in the city protests strenuously. They claim that busing, in effect, discriminates against them by undermining their special way of life.

• Medical missionaries and health officers dedicate their lives to the service of underdeveloped peoples. Medicine, surgery, and sanitation are introduced. The death rate falls dramatically. Babies live, grow, marry; men and women who once would have died at 35 live to the age of 50 or 60. Suddenly there are too many people. The farms have been divided too many times, and the pastures are eroded from overgrazing. The new national governments struggle to increase production just fast enough to keep up with the mushrooming population. Just raising the standard of living for more than a tiny minority seems beyond hope.

• After World War II the United States government, concerned about the hostile stance of the Soviet Union, concluded that for its national defense it must resolutely oppose communism. Money was appropriated for weapons research, and for organizations to counter Soviet propaganda; a new intelligence network was created; the armed forces were kept in readiness. More than 30 years later the arms race costs the nation billions of dollars a year; thousands of Americans have died in an undeclared war in a small Asian country; and political opinion on the subject of national defense has become severely polarized.

• On June 17, 1972, in Washington, D.C., burglars were discovered breaking into the Democratic party headquarters at the Watergate complex. Investigation of the event and the attempted cover-up resulted, more than two years later, in the resignation of President Richard M. Nixon and the imprisonment of many of his aides on charges of conspiracy, perjury, and obstruction of justice. Subsequent congressional investigations, sparked in part by the Watergate burglary, revealed extensive evidence of illegal corporate contributions to political campaigns, CIA involvement in attempts to assassinate foreign leaders, and FBI harassment of U.S. citizens.

• In the late nineteenth century, unskilled factory laborers often worked 12 hours a day, 7 days a week. Eighty or ninety years later, after bitter battles in the streets and in governmental chambers, the 8-hour day and the 5-day week have become standard—and the 4-day week has become an alternative. Sociologists are becoming aware of a potential problem; soon large numbers of workers may have more leisure time than they know how to use.

How Does a Social Condition Become a Social Problem?

Cited above are some examples of what most would agree are our society's problems. What is not clear, however, is how these problems and others like them have come to be regarded as something to be solved or alleviated. When did the isolation of the aged change from a "condition" to be deplored from afar to a "social problem" in need of reform? Why do we view corruption among elected officials as something to be punished and prevented rather than accepted or, at least, tolerated?

The answer is simple, although the process is complex. Conditions become "social problems" when society decides that they need improvement. For a social condition to become a social problem, a significant number of people—or a number of significant people—must agree both that the condition violates an accepted value or standard *and* that it should be eliminated, resolved, or remedied through collective action.

For a social problem to be recognized, there must be both an "objective" and a "subjective" element. The objective element is the condition itself; the subjective element is the belief that the condition should be changed. The process causing this subjective belief to arise is a complex one, involving both individual and historical forces affecting the evolution of a society's values.

Until the eighteenth century, for example, most people worked under poor conditions for long hours at arduous tasks; they lived in deprivation and often died young, sometimes from terrible diseases—no one considered these "social problems." They were accepted as a natural, inevitable condition of life, decreed by divine providence that would some day be understood. As philosophers like Locke and Rousseau developed the democratic theory that every person was created equal, and as others acquired the scientific knowledge enabling them to improve their environment, people began reassessing their living conditions. In France and England certain "enlightened" thinkers began to argue that poverty was not inevitable, but was the result of an unjust social system. Poverty could, therefore, be alleviated by a democratic reorganization of society, a redistribution of wealth, and the determination of a person's station in life by individual merit, rather than by inherited social position.

Although this awareness began in the late eighteenth century, similar reassessments are still being made. Changes in judgment often occur when a traditional "misfortune" is suddenly considered an "injustice"—when a significant number of people realize that certain conditions have social or institutional causes. Before the nineteenth century, poverty was considered a misfortune since people felt helpless to do anything about it. It could be deplored, written about—even alleviated in particular cases—but not prevented. Poverty was "God's will," a result of humanity's original sin, a stroke of fate, or bad fortune. Only when people began to believe that they could improve society and provide better living conditions were they able to reevaluate poverty not as a misfortune but as an injustice. Even today, however, some people continue to hold the earlier view.

What was once considered a desirable social norm may now take on a negative appearance. For example, when there were few labor-saving devices and most work had to be done by hand, an accepted social norm was that men should procure food and other necessities. The care of home and children, usually requiring somewhat less physical strength, was a woman's responsibility. As society changed, the nature of outside work changed, too. The realm of business came to be considered a man's world, while a woman's place was in the home. With the growth of technology and the increase of outside child-care agencies—schools, recreational facilities, and others—the practical need for women to stay at home was lessened, and changes in the education of women made them less willing to stay there. The norm began to seem less acceptable, so that today much of society regards the traditional restrictions on women in the business world as a social problem and urges new hiring practices, provisions for day care, equal pay for equal work, and other measures designed to give women equal status.

Assumptions about Social Problems

People have their own ways of looking at things, and their own points of view. We all make certain assumptions about the world to give us a framework for understanding our experience, for making sense out of all the different things that happen to us and around us, helping us decide how to respond. Sometimes, of course, we discover that our point of view no longer provides us with a useful framework, so we may change it.

When sociologists consider social problems, they make basic assumptions about why things happen as they do. These assumptions, or premises—described below—are a starting point for studying some very complicated problems:

Social problems are, to some extent, the result of indirect and unexpected effects of acceptable patterns of behavior.

There are numerous examples of this phenomenon; the population explosion is one. Having many children has been a valued practice in many places for a long time, and for most of that time it was a necessity. Throughout history, most children died in childhood. Now, because better ways of sustaining human life have been discovered, most countries have too many people. India has far more than can be fed properly; demographers warn than other nations will soon face a similar situation. The population problem is more than a question of food supply, although severe malnutrition has been endemic in overcrowded countries, but clean air, adequate housing, education, employment, and the intangible called "quality of life" are also involved. Consequently, what was once the revered norm of having many children has become a social problem.

Consider the use of insecticides. These chemicals were once considered a boon to farmers and consumers; they destroyed insects and helped to preserve crops. Farmers could produce more food for more people at less cost than before. Recently, however, ecologists have demonstrated that some insecticides destroy the soil, damage plants, and taint the food produced. Insecticides have, therefore, created new problems—for the farmers now dependent upon them to protect their crops, for the consumers eating the foods affected by them, for the government that must decide whether to restrict their use and prohibit the sale of certain foods, and for the scientists who must find new substances to replace them and ways to undo whatever harm that was caused. Once again, a beneficial innovation has created new and unexpected problems.

This will give some idea of how different social problems may arise—not because of bad deeds, bad people, or bad luck, but as unintended consequences of accepted ways of doing things, particularly as these interact with subsequent technological change. While many religions and philosophies have considered crime and poverty the result of human wickedness or fraility (the "bad seed" idea), this explanation is no longer adequate.

Not only are social problems not caused by evil intent, they may even be the result of extremely well meaning actions. For example, Prohibition laws (outlawing the sale of liquor) went into effect in 1919 to protect people from the "evils" of alcohol. But Prohibition, in effect, promoted bootlegging and the rise of modern organized crime.

Why do people with good intentions tend to create problems or cause others to do so? The answer gives us our second premise:

A certain social structure and culture induce most people to conform, but can also cause some people to deviate.

Property rights, a major element in the social structure of the United States, are associated with the perennial problem of the "haves" and the "have-nots." We regard it as possible and legitimate to become the owner of some portion of the land, money, or other goods of society; and also consider that such ownership confers a right to keep this property, or to dispose of it as the owner chooses, subject to certain socially determined limitations. Many ways of acquiring property are socially approved—working to earn money, buying a car from a dealer, growing vegetables on one's own land, or writing a book and copyrighting it. Other ways of acquiring property, stealing or fraud, for example, are considered deviant.

Most Americans conform, in general, to the established pattern regarding property rights. They may stretch the limits occasionally—a little deceit, an occasional "liberation" of some company property—but not beyond the degree that society will tolerate. The average middle-class wage-earner wants to own a home, is willing to work at a steady job and pay interest on a mortgage to pay for it, and claims the right to remodel, enlarge, or sell it, once it is bought.

Some people, however, are unable, and/or unwilling, to acquire property by approved means. They may be unable to find work paying an adequate salary, have too many children, high medical bills, and/or other expenses eating up their earnings. These people may resort to deviant means to obtain money and goods. Thus we have the shoplifter, the embezzler, the burglar, the mugger, and the armed robber—all are deviant from cultural norms, yet in a sense all are created by the cultural pattern.

In this connection, it is worth noting that deviant behavior to the eyes of one group within a society may be approved or, at least tolerated, by another. What middle-class merchants call "stealing" may be "taking" to lower-class youngsters who reason that they need the object more than the merchant does.

This leads to a third premise:

Every social structure, or society, is composed of different categories of people who have similar levels of income, amounts of education, ethnic background, and occupations; these various groups constitute "strata" or layers of society. Those in different strata experience the same problems differently and are therefore likely to understand them differently.

In other words, one's attitude will be influenced by background, education, level of income, occupation, and personal experience. Since a person may occupy more than one position (a middle-class Jewish lawyer or an upper-class Protestant lawyer), an individual's attitude is seldom wholly determined by any single factor. Chances are that a person earning $50,000 a year will react differently to the problems in a ghetto slum than will the person living in one. A Jewish corporation president, on the other hand, may have the same attitude toward Israel as his or her Jewish secretary.

A person's attitude toward a certain problem moreover may change when moving from one position to another. In their study of Poles in Chicago, William I. Thomas and Florian Znaniecki pointed out that years ago most Chicago residents considered the Poles (poorly paid immigrants) a threat to law, order, and middle-class morality, since they had an unusually high rate of delinquency and crime. Later when those same Poles achieved well-paying jobs, suburban homes, and social respectability, they were in turn similarly hostile toward the poor blacks now living in the ghetto areas of the city.[1] The same thing has happened with other ethnic groups—Italians, Irish, and Russians—all of whom today react to black and Spanish-American ghetto residents very much as white Anglo-Saxon Protestants once reacted to them and their parents.

In order to assess people's attitudes toward social problems, therefore, one should consider their social background and previous experience. These factors not only affect the understanding of a particular problem, but they also influence the solution proposed to remedy it. This leads to our fourth major premise:

People in different social strata propose different solutions to social problems. Since these solutions usually favor their particular interests and values, it is often difficult to reach agreement on or to implement a solution to a given problem.

Any number of common events in today's world illustrate this premise. If the problem is one of improved housing for the poor, it is likely that the poor will favor public financing and scatter-site housing in middle-class neighborhoods. Residents of these neighborhoods, fearful of crime, new taxes, and the decline of property values, will advocate private financing and rebuilding the present slums. Minorities may demand open admission to a college for their applicants, regardless of academic qualifications, as a means of raising minority status, while the administration maintains that the same end will be best accomplished by holding minority students to the same standards required for others.

In other situations, a group may actually prefer *not* to see certain problems solved, since that group may benefit from their perpetuation. Many landlords, for example, benefit from housing shortages among the poor and even middle classes—a shortage allows them to impose high rents without providing adequate (and costly) services.

These premises imply two vital points. First, every social structure can

---

[1]William I. Thomas and Florian Znaniecki, *The Polish Peasant in Europe and America* (New York: Octagon, 1971).

generate social problems, creating new problems and new deviations. Second, much of a person's behavior, perception, and attitude is influenced by his or her social position. The environment and background of the groups involved, therefore, are significant factors in the origin and elimination of social problems.

The Study of Social Problems: Related Disciplines

Persons other than sociologists have concerned themselves with social problems. Philosophers since antiquity have speculated on the causes of social problems and offered solutions; religious leaders, philanthropists, revolutionaries, and writers have likewise strived to lessen the suffering of individuals or groups. It is impossible to consider here all the theories or all the ways in which people have worked for social improvement. We will discuss only the various approaches to social problems of some of the disciplines within the social sciences. History, political science, economics, social psychology, anthropology, and even biology all share to some extent with sociology the analysis of human behavior, and each approaches a given problem from a somewhat different viewpoint.

History.   History is the study of the past. Historical data can be used by the sociologist to understand present social problems. Indeed, a knowledge of historical background, or the forms taken by social institutions in the past, can be extremely helpful. For example, historical factors played an important part in shaping the present situation of American blacks. Since most American blacks are descendants of slaves, it is very difficult not only for whites but even for blacks to be free of a negative attitude. Many factors for this attitude can be considered: the peculiarity of the English law of slavery that treated the slave as wholly dehumanized property; the technological developments that created a rapidly expanding market for cheap, slave-grown cotton; the widespread fear of slave revolts that led to severe legal restrictions even on freed slaves; and the whole course of post-Civil War economic and political developments in the South. All of these factors need to be considered if we are to understand why black Americans have for so long been second-class citizens in our country, and why often they have been not only poor and uneducated but "shiftless," "improvident," and plagued by a high crime rate. The environment of the past and the consequent self-image are two important factors that created the present situation. For these and other reasons historians can make enormous contributions to our study and our understanding of such social problems.

Cultural Anthropology.   Cultural anthropology studies the social organization and development of primitive societies both past and present. Since cultural anthropology is closely related to sociology, many of the same techniques can be used in both fields, and the findings of cultural anthropologists regarding primitive and traditional cultures shed light on related phenomena in more complex modern societies.

Suicide is one of the modern social problems about which anthropologists have contributed some insights. It has been shown that suicide rates vary from one culture to another, and that societies differ in their attitudes toward suicide. Some societies regard it as laudable, some absolutely forbid, it while others cannot even conceive of it. Ritual suicide, the Japanese *hari-kiri*, the Indian *suttee*, the older forms in which kings or religious leaders killed themselves, were to ensure some needed good fortune for the people. On the basis of anthropological observations, today's sociologists can recognize that calling suicide a product of modern life, city life, or technological and depersonalized culture is overly simplistic.

The role of women in society, of particular interest today, is a subject on which anthropologists have much to contribute; they are able to report on the role of women in differing cultures around the world. Studies show that women seem to occupy a generally subordinate position in most societies, but occasionally do exercise some authority. A particularly interesting subordinate pattern appears in a study of village life in Taiwan in 1959–1960.[2] In the village of Peihotien, the only careers for a woman were those of wife and prostitute. Children were valued largely on the basis of what they could contribute to the family, so a girl, who would normally be marrying into another household at about the age when she begins to be economically useful, was considered a liability. Poor families, therefore, frequently gave or sold their infant daughters to other families who would adopt the girls as future wives for their sons.

A wife's status in the world depended entirely on her husband's family, and her ability to bear sons. If not adopted in infancy, a woman married into a home in which she was a stranger and a servant; only when she had borne a son did she really become a member of the family. If a daughter did not marry, it was usually because she was needed to support her parents; since there were few paying jobs available to young women (working in a small local factory might be one), the only way a girl could earn a substantial income was prostitution. She could do this and remain respectable as long as she carried on her professional activities outside the village and turned over most of her earnings to her parents. Prostitution would enable her to dress better and eat better than most of the villagers. She might even marry, later on, into a quite respectable family, since there was a tendency to feel that such a woman was less likely than most to be unfaithful after marriage. Nevertheless, few ever became prostitutes except from necessity.

Among certain Pacific-island societies, women have been found to hold positions of almost chiefly dignity; frequently, in fact, family descent is passed on through the female line. Cross-cultural comparisons, as a result of anthropological studies, question how much the relative positions of women and men are the result of nature or social convention.

Psychology and Social Psychology. Psychology deals with human mental and emotional processes, focusing primarily on individual experience. Rooted in biology, it is more experimental than the other social sciences. An understanding of the psychological pressures underlying individual responses to societies' pressures can illuminate social attitudes and behavior. Studies of the childhood experiences of child abusers, for example, have found they themselves were beaten, neglected, or otherwise abused as children.

---

[2]Margery Wolf, *The House of Lim: A Study of a Chinese Farm Family* (Englewood Cliffs, N.J.: Prentice-Hall (ACC), 1960).

Knowledge of such factors can shed light on child abuse as a social, as well as an individual, problem.

Social psychology, the study of how the psychological processes, behavior, and personalities of individuals influence, or are influenced by, social processes and social settings, is of particular value for the study of social problems. For example, studies of the personality that show minority prejudice—anti-Semitism, white racism—are frequently "authoritarian" types. Authoritarian personalities have little insight into their own behavior and feelings, and try to stifle or deny their emotions. Unable to admit to themselves their hatred, resentment, or fear of their parents or other childhood authority figures, they project these emotions onto others, becoming submissive toward, or even fearful of, those with authority over them, and harshly aggressive toward those beneath them.

Other prejudice appears to be a function of social conformity on the part of those whose need to be liked and approved of is strong. For the authoritarian personality, prejudice and discrimination stem from and fulfill a personal need.

Other studies have investigated the psychological characteristics of youth protest. A correlation has been indicated between leftist activists and permissive, mother-dominated families, conservative activists and authoritarian, father-dominated families. The evidence, however, is far from conclusive. Family correlations have also been suggested between the politically radical and the culturally renunciatory ("hippie," "dropout") types of protester against "the establishment." This field of study is still so new that many of the findings remain tentative.

Biology. The relationship of biological inheritance and biological processes to social behavior has long been a subject of speculation; the annals of prejudice are rich in supposed biological justification. For example, certain ethnic minorities are regarded as being "highly sexed." Actually, it is quite reasonable to conceive of a biological influence on behavior, but difficult to establish scientific proof of it. For example, it has been suggested that many American Indians may suffer from an inherited genetic vulnerability to the effects of alcohol, and may therefore be more likely, under given circumstances, to become alcoholics. Since it is difficult to find situations in which all conditions except heredity are the same for Indians and non-Indians, this thesis has been impossible to prove.

Criminal behavior is another social problem in which the possibility of biological influence has been systematically investigated. During the nineteenth century, Cesare Lombroso, an Italian, developed a theory of the "born criminal"—people born with traits predisposing them to criminal activity, who can be recognized by their bestial appearance. In its original form, the theory was too simplistic and could not ultimately be maintained. More recently some studies have found, however, that men with a genetic disorder known as the "XYY Syndrome" (in which they possess an extra Y chromosome) are somewhat overrepresented in prison populations. This does not mean that all victims of the disorder will become criminals (most do not); however, such men may be unduly sensitive to environmental factors that encourage crime.

While possible biological influences on specific types of social behavior are worth investigating and may turn out to be significant, as yet we have very little hard data about their nature and importance. We see that there are numerous approaches to the study of social problems besides the sociological. Rather than regard these various approaches as rivals, to be pitted against each other, it is necessary to consider all of them to develop the fullest understanding of social problems and a comprehensive way of finding solutions.

The Sociological Perspective

Social problems, directly or indirectly, affect everyone's lives, some even cause serious social damage. Sociologists, and other social scientists, are trying to determine how our society works satisfactorily and how it fails, hoping to find ways of intervening in problem situations, so that the quality of life can be improved for everyone.

Sociology is a relatively young discipline; its focus is on people's social behavior and organization. Unlike psychology, which deals primarily with the individual, sociology studies *patterned social relationships*, how they are maintained and how they change. For instance, sociologists might study protest movements on college campuses, to discover the patterns of relationship within protest groups (do the groups have strong leadership? are they loosely or tightly organized? how do they arrive at decisions? how do they handle dissent?), and the relationships between these groups and others, such as college administration and police (is hostility expected? how is it expressed? how do the various groups communicate?). They would investigate the roles—the patterns of expected behavior—of groups and individuals in these relationships, and how these roles and relationships originate and change in response to surrounding social forces. They would not be particularly concerned, however, with the psychological motivations of individual participants nor with the features unique to the situation of one particular group.

While sociology is concerned with social behavior patterns in general, a social problem is one concerned primarily with behavior that departs from established norms (deviance) and social structures when disruption and conflict arise because individual and collective goals are not being achieved. For example, a student of social problems might try to determine why, in a society with the world's highest standard of living, over 30 million people are living in poverty. This student might also try to determine why, in a society that stresses a high level of education, many highly educated people are unable to find jobs. By collecting data on such phenomena, the student of social problems would hope to help remedy the situation so that more people could lead satisfying lives. He or she also hopes to obtain insight about human behavior in varying conditions which will illuminate general sociological questions.

Drug abuse, for example, has become one of the most persistent and oppressive problems in the United States. The continued abuse of narcotic drugs often destroys individual initiative, self-control, and sometimes even life itself; in addition, it is linked with large-scale organized crime. Several approaches have been developed to fight the problem. A religious teacher might preach that using drugs is spiritually debilitating; a lawmaker might impose severe penalties on the user or dealer; a journalist might write about the number of addicts who are arrested and jailed each year, or the number who die from the effects of drugs; and a filmmaker might portray the terrifying and torturous aspects of addiction. Sociologists attempt to discover the causes and effects of addiction by analyzing its effects on certain groups of people under various sociocultural conditions. By so doing, they hope society will obtain a realistic and accurate view of the drug problem and will be able to make informed decisions about it.

Drug abuse is only one example of the many types of so-called deviant behavior to be found in any society. The term "deviant" carries for some people unfortunate connotations of sickness, mental illness, or unnaturalness not intended by the sociological meaning. It may be useful here to give some idea of what sociologists actually mean when they speak of deviance.

Deviant behavior is simply behavior that varies from an accepted norm. All of us have or will eventually deviate from some behavioral norm, either by choice or by necessity, but will not, as a result, be labeled "deviants." On the other hand, almost no one will deviate from all norms, and few will deviate from any norms all the time. The embezzler may be a faithful marriage partner, the prostitute may be quite conventional except for occupation. Deviance and conformity, then, are not generalized traits—no one is either totally "normal" or totally "deviant."

Society does not react to deviance with perfect consistency; deviance from the norm is usually tolerated within certain limits, only when those limits are exceeded is the label "deviant" applied. In most cultures, for example, moderate drinking is accepted and approved. People can drink a little more than the accepted norm, and occasionally get drunk, without being called alcoholics or drunkards. If they begin getting drunk two or three times a week, however, they have passed the allowable limits and will be labeled alcoholics. An additional factor in society's judgment will be the degree to which these people adhere to other norms. If they are frequently absent from work, appear dirty and sloppily dressed in public, or are arrested for disorderly conduct, they are more likely to be considered alcoholics than if they manage to remain neat, punctual, and courteous, although they may be dependent on alcohol.

Further, it is possible to deviate by overconformity. In a business office there is often one employee who observes all the rules so minutely as to be a nusiance. In most cases overcomforming deviants are probably more easily tolerated than the nonconforming ones, since they usually cause less trouble—teetotalers may pose more problems at a party, but they are not likely to cause the breakup of their families.

We see that deviant and normal behavior cannot be set against each other as absolute opposites; deviance is part of a behavioral continuum, shading into both ends of normality, the boundaries between them being exceedingly flexible.

It should also be pointed out that both the norms and the degree of tolerance for deviation vary considerably between societies and at various times. What is considered promiscuous behavior in the United States may be acceptable in Sweden. A degree of dependence on narcotic drugs labeled abusive in the 1970s might have been considered necessary treatment for poor health in 1910. As indicated earlier, the norms of any given social structure tend to foster deviance in certain respects, since the means of attaining approved goals are unequally distributed among the society's members. Just as a society that places a high value on property may promote crimes against property, one especially concerned about female chastity may have a high incidence of rape and prostitution. One that exalts education may cause those without approved educational background to patronize "diploma mills" or use other fraudulent, or even violent, means to attain the ends to which education is supposed to lead. In order to understand what a society regards as deviant behavior, the sociologist must study the norms of that society and the values supporting them.

Useful Deviance and Social Change

It is important to note that deviant behavior, under some circumstances, can have constructive consequences.[3] Our society, for example, is dominated by complex organizations prescribing a bewildering variety of rules and procedures to be followed. Frequently these become overly time-consuming and counterproductive. It may be necessary to circumvent these rules if effective action is to be taken. Cutting a class to study for an exam or staying home from work to complete an assignment are minor examples of constructive deviance.

Occasional deviance may also be a kind of safety-valve. There is usually some frustration when people curb their own desires to conform to society's rules; these frustrations may eventually accumulate to dangerous levels. In all social systems, large and small, occasional deviance occurs to express and relieve frustrations. All societies, in fact, provide periodic recognized occasions (called "saturnalia" by anthropologists) when the normal rules of conduct are suspended. A familiar example would be snowball or water balloon fights on a college campus. On a more complex level, prostitution can be useful to society: it provides extramarital sex (for those who want it) without really threatening the institutions of marriage and the family.

Kai Erikson has pointed out that one of the most important functions of deviance in any organization or society is to clarify norms.[4] People do not learn about acceptable behavior by memorizing lists of rules, but instead by "testing the limits" or by watching what happens when others test them. Most children, for example, experiment with stealing at least once, but when their parents scold or punish them for it they quickly give it up. Some children may not even attempt stealing after observing the punishment given to a brother or sister for stealing. In either case, they learned what society will or will not tolerate by seeing the consequences of deviant behavior. On a much larger scale, institutions in society often have elaborate procedures (such as the media publicity and courtroom rituals that accompany criminal trials) to identify and label deviants. These often serve to mark the boundaries of permissible behavior for society. Finally, deviant acts also may promote group cohesiveness and solidarity by causing members of the group to perceive such acts as a common threat.

It is important to note that society's strong interest in identifying deviants results in an unfortunate consequence: people who are labeled deviants often remain stigmatized long after the label has lost whatever validity it may once have had. Ex-convicts or former mental patients, for example, often encounter many forms of discrimination after release from an institution.

Deviance can also warn society that certain rules are not just or reasonable. Rosa Parks refused to relinquish her seat to a white man on an

---

[3]Albert K. Cohen, *Deviance and Control* (Englewood Cliffs, N.J.: Prentice-Hall, 1966).

[4]Kai T. Erikson, "Notes on the Sociology of Deviance," *Social Problems* 9 (Spring 1962), 307-314.

Alabama bus, for example, a gross violation of Southern etiquette in the 1950s; yet, this black woman's act was an important landmark in the civil rights movement and sparked the Montgomery bus boycott that brought Dr. Martin Luther King, Jr., to national prominence. The liberalization of divorce laws, the gradual acceptance of premarital sex, and the growing equality between the sexes are other examples of social changes that have occurred as a result of widespread deviance from traditional standards of acceptable behavior. Deviance, therefore, can be one of the factors that effect needed changes in the organization of society.

Five Perspectives on Social Problems

Sociology, as we have suggested, is committed to the study of social behavior and social organization. Because it is a young science, it lacks a solid set of propositions and laws comparable to those used by natural scientists. Instead, sociologists have a frame of reference that guide them in their study of human behavior. This orientation is reflected in the premises discussed earlier, and contain two basic postulates: first, certain kinds of social problems may be an inevitable, but unplanned, development of *any* social organization; second, people in different social strata react to these problems differently and propose different solutions. These two factors imply that many problems can be alleviated by reorganizing the social structure that generated them.

Guided by these assumptions. sociologists try to establish comprehensive theories of human social behavior that will enable them to understand the nature of societies. Since the knowledge that guides them is often both new and fragmented, such theories must be considered empirical generalizations rather than scientific laws. These generalizations are based on repeated observations of certain behavior (for example, juvenile delinquency rates are often higher in low-income than in middle- and upper-income areas). By testing these generalizations in other situations (by studying the relationship between juvenile delinquency and poverty in many societies), sociologists try to develop a set of laws and principles that will explain how and why social problems occur.

In the sections that follow we describe five of the most significant sociological perspectives for the study of social problems.[5] Each theory emphasizes a different aspect of a social problem and offers differing explanations as to why social problems occur and how they may be alleviated. (See Table 1-1.)

The Social Pathology Perspective

As we pointed out earlier, the possibility of correcting social problems is relatively new. The Civil War caused a host of urban problems, brought about by rapid industrialization, the migration from farms to cities, and a large influx of European immigrants. Early sociologists, impressed by the success of the scientific method in technical fields, attempted to develop a scientific

[5]The following discussion is based on Earl Rubington and Martin S. Weinberg, eds., *The Study of Social Problems: Five Perspectives* (New York: Oxford University Press, 1971). For alternative ways of discussing sociological perspectives on social problems see Amitai Etzioni, *Social Problems* (Englewood Cliffs, N.J.: Prentice-Hall, 1976).

Perspective	Definition	Causes	Conditions	Consequences	Solutions
Social pathology	Violation of moral expectations	Failure in socialization Can't be taught, or rejects values and beliefs	Innate defects—immoral properties of individuals or societies	Costly Dehumanizing	Eugenics Moralizing individuals Education
Social disorganization	Failure in expectations Normlessness Culture conflict	Social change—disharmony	Anything technical, social, etc. that causes change	Personal stress and disorganization System change or failure	Equilibrate parts of system (slow down technology, for example)
Value conflict	Any conditions incompatible with values	Value conflict	Competition and contact	Costly—sacrifice of values	Consensus Trading Power
Deviant behavior	Departure from norms	Learning and being committed to deviant ways	Restricted conventional means Accessible deviant means Restricted societal ends	Many possible consequences depending on nature of illegitimate world	Resocialization Increase legitimate means and ends
Labeling	Conditions under which society defines social problems	Awareness	When labeler stands to gain	Reordering relations Secondary deviance	Change definitions Take profit out of labeling

Source: Earl Rubington and Martin S. Weinberg, eds., *The Study of Social Problems: Five Perspectives.* New York: Oxford University Press, 1971.

Table 1-1
Five Perspectives on Social Problems

approach to the study and solution of these social problems in the United States.

The premises of the sociological theory developed by these sociologists were rooted in the "organic analogy," that compared human society to the human body, and saw both as a vast organism, all of whose complex, interrelated parts should work together for the health and stability of the whole. Social problems arise when either individuals or social institutions fail to keep pace with changing conditions and thereby disrupt the healthy operation of the social organism; such individuals or institutions were considered "sick" (hence the term "social pathology"). European immigrants who failed to adjust to American urban life, for example, were considered to be a source of "illness," at least insofar as they affected the health of their adopted society. Underlying this concept of illness was the concept of morality—social problems ultimately violated the moral expectations of social order and progress.

Early social pathologists tended to identify individuals as the source of society's problems. Problem individuals were those who could not be properly socialized or who rejected society's values and beliefs because of some innate defect. Modern social pathologists tend to focus more on defects in society and its institutions. In other words, they feel that immoral societies produce immoral individuals, who in turn produce social problems.

Social problems, according to social pathologists, increase the cost of maintaining social order; if left unsolved, they may also gradually dehumanize society. Because, they thought, social problems resulted from innate defects in individuals, early social pathologists recommended programs to prevent the transmission of these defects to succeeding generations. Modern social pathologists focus on changing the morals of individuals and societies, and emphasize education as the solution to social problems.

Immigration, urbanization, and industrialization increased rapidly after World War I. Many new arrivals to the cities failed to adapt to urban life. European immigrants, rural whites, and Southern blacks were often crowded together in degrading slums, and had difficulties learning the language, manners, and norms of the dominant urban culture. Many who managed to adjust to the city were discriminated against because of their religion or race, while others lost their jobs because technological advances made their skills obsolete. Because of these conditions, many groups formed their own subcultures or devised other means of coping. Alcoholism, drug addiction, mental illness, crime, and delinquency rates rose drastically. Some sociologists of the time believed the social pathology perspective could not adequately explain the widespread existence of these social problems, and developed a new concept that eventually became known as the social disorganization perspective.

The Social Disorganization Perspective

This new perspective viewed society as being organized by a set of expectations or rules. Social disorganization, according to this theory, results when these expectations fail, and was manifested in three major ways: through *normlessness*, when people have no rules that tell them how to behave; through *culture conflict*, when people feel trapped by a contradictory set of rules; and through *breakdown*, when obedience to a set of rules results in no rewards or in punishment. Rapid social change, for example, might make traditional standards of behavior obsolete without providing new standards (normlessness). The children of foreign immigrants might feel trapped between the expectations of their parents' culture and the expectations of their new society (culture conflict). The expectations of blacks might be frustrated when they do well in school but encounter job discrimination (breakdown).

Stress experienced by victims of social disorganization may result in a form of "personal disorganization," such as drug addiction or crime. The social system as a whole also feels the force of disorganization, and may respond by changing its rules, by keeping contradictory rules in force, or by breaking down. Disorganization can be halted or reversed by isolating its causes and correcting them. For example, technological change cannot be reduced until society makes new rules and expectations.

The Value Conflict Perspective

The value conflict perspective arose after the Depression and World War II, when there was the need to make sociology more objective and useful to society. According to value conflict theorists, previous concepts of "sickness" or "social expectations" were largely subjective. They pointed out that deviance from the rules was not necessarily due to the failure of the individual or of society's rules. What is problematic to society as a whole may well be normal or justifiable to a particular group. Thus value conflict theorists define social problems simply as "conditions that are incompatible with group values."[6] Such problems are normal, they add, since there are many groups in a complex society whose interests and values are bound to differ.

Social problems, according to the value conflict theory, occur when groups with different values meet and compete. For example, landlords may want to raise rents, while tenants want to keep them low. This situation results in conflict. The consequences of conflict can be costly: as groups become polarized, higher goals (victory) may be sacrificed for lower ones (compromise). Conflicts are generally settled in one of three ways—consensus, trading, or power. Landlords and tenants may agree that a smaller rent increase is justified (consensus); tenants may require that landlords do less for their buildings in return for a lower rent increase (trading); or, landlords might evict tenants who do not pay the demanded rent increase (power).

The Deviant Behavior Perspective

The deviant behavior perspective is one of the most influential perspectives for the study of social problems. It was developed, first, because previous theories of social problems proved too broad for useful empirical research. It was more practical, or at least easier, to study people who deviated from accepted norms—such as hobos or delinquents—than to study "morals," "rules," or "groups." Second, many sociologists felt obliged to explain why higher rates of deviance seemed to exist among certain groups and certain social classes, and why not all members of these groups or classes became deviant.

Social problems, according to the deviant behavior perspective, are defined as behaviors or conditions that are deviant from the norm; they arise when the legitimate means of achieving cultural goals are blocked. Working-class youngsters, for example, whose access to jobs is limited, may form delinquent subcultures to obtain and maintain status within their group. Not everyone with limited legitimate opportunities will become deviant, however; there must also be a stimulus. If delinquency is admired among group members, and individuals are delinquent, then group members will have many reasons to become delinquent.

Deviant behavior can have various consequences to society, depending on the specific deviance. (Some of these consequences, such as the fear of crime, are obvious.) The best way to reduce deviance is to "resocialize" deviants by increasing their contacts with accepted patterns of behavior.[7] In addition, the social system must also be made less rigid, so legitimate opportunities and goals become more attainable.

The Labeling Perspective

The labeling perspective is the most recent major sociological approach to the study of social problems. It questions many assumptions made by other sociological theorists. Other perspectives assume that poverty, delinquency, addiction, and crime will be defined as social problems and are concerned with explaining why and under what conditions such problems occur. Labeling theorists feel that accepted definitions of deviance or social problems

[6]Rubington and Weinberg, *Study of Social Problems*, p. 86.
[7]Rubington and Weinberg, *Study of Social Problems*, p. 127.

are subjective and are interested in explaining why and under what conditions certain acts and situations came to be defined as problematic or deviant.

This implies that the label "deviant" reveals more about the society applying it than about the act or person so labeled. In certain societies, for example, homosexuality is far more accepted than in our own. Labeling theorists suggest that there are repressive forces in American society that benefit from labeling homosexuals as deviant (for example, institutions that profit from the strong emphasis on marital and family ties). Similarly, deviant acts are not always judged in the same way—prison sentences for black criminals, for example, tend to be longer than sentences for white criminals who commit the same crimes. This would suggest to labeling theorists something about the distribution of power in our society. In short, labeling theory separates deviant people and nondeviant people not by what they do but how society reacts to what they do.

According to labeling theorists, social problems are conditions under which certain behaviors or situations become defined as social problems. The cause of a social problem is simply society's awareness that a certain behavior or situation exists. (Obviously, society could not react to something it knows nothing about.) A behavior or situation becomes a social problem when someone somehow can profit by applying the label "problematic" or "deviant" to it. Such labeling causes society to suffer in two ways. First, one group unfairly achieves power over another group—"deviants" are repressed either through discrimination, social prejudice, or force. Second, those labeled as deviants may accept this definition of themselves—the label may then become a self-fulfilling prophecy. The number and variety of deviant acts may be increased in order to reinforce new roles as deviants. A person labeled as a drug addict, for example, may adopt what is popularly considered to be a drug addict's life style—resisting employment or treatment, engaging in crime, and so on. (Sociologists call this elaboration on the original deviant act "secondary deviance.")

Solutions to social problems, according to labeling theory, lie in changing definitions of what is considered deviant and in taking the profit out of the label.[8] Accepting a greater variety of acts and situations as normal will automatically eliminate these acts or situations as objects of concern. (The legalization of small amounts of marijuana for personal use is an example of how changing the definition of deviance removes a social problem.) Similarly, discouraging the tendency to impose labels for personal gain or satisfaction reduces the labeling process and can cause former problems to become less significant. Communism, for example, was an issue of great concern to Americans in the 1950s; many people won popularity or power by applying the label "Communist" to others. When it became clear that the label was being misapplied and that monolithic Communism was a false fear, the Communist label lost its significance—and the "social problem" of internal Communist influence virtually disappeared.

Each of the above perspectives attempts to supply a coherent explanation for the existence of social problems. Considering the differences between them, however, it is not surprising that these perspectives have had different effects on the discipline of sociology. The social pathology perspective has proved to be of limited usefulness in generating empirical research; its

[8]Rubington and Weinberg, *Study of Social Problems*, p. 169.

concepts of "sickness" and "morality" are too subjective to be meaningful to many sociologists. When moral considerations are most important, however, the social pathology perspective can still be applied. In modern times, for example, this perspective has provided a meaningful way of studying extreme or pathological conditions, such as concentration camps or the widespread indifference to mass starvation.

The social disorganization perspective developed when the United States was undergoing rapid social change and social problems seemed localized among immigrant groups. Later sociologists criticized the value judgment inherent in the term "disorganization" and pointed out that a diverse society is not necessarily a disorganized one. Today the social disorganization perspective is best used to study the effects of rapid industrialization on technologically underdeveloped societies.

The value conflict approach was and is felt by many sociologists to be of limited relevance because of the difficulty in demonstrating its validity for most social problems. When values of contending groups are clearly a factor in causing a problem, the value conflict perspective is, of course, highly applicable. The so-called generation gap, for example, frequently has its basis in a conflict of values.

Of the five, the deviant behavior perspective has sparked the greatest amount of research. It was developed when there was widespread agreement as to what constituted a social problem and also when there was a need for practical solutions to social problems. Indeed many of the social programs of the 1960s and 1970s were based on the concepts of the deviant behavior perspective and on the research it generated. Laws requiring busing to achieve educational equality, for example, were based on research that suggested black students would benefit from integrated classes.

The labeling perspective developed as a counterweight to several of the other perspectives in that it stressed the subjective nature of labels like "immoral" or "deviant" and described how such labels could aggravate social problems. Because it represents a relatively new approach to the study of social problems (and indeed is rather controversial among sociologists), it is not yet certain how great its impact will be. It has already proved useful in discussing areas that do not involve clearly defined values or norms, such as drug use, mental illness, and sexual behavior. It should be noted that many of the fundamental social problems we will be discussing in this book have their origin in a multiplicity of causes. They may require the application of several sociological perspectives in order to be completely understood and resolved. For this reason in this book we take an eclectic approach to the study of social problems, and use those perspectives that seem to apply most reasonably to each specific problem.

Organization of the Book

Sociologists have become increasingly aware of the interdependence of many social problems. In this volume, therefore, we do not group chapters according to the traditional divisions of deviant behavior and social disorganization. Instead, our chapter sequence follows a logical "micro" to "macro" pattern that suggests the interrelationships of social problems and offers both teachers and students maximum flexibility in the use of the text. In early chapters, for example, we focus on individual behaviors such as drug use or crime. Of course, the societal factors affecting these behaviors are noted and described. The middle section of the book focuses on discriminatory social institutions and norms, with chapters on such topics as prejudice, sexism, and age discrimination. We make every attempt, however, to indicate the effects of large-scale discrimination on individuals. In later chapters we discuss problems common to many societies, such as those relating to cities, families, and work. In the final chapters on population and environment we focus on matters of global significance. It seemed best to discuss each subject in a separate chapter in order to deal with it comprehensively and in depth. We have tried to indicate where different problems overlap and how they are interrelated.

In order to make the book easier to use, the organization of each chapter follows a fairly consistent pattern: (1) the specific aspects of the problem to be considered; (2) the important sociological theories or hypotheses relating to it; (3) factors that seem to correlate with it; (4) possible means of intervention to control or alleviate the problem; (5) prospects for the near future—that is, how the problem seems likely to develop in the next few years; and (6) a concise summary that reviews the essential concepts and facts of the chapter. In addition the comprehensive bibliography at the end of each chapter can be used as a study and research aid.

Summary

Social problems are conditions in society that are widely regarded as needing improvement or remedy. The idea that something can or should be done about social problems is a relatively recent development, coinciding with the evolution of enlightened rationalism and the scientific revolution.

Conditions defined as social problems vary from society and with changes in a society. Certain generalizations about social problems can be made, however: They often result unexpectedly from acceptable patterns of behavior (such as having large families resulting in overpopulation); they may arise as a result of accepted social principles (such as the desirability of private property, which may cause poor people to steal); they are likely to be perceived differently by people in different layers of society; and solutions proposed for them are likely to reflect the interests of the people offering the solutions. Thus the social and cultural environments of groups or individuals are important factors in the origin and elimination of social problems.

Several disciplines in the social sciences, other than sociology, contribute to our understanding of social problems. *History* can help us understand what factors in the past led to present conditions. *Cultural anthropology* can tell us how our own problems differ from or are similar to those in other societies. *Psychology* and *social psychology* can help us understand how individual experiences and personality types can affect the incidence of social problems. Finally, *biology* can offer insight into how individuals can be naturally disposed to behaviors that society considers problematic.

Sociology focuses generally on people's social behavior and social organization. The study of social problems focuses specifically on behavior that departs from established norms (*deviance*) and on social organizations that experience difficulties to the extent that their goals are not being achieved. Sociologists attempt to determine why these problems occur and how they can best be remedied. Though they often study so-called deviant behavior, sociologists are aware that both "deviant" and "normal" behaviors are difficult to isolate and that deviance often has constructive consequences, such as clarifying social norms and bringing about necessary changes in society.

Five theoretical sociological perspectives for the study of social problems have been identified. They are the *social pathology* perspective, which sees social problems as violating society's moral expectations; the *social disorganization* perspective, which stresses the failure of rules as a source of social problems; the *value conflict* perspective, which considers problems to be "conditions incompatible with social values"; the *deviant behavior* perspective, which focuses on acts or conditions that deviate from social norms; and the *labeling* perspective, which is concerned with the conditions under which society defines social problems. Each perspective generally offers insights into different kinds of social problems. When social problems have many, complex causes, however, several perspectives may apply.

Bibliography

Bates, Alan P. *The Sociological Enterprise.* Boston: Houghton Mifflin, 1967.

Becker, Howard S. *Outsiders: Studies in the Sociology of Deviance.* New York: Free Press, 1963.

————, ed. *Social Problems: A Modern Approach.* New York: Wiley, 1966.

Bell, Robert R. *Social Deviance.* Homewood, Ill.: Dorsey Press, 1971.

Berger, Peter L. *Invitation to Sociology: A Humanistic Perspective.* New York: Overlook Press, 1973.

Clinard, Marshall B. *The Sociology of Deviant Behavior*, 4th ed. New York: Holt, Rinehart and Winston, 1974.

Cohen, Albert K. *Deviance and Control.* Englewood Cliffs, N.J.: Prentice-Hall, 1966.

Dinitz, Simon, et al., ed. *Deviance.* New York: Oxford University Press, 1969.

Douglas, Jack D., ed. *Observations of Deviance.* New York: Random House, 1971.

Elliot, Mabel A., and Merril, Francis E. *Social Disorganization.* 4th ed. New York: Harper, 1961.

Freeman, Howard E., and Kurtz, Norman R., eds. *America's Troubles*, 2nd ed. Englewood Cliffs, N.J.: Prentice-Hall, 1973.

Gouldner, Alvin W., and Miller, S. M., ed. *Applied Sociology.* New York: Free Press, 1965.

Hornstein, Harvey, et al., ed. *Social Intervention.* New York: Free Press, 1971.

Inkeles, Alex, ed. *What is Sociology? An Introduction to the Discipline and Profession.* Englewood Cliffs, N.J.: Prentice-Hall, 1964.

Lindenfeld, Frank, *Radical Perspective on Social Problems*, 2nd ed. London: Macmillan, 1973.

Merton, Robert K. "Social Structure and Anomie." *American Sociological Review*, 3 (October 1938), 672-682.

Offenbacher, Deborah I., and Constance Poster, eds. *Social Problems and Social Policy.* Englewood Cliffs, N.J.: Prentice-Hall, 1970.

Perrucci, Robert, and Pilisuk, Marc, ed. *The Triple Revolution Emerging.* Boston: Little, Brown, 1971.

Rosenberg, Bernard, et al., ed. *Mass Society in Crisis.* 2nd ed. New York: Macmillan, 1971.

Schur, Edwin. *Labeling Deviant Behavior.* New York: Harper & Row, 1971.

Sutherland, Edwin H., and Cressey, Donald R. *Criminology,* 9th ed. Philadelphia: Lippincott, 1974.

Physical and
Mental Health

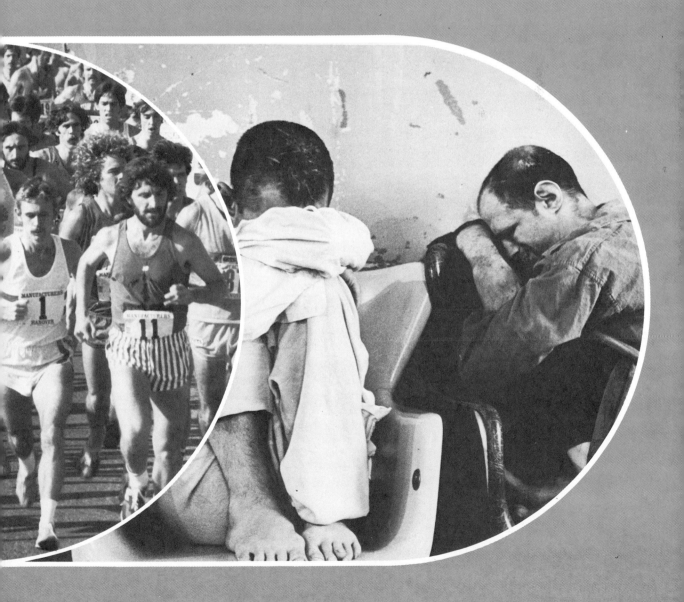

Facts about Physical and Mental Health

- In the past 5 years, physical health-care spending has almost doubled.
- Nearly one-third of the hospitals in the United States fail to meet minimum standards of safety and adequacy.
- An estimated 40,000 people die each year in the United States as a result of unnecessary or harmful medical treatment.
- More than 6 million people in the United States are treated for mental illness each year, about 25 percent of the total estimated to need such treatment.
- About 800,000 people are in the nation's 500 mental hospitals; an estimated 250,000 of these are untreated, harmless, and able to function on their own.

Health is essential to all societies. For societies to survive and perpetuate themselves, their members must attain and maintain some degree of good health. Precise definitions of health and illness, however, vary from society to society. As David Mechanic has stated:

> Implicit in all ideas of health and disease—whether specific or more general—is some concept of normal fitness and behavior, but concepts of health fitness and acceptable behavior, as well as those of disease and disability, depend on the state of health institutions and health science and on the social and cultural context within which human problems are defined. A wide variety of diseases are not defined by particular groups as illness conditions because they occur frequently and are regarded as the common state of man. In some tropical countries, yaws, an infectious disease characterized by skin eruptions with a raspberry-like appearance, was so pervasive that individuals did not regard it as deviant. Dyschromic spirochetosis, a disease characterized by spots of various colors that appear on the skin, was so common in a particular South American tribe that Indians who did not have it were regarded as abnormal. In short, health and disease, as well as their definitions, are often molded by the social context within which they occur.[1]

In the United States health and happiness are among the most highly prized values. "To your health" is a common toast; "Have a happy and healthy New Year" is a common year-end expression. As Lerner put it: "One indication of the importance of health in our society is the enormity of the industry which has developed to maintain it."[2] The health industry today employs some 5 million people and accounts for almost 9 percent of the gross national product (GNP). Americans spent over $142 billion on health care in 1977, 13 percent more than in 1976.[3]

Most of us, in fact, have come to consider proper medical care as a basic

---

[1] David Mechanic, *Medical Sociology*, 2nd ed. (New York: Free Press, 1978), p. 26.

[2] Monroe Lerner, "Health as a Social Problem," in *Handbook on the Study of Social Problems*, ed. Erwin Smigel (Chicago: Rand McNally, 1971), p. 295.

[3] R. M. Gibson and C. R. Fisher, "National Health Expenditures. Fiscal Year 1977," *Social Security Bulletin*, vol. 41, no. 7 (July 1978), 6.

human right, not as a privilege. This, however, was not always true. As late as 1967, the president of the American Medical Association (AMA) maintained that health care should be available only to those who could afford it. Today, however, polls show that Americans, in all segments of society and from every political persuasion, consider medical care their right.[4] This opinion is reflected at all levels of government. Richard Nixon expressed the prevailing viewpoint in his "Health Message of 1971":

> Just as our National Government has moved to provide equal opportunity in areas such as education, employment, and voting, so we must now work to expand the opportunity for all citizens to obtain a decent standard of medical care. We must do all we can to remove any racial, economic, social or geographic barriers that now prevent any of our citizens from obtaining adequate health protection. For without good health, no man can fully utilize his other opportunities.[5]

If Americans spend large amounts of money on health care, if there are a large number of health personnel, if a philosophy of health care as a right has developed and spread—then why is health care in the United States, as the late Robert Kennedy described it, "a national failure"? America, he insisted, is "providing poor quality care at high costs," costs that are "staggering." Despite this extraordinary investment, Kennedy said, "in 1950, we ranked fifth in the world in our infant mortality rate. Today we rank fifteenth—below all of the industrialized nations of Europe. Twelve other nations have higher life expectancy rates than we do."[6] These statistics have improved somewhat, but the fact is that although our health-care resources have the *potential* for delivering the highest quality care to all citizens, in *actuality* they leave much to be desired. One reason for this is that our health resources are designed largely to *treat* disorders rather than to *prevent* them from occurring. Few of us, for example, receive reminders from our physicians that we are due for an annual checkup (the way we might from our dentists). The emphasis on treatment violates the common-sense notion that "an ounce of prevention is worth a pound of cure." It also makes medical care much more problematic and expensive, and leaves many of us—and not only the poor or disadvantaged—feeling mentally or physically unfit much of the time.

Health care services are not equally distributed. As Lerner put it, medical care is still "a scarce product . . . rationed by society according to the individual's ability to pay."[7] Illness and disability are much more common among the poor than among the affluent, although only the affluent have sufficient access to proper medical care. Finally, costs for health care, including health insurance, are extremely high and rising sharply. Today, even many members of the middle class are not protected against the cost of a debilitating illness, and many others cannot afford even the most essential medical services.

In this chapter we will discuss these and other problems of America's health-care resources in greater detail. We will concentrate in the first part of

---

[4]Herbert E. Klarman, *The Economics of Health* (New York: Columbia University Press, 1965), p. 336
[5]Richard Nixon, "Health Message of 1971," February 18, 1971, White House.
[6]Quoted in John A. Denton, *Medical Sociology* (Boston: Houghton Mifflin, 1978), p. 65.
[7]Lerner, *"Health as a Social Problem,"* p. 287.

the chapter on physical-health problems. We will try to describe why and how these problems developed, and what can be done to help remedy them.

Problems of Physical Health

America's health-care resources are impressive. Many of our more than 7,000 hospitals are among the most modern in the world, and our approximately 400,000 physicians have been rigorously trained. In recent years, the physician-to-population ratio has been expanding, even though the geographic distribution of doctors is still heavily weighted in favor of metropolitan areas. New medical schools, more students, and an influx of foreign medical-school graduates are responsible for this increase in physicians. Assuming that there are no drastic changes in the size of medical-school graduating classes or in the American population, the doctor-to-patient ratio might be 50 percent greater by the year 1990 than it is today.[8]

Despite these figures, we are not as healthy as we could or should be. For example, our life expectancy is lower than that of Sweden, Norway, the Netherlands, France, Japan, or Denmark, and our infant-mortality rate is higher than that of 13 other countries.[9] The death rate from heart disease in the United States is by far the highest in the world. The incidence of cancer and the death rate from cancer rank among the highest. Part of this comparatively poor health picture results from the way we live. The growing number of people in sedentary occupations, the overwhelming presence of fattening, nonnutritious foods in our diet, and the widespread lack of proper exercise have undoubtedly contributed to our high incidence of heart disease and other ailments. Similarly, it is probable that environmental pollution (see Chapter 16) and cigarette smoking have contributed to the already high and still rising cancer incidence. There can be little doubt, however, that many of our health problems are aggravated because of the kind of medical care that is—or is not—available. As two analysts of our health-care resources stated:

> Every day three million Americans go out in search of medical care. Some find it; others do not. Some are helped by it; others are not. Another twenty million Americans probably ought to enter the daily search for medical help, but are not healthy enough, rich enough, or enterprising enough to try.[10]

Inequality in Access to Health Services

The use and availability of medical care are directly related to socioeconomic class and race. The racial aspect is most directly illustrated by a comparison of life expectancy for whites and nonwhites: on the average, the life expectancy for white males is about 7 years longer than for nonwhite males and about 6 years longer than for females.[11] In addition, the infant-mortality rate for nonwhites is almost twice that of whites: 24.6 per 1000 live births, as compared to 14.7. Although infant mortality has been on the decline in this

[8]Howard D. Schwartz and Cary S. Kart, *Dominant Issues in Medical Sociology* (Reading, Mass.: Addison-Wesley, 1978), p. 385.

[9]*United Nations Demographic Yearbook, 1976* (New York: United Nations, 1977).

[10]Barbara Ehrenreich and John Ehrenreich, *The American Health Empire* (New York: Vintage Books, 1971), p. 3.

[11]Mechanic, *Medical Sociology,* p. 165.

country since 1900, the rate for nonwhites has continued to remain approximately two-thirds higher than that for whites.[12] Nonwhites suffer proportionately more from almost every illness than do whites; and, because they are less likely to have been immunized, nonwhites suffer higher rates of death from infectious diseases. Such differences cannot be ascribed to income differences alone, since, even when income is the same, death rates are still higher for nonwhites.[13]

From a socioeconomic point of view, there is a strong relationship between membership in a lower class and a higher rate of illness. People in the lower classes tend to feel sicker and have higher rates of untreated illness than those in the middle and upper classes. They also tend to be disabled more frequently and for longer periods than do members of the middle and upper classes. Furthermore, mortality rates for almost all diseases are higher among the lower classes. For example, contrary to the popular belief that top executives have higher rates of heart disease caused by stressful jobs, the highest rate of heart disease actually occurs among the lowest salaried; the lowest rate occurs among top-level managers and executives. Persons in families with an income of less than $3,000 per year had over 3 times more disability than those in families with an income greater than $25,000 per year.[14]

Which factors account for these disparities in health? Perhaps, as Seham points out,

> for the most part, delivery of health care services is geared to the upper- and middle-class culture because these services take on all the qualities of a commodity for sale and the affluent are the preferred and often the only market. This is especially true in the preventive areas.[15]

Thus, the high infant-mortality rate among the poor is largely due to their high incidence of infectious diseases. Unlike those in the middle and upper classes, poor parents simply cannot afford a private or family physician to make sure that their infant is properly immunized. In all age groups, the health of the poor is adversely affected by their inability to afford private, high-quality medical care. As Lerner states, the illnesses of the poor "are much more likely to remain untreated and, consequently, to increase in severity, because the poor generally remain outside the private medical-care system.[16] Not only are the poor unable to afford proper care, they also have limited care available in their own neighborhoods. Rural or poor urban areas suffer from a chronic, severe shortage of physicians and other medical services.

When poor people do seek treatment for an illness—often only when a crisis is reached—they tend to visit a clinic rather than a private physician, and they must travel at some cost and inconvenience to the nearest medical facility. At the clinic, they receive the most impersonal kind of treatment,

[12]"The Forward Plan for Health," reprinted in Schwartz and Kart, *Dominant Issues*, p. 380.
[13]Max Seham, *Blacks and American Medical Care* (Minneapolis: University of Minnesota Press, 1973), p. 10.
[14]*Source Book of Health Insurance Data, 1977–1978* (Washington, D.C.: Health Insurance Institute), p. 65; also S. Leonard Syme and Lisa F. Berkman, "Social Class, Susceptibility, and Sickness," *American Journal of Epidemiology*, vol. 104 (July 1976), 1–8.
[15]Seham, *Blacks and American Medical Care*, p. 20.
[16]Lerner, "Health as a Social Problem," pp. 308–309.

often waiting many hours in crowded waiting rooms and seeing different physicians on successive visits. A trusting relationship with a physician, therefore, is never established, and health-care becomes fragmented. Furthermore, physicians at the clinic almost always come from a white, middle- or upper-class background that differs markedly from that of the poor white, black, or Spanish-speaking person. And, as Seham put it:

> In general, health professionals have little—if any—understanding of the life style of the poor. For a doctor to advise a patient who is living in poverty to increase his intake of protein, without helping him to work out how to do it, is useless. Similarly, to suggest to a working mother than she come to the clinic for weekly treatments, when the clinic hours coincide with her working hours, is tantamount to not providing treatment at all.[17]

In sum, poor people, white and black, are shut off from private medical care by their inability to pay for it. They become distrustful of public-health clinics, as well, and avoid them as long as possible. This lack of proper medical care among the poor leads to higher rates of illness that result in death. It is for this reason that class or race, in the words of one observer, "influences one's chances of staying alive."[18]

The High Cost of Health

From 1960 to 1969, health-care costs increased by 42.5 percent, while the cost of living rose only 23.8 percent. By 1977 health-care costs had risen another 77 percent, outstripping the inflationary rise in the cost of living by more than 13 percent. Today, hospital and physician costs are rising almost twice as fast as the overall inflation rate. In 1974, for example, the overall inflation rate, as measured by the increase in the consumer price index, was almost 6 percent. In that same year, physicians' fees rose 8.5 percent, hospital services rose 9.26 percent, and the cost of a semiprivate hospital room rose 12.4 percent. Overall, in 1977 the national health expenditure per capita was $736.92, up from $33.57 in 1970.[19]

Hospitals. Why have health-care costs risen so sharply? Figure 2-1 shows that hospital charges have gone up dramatically—exceeded only by nursing-home care in percentage of increase. Hospital charges now account for almost 40 percent of all health costs; the average cost of a day in a hospital is over $118 nationwide. The use of technologically-advanced—and expensive—equipment and the wage increases won by hospital workers explain only some of the rise in hospital fees. Also, a greater consumer demand now exists.

Most important to the rise in costs, however, has been inefficient hospital management and the fact that hospitals, unlike other businesses, feel no need to keep costs down. Patients and physicians, for example, are often discouraged from using hospitals on an outpatient basis, although perhaps one-third of all hospital procedures could be performed as effectively—and

[17]Seham, *Blacks and American Medical Care*, pp. 22–23.
[18]Aaron Antonovsky, "Class and the Chance for Life," in *Inequality and Justice*, ed. Lee Rainwater (Chicago: Aldine, 1974), p. 177.
[19]U.S. Bureau of the Census, *Statistical Abstract of the United States, 1977* (Washington, D.C.: U.S. Government Printing Office, 1978), pp. 478–479; Gibson and Fisher, "National Health Expenditures," p. 5.

Hospital care $65.6 billion or 46%	Hospital care $339–$432
Physicians' services $32.2 billion or 22.6%	Physicians' services $162–$207
Drugs $12.5 billion or 8.7%	Drugs $ 66–$ 85
Nursing-home care $12.6 billion or 8.8%	Nursing-home care $ 66–$ 85
Dentists' services $10.0 billion or 7%	Dentists' services $ 52–$ 66
Other $9.7 billion or 6.8%	Other $ 53–$ 64
	Total $738–$939

more economically—in this way. Hospitals, however, may not be totally at fault for this wasteful use of their facilities. Physicians, after all, usually regulate admissions to hospitals and determine how long their patients will stay, thereby contributing to unnecessary hospitalization. In a sense, they share the responsibility with the hospitals that offer few self-care facilities for patients admitted for limited tests or procedures, and who can look after themselves. In addition, few hospitals provide preventive services designed to head off health problems before they arise; this may occur because the physicians who service the hospital's patients have never demanded these services.[20] In addition, hospitals in a given community often compete with one another over which facility has the most prestigious and costly equipment. This usually results in the duplication of expensive, seldom-used equipment, the costs of which are passed on to every patient.

Another important consideration is that hospitals, like most health services, do not operate according to normal patterns of supply and demand. People use medical care because they need to; they cannot reduce the costs of care by avoiding treatment. Thus the fees for health services are controlled by the suppliers—hospitals, physicians, and drug companies—rather than by consumers. People have no choice but to pay what health care costs; they cannot go without it.

This already unequal situation has been further biased in favor of health-service providers by public and private insurance programs. Blue Cross, for example, which provides hospital insurance, was originally designed to protect against the high, and often sudden, costs of hospital care through the prepayment of low premiums that ensure the payment of hospital fees. The system proved so successful that hospitals were able to raise their fees at will, assured that Blue Cross would pay the higher fees. Costs were passed on to the consumer by raising the premiums. The result was increasingly high premiums for those covered by Blue Cross with no increase

Figure 2-1
(Left) United States Medical Expenditures (Fiscal Year 1977); (Right) Projected United States Medical Expenditures (in billions of dollars) for the Year 2000.

Source: United States Department of Health, Education and Welfare, *Social Security Bulletin,* vol. 41, no. 7 (July 1978), 6; and Public Health Reports, vol. 93, no. 5 (September-October 1978), 529.

[20]Rodney M. Coe, *Sociology of Medicine* (New York: McGraw-Hill, 1978), pp. 384–389.

in service. (Blue Shield, which offered similar coverage for physicians' fees, developed on much the same pattern.) Furthermore, until recently, Blue Cross would not pay medical expenses incurred during outpatient care; it actually became less expensive for a patient to be hospitalized than to be treated and sent home. As a consequence, alternatives to hospitalization, such as preventive medicine and outpatient care, were never fully developed.[21]

Physicians.   Over the past 30 years, physicians have had the highest median income of any occupational group. Since 1965, physicians' fees have increased by more than 150 percent to a total of more than $46 billion annually.[22] One factor in the increase has been the part played by Blue Shield and other insurance programs. Physicians, in addition, have felt no need to reduce their costs, since the nature of their occupation assures them a steady supply of patients, and medical insurance guarantees that their bills will be paid.

Members of a successful Tennessee commune have established their own clinic to combat the rising costs of health care.

UPI

[21]Sylvia A. Law, *Blue Cross: What Went Wrong?* (New Haven, Conn.: Yale University Press, 1974).

[22]Coe, *Sociology of Medicine*, p. 384.

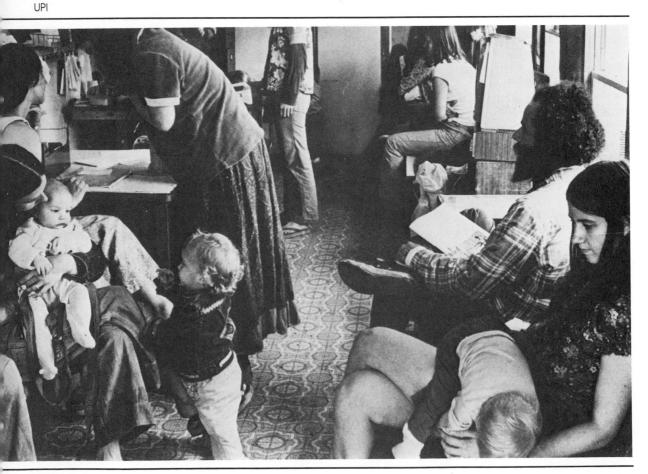

Another factor is the shortage of physicians that developed during a time when the demand for medical services increased. In 1950, for example, there were about 109 physicians for every 100,000 people in the United States; today there are about 95 physicians providing private care for every 100,000 people. The ratio in metropolitan areas is much better, with about 233 doctors available for every 100,000 people in those communities with populations of 5 million or more. The ratio, however, declines sharply with the size of the community. Some small towns and rural areas suffer from severe shortages of medical personnel, particularly specialists. In urban areas, poor sections, although surrounded by well-serviced communities, may lack medical facilities. In all areas, however, doctors find increasing demand for their services and are able to raise their fees almost at will.

The growing willingness of many patients to sue if they feel they have been badly treated—perhaps reflecting the rise of the consumer movement—and the tendency of juries to award large sums of money in malpractice cases have also affected physicians' fees. Most physicians are required by law to carry malpractice insurance, with annual premiums ranging from $3,000 to $35,000. (The highest premiums are paid by

In some areas of the country, the physician shortage is so acute that communities must advertise for physicians. This sign appears along a highway only about 50 miles from Chicago.
Paul Sequeira/Photo Researchers, Inc.

anesthesiologists, whose job is considered to carry the greatest risk.) The costs of these premiums, of course, are passed on to the consumer in the form of higher physicians' fees.

Perhaps the greatest cause of the increase in physicians' fees, however, has been the growing tendency toward specialization. Of the nation's 366,000 physicians, 84 percent are in a specialty and only about 14 percent are in general practice. (This compares to about 30 percent who were general practitioners (GP) in 1960.) One reason for this growth in specialization is, of course, the advances in medical knowledge. Physicians today can become competent only in increasingly limited areas, and so they tend to specialize. Another reason, however, is that specialists receive more income than general practitioners, because it is assumed that their longer training and expertise entitle them to higher fees. Thus specialists can make up to one and one-half times what a GP earns.[23] The extra income comes directly from patient fees. Specialization also increases costs in another way; patients are forced to consult several physicians for a variety of ailments, instead of being able to see one physician for all of them. These repeated visits to different physicians multiply the cost of treatment many times. (An additional side effect is that medical care becomes fragmented and impersonal, since patients rarely establish a long-term relationship with one physician.)

Health Insurance.   The high cost of medical services has made some form of health insurance a necessity for all except the wealthy. Poor people cannot afford even out-of-pocket expenses for the most minimal care; and while middle-income people can pay most ordinary expenses, a severe or prolonged illness can mean financial ruin.

About 80 percent of the United States population was covered by some form of health insurance in 1975. However, one-third of the costs of medical care during that year were still paid by consumers, either to cover the deductible portion of their expenses (the amount the individual must pay before the insurer takes over) or for services not covered by insurance policies.

There are four categories of insurance: commercial insurance companies selling both individual and group policies, Blue Cross–Blue Shield, independent pre-paid groups such as Kaiser–Permanente and the Health Insurance Plan of New York (which will be discussed later in this chapter), and public insurance such as Medicare and Medicaid. During the last decade, public insurance has grown more rapidly than any other source of payment. More than half of the hospital costs for 1974 and more than 25 percent of the total doctors' fees were paid through public insurance.

Almost all these forms of insurance have their shortcomings. Subscribers to Blue Cross and private plans have complained about the steadily increasing costs of their premiums, which have not been accompanied, they feel, by a corresponding increase in benefits. One study showed that holders of health insurance policies felt that insurance was merely a form of economic protection and had no effect on the quality of care they could hope to receive. Doctors argue that it does, since patients who are insured tend to be more willing to be hospitalized, purchase drugs, and make other expenditures required for treatment. Studies have shown that the insured *do* use medical care more than the uninsured. Still, consumer dissatisfaction with insurance

[23]*Statistical Abstract of the United States, 1977*, pp. 100, 101.

remains high since benefits have not kept pace with rising costs and a serious illness can threaten the financial security of most middle-class families.[24]

Two programs designed to help the medically needy obtain health care—Medicare and Medicaid—were passed by Congress in 1965. Medicare, a public health insurance program, is paid for by Social Security taxes. It is designed to cover some of the medical expenses of those 65 or over. Those (over 65) who are ineligible for Medicare may voluntarily enroll in the program by paying premiums. Medicaid, an assistance program financed from federal and state tax revenues, is designed to pay the medical costs of those unable to afford even basic health care. Although these two programs have been significantly helpful to many Americans, there have been many problems.

First, there is inequity in the distribution of Medicare services. The poorest people continue to receive the fewest services. For example, people with incomes over $15,000 per year receive twice the amounts for physicians' services as do those with incomes of $5000 or less. Whites have 30 percent more payments for hospital care and 60 percent more for physicians' care than do nonwhites. There are also inequities in geographic distribution. A number of factors have caused the Medicare program to fail to reach its goal of full accessibility of health care for the nation's elderly. One of the reasons is the existence of requirements for deductible payments and co-insurance. The financially secure can make these. The poor can turn to Medicaid for this portion of their expenses. But the near-poor aged—and this is a very large group—still must go without the care they need because they cannot pay for it.

The second major problem with Medicare and Medicaid is their cost to the public and their impact on inflation of health care costs in general. Both programs have been criticized for waste and for abuse by administrators and physicians, who have no incentive to keep costs down and few auditing controls to keep them ethical. Hospitals, for example, have used Medicare funds to construct new buildings, purchase superfluous equipment, and hire such nonmedical personnel as public relations directors. Physicians have operated "Medicaid Mills"—clinics that service the poor—often with tests and treatments that are unnecessary. Many physicians refuse to treat patients under Medicaid because of the paperwork or regulations involved, and since many physicians' offices are geographically inaccessible, these "Medicaid Mills" are often the only source of health care to the poor. Blue Cross, which administers a majority of the Medicare and Medicaid reimbursements to physicians and hospitals, has been attacked recently for not taking a more active role in identifying and reporting suspected abuses of public money, and for not developing cost-control incentives.[25]

Medicare and Medicaid also have been a major factor in the rise in health-care costs because they have sharply increased the demand for health services. Moreover, the maximum fees that Medicare sets for specific health services (Medicaid offers blanket coverage) became the minimum that physicians and hospitals were willing to charge—driving up the costs of care still further. The costs of Medicare have also increased as a result of the many abuses it has suffered by physicians, hospitals, and nursing homes. For

[24]Coe, *Sociology of Medicine*, pp. 388–392.
[25]Mechanic, *Medical Sociology*, pp. 496–497; Denton, *Medical Sociology*, p. 302.

example, patients are frequently—and unnecessarily—sent from one specialist to another, so that each physician can bill the government. It has been estimated that such overcharges totaled $27 million over a 5-year period.[26]

The Problems of Unnecessary or Harmful Treatment

In a significant number of cases, patients receive treatment that is either unnecessary or harmful to their health or even their lives. Sometimes this treatment is psychologically harmful—that is, it makes the patient feel abused and resentful. Members of minorities and women are often mistreated in just this way. As one analysis of the American health system stated:

> Since blacks are assumed to be less sensitive than white patients, they get less privacy. Since blacks are assumed to be more ignorant than whites, they get less by way of explanation of what is happening to them. And since they are assumed to be irresponsible and forgetful, they are more likely to be given a drastic, one-shot treatment, instead of a prolonged regimen of drugs, or a restricted diet. . . . Women are assumed to be incapable of understanding complex technological explanations, so they are not given any. Women are assumed to be emotional and "difficult," so they are often classified as neurotic well before physical illness has been ruled out. (Note how many tranquilizer ads in medical journals depict women, rather than men, as likely customers.) And women are assumed to be vain, so they are the special prey of the paramedical dieting, cosmetics, and plastic surgery businesses.[27]

Many other forms of mistreatment are physically harmful, sometimes resulting in disability or death. Patients have been increasingly reacting to such incidents of medical malpractice with lawsuits. Malpractice litigation is on the rise for several reasons that are only indirectly related to the competence of physicians. Our ineffective insurance programs play a significant role. If people were adequately covered for disabilities or for procedures necessary to correct conditions stemming from malpractice, they might be less anxious to take up a time-consuming, often emotionally difficult, lawsuit. The increasing sophistication of modern medical technology also plays a part. While recent scientific advances enable doctors to perform treatments that once would have seemed miraculous, these same treatments can also be more hazardous for the patient if they are used incorrectly or with less than expert skill and care. Public expectations about the powers of modern medicine also aggravate the possibility of malpractice suits. People believe strongly in the new technology. When it fails they are apt to feel angry and frustrated, blaming the most available representatives of medical science—their physicians and hospitals. Another significant contribution is made by the highly specialized medical profession itself. Specialization has broken up services and eroded the traditional doctor-patient relationship. There is an absence of trust and communication between patients and their physicians, and this atmosphere can result in patient-instigated legal actions.[28]

Unnecessary surgery spawns, perhaps, the most malpractice suits. Several studies have found, for example, that about 2.4 million unnecessary

[26]"Health Care in America—Progress and Problems," *U.S. News & World Report,* June 16, 1975, pp. 50–51.
[27]Ehrenreich and Ehrenreich, *The American Health Empire,* pp. 14, 16.
[28]Mechanic, *Medical Sociology,* pp. 503–515.

operations are performed each year. Most of these operations are hysterectomies and tonsillectomies, of which 260,000 and 500,000 respectively are estimated to be unnecessary; of these, at least 11,900 kill the patient. These deaths would not have occurred without unnecessary surgery. About 30,000 additional deaths each year are caused directly by reactions to antibiotics and other prescribed drugs. Such bad reactions also cause some 300,000 side effects that result in hospitalization. Thus the overprescription of antibiotics and other drugs is in itself a major cause of illness and death in the United States.[29]

Considering the high level of training required of physicians and the many modern health facilities that exist, why does such shocking mistreatment occur? Perhaps the most important reason is that M.D.s generally are not required to keep up with medical knowledge once they complete their training; only a limited number of states (Washington, for example) requires a relicensing examination of their physicians. Usually, once an M.D. is licensed, he or she is not made to read another medical text or journal, or attend a medical conference, in order to remain in practice.

This bad situation is made worse because few states have an agency where incompetence can be reported and acted upon. Furthermore, since patients rarely know that they are being poorly treated, the responsibility for reporting incompetence lies with other physicians, yet most physicians are reluctant to report on their colleagues, even when they know that patients' lives are being endangered. Thus, only about 72 doctors a year lose their license for incompetence—a tiny fraction of the total that is believed to exist.[30]

The many deaths due directly to surgery largely reflect the unnecessary nature of much of the surgery performed in the United States. Americans have the highest rate of elective (optional) surgery in the world; they undergo about 14.4 million such operations annually. Yet, it has been estimated that one-fifth of all elective surgery is not in the patient's best interests. No surgical procedure is without its risks. Even in a simple operation such as a tonsillectomy, approximately 2 out of every 1,000 patients die; the death rate for more complex operations in much higher. (See Table 2-1.)

Why is the rate of surgery so high in the United States? One simple reason is that there are too many surgeons. It has been estimated that there are 22,000 more physicians who do surgery than are necessary. Since their livelihood depends on performing operations, surgeons are less likely to recommend a nonsurgical treatment to a patient. This is demonstrated by studies that show that rates of surgery are higher in those states that have proportionately more surgeons, and lower where there are proportionately fewer surgeons. Presumably, patients in those states with less surgery are finding other forms of treatment. Another, related, reason for excess surgery is the American system of fee-for-service. Since most surgeons—and physicians—are paid each time they treat a patient, they are encouraged to see and treat as many patients as they can; patients often do not receive the individual attention they need, and more surgeries are performed, sometimes

[29]"Incompetent Surgery Is Found Not Isolated," *New York Times*, January 27, 1976, pp. 1 ff.; "Thousands a Year Killed by Faulty Prescriptions," *New York Times*, January 28, 1976, pp. 1 ff.
[30]"Unfit Doctors Create Worry in Profession," *New York Times*, January 29, 1976, pp. 1 ff.; "Few Doctors Ever Report Colleague's Incompetence," *New York Times*, January 29, 1976, pp. 1 ff.

Surgery				
14 million nonemergency operations annually	of which	2.38 million deemed unnecessary	during which	11,900 people died
Antibiotics				
6 billion doses estimated consumed in United States	of which	22 percent deemed unnecessary	during which	10,000 fatal and near-fatal reactions to antibiotics occurred
Regulation of Doctors				
320,000 licensed physicians in United States	of which	16,000 deemed in-competent or unfit	of these	66 licenses revoked each year, on the average, in the United States

Source: *The New York Times*, January 26, 1976, p. 20. © by the New York Times Company. Reprinted by permission.

Table 2-1
Indications of Medical Incompetence in the United States

with less than adequate carefulness. For example, studies by the Department of Health, Education, and Welfare and the Social Security Administration found that patients covered by fee-for-service insurance plans such as Blue Cross were undergoing significantly higher rates of surgery than patients covered by prepaid plans.[31]

The Roots of Health Problems

General Problems   Every society is faced with the problem of distributing health-care services among its people; the United States uses a marketplace approach, which views health care as a commodity subject to the demands and spending power of consumers. Reformers have stressed the advantages of the planning model of health-care distribution, under which needs are determined by experts and met according to the directions of some governing body. This approach is based on the premise that the general interest is best satisfied by some force beyond the individual.

Though the planning model presents some problems, so does the marketplace approach. Its greatest failure in the United States has been the unequal distribution of a service that has come to be viewed as a right. There are a number of reasons why health care cannot be treated as a commodity. These include:

- Information—A consumer is not in a position to shop for medical treatment as he or she would for any other product or service, since personal needs cannot be gauged.
- Product Uncertainty—The consumer does not have sufficient knowledge to judge the effectiveness of sophisticated treatments.

[31]"Incompetent Surgery Is Found Not Isolated."

- Norms of Treatment—Medical care is performed under the control of a physician. A patient does not direct his or her treatment.

- Lack of Price Competition—Prices for doctors' services are not advertised and are not subject to the competition that is inherent in the true marketplace.

- Restricted Entry—Though there have been recent attempts to graduate more doctors, there are still numerous barriers to entering medical school. Many qualified applicants continue to be turned down because of a limited number of places. And there are relatively few women, minority students or students from disadvantaged backgrounds.

- Professional Dominance—Many health-care services now restricted to physicians could be performed by trained technicians. This has created a monopoly.

- Misallocated Supply—An abundance of specialists and subspecialists encourage the use of expensive and sophisticated treatments when simpler ones would be just as effective.[32]

The weakness of the American system, as it is, has been described in a report to Congress by the Health Services and Mental Health Administration:

> The pervasive influences of the medical profession over almost all facets of the health care delivery process, including the management of hospitals and admission policies of medical schools, has tended to make the health system more responsive to the interests of the profession than to the needs of consumers.[33]

The "pervasive influence of the medical profession" described in the report is exemplified by the role played by the American Medical Association in limiting the number of physicians in this country. During the first half of this century, stringent licensing requirements and strict standards for medical school admissions reduced the doctor-to-population ratio to a critical low. Scarcity of doctors allowed physicians to raise their fees almost at will. Recently, as discussed earlier, the scarcity problem has been somewhat alleviated, although medical schools still tend to restrict the number of places available to applicants. Since the expenses of medical schools are largely subsidized by public funds, they have been attacked for not being responsive to public needs. It is felt that minority-group members, women, and people from disadvantages backgrounds, who might work as doctors among poorly served segments of society, are underrepresented in medical school. In addition, the medical establishment restricts the activities of other practitioners who, though trained and capable, might encroach on their responsibilities. The AMA has been active in establishing legal and licensing barriers that limit the scope of other health occupations.[34]

Private insurance plans, like Blue Cross and Blue Shield, and federal ones, Medicaid and Medicare legislation, were originally intended to solve many of the problems and inequities of the American health-care system.

---

[32]Mechanic, *Medical Sociology*, pp. 335–370.

[33]U.S. Department of HEW, *Toward a Systematic Analysis of Health Care in the United States* (Washington, D.C.: U.S. Government Printing Office, 1972), p. 6.

[34]Mechanic, *Medical Sociology*, pp. 345–349.

However, these plans, as have already been suggested, have merely compounded existing difficulties. In the words of one analysis, "They are at one and same time the major cause of the runaway costs of the medical system, and a major source of power defending the status quo and preventing major reorganizations of the medical care system from occurring." These plans leave control of the system in the hands of health-care suppliers: it is the physicians and hospitals that decide what and how much treatment each patient needs. Moreover, it is the physicians and the hospitals that decide how much to charge; there are no restrictions on fees, because the insurance plans guarantee that they will be paid no matter how inflated they are. Thus the costs of health care keep going up. And as the above analysis noted,

> Meanwhile, in the face of rising health care costs, the cost of . . . health insurance has soared, too. As a result, an increasing number of people fall into no man's land—too rich for Medicaid, too young for Medicare, too poor to buy private health insurance, and certainly too poor to pay hospital bills.[35]

The Problems of Poverty

We have already suggested that lack of access to proper medical care causes higher rates of illness and death among the poor. Antonovsky, in his analysis of the relationship between class and illness, suggests that the problem of access has become even more significant for the health of the poor than in the past. Until the early twentieth century, the ill health of the poor was largely caused by infectious diseases, which were rampant in the crowded, unsanitary, and debilitating conditions in which they were forced to live. Though these conditions have not changed much, medical science today is able to control and cure infectious diseases much more effectively. Thus, except among the extremely poor (who rarely receive medical attention) and among the infants of the poor (who are usually in a weakened condition), infectious diseases by themselves no longer account for the tremendous differences in health between the poor and the nonpoor. Instead, as Antonovsky stated,

> Access to good medical care, preventive medical action, health knowledge, and limitation of delay in seeking treatment have become increasingly important in combating mortality, as chronic diseases have become the chief health enemy in the developed world. In these areas, lower class people may well be at a disadvantage.[36]

Antonovsky predicted, in fact, that as control of chronic diseases (cancer, for example) became more important, the differences between the health of the poor and the nonpoor would increase—that is, that the poor would have still higher rates of illness and death compared to the nonpoor.

Lee Rainwater, in his analysis of the relationship of class to ill health, suggests that lack of access to medical care is not the only factor that affects the health of the poor; just being poor promotes poor health. The poor, for example, cannot afford to eat properly, and so their bodies are likely to be weak. They often live in the most polluted areas, and are susceptible to respiratory diseases. They cannot afford proper housing, and are exposed to disease-carrying refuse and rodents. Perhaps most important, their lives are

[35]Ehrenreich and Ehrenreich, *The American Health Empire*, pp. 130–132.
[36]Antonovsky, "Class and the Chance for Life," p. 178.

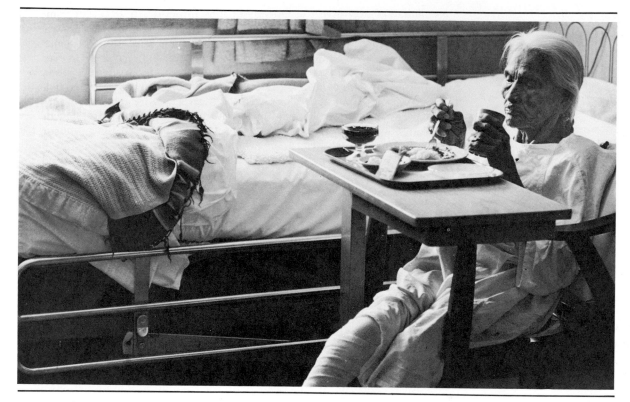

filled with stress—they are always worried about getting enough money to pay for essential needs. Such long-term stress can cause both physical and mental illnesses. It also makes it difficult to react to minor signs of ill health. A cough, for example, is likely to be dismissed if one doesn't have enough to eat; only a much worse cough will prompt a visit to a clinic, and by then it may be too late. The poor also seem to feel middle-aged earlier than the nonpoor. As such, the poor are likely to accept illness and disability as somehow natural—even in their thirties. Finally, the poor are frequently treated with contempt and hostility by the physicians and medical personnel whom they encounter, and they are therefore more likely to avoid professional treatment—either preventive or curative—becoming ill more frequently and remaining ill longer.[37] (See Chapter 7 for an additional discussion of poverty and health.)

Health care in the 1980s: Many of the aged need constant care which can only be provided at great expense in a hospital environment.
Woodfin Camp & Assoc.

Social Policy and Action

Recent public opinion polls suggest that a significant majority of Americans are now eager for changes in the delivery of health care. Although this is a long-standing sentiment—the clamor for government-mandated reform goes as far back as Theodore Roosevelt's presidency—the present national concern

[37]Lee Rainwater, "The Lower Class: Health, Illness and Medical Institutions," in Rainwater, *Inequality and Justice*, pp. 179–187.

over inflation may give the movement new impetus. In 1977, for example, Americans spent 8.6 percent of the GNP on health care, more than any other industrialized nation. Indications such as the infant mortality rate show that Americans are not getting the best possible return on their investment.[38]

While changing the health-care delivery system is a formidable task, it is complicated by the competing interests of consumers, labor, minorities, the medical profession, and the pharmaceutical, health-care, and insurance industries. Suggestions for solving the problem have ranged from socialized medicine to voluntary cost controls. Implicit in almost all the proposals has been an expansion of government's role in supervising and financing health services through alternative provider organizations or alternative financing systems.

Alternative Provider Organizations

Health Maintenance Organizations.   The Health Maintenance Organization (HMO) provides complete medical services to subscribers within a specific region who pay an annual fee to join. Members are entitled to all the medical services provided by the HMO, which may, depending on the plan, include everything from a vaccination to major surgery. The HMO is based on the concept of group practice: several doctors working together and sharing facilities and patients. General practitioners see all patients first and refer them to specialists only if their case warrants it.

HMOs were developed to correct two major problems in the present health-care system: high costs and lack of emphasis on preventive medicine. HMOs stress ambulatory care rather than hospitalization and generic drugs rather than expensive name brands. General practitioners, rather than more expensive specialists, are the primary physicians. Physical examinations, early detection and treatment, and innoculation are all emphasized to maintain health and avoid serious, costly illness.

Proponents claim that HMOs have been especially effective in curbing unnecessary hospitalization, tests, and surgery. Critics argue that they provide "assembly-line" care, are bogged down in bureaucratic red tape, and that their centralized location makes them inaccessible to many people, so that the best care is still provided to the educated and affluent members.

The first HMOs, Kaiser-Permanente and the Health Insurance Program of New York, were established in the 1930s. HMOs received a new boost from the Health Maintenance Act of 1973 which provided funds for establishing new HMOs, gave employees the right to choose HMOs over group insurance plans, and abolished numerous state restrictions against these programs.[39]

Planned Regional Health Systems

The National Planning and Resources Development Act of 1974 established Health Systems Agencies (HSAs) in every state to plan and administer local health services. This system is intended to remedy the economic and geographic problems that prevent equitable delivery of health care.

Like the HMOs, the HSAs emphasize preventive medicine and rely on staffs of general practitioners for primary care and referral. Unlike the HMOs,

[38]Richard J. Margolis, "National Health Insurance—The Dream Whose Time Has Come," in Schwartz and Kant, *Dominant Issues*, p. 508.

[39]David Mechanic, "The HMO: Background Considerations," in Schwartz and Kant, *Dominant Issues*, pp. 499–507.

they are financed through government subsidies and business and employee taxes. HSA opponents like to point out the similarities between HSAs and Great Britain's controversial National Health Service (NHS). This centrally organized, government subsidized system of socialized medicine has been providing service-on-demand in Great Britain since 1948. Although the NHS has vastly improved Britain's health care, its opponents say the costs have been prohibitive. In NHS's first year of operation, its expenses were double that of its estimated budget. It has also been attacked for impersonal care, for bureaucratic inefficiency, and waste. Many physicians appear dissatisfied with the system. The general practitioners, who form its backbone, recently threatened a catastrophic strike. Meanwhile, its critics insist, there is still a two-tiered system of health care, with the affluent receiving superior treatment from private, fee-for-service practitioners.[40]

Medicare and Medicaid.   Medicare, the system under which the government pays for the medical care of people over 65, is the culmination of a design for reform that began during Franklin Roosevelt's New Deal. More of the economic barriers to health care were lowered with the subsequent passage of Medicaid, which provides publicly subsidized health care for those below a certain income level. Although these programs have improved, the health of America's poor and elderly and have reinforced the belief in medical care as a human right, they have also been criticized by both liberals and conservatives for inefficiency and for contributing to inflation. One of the chief targets of criticism is the method of reimbursement used by both systems. This system, which allows providers to charge whatever is reasonable and customary, critics claim encourages price hikes and fraud. Since the passage of Medicare and Medicaid, medical costs have taken a quantum leap: prices have more than tripled and per-capita expenditures have increased by 250 percent. Despite these abuses and problems, Americans still seem to want government to take some action to curb health-care costs and improve services. Eighteen different bills, for example, were submitted to the 94th Congress, each offering a different solution to this problem.

National Health Insurance.   The proposals that attracted the widest support called for some form of national health insurance. The most sweeping of all is the Health Security Bill, sponsored by Senator Edward M. Kennedy and Representative James C. Corman; it calls for a federalized system of health care, managed by the Department of Health, Education and Welfare (HEW) and funded by payroll taxes and general revenues. The unique features of this proposal are its guarantee of comprehensive care for all Americans and its nationalized health care budget. Under this plan, the annual health-care budget cannot exceed the projected revenues allotted for it. If it does, the resulting burden would be borne by doctors and hospitals, who would have to reduce their fees, instead of their services, to balance the budget.

The Catastrophic Health Insurance and Medical Association Reform Act, sponsored by Senators Russell Long and Abraham Ribicoff, offers protection from the financial burden of serious illness. Under this program, financial subsidies begin after a patient has spent $2000 or 60 days in the hospital.

Alternative Financing Systems

[40]Coe, *Sociology of Medicine*, pp. 399–404.

Financing would come from payroll taxes, government sponsored insurance, and private insurance plans. Other proposed measures include the Comprehensive Health Insurance Plan, the National Health Care Services Reorganization and Financing Act, and the National Health Care Insurance Act. All of these provide relief from major medical expenditures and require patient cost-sharing; most would work through the insurance industry.[41]

Improving the Existing System

It seems likely that the present system of health-care delivery will require a complete overhaul before its inefficiency, inequity, and exorbitant costs can be remedied. Meanwhile, certain preliminary measures could make this system more responsive to America's current health-care needs. Some of the suggestions that have been offered include:

1. Expand outpatient facilities, so that illnesses can be detected and treated *before* hospitalization is required.

2. Build more medical schools and admit more applicants to insure an adequate supply of physicians.

3. Encourage medical schools to graduate more GPs to curb reliance on expensive specialists. Encourage medical students to become GPs through grants, fellowships, and other incentives.

4. Provide special training to make physicians more sensitive to the needs of minorities and the poor. Recruit more minority applicants to medical schools, since statistics indicate that these doctors usually practice among minority patients neglected by other physicians.

5. Train paramedics to relieve doctors of routine work, to provide preventive medical services, and to service regions without physicians. Many observers have suggested that the United States adopt the "barefoot doctor" program which has been highly successful in the Peoples' Republic of China. These barefoot doctors are laymen trained to provide basic medical services. They work in both the inner cities and in remote rural areas, performing simple diagnostic tests, administering innoculations, teaching nutrition and birth control. They are trained to diagnose illnesses and recognize serious symptoms for referral to physicians.[42]

6. Institute programs to attract physicians to practice in such underserviced areas as the inner cities and rural regions. Most doctors are now clustered in affluent areas, while many rural communities have no physicians at all.

7. Encourage insurance companies to refuse to pay unreasonable charges and to set lower maximum payments for doctor and hospital services.

8. Permit physicians to advertise their fees and services as other professionals—dentists and lawyers—do in many states. Competition, many people argue, is an excellent method of cost control.

Additional proposals involve improving the quality of health care. Senator Edward M. Kennedy has suggested, for example, all U.S. physicians

[41]Margolis, "National Health Insurance," pp. 514–517.
[42]Victor W. Sidel, "Medical Care in the People's Republic of China: An Example of Rationality," in Schwartz and Kant, *Dominant Issues*, pp. 477–489.

be required to take a national relicensing exam every three or four years. This will make it necessary for physicians to keep up with advances in medical knowledge, and will also make it easier to keep incompetent physicians from practicing.

An important step toward the monitoring of physicians' performance was taken in 1973 when Professional Standards Review Organizations (PSROs) were set up by federal amendments to the Social Security Act. The legislation provided that, starting in 1976, review boards composed of physicians would review the treatment given to all Medicare and Medicaid patients. Any physician treating such patients may have to register with a local PSRO; the PSRO approves or disapproves the physician's treatment of these patients. If a less expensive form of treatment can be used, the PSRO suggests it and costs are thus kept down. In addition, because the PSRO is made up entirely of physicians, proper treatment of Medicare and Medicaid patients has become much more likely.

Increasing the number of medical groups, which now are scattered throughout the country, would also do much to reduce costs and the possibility of mistreatment. A medical group generally consists of a GP or internist working and sharing facilities with a number of different specialists. Members of the group share the expenses of overhead and equipment, and can afford to charge lower fees. Because the physicians work together, they tend to monitor and learn from each other, reducing the chance of malpractice.

The Disabled and Handicapped

Although pitied and given some sympathy, the disabled and handicapped are regarded by American society as deviants and minorities. The one in eleven Americans who are blind, lame, deaf, mentally ill, mentally retarded, or otherwise physically disabled or handicapped make most of us uncomfortable, self-conscious, and angry. Because they do not conform to the American model or ideal, the disabled and handicapped are stigmatized as freaks, losers, partial persons, and the like. It is assumed, for example, that they are childlike and innately incapable and are frequently discriminated against at every turn.

America's handicapped have literally been a forgotten people. They have been excluded from work, school, and society, by both active discrimination and by the barriers imposed by a world designed for the able-bodied. Steps, curbs, narrow doorways and aisles—impassable obstacles to many of the disabled—are but a few of the aspects of everyday life that impede the physically handicapped.

The disabled suffer from the highest unemployment rate of any group—possibly as high as 40 percent of those who are able to work. In addition, many handicapped people are underemployed—assigned to low-level, low-paying jobs because employers and sometimes rehabilitation counselors are afraid to offer them challenges. In many instances, Social Security regulations keep the handicapped unemployed by limiting the amount of money they can earn and still retain benefits. As little as $200 a month in salary will cause a handicapped person to lose the government subsidy that is desperately needed for medical treatment or special attendants. For all these reasons, the majority of the handicapped exist at poverty levels. The 1970 Census indicated that the proportion of the disabled living in poverty was almost twice as high as that of the general population.[43]

Numerous studies have shown that when the disabled are hired, they usually dispel all the negative myths that surround them. An overwhelming majority prove to be dedicated, capable workers, they have only a slightly higher-than-average absentee rate, and their turnover rate is well below average. The disabled are neither slower nor less productive than other workers and have excellent safety records.[44]

There are an estimated 35 million physically handicapped Americans— and their number is growing. Vietnam War veterans added 490,000 to the disabled population. In addition, advances in medical science now permit many people to survive serious accidents, usually with handicaps. Technology is also making it possible for many disabled people, who would have been bedridden or housebound in the past, to enjoy new mobility and acquire new skills. Improved health care and prevention of disease have meant that more people than ever before are living to an old age—and incurring the disabilities that come with advanced years. (See Chapter 10.)

These handicapped people have emerged as a recognized minority. Like women and blacks, they are demanding an end to the discrimination that keeps them out of jobs and out of the mainstream of life. They are vigorously opposed to any attempt to place them in special programs or schools, except during the necessary phases of rehabilitation or therapy. Special programs,

[43]Sonny Kleinfeld, "The Handicapped: Hidden No Longer," *Atlantic*, vol. 240, no. 6 (December 1977), 90. Robert Bogdan and Douglas Bisklen, "Handicapism," *Social Policy* (March/April 1977), 155–160.

[44]Robert B. Nathanson, "Ideas for Action," *Harvard Business Review*, vol. 55, no. 3 (May-June 1977), 7.

Contestants in the Wheelchair Basketball Tournament prove that the physically handicapped needn't lead crippled lives.
UPI

they insist, are the ghettoes of the handicapped, and they refuse to be confined there any longer.

In 1973 Congress responded to their demands with the sweeping Rehabilitation Act which prohibited government agencies and contractors from discriminating against the handicapped and mandated affirmative action plans for their hiring and promotion. The Act also created a board to oversee the Architectural Barriers Act of 1968, which requires all new public facilities built with federal funds to be accessible to the disabled.

In 1977, the Rehabilitation Act received new clout when HEW Secretary Joseph P. Califano authorized regulations requiring all recipients of HEW funds to provide the handicapped with equal access to their employment or services—or lose their subsidies. The new regulations extended the term handicapped to include the disfigured, retarded, mentally ill, emotionally disabled, drug and alcohol addicted, and persons with histories of cancer and heart disease.

In practical terms, the HEW rulings mean that new buildings constructed with HEW grants must be equipped with such features as ramps and elevators. Old buildings had to be remodeled. Employers had to provide assistance for handicapped employees or potential employees, such as braille literature, telephone amplifiers, special parking or furniture. Public schools must "mainstream" or integrate handicapped students into regular classrooms. Officials estimated that it would cost more than $2.4 billion annually to implement the plan. Its supporters pointed out the substantial reduction in welfare costs that it would achieve.

The impact of the ruling has thus far been felt most strongly by educational institutions—from elementary schools to medical schools—many of which are both financially beleaguered and dependent on HEW for subsidies. It will cost approximately $2800 a year to educate a handicapped child in the public school system—twice that of a normal student. And HEW will be providing only a small portion of the necessary funds. The problems of handicapped children are enormous. There are approximately 8 million of them, 12 percent of the school-age population, and only 40 percent of this 8 million are now in special education classes. A million disabled children, it is estimated, do not attend school at all because their parents cannot afford private institutions and because the public schools either cannot accommodate or are physically inaccessible to them. The new regulations seem to guarantee their right to education.

On the other hand, the regulations pose complex problems beyond the question of who will pay the added costs of educating these children in the regular school system. Critics argue that mainstreaming will harm both the handicapped and the able-bodied. The handicapped, they say, will not get the attention they should from teachers untrained to cope with their special problems. They feel this situation will be particularly difficult with emotionally disturbed, learning disabled, or retarded children. Normal students, they contend, will suffer because the pace of learning will have to be slowed to accommodate the handicapped.

In some schools, where the regulations were implemented on schedule, September 1978, reports are encouraging. Teachers say that both the handicapped and the nonhandicapped have benefited from the experience. The program is still too new and too untested to draw firm conclusions.[45]

[45]Kleinfeld, "The Handicapped," p. 29.

While the struggle for equal educational opportunity continues, the disabled are also working, with special interest groups and large organizations like the Veteran's Administration, to battle job discrimination and to make the everyday life of the emerging handicapped more livable. Buses and subways that the handicapped can use, telephones and water fountains that they can reach, the right to enter restaurants and movie theaters in wheelchairs or with seeing-eye dogs—these are some of the everyday things they want for themselves. Perhaps most important is the campaign of the disabled to alter their own image. The civil rights' and women's movements have demonstrated the importance of image in fostering unconscious attitudes of discrimination. With this in mind, the handicapped want to replace the traditional advertising poster of the child on braces or crutches with pictures of competent, active handicapped people.

Prospects

As this book goes to press, it is still unclear which, if any, of the health bills before Congress will pass. There is, however, widespread agreement that the nation's health system needs to be reformed; and some new form of health financing—either through national health insurance or through a prepayment system—will eventually have to be passed. There is also a belated recognition on the part of the AMA that the shortage of GPs must be alleviated. As a result, medical schools are beginning to graduate more GPs; whether there will be enough of them to meet the need remains to be seen.

It is likely, in any case, that health and health care will remain social problems in the foreseeable future. Aspects of the American life style that contribute to illness—such as smoking and pollution—will not be eradicated overnight. And even if health services are made available to all, class and racial inequality in health care will continue to exist. As long as the poor and those who suffer the effects of discrimination are deprived in other areas of life, they will be deprived of proper health-care; it is difficult for those living outside the mainstream of society, with limited access to food, shelter, and comfort, to maintain optimum levels of physical and emotional health. No health-care system, however equitable and efficient, can cure the ills caused by poverty, prejudice, and discrimination.

One new problem that has recently begun to receive much-needed attention is how to control our new power over health and the life span. Advances in medical technology have raised many complex ethical questions: How should a limited number of organ transplants be allocated? Should abortion be mandatory if genetic defects are detected in the fetus? Indeed, should we allow abortion on demand? Who decides when to terminate life-prolonging efforts, or, in the common, inelegant phrase, when to "pull the plug"? If machines can keep people breathing and their hearts beating indefinitely, when does death occur? Under what conditions, if any, can experimentation on human subjects be allowed? It is obvious that new codes and guidelines will have to be developed to cope with these issues. Today, no clear standards for the medical and research industries exist in many complex, delicate areas. Experts testifying before a congressional committee in 1973 recommended that a national board of ethics be created to supervise all federally funded research on human subjects. Others suggest that local ethics boards be created to supervise the medical and research practices within a local area.[46] Physicians and researchers strongly resist such suggestions, fearing that they will lose their present freedom. It is therefore likely that a code of ethics, if one is ever developed, will come from within professional medical societies rather than from any outside regulatory agency.

Problems of Mental Health

The problems of physical health we have discussed seem serious and widespread, but mental illness, afflicting at least 10 percent of the population, is "America's primary health problem," according to the National Institute of Mental Health. Every year more than 6 million people, including perhaps half a million children, are treated for some kind of mental disorder. Nearly half are hospitalized, either in mental or in general hospitals. Most are discharged after a brief stay, many are long-term chronic patients, and others will be hospitalized until they die. Over 2 million patients are treated in outpatient clinics or by psychologists and psychiatrists in private practice.[47] Another 15 million who are not under any treatment suffer from some degree of mental disorder, often unrecognized as such. The total cost of all this, in tax money, private fees, losses to business through employee illness, and other expenses, is estimated to exceed 20 billion dollars per year.[48]

Clearly, mental health is a problem we cannot afford to neglect. It has not been ignored in professional circles; research as to its causes, and experiments in developing more effective treatment, have been proceeding for more than a century. Until recently, efforts at systematic, concerted programs foundered on public fear, ignorance, and apathy. Few wanted to know about the problem or were willing to spend the necessary money to solve it. But in recent years public awareness of the possibilities for helping the mentally ill has grown, aided by television programs, magazine articles, and books dealing with various aspects of mental health.

The Nature of Mental Health

Some of the language of mental disorder has become a familiar part of everyday vocabulary. We use the terms "neurotic," "psychotic," "paranoid," and perhaps "psychosomatic" to express judgments, usually unfavorable, about the behavior of other people. Those who, we feel, are convinced that their co-workers are out to get them are paranoid; others who keep their teenage children home from school every time they sneeze are neurotic. Sometimes we substitute more general colloquial terms, such as "spaced out," "uptight," or simply "sick." Whatever the terms we use, we are apt to have only a vague idea as to their precise meaning.

In part, this imprecision reflects the extreme difficulty in precisely diagnosing mental disorders. Whereas many physical illnesses have agreed-

---

[46]Amitai Etzioni, *Genetic Fix* (New York: Macmillan, 1973).

[47]U.S. Bureau of the Census, *Statistical Abstract of the United States, 1975* (Washington, D.C.: U.S. Government Printing Office, 1976), p. 82.

[48]*The High Cost of Mental Illness* (pamphlet) (New York: National Association for Mental Health, n.d.).

upon determinants whose presence can be revealed by objective tests, the identification of mental disorders largely depends on behavioral symptoms, and on the relative importance assigned to them by the person making the diagnosis. In a few cases, a specific disorder has been found to have a specific organic cause; generally, however, there is less consensus about mental disorders. Furthermore, an erroneous medical diagnosis often does not have the same consequence as an erroneous psychiatric diagnosis. A person who is told that the diagnosis of heart disease was incorrect feels relieved; a person who is told that the diagnosis of schizophrenia was incorrect often still remains labeled as mentally ill, no matter what the doctor says. Moreover, the diagnosis of mental illness—correct or incorrect—carries a greater stigma than a diagnosis of physical illness. Senator Thomas Eagleton, for example, was forced, by public demand, to forego his candidacy for vice-president in 1972 after it was revealed that he had undergone shock treatments for depression; Franklin Roosevelt, on the other hand, was elected president four times even though he had had polio.

This is not to say that the diagnosis of mental disorders is useless or impossible. Practical experience has shown that certain sets of symptoms seem to occur together, and numerous tests have been developed to indicate a patient's underlying motivations. These tests plus personal sensitivity and patience can help trained, experienced, and skilled practitioners to learn much about a patient's problems. But in the nature of the process, much more depends on the orientation of the practitioners than is usually thought to be true for medical doctors. How do these practitioners decide which symptoms are significant? For that matter, how do they decide what *is* a symptom? What fundamentally, do they believe a mental disorder is?

There are two, and perhaps three, different ways to answer this last question, and each has its implications for prevention and treatment.

Mental Illness.   The most familiar school of thought holds that a mental disorder is properly considered an illness. That is, a mental disorder is primarily a disturbance of one's normal personality analogous to the physiological disturbance caused by physical disease, and is to be remedied primarily by treating the person affected. Attention is centered on the pathology—the anxieties, hostilities, maladjustments, and other tensions underlying abnormal behavior—and the aim of treatment is to relieve or remove these personal tensions, on the assumption that once this is done, patients will be able to function adequately in their external lives.

The illness concept, or medical model, of mental disorder arose in reaction to the older notion that the mentally disturbed were mad, possessed, blameworthy, to be locked up, beaten, or killed. It made possible serious and scientific investigation of possible causes and cures of mental disorder, and was responsible for the development of practically all the systems of mental health care and therapeutic treatment in existence today—systems which are still largely in the hands of medically oriented personnel. It has helped to lessen, at least among the sophisticated, the stigma and shame of mental disorder, since, after all, "illness can happen to anyone."

Nevertheless, the concept of mental disorder as "illness" has certain disadvantages. In concentrating on individuals and their immediate environment (often their childhood environment), it tends to disregard the wider social environment as a possible, major source of difficulty. In addition, especially for hospitalized patients, the "illness" concept can lead to impractical criteria of "recovery"—people may have gained considerable insight into their inner tensions, but still be unable to function adequately when they return to the outer tensions of a perhaps unsatisfactory home, job, or society. Conversely, people who no longer have any abnormal behavioral symptoms may remain hospitalized because it is felt that their "illness" may resurface.

Deviance.   The concept of mental disorder as illness holds that something about a person is abnormal, and that the fundamental problem lies in his or her interior emotional makeup, which was twisted, repressed, or otherwise wrongly developed as a result of genetic or chemical factors or events early in life. While this seems to explain some mental disorders, a feeling has gradually developed that other factors need to be taken into account, especially the constant pressures exerted by society. Out of this has grown the view that mental disorder represents a departure from certain institutionalized expectations of society—that it is a form of social deviance or maladjustment.

It is worthwhile to emphasize the slightly differing implications of the two terms "maladjustment" and "deviance." The first, with the prefix "mal–," which means "bad," assumes the rightness of the norms being violated; it is in the violators that something is wrong, something that is perhaps not their fault but that for their own sake needs to be corrected, or "readjusted." "Deviance" is much more dependent on how society regards the particular norms that have been violated. Here the idea of *residual deviance*, formulated by Thomas Scheff, may be useful. According to Scheff,[49] most social conventions are recognized as being such, and their violation carries fairly clear, often moral, labels: people who steal another's wallets are thieves, people who act haughtily toward the poor are snobs, and so on. But there is a large residual area of social convention that is so completely taken for granted that it is assumed to be more or less part of human nature. In Scheff's example, it seems natural for people holding a conversation to face each other, rather than to look away. Violating this norm seems frightening since it seems contrary to human nature. After all, it is perfectly "natural" for wallet-thieves to want money, they merely acquire it illegally. But what natural reason could there be for someone to stare at the ceiling while talking to people, or to retreat to the far side of the room and shout at them? There must be something wrong with such people—they must have mental problems.

Scheff suggests that this residual deviance occurs in many, even most, people at one time or another, and usually passes without treatment. What causes it, in some cases, to become a stabilized mental disorder is that *society decides to label it as one*. When this happens, the *role* of "mentally ill person" is offered to deviants. Since they are often confused and frightened by their own behavior during a time of stress, and by other people's reactions to it, they are apt to be particularly impressionable, and may accept the offered role. Once this happens, it becomes difficult for them to change their behavior and return to their "normal" role.

Scheff admits that this theory is not fully developed, but he supports it with certain evidence from the military:

[49]Thomas J. Scheff, "The Role of the Mentally Ill and the Dynamics of Mental Disorder," *Sociometry* (1963), pp. 436-453.

The experience of battlefield psychiatrists can be interpreted to support the hypothesis that residual deviance is usually transitory. Glass reports that combat neurosis is often self-terminating if the soldier is kept with his unit and given only the most superficial medical attention . . . [But] soldiers who are removed from their unit to a hospital . . . often go on to become chronically impaired. That is, their deviance is stabilized by the labeling process, which is implicit in their removal and hospitalization.

If this is so, behavior considered to show mental disorder will vary from one society or culture to another. More important, mental disorder may actually be caused by some of the attempts to cure it. As Levine and Levine point out, commenting on Scheff:

The mental health professions, and psychiatry in particular, are viewed as contributing to the development of mental illness by providing the doctor role. In effect, by treating a patient in a separate treating institution, the doctors certify that the patient is indeed a patient and is indeed mentally ill.[50]

A further implication of Scheff's thesis, again emphasized by Levine and Levine, is that by regarding residual deviance as evidence of mental illness, the psychiatrist may be creating personal conflict and attempting to hold up social change.

Not only is the mental health professional the one who identifies the deviant; in the very doing he confirms the validity of the social norm violated. . . . In periods of relative social stability, there may be little problem in the mental health professional acting to confirm social norms. However, in periods of acute social change, the mental health professional may contribute to the exacerbation of the dislocations people endure by becoming part of the process which induces and maintains cultural lag. The mental health professional may be confirming social norms which no longer have validity in terms of the way people actually live in a changing society.[51]

The point of the concept of mental disorder as deviance is that such disorder may be the function of one's inability to comply with societal expectations, and of the label which society attaches to those who deviate.

Problems in Living. A third approach to the nature of mental disorder is offered by Thomas Szasz, a psychiatrist who has caused considerable controversy by contending that mental illness is a myth.[52] By this, he means not that the social and psychological disturbances commonly called mental illness do not exist, but that it is dangerously misleading to call them illnesses. Rather, he believes, they should be regarded as manifestations of unresolved problems in living.

The significance of Szasz's basic argument is that it concerns justice and individual liberty. As he sees it, a diagnosis of mental disorder involves a value judgment, based on the behavioral norms held by the psychiatrist; and to call

[50]Murray Levine and Adeline Levine, "The Climate of Change," in *Clinic, Court, School and Community: A Social History of Helping Services,* ed. Murray Levine and Adeline Levine (Englewood Cliffs, N.J.: Prentice-Hall, 1970).

[51]Levine and Levine, "The Climate of Change."

[52]Thomas S. Szasz, *The Myth of Mental Illness: Foundations of a Theory of Mental Illness* (New York: Harper & Row, 1971).

it illness allows the doctor to use medicine to correct what are essentially social, ethical, or legal deviations.

Not only is this logically absurd, claims Szasz, it is dangerous. In "Justice in the Therapeutic State," he discusses the divergent concepts of the Legal State and the Therapeutic State. The business of the Legal State is "the maintenance of peace through a system of just laws justly administered." The Legal State has no claim on its citizens beyond what is set down in the law; whatever else citizens do is none of the State's business. By contrast:

> In the scientific-technological conception of the State, therapy is only a means, not an end. The goal of the Therapeutic State is universal health, or at least unfailing relief from suffering. This untroubled state of man and society is a quintessential feature of the medical-therapeutic perspective on politics. Conflict among individuals, and especially between the individual and the State, is invariably seen as a symptom of "illness" or psychopathology, and the primary function of the State is accordingly the removal of such conflict by "therapy"— "therapy" imposed by force, if necessary. It is not difficult to recognize in this imagery of the Therapeutic State the old Inquisitorial, or the more recent Totalitarian, concept of the State, now clothed in the garb of psychiatric treatment.[53]

In short, Szasz believes, liberty can be unwittingly sacrificed by a too great concern for the "cure" of "mental illness."

Classification of Mental Disorders

There have been many attempts to classify mental disorders, but none has been fully satisfactory. As was pointed out previously, diagnosis of these disorders is a complicated matter, depending largely on the surface evidence of emotional and behavioral symptoms, which rarely occur in clear-cut, easily distinguishable patterns. The traditional medical model of mental illness distinguishes certain major categories, in which different types of emotional disturbances are grouped. Labeling theory, on the other hand, sees such categories as reflecting the biases of those who make them up, rather than any objective set of behaviors. We will discuss both schools of thought below.

The Illness Model

Here we shall briefly described four of the major categories in the illness model:

Neurosis.   The term "neurosis" refers to a general type of disorder in which the individual suffers from severe anxiety but continues to try to function in the real world, usually through the use of various subterfuges or defense mechanisms. These may hamper normal activities—for example, constant hand-washing or repeated, objectively needless checking and rechecking of minor calculations. However, most persons who are neurotic never seek treatment, because they can usually still function somewhat realistically.[54]

[53]Thomas S. Szasz, "Justice in the Therapeutic State," *Comprehensive Psychiatry*, 11 (1970), 433–494.

[54]John A. Clausen, "The Sociology of Mental Disorder," in *Handbook of Medical Sociology*, ed. Howard E. Freeman, *et al.* (Englewood Cliffs, N.J.: Prentice-Hall, 1972), p. 172.

Psychosis.   Psychosis is a condition in which a person's mental functioning is severly impaired. *Schizophrenia,* the most common, varies considerably in its symptoms. Schizophrenics may withdraw from reality or distort it to suit themselves; their emotional responses may be either apathetic or inappropriate and inconsistent; their thought and speech may be disorganized, and they may make bizarre associations of ideas; they may suffer from delusions or hallucinations; they may believe that they, or a part of them, are nonexistent or dead. One or another type of symptom may predominate at different times in the same person. *Manic-depressive illness* is another form of psychosis in which the sufferer shows moods of extreme excitement or depression.

Organic Psychosis.   This is psychotic behavior resulting not from some emotional difficulty but from damage to the central nervous system. One of the most common forms is *senile psychosis*, believed to result from a diminished oxygen supply to the brain associated with cerebral arteriosclerosis in advanced age. *Alcoholic psychosis*, often found in long-term alcoholics, is another organic psychosis. In rare cases, infection or tumor of the brain, or repeated injury to the head, may cause organic psychosis.

Psychosomatic Illness.   Probably because of the physical tension created by fear and anxiety, or because of the chemical secretions induced in the body by these emotions, continued emotional stress can result in physical illness. These psychosomatic disorders involve genuine organic harm. Common forms are headaches, stomachaches, backaches, ulcers, high blood pressure, and allergies. They may be learned, perhaps unconsciously, as defenses against specific threats; a person who dislikes parties, for example, but does not quite want to admit it, may develop a headache whenever a party threatens.

Labeling Theory   As we noted at the beginning of this chapter, just as some physical illnesses may be culturally defined, such is the case for certain mental disorders. The medical model assumes that patients present symptoms, that those symptoms comprise diagnosable categories of mental illness, and that we may distinguish the mentally healthy from the mentally unhealthy. But there is a growing belief that at least some psychiatric diagnoses of mental illness are pigeonholes into which certain behaviors are arbitrarily placed.[55] Szasz believes, for example, that the customary psychiatric diagnoses are not distinct categories of diseases, but rather labels describing behavior that is contrary to accepted social and psychological norms.

The diagnosis of schizophrenia, according to labeling theorists, has been particularly misused. Although there is little agreement about its origins, causes, and symptoms, it is the most commonly used diagnosis for severe mental illness. To labeling theorists, this suggests that diagnoses of mental illness tend to reflect cultural values, not scientific analysis. Persons are not "schizophrenic" in the sense that they manifest definite symptoms, but that their behavior violates society's norms and expectations. For example, a person who sees visions might be considered perfectly normal, even admirable, in many cultures, although we would probably regard him or her as disturbed.

[55]See T. R. Sarbin, *Psychology Today*, vol. 6, no. 18 (1972); and E. Schur, *American Journal of Sociology*, vol. 75, no. 309 (1969).

One recent study comparing Germans and Americans reflected the degree to which culture influences the perception of mental illness. In this study, German psychiatrists, laymen, and even mental patients tended to hold the same concept of mental illness; it is an organic, probably incurable problem. Similar American groups all tended to view mental illness as curable and related to environment and experiences. Both groups of psychiatrists, although they had been thoroughly trained, tended to reflect the concepts of their society, more than that of established scientific thinking.[56]

The problem with labeling people mentally ill is threefold: it makes us perceive certain behavior as "sick," something to be eliminated rather than understood; it gives public agencies the right to incarcerate people against their will simply for not conforming; and it causes these people to define themselves as rule-breakers and undesirables, and allows them to fulfill that image.

Many studies have demonstrated the influence of societal factors on a diagnosis of mental illness and the vagueness of such a diagnosis. Rosenhan, in a study we shall describe more fully later, found that psychologists and psychiatrists on the staffs of several mental hospitals were unable to determine accurately which of the people they interviewed were mentally healthy or unhealthy.[57] Greenley found that the attitudes of the families of patients in a mental hospital were critical factors in how the illnesses of these patients were defined. If the family insisted that the patient be released, the psychiatrist in charge would generally agree. The patient, upon discharge, would then be defined in the doctor's conversation and in official records as "well enough to leave." In cases where there were no pressures for a patient to be released, the patient generally stayed in the hospital, defined as "too sick to leave."[58]

This drawing, done by a schizophrenic patient, captures the frightening and distorted reality of the psychotically ill.
UPI

Mental Disorder and Social Structure

Sociologists try to investigate the relationship between social factors and the incidence of mental disorders. For instance: Is mental disorder associated with social class? Does it occur more frequently in urban centers than in rural areas or suburbs? Among what age group is it most prevalent? Would changes in social conditions preclude or alleviate certain mental disorders?

The study of these relationships, however, is complicated by the difficulty of ascertaining the prevalence of mental disorder. We can count the number of patients in mental hospitals, and, somewhat less accurately, those receiving treatment in clinics and other outpatient facilities. It is far more difficult, however, to obtain reliable statistics about the number being treated in private practice. Moreover, any number of persons who would qualify as emotionally disturbed are not under treatment at all, and so do not appear in most estimates of mental disorders. Consequently, any statistics on treated mental disorder must be regarded as providing only a very rough estimate of the total number of people suffering from such problems. Nevertheless,

[56]J. Marshall Townsend, "Cultural Conceptions, Mental Disorders, and Social Roles: A Comparison of Germany and America," *American Sociological Review*, vol. 40, no. 6 (December 1975) 739–751.

[57]D. L. Rosenhan, "On Being Insane in Insane Places," *Science*, vol. 179, no. 4070 (January 19, 1973), 250–258.

[58]James R. Greenley, "Alternative Views of the Psychiatrist's Role," *Social Problems*, vol. 20, no. 2 (Fall 1972), pp. 252–262.

sociologists have been able to establish several tentative conclusions about the relationship between mental disorders and social structure.

Social Class and Mental Disorder

Much scientific knowledge originated in folk wisdom and common sense. Long before sociologists began to make systematic studies of social conditions and mental disorder, the connection between the two had been recognized. It was only in the 1930s, however, that a serious sociological study of this relationship began, and while the results are not in perfect agreement, they offer some useful information.

One of the earliest studies investigated the residential pattern for 35,000 hospitalized mental patients from Chicago. The highest rates of mental disorder were found near the center of the city, where the population was poor, of very mixed background, and highly mobile. While this number included many cases of organic psychosis, due to syphilis and alcoholism in the "skid row" districts, it also included a significantly high rate of schizophrenia throughout the area. Conversely, the lowest rates of mental disorder were found in stable residential areas of higher socioeconomic status. Manic-depressive psychoses, however, were more randomly distributed than schizophrenia. The authors concluded that the seriously disorganized character of life in the central city was largely responsible for the high incidence of personal disorganization and mental illness.[59]

A later study sought to determine the relationship between social class and treated mental illness in New Haven, Connecticut.[60] Whereas the Chicago study only included hospitalized patients, the New Haven researchers obtained reasonably complete data on clinic and private patients as well. Using a socioeconomic scale running from class I (highest) to class V (lowest), they determined that the *incidence* (rate of occurrence in a year of new cases) and *prevalence* (number of cases existing on a given date) of psychosis were significantly higher in class V than in the other four classes. Schizophrenia was the most common psychosis in all classes, but it was especially prevalent in class V. The study also revealed that the types of treatment and opportunities for rehabilitation available to the lower classes were much less satisfactory than those for the upper classes, which may have contributed to the proliferation of schizophrenia in class V. Another possible factor is that "the same set of presenting symptoms is diagnosed as more severe when the patient is perceived . . . to be a working class person than when he is seen as middle class."[61] Such inconsistency in diagnosis could have inflated the figures for class V. (See Figure 2-2.)

A third study, by William Rushing, which tended to confirm the relationship between mental disorder and social class included a relatively large number of cases occurring over an extended interval. Rushing studied 4,650 males admitted for the first time to mental hospitals in Washington, D.C., between 1954 and 1956. He found that the rate of hospitalization for lower-class males was higher than that for all others; that hospitalization

---

[59]Robert E. L. Faris and H. Warren Dunham, *Mental Disorders in Urban Areas* (Chicago: University of Chicago Press, 1938).

[60]August B. Hollingshead and Frederick C. Redlich, *Social Class and Mental Illness: A Community Study* (New York: Wiley, 1958).

[61]See S. M. Miller and Elliot G. Mishler, "Social Class, Mental Illness, and American Psychiatry: An Expository Review," *Milbank Memorial Fund Quarterly* 37 (April 1959), 1–26.

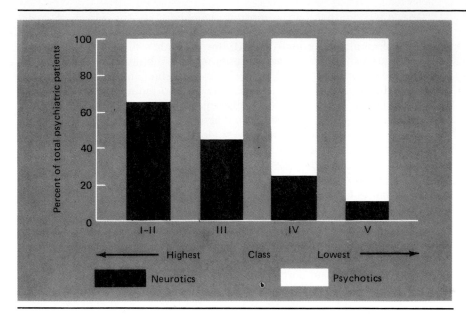

Figure 2-2

Percentage of Neurotics and Psychotics among Total Psychiatric Patients, by Class

Source: August B. Hollingshead and Frederick C. Redlich, *Social Class and Mental Illness: A Community Study,* © 1958, John Wiley & Sons. Reprinted by permission of John Wiley & Sons, Inc.

varied inversely with class; and that while the rate increased steadily with each drop in social class, the increase from the next-to-lowest to the lowest class was disproportionately large. Rushing considered that the high incidence in the lowest class might be explained by the frequent contact that members of this class have with the courts, welfare workers, and other officials who can refer them for hospitalization; moreover, they are less likely to be protected, tolerated, or financially supported by their families, to whom they have become a burden.[62]

All of these studies, then, agree that psychosis in general, and schizophrenia in particular, are much more common at the lowest socioeconomic level. They do not indicate, however, whether most of these schizophrenics originated in class V, or whether they drifted down to it as their disorder increased. In other words, they fail to make clear whether low socioeconomic status is primarily a cause or an effect of serious mental disorder. One other study bears on this point.

The Midtown Manhattan Study went beyond treatment to include a random sample of 1,660 adult residents of Manhattan's midtown area.[63] The researchers found that almost 23 percent were significantly impaired in mental functions, including many persons not under treatment. One of the factors investigated was the socioeconomic status, not only of the subjects, but also of their parents. Among subjects considered seriously impaired in their mental functioning, twice as many had lower-class as upper-class parents. Among those considered healthy, more than twice as many had upper-class parents. This suggests a definite influence of socioeconomic status on the mental health of children.

[62]William Rushing, "Two Patterns in the Relationship Between Social Class and Mental Hospitalization," *American Sociological Review* 34 (August 1969), 533–541.

[63]Leo Srole, *et al., Mental Health in the Metropolis: The Midtown Manhattan Study,* rev. ed. (New York: Harper & Row, 1975).

One question that has interested sociologists is the effect of social mobility—movement from one socioeconomic level to another—on the incidence of mental disorders. The Midtown Manhattan Study suggested a stronger relationship of downward than of upward mobility to severe mental disorder. However, in a research review, Robert Kleiner and Seymour Parker[64] distinguish between *social mobility* (actual achieved mobility of the individual) and *mobility orientation* (the discrepancy between the individual's aspirations and status). They suggest that orientation is significantly more related to mental disorder than mobility alone. Presumably, those who feel they should have attained a higher (or a lower) status are more likely to become disturbed than those who accept their status, whatever it may be. Kleiner and Parker caution, however, that unrealistic aspirations (high or low) may be a result of mental disorder as well as a cause of it.

Social Class and Treatment. We have already mentioned Rushing's speculation that lower-class patients are more likely to be hospitalized, because they are more often in contact with the courts, welfare workers, and others likely to think in terms of treatment by hospitalization. The New Haven study seems to support this. Among the lowest class, 52 percent of the psychotic patients were referred for treatment by the police and courts and 20 percent by social agencies; whereas in the highest class over 70 percent were referred by themselves or by family and friends.

Even when lower-class people actively seek treatment, their socioeconomic position may be against them. A study by Jerome Myers and Leslie Schaffer of class differences in a community clinic illustrates this. The clinic in question, which treated mainly neurotics, had a system of nominal and scaled fees, so that, in theory, it should have been equally available to everyone. And, in fact, persons from all but class I did apply for treatment. However, of the class V persons who applied, only about one-third were recommended for acceptance by the interviewing staff, compared to about four-fifths in class IV and nine-tenths in classes II and III. Moreover, lower-class persons who were accepted were likely to be treated for shorter periods and by less-qualified personnel—psychiatrists in training, or medical students taking a four-week course—than were the upper-class patients. Myers and Schaffer suggest that some of this may have resulted from communication and value differences— that the psychiatrists, who were mainly from classes I and II, found it difficult to relate effectively to class IV and V patients. The staff is reported to have found that these applicants were often "not psychologically minded" or "lacked motivation for psychotherapy." The authors suggest that "perhaps psychiatrists need to acquire new symbols and values in dealing with lower-class patients; or perhaps new approaches are necessary to bring psychotherapy to such persons."[65]

It is not unreasonable to suppose that class differences in treatment would affect recovery rates. A ten-year follow-up of the New Haven study reported on the 1960 treatment status of all patients included in the original sample. It was found that among those who had been hospitalized in 1950, more lower-class than upper-class patients remained hospitalized in 1960.

[64]Robert J. Kleiner and Seymour Parker, "Goal Striving, Social Status, and Mental Disorder," *American Sociological Review* 28 (April 1963), 169–203.

[65]Jerome K. Myers and Leslie Schaffer, "Social Stratification and Psychiatric Practice: A Study of an Outpatient Clinic," *American Sociological Review* 19 (June 1954), 307–310.

Particularly low rates of release were found for those who had received primarily custodial care, and for state hospitals, as opposed to patients of private or veterans' hospitals. Members of the lower-class, of course, are likely to fall into the categories with low rates of release. The authors also suggest that social factors in the community are partly responsible for the different release rates: Middle- and upper-class families are more apt to have resources for consultation and outpatient treatment of family members who still require some amount of care and supervision, and, therefore, may be more willing to take them back.[66]

It seems clear that whether or not lower-class persons are in greater danger of becoming emotionally disturbed, once they have become so, their chances for quality treatment and eventual recovery are substantially lower than those of their upper- and middle-class counterparts.

Urbanization

Cities have always had a rather bad press in America. It is one of our cultural predispositions to believe that most of what ails city dwellers can be remedied by getting them off the streets and into the country. Hence, it is not surprising that we tend to assume a connection between city life and mental disorder. Unfortunately, since there has been little research on mental disorder comparing urban and nonurban areas, no conclusive test of the assumption is yet available. Investigation is rendered more difficult because mental disorder is more likely to be diagnosed and treated where facilities are readily accessible—which usually means in and around cities. Studies of treated mental disorder, therefore, can only be used with great caution for urban-rural comparison.

The Midtown Manhattan Study, the major urban study dealing with how mental disorder is distributed among a general population, revealed a high percentage of disturbance within an adult sample. Only about 18 percent of the respondents were rated as "well"; roughly 60 percent showed mild to moderate symptoms of disorder, and slightly over 20 percent were significantly impaired in their functioning. However, a study of the rural Hutterite communities of Montana, the Dakotas, and Canada revealed about the same rate of hospitalized mental illness as in New York City[67]. The Hutterites differed from the usual urban group by having a higher proportion of manic-depressive than schizophrenic individuals; and they tended to keep their mentally ill at home rather than in hospitals. Other studies have suggested that it is not urban life *per se*, but the deteriorated quality of life which often develops in the central city that creates a high level of mental disorder—the dirt, noise, transportation problems, inadequate housing, and so on.[68]

Other Social Factors

Other factors which have been investigated for their relationship to mental disorder include race and sex. Studies have found, for example, that there are proportionately about 35 percent more blacks in mental hospitals than

---

[66]Jerome K. Meyers, Lee L. Bean, and Max P. Pepper, "Social Class and Psychiatric Disorders: A Ten Year Follow-up," *Journal of Health and Social Behavior* (Summer 1965), pp. 74-79.

[67]Joseph W. Eaton and Robert J. Weil, *Culture and Mental Disorders* (New York: Free Press, 1955).

[68]Jonathan Freeman, "The Effects of Crowding on Human Performance and Social Behavior," in *Contemporary Studies in Psychology*, ed. F. J. Mcgulgan and Paul J. Woods (Englewood Cliffs, N.J.: Prentice-Hall, 1972) pp. 195–219.

whites.[69] Such differences can largely be explained in terms of factors we have already described: Blacks (and poor people, a large number of whom are black) are much more likely to be seen as requiring hospitalization rather than whites, who are seen as best suited for psychotherapy. Blacks are also much more likely to deal with social agencies, including mental health officials. Finally, blacks are more likely than whites to live in deprived urban environments.

Scott's review of research on the social-psychological correlates of mental illness mentions findings that blacks have a higher incidence of psychosis than whites, but that among blacks there is less association between psychosis and low-prestige occupations.[70] The different relationship between occupational status and psychosis for blacks and for whites in America can be explained in part by a lesser importance attached to upward social mobility in the traditional black society. After all, when most middle-class jobs were closed to blacks by the very color of their skin, black people with any steady job could feel that they were proving their worth fairly well. However, most blacks today are refusing to accept the lower rank long assigned to them by American culture, and are aspiring to opportunities long enjoyed by the dominant white majority. It may be expected that some types of disorder will increase among blacks as their aspirations outstrip their present achievements, pushing them to strive for more education, better jobs, and social acceptance. And some of the most successfully mobile blacks may suffer most, by being cut off from their black-culture background.

Women and Mental Disorders.   According to Phyllis Chesler, women have much higher rates of admission to mental hospitals than men, and also have much higher rates of depression.[71] Chesler suggests that the nature and incidence of mental disorder among women are a reflection of women's secondary status and restricted roles in our society. Women are expected to conform to rigidly defined standards of behavior—to be passive, dependent, and emotional, for example, in accordance with traditional feminine roles. Women are therefore more likely than men to find their roles restrictive and to become depressed if they cannot conform to them. Also, because the range of behaviors they are permitted is narrow, women are more likely than men to behave in ways that are considered unacceptable—especially to men. Since mental health professionals are predominantly male, women who behave in nontraditional ways are more likely to be defined as mentally disturbed. (See Chapter 8.)

Chesler cites one study in which mental health clinicians were asked to identify healthy male traits, healthy female traits, and healthy adult traits. It was found that most clinicians hold different standards of mental health for men and women, and that these standards followed traditional sex-role stereotypes. Thus, healthy women were considered to be unaggressive, submissive, excitable, and vain. Other studies, cited by Chesler, confirm that such attitudes are indeed acted upon by mental health professionals. For example, it was found that the major difference between female ex-mental patients who were rehospitalized and those who were not was that the rehospitalized patients had refused to perform their domestic "duties"—

---

[69]Seham, *Blacks and American Medical Care*, p. 11.

[70]William A. Scott, "Social Psychological Correlates of Mental Illness and Mental Health," *Psychological Bulletin* 55 (March 1958), 65, 72–87.

[71]Phyllis Chesler, *Women and Madness* (New York: Avon, 1972).

cleaning, cooking, and the like. Females were also more likely to be called schizophrenics for behavior that was considered acceptable in men. In a study of depression among middle-aged women, Bart found that women who accepted their traditional female roles became depressed when these roles were no longer useful—when children grew up and left home, for example.[72] It is likely that as the social climate changes, fewer women will feel required to fulfill traditional expectations.

The Treatment of Mental Disorders

Having considered the nature and some of the causes of mental disorder, we now consider the matter of treatment—the principal techniques, and the social institutions through which these are made available. A brief sketch of the history of mental health care will enable us to understand the picture today.

[72]Pauline B. Bart, "Depression in Middle-Aged Women," in *Women in Sexist Society*, ed. Vivian Gornick and Barbara K. Moran (New York: Basic Books, 1971), pp. 163–186.

As long as patients do not cause trouble, they may be left largely to their own devices in the bare wards of many huge, understaffed mental institutions.
Jerry Cooke/Photo Researchers, Inc.

The Historical Background

It is only recently that mental disturbance has been considered an illness which could be cured. For centuries people held the Medieval notion that mental aberration was a sign of sin or of some supernatural influence. A decisive change began during the French Revolution when Philippe Pinel, a physician, unchained the patients in mental asylums and proved that they could respond positively to kindness and concern. Later in the United States, the humanitarian reformers Dorothea Dix and Clifford Beers, who had been a mental patient himself, fought for humane treatment of the mentally disturbed.

The emergence of professional social casework in the 1920s gave further impetus to public support of mental health care. But it was the Depression of the 1930s that forced society to admit that mental disorders were often the result of unhealthy social forces. World War II brought increased awareness of emotional health when many psychiatrists were trained and mobilized to treat soldiers suffering from the stress and horror of combat. The government began to devote more money to research and treatment of mental problems, and in 1946 the National Mental Health Act was passed, followed three years later by the establishment of the National Institute of Mental Health.

Recently, there has been a shift from the construction of mental hospitals to an emphasis on outpatient care and treatment in community health centers. The development of psychotropic drugs that control mood and behavior has permitted many patients to return to their communities. This has had some positive effects, but has also unleashed a flood of new problems for the mentally disturbed and for the people who now have to live with the disturbed. The mental health establishment and the government are still attempting to solve this problem.

Modern Approaches

The scientific treatment of mental disorder began with attention to the individual sufferer. Despite our more recent realization of the importance of social factors, the traditional individual methods, and variations of them, continue to be employed, whether in the hospital and private-office framework or in the context of the new community orientation. We shall look briefly at several of the main techniques of therapy, then consider the treatment structure itself, and some of the ways in which it can facilitate, or impede, the patient's recovery. It should be stressed that most modern therapists do not restrict themselves to any one school or approach, but rather use a variety of methods to suit the special needs of each patient.

Psychotherapy. Most major types of treatment fall into the general category of psychotherapy. With this approach, patients are helped to understand the underlying reasons for their problems, and in the light of that understanding, try to work out a solution. The process involves some form of personal interaction between the patient and the therapist or between patients in groups. Some of the major approaches to psychotherapy include:

- Psychoanalysis—Developed by Sigmund Freud in the late nineteenth century, psychoanalysis seeks to uncover unconscious motives, memories and fears that prevent the patient from functioning normally. Patients may use a number of avenues of exploration and discovery, including dreams and free associations.

• Client-centered therapy—Developed by Carl Rogers in the 1940s, this approach emphasizes current problems rather than unconscious motives and past experiences. Unlike psychoanalysis, the patient sets the course of the therapy, while the therapist provides support.

• Group therapy—This popular and recent innovation provides a forum in which people can solve their problems through interaction with one another. Some therapy groups are led by professionals, while others are organized by someone who has experienced the same problems of the patients—for example, Alcoholics Anonymous, Weight Watchers, or Gamblers Anonymous. Another important type of group therapy is family therapy in which family members work with a trained professional to overcome their difficulties.

Hypnosis, Shock Treatment, and Chemotherapy. In addition to therapy, other forms of treatment may be used. Sometimes these treatments may be combined with one another or with some form of psychotherapy. The most commonly used are:

• Hypnosis—which may help patients to remember deeply repressed but significant memories that may be blocking their progress.

• Shock treatment—is an electric shock which produces a convulsion and brief unconsciousness. Although frightening and potentially dangerous, it has produced dramatic results with deeply depressed and some schizophrenic patients.

• Chemotherapy—may include a variety of drugs from mild tranquilizers to anti-depressants. It is generally believed that chemotherapy should be used in conjunction with some form of therapy, since drugs alone can rarely effect significant and long-term changes in behavior.

Behavior Modification. The theory behind psychotherapy holds that unacceptable behavior is the result of a maladjusted personality. Another school of thought takes the reverse position—that behavior is the cause, personality the result. Somehow a person has learned—has been conditioned—to respond unsatisfactorily, and thus has been prevented from achieving a healthy relationship to society. Thus a child may have been taught always to behave aggressively, or always to be silent and withdrawn. If the child can learn a more effective pattern of behavior toward other people, he or she will have a better chance of having normal relationships and a healthy personality. Therapy, according to this approach, is a matter of learning—in fact, it is reconditioning. The behavior therapist may use any one of a number of learning techniques in order to replace the patient's maladaptive behavior with more useful responses.

Mental Hospitals. From Pinel's time until well into the twentieth century, mental health care meant, in practice, mental hospitals. The insane were to be sheltered within protecting institutions from the buffets of a hostile world, they were kept from harming themselves or others, and were given the help and treatment that was available. Some early hospital administrators

The Organization of Treatment

recognized the importance of individual care and a positive atmosphere. Charles Dickens, describing one small New England "retreat" that he visited in 1842, speaks "of the evening lectures and concerts, of the gardening, fishing, and hunting, of the availability of horses and carriages for drives in the country."[73]

Such an approach was possible only in an era of small private hospitals. As the government began to take over responsibility for the care of the mentally disturbed, the ideal of a "retreat" remained; hospitals were built in secluded spots and surrounded by high walls and locked gates. Within the walls, all the patient's needs were to be met. But the purpose of the hospital was not merely to protect patients from society, and if possible to cure them, it was also to protect society from the patients. The old stereotype of the "raving lunatic" persisted, and imperceptibly security came to be treated as more important than therapy.

In the interest of economy and efficiency, the system of enormous hospitals developed, each housing several thousand patients, staffed largely by aides whose main job was to keep things quiet on as low a budget as a state legislature could decently supply. Staffing these hospitals is a perennial problem. Salaries are usually low, conditions of work are often unattractive or discouraging, and professionally trained personnel are almost irresistibly tempted by private hospitals, clinics, or private practice, where the rewards, both monetary and in visible therapeutic achievement, are much greater. Consequently, public institutions must depend heavily on partially trained personnel, and particularly on the attendants, or nursing aides. These attendants, though not fully qualified, are the persons most constantly in contact with patients, and typically control most aspects of their daily lives, including access to doctors.

It is also becoming increasingly clear that the design of many of these older buildings may actually do emotional harm to patients. High ceilings, endless maze-like corridors, huge wards lined with rows of matching beds, lack of color, lack of privacy—all may increase depression or disturbance and undo any benefits of therapy. For these reasons, mental hospitals now being built often aim at a maximum degree of flexibility, while incorporating current insights into the needs of those suffering from mental disorders. Construction is low and open, space is planned to allow for small-group relationships, for normal and constructive activities, and to provide the necessary minimum of security without simulating a prison. Building mental hospitals, however, entails enormous expense, and, since the problems of the institutionalized mentally ill have a low priority in our society, a sufficient number of new hospitals are not being built.

There is increasing evidence that hospitalization may not always be the best solution, even in good hospitals. Long-term studies have shown that patients who do not improve enough to be discharged within a short period of time are likely to remain for a very long time, if not indefinitely. This results partially from the hospital's inadequacies already discussed, but also seems to be a consequence of the very fact of hospitalization. This is the position taken by Erving Goffman, who developed the concept of the "total institution" as

[73]Harold L. Raush with Charlotte L. Raush, *The Halfway House Movement: A Search for Sanity* (Englewood Cliffs, N.J.: Prentice-Hall (ACC), 1968), pp. 3–4, 11.

a place of residence and work where a large number of like-situated individuals, cut off from the wider society for an appreciable period of time, together lead an enclosed, formally administered round of life.[74]

The mental hospital is a prime example of the total institution; because inmates are constantly subject to its control, it profoundly shapes their sense of self. In general, mental hospitals downgrade the patients' feelings of self-esteem and emphasize their failures and inadequacies. Uniform clothing and furniture, regimented routine, and the custodial atmosphere of the hospital make patients docile and unassertive. Since the psychiatric approach requires cooperation, the staff often encourages patients to view themselves as sick and in need of help. Any act of self-assertion or of rebellion against the institutional arrangements will probably be interpreted as further evidence of illness, and patients will be expected to take that view of it themselves. Release from the hospital is often contingent upon their acceptance, or apparent acceptance, of the official interpretation of their hospital and prehospital life. Finally, Goffman concludes that in most cases the probability is high that hospitalization will do more harm than good.

Recently, a civil rights movement for the mentally ill has developed. It has attacked both the process by which people are committed to mental hospitals and their right-to-treatment once they are there. Too often, the movement insists, people are committed as a means of social control or to isolate them from a community that finds them dangerous or annoying. Sometimes this is necessary, but many commitments are made by courts, judges, and psychiatrists who have not investigated the case thoroughly or considered other alternatives.

Too often mental hospitals serve as warehouses for the emotionally disturbed; their emphasis is on custody, not treatment. A recent court case in Alabama, *Wyatt v. Stickney*, established a patient's rights to therapeutic treatment while he or she is incarcerated and mandated standards for that state's hospital programs and staffs.

The Rosenhan study, mentioned earlier in this chapter, illustrates the conditions within mental hospitals. This research project involved eight normal people, "pseudopatients," who were admitted to a mental hospital and diagnosed as schizophrenics. Their only "symptom" was that they had heard voices on one occasion. Though they spent some time in the institution and were recognized as normal by their fellow inmates, the staff continued to think of them as schizophrenic. They were released with the diagnosis of "schizophrenia in remission." In a follow-up study, a hospital that had heard of these findings was told that over a period of three months, some pseudopatients were going to attempt to gain admission into the hospital. Staff members were asked to judge which applicants to the hospital were faking illness. Over this three-month period, at least 41 patients were judged to be pseudopatients. In fact, none were.

The results of this study were widely cited as evidence of the labeling theory, in that the diagnosis of illness—or health—was applied regardless of the actual condition of the patient. But it is what the pseudopatients observed

[74]Erving Goffman, *Asylums: Essays on the Social Situation of Mental Patients and Other Inmates* (Garden City, N.Y.: Doubleday, 1961), p. xiii.

while in the hospital that interests us. Though staff members were helpful and even dedicated, their behavior toward the patients left much to be desired. Staff members were kept apart from patients, as much as possible, behind a glass enclosure; psychiatrists, in particular, almost never appeared on the wards. When staff members were approached by pseudopatients with questions, their most common responses were to ignore the questions or to mumble something—avoiding eye contact all the while—and quickly move on. Patients were sometimes punished excessively for misbehavior, and in one case a patient was beaten. The entire atmosphere was characterized, in Rosenhan's words, by "powerlessness and depersonalization."

Some recent reforms in hospital procedures have sought to deal with the problems caused by hospitalization, and progress has been made. But a more revolutionary development is the idea, made practical by the existence of therapeutic drugs, that mentally disordered persons should be treated in their own community, within as nearly normal a pattern of everyday life as possible. This brings us to the growing field of community psychology.

Community Psychology.   Outpatient treatment for mental disorders is far from new, but until recently it was largely confined to neurotic disorders and to the upper and middle classes. With the passage of the Community Mental Health Centers Construction Act, the idea of easily accessible, locally controlled facilities that could care for people in their own communities was established. In 1978, there were more than 1,000 of these centers in the United States, and their number is growing.

The community psychology movement seems to have arisen from two basic sources: the awareness that social conditions and institutions must be taken into account when dealing with individual mental health problems, and the idea that the psychologist or psychiatrist should be able to contribute something useful to the understanding and solution of social problems. The guidelines laid down for the centers provided for a wide range of mental health care within the community and for coordination with, and consultative assistance to, other community agencies. Unfortunately, the "illness model" was still strong—the Joint Commission's central concern was defined as being with treatment rather than with prevention. Closely related problems such as alcoholism, juvenile delinquency, and mental retardation were largely ignored.

Nevertheless, there are certain encouraging developments. In Caplan's technique of mental health consultation, psychologists or other professionals spend much of their time in consultation with community care-givers—the doctors, teachers, clergy, law enforcement personnel, and others who by virtue of their professional roles are most likely to be in contact with people who need help.[75] These people are apt to encounter problems of mental disorder at a very early stage; if community care-givers are taught to recognize disorders and are provided with information and resources, they can often handle such early problems themselves, or refer them to professional therapists before they become serious and chronic. They may also be able to contribute valuable knowledge from their own professional fields, once they

[75]See G. Caplan, *Principles of Preventive Psychiatry* (New York: Basic Books, 1964). See also discussion in Emory L. Cowen, Elmer A. Gardner, and Melvin Zax, *Emergent Approaches to Mental Health Problems* (Englewood Cliffs, N.J.: Prentice-Hall, 1967), pp. 412–415.

are encouraged to see themselves as participants in the mental health care process.

At the other end of the treatment continuum are ex-mental patients discharged from a hospital and attempting to reestablish themselves in the community. If they have been hospitalized for a long time and in a large custodial-type institution, they may need considerable help in relearning the skills of everyday life and social contact in the ordinary world. To help meet this need, various expedients are being tried, one of the most interesting of which is the halfway house. This is a small residential community, usually under private auspices and most often in an urban area, in which for weeks or months ex-patients are helped to adjust from hospital to normal life. They may receive therapy from a psychiatrist, may be trained for a job and helped to obtain or keep one, and in any case get needed practice in fitting into a community where behavior is not subject to hospital regulations.

Prospects

Mental disorder has probably existed since the beginning of time; in today's crowded, complicated, high-pressure world it persists, possibly to a more serious degree. The nature of the problem, however, has changed. Where once insanity was a mysterious, incomprehensible affliction, and its victims were dismissed as hopeless objects of pity or abuse, today mental disorder is known to have understandable (though not yet fully understood) causes and a substantial chance of prevention and cure. The modern frustration arises because many of the causes of mental disorder are recognized as being so deeply rooted in human social organization, so interwoven with economic and political institutions, that any attempt to deal with them at a fundamental level is bound to have frightening effects on the status quo and may well create new dislocations with their accompanying ill effects—not to mention the sheer cost in dollars and cents. Nonetheless, recent decades have seen a dramatic increase in awareness of these problems and in attempts to meet them by government and private agencies. Much of the effort is going into fairly traditional training and treatment, but innovative experiments are also under way, as the need for an interdisciplinary, community-wide approach is being recognized. In particular, there is a growing realization that effective mental health care for the poor requires new concepts and techniques.

One sign that attitudes toward the mentally ill are beginning to change was the 1975 Supreme Court decision that mental patients cannot be held in institutions against their will if they are not dangerous and can survive on their own. The decision demonstrated that the mentally ill have legitimate civil rights that must be protected and that mental illness does not, of itself, imply an inability to function within the community.

But, even today, much of the knowledge about mental illness remains mysterious to a great number of people who still tend to regard such disorders as alien, frightening, and shameful. Consequently, it is hard for them to sympathize with new approaches to treatment. Where the psychologist sees a mentally ill person who could be treated in the community, many others see a dangerous lunatic who must be "put away" to protect society. Where the professional sees a depressed neurotic in need of understanding and psychotherapy, the public may see a weakling who needs to stop sponging off other people and get to work. Conversely, where some sociologists see nonconformity, many psychiatrists and psychologists see mental disorder. And where the sociologist sees people trapped in a slum environment which predisposes them to mental disorder, riots, and crime, too many honestly worried citizens see unreasonable demands, unwillingness to work, and the influence of outside agitators. An effective attack on mental disorder in our society must include—perhaps must begin with—an enormous amount of reeducation. Only as the majority of American citizens gain some genuine understanding of what mental disorder is, and why it happens, are they likely to assume the responsibility for dealing with it. A major responsibility of sociology is to build this understanding.

Summary

Although health is an essential requirement of all societies, definitions of health and illness vary; in the United States, health is a highly prized value. However, medical care in the United States has traditionally been a product available at a price through private enterprise, and has only recently come to be regarded as a right rather than a privilege.

Nevertheless, gross disparities continue to exist in the use and availability of health services. Members of minorities and the poor have considerably higher rates of illness and death than have white and more affluent people. Even the more affluent have problems obtaining quality health care, however, since hospital, physician, and health insurance costs have increased enormously, and much medical treatment is unnecessary or harmful. In large part these problems exist because the nation has no unified health-care system, such as those that exist in other industrialized nations. Suggestions for solving the problems of health care focus on alternative provider organizations, such as Health Maintenance Organizations, and alternative financing systems.

Mental illness is "America's primary health problem," but only about 25 percent of those with some mental problem receive treatment. Traditional definitions of mental disorder favor the "medical model" of mental illness, seeing disturbance of the personality system as analogous to the disturbance of the physiological system by physical disease. Major categories of illness in the medical model include neurosis, psychosis, organic psychosis, and psychosomatic illness. Scheff's social deviance model holds that the disturbed person is departing from certain societally defined norms of behavior; however, that "rule-breaking" behavior is not illness. Still another concept ascribes mental disorders to problems in living. According to Szasz, human relations are inherently difficult and inevitably involve interpersonal conflicts; by defining problems of adjustment as symptoms of "illness," we may impose therapy by force and deprive people of liberty.

Labeling theory holds that behaviors cannot be categorized in the same clear-cut way that physical symptoms can. It suggests that if deviant behavior is overlooked, it is likely to be transitory, but if it is publicly labeled, it may become stabilized.

The relationships of social variables—socioeconomic class, urbanization, race, and sex—in the incidence of mental disorders have been investigated in numerous studies, and some correlations have been found. It has also been found that similar symptoms may receive different diagnosis and treatment according to the socioeconomic status and sex of the patient.

While in the past hospitalization was the major form of treatment for the mentally disturbed, most treatment today involves psychotherapy in any of several forms; increasingly, chemotherapy is being used as an adjunct. The more severely impaired are still hospitalized, however, usually in large, impersonal and inadequately staffed institutions. There is a new trend toward community treatment, which encourages patients to resume their daily lives in the community and to continue care on an outpatient basis.

Bibliography

Chesler, Phyllis. *Women and Madness*. New York: Avon, 1972.

Driver, Edwin D. *The Sociology and Anthropology of Mental Illness: A Reference Guide*. Amherst: University of Massachusetts Press, 1972.

Ehrenreich, Barbara, and Ehrenreich, John. *The American Health Empire*. New York: Vintage Books, 1971.

Freeman, Howard E., et al. *Handbook of Medical Sociology*. Englewood Cliffs, N.J.: Prentice-Hall, 1972.

Friedson, Eliot. *The Profession of Medicine*. New York: Dodd, Mead & Co., 1968.

Hollingshead, August B., and Redlich, Frederick C. *Social Class and Mental Illness*. New York: Wiley, 1958.

Jaco, E. G., ed. *Patients, Physicians, and Illness*. 2nd ed. New York: Free Press, 1972.

Jones, Kathleen. *History of the Mental Health Services*. London: Routledge & Kegan Paul, 1972.

Rose, Arnold M. *Mental Health and Mental Disorder: A Sociological Approach*. New York: Norton, 1955.

Rosen, George. *Madness in Society: Chapters in the Historical Sociology of Mental Illness*. London: Routledge & Kegan Paul, 1968.

Scheff, Thomas. *Being Mentally Ill: A Sociological Theory*. Chicago: Aldine, 1966.

———. *Mental Illness ans Social Processes*. New York: Harper & Row, 1967.

———. ed. *Labeling Madness*. Englewood Cliffs, N.J.: Prentice-Hall, 1975.

Seham, Max. *Blacks and American Medical Care*. Minneapolis: University of Minnesota Press, 1973.

Srole, Leo, et al. *Mental Health in the Metropolis: The Midtown Manhattan Study*. Rev. ed. New York: Harper & Row, 1975.

Stevens, Rosemary. *American Medicine and the Public Interest*. New Haven: Yale University Press, 1971.

Szasz, Thomas. *The Myth of Mental Illness*. Rev. ed. New York: Harper & Row, 1974.

U.S. Department of HEW. *Toward a Systematic Analysis of Health Care in the United States*. Washington, D.C.: U.S. Government Printing Office, 1972.

Wilson, Robert Neal. *The Sociology of Health—An Introduction*. New York: Random House, 1970.

Variations in
Human Sexuality

Facts about Variations in Human Sexuality

- In more than half of contemporary societies, some homosexual activity is considered acceptable, under certain circumstances or for certain members of the community.

- No detectable personality differences have been found between homosexuals and heterosexuals.

- Thirty-one states still prohibit homosexual acts between consenting adults; a majority of states also prohibit heterosexual oral-genital contact.

- In 1977 there were 85,900 arrests for prostitution in the United States.

- About 80,000 to 100,000 children are sexually molested each year.

There is no evidence that pornography leads to sex crimes. Until fairly recently, the commonly accepted American attitudes toward sexual behavior were traditional and easy to define: Normal sex was that which tended to the procreation of children within a socially legitimate family. Premarital intercourse might be allowed within the narrowly defined range of acceptable behaviors, but only if it led to marriage fairly quickly. All other sexual acts, such as oral-genital contact between man and wife or any act between consenting adults of the same sex were condemned and prohibited. The possibility of allowing for variations in sexual tastes, or even the idea that such differences were perhaps a legitimate reflection of human individuality, was ignored. Today, although sexual matters are being discussed more openly than ever before, our attitudes toward sex are much more ambiguous, ambivalent, and inconsistent. On the one hand, a considerable variety of sexual behavior is available in the media, on the streets, in schools, and, for many, in their bedrooms. On the other hand, many people decry our new sexual freedom as "permissive," "abnormal," or even "degenerate." Many communities oppose even basic sex education in their schools. And, in most states, laws not only prohibit many sex acts of a nonheterosexual or a nonmarital nature, but even some sex acts between husband and wife.

If our present sexual norms are complex, inconsistent and contradictory, it is partly because they are rapidly changing. Already, behavior and situations that were once unmentionable in the United States are now commonly discussed—and openly practiced. Surveys taken in 1937 and 1959 indicated that only 22 percent of respondents approved of premarital sex; in a 1973 survey comparable to Kinsey's studies, more than three-fourths of men and over half of women found premarital intercourse acceptable. This same 1973 survey also found greatly increased acceptance and practice of oral and anal sex since Kinsey's studies of 1948 and 1953.[1] Sex-change operations, which first took place in the early 1930s, were not widely publicized until 1952, when the revelation of Christine Jorgensen's sex-change operation met with

[1]Morton Hunt, *Sexual Behavior in the 1970s* (New York: Dell, 1974), pp. 11, 21, 23.

widespread shock and disapproval. Yet recent estimates are that some 2,000 people have now undergone such operations.[2]

Despite the seemingly radical nature of such developments, many traditional sexual attitudes are still present—not only in our laws, but also in our behavior. For example, while more of us have become permissive toward premarital, oral, and anal sex, we still prefer these and other practices within the context of close and affectionate relationships. As Hunt comments:

> A growing body of research literature has established the fact that much of the current premarital coitus on campuses and in the big cities takes place between males and females who live together in what are essentially trial marriages or companionate marriages with firm emotional ties, conventional standards regarding fidelity, and a definite social identity as a couple. . . . The new sexual freedom operates largely within the framework of our longheld cherished cultural values of intimacy and love.[3]

In short, we seem to be moving toward a new sexual order through reform (gradual, partial change), rather than through revolution (sudden, radical change). Our traditional values often coexist with—or at least help shape—our contemporary values.

As suggested in Chapter 1, social change and conflict are often accompanied by social problems; the changes and conflicts in our attitudes toward human sexuality are no exceptions to this principle. Our growing sexual freedom, for example, has been accompanied by rapidly increasing rates of venereal disease. And while more teenagers engage in sexual intercourse, studies have found that many of them only rarely—if ever—use contraceptives, and are misinformed about the time during the menstrual cycle when pregnancy is most likely to occur. Conversely, many people are still quite concerned about sexual behavior that departs from traditional norms—such as homosexuality and prostitution—and would like to see such behavior suppressed. We shall be discussing these problems in this chapter; before we begin, however, it would be helpful to review the origins of our current views on sexuality and briefly to examine attitudes toward sexuality in other cultures. In this way, variations in human sexuality in our society can be seen in perspective and can be better understood.

Origins of Today's Attitudes

What is defined as acceptable or nonacceptable sexual behavior varies from culture to culture and from one period to another. A major part of our own sexual legacy comes from our Puritan and Victorian forebears, who elaborated on certain aspects of Judeo-Christian tradition.

The Old Testament and traditional Judaism approved of coitus only within the context of marriage and only for begetting children; it also strongly condemned masturbation, homosexuality, and various other practices. Jewish tradition, however, validated sex—within permitted boundaries—as pleasurable. Early Christianity took a more ascetic view and, following St. Augustine,

---

[2]Deborah Feinbloom, *Transvestites and Transsexuals: Mixed Views* (New York: Delta, 1977), p. 25.

[3]Hunt, *Sexual Behavior in the 1970s*, pp. 153–154.

regarded sex as degrading or evil. Graeco-Roman sexual mores, which had tolerated or even encouraged a wide range of sexual behavior, were condemned[4] and sexuality was seen as the irrational part of human nature that had to be controlled. It existed only for the purpose of procreation. In practice, such attitudes naturally prevailed infrequently over the next 1,000 years. Particularly during the Renaissance, sexual behavior among all classes and even among the religious hierarchy often strayed far from the stated standards of the Judeo-Christian tradition.

The Protestant Reformation that began in the sixteenth century produced a stricter and even more repressive sexual code. The ethic of hard work and austerity emphasized the importance of self- (and sexual) denial as a virtue. Puritanism, which was for a while dominant in England, also emphasized rigid adherence to religious law and a life of asceticism. The Puritan tradition eventually became extremely influential in the United States, because the Puritans were among the first to colonize America in the seventeenth century.

The sexual codes of the major Western religions, already firmly entrenched, were further reinforced by the rise of capitalism during the eighteenth century when:

> . . . sex got bound up in the economic ethic—prudence instead of profligacy, privatization instead of public display, savings instead of expenditures. The Puritan-dominated sex ethic became that of penny-pinching Adam Smith. . . . The moral values of the new middle classes, with their belief in hard work, delayed gratification, and avoidance of pleasure, including the sexual, were to triumph during the Victorian age, not only in England but in most of Western Europe.[5]

Such influences, of course, were also felt in the United States. In fact, the Victorian moral system, which grew out of the religious and economic values we have described, was the most direct antecedent of our traditional sexual code. Victorian values stressed the importance of self-control; "giving in" to one's sexual desires was seen as a weakness. Perhaps more important, in terms of our own culture, the Victorians had strong ideas about the proper status and behavior of women:

> The good woman was virginal before marriage—undamaged property—had many children, and exhibited no pleasure in sexuality. The bad woman willingly "gave it away," wasted her sexual capital, and lost the opportunity to marry.[6]

The sexual activities of men, on the other hand, were tolerated, if they took place not with "respectable" women but with servants or prostitutes. This denial of female sexuality, and the setting of different standards of behavior for men and women, formed the basis of the "double standard" that characterized American society and, to some extent, still persists today.

Formal Study of Human Sexual Conduct

Whatever their attitudes toward sexual behavior, people have rarely been able to ignore that sexuality exists. The art of primitive peoples abounded with

[4]K. J. Dover, *Greek Homosexuality* (Cambridge, Mass.: Harvard University Press, 1978).

[5]John Gagnon and Bruce Henderson, *Human Sexuality: The Age of Ambiguity* (Boston: Little, Brown, 1975), p. 16.

[6]Gagnon and Henderson, *Human Sexuality*, p. 16

phallic symbols and other sexual imagery; the Victorians did a brisk trade in erotic drawings and novels. We know today that sexuality plays an important—possibly even a central—role in the human experience. It was perhaps inevitable that people's preoccupation with the subject would eventually lead to its formal study. And as we shall see, such formal studies of human sexuality in the late nineteenth and early twentieth centuries contributed to the current liberalization of sexual behavior.

The first major modern student of human sexuality was Sigmund Freud. The insistent intrusion of sexual material in the recollections of his patients led Freud, in the 1890s, to postulate that the sex drive was a fundamental part of human life, and was present at birth or perhaps even in the developing fetus. Such a view was courageous and innovative, since sexuality was considered an abnormal part of human nature that appeared only in adolescence when procreation became possible. His new idea that sexuality was a critical part of human development provoked shock and outrage at the time, but eventually Freud's ideas were to have a liberating effect on Western society. Not only did sexual feelings become more acceptable, but the entire subject of sexuality was legitimized as a subject of research. Some of Freud's ideas, however, are considered antiquated today—particularly those on female sexuality. (See Chapter 9.)

More practical researchers in Freud's time (such as Havelock Ellis) and after were concerned more with dispelling ignorance about sexual matters than with proposing new theories of sexuality. In the late 1930s, Alfred C. Kinsey, an American zoologist, began a systematic study of sexual practices in the United States. His *Sexual Behavior in the Human Male*, published in 1947, reported on interviews with 5,300 white American men and documented that our national sexual behavior did not conform to our stated moral values. Some 83 percent of Kinsey's subjects had experienced premarital intercourse, half of those who were married had committed adultery, nearly all (92 percent) had masturbated to orgasm, and one-third had had at least one homosexual experience since puberty, mostly in early adolescence. Five years later *Sexual Behavior in the Human Female* was published, detailing interviews with 5,940 white American women. This volume showed that, while the old double standard was still alive and well, women were not as asexual as many people thought. More than half of all women interviewed had had premarital intercourse, and one-fourth of those who were married had had extramarital intercourse. Such statistics on female sexuality were particularly shocking during a time when women were expected to be "ladies." But all of Kinsey's material on masturbation, premarital intercourse, adultery, and homosexuality was disturbing and controversial. Kinsey's data were widely disseminated in the press, and for the first time, people in the United States were confronted with the wide gap between their sexual practices and their sexual mores. One probable effect of these studies was that many people became more free in their sexual behavior—or at least felt less guilty about it—secure in the knowledge that they were joining sizable numbers of other citizens behaving in a similar way.

In the late 1950s two American researchers, Dr. William H. Masters and Virginia Johnson, began to investigate the physiology of sex. Their findings have influenced the present climate of sexual and sex-role change. Freud had asserted that vaginal orgasm was the superior form of female response;

however, by means of ingenious laboratory equipment and procedures, Masters and Johnson found no physiological difference between the clitoral and vaginal orgasm. With the publication of this and other information in *Human Sexual Response* (1966), they enhanced the sex lives of many women who had previously believed themselves to be inadequate because their bodies did not live up to the Freudian ideal. With the additional, verified facts that some women are able to enjoy numerous orgasms in succession, and that both men and women are capable of enjoying sexual activity into advanced age, sexual expectations for both sexes were transformed. Turning their attention next to the great amount of human unhappiness caused by various forms and degrees of sexual incompatibility or dysfunction, Masters and Johnson went on to research and publish *Human Sexual Inadequacy* (1970), and to establish a sex treatment center for couples with severe adjustment problems. Sex treatment clinics (not all of them legitimate) proliferated in the 1970s, as well as numerous "do-it-yourself" books such as *The Sensuous Woman* and *The Sensuous Man*.

From a Puritan-Victorian ethic, in which an educated woman at the turn of the century was taught to believe that it was "more wholesome to sleep alone and avoid the temptation of too frequent intercourse,"[7] we have come to believe that everyone has a right to the full enjoyment of sex. While, to many observers, it seemed that there were notable changes in the national sex life since Kinsey, no one had measured the distance traveled. That gap was closed in 1973, when Morton Hunt undertook an extensive national survey on sexual practices. Hunt found what many had suspected: Today premarital sex begins at an earlier age and is more frequent than in Kinsey's era. Over half of the college men interviewed had had intercourse before they were 17. About three-fourths of single women under 25 in Hunt's sample—compared with only one-third in Kinsey's—had had intercourse. Some 80 percent of young married women (ages 18 to 24) were not virgins at marriage, a significant increase from just over half of all wives, as reported by Kinsey. Hunt also found the practice of oral sex to be increasing, especially among the young. Contrary to expectations, he also found that homosexuality had not become more prevalent since Kinsey's time.

It would seem that much has changed in the 80 years since Freud first proposed his revolutionary theories, and we need not rely solely on Kinsey's and Hunt's studies to tell us how much has changed. Street clothes have become more varied, colorful, and revealing; bathing suits have become flimsier; sex is discussed fully and frankly on television; and films in legitimate theaters depict in full detail a great variety of sex acts. But, as we have already suggested, the change has not yet been completed. There is still widespread ignorance about sexual matters, as our high rates of illegitimacy and venereal disease indicate. Many of our sex laws still reflect ancient religious attitudes. The Supreme Court struggles—almost annually—to define pornography. (Its 1975 decision states that a work must meet "community standards" of decency—which at best leaves the issue unresolved.) And in a 1976 decision, the Supreme Court upheld the right of states to make homosexual acts (and, by implication, all acts of sodomy) between consenting adults illegal. Clearly, despite the general liberalization of our sexual practices, many of us still perceive certain aspects of our sexual behavior as social problems.

[7]"A Sex Poll (1892–1920)," *Time*, October 1, 1973, p. 63.

The Varieties of Human Sexuality

One way to get a perspective on sexual norms in our society is to remember that virtually every conceivable sexual activity and orientation have, at some time and place, to some degree, by at least some people, been socially acceptable. Premarital sex, sex only to procreate, homosexuality, lifelong celibacy, adultery, monogamy, polygyny (more than one wife), polyandry (more than one husband)—each has been a behavior standard for some human community. Not even incest, which is the most widely proscribed sexual relationship, has been universally tabooed; it was institutionalized among royal families in some ancient cultures as a way to maintain the purity of the royal line. (In 1976 a government committee in Sweden recommended that all laws prohibiting incest be dropped, on the assumption that its social genetic harm had been exaggerated.[8])

Perhaps the most outstanding characteristic of human sexuality, then, is that its manifestations are extraordinarily varied; and the kinds of sexual behavior defined as appropriate vary from place to place and from time to time. For example, only a small minority (the United States among them) of the 190 contemporary societies studied by Clellan Ford and Frank Beach prohibit sexual expression in children. Trobriand Islanders encourage premarital sex as an important preparation for marriage; the Ila-speaking peoples of Africa permit boys and girls to play man and wife even before puberty;[9] and the Lepcha people of Asia believe that girls need sexual intercourse in order to mature.[10] Conversely, in many South American and Moslem societies, premarital chastity for women is highly regarded. A woman who is not a virgin upon marriage is likely to be shamed and ostracized.

Sexual attitudes in the United States have been shaped not only by the religious and economic influences described earlier, but also by a frontier tradition that places great emphasis on conformity to a rigid masculine stereotype. As a result, male homosexuals have been among the most harassed and despised people in our society. In most other societies, however—past and present—homosexuals have been tolerated and often respected. Male and female homosexuality was an accepted, even honored part of life in ancient Greece. Today, among some peoples in Africa and New Guinea, anal intercourse is a normal part of a young boy's life. Female as well as male homosexual practices are encouraged in northern Sumatra, where adolescents of each sex live in peer group residences until they are ready for marriage. During this period, all youngsters learn homosexual techniques from older adolescents of the same sex.[11] Interestingly enough, where homosexuality is considered a normal part of adolescent development, the transition to a heterosexual relationship in marriage is apparently not impeded.

Given the great variety of human sexual expression, there seems little doubt that human sexual behavior is learned. Being born male does not automatically produce the "red-blooded American he-man," interested only

[8]*New York Times,* March 7, 1976.

[9]Clellan S. Ford and Frank A. Beach, *Patterns of Sexual Behavior* (New York: Harper & Row, 1951).

[10]Gagnon and Henderson, *Human Sexuality,* p. 14.

[11]Gagnon and Henderson, *Human Sexuality,* p. 11.

in sports and women; being born female does not automatically produce the docile Moslem woman, content to veil her face. The attitudes of others, the acceptable role models available, rituals, schools, and eventually society as a whole all influence the sexual behavior that one will find acceptable. Males and females in every society must *learn* what "turns them on"—the psychosexual stimuli to which they respond have far more to do with cultural expectations than with their biological sex. (See Chapter 9.) As Gagnon and Henderson comment,

> We assemble our sexuality beginning with gender identity, and we build upon that the activities that we come to think of as fitting to ourselves. Our belief in what is correct and proper results more from our social class, religion, style of family life, and concepts of masculinity and femininity than from the specifically sexual things that we learn.[12]

Classifying Variance in Human Sexuality

We have seen that sexual practices in other cultures have differed markedly from our own, and that our own sexual norms have evolved from our unique religious, economic, and cultural experience. It will be helpful to remember this as we consider the sexual practices that are regarded by our society as variations from the sexual norm.

Defining Sexual Social Variance

As we stated in Chapter 1, social problems are acts which depart from a norm or value to such an extent and in such a way that a significant number of people or a number of significant people feel that something should be done about them. The difficulty with applying this definition to sexual acts is that it is hard to say which norms are really operative or enforced. Even in Kinsey's time, there was a great difference between the purported norms of our society and people's actual behavior. Today, it has become even more difficult to define sex-related social problems. Sexual behavior that was once condemned is now believed by most people to be fairly, or even completely, acceptable. Not long ago, for example, cunnilingus and fellatio were considered wrong or immoral acts; today, the vast majority of young people have engaged in them. Until recently, masturbation was considered sinful, socially harmful, and unhealthy; today it is widely assumed that masturbation is not only normal but beneficial for an individual's sexual development.

Nevertheless, there are still sex-related acts or conditions that many people have difficulty accepting: illegitimacy (discussed in Chapter 11), homosexuality, prostitution, and pornography are considered social problems by many people. In the past, such behavior was termed "deviant," meaning behavior that does not conform to norms. We now avoid this term whenever possible, since it implies a value judgment that there is a normal and therefore proper form of sexual expression, and also because it connotes the same stigma as "degenerate," "perverted," or "sick." We prefer instead to refer to

---

[12]Gagnon and Henderson, *Human Sexuality*, p. 30.

those sex-related acts or conditions which are perceived as social problems as sexual variance or in some cases as sex-related social problems.

One way to try to determine precisely what sexual matters are considered variant, or are social problems, is to look at the legal system. Presumably, acts or conditions that depart extensively from social norms or values will be declared illegal. Most sex laws in the United States take into account four elements in a sexual relationship: the degree of consent (forcible rape, for example); the nature of the object, restricting legitimate sex objects to human beings of the opposite sex, of a certain age, of an acceptable distance in kinship, and to the spouse; the nature of the sexual act, restricting behavior to certain practices in heterosexual intercourse; and the setting in which the behavior occurs, generally prohibiting public sexual activity.[13]

Sex Crimes

There are, however, many difficulties caused by using these laws to help define sexual variance. According to the studies previously mentioned, a substantial portion of the adolescent and adult population of this country is already violating them. Thus, some of these laws do not seem to be directly related to people's real sexual attitudes and behavior. In addition, many of these laws are anachronistic, dating from the very beginning of American history, when sexual norms were far different from what they are today. The prohibitions against adultery, for example, which are on the books in almost all states, date back to the seventeenth-century Puritans of the Massachusetts Bay Colony who made adultery a crime punishable by death. Other laws seem even more antiquated. As Herant Katchadourian and Donald Lunde point out: "Almost all sexual activity that may occur between husband and wife, with the exception of kissing, caressing, and vaginal intercourse, is defined as criminal in every state of the union."[14] It is not clear how such laws are related to contemporary sexual attitudes; they seem to be of limited usefulness in helping determine what sex-related matters are social problems.

One final reason sex laws are unreliable indicators of sexual norms is that they vary from state to state. In Texas, for instance, two unmarried adults who have intercourse can be fined $500; in Rhode Island the penalty for the same behavior is $10; and in Arizona this behavior constitutes a felony with a potential sentence of up to three years' imprisonment. In many states, married women who engage in extra-marital sex with single men would probably be charged with adultery, but married men who do the same with single women are more likely to be charged with fornication, which usually carries a lesser penalty and in some states is not a crime at all. Still other inequities show up in the standards used in different jurisdictions. Los Angeles, for example, which has the highest rate of forcible rape in the nation, defines almost any approach of a man to a woman who is a stranger for purposes of "sexual gratification" as rape.

In short, because the laws are so inequitable and variable, because they prohibit some forms of private behavior between consenting adults, and because differing standards are used in defining the same offense, the legal

[13]See Marshall B. Clinard, *Sociology of Deviant Behavior*, 4th ed. (New York: Holt, Rinehart and Winston, 1974).

[14]Herant Katchadourian and Donald T. Lunde, *Fundamentals of Human Sexuality*, 2nd ed. (New York: Holt, Rinehart and Winston, 1975).

definitions of sexual social problems are unreliable as an analytical tool for sociological purposes.

Types of Sexual Social Problems

A more useful classification of sex-related social problems is offered by Gagnon and Simon, who distinguish between three categories of sexual variance or problems. We will use our own labels for the three categories.

Tolerated Sex Variance.   This category includes such acts as heterosexual oral-genital contact, masturbation, and premarital intercourse. These acts "are generally disapproved, but . . . either serve a socially useful purpose and/or occur so often among a population with such low social visibility that only a small number are ever actually sanctioned for engaging in [them]."[15] Such acts are minor problems at worst; they arouse little special interest or social pressure for their regulation. It is likely that as our society becomes more tolerant, these acts will become socially acceptable and cease to be regarded as social problems.

Asocial Sex Variance.   This category includes incest, child molestation, rape, exhibitionism, and voyeurism. These acts are usually committed by one individual or, at most (as in gang rape), a small number of persons. While there are social influences on the incidence of such acts, on an individual basis they must be understood primarily within a psychological or social-psychological viewpoint. (See Chapter 1.) Persons who engage in them do not have a social structure that recruits, socializes, and provides social support for these acts. Major forms of asocial sex variance—incest, rape, and child molestation—elicit widespread, strong disapproval even among other law-breakers.

Incest—sexual relations between persons so closely related that they are by law or custom forbidden to marry—is nearly universally prohibited. According to Herman and Hirschman,

> The incest taboo is universal in human culture . . . . All cultures, including our own, regard violations of the taboo with horror and dread. Death has not been considered too extreme a punishment in many societies. In our laws, some states punish incest with up to twenty years' imprisonment.[16]

Weinberg found that where father-daughter incest occurs, which is the pattern in most cases, the family is likely to be characterized by paternal dominance, with the father intimidating and controlling the other family members. When sibling incest occurs, the parents are not dominant and do not "restrain the siblings from mutual sex-play." In cases of mother-son incest, the family is characterized by maternal dominance, with the father either absent or extremely subservient. In any case, Weinberg found, incest confuses family roles and creates rivalries within the family. It also creates personal conflict within the involved child or children and disturbs even those family members who may be only subliminally aware of what is occurring.[17]

---

[15]John H. Gagnon and William Simon, "Introduction: Deviant Behavior and Sexual Deviance," in *Sexual Deviance*, ed. John H. Gagnon and William Simon (New York: Harper & Row, 1967), p. 8.

[16]Judith Herman and Lisa Hirschman, "Father-Daughter Incest," *Signs: Journal of Women in Culture and Society*, vol. 2, no. 4 (1977), 735.

[17]S. Kirkson Weinberg, *Incest Behavior* (New York: Citadel Press, 1955).

Incest is not common in the United States; if the definition of incest is broadened to include noncoital acts such as petting and sexual acts between relatives outside the nuclear family, then the incidence of incest is high. Well over half of these contacts, however, involved relatively isolated cases of petting between children or adolescents. Hunt also suggests that the common belief that incest occurs more frequently among families of low socioeconomic status is erroneous. He found that incestuous acts were more common among higher socioeconomic levels. Higher rates of incest among lower socioeconomic groups are reported because

> the poor, the ignorant and the incompetent come to official attention, while people of higher socioeconomic status are either able to keep their incestuous acts hidden or, if discovered, to keep the discovery from becoming part of the official record.[18]

Child molestation in most societies, including our own, is deplored and feared, and results in humiliation and loss of status for the participating adult. Contrary to popular belief, heterosexual child molestation is far more common than homosexual child molestation. The child molester is not the stereotypical "dirty old man"; the average age of the male heterosexual offenders studied by Gebhard and his colleagues[19] was 35, only one in six was over 50.

In the cases studied by Gebhard and his colleagues, most young girls who were molested knew their molesters. In Gebhard's words,

> Contrary to general opinion and to parental fears, it seems that the immature female is more vulnerable to friends and acquaintances than to mythical strangers lurking in concealment.

Approximately 31 percent of the child molesters were married, almost as many were widowed or divorced; 40 percent had never married. In about 30 percent of the cases, alcohol was involved. These men were not physically dangerous, however; they did not use force, and seldom attempted coitus. They were, psychologically, apparently "unable to defer the gratification of their impulses."[20] The role of alcohol in these cases is apparently to release inhibitions that otherwise would stand in the way of a person's accosting a child. (See Chapter 4.)

Forcible rape—coercive heterosexual coitus with a woman of legal age—is the most frequently committed violent crime in the United States, with more than 63,000 cases reported annually and, according to various estimates, perhaps three and a half times as many cases unreported. Our concern here is with some of the psychosocial factors involved in the committing of rape. (See Chapters 5 and 6 for a discussion of rape as violent crime, and Chapter 9 for further analysis of rape as a reflection of traditional male-female sex roles.)

Many studies have found that rapists are young and unmarried; some studies also suggest that a disproportionate number of convicted rapists are

---

[18]Hunt, *Sexual Behavior in the 1970s*, pp. 341, 343, 347.

[19]Paul H. Gebhard, *et al.*, "Child Molestation," in *Problems of Sex Behavior*, ed. Edward Sagarin and Donal E. J. MacNamara (New York: Crowell, 1968).

[20]Gebhard, *et al.*, "Child Molestation," pp. 245, 247, 258.

According to legend, Ancient Rome was originally an all-male society until the Romans abducted their first wives as depicted in David's famous painting, *The Rape of the Sabine Women*. Feminists would cite this myth as evidence of the age-old use of sexual force in male-female relations.

Musée du Louvre

physically handicapped in some way.[21] Ostensibly, then, sexual deprivation is a key causative factor in rape. Most analysts believe, however, that the desire for sexual gratification is at most a secondary motive for rape. In this view, rape is an act of aggression or sadism that a person engages in in order to bolster a weak self-image and to feel powerful and omnipotent.[22]

Whether or not rape is chosen as the means for such ego-bolstering seems to be related to culture's views of sexuality and its attitudes toward men and women. There are some societies in which rape is unknown. Among the Arapesh of New Guinea, for example, the masculine role is so nonaggressive and peaceful that the concept of rape is incomprehensible. Conversely, some societies have an even higher incidence of rape than the United States. The Gussi tribe in Kenya, for example, has a rape rate at least five times higher than the United States. Men and women of the Gussi tribe traditionally

[21]Duncan Chappell, *et al.*, "Forcible Rape: A Comparative Study of Offenses Known to the Police in Boston and Los Angeles," in *Studies in the Sociology of Sex*, ed. James H. Henslin (Englewood Cliffs, N.J.: Prentice-Hall, 1971), p. 172.

[22]Manfred S. Guttemacher, *Sex Offenses* (New York: Norton, 1951).

regard each other as competitors, and women typically resist intercourse even with their husbands.[23]

In the United States, there are various theories of the relationship of rape rates to the social climate. One, suggested by Merton's theory of anomie (See Chapter 5), is that where heterosexual contact is valued, but where access to such contacts are restricted, the rape rate will be higher. According to this hypothesis, the more sexually permissive a society, the lower will be its rape rate. Another theory, advanced by feminists, holds that rape is the result of the traditional, patriarchial structure of American society in which heterosexual love is expressed by male dominance and female submission. As Griffin puts it:

> A man who derives pleasure from raping a woman clearly must enjoy force and dominance as much or more than the simple pleasures of the flesh. . . . If a man can achieve sexual pleasure after terrorizing and humiliating the object of his passion, and in fact while inflicting pain upon her, one must assume he derives pleasure directly from terrorizing, humiliating, and harming a woman.[24]

Minor forms of social sex variance are exhibitionism—the deliberate exposure of one's sex organs, and voyeurism—watching persons who are undressing or undressed or performing a sexual act. "Flashers" and "peeping Toms" may be somewhat annoying, but perhaps because they are not as threatening as the other forms in this category these behaviors have not received much analysis.

Structural Sex Variance. Behavior in this category is fairly well organized, participated in by substantial numbers of people, and involves several different roles and supportive social structures. Although supported and engaged in by large numbers of people, these behaviors run counter to prevailing norms and legal statutes, and thus lend themselves readily to sociological analysis. Three examples of structural sexual variance that we shall examine in some detail are homosexuality, prostitution, and pornography.

Homosexuality

Homosexuality is a sexual preference for members of one's own sex. Some people are exclusively homosexual, others may engage in homosexual behavior only under special circumstances, such as imprisonment, while still others have both homosexual and heterosexual experiences. Both males and females may be homosexuals—female homosexuals are usually referred to as lesbians. To date, much more research has been done on male homosexuality than on lesbianism.

Homosexuality has alternately been regarded by our society either as a sin or as the effect of some physical or mental disturbance; not so long ago it was generally considered too shameful and indecent to be spoken of openly. Although society has lately become more tolerant of open discussion of

---

[23]Chappell, *et al.*, "Forcible Rape," pp. 174–175.

[24]Susan Griffin, "Rape: The All-American Crime," in *Sexual Deviance and Sexual Deviants,* ed. Erich Goode and Richard R. Troiden (New York: William Morrow, 1974), p. 310.

homosexuality, many prejudices still prevail. According to the Harris Survey, almost half of the American people believe that homosexuals should be barred from certain jobs for which they are qualified, particularly those involving the young, simply on the basis of their homosexuality.[25]

It is difficult to determine, with any accuracy, the number of homosexuals in the United States. In the past, most estimates were based on Kinsey's studies that found about 4 percent of white males, and 2 percent of white females exclusively homosexual. He estimated that 37 percent of American males have some homosexual experience to the point of orgasm between adolescence and old age, and that 10 percent of American males have long periods of more or less exclusive homosexuality. However, because Kinsey had to make special efforts to locate and interview homosexuals, most experts believe that Kinsey's statistics are overestimates. The most reliable estimate is that more than 4 percent of American males and less than 2 percent of females are predominately homosexual.[26]

One problem, of course, is that many homosexuals are secretive about their sexual preference and may never be included in any statistics. For example, even though homosexuals are supposed to be barred from the armed forces—and efforts are made to find them prior to enlistment—studies (and the recent case of Air Force Sergeant Matlovitch) have found that many homosexuals succeed in completing military service without being discovered.[27]

One of the most common misconceptions about homosexuals is that they are easily identifiable. The typical male homosexual is thought to be obviously effeminate in manner, dress, and speech, and to work in the creative arts. In reality, there is as wide a divergence among homosexuals as among heterosexuals, and they can be found in any occupation, including such stereotypically "masculine" activities as sports. It has been estimated that only about 15 percent of all homosexuals are easily identifiable, conforming in appearance or manner to the stereotype.[28] Many of these may do so only for a brief period, when they have first publicly acknowledged their homosexuality and feel compelled to act it out.[29] Nor do homosexuals share any evident pattern of personality characteristics. Evelyn Hooker administered three common clinical projective tests to both homosexuals and male heterosexuals. Experts who examined the results of the tests found that they did not distinguish reliably between homosexuals and heterosexuals.[30] Other psychologists administered similar tests to lesbians and female heterosexuals, and could find no personality differences between these two groups.[31]

The one thing which homosexuals do have in common is their sexual preference and the resulting social and psychological strains imposed by a

[25]*The Harris Survey,* July 18, 1977.

[26]Paul H. Gebhard, "Incidence of Homosexuality in the United States and Western Europe," *National Institute of Mental Health Task Force on Homosexuality: Final Report and Background Paper.*

[27]Robert R. Bell, *Social Deviance* (Homewood, Ill.: Dorsey Press, 1971), p. 282.

[28]C. A. Tripp, *The Homosexual Matrix* (New York: McGraw-Hill, 1975), p. 99.

[29]William Simon and John H. Gagnon, "Homosexuality: The Formulation of a Sociological Perspective," *Journal of Health and Social Behavior* 8 (September 1967), 177–185.

[30]Evelyn Hooker, "The Adjustment of the Male Overt Homosexual," *Journal of Projective Techniques* 21 (1957), 18–31; and Evelyn Hooker, "Male Homosexuality and the Rorschach," *Journal of Projective Techniques* 22 (1958), 33–54.

[31]"Lesbians' Life Adjustments—Same as Straights," *Psychology Today,* December 1975.

society which powerfully disapproves of it. The ways in which they satisfy their desires and cope with the attendant problems vary—to some extent along socioeconomic lines.[32]

One important difference among homosexuals is how willing they are to "come out" and live their homosexuality openly. Some are completely candid about it. These may have relatively low-status and/or low-visibility jobs, which they are in no danger of losing because of their homosexuality; they may work in fields where homosexuality is frequently taken for granted, such as the arts, or they may be the young who have not yet made family and career commitments, and who believe that their sexual, psychological, and emotional needs are more important than their jobs and/or social position. These people may have made the most definite commitment to the homosexual life. More than others, their social lives may revolve almost completely around their homosexuality and are usually the ones, for example, who frequent "gay" bars. Others may come out for idealistic reasons—to confirm their identity publicly, to live truthfully, and in a small number of well-publicized cases, to change public opinion or challenge legal proscriptions. Many homosexuals, however, lead quite conventional, stable lives that are simply homosexual counterparts to conventional heterosexual patterns. They have steady jobs, and a regular social life, which may center around groups of homosexual friends; they generally avoid public settings like bars.[33]

Many homosexuals who do remain covert do so out of fear for their jobs—such as teaching, the ministry, or other professions—where discovery of their homosexuality would mean instant dismissal; some may be married with children. These ties to the "straight" world influence their homosexual contacts. They avoid gay bars—where it is more difficult to remain anonymous—in favor of public toilets, known by homosexuals as "tearooms," or Turkish baths, where sexual encounters are usually impersonal. Some married men may stop briefly at these places on the way home from work. They may not admit even to themselves that these encounters are homosexual, since they may make a distinction between whether they take an active or passive role in the exchange. It is likely that their wives are totally unaware of the situation.[34]

Some married homosexuals may enjoy intercourse with their wives; a few may be genuinely bisexual, enjoying the sex act with either male or female partners. Most are more comfortable in homosexual relationships, but are married for domestic stability, companionship, and respectability. Barry M. Dank studied fifteen marriages in which the husband was a homosexual and found that while all of these men had been homosexually oriented before their marriages, and most had had homosexual relations, 80 percent refused to consider themselves homosexual at the time they were married. Some expected to outgrow their homosexual desires with age while others married explicitly to escape them. Their refusal to accept their own homosexuality sprang from ignorance and abhorrence at being identified with a socially outcast minority. Although more than half of these men were able to function sexually with their wives, most continued to have sex with other men while

[32]Allen P. Bell and Martin S. Weinberg, *Homosexualities: A Study of Diversity Among Men and Women* (New York: Simon and Schuster, 1978).

[33]Bell and Weinberg, *Homosexualities*, pp. 129–131.

[34]Laud Humphreys, *Tearoom Trade: Impersonal Sex in Public Places* (Chicago: Aldine, 1975).

they were married, and only one of the marriages survived the wife's knowledge of her husband's homosexuality.[35]

While some male homosexuals have many sexual partners, most seek and achieve a stable relationship with only one other male. A study by Saghir and Robins showed that 61 percent established deep emotional relationships with at least one other male for a relatively long time.[36] These relationships often parallel the traditions and symbols of heterosexual marriages. Homosexuals may exchange rings, celebrate wedding anniversaries, and dream of raising a child. However, contrary to popular belief, it appears that roles within homosexual marriages are not clearly divided into "masculine" and "feminine," or dominant and submissive.[37]

A special category of homosexuality is the situational—that is, homosexual activity which takes place in circumstances where heterosexual contact is virtually impossible. Such behavior, for example, is the rule in prisons, where some of it can only be characterized as rape.[38] Homosexuality also tends to be relatively frequent in sex-segregated schools, mental hospitals, and military installations, when students, inmates, or military personnel are essentially isolated from contact with members of the opposite sex. Probably the majority of people who take part in homosexual acts in such settings do not continue to do so once they return to the outside world, although for some the pattern may become permanent.

Another form of situational, transitory homosexuality occurs among lower-class delinquent youths, who engage in homosexual prostitution with an adult male fellator. Reiss found that many boys from the lowest socioeconomic stratum in large cities are taught this behavior and are encouraged in it by a delinquent peer group or gang, whose older members know how to locate potential clients.[39] These encounters occur at places well known in the community, such as certain street corners, parks, public toilets, or movie houses. Not all lower-class boys will accept such relationships. There are several prerequisites for those who do—the boy must belong to a group which accepts and encourages this behavior; the group must indoctrinate him into it; he enters such relationships strictly to make money and never for sexual gratification ("easy money," as one boy put it). Certain specific expectations govern the transaction itself: only oral-genital fellatio, with the adult client the fellator, and no other sexual act, is permitted; the client must pay for the service; and no close or ongoing relationship should develop. The boy and/or his peer group will resort to violence if the adult does not conform to the established customs for such transactions. If the boy stays within this pattern, he will not be defined by the peer group as a homosexual, and therefore he will not define himself as one. Because the boys do not view themselves either as prostitutes or homosexuals, this is a transitory role for the participants and "simply another one of the activities which characterizes a rather versatile

[35]Barry M. Dank, "Why Homosexuals Marry Women," *Medical Aspects of Human Sexuality* (August 1972), 14–23.

[36]Marcel. T. Saghir and Eli Robins, *Male and Female Homosexuality* (Baltimore: Williams and Wilkins, 1973), p. 72.

[37]Joseph Harry and William B. DeVall, *The Social Organization of Gay Males* (New York: Praeger, 1978), p. 82.

[38]Edwin Johnson, "The Homosexual in Prison," *Social Theory and Practice*, vol. 1, no. 4 (Fall, 1971), 83–92.

[39]Albert J. Reiss, Jr., "The Social Integration of Queers and Peers," in *The Other Side: Perspectives on Deviance*, ed. Howard S. Becker (New York: Free Press, 1964), pp. 181–210.

pattern of deviating acts," according to Reiss. The boys never become part of the homosexual community, and their adult clients are apparently not active members of that community either; they are likely to include secretly homosexual husbands.

In addition to the variety of behavior patterns among different individuals, the same individuals may deal with their homosexuality in different ways at different stages of their lives. The most important distinction here seems to lie in whether or not individuals recognize themselves as homosexuals, and how they react to that knowledge. Mary McIntosh[40] has noted that a major influence on how individuals deal with their homosexuality is society's attitude toward it. She suggests that homosexuality should be regarded as a social role, rather than as a condition or trait, because how it is expressed reflects social expectations. As we have already suggested, personality traits of homosexuals and heterosexuals are generally indistinguishable, and homosexuals can be found in all social strata and occupations. Yet society does not see homosexuals as individuals. It expects that all those who engage in any homosexual activity will share specific traits: that they will be exclusively or predominantly attracted to people of the same sex; that in personality and appearance, they will be effeminate if male and masculine if female; that all their relationships with members of the same sex will be sexually loaded; and that they will be attracted to and probably try to seduce younger people of the same sex. Such expectations inevitably influence the self-image of anyone who identifies as a homosexual, leading these individuals either to assume that they should adopt some of these behaviors to conform to the homosexual "role" as defined by their society or to lead unnecessarily lonely lives isolated both from "straight" society to which they do not conform and from a "gay" world with the image of which they do not feel comfortable.

The phenomenon of "coming out"—defined by Simon and Gagnon as "that point in time where there is self-recognition by the individual of his identity as a homosexual and the first major exploration of the homosexual community"[41]—has been the subject of an important study by Barry Dank.[42] Dank found that most people did not make the identification for some time after they first became aware of homosexual desires in themselves. The average interval was six years, but it might be considerably longer. Usually this lag occurs because society has provided no conceptual meaning for the term "homosexual" with which people can relate. As one of Dank's subjects said:

> I really didn't know what a homosexual was. In the back of my mind, my definition of a homosexual or queer was someone who wore girls' clothes and women's shoes, 'cause my brother said this was so, and I knew I wasn't.

Or:

> I had always thought of them as dirty old men that preyed on 10–, 11–, 12–year-old kids.

[40]Mary McIntosh, "The Homosexual Role," *Social Problems*, vol. 16, no. 2 (Fall 1968), 182–192.

[41]Simon and Gagnon, "Homosexuality," pp. 177–185.

[42]Barry M. Dank, "Coming Out in the Gay World," *Psychiatry* 34 (March 1971), 180–197.

Consequently, people may carry on homosexual relationships for years while defending themselves by various mental expedients, and usually with some degree of self-rejection, from calling themselves homosexuals.

Generally it is through contact with admitted homosexuals that coming out finally takes place. Gay bars, tearooms, YMCAs, and such one-sex environments as prisons, mental hospitals, the military, and some schools are frequent settings for this experience. Occasionally, a person comes out as a result of reading, rather than through interpersonal contact, but this is the exception. In either case, the significant fact is that homosexuals encounter a concept of their homosexuality with which they can identify, unlike the highly negative concept usually instilled in them by "straight" society. For nearly all homosexuals, this discovery comes as a great relief, as one of Dank's subjects described:

> I knew that there were homosexuals, queers and what not; I had read some books, and I was resigned to the fact that I was a foul, dirty person, but I wasn't actually calling myself a homosexual yet. . . . The time I really caught myself coming out is the time I walked into this bar and saw a whole crowd of groovy, groovy guys. And I said to myself, there was the realization, that not all gay men are dirty old men or idiots, silly queens, but there are some just normal-looking and acting people, as far as I could see. I saw gay society and I said, "Wow, I'm home."

In some ways, the most troubled homosexuals are those whom Dank calls the "closet queens"—the persons with homosexual desires and perhaps homosexual activities, who never make the contacts which will enable them to accept themselves as homosexuals.

In view of the increasingly free circulation of positive and objective information about homosexuality, and of the increasing visibility of the homosexual community, Dank hypothesized that more homosexuals than in the past will be able to identify themselves as homosexuals, and will do so at an earlier age. This may make it easier for homosexuality to be regarded as a way of life rather than as a crime or a mental illness, and may in turn facilitate greater integration of homosexuals into the general society.

People have always wondered what causes someone to be a homosexual, but no one has found a definite answer. Some authorities have posited a biological determination, and studies with identical twins suggest a genetic, or inherited hormonal, determinant. W. S. Schlegel, for example, found that in 95 percent of his identical twin pairs, both subjects were homosexuals, while among fraternal twins the figure was only 5 percent.[43] Biological studies, however, have generally been inconclusive, and the twin studies are confused by environmental factors. To date, there is no strong evidence that homosexuality is biologically determined—although, according to Evelyn Hooker, a large proportion of homosexuals themselves believe that it is.[44]

More important than any biological factor, probably, is the social environment in which a person grows up. As we have suggested, the crucial

[43]W. S. Schlegel, "Die konstitutionbiologischen Grundlagen der Homosexualitat," *Zeitschrift für menschliche Verebung. Konstitutionslehre* 36 (1962), 341–346; *American Journal of Human Genetics* 4 (1952), 136–146.

[44]See Evelyn Hooker, "The Homosexual Community," in *Perspectives in Psychopathology: Readings in Abnormal Psychology*, ed. James O. Palmer and Michael J. Goldstein (New York: Oxford, 1966).

thing about human sexual behavior is that it is learned. Human beings may or may not have a basic need for sex, but its expression is shaped by experience. Psychiatrists and psychologists have not been particularly successful in identifying any early experiences which result in homosexuality. Certain situations do seem to be frequent in the case histories of homosexuals: the family often includes a dominant or seductive mother, and a weak, detached, or overly critical father—factors which prevent the male child from identifying with the masculine role. Yet it is not clear why homosexuality develops only in some, and not in all, children reared under these conditions; many researchers, in fact, question entirely whether homosexuality is caused by a pathological family situation. While some personality problems seem to be shared by homosexuals, many homosexuals themselves often make the point that these are due mainly to excessive societal pressures on them to conform to arbitrary norms. That is, it is society's stigmatizing of homosexuals which causes them to develop certain traits sometimes identified with homosexuality; these traits are not the cause of their becoming homosexuals. [45]

Psychology has had little success in changing the sexual orientation or life style of homosexuals; in 1973, the American Psychiatric Association voted to remove homosexuality from the list of mental disorders in its diagnostic manual. Bell and Weinberg found that only about 25 percent of male homosexuals regretted their homosexuality. [46] Few homosexuals sought counseling from traditional therapists, since the professional bias tended to view the problem as a mental illness affecting sexual behavior. Many psychologists now emphasize helping troubled homosexuals to accept themselves and their life style with minimal conflict, instead of attempting to "cure" them.

The particular concern of the sociologist is less with the psychology of the homosexual than with homosexuality as a life style or career, to be studied like any other life style in which the question of original causes is only one element. The social forces which influence the development of the homosexual life style at all its stages are equally important, as is the reciprocal influence of the homosexual presence on society in general. To learn something about these influences, we shall look more closely at the homosexual subculture.

Subcultural Aspects of Homosexuality

Like many other groups, homosexuals share significant activities and possess group norms and a "special language."

The homosexual subculture exists in most large cities in the United States—all of which have large homosexual populations in certain neighborhoods, streets, or buildings. Sociologists frequently use the term "gay ghetto" to define such an area. According to Martin Levine, a gay ghetto "must contain gay institutions in number, a conspicuous and locally dominant gay subculture that is socially isolated from the larger community, and a residential population that is substantially gay." [47] Two of the largest gay ghettos are in Greenwich Village in New York City and the Castro Street district of San Francisco. Gay institutions in these neighborhoods, which

[45]M. T. Saghir, et al., "Homosexuality: III. Psychiatric Disorders and Disability in the Male Homosexual," American Journal of Psychiatry 126, vol. 9 (March 1970), 1079–1086.

[46]Bell and Weinberg, Homosexualities, p. 125.

[47]Meredith Gould and Martin Levine, Gay Men: The Sociology of Male Homosexuality (New York: Harper and Row, 1979), p. 160.

provide services and act as common meeting places, include certain parks, restrooms, cinemas, public baths, gyms, and bars. Cities with a large gay population also support an increasing number of gay businesses—restaurants, boutiques, barber shops, bookstores, travel agents and repair shops—which cater primarily (though by no means exclusively) to a gay clientele. Certain doctors, dentists, and lawyers also have a largely gay practice. Many of these businesses and services advertise in the *Gay Yellow Pages,* that covers most of the United States and Canada, and in several national and regional magazines and newspapers that are published primarily for a gay readership. This proliferation in number and scope of such businesses has helped foster a tangible sense of community among homosexuals. In New York and San Francisco, for example, it is possible for a homosexual to live, work, shop, and be entertained in a primarily gay milieu.

A minority of the homosexual subculture frequent the public restroom or "tearoom" in which impersonal sex is readily available. Laud Humphreys believes that the accessibility, invisibility, variety, and impersonality of the tearooms make sexual encounters there particularly attractive to covert male homosexuals.[48] These places are in locations accessible to men before and after work and during the lunch hour, while other places for casual sex, such

[48]Humphreys, *Tearoom Trade.*

Two gay men stroll down New York's Christopher Street. Many men and women have decided to live openly as homosexuals, whether or not they experience social disapproval.

Jan Lukas/Photo Researchers, Inc.

as bars and baths,[49] are usually open only at night and may be in less convenient neighborhoods; further, they would require more time spent in socializing, and could not be as readily fitted into a work-and-commuting schedule. Public restrooms also provide alibis for someone found there; there is a constantly changing population, providing a variety of potential sexual partners; sex without relationship or emotional involvement is appealing to the man who is maintaining a heterosexual life style.

The gay bar, however, provides a much more significant gathering place for the homosexual community. Once clandestine establishments, gay bars are no longer likely to be targets of police harassment; they have proliferated throughout the country, and now number about 4,000.[50] Because homosexuals frequently patronize several bars in a single evening, the bars are conveniently clustered together. This may influence residential patterns, or may be a response to such patterns. The bars, and what they tell about the neighborhood, are especially useful to homosexuals who have just arrived in a new city; they make it easy and relatively safe for them to find new friends and partners. One of the most significant functions of the gay bar, however, is that it provides a setting for coming out, and for socializing new members into the subculture. Many men come out in gay bars, because that is where they are able to observe and meet other homosexuals with whom they can identify.

Furthermore, the subculture provides homosexuals with a language they can use to communicate with and recognize one another. A homosexual who is "cruising," or looking for a sexual partner, can tell by fairly standardized behavioral gestures which of the men he meets are interested in a pickup, and even what kind of sexual activity they are willing to engage in. Since the danger of detection and arrest is never far from the homosexual in a public place, knowledge of such in-group language is important in order to make any contacts at all.[51]

One of the most important functions of the homosexual subculture is to provide its members with a way of understanding and accepting their sexual orientation. This function is performed not only by the gay bar and similar meeting places, but also by some homosexual organizations, which, in recent years, are becoming increasingly vocal. Among the best known of these groups are the Mattachine Society, founded in the early 1950s, and the newer National Gay Task Force. These groups work to abolish laws which discriminate against homosexuals, and to persuade homosexuals themselves and society in general that there is nothing shameful or harmful about being homosexual.

Lesbianism

It is harder to accurately estimate the number of lesbians in the United States than the number of male homosexuals. Lesbians are less conspicuous, they are generally less publicly active and have fewer sex partners than male homosexuals, they are less likely to cruise or to frequent bars, and they are less likely to be arrested by the police. In addition, social custom makes it easier to conceal female than male homosexuality. A single woman who does not date men is usually assumed to be simply uninterested in, or afraid of, sex,

[49]Martin S. Weinberg and Colin J. Williams, "Gay Baths and the Social Organization of Impersonal Sex," *Social Problems*, vol. 23, no. 2 (December 1975), 124–136.
[50]"Gays on the March," *Time*, September 8, 1975, p. 33.
[51]Bell, *Social Deviance*, p. 274.

rather than suspected of lesbianism. Also, it is considered more acceptable for two women to share an apartment, or kiss or touch in public, than it is for men.[52]

Finally, the laws against homosexuality are usually concerned primarily with male actions. As Bell points out, the legal controls over sexual behavior have generally been developed by men, and men have rarely seen female homosexuality as a serious threat.[53] This, plus the tendency of lesbians to be less publicly active than their male counterparts, has usually kept the police from paying very much attention to them, so that they seldom appear in arrest records and official statistics.

While female homosexuals are as individually different as male homosexuals, there are some general differences between how males and females manage their homosexuality. Many of these differences appear to arise from the differing socialization of males and females in general. Homosexuals, as much as heterosexuals, are affected by society's expectations about the kind of behavior that is appropriate to each sex. Well before a girl begins to experience homosexual tendencies, she is absorbing society's assumptions about how females should act—for example, that they should be less aggressive and that sex is permissible only as part of a lasting emotional relationship.

Further, sexual experience, of whatever sort, usually begins later for females than for males. A boy is likely to have sexual experience to the point of orgasm—usually by masturbation—relatively early in adolescence, while the corresponding experience for a girl is likely to come late in adolescence or early in adulthood (at least in the past—today the pattern may be changing).[54] It is, therefore, likely that a girl learns to think in terms of emotional attachment and permanent love relationship before she develops any strong commitment to sexuality; when that commitment appears, whether heterosexual or homosexual, it is fitted into the total "love" context. For boys, with their earlier experience, sex is apt to remain much more an independent and autonomous drive, possibly, but not necessarily, linked with love. Thus, for most of the lesbians that Gagnon and Simon studied, the first actual sexual experience came late, during an intense emotional involvement.[55]

These differences in development and socialization underlie many of the subsequent behavioral differences between male and female homosexuals. The lesser sexual activity of the lesbian, for example, has simply paralleled the behavior of women in general in our society. Lesbians typically, though not always, come out at a later age than do male homosexuals. When a lesbian does come out, she usually looks for one partner and remains with her as long as the relationship is satisfying. When she is between partners, she is less likely than a male to look for "one-night stands" to satisfy her purely sexual needs—and thus spends less time in the gay bars and other gathering places which are so important to the male homosexual.

A lesbian subculture does exist, particularly in large cities, but for women, the gay bar is less a source of pickups than a place to socialize. The subculture may also remove inhibitions, overcoming some of the sexual-

---

[52]Goode and Troiden, *Sexual Deviance and Sexual Deviants*, p. 234.

[53]Bell, *Social Deviance*, p. 288.

[54]Ibtihaj S. Arafat and Wayne R. Cotton, "Masturbation Practices of Males and Females," *The Journal of Sex Research*, vol. 10, no. 4 (November 1974), 299.

[55]Gagnon and Simon, *Sexual Conduct*, pp. 176–216.

repression training of childhood, and teaching the woman how to express her sexuality more freely and directly. But probably its major contribution is as a locus of companionship, a setting in which the lesbian can relax and be open with friends from whom she need not conceal what she is.[56]

Just as the stereotype of the male homosexual includes effeminacy, so does the lesbian image includes masculinity. Actually, it appears that "male" and "female" roles are seldom sharply defined in lesbian relationships. There are masculine, or so-called "butch," lesbians, but they seem to be the exception. Saghir and Robins, for example, found that more than two-thirds of lesbians have an appropriately feminine appearance.[57] Like her male counterpart, the lesbian who has newly come out may feel a need to act out her variant role for a time by adopting distinctive behavior, in order to redefine her identity. However, lesbians may have another and quite different reason for adopting some masculine characteristics: as unmarried, self-dependent women, they frequently must shoulder responsibilities which in many families or households would fall to the male. It is largely because these are socially defined as male functions that women who perform them appear masculine.

As with male homosexuality, a special category of lesbianism is found in prisons. Rose Giallombardo, in her study of social organization in a women's prison,[58] found that prisoners engaged widely in homosexual activity, and most maintained that it was legitimate to do so since heterosexual contacts were unavailable.

Research on lesbiansim has been especially scant, and much of our knowledge is based on limited data and what might be called "educated speculation." As with most varieties of sexual behavior, further study is needed.

Social Control

Recently, there has been a growing debate over homosexuality's place in society; however, through its laws, and various employment policies, society has sought to repress it. In most states, homosexual behavior is illegal, both in public and in private; penalties range, in some states, from ten years to life imprisonment. As yet, only Colorado, Connecticut, Delaware, Hawaii, Illinois, New York, North Dakota, Arkansas, Ohio, Oregon, California, New Mexico, Maine, Washington, and New Jersey do not restrict private sexual acts between consenting adults. Obviously, laws against homosexual behavior are difficult to enforce in cases of private encounters between two consenting individuals, when no complaint is lodged. In general, homosexuals who are arrested today are those who have been cruising or soliciting in public places.

Today also, particularly as homophile organizations become more militant and politically oriented, restrictive laws are coming under attack as violating constitutional rights and attempting to legislate private morality. Those who support restrictive laws usually argue that they are necessary to protect young boys from seduction, and that legalizing homosexual behavior will encourage more people to become homosexuals. Against this must be set the incalculable loss to society when homosexuals are legally or informally

[56]For a fuller discussion of the lesbian subculture, see Bell, *Social Deviance*, p. 294.

[57]Saghir and Robins, *Male and Female Homosexuality*, p. 268.

[58]Rose Giallombardo, "Social Roles in a Prison for Women," *Social Problems* 13 (Winter 1966), 266–288.

banned because of their sexual preference from pursuing certain careers, and the cost of the enormous personal suffering imposed on them and their families by society's moral rejection.

In 1957, in England, the Wolfenden Committee released a report on homosexuality that urged that homosexual behavior in private between consenting adults be legalized. The committee found that

> the law itself probably makes little difference to the amount of homosexuality which actually occurs; whatever the law may be, there will always be strong social forces opposed to homosexual behavior. . . . There is no valid reason for supposing that any considerable number of conversions would follow the change in law.[59]

The committee also found no evidence to indicate that homosexuals who start with adult partners will at any stage of their life attempt to seduce young boys. In 1967, the British Parliament adopted a law incorporating the recommendations of the Wolfenden Committee.

In the United States, legal restrictions against homosexuals have not been lessened, except in the few states just mentioned; in fact, in recent years some states have increased the penalties for homosexual behavior. Georgia recently broadened its sodomy law to include lesbian sexual relationships.[60] And the March 1976 decision of the United States Supreme Court, declining to hear arguments on a lower court ruling, in effect held that states may prosecute and imprison people committing private homosexual acts, even when both parties are consenting adults. While the Supreme Court action did not require states to reinstate sodomy prohibitions or to enact them, the decision reduced pressure on states to repeal such laws, and slowed the movement for homosexual rights in employment, housing, and other areas. In fact, local ordinances which prohibited discrimination on the basis of sexual preference have been repealed by popular referenda in Dade County, Florida, and St. Paul, Minnesota.[61]

Many experts, however, continue to urge liberalization. In its 1969 report, the National Institute of Mental Health's Task Force on Homosexuality recommended that homosexual behavior between consenting adults be legalized. As did the Wolfenden Committee, the task force found that while these laws do not prevent homosexual behavior, they may contribute to the mental health problems of many homosexuals. The task force also recommended that the employment policies of some government agencies, in which homosexuality is a ground for barring from hiring or for instant dismissal, be changed. The usual justification for these policies is that a homosexual in a high position is subject to blackmail and is, therefore, a security risk. The task force noted that this would not be the case if the laws against homosexuality were changed, and that these regulations also cause mental stress in homosexuals and block their hopes for careers.

Some careers, noticeably medicine, law, teaching, and the military, have been virtually out of the question for acknowledged homosexuals, although

---

[59]*Report of the Committee on Homosexual Offenses and Prostitution,* par. 58, 1957. The American edition, *The Wolfenden Report,* was published by Stein and Day, Briarcliff Manor, New York.

[60]*Time,* September 8, 1975, p. 35.

[61]Jean O'Leary and Bruce Voeller, "Gay Rights Law: Confusion En Route to Equality," *Juris Doctor* (June/July 1978), pp. 36–41.

medical and law schools are beginning to accept homosexual applicants. According to Williams and Weinberg, 2,000 to 3,000 persons discovered to be homosexuals or to participate in homosexual acts are separated from the armed forces annually, usually with an "undesirable" discharge, which does not entitle them to certain benefits and may deter subsequent employers or otherwise handicap their civilian lives.[62] Homosexuals often have difficulty obtaining insurance, because they may be considered insurance risks; they also can be evicted from privately owned housing, and are usually unable to obtain security clearances in either government or industry, for fear of blackmail.

Some recent court decisions have upheld the rights of homosexual teachers, and a few school boards, including those of the District of Columbia and San Francisco, prohibit discrimination against homosexuals in hiring. Some corporations have also announced an antidiscrimination hiring policy, and the Federal Civil Service Commission has reversed its previous position that homosexuals were unfit for public service.

Nowhere is homosexuality itself a crime; only are certain acts, usually referred to as sodomy and including both oral-genital and anal-genital contact, defined as crimes. These laws have been used primarily against male homosexuals. In 1973 the American Bar Association called for repeal of all state laws defining any form of private noncommercial sex between consenting adults as criminal.[63] Peter Fisher states that very few nations, Russia and China among them, join the United States in punishing homosexuals. He also notes that numerous Western nations, including Mexico, Switzerland, Great Britain, and Canada, and all other countries whose legal systems are based on the Napoleonic Code, first adopted in France in 1804, do not consider homosexual acts a crime, nor do they include private homosexual acts between consenting adults in their penal codes.[64]

Prostitution

Prostitution can be defined as sexual intercourse on a promiscuous and mercenary basis, with no emotional attachment; prostitutes make a living by selling sexual favors to those who will pay. Although most prostitutes are female, there is also a small, but growing number of male prostitutes. Both groups cater to a male clientele.

Prostitution has existed since the dawn of history—it is sometimes referred to as "the oldest profession"—but its place in society and the prevailing attitudes toward it have varied. In early societies it often served religious functions; groups of prostitutes might be attached to the temples, and respectable women might "serve the good" in this way during part of their lives. Occasionally secularized prostitution has been legitimized—with a certain amount of reluctance—as it is today, in some parts of Nevada. The usual rationale for this has been that there are going to be prostitutes, and that men are going to patronize them, so it is better to have the practice out in the open where some supervision can be exercised. More often, especially during

[62]Colin J. Williams and Martin S. Weinberg, *Homosexuals and the Military: A Study of Less Than Honorable Discharge* (New York: Harper & Row, 1971).

[63]Sandra Stencel, "Homosexual Legal Rights," *Editorial Research Reports*, no. 10 (March 8, 1974), 181–200.

[64]Peter Fisher, *The Gay Mystique: The Myth and Reality of Male Homosexuals* (Briarcliff Manor, N.Y.: Stein and Day, 1972), p. 128.

the past century, prostitution has been banned—with greater or lesser efforts to enforce the ban—and the female prostitute was considered a "fallen woman," degraded and disreputable. Late Victorian ideals of womanhood were particularly conducive to this view: "nice" women were expected to regard sex as a disagreeable duty, and the woman who knew too much about it, practiced it often, and was even prepared to enjoy it was necessarily suspect, debased, and un-womanly. Today the female prostitute is still looked down on, but less for her sexual proficiency and more for her exploitative, loveless use of it.

It is difficult to estimate the number of prostitutes in the United States today, particularly because many of them have part-time or full-time legitimate jobs that camouflage their activities as prostitutes. Marshall Clinard has estimated that there are about 275,000 women in America today whose full-time occupation is prostitution.[65] There are no available statistics on the number of full-time male prostitutes.

Prostitutes do not constitute a homogeneous category. There are several fairly well defined professional levels among them, with typical differences in education, fees, methods of attracting customers, and types of customers served. Fees for services vary not only according to the "class" of the prostitute, but also the community or neighborhood, and such other factors as inflation.

The aristocrats among prostitutes are the "call girls" and "call boys." These are the best educated, best dressed and most attractive, and may often work part-time in modeling or the theatre. This type of prostitute never solicits; clients come through personal references, and arrangements are usually made by telephone. The going rate is $100 for an evening, but could easily be twice as much, and the evening may include dinner at an expensive restaurant. Their clients, predictably, come from the upper-middle and upper classes. Male houses of prostitution cater to homosexuals and bisexuals and have a lower visibility than female houses of prostitution. This is chiefly due to the secretiveness of the activity, the general societal stigma, and the eliteness of the call boy within the male homosexual subculture.[66] Both call boys and call girls consider themselves totally distinct from other prostitutes, and in fact never refer to themselves as prostitutes.

Like call girls, "female hustlers" are attractive and place great value on the status symbols, such as good clothes, which separate them from other types of prostitutes. Unlike call girls, however, hustlers solicit directly, working from night clubs and bars, and they are paid less, getting about $40 for "turning a trick"—performing sexual intercourse. Unlike call girls, they may have several clients each night.

A "house girl" works in a brothel, or house of prostitution, and is in the position of employee to the madam who runs the house. She must accept any client whom the madam assigns to her, and is allowed to keep half of the $25 or more fee for each trick.

Somewhat looked down upon by all other prostitutes is the "street walker." She solicits customers wherever she can find them, and charges about $20 a trick. In small towns, under highly competitive conditions, or if she is desperate, a woman may charge less.

[65]See Clinard, *Sociology of Deviant Behavior.*
[66]David J. Pittman, "Call Boys' Now Also Coming into Vogue," comment on Martin Hoffman, "The Male Prostitute," *Sexual Behavior* (August 1972), 17–21.

Prostitutes at these various levels have little to do with each other; they work in different places and attract different clients. The only movement between the groups is generally downward; when a call girl begins to lose her looks and is less in demand, she may be forced to solicit directly, while hustlers and house girls may eventually be reduced to walking the streets.[67]

There is a similar hierarchy among male prostitutes although there are fewer types. The most visible male prostitute is the "hustler." Typically, he wears the "masculine" uniform—levis, a leather jacket, and boots. To most of his clients, or "scores," it is important to believe that the hustler is heterosexual, or straight. And, in fact, research has shown that the majority of hustlers are straight. In a study of prostitution in Sweden, only seven out of 300 male prostitutes interviewed were homosexual.

Other researchers have determined that sexual self-definition is extremely important to the male prostitute, whether he is a call boy, hustler, a delinquent youth out to make a quick buck, or "chicken," the child prostitute who appeals—as does his young female counterpart—to a primarily well-to-

[67]Pittman, "Call Boys," p. 21.

do, but not necessarily middle-aged or elderly, male clientele.[68] Some male prostitutes have no difficulty accepting their homosexuality. But those to whom a heterosexual self-image is necessary, however, follow a clearly defined set of rules to maintain that image.

The first rule relates to motivation. The goal must be monetary; to seek sexual gratification would be to admit homosexuality. The second rule relates to "masculinity"; although many male prostitutes, both straight and gay, will perform any sexual act for the right price, many straight hustlers set limits on what they will do with a client, and perform only in the traditionally masculine role. Hustlers who at one time were able to fool themselves into believing they were not gay because they (a) remained emotionally uninvolved during sex or (b) maintained a masculine posture throughout the encounter, may later define themselves as gay and view their hustling period as a time of self-deception.[69]

A recent mode in prostitution, the massage parlor, has lately become a national phenomenon. In these establishments a man can pay to not only be stimulated to ejaculation, a procedure known as a "local," but more extensive services are also available. Velarde and Warlick studied owners, masseuses, and customers in a suburban West Coast community.[70] Fees ranged from $10 to $15 for an hour's massage, although the plusher places charged more. There was also usually an extra fee or tip to the girl; the more services she performed, the higher was the extra fee, usually $5 per service. Virtually all of the girls were young and unskilled, and had taken this job to earn money. They had to become licensed masseuses first, and were instructed by the owners in the local solicitation laws, which make it illegal for the girl to solicit. The girl had to become expert in getting the customer to solicit her services and in detecting undercover policemen.

Velarde and Warlick found few typical characteristics among masseuses. Many, however, had a low opinion of other masseuses and rationalized extensively to avoid defining themselves as prostitutes. Most were either married or had boyfriends, and apparently none were lesbians. There was a high rate of employee turnover due to conflicts with the owners, as the girls went to other parlors in search of a better, less exploitative boss. Most customers were white middle-class businessmen over 35. A second category was transients such as traveling salesmen, men new to the area, or younger married men who were having marital problems. A third category consisted of men who were physically or mentally unattractive, men with deformities, or men seeking debasing treatment along with sex.

Many of the customers were regulars who returned week after week, usually at the same time of day, either on their way to or from work, or during a lunch or coffee break.[71] Although the majority of masseuses held a positive or at least nonnegative opinion of their customers, they also felt that it was unacceptable to become sexually aroused by the client—an attitude shared by

[68]H. Benjamin and R. Masters, *Prostitution and Morality* (New York: Julian Press, 1964), p. 296–297.

[69]Pittman, "Call Boys," p. 18.

[70]Albert J. Velarde and Mark Warlick, "Massage Parlors: The Sexuality Business," *Society,* vol. 11, no. 1 (November–December 1973), 63–64.

[71]Clifton D. Bryant and C. Eddie Palmer, "Tense Muscles and the Tender Touch: Massage Parlors, 'Hand Whores,' and the Subversion of Service," in *Sexual Deviancy in Social Context,* ed. Clifton D. Bryant (New York: New Viewpoints, 1977), p. 140.

other types of prostitutes, both male and female. In order to maintain a professional self-image, the women sought to deny their own sexual response.

There are several factors that make the life of a masseuse very attractive. The pay and working conditions are favorable: during one 8-hour shift, a masseuse will have anywhere from two to six customers, at an average of $25 each. Daily income is thus computed at $50 to $150, or $12,000 to $36,000 per year.[72]

Sociologists have investigated the function of prostitution. This inquiry really has two facets: first, why prostitution as an institution has persisted, which encompasses why men frequent prostitutes; and, second, why individuals become prostitutes.

Prostitution as Socially Functional. The classic study of the causes of prostitution as an institution was done by Kingsley Davis in 1937. He related prostitution to several fundamental aspects of human physical nature and of society. First, unlike most female animals, which have well-defined periods of fertility that correspond to sexual responsiveness, human females can be sexually receptive at all times. Second, a relatively long time is required to rear and socialize human young. Given these facts, he thought it was imperative for society to control the sex drive and to make it compatible with the nurturing of children; otherwise, society could not perpetuate itself. As Davis put it: "Erotic gratification is made dependent on, and subservient to, certain cooperative performances inherently necessary to societal continuity."[73]

Most human societies control the sex drive primarily through the family unit, making sexual gratification permissible chiefly within the family, in which the young are reared. Sexual expression which contributes to the family's existence or cohesion is approved and recommended; in proportion with its failure to do so, it is disapproved.

Feminists argue that prostitution is derived from the attitude that women are the sole sexual property of the male. Coupled with the general economic dependence of women, this attitude creates a situation in which women have the choice either of becoming domestic slaves within marriage or of submitting to sexual relations for wages. Either alternative results in the same situation—both groups of women submit to sexual relationships for economic gain.[74]

The mercenary and impersonal nature of prostitution, which makes it contrary to the stated values and norms of society, also makes it functional. Many people feel unable to satisfy their sexual needs within the family structure. Not only do unmarried men and widowers have no legally recognized outlet in this framework, but some married men want more (or more varied) sexual satisfaction than their wives want to or can supply. Others, such as members of the armed forces, or salesmen whose work entails much traveling, may be absent from their families for extended periods. Such men may be unable or unwilling, because of possible complications, to set up

[72]Paul K. Rasmussen and Laurens L. Kuhn, "The New Masseuse, Play for Pay," in *Sexuality: Encounters, Identities, and Relationships,* ed. Carol Warren (Beverly Hills: Sage, 1976), p. 13.

[73]Kingsley Davis, "The Sociology of Prostitution," *American Sociological Review* (October 1937), p. 746.

[74]Harold C. Barnett, "The Political Economy of Rape and Prostitution," *Union for Radical Political Economies,* vol. 8, no. 1 (Spring 1976), 63.

a permanent liaison with any one woman, and the brief, impersonal, non-obligating relationship with a prostitute fulfills their immediate needs. There are those, too, who desire unconventional forms of sexual activity— sadomasochistic practices, for example—which they hesitate to reveal to their wives or friends, or who suffer from physical deformities which, rightly or wrongly, lead them to suppose that they have to buy sex. For such men, anonymity is highly valuable. A prostitute is quickly available, she is knowledgeable enough to provide a variety of sexual satisfactions, and when the business is done, she can be paid off and forgotten. Emotional complications and possible pregnancy are her concern, not the customer's.

Another concern for the prostitute, of course, is how to bear the main burden of social efforts to enforce morality. While others violate the law by directing prostitutes to illegal acts, by providing them with hotel rooms and installing them in massage parlors, the prostitute is most likely to be arrested, fined and jailed.

Particularly in societies such as the United States, which emphasize women as sex objects and where men desire to purchase the illusion of a sexual relationship in which the woman is passive and concerned only with a man's satisfaction, one may experience a high potential monetary return to prostitution. Thus prostitution endures. According to Davis, the only society in which it could conceivably disappear would be one of complete sexual permissiveness. Such a society is highly unlikely, however, because total sexual freedom could destroy the family, making it virtually impossible to raise children. Prostitution is therefore less threatening to society than the conditions that it would eliminate. In any case, Davis points out that even a totally permissive society could not eliminate prostitution unless all desires were complementary. Since there will always be an unequal distribution of good looks and desirability, some people will always desire others who do not return their interest, and the less favored would be driven to try to purchase the sexual favors of others.

Why People Become Prostitutes.   Since society considers prostitution unacceptable and degrading, why do people become prostitutes? It is usually assumed that because of society's disapproval, asking why someone becomes a prostitute is different from asking why someone becomes a lawyer. Robert Bell, however, suggests that the answers to the two questions may not be so different, and that more attention should be paid to the answers that prostitutes give when asked why they enter their line of work. If good pay, association with glamorous people, and the chance to form a romantic relationship with a client are acceptable reasons for becoming an administrator, why should they not apply to becoming a prostitute? Kingsley Davis has suggested that perhaps the truly puzzling question is why more people do not become prostitutes—why so many people stick with such tedious jobs as secretaries and clerks, waiters and waitresses, when they could make more money in less time as prostitutes? Evidently society's norms against prostitution work very strongly for most women, just as norms against prostitution and homosexuality work very strongly for most men.

Some studies approach the question psychologically. Such studies consider two things—the unique life history and psyche of an individual, to see what factors might predispose him or her to become a prostitute; and the psychological defenses or mechanisms which he or she develops after becoming a prostitute to maintain an acceptable self-image in the face of society's disapproval.

In one study that touched on both these questions, fifteen female prostitutes, all streetwalkers, were interviewed, and certain common background characteristics were identified.[75] The women, generally, were alienated from their parents and had usually had a total break with their fathers, toward whom they expressed hostility. Before becoming prostitutes, they had felt themselves to be isolated in an urban society, without any real friends. Similar findings are reported by Nanette Davis in another study of streetwalkers. Most of her subjects had felt, since early childhood, that they were considered either "bad," "slow," "troublemakers," or "different" by their families and teachers.[76] Davis concluded that this early negative informal labeling contributed to the later emergence of an identity as a prostitute.

Studies of male prostitutes have disclosed similar findings—a high percentage of broken homes, and a feeling of being either unwanted or misunderstood.[77] Hoffman, among others, has noted that male prostitutes possess a distinct desire for affection—often unrecognized—and a strong disdain toward their "scores."

Prostitutes, nevertheless, have a problem maintaining their self-respect. Jackman and his co-workers found that prostitutes commonly claim to be no more immoral than anyone else, but simply less hypocritical. As evidence they cite their customers, who are often respected men cheating on their wives. They also say that society only pretends to scorn prostitutes, whereas in reality they are needed and depended upon. Another common defense is to exaggerate other values, such as the financial rewards of prostitution.

Not all of Jackman's subjects adopted the same defense. The prostitutes had different "reference group orientations"—that is, different groups with whom they identified and whose standards they adopted. The first of these reference groups was what the authors called the "criminal world contraculture"—pimps, other prostitutes, racketeers, and hustlers. By identifying with this group, a prostitute could show contempt for the rest of society and identify it as hopelessly square, hypocritical, and dead, and could also place supreme value on money, flashy possessions, and a swinging nightlife.

Other prostitutes manifested a "dual world" reference group orientation; they separated their work from the rest of their lives, associated little with other prostitutes, professed solid middle-class values, identified strongly with their families, and were eager to be considered good mothers. Unlike prostitutes oriented toward the criminal world contraculture, and who often said they enjoyed sex, those in the second group dissociated themselves from the sexual acts in which they engaged, and showed a strong unwillingness to discuss sex at all.

Still other prostitutes fell into neither group and were categorized as "alienated." They were apathetic, identified with no one, and were often

[75]Norman R. Jackman, Richard O'Toole, and Gilbert Geis, "The Self-Image of the Prostitute," *The Sociological Quarterly* 4 (April 1963), 150–161.

[76]Nanette J. Davis, "The Prostitute: Developing a Deviant Identity," in Henslin, *Studies in the Sociology of Sex.*

[77]Kenneth N. Ginzburg, "The 'Meat-Rack': A Study of the Male Homosexual Prostitute," in Bryant, *Sexual Deviancy in Social Context*, pp. 160–161.

heavy drinkers. In effect, this group was the least successful in maintaining a satisfactory self-image; they did not resolve the problem at all.

A more directly sociological approach has focused on the types of structures, particularly informal ones, that exist to direct a girl into prostitution. They deal more with the "how" than with the "why" of becoming a prostitute.

Nanette Davis, in the study of streetwalkers previously referred to, interviewed 30 prostitutes in correctional institutions and found a typical three-stage pattern by which her subjects had progressed from casual promiscuity through a transitional phase to full-fledged prostitution. Her findings led her to conclude that the crucial influences in this process are those that lead someone to identify herself as a person who has departed from the values and norms of society and to organize her behavior accordingly.

The first stage in the process, a period of gradual drift from promiscuity to the first act of prostitution, might take several years, but typically began at an early age. Of Davis' subjects, 19 had had intercourse by age 13. The mean age for the first act of prostitution was 17.3, but the earliest age was 14. In the three cases in which sexual intercourse did not occur until age 17 or 18, the families were very strict, with strong control and a rigid attitude toward sex, so that sexuality became an avenue of rebellion for the girls. But most of the girls' families were highly permissive, exercising little or no supervision, and peer group norms favored early sexuality, so that both the opportunity and encouragement for promiscuity were present.

During adolescence and even earlier, most of the girls were already considered "bad," "different," "troublemakers," "slow," and otherwise unsatisfactory by parents, teachers, and others. In most cases family life was unstable, and more than half had spent part of their childhood separated from their family. Twenty-three were sentenced during adolescence to correctional institutions for truancy, sex delinquency, or other causes, where they met more experienced inmates who made prostitution seem prestigious. Since the girls were usually confused about their own identity at this point, they were glad to learn a new and attractive role.

The girls who were not institutionalized generally experienced peer group pressures toward prostitution—"everyone was doing it." Some of the girls were encouraged by pimps who provided clients and the kind of secure relationship that the girls badly needed; this was the precipitating factor in their choice of prostitution as a career. And those from overly strict families reacted by doing what their suspicious parents apparently expected they were already doing.

During the second stage, which Davis calls "transitional deviance," the girl was learning the skills of prostitution, engaging in prostitution on an occasional basis, but not yet thinking of herself as a "prostitute." She usually retained some commitments to the straight world—a job, marriage, nonprostitute friends—but rationalized her behavior by various expedients. Economic motivation now became primary, together with in some cases loneliness and/or entrapment by the pimp. Eventually this stage culminated in some situation, such as arrest, that forced the girl to perceive herself unequivocally as a prostitute.

Professionalization is the final stage. Labeled by society as a prostitute, perceiving herself as one, the girl makes sex her vocation and shapes her whole life around it. Most of Davis' subjects claimed that they would not want to go back to the "square" life, though some maintained that prostitution was only transitional, a road to another career, such as modeling or dancing. Only a few actually succeeded in retaining a home with children, and these few had to keep their "respectable" and "unrespectable" lives and associates strictly separated.

It would appear, then, that the low-status prostitute typically drifts into her profession through a combination of circumstances, facilitating social structures, and the internalization of social labeling. Rarely has she set out deliberately, with free choice, to become a prostitute.

The case of the higher-status prostitute may be somewhat different. James Bryan has studied the recruitment of call girls.[78] He found that most call girls get their start from a personal contact with someone else in the field, by approaching a known call girl directly, or associating with a pimp. Before going out on their own, most girls have a period of training or apprenticeship, usually lasting two to three months. The training may be given by the pimp, or by an experienced call girl, in which case the trainee usually lives in another call girl's apartment. During this time, she is taught a certain philosophy toward her work, including the attitudes she should take toward prostitution and her customers. She is taught, for example, that males are exploitative and that it is right to exploit them in return. Such values create an *esprit de corps* among call girls and a shared contempt for the rest of the world. The training also covers practical business matters—how to converse with a client or arrange a fee. Very little is taught about direct sexual techniques. The chief function of the apprenticeship is to let the novice call girl develop a clientele. Once she has achieved this, she moves out on her own.

The Prostitute Subculture

Like members of other subcultures, prostitutes usually develop their own specialized knowledge, language, folklore, and network of relationships, in this case with other prostitutes, pimps, customers, and police. Becoming a prostitute means more than selling sex for money; it means becoming part of a well-defined, distinct world. Robert Bell has described some of the features of the prostitute subculture.[79]

A major part of this subculture involves the roles of those who participate in it. One important role, obviously, is that of the customer.[80] The prostitute learns to see the customer in strictly economic terms, as her source of income. This is facilitated by the attitude that the customer is basically corrupt—a belief that, as discussed earlier, prostitutes adopt as a way of maintaining their self-image.

Another subculture figure important to many prostitutes is the pimp. A pimp lives off the earnings of one or more prostitutes, and he serves as manager, protector, and companion/lover. According to Jennifer James, who studied 72 prostitutes and 38 pimps, virtually all streetwalkers have a pimp, who may be a husband or boyfriend, usually referred to as "my man."

[78]James H. Bryan, "Apprenticeships in Prostitution," *Social Problems* 12 (Winter 1965), 278–297.

[79]Bell, *Sexual Deviance*, pp. 237–247.

[80]An insightful and often amusing account of a sociologist's first visit to a brothel is provided in George Lee Stewart, "On First Being a John," *Urban Life & Culture*, vol. 1, no. 3 (October 1972), 255–274.

Although in the past pimps often acquired customers for their girls, now their responsibilities are primarily financial, and they almost never appear on the street, except occasionally, to check up on their women. Although most of the prostitutes in James' sample claimed to have previously worked as waitresses, nurses' aides, or clerks, the pimps generally had not had previous job experience and appeared "totally uninterested in traditional occupations." The mean age of the pimps was 30.2 years, a few years older than their girls, whose mean age was 22.6 years. James believes this age differential reflects the traditional male-female role relationship—an "older male is more likely to exercise authority over a younger female."[81]

A study by two anthropologists[82] found that part of the attraction of pimping was the pimps' delight in exercising total control over women who they felt should be completely subservient to men. This feeling might have been enhanced by the fact that many of the pimps studied were black, and many of their prostitutes were white. Another considerable attraction, of course, was the chance to make a great deal of money while doing virtually nothing. The study found that pimps put great value on material possessions, lavish parties, and expensive jewelry and clothing, and in general on living an elegant life, free from strain and drudgery.

Although pimps exploit their prostitutes, it is clear that these women derive something from this relationship that they feel they need. James found that a streetwalker's status within the subculture was derived from her pimp—how good-looking and well dressed he was, and whether he drove a flashy, prestigious car. Without a pimp, she was an "outlaw," likely to be harassed, or threatened with assault or robbery on the street; the pimp, also, took care of business matters—paying bills, arranging bail and lawyers' fee when necessary, and so on.

Another pertinent element is that a prostitute and her pimp are usually lovers. Common belief has it that the pimp simply uses a prostitute for his own pleasure, while she gets no sexual satisfaction from him. This is related to the myth that women become prostitutes because they are frigid. Probably, however, most prostitutes achieve orgasm at least as often as most wives. If prostitutes do become sexually unresponsive, it is generally an effect of their disillusionment with men. The same applies to the common belief that women become prostitutes because they are lesbians: the prostitutes who become homosexual generally do so as a result of their prostitution experiences that have caused them to become disillusioned with men.

Besides sexual satisfaction, the pimp also provides his prostitutes with a sense of roots, of family, and of being taken care of. It has been pointed out that the pimp-prostitute relationship is similar to a traditional husband-wife relationship, with the economic roles reversed; the prostitute makes money and the pimp provides her with a sense of security and family.

James discusses several myths about prostitutes and their pimps. It is widely believed, for instance, that pimps use force to get prostitutes to work for them. In fact, they will most likely talk a woman into working, because streetwalkers will not stay with a man who abuses them. Again, with very few exceptions, pimps are not likely to seduce young girls, because the legal

[81]Jennifer James, "Prostitute-Pimp Relationships," *Medical Aspects of Human Sexuality* (November 1973), pp. 147–163.

[82]Christina Milner and Richard Milner. Their study was briefly described in *Time*, January 11, 1971.

problems of involvement with underage females are too much trouble. It is also widely believed that pimps control women by getting them addicted to heroin. According to James, however, an addict is not of much value as a prostitute, since she will usually not want to work unless she needs a fix; many women do turn to prostitution after becoming addicts, in order to pay for their drug supply. (Winick, who studied prostitutes in the New York area, disagrees; according to his research, substantial numbers of the girls in the East are narcotics addicts, and pimps are very likely to be the major source of drugs for them. He suggests that this and other differences between his and James' findings, that were based on a West Coast area study, perhaps reflect regional differences in the subculture.[83])

Currently prostitution is illegal everywhere in the United States except in some Nevada counties. While there does not seem to be any strong movement afoot in any of the other states to follow Nevada's example, many arguments have been offered in support of legalization. It is claimed that prostitution exists and will continue to exist regardless of the law. Recognizing this fact will bring many benefits; legislation would make prostitutes' income taxable; it could eliminate, or reduce, the frequent connections of prostitution with crime and governmental corruption, and health regulations for prostitutes could be enacted and enforced reducing the incidence of venereal disease. It has been suggested that legalization of brothels would result in the reduction of streetwalking and public solicitation, which disturbs neighborhood residents.

Social Control

Many advocates of legalization point out the class differential with which the laws are enforced. Unless very indiscreet, call girls and their upper-middle-class customers are seldom the targets of police action. It is the lower-class practitioners, with their lower-class customers, who bear the brunt of antisolicitation laws. It has also been pointed out that prostitution is usually a victimless crime, since the customer participates willingly and generally has few complaints.

Since most laws against prostitution and solicitation require specific evidence of an offer to exchange money for sexual services, a major means of curbing prostitution has been for plainclothes policemen to pose as customers. Objections are that this method is unjust in that it singles out only one partner in the crime; if a prostitute commits a crime, so does her equally liable customer. Oregon and New York (as well as a few other states and some cities) now have laws stating that a man can be jailed for as much as a year and fined up to $1,000 for offering to pay for sexual services. The city of Portland, Oregon, has female police officers pose as streetwalkers. Even so, the law isn't enforced equitably, and far fewer customers are arrested by female officers than are prostitutes by male officers.[84] Entrapment of participants of either sex is protested by civil libertarians, who argue that this is a violation of the right to privacy, they favor legalization on the grounds that sex for a fee is a private matter between consenting adults. Supporters of legalization argue that it is harmful to the social order to have laws on the books that are

[83]Commentary on James, *Medical Aspects of Human Sexuality*, in Charles Winick, *The Lively Commerce: Prostitution in the United States* (Chicago: Quadrangle, 1971), p. 160.

[84]Joan Libman, "Prostitution Law in Oregon May End a Double Standard," *Wall Street Journal*, October 18, 1974, pp. 1 ff.

regularly flouted; since laws against prostitution are not effectively enforced, it would be better not to have them at all.

Still another reason why it might be worthwhile to legalize prostitution is that prostitutes would no longer be "law breakers." This change in status might go a long way toward reducing the tension and stress to which most prostitutes are subject. Legally, at least, they would no longer have to define themselves negatively, and they would no longer be constantly in fear of arrest, even though by other norms prostitution would still be regarded as a social problem.

In Nevada, legalized prostitution seems to work quite well. There are about 30 to 40 legal brothels, with 7 to 10 girls in each. The brothels do a brisk business, bring in considerable tax revenue, and are inspected regularly by physicians. There seems to be no greater amount of prostitution in counties in which it is legal than in those in which it is not.

Pornography

A third area which needs to be discussed in relation to sex-related social problems is pornography, that may be defined as depicting sexual behavior so as to sexually excite the viewer. Pornography has existed for centuries—the covert vendor of "feelthy pictures" is an old cartoon staple—but has become a social problem today. The vast increase and unprecedented openness of its distribution, and its tendency to concentrate in a particular area and thereby adversely affect whole neighborhoods, have caused serious disagreement, even among responsible thinkers, both about what actually constitutes pornography and about the wisdom of permitting or suppressing it.

Gagnon and Simon point out that simply to describe a book, a film, or an event as "pornographic" or "obscene" defines it as being sexually stimulating, and

> can produce a psycho-sexual response in the labeler and his audience very similar to that produced by the pornographic object itself. The very act of labeling generates a sense of sexual anticipation and engages our fantasies about the business of pornography and the erotic character of those who produce it.[85]

Sexual attitudes and behavior are, as we have seen, learned. Among the things we learn is that anything "pornographic" is something other than an appropriate sex object that has the capacity to arouse us. This belief in the power of pornography is related to the view of sex as innate, overwhelming, and instinctive. Pornography is considered able to release the sexual beast in all of us (especially males), and to have, as Gagnon and Simon put it, "a magical capacity to push men into overt sexual action." In their view, pornography deals with illicit sex; it does not describe "conventional sexual activity that occurs within a marital relationship. The rule is: if the activity is conventional, the context is not (the relationship, the motives, etc.); if the context is conventional, the activity is not." It is this illicit emphasis that makes pornography controversial.

Any discussion of pornography must include censorship, and, in the

[85]Gagnon and Simon, *Sexual Conduct*, pp. 260–282.

United States, the issue of First Amendment rights under the Constitution. Today, when many feel that there has been an increasing attempt by government to curtail the exercise of these rights, freedom of speech becomes a particularly sensitive issue. Serious arguments both for and against the suppression of pornographic material can be made. The following arguments are made against limiting pornography: that censorship is damaging to artistic and literary efforts, since past experience has shown that works of sound artistic value are apt to be judged pornographic or obscene if they contain any explicit sexual material, no matter how it is used; that the vagueness of all existing legal definitions of pornography gives too much latitude to judges or other authorities, enabling them to suppress material, in effect, merely because they themselves consider it offensive; that the reading or viewing of pornographic material is a private act, which does no harm to society and therefore cannot legitimately be prohibited by society; if pornography is freely available, people of sophistication and critical judgment will soon become bored with it and turn to more worthwhile entertainment. When arguing against pornography, the claim is made that habitual exposure to pornography is indeed harmful, particularly to the young, and therefore to the society of which they are a part; and that when pornography becomes so widespread that those, presumably a majority, who wish to avoid it find it excessively difficult to do so, it is legitimately a matter for social control. It is this argument that has prompted several Supreme Court attempts to define and control pornography, culminating in the June 1976 decision that it is constitutional for municipalities to restrict the proliferation of pornographic theaters and bookstores through zoning regulations.

Unfortunately for the objectivity of these discussions, there has until recently been a serious lack of empirical research into either the effects of pornography or the extent of exposure to it. The surface has barely been scratched; however, over the past decade, some studies have been made, notably in connection with the work of the U.S. Commission on Obscenity and Pornography, reported in 1970. On the basis of these studies, the commission concluded—although not unanimously—that no social or individual harm could be traced directly to exposure to pornographic material. The Commission therefore recommended the relaxation of most existing restrictions on such material. The sharp, and largely nonrational, rejection of these findings and recommendations, both in government and elsewhere, suggests the degree to which empirical study in this area must contend with the deeply ingrained fears of the population at large.

What, exactly, have the investigations of the last decade revealed? For one thing, they have made clear that some degree of exposure to pornographic material is quite common in our society, and apparently has been for a long time. The study of Abelson and his colleagues, done under the auspices of the Obscenity Commission, showed that, of a nationwide representative sample of 2,486 adults, 84 percent of the men and 69 percent of the women had been exposed to some kind of explicit sexual material.[86] Other studies show similar results. Younger adults and people with some college education were more likely than older adults and people with only high school education to have encountered sexual materials. Among men, but not women, geographic

[86]H. Abelson, et al., "Public Attitudes toward Erotic Materials," *Technical Reports of the Commission on Obscenity and Pornography*, vol. 6 (Washington, D.C.: U.S. Government Printing Office, 1970).

location made a difference—the greatest exposure was in large metropolitan areas and in the northeast, the least in the north central states.

The number of persons reporting extensive experience with erotic materials, however, was relatively small. Of Abelson's subjects, only 14 percent of the men and 5 percent of the women reported having seen specific types of sexual pictures as often as five times in a two-year period. Since the design of the study made it likely that this was a somewhat low figure, the Obscenity Commission concluded that probably "somewhere around one-fifth or one-quarter of the male population in the United States has somewhat regular experience with sexual materials as explicit as intercourse,"[87] and a somewhat smaller number has regular experience with depictions of oral-genital or sadomasochistic activities.

How early does this exposure begin? In Abelson's study, 74 percent of the men and 51 percent of the women had encountered explicit sexual materials before age 21, 54 and 44 percent before age 18, and 30 and 17 percent before age 15. Other studies tend to confirm this pattern. The replies of those questioned suggest that early exposure has been more common among younger adults than among an older generation, but, the Commission points out, older people often have trouble recalling the exact year when a

The open marketing of pornography: a dizzying display of films, peep shows, books, and novelties all available within a few blocks of New York's Times Square.

Geoffrey Gove/Photo Researchers, Inc.

[87]*The Report of the Commission on Obscenity and Pornography.* Section F: "Patterns of Exposure to Erotic Material" (Washington, D.C.: U.S. Government Printing Office, 1970).

given event in their youth took place, so that this may not be a reliable difference.

Apparently, neither adults nor teenagers generally experience pornographic material directly through a "dirty book" store. Most reported having obtained the material through friends, and viewed it in company, not in solitude. Those who do patronize the "adult bookstores" are apt to be white, male, age 26 to 55, middle class, married, and shopping alone. The average patron of sexual movies is similar, except that he may be somewhat more likely to attend with companions—the literature seems to disagree on this last point.[88]

Why people want pornographic material is an unresolved question; many of the adult-movie patrons surveyed by Nawy said that such movies enable them to enhance their own (largely heterosexual) sex lives. A lesser but still large number simply enjoyed the viewing. Substantial numbers of Abelson's subjects said that pornographic material excited them sexually, provided entertainment and information, and in some cases helped to improve their marriage relations. These may be true effects of pornographic experience, or they may be rationalizations developed by the users to justify their activity to themselves; the available evidence leaves the question open.

Probably the most widespread assumption, however, and the greatest fear, is that pornography leads to crime, specifically to sex crimes. The former head of the FBI, J. Edgar Hoover, asserted in a 1956 statement to a congressional committee that "the circulation of periodicals containing such salacious materials plays an important part in the development of crime among youth of our country."[89] Most people might have agreed with him then, and many still would, yet the evidence we have today simply does not prove anything of the sort. In a 1971 survey of the major studies of pornography-crime correlation, W. Cody Wilson pointed out that most sex-crime offenders had significantly less experience with, and later introduction to, pornographic materials in their youth than their control normals.[90] Similar results were found by Goldstein and his associates in a California study of institutionalized sex-crime offenders.[91] Child molesters and rapists had significantly less exposure to pornography during adolescence than a control group of nonoffenders outside the institution. Those offenders with excessive exposure to pornography had already formed unorthodox sexual identities prior to such exposure. Less information is available about sex crimes among juveniles, but from 1960 to 1969, when sexual materials generally became far more widely available than they had been before, juvenile arrests for sex crimes decreased.[92] These statistics appear to justify the Commission's rejecting an association between pornography and criminal acts.

Similar data are reported from Denmark, where first the liberalization (in

Residents of New York's Time Square protest pornography. Besides the usual concern for moral issues, these demonstrators point out pornography's debilitating effect on the neighborhood's economy.

Leif Skoogfors/Woodfin Camp & Assoc.

---

[88]See Abelson, *et al.*, "Public Attitudes toward Erotic Materials"; also H. Nawy, "The San Francisco Erotic Marketplace"; M. M. Finkelstein, "Traffic in Sex-Oriented Materials: Part I," and C. A. Winick, "A Study of Consumers of Explicitly Sexual Materials: Some Functions Served by Adult Movies," *Technical Reports of the Commission on Obscenity and Pornography.*

[89]In "Obscene and Pornographic Literature and Juvenile Delinquency," *Interim Report of the Committee on the Judiciary*, 84th Congress, 2nd Session, June 28, 1956, p. 2.

[90]W. Cody Wilson, "Facts Versus Fears: Why Should We Worry about Pornography?" *Annals of the American Academy of Political and Social Sciences* 397 (September 1971), 105–117.

[91]Michael J. Goldstein, Harold S. Kant, and John J. Hartman, *Pornography and Sexual Deviance* (Berkeley: University of California Press, 1974).

[92]Wilson, "Facts Versus Fears," p. 113.

1967) and then the repeal (in 1969) of the obscenity statute made it possible to compare the incidence of sex crimes in a before-and-after situation. As summarized by Wilson, the Danish study showed that

> the number of sex crimes decreased by 40 percent in the two years following the first liberalization of the availability of pornography as compared with the relatively stable average of the previous nine years; the number of sex crimes reported to the police decreased 30 percent further in the year in which the second liberalization of the pornography law occurred.

However, the decrease was only in such "passive" crimes as voyeurism and exhibitionism; more aggressive sex crimes showed no significant diminution. While Wilson warns that this decrease may reflect, in part, a decreased inclination to report minor sex crimes to the police, he believes that it also reflects an actual reduction in the number of such crimes. In this instance, we can theorize that the stimulation provided for some people by pornography is, in its absence, sought in certain forms of public sexual acting-out behavior. Pornography is, therefore, a functional substitute for such behavior, and to this extent at least it may even be socially beneficial.

Insofar as the case for suppression of pornography rests on the supposed relationship between pornography and crime, it can be regarded as at least tentatively disproved. But a number of thoughtful writers question whether pornography, or at least the wide and open dissemination of it, may not result in more subtle harm, which society cannot safely afford to ignore. Irving Kristol sums up the problem rather succinctly:

> The question we face with regard to pornography and obscenity is whether, now that they have such strong legal protection from the Supreme Court, they can or will brutalize and debase our citizenry.[93]

It is foolish to claim that frequent exposure to pornography, and to an environment presupposing it, will have no effect on one's tastes and outlook. This would be equivalent to saying that no experience or encounter affects human development—that, in fact, no learning is possible. The question, then, is whether pornography has harmful effects—whether society has a legitimate interest in preventing what is to be learned from it. Kristol argues that pornography offers a degraded view of human beings, depriving them of their specifically human character by depicting sex not as part of a personal relationship between two people but as a mere physical act, "animal coupling . . . a public spectacle . . . ." He asserts that pornography "appeals to and provokes a kind of sexual regression," because "it is a masturbatory exercise of the imagination." It thereby discourages the mature development of healthy adult relationships, and has an infantilizing effect on society. It was this, he argues that led people of an earlier age to supress pornographic material: they "took care not to let themselves be governed by the more infantile and irrational parts of themselves."[94] Walter Berns, writing in *The Public Interest*, makes essentially the same point from a slightly different

[93]Irving Kristol, "Pornography, Obscenity, and the Case for Censorship," *New York Times Magazine*, March 28, 1971, p. 24.
[94]Kristol, "Pornography, Obscenity and the Case for Censorship," pp. 112–113.

angle. He connects shame to self-government and democracy: "To live together requires rules and a governing of the passions, and those who are without shame will be unruly and unrulable." Those "who had carried liberty beyond any restraint" have lost the capacity for self-government, and are likely to succumb to tyranny or enforced restraints imposed by others.[95]

Several counter-arguments favor permitting the unhindered distribution of pornography. First, as we have already indicated, the alleged negative social impact of pornography is difficult if not impossible to prove; in fact, existing evidence seems to show no clear association. The danger of censoring ideas, however, is clear and real, therefore, the burden of proof should be upon those who would censor pornography, to demonstrate conclusively that it does have significant negative impact to justify censorship. Second, censorship of sexually explicit materials has, in the past, led to censorship of great literature and art. We laugh now at adding fig leaves to nude Greek and Roman statues, or shadows to Breughel's paintings, yet in some areas of the country, even today, books are routinely banned for being too sexually explicit. Sexually explicit films—whatever their merit—are still rated with an "X," a symbol with strong, negative connotations. Censorship directed at works of art may also produce censorship of unpopular ideas, and threaten the foundations of democracy. Many claim, with justification, that the right to produce pornography is a constitutionally protected freedom of speech. Finally, our sexual mores are now generally more permissive and liberated. Part of the reason, perhaps, is the recognition that freedom from sexual inhibition is far better than the repression of sexuality, that has caused severe problems for many people, including guilt and difficulties in sexual adjustment.

Empirical studies have not shown, and probably cannot show, the effects of a more or less pornography-suffused, or at least very pornography-permissive, atmosphere either on individuals or on society as a whole. Yet there have to be some effects, good, bad, or socially irrelevant. To deal rationally with the question requires resorting to such other disciplines as psychology, history, and even philosophy, in which exact knowledge is rarely possible. We shall probably have to decide, without the aid of precise scientific proof, for or against the effects of pornography in this wide sense, and in the absence of such proof we are not likely to reach a consensus.

Prospects

In recent years, society—or at least substantial parts of it—seems to have been taking an increasingly liberal attitude toward sexual expression. Magazines regularly publish articles on such sexual phenomena as group sex, there is abundant nudity on screen and on stage, the double standard for men and women is gradually being dropped or eased, and, occasionally, respectable authorities support the idea of trial marriages for young couples. Hunt's investigations indicated to him that "the average American now holds many opinions about sex that a generation ago were rarely held by any but highly educated big-city sophisticates and bohemians."

[95]Walter Berns, "Pornography vs. Democracy: The Case for Censorship," *The Public Interest* (Winter 1971), pp. 3–24.

> Almost all human societies . . . educated their young in sexual matters, including the mechanics of copulation. In some societies, parents, other elders or priestly persons have explained the sex act in words. In others, songs, drawings and sculpture have been used to explain what happens in intercourse. In still others, the young have had ample opportunity to see or overhear adults doing it. And in some, the sexual act has been publicly demonstrated during fertility rites or orgiastic celebrations. American society, however, has long been without any officially sanctioned system of teaching the young sexual skills.[96]

His survey showed that for most people, information about sex had been learned from friends. Neither the fathers of two-thirds of the men and of more than four-fifths of women nor the mothers of three-quarters of the men and of nearly half of the women had ever discussed sexual matters with their children before or during their children's high school years.

The lack of readily available and accurate information has consequences for individuals and for society. Hunt believes that "countless cases of psychosexual disability or limitation of function . . . innumerable flawed marriages and . . . an unmeasurable amount of needless human unhappiness and frustration" can be traced to "defects in the sexual education of young Americans."[97] Zelnik and Kantner, who studied sexually active teenage girls, found that ignorance and misinformation about their chances of becoming pregnant resulted in more than three-fourths of them using contraceptive methods only irregularly if at all.[98] Yet, despite the seemingly widespread approval of sex education, many communities still lack sex-education courses in their school curricula. Those who attempt to make sex education part of a school program continue to encounter strong community opposition in many parts of the country.

What effect, if any, will current sexual attitudes have on homosexuals? Again, prospects are uncertain; in many parts of the country, it seems probable that in the near future homosexuals will gain greater acceptance. Organized homophile groups are doing much, at least in major cities, to make the public recognize the discrimination that homosexuals face. Possibly this will help remove some, if not all, legal restrictions in many areas. On the other hand, as we have seen, most states continue to prohibit certain sex acts between consenting adults and have received Supreme Court justification for their ban.

It does not seem as if the general change in sexual attitudes is having much of an effect on attitudes toward prostitutes except, perhaps, to decrease the demand for their services, as the double standard becomes weaker and sex becomes increasingly available. Prostitutes have been proclaimed by some women's liberationists as the only honest women, but prostitutes themselves do not seem to relish this championship; generally, they have been largely ignored by social movements. For this reason, some prostitutes have organized on their own (in a movement called "Coyote") to fight for the decriminalization of prostitution. It is possible that as public attitudes become generally more liberal, prostitutes will suffer less from legal sanctions;

[96]Hunt, *Sexual Behavior in the 1970s*, p. 24.
[97]Hunt, *Sexual Behavior in the 1970s*, pp. 120–131.
[98]Melvin Zelnik and John Kantner, "Sexuality, Contraception, and Pregnancy among Young Unwed Females in the United States," in *U.S. Commission on Population Growth and the American Future, Demographic and Social Aspects of Population Growth* (Washington, D.C.: U.S. Government Printing Office, 1972).

widespread acceptance of prostitution, however, seems unlikely in the forseeable future.

It is clear that in only a few places have attempts been made to change sex laws (and sex education) to conform with present behavioral realities. Even as more people espouse a more permissive attitude, the national ambivalence toward sexual matters, noted at the beginning of this chapter, shows few signs of abating.

Summary

Although there has been a far-reaching liberalization of sexual attitudes in the United States, traditional attitudes still influence our sex laws and behaviors. These traditional attitudes stem from the Judeo-Christian tradition, which accepted sex only with the context of heterosexual marriages; the influence of capitalism, with its emphasis on delayed gratification, reinforced repressive sexual attitudes; and the Victorians, who stressed self-control and promoted a "double-standard" of sexual behavior.

Formal study of human sexuality helped to liberalize our sexual attitudes, starting with Freud's theory that sexuality was an integral part of human development through Kinsey's revelations that American sexual behavior differed from its professed norms. Studies of sexual behavior in other cultures indicate that virtually every form of sexual activity has at some time and place been acceptable, suggesting that human sexual expression is largely learned, not instinctive.

Gagnon and Simon distinguish between three categories of sex-related problems. *Tolerated sex variance* refers to acts that are disapproved but that are rarely considered criminal. *Asocial sex variance* includes acts such as incest, child molestation, and rape, which are not reinforced by a social structure. *Structural variance* is problematic sexual behavior that has supportive social structures.

Homosexuality is a sexual preference for members of one's own sex. Not everyone who engages in homosexual acts identifies as a homosexual, nor are homosexuals an easily identifiable group; they are found in every occupation and social stratum. They also differ in how they deal with their homosexuality. The homosexual subculture does, however, share certain activities and norms. Differences in the way male and female homosexuals manage their homosexuality reflect society's different patterns of socialization for men and women.

Prostitution is sexual intercourse on a promiscuous and mercenary basis. There are several levels among prostitutes, ranging from the call girl or call boy to the streetwalker. Prostitution exists largely because it is socially useful. Early self-identification as someone who varies from social norms is apparently an important influence in the background of many prostitutes.

Pornography is the depiction of sexual behavior, usually illicit, in a way intended to sexually stimulate the viewer. Although the connection between pornography and sex crime has largely been disproved, controversy still exists about the social effects of pornography.

Although sexual attitudes in the United States have become more liberal and some restrictive sex laws have been repealed, in many areas all except the most traditional sex behaviors are still prohibited.

Bibliography

Altman, Dennis. *Homosexual: Oppression and Liberation.* New York: Piterbrodge and Diemstfrey, 1971.

Becker, Howard S., ed. *The Other Side,* New York: Free Press, 1964.

Bell, Robert R., and Gordon, Michael. *The Social Dimensions of Human Sexuality.* Boston: Little, Brown, 1972.

Bell, Alan P. and Weinberg, Martin S. *Homosexualities: A Study of Diversity Among Men and Women.* New York: Simon and Schuster, 1979.

Benjamin, H., and Masters, R. *Prostitution and Morality.* New York: Julian Press, 1964.

Benson, R. *In Defense of Homosexuality: Male and Female; A Rational Evaluation of a Social Prejudice.* New York: Julian Press, 1965.

Cappon, Daniel. *Toward an Understanding of Homosexuality.* Englewood Cliffs, N.J.: Prentice-Hall, 1965.

Cory, Donald W., and LeRoy, John R. *The Homosexual and His Society: A View from Within.* New York: Citadel Press, 1963.

Gagnon, John H., and Simon, William, eds. *Sexual Deviance* Chicago: Aldine, 1973.

————. *Sexual Conduct.* Chicago, Aldine, 1973.

Goldstein, Michael J., and Kant, Harold S. *Pornography and Sexual Deviance.* Berkeley, Calif.: University of California Press, 1974.

Greenwald, Harold. *The Elegant Prostitute: A Social and Psychoanalytic Study.* New York: Walker, 1970.

————. *The Call Girl.* New York: Ballantine, 1958.

Hoffman, Martin. *The Gay World: Male Homosexuality and the Social Creation of Evil.* New York: Basic Books, 1968.

Hunt, Morton. *Sexual Behavior in the 1970's.* New York: Dell, 1974.

Johnson, Cecil. *Sex and Human Relationships.* Columbus, Ohio: Charles E. Merrill, 1970.

Karlen, Arno. *Sexuality and Homosexuality: A New View.* New York: Norton, 1971.

Masters, William H., and Johnson, Virginia, *Homosexuality in Perspective.* Boston: Little, Brown, 1979.

Ponse, Barbara. *Identities in the Lesbian World.* Westport, Conn.: Greenwood Press, 1978.

Ruitenbeck, Hendrick M., ed. *Homosexuality: A Changing Picture.* Atlantic Highlands, N.J.: Humanities Press, 1974.

Sagarin, Edward, and MacNamara, Donald E., eds. *Problems of Sex Behavior.* New York: Thomas Y. Crowell, 1968.

Schofield, Michael G. *Sociological Aspects of Homosexuality: A Comparative Study of Three Types of Homosexuals.* Boston: Little, Brown, 1965.

Schur, Edwin M., and Beday, Hugo A. *Victimless Crimes: Two Sides of Controversy.* Englewood Cliffs, N.J.: Prentice-Hall, 1974.

Sheehy, Gail. *Hustling.* Dell Publishing Co., 1977.

Teal, Donn. *The Gay Militants*. New York: Stein and Day, 1971.

Tripp, C. A. *The Homosexual Matrix*. New York: McGraw-Hill, 1975.

Weinberg, Martin S. and Williams, Colin J. *Male Homosexuals: Their Problems and Adaptations*. New York: Oxford University Press, 1974.

Williams, Colin J., and Weinberg, Martin S. *Homosexuals and the Military: A Study of Less Than Honorable Discharge*. New York: Harper & Row, 1971.

Winick, Charles. *The Lively Commerce: Prostitution in the United States*. Chicago: Quadrangle, 1971.

Report of the Committee on Homosexual Offenses and Prostitution. *The Wolfenden Report*. Briarcliff Manor, N.Y.: Stein and Day, 1963.

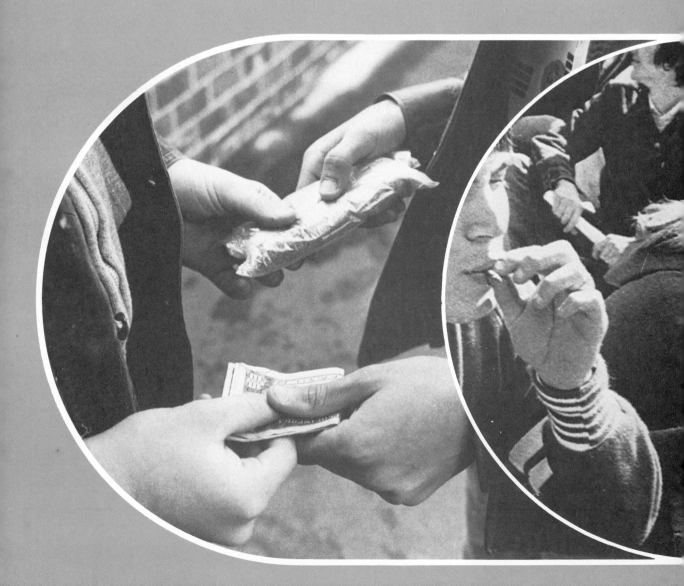

Problems of
Chemical
Dependency

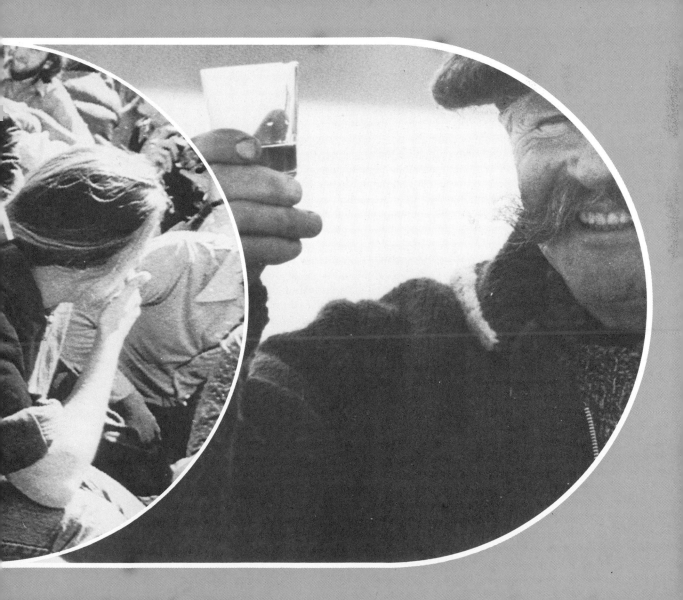

Facts about Alcohol and Drugs

- The average American drinker consumes nearly 3 gallons of pure alcohol a year.
- The economic cost of alcoholism is nearly $43 billion per year.
- Almost 44 million Americans used marijuana at least once in 1977.
- 70 percent of all U.S. prescriptions are for psychoactive compounds.

Ours is a drug-using society—to ease pain, to increase alertness, to relax tension, to lose weight, to fight depression, to prevent pregnancy, Americans of all ages and at all socioeconomic levels consume vast quantities of chemical substances every year. Most of these drugs are socially acceptable, and most people use them for socially acceptable purposes. Alcohol is pharmacologically a drug, as are caffeine and nicotine; these are commonly and widely used as simple aids to sociability and ordinary activity. But some drugs, and some users of other drugs, are socially defined as unacceptable, and it is these drugs and users that are believed to constitute the "drug problem."

The uses, and abuses, of alcohol and other drugs are combined in this chapter for a number of reasons. For one thing, through personal and social effects, alcohol abuse is probably more harmful than the abuse of less socially accepted drugs. Alcohol and other drugs offer satisfactions which make them attractive to many people, but both can be habit-forming, sometimes with destructive consequences to users as well as to nonusers, and, in both cases, there are controversies over the causes, consequences, and moral implications of use.

The rationale determining the acceptability of a given drug is illogical. Frequently a drug favored by the dominant culture is approved, while another, associated with a subculture, is outlawed. Frederick H. Meyers, among others, has pointed out that

> the effects of marijuana, both operationally and in its mechanism of action, correspond . . . to those of other sedatives and anesthetics, especially alcohol. . . . One is driven to the conclusion that the differences between the dominant attitudes and consequent laws toward marijuana and alcohol are unrelated to the pharmacological effects of the drugs but are due to a conflict between the mores of the dominant and one or more of the subcultures of the country.[1]

Along the same lines, a poll taken by the National Institute on Alcohol Abuse and Alcoholism (NIAA) found that a majority of parents considered hard liquor less dangerous than most drugs to the future health and safety of their children; only 16 percent of parents considered it a greater threat than marijuana. A survey by the National Commission on Marihuana and Drug Abuse found that alcohol was regarded as a drug by only 39 percent of adults and 34 percent of young people.[2] Morris Chafetz put it this way:

[1]Frederick H. Meyers, "Pharmacological Effects of Marijuana," in *The New Social Drug,* ed. David E. Smith (Englewood Cliffs, N.J.: Prentice-Hall, 1970), p. 39.
[2]Sandra Stencel, "Resurgence of Alcoholism," *Editorial Research Reports* 2 (December 26, 1973), 990–991.

Nonalcoholic drugs are somehow foreign and frightening, because their use, except as medicine, is not yet accepted as part of the mainstream of American culture. Alcohol, on the other hand, is so common a drug that we tend to ignore it—and its victims—as we have done for far too long.[3]

Other observers have noted that increased drug use in the 1960s coincided with a period of cultural ferment—political disturbances and sexual freedom—especially involving young people. Increasingly, adults from the dominant culture consider youth itself as "a separate and separable" cultural subgroup, and while alcohol use is "interpreted as part of growing up, as an act of socialization, [some drug use] is viewed as 'growing away' rather than growing up."[4] Similarly, there has been excessive use of amphetamines and barbiturates, drugs which were long regarded with much less concern than even the occasional use of heroin (which typically has been a lower-class drug). Many authorities, however, regard abuse of amphetamines and barbiturates as more widespread and dangerous than the occasional use of heroin.

What Is a Drug?

From a strictly pharmacological viewpoint, a drug is simply any substance which chemically alters the structure or function of a living organism. So inclusive a definition, however, encompasses everything from food, vitamins, and hormones to laxatives, snake and mosquito venom, anti-perspirants, insecticides, and air pollutants. Obviously, this definition is too broad to be of practical value. Definitions that depend on context are more useful. In the medical sense, for example, a drug may be any substance prescribed by a physician or manufactured expressly to relieve pain or to treat and prevent disease. In the sociolegal context, "drug" denotes any habit-forming substan-

[3]Morris E. Chafetz, U.S. Department of Health, Education and Welfare, *Alcohol and Alcoholism* (Rockville, Md.: National Institute on Alcohol Abuse and Alcoholism, 1972), p. iii.

[4]Joseph R. Gusfield, "The (F)utility of Knowledge?: The Relation of Social Science to Public Policy toward Drugs," *Annals of the American Academy of Political and Social Science* 417 (January 1975), 1–15.

Even the most common household drugs have a place in the realm of legal drug abuse. Overdoses of seemingly innocuous vitamins or laxatives can cause serious side effects.
Louis Goldman/Photo Researchers, Inc.

ces that directly affect the brain or nervous system. More precisely, it refers to any chemical substance that affects bodily function, mood, perception, or consciousness; that has a potential for misuse; and that may be harmful to the user or to society.

Although this last definition is more satisfactory for our purposes than the original broad one, it omits the social bias which traditionally has determined what is labeled a drug. When society has for centuries used a habit-forming substance, this substance may not be classified as a drug, even if it has been scientifically proven to be harmful. Alcohol and tobacco (nicotine) are cases in point.

The Abuse of Legal Drugs

We can define drug abuse as the use of unacceptable drugs, and the excessive or inappropriate use of acceptable drugs, so that physical or psychological harm can result. (See the discussion of drug dependence later in the chapter.) From this definition, there can be little question that the abuse of legal drugs—excluding alcohol—causes more harm than the abuse of illegal drugs.

The most widely abused of all drugs is aspirin—$438 million in annual retail sales; about 27 million pounds of aspirin, several billion tablets—are consumed each year in the United States. Aspirin is often taken in excessive dosages for every physical or mental discomfort, real or imagined. It is far from harmless, however, and, in fact, can and does cause ulcers, gastrointestinal bleeding, and other ailments. Many other substances that can be obtained without a prescription are also widely abused. The American preoccupation with "regularity," for example, causes millions of people to use laxatives unnecessarily, with resultant harm to their digestive systems. The fear that they are not getting enough vitamins causes many people to take excessive doses of vitamin supplements—yet, large doses of vitamins A and D are toxic.

More serious is the abuse of prescription drugs. The flow of tranquilizers, sedatives, pain killers, and stimulants to the public is supposedly controlled by physicians and pharmacists; nonetheless, these drugs are easily obtained— legally and illegally. Some physicians, pressured by patients who demand quick and easy relief, dispense drugs with great facility—more than 1.5 billion drug prescriptions at a cost of some $8 billion are filled each year.[5] Yet only a few doctors (about 2 percent of America's 500,000 practicing physicians) knowingly deal in false prescriptions.[6] More often, prescription drugs enter the illegal market through other channels: individuals falsify ailments or forge prescriptions in order to reap enormous profits by reselling drugs on the street. Another legal sedative, alcohol, produces dangerous and unpredictable effects when taken in conjunction with other drugs. The chemicals mingle in the bloodstream, and the result is far more powerful than the user expects. In the twelve months prior to May 1, 1977, the National Institute on Drug Abuse reported that 47,700 people were treated for mixing drugs and alcohol; of these, there were 2,500 fatalities. For those who mix drugs and alcohol, cross-addiction is also a problem. Dr. Jack H. Mendelson of the Harvard Medical School notes that people who suffer from one addiction may be

[5]U.S. Bureau of the Census, *Statistical Abstract of the United States, 1977*, 98th ed. (Washington, D.C.: U.S. Government Printing Office).

[6]"Boom in Illegal Pills," *Newsweek*, August 14, 1978, p. 22.

especially susceptible to forming a second dependency.[7] Drugs and alcohol, both legally obtainable, pose a threat that is equal to that of illegal drugs.

Perhaps so many legal drugs are abused because they are so easily available; of the approximately 50 barbiturates on the market today, for example, only about 6 are needed for medical purposes, the remainder having been created by drug companies only to increase sales. The pervasive advertising of drugs also leads to their abuse. Drug companies spend one-fourth of their income on advertising, trying to convince consumers that there is something wrong with them—that they take too long to fall asleep, for example, or that they are too tense—and then suggest that their medications will solve these problems. As a result many people use unnecessary drugs excessively, and others with serious ailments fail to seek treatment. Finally, the common desire for convenient, short-term solutions to problems may lead to excessive drug use. For many people, taking (or offering) a pill is simply easier than working a problem out or learning to endure it. It is safe to say that the easy availability of drugs, their persistent promotion, and the popular desire for instant cures for symptoms or difficulties make the abuse of legal *and* illegal drugs much more likely.

Alcohol Use and Abuse

It is one of the cultural peculiarities of our society that the problems specific to alcohol—chronic inebriation, "skid row" vagrancy, drunken driving—arouse less interest and concern than abuse, or even use, of other drugs. In part, as we have already suggested, alcohol—in contrast to other drugs—is thoroughly integrated into Western mores. It may also be better adapted to our complex life style, since, besides relieving tension and lessening sexual and aggressive inhibitions, it seems to facilitate interpersonal relationships, at least superficially, whereas other drug experiences, even in groups, are often highly private.

It has been estimated that the "Average American Drinker" consumes 2.69 gallons of absolute alcohol in the course of a year. This represents the equivalent of a total annual consumption of 2.58 gallons of whiskey, 2.24 gallons of wine, and 28.08 gallons of beer per person.[8] For some of America's 112 million drinkers, the use of alcohol is a normal, pleasant, sociable activity; for others it is a spur to enable them to work, a sedative to calm them down, or a kind of anesthetic to dull the pain of living. For still others, it seriously impedes normal functioning and creates major problems, both for themselves and for those close to them.

Our society approaches alcohol with mixed feelings. On the one hand, it creates warmth and "high spirits," promotes interpersonal harmony and agreement ("happy hour," "Let's drink to that"). It has long been used in informal rituals (such as Christmas eggnog) and formal rites (wine as the blood of Christ), and has been important to the economy of many nations. The growing and harvesting of grapes, grain, and other crops, and the brewing, fermenting, distilling, and sale of alcoholic beverages have provided employ-

---

[7]William Stockton, "New Clue in the Cancer Mystery," *The New York Times Magazine*, August 2, 1978, pp. 18 ff.

[8]Mark Keller and Carol Gurioli, *Statistics on Consumption of Alcohol and on Alcoholism* (New Brunswick, N.J.: Rutgers Center of Alcohol Studies, 1976), pp. 3–5.

ment, trade, and national revenue from the heavy taxation of alcohol. On the other hand, the problems created by the abuse of alcohol have been staggering: public drunkenness and disorderly behavior, traffic and industrial accidents, poor social functioning, broken marriages, and exacerbation of poverty, mental and physical illness, crime, and suicide.

Problem Drinkers and Alcoholics

There are an estimated 12 million problem drinkers and almost 6 million alcoholics in the United States: about 83 percent are men, and 16 percent are women.[9] Almost one out of every ten drinkers is a problem drinker or alcoholic. Yet the terms "problem drinker" and "alcoholic" elude clear-cut definition. According to sociologist Robert Straus, a distinction should be drawn between addictive and non-addictive alcoholism.[10] Non-addictive alcoholics may be chronic drinkers who drink to the point of stupefaction and whose frequent imbibing interferes with their health, interpersonal relationships, and economic functioning; they are not, however, addicted to alcohol. The roots of their drinking are usually psychological or social, and their goal is to help them escape reality—alcohol produces a desired oblivion and euphoria. They are thus problem drinkers, rather than alcoholics.

In contrast, alcohol addicts have an uncontrollable need to achieve a peak of intoxication, and if this need is frustrated they will develop acute withdrawal symptoms, like those of narcotics addicts—uncontrollable trembling, nausea, rapid heartbeat, and heavy perspiration. Some alcohol addicts have bodily symptoms after abstaining for only one day; and, in fact, alcohol withdrawal is even more likely to kill than is narcotics withdrawal.

Alcoholism may develop after ten or more years of problem drinking; however, many alcoholics go directly from total abstinence into chronic alcoholism. In some cases, it is believed, this may be due to biochemical predispositioning. For example, a genetic cause of alcoholism was suggested by the results of a study of Danish men who had been adopted and raised apart from their biological parents. The men whose biological parents were alcoholic had significantly greater drinking problems, more psychiatric treatment, and higher divorce rates than the adopted men in a matched control group.[11] Most authorities believe, however, that a single cause for problem drinking or alcoholism is rare. Instead, a complex variety of physiological, psychological, and sociological factors seems to be involved. According to one study, a problem drinker is most likely to be one who

> (1) responds to beverage alcohol in a certain way, perhaps physiologically determined, by experiencing intense relief and relaxation, and who (2) has certain personality characteristics, such as difficulty in dealing with and overcoming depression, frustration, and anxiety, and who (3) is a member of a culture in which there is both pressure to drink and culturally induced guilt and confusion regarding what kinds of drinking behavior are appropriate.[12]

[9]Keller and Gurioli, *Statistics on Consumption*, pp. 4, 12.

[10]Robert Straus, "Alcohol and Alcoholism," in *Contemporary Social Problems*, 3rd ed., ed. Robert K. Merton and Robert Nisbet (New York: Harcourt Brace Jovanovich, 1971), pp. 247–248.

[11]Donald W. Goodwin, *et al.*, "Alcohol Problems in Adoptees Raised Apart from Alcoholic Biological Parents," *Archives of General Psychiatry* 28 (February 1973), 238–243.

[12]Report of the Cooperative Commission on the Study of Alcoholism, in Stencel, "Resurgence of Alcoholism," pp. 1001–1002.

Scarcely any society, past or present, has lacked some alcoholic beverage. For thousands of years wine has accompanied food in the diets of Mediterranean peoples. Among Jewish families, wine is part of the weekly Sabbath and yearly Passover rituals. In northern Europe, beer, whiskey, and hard cider are traditional. The Orient has rice wine. The tropics have palm wine, orange beer, and other quick-fermented beverages. Nomadic herdspeople of the past sometimes made use of fermented mare's milk. Of the world's major religions, only Islam forbids wine as a ritual or social beverage.

Among some groups, alcoholic beverages are normally drunk in moderate amounts at meals. Others drink after meals, or independent of them, and perhaps to drunkenness. It is the latter custom which seems to promote alcoholism, as is illustrated by a comparison of American Jews and Italian-Americans, who customarily drink with meals and in the home, and Irish-Americans, who are more likely to drink outside the home and/or not at meals. Among the Jews and Italians, most adults use alcohol and report having done so since childhood, but the rate of alcoholism is quite low; while among the Irish, childhood drinking is less likely, and alcoholism rates are much higher.[13]

This correlation between familial drinking patterns and alcoholism rates has been found to hold true for other groups as well. For ethnic groups in which drinking habits are established by cultural custom, alcohol abuse is rare. But in those groups with ambivalent attitudes toward alcohol, including American Protestants, alcoholism rates are high—in particular, drinkers from those groups in which alcohol is seldom used are most likely to encounter problems.[14] In general, when children grow up with routine, comfortable, intrafamilial exposure to alcohol, they are very unlikely to become excessive drinkers when they become adults.

Significantly, in the United States generational status is becoming as important as ethnic background in determining drinking patterns. Among first-generation Italian-Americans, for example, frequent and even daily wine drinking is customary, but there are few alcohol-related problems; later generations have higher rates of heavy drinking and favor drinks of higher alcoholic content.[15]

A study published by the Department of Health, Education, and Welfare (HEW)[16] lists some of the characteristics of the American drinker. Age, sex, ethnic and religious background, education, occupation, and place of residence all seem to be related to whether, how much, and how an individual will use alcohol. For instance, heavy drinking among men is most common at ages 30 to 34 and 45 to 49, among women at ages 21 to 24 and 45 to 49. Men of the youngest age group for which data are available, 18- to 20-year-olds, are heavier drinkers than 21- to 24-year-olds. In general, older people drink less, even if they have been drinkers when young.

The last three decades have seen a dramatic increase in alcoholism among

[13]U.S. Department of Health, Education and Welfare, *Alcohol and Health* (Rockville, Md.: U.S. Public Health Service, 1974), pp. 15–16.

[14]Chafetz, *Alcohol and Alcoholism*, pp. 10, 16.

[15]HEW, *Alcohol and Health*, p. 15.

[16]U.S. Department of Health, Education and Welfare, *First Special Report to the U.S. Congress on Alcohol and Health* (Rockville, Md.: U.S. Public Health Service, 1971).

Figure 4-1
Source: Reprinted by permission from *Journal of Studies on Alcohol,* vol. 36 (1975), pp. 144–1451. Copyright by Journal of Studies on Alcohol, Inc., New Brunswick, N.J. 08903.

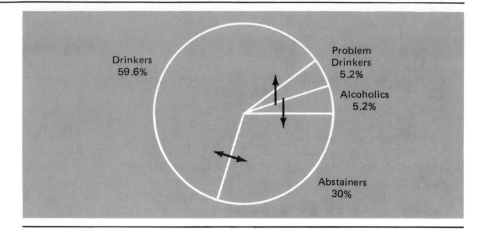

adult women. In the 1950s, one in six alcoholics was female; today, according to the National Institute of Mental Health (NIMH), the rate is nearly one in five. There are several possible explanations for the rising statistics, but new research has focused on the differences between female and male alcoholics. As with male alcoholics, social factors—the presence of alcoholism in the family, childhood unhappiness, and trauma—are important influences. But for women, increasing rates of alcoholism seem to be related to their massive influx into the work force. When women seek—and feel compelled to seek—careers outside (and often in addition to) their traditional role as housewife and mother, they encounter new and heavy pressure. One study found that working-married women are more likely to become alcoholics than housewives or single-working women. Yet the statistics on female alcoholism may be misleading. As women have become more visible in society, their drinking patterns have become more noticeable. Perhaps researchers are only now learning to identify the female alcoholic, and many women may still be hiding their drinking problems at home.[17]

In regard to socioeconomic status, drinking appears to be most frequent among younger men at the highest socioeconomic level and least frequent among older women at the lowest level. The higher socioeconomic classes drink to excess less often; heavier drinking for escape is found at the lower socioeconomic levels and among young people.[18]

Occupationally, business and professional men rank high on heavy drinking, while farmers rank low. Among women, service workers have the highest proportion of heavy drinkers. Regular churchgoers drink less than nonchurchgoers; but among this group, Jews and Episcopalians are the highest drinkers, conservative and fundamentalist Protestants the lowest. But Jews have a low proportion of heavy and escape drinkers, and more Catholics than others are both drinkers and heavy drinkers. Regionally, the South has a below-average proportion of drinkers, which may correlate both with rural

[17]"Causes of Female Alcoholism," *Intellect* (January 1977), p. 213; "Working Wives: Driven to Drink?" *Newsweek,* September 16, 1978.

[18]Gary L. Albrecht, "The Alcoholism Process: A Social Learning Viewpoint," in *Alcoholism: Progress in Research and Treatment,* ed. Peter G. Bourne and Ruth Fox (New York: Academic Press, 1973), pp. 26–27.

and small-town status, and with the more conservative religious affiliations of the "Bible Belt." There are no significant racial differences in drinking behavior.[19]

Throughout the 1970s there was a marked increase in alcohol consumption among teenagers and young adults. As early as 1974 Morris Chafetz noted: "The switch is on. Youths are moving from a wide range of other drugs to the most devastating drug—the one most widely misused of all—alcohol."[20] Unfortunately, teenage drinking has been abetted by parents who, frightened by the specter of drug abuse, regard drinking as the lesser of two evils. The failure to assess the dangers of alcohol abuse has contributed to today's high statistics and, although the exact extent of the problem is unclear, there can be no doubt that teenage and pre-teenage drinking is widespread.[21] Estimates by the NIAAA indicate that 3.3 million teenagers have encountered difficulties because of their drinking. A recent national survey found that 74 percent of all students in grades 7 through 12 were regular drinkers—70 percent of the girls and 79 percent of the boys. Nineteen percent of the students—15 percent of the girls and 23 percent of the boys—were defined as problem drinkers, being drunk at least six times in the previous year or being in trouble because of drinking twice during the same period. Even the more conservative estimates place the number of problem drinkers among America's young at more than a million.[22]

Drinking among Young People

Teenagers are drinking more, and they are drinking at an earlier age. The NIAAA reports that the average child now takes his or her first drink before age 13. In the past, significantly more young boys drank than young girls, and drinking was heaviest in the Northeast and along the West Coast. Though these distinctions still exist, the gaps are closing. As the statistics in the preceding paragraph suggest, young women are drinking nearly as much as their male counterparts, while teenagers in the South and Midwest are catching up with other parts of the country.

The growing popularity of alcohol among the young is attributed to many factors: the difficulty, expense, and danger of procuring other drugs; lowered legal drinking ages; the manufacture and advertisement by the alcoholic beverage industry of products that are especially appealing to the young, such as sweet wine and milkshake-type drinks. Very recently, alarmed at the increase in traffic fatalities involving young drunken drivers, some states have enacted legislation raising the drinking age from 18 to 19, 20, or 21.

The estimated 3.3 million teenagers defined as problem drinkers include those who have had difficulties with teachers or the police because of their drinking. Of these, only a relatively small percentage can be defined as chronically alcoholic. Alcoholic teenagers differ from other adolescent drinkers. They drink more often and consume greater quantities, often specifically to get drunk; they are more likely to drink alone, to display aggressive or destructive behavior, and to have severe emotional problems.[23]

[19]HEW, *Alcohol and Health*, pp. 17–18; see also Albrecht, "Alcoholism Process."

[20]"Alcoholism: New Victims, New Treatment," *Time*, April 22, 1974, p. 75.

[21]Daniel Yankelovich, "How Students Control Their Drug Crisis," *Psychology Today*, (October 1975).

[22]Ernest P. Noble, ed., *Alcohol and Health: Third Special Report to the United States Congress* (Rockville, Md.: U.S. Public Health Service, June 1978), pp. 23–26.

[23]Stencel, "Resurgence of Alcoholism," pp. 990–991.

Alcohol and young
people: an accepted
step in the socialization
process.
Christa Armstrong/Photo
Researchers, Inc.

Many young people turn to alcohol for the same reasons their parents do—to have a good time, to escape from the stress of everyday life, and to conform to normative social behavior. As Albrecht points out:

> Both their peer group and the adult society that they are being socialized to enter encourage and reward drinking behavior. Learning to drink for the adolescent is but present and anticipatory socialization. . . . The major influences on whether or not an individual drinks are the principal agents of socialization in his life, his parents and his peers.[24]

Whether due to hereditary or environment, the children of drinkers tend to become drinkers themselves. According to Robert A. Unger of the ACCEPT Alcoholism Clinic in New York, 50 percent of the children of alcoholics may have drinking problems sometime in their lives.[25]

Drinking among young people can also be construed as a rebellion against the adult world—an attempt to assert independence and copy adult behavior. Some authorities believe that extremely strict regulations against drinking only make it more appealing, and prohibition is extremely difficult in a society in which alcohol is widely used and relatively easy to procure.

[24]Albrecht, "Alcoholism Process," pp. 30–31.
[25]"Adolescent Alcoholics: How to Sell Teen Sobriety," *Human Behavior* (August 1978), p. 57.

Alcohol-Drug Interaction.   Like adults, teenagers often mix alcohol with other drugs, yet, like many adults, are ignorant of the effects of such combinations. Besides the possibility of cross-addiction (dependence upon both drugs and alcohol), some alcohol-drug combinations are lethal, and the results are not always predictable. Metabolic factors cause the user's tolerance to fluctuate. An intake that is harmless one day can later, even in smaller quantities, cause coma or death. Aside from the purely physiological effects, the drug-alcohol combination can change the user's mood, causing temporary instability or severe depression.

Drugs (including alcohol) interact in the system in two basic ways—synergistically and antagonistically. In a synergistic interaction, two or more drugs exert a mutual influence upon each other to produce an effect much greater than either would cause alone. Certain vitamins, for instance, can only be utilized by the body when they are taken in conjunction with other vitamins. With toxic substances, which all drugs essentially are, the synergistic reaction can be fatal. Sedatives like barbiturates (found in prescription sleeping pills) or methaqualones (known by their brand name, Quaaludes) are especially dangerous when taken with alcohol. Both substances depress the

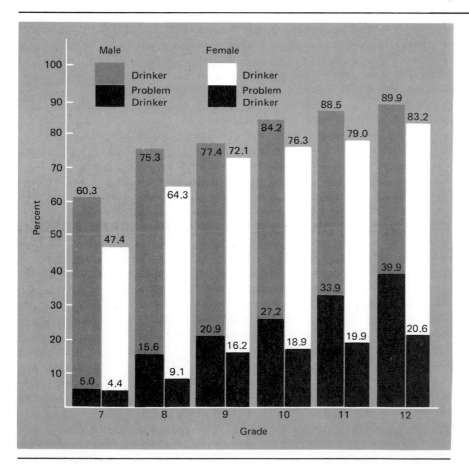

Figure   4-2
Source: Ernest P. Noble, ed., *Alcohol and Health: Third Special Report to the United States Congress*, (Rockville, Md.: U.S. Public Health Service, June 1978), p. 24.

central nervous system, and the poisoning that results can leave the user mildly sedated—or in a coma. Antagonism, the reverse of synergism, occurs when one drugs negates the effect of another. If a person overdoses on heroin, for example, a narcotic can induce an antagonistic response. Yet antagonistic interactions can also work to the body's detriment. Alcohol, even in moderate quantities, can block the beneficial effects of prescribed antibiotics and other medicines.

There are four major factors that govern how drugs and alcohol will interact in the system: absorbtion (incorporation of the substance into the bloodstream), distribution (the movement of the substance from the bloodstream to the part of the body on which it works its most profound effect), excretion (the substance's passage through the system and its eventual elimination), and biotransformation (or metabolism—the rate at which a substance reaches peak concentration in the bloodstream). Each of these four factors can in turn be effected by such other conditions as the amount of sleep the user has had, what food has been eaten and when, and the body's overall health and tolerance. In short, drug-alcohol interaction can change on a day-to-day—even hour-to-hour—basis.[26]

As more is learned about the hazards of combining drugs and alcohol, physicians are beginning to recognize the role of alcohol in their patients' lives. Many doctors caution patients not to drink while taking certain antibiotics since the alcohol will reduce or wholly destroy the beneficial effects of the drug. Similarly, doctors prescribing sedatives forbid the use of alcohol, since the interaction of the two substances produces a multiple, potentially lethal, result. The relationship between drugs and alcohol is unique, and the medical world is only now beginning to grasp it. As was noted in the first part of this chapter, alcohol actually a drug in itself, is a depressant. This fact was ignored for many years. Alcohol withdrawal, for example, was often treated with diazepam (or Valium); however, new understanding of alcohol as a drug threw this practice into question. If one drug was simply replacing another, little was in fact being done to help the patient recover.

Social Problems Related to Alcohol

Health   On the average, alcoholics can expect to live 10 to 12 years less than nonalcoholics. There are several reasons for this shortened life span. First, alcohol contains a substantial number of calories, containing no vital nutrients, except water. Thus, alcoholics generally have a reduced appetite for nutritious food, and inevitably suffer from vitamin deficiencies; as a result, they have a lowered resistance to infectious diseases. Second, over a long period of time, large amounts of alcohol destroy liver cells and cause them to be replaced by scar tissue; this condition—cirrhosis of the liver—is the sixth most frequent cause of death (approximately 33,000 a year) in the United States. Heavy drinking also contributes to a wide range of heart ailments, and there is some evidence that alcohol contributes to the incidence of cancer. Finally, studies indicate that alcohol is implicated in more than 10,000 suicides annually. It is

[26]Dominick A. Labianca, "Hazards and Benefits of Drug Interaction," *Intellect* (April 1978), pp. 401–403.

Average Annual Death Rate per 100,000						
	1963-64		1973-74		Percent Increase 1963-64 to 1973-74	
Sex and Age	White	Nonwhite	White	Nonwhite	White	Nonwhite
Male						
Ages 20 and over	11.5	20.6	16.8	42.6	46	107
20-29	.6	4.9	1.1	7.3	83	49
30-39	4.9	23.1	7.0	39.7	43	72
40-49	15.2	33.4	22.9	70.6	51	111
50-59	25.1	29.2	34.9	76.0	39	160
60-69	25.9	24.3	40.0	48.7	54	100
70 and over	13.7	10.4	18.5	22.3	35	114
Female						
Ages 20 and over	4.2	9.5	5.7	16.2	36	71
20-29	.2	2.6	.2	2.5	–	–4
30-39	2.4	12.9	2.3	15.2	–4	18
40-49	7.5	16.0	9.2	30.5	23	91
50-59	9.2	12.5	13.4	27.7	46	122
60-69	6.0	7.0	10.4	15.5	73	121
70 and over	2.5	–	3.3	4.8	32	–

Source: Metropolitan Life Insurance Company, *Mortality from Alcoholism, Statistical Bulletin* (December 1977), p. 2.

Table 4-1
Mortality from Alcoholic Disorders

interesting that there is some evidence that, for unknown reasons, the life expectancy for light-to-moderate drinkers exceeds even that of total abstainers.[27]

Drinking and Driving

The statistical connection between alcohol and driving accidents is staggering. Wherever studies have been undertaken to measure the alcoholic level of drivers involved in accidents, the same distressing conclusions are reached: alcohol is a factor in about 50 percent of all fatal vehicular accidents and serious automobile accident injuries. That is, alcohol is implicated in almost 23,000 deaths and about 500,000 serious injuries resulting from auto accidents each year. In 1977 there were 1,262,200 arrests in the United States for driving while under the influence of alcohol.[28]

Other studies have shown that the dimensions of the problem may be even greater. Statistics released by the Secretary of Transportation, for example, based on investigations conducted over a number of years, indicate that at least 800,000 traffic accidents a year are the result of drinking.[29] One

[27]Noble, *Alcohol and Health,* pp. 10–12; *Recent Trends in Mortality from Cirrhosis of the Liver* (New York: Metropolitan Life Insurance Company, February 1977), pp. 7–11.
[28]Noble, *Alcohol and Health,* p. 13; *Uniform Crime Reports* (Washington, D.C.: Federal Bureau of Investigation, October 18, 1978), p. 172.
[29]*Alcohol and Highway Safety: A Report to the Congress from the Secretary of Transportation* (Washington, D.C.: U.S. Department of Transportation, 1968).

study of fatal motor accidents in New York showed that the blood-alcohol level of 75 percent of the drivers was above 0.1 percent. A study of drivers and pedestrians involved in fatal accidents in California during one year similarly demonstrated that alcohol contributed to the death toll. Alcohol levels of more than 0.1 percent were found in 53 percent of the drivers and 32 percent of the pedestrians.[30]

The prosecution of persons involved in accidents attributable to alcohol is seriously hampered by the general attitude toward drinking. An Indiana report asserts that juries are found to be reluctant to render guilty verdicts in drunken-driving cases because the jurors themselves identify and sympathize with the defendant. Even when drunken-driving laws are rigidly enforced, however, the problem is not always solved; in some European countries, for example, vigorous attempts by the governments to curb drunken driving have met with little success. The attitude that it is acceptable to drive after drinking is apparently too widespread for law enforcement to have much effect.

Alcohol and Arrest Rates

In 1977 the FBI reported that 1,727,200 arrests, or about a third of the national total, involved drunkenness or an offense related to violations of the liquor laws.[31] These criminal acts were minor, involving breaches of the peace, disorderly conduct, vagrancy, and so on. In arrests for major crimes, drunkenness generally does not appear in the charges, yet alcohol often contributes to crime.

Among 588 cases of homicide in Philadelphia, alcohol was found in either the victim, the offender, or both, in 64 percent of the cases. Among 100 male sex offenders in another study, "8 percent were chronic alcoholics, and 35 percent were drinking at the time of the offense." The rates for drinking in relation to skilled property crimes, such as forgery, appear to be somewhat lower than for violent and sexually related crimes.[32]

Other studies have shown that alcohol was used by up to 80 percent of offenders immediately prior to their committing a homicide and other assaultive offenses, and that alcohol was a factor in 67 percent of sexual crimes against children and 63 percent of sexually aggressive acts against women. Still other studies have indicated that young people who used alcohol were responsible for significantly more crimes of assault than their nondrinking peers, and that the use of alcohol correlated significantly with other forms of antisocial behavior, such as poor school attendance, unsatisfactory work records, and excessive fighting.[33] (See also Chapter 5.)

The reasons for the high correlation of drinking with arrests for serious crimes are not fully understood. It has been pointed out that alcohol, by removing some inhibitions, may lead people to behave as they would not ordinarily do. Likewise, as with other drugs, the need to obtain supplies may lead to theft or other property crimes, sometimes with violence, such as armed robbery. Since chronic alcoholics may be unable to hold steady jobs,

[30]Chafetz, *Alcohol and Alcoholism*, p. 11.

[31]*UCR*, p. 172.

[32]The President's Commission on Law Enforcement and Administration of Justice, *Task Force Report: Drunkenness, Annotations, Consultants' Papers, and Related Materials* (Washington, D.C.: U.S. Government Printing Office, 1967), pp. 40–41.

[33]National Commission on Marihauna and Drug Abuse, *Drug Use in America: Problem in Perspective*, Second Report (Washington, D.C.: U.S. Government Printing Office, March, 1973), p. 157.

their financial difficulties are compounded, perhaps increasing the temptation to commit crimes.

Also, the values and self-concepts of chronic heavy drinkers are apt to change as their condition progresses. They are more likely to associate with delinquents or criminals, which may lead them to commit criminal acts themselves.

Excessive drinking may also be not the cause of crime, but an effect of other underlying conditions, such as a disordered social environment. As the President's Commission on Law Enforcement and Administration of Justice has said:

> At the very least a criminal outcome is the consequence of alcohol . . . plus personality, plus group or subcultural membership plus opportunity plus drinking circumstances plus other events. Even this addictive scheme is insufficient, for the likelihood is one of interplay or interaction with differing outcomes each time one element in the drama of conduct is altered.
>
>   Finally . . . one does not know that the relationship now shown between alcohol use and crime is not, in fact, a relationship between being caught and being a drinker rather than in being a criminal and being a drinker.[34]

In addition to its involvement in serious crime, alcoholism creates another problem by straining the law-enforcement machinery, with the processing of petty offenders. The arrest, trial, and incarceration of offenders costs the taxpayer billions of dollars each year. And many of these arrests involve only a small segment of the community—the neighborhood drunk or derelict—who may be repeatedly arrested and imprisoned during the year.

Effects on the Family

If the only victims of alcoholism were the alcoholics themselves, the social effects would be serious enough, but others, especially the families of alcoholics, also suffer. The emotional effect, which is part of any family crisis, is heightened when the crisis itself is socially defined as shameful. Fire, illness, and accident—so-called "acts of God"—are tragedies that cannot be helped, but alcoholism somehow reflects on the people affected by it. The children of an alcoholic parent frequently develop severe physical and emotional illness, and marriage to an alcoholic often ends in divorce or desertion. An alcoholic parent may eventually become unable to provide financial support, and poverty may ensue. (See Chapter 1.)

If the families of alcoholics attempt to stand by them and help them overcome their condition, certain typical stages of adjustment are likely to occur. These stages were examined by Joan K. Jackson in a study of the families of alcoholic men.[35] She found that the first stage was a denial by all concerned that the problem existed—an attempt to pretend that excessive drinking was somehow normal. When this became impossible, there were various attempts to eliminate the problem, followed by progressive family disorganization. At some point the wife began to take over the husband's roles, and gradually a reorganization, with the alcoholic husband more or less excluded, took place. Eventually, in some cases, it appeared necessary to exclude the husband, and a further degree of reorganization occurred.

[34]President's Commission, *Task Force Report: Drunkenness*, p. 43.
[35]Joan K. Jackson, "The Adjustment of the Family to Alcoholism," *Marriage and Family Living* 18 (November 1956), 358–370.

Finally, if the husband obtained help and succeeded in controlling his alcoholism, he was reintegrated into the family, with the new redefining of roles and groping after renewed trust and confidence that this entailed. Not all families complete this cycle, and even in those which do, permanent scars may remain.

Skid Row Alcoholics

"Skid row" alcoholics constitute only a small percentage of alcoholics, but because of their visibility and low status, they account for a high percentage of those arrested for drunkenness.
Charles Gatewood

Contrary to popular belief, only about 5 percent of all alcoholics and problem drinkers are of the "skid row" category; most alcoholics appear to be average people with jobs and families.[36] Several theories have been advanced by sociologists to explain the differences between the alcoholics sunk in the anonymity of skid row, and those who remain at home. Skid row alcoholics clearly wish to divorce themselves from their past as well as to drink. Howard M. Bahr concludes that neither alcohol nor the lack of a home or family impels a person to become a skid row alcoholic. Rather, the cause is a "lack of social affiliation," a feeling that usually long preceded the actual decision.[37] Skid row derelicts have a great need to escape the realities of social living—an escape that chronic drinking can intermittently provide.

In a sample study of men who were repeatedly arrested for inebriation, disorderly conduct, vagrancy, and other similar offenses, about 96 percent of the offenders were either single or had broken marriages, compared with 11 percent of the total male population of the United States. Most offenders were also uneducated, 70 percent had not gone beyond eighth grade, 68 percent were unskilled workers. Many were accustomed to institutionalized living and such semiprotective environments as the Civilian Conservation Corps, the Army, railroad gangs, lumber and fruit camps, or the Salvation Army and similar shelters. They were chronic dependents.

> The chronic drunkenness offender is the product of a limited environment and a man who has never attained more than a minimum of integration in society. He is and has always been at the bottom of the social and economic ladder; he is isolated, uprooted, unattached, disorganized, demoralized and homeless, and it is in this context that he drinks to excess. As such, admittedly through his own behavior, he is the least respected member of the community, and his treatment by the community has, at best, been negative and expedient. He has never attained, or has lost, the necessary respect and sense of human dignity on which any successful program of treatment and rehabilitation must be based.[38]

Social Control

Because of the many facets of human motivation and the diverse social conditions leading to alcoholism and excessive drinking, these problems are complex and no one solution can be applied to all cases. Repeated arrests of chronic inebriates seem merely to perpetuate a deviancy-reinforcement, or "revolving door," cycle. Offenders are arrested, processed, released, then arrested again, possibly only hours after their release. Each such arrest, involving police, court, and correctional time, is expensive and may actually

---

[36]Stencel, "Resurgence of Alcoholism," p. 989.
[37]Howard M. Bahr, *Homelessness and Disaffiliation* (New York: Columbia University Press, 1968).
[38]President's Commission, *Task Force Report: Drunkenness*, pp. 11–13.

contribute to an excessive drinker becoming an alcoholic and encourage the inebriate to act out secondary deviances.[39]

It is increasingly being recognized that alcoholism is a sickness, with a variety of psychological and physiological components, and that through an equal variety of treatments it is possible to rehabilitate, although not completely cure, many chronic inebriates. There have been nonpunitive attempts—some more successful than others—to assist alcoholics to overcome their addiction or habituation and to create alternatives to enable alcoholism-prone individuals to handle disturbing emotions and anxieties. **Treatment and Rehabilitation**

This represents a significant shift of public opinion. Not long ago the alcoholic was considered an outcast, untreatable (and therefore not to be treated), intractable, and, if he or she happened to be a relative, unacknowledged. It is now believed that:

> No miracle cure, no equivalent of the Salk vaccine is in sight for the alcoholic, and none is ever likely to be found . . . but for every one of the many alcoholisms there is at least one treatment or combination of treatments that offers a good chance of cure.[40]

One reflection of this changed attitude was the Comprehensive Alcohol Abuse and Alcoholism Prevention, Treatment and Rehabilitation Act of 1970, which created both the National Institute on Alcohol Abuse and Alcoholism to coordinate federal activities and the National Advisory Council on Alcohol Abuse and Alcoholism to recommend national policy. The act provided more immediate aids as well, such as grants to individual states for developing comprehensive programs for alcoholism, grants and contracts for specific projects on prevention and treatment, and incentives for private hospitals admitting patients with alcohol-related problems.

Traditionally, hospitals have offered little beyond immediate "drying out" and release of the specifically alcoholic patient, or treatment of a specific medical problem but not its alcoholic cause. This too is changing. The American Hospital Association is now advocating alcoholism programs that would be regularly available in the nation's general hospitals, and is attempting to utilize the resources of general hospitals in community systems of alcoholic treatment.[41] Unfortunately, many hospitals still do not provide such care for alcoholics, and most health insurance programs do not yet cover this illness.

Unquestionably, the most dramatic successes in coping with alcoholism are achieved by Alcoholics Anonymous (AA). The effectiveness of this group in reforming individual alcoholics is based on what amounts to a conversion, a profound and quasi-religious phenomenon. Alcoholics are led to this experience by a fellowship with other individuals like themselves, some of whom have already mastered their problem, while others are in the process of mastering it. **Alcoholics Anonymous**

[39]President's Commission, *Task Force Report: Drunkenness*, pp. 8–9.
[40]"Alcoholism," *Time*, p. 78.
[41]HEW, *Alcohol and Health*, p. 148.

AA insists that drinkers face their shortcomings and the realities of life and, when possible, make amends to persons they have injured or aggrieved in the past. The movement also concentrates on building up the alcoholics' self-esteem and reassuring them of their basic worth as human beings. Since its founding in 1935, the group has evolved a technique by which reformed alcoholics support and comfort the drinker attempting rehabilitation. This support is available to the alcoholic during crises when he or she feels in danger of a relapse to drinking.

There are more than 320,000 members in some 16,500 groups in the United States. Almost four hundred groups have been created to deal specifically with the growing number of teenage and young adult drinkers.[42] AA has spawned Al-Anon, a program to aid the nonalcoholic spouse, and Alateen, to help the children of alcoholics with their common problems or understanding the sick family member and coping with their own troubling emotions. The alcoholic family member need not be a participant in Alcoholics Anonymous for relatives to participate in these offshoot programs, which grew from the recognition that an entire family is psychologically involved in the alcohol-related problems of any one of its members.

AA appears to be the most successful large-scale program for dealing with alcoholism. It is essential, according to AA precepts, for addicts to acknowledge their lack of control over alcohol and to abstain completely from all alcoholic beverages. This approach sees alcoholism as an "allergy" in which even one drink can produce "an intolerable craving for more."[43] While precise figures are not available, it seems that more than half of those who join the group with serious intentions are rehabilitated.[44] The voluntary character of the program probably contributes to its rate of success; whether the AA approach—particularly its insistence on total abstinence—could successfully be applied to all alcoholics is debatable.

Antabuse Programs

Antabuse, a drug developed in Copenhagen in 1947, is one of the newer weapons against alcoholism. It is a prescription drug that sensitizes the patient's system, so that consuming even a small quantity of alcohol causes strong and uncomfortable physical symptoms. Drinkers become intensely flushed, their pulse quickens, and they feel nauseated.

Before beginning treatment with Antabuse, an alcoholic is detoxified. Then the drug is administered to the patient for several consecutive days, along with doses of alcohol. The patient continues to take the drug for several more days, and at the close of the period another dose of alcohol is administered. The trial doses of alcohol condition the patient to recognizing the relationship between drinking and the unpleasant effects. Other techniques similar in principle depend on different nausea-producing drugs, or on electric shock, to condition the patient against alcohol; this basic process is variously known as aversion therapy or behavior conditioning.

Antabuse, which the World Health Organization (WHO) has named Disulfiram, has gained only limited acceptance in the treatment of alcoholics. Critics claim that its effect is too narrow, and that the personality problems of

[42]Diane Withers, *et al.*, "The Latest Teen Drug," *Newsweek*, January 8, 1978, pp. 43–44.
[43]From the AA credo, in Stencel, "Resurgence of Alcoholism," p. 1004.
[44]Morris E. Chafetz and Harold W. Demone, Jr., *Alcoholism and Society* (New York: Oxford University Press, 1972).

the drinker are neglected. They also maintain that the drug does not work for persons suspicious of treatment or for those with psychotic tendencies. Nevertheless, it is a useful tool for a skilled practitioner.

Sanford Billet regards Antabuse as part of a total treatment program including psychotherapy, drug therapy, and vocational and social rehabilitation. He believes that Antabuse, by providing a concrete, immediate reason not to drink, helps the patient to stop drinking entirely, so that he or she can profit from all phases of the treatment program. In a sample study, 64 percent of the alcoholics who used Antabuse (together with the rehabilitation program) improved "markedly"; 35 percent improved "moderately." Without Antabuse (but with the rehabilitation program), 31 percent improved "markedly" and 42 percent improved "moderately."[45]

Community Programs

The problem drinker or alcoholic who receives medical help while remaining part of a family unit usually responds better than one who is institutionalized. In community-care programs, many of which are being set up, not only the problem drinkers and alcoholics, but also the family members are treated. The approach here resembles that used in family therapy in community mental health programs (see Chapter 2). The need to deal with the problem drinker's, or alcoholic's, family, both in their attitude toward the patient and in their own adjustment, is an essential part of the therapy. Besides getting medical help, problem drinkers and alcoholics need to develop a healthy image both of themselves and their families and a feeling of security. Consultations with the families aim to persuade patients that they are trusted and respected—feelings they must develop if they are to obtain satisfaction from a nondrinking life.

Since the vast majority of problem drinkers and alcoholics are still living with their families and working, rehabilitation—not total abstinence—is often the goal of treatment. The NIAAA considers this goal achieved "when the patient maintains or reestablishes a good family life and work record, and a respectable position in the community, and is able to control . . . drinking *most of the time*." The institute reports that "a successful outcome can be expected in at least 60 percent, and some therapists have reported success in 70 or 80 percent, depending on the motivation and intelligence of the patient and his determination to get well; the competence of the therapists; the availability of hospital or clinic facilities and tranquilizers and other drugs; and the strong support of family, employer, and community."[46] One relatively new development is transitional intermediate care facilities that help problem drinkers and alcoholics who are undergoing rehabilitation to rejoin their communities.

Company Programs

Another relatively new development, and one that has been demonstrably successful, is for companies to sponsor alcohol treatment programs for their employees. The aims of such programs are twofold: early identification of a drinking problem and therapeutic intervention before it is too late. Company programs have been resisted by employees who resented having their privacy

---

[45]Sanford L. Billet, "Antabuse Therapy," in *Alcoholism: The Total Treatment Approach*, ed. Ronald J. Cantanzaro (Springfield, Ill.: Charles C. Thomas, 1974), pp. 167–174.

[46]Chafetz and Demone, *Alcoholism and Society*, p. 17.

invaded or being stigmatized as alcoholics. Successful programs, however, have overcome these objections by making counseling by a social worker-therapist available to deal with personal problems as they surface instead of appearing to concentrate specifically on alcoholism. As problems are identified, they can be referred to appropriate community resources. Since there is no stigma attached to an employee's seeking help or being called in for a conference under such multifaceted programs, they have met with notable success.

It is estimated that problem drinkers in business and industry may have a rehabilitation rate as high as 80 percent. An important factor in that rate is the motivation of the worker to remain in the community and to keep working.[47]

Educational Programs   Alcohol education, like drug education, is most helpful when it imparts accurate information instead of exploiting fears and overdramatizing effects. Because of recent evidence that adolescents have begun drinking at younger ages and that peers and the family are decisive in determining drinking attitudes and behavior in young people, information programs on alcohol have been started in many elementary schools and high schools.

Rupert Wilkinson points out that changes in public attitude can help considerably to prevent alcoholism. One of the key influences is advertising campaigns for alcoholic beverages that invest alcohol with a certain mystique symbolizing virility and romance. Instead, he maintains, advertising should show alcohol being drunk in a family setting, as a natural part of home life. In this way the myths of alcohol use could be eliminated.[48]

The most significant educational programs, however, should try not only to demythologize alcohol and disseminate information about its effects, but also to change the public attitudes toward problem drinking and alcoholism. For too long we have emphasized the abuse of illegal drugs and ignored "the most serious drug problem facing this country today"[49]—the problem of alcohol abuse. Only when we better understand how widespread and harmful alcohol abuse is, and learn to regard alcohol abusers as people needing help rather than as outcasts, will we begin to make significant headway toward solving the problems of alcohol abuse in our society.

Drug Use and Abuse

Like the term "drug," the term "addiction" is used rather loosely to denote any habitual or frequent use of a drug, with or without dependence on it. In fact, addiction is a complex phenomenon involving the drug user's physical and psychological condition, the type of drug used, and the amount and frequency of use. Similarly, precise degrees of dependence are difficult to define because of the physiological and psychological complexity of drug use. Nevertheless, a limited consensus has developed among some experts and certain definitions are considered acceptable: Physical dependence occurs

[47]Chafetz and Demone, *Alcoholism and Society*, p. 28; HEW, *Alcohol and Health*, p. 154.
[48]Rupert Wilkinson, *The Prevention of Drinking Problems: Alcohol Control and Cultural Influence* (New York: Oxford University Press, 1970).
[49]National Commission on Marihuana and Drug Abuse, *Drug Use in America*, p. 142.

when the body has adjusted to the presence of a drug and will suffer pain, discomfort, or illness—the symptoms of withdrawal—if its use is discontinued. The word "addiction" is used to describe physical dependence; psychological dependence occurs when a user needs a drug for the feelings of well-being it produces. The word "habituation" is sometimes used to mean psychological dependence.

Other experts prefer not to make the distinctions between physical and psychological dependence, since these are so often interrelated and since words like "addiction" have come to connote something alien or evil. These experts prefer to characterize the compulsion to use a drug simply as "drug dependence," without attempting to define its physical and psychological components.

It is important to note that not all drug use is considered drug abuse, in the sense that it impairs health. A person suffering from an illness that required treatment with morphine, for instance, might be addicted but would not be considered an abuser. In a survey of drug use among students, Daniel Yankelovich found it necessary to distinguish between nonusers, regular users, and abusers.[50] About 58 percent of high school and college students were nonusers of illegal drugs, and about a third used illegal drugs (usually marijuana) regularly, generally on social occasions; less than 10 percent manifested an inordinate preoccupation with and a dependence on drugs.

Most adult Americans use drugs; many use a wide variety frequently; and the term "drug user" might justly be applied to nearly all of us. A survey of regular and occasional users of both legal and illegal drugs—persons not chronically dependent on drugs—showed a correlation of broad drug experience with higher education, high-average income, and liberal or independent political beliefs. From the group with the least drug experience to that with the most intensive drug use, there was a steady shift up the social scale, as well as increased education, a higher divorce rate, a younger average age, and a higher proportion of white persons.[51]

Except for the opiates and alcohol, we have no precise knowledge about the rate of use of mind-altering drugs, the kinds of users, and the dosages and effects of long-term ingestion. In some instances, the pharmacological properties and effects of these drugs on the user are not fully understood; thus a definitive judgment on the risks and dangers involved is not always possible. Nevertheless, some general statements can be made.

Marijuana

While those who regard every young person as a regular user of marijuana are evidently exaggerating the facts, there is no question that marijuana use is widespread. A 1977 study of high school seniors by HEW found that 56 percent had used marijuana at least once and that 9 percent used it daily. The National Institute on Drug Abuse estimates that 60 percent of college students had tried the drug and that 28 percent smoked it frequently.[52]

Since such surveys depend on self-reports about illegal behavior, the true

[50]Yankelovich, "How Students Control Their Drug Crisis."

[51]Richard H. Blum et al., *Society and Drugs: Social and Cultural Observations* (San Francisco: Jossey-Bass, 1969), pp. 272–275.

[52]Lloyd B. Johnson, et al., *Drug Use Among American High School Students, 1975–1977* (Rockville, Md.: U.S. Public Health Service, 1978), pp. 7, 10; Ira Cisin, et al., *The National Survey on Drug Abuse: 1977* (Rockville, Md.: National Institute on Drug Abuse, 1978), p. 5.

percentage of drug use may be somewhat higher than these figures suggest. But it is apparent, in any case, that the degree of frequency of use varies widely. Helen H. Nowlis, in her book on drug use on college campuses, distinguishes three categories of users; (1) the *experimenters,* who have tried one or more drugs, usually marijuana or LSD, once or twice; (2) the *users,* who use one or more drugs occasionally; and (3) the *heads,* for whom drug-use dominates their lives.[53] To lump together and condemn persons in all three categories, as is sometimes done by the popular media and the opponents of drug use, is to obscure the true issues.

A generation ago, the drug most favored by students and young adults seems to have been alcohol, and there were many who regarded college drinking as a fairly serious social problem. About a decade ago the concern shifted to those drugs legally designated as narcotics; and some social scientists believed that marijuana in particular was becoming a replacement drug for alcohol, being used by a generation developing new ways of expressing itself. But it is now apparent that marijuana did not replace alcohol, but was adopted in addition to, and frequently along with, alcohol. In fact, as stated earlier, alcohol is by far the most commonly used drug among all students.

Probably because of the illegal status of marijuana and other mood-altering drugs, their use during the 1960s became almost the hallmark of that group of young people who were rebelling against existing social norms—rebelling far more deeply than the earlier alcohol generation usually did. Today, however, marijuana is popular among young people largely because, like alcohol, it is a social drug. It is generally used as part of group activity, and apparently contributes to a heightened feeling of warmth and unity among those present. In fact, in some circles, the student who abstains from marijuana is likely to encounter considerable social pressure.

For years, heated debates about the hazards of long-term marijuana use have been raging, and there appears to be no end in sight. Some studies that apparently show lowered male hormone levels, brain damage, and other ill effects as a result of marijuana use have been questioned on the grounds of poor research techniques and methodology. In one often-cited hormone-level study, for example, all of the 10 marijuana smoking subjects had used LSD, and most had also used amphetamines and/or other drugs; obviously these drugs, or the multiple-drug combination, might have been responsible for any long-range ill effects.

One study by the NIMH analyzed the effects of long-term marijuana smoking in Jamaica, where many heavy users smoke at least eight "spliffs" (a more potent marijuana cigarette than the typical American "joint") a day. The researchers found that field workers expended more energy after smoking a spliff than before, but appeared to accomplish less actual work. They noted "no significant physical abnormality" attributable to the drug in any of the smokers or in the control group. Neither were there significant chromosome abnormalities or differences in brain-wave recordings. When the long-term marijuana users were deprived of the drug for two or three days, there were no "demonstrable intellectual or ability deficits . . . there is no evidence . . . of brain damage." At worst, the Jamaica study indicates, there may be

---

[53]Helen H. Nowlis, *Drugs on the College Campus* (New York: Doubleday, 1969), p. 62.

impaired lung function due to smoke (marijuana or tobacco) inhalation. Other studies tend to support these findings.[54]

One of the public's greatest fears about marijuana is that its use will lead to the use of other drugs (the "stepping-stone" theory); however, this appears to be a myth. Persons are most likely to become multidrug users as a result of peer pressure, not because of the effects of one specific drug. If any drug is associated with the use of others, including marijuana, it is tobacco, followed closely by alcohol. Many studies have revealed a close association between the use of tobacco and, to a lesser extent, of alcohol, and the use of marijuana and other mind-altering drugs. In fact, some studies indicate that marijuana abstainers tend to have been raised by parents who use no drugs.[55] It should be emphasized that although many opiate users may at some time have used marijuana, the overwhelming majority of marijuana users do not progress to other drugs. In particular, no causal relationship has been shown to exist between marijuana use and subsequent heroin use.[56]

Despite a general lack of convincing data on the ill effects of marijuana, the drug continues to be outlawed. It was first introduced in the United States in 1920, and its general use was outlawed by the federal government in 1937.

[54]Edward M. Brecher and the Editors of Consumer Reports, "Marijuana: The Health Questions," *Consumer Reports* (March 1975), pp. 143–149.

[55]See, for example, the articles by Denise Kendal, *et al.*, in *Journal of Social Issues*, vol. 30, no. 2 (1974) and *Journal of Health and Social Behavior*, vol. 15, no. 4 (December 1974).

[56]*Marihuana: A Signal of Misunderstanding, First Report of the Commission on Marihuana and Drug Abuse* (Washington, D.C.: U.S. Government Printing Office, 1972), p. 109.

Table 4-2
States That Have Decriminalized Marijuana

State	Effective Date	Amount	1st Offense	2nd Offense	Classification
Alaska	9-1-75	private use 1 oz	$100	—	civil
		public - 1 oz	$1,000	—	
California	1-1-76	1 oz or less	$100	—	misdemeanor
		1 oz or more	0-6 mos./$500	—	no permanent record
Colorado	7-1-75	1 oz or less	$100	0-2 yrs	class 2 petty offense,
		1 oz or more	0-1 yr/$500	$500-$1000	no permanent record
Maine	3-1-76	1½ oz or less	$200	—	civil
		1½ oz or more	0-1 yr/$500	—	
Mississippi	7-1-77	1 oz or less	$100-$250	$250/5-60 day, drug education	noncriminal offense
		1 oz to 1 kilogram	felony or misdemeanor	discretion of courts	
Minnesota	4-10-76	1½ oz or less	$100	0-90 days/$300	civil
		1½ oz or more	0-3 yrs/$3000	0-6 yrs/$6000	
Ohio	11-22-76	100g (3.5 oz)	$100	—	minor misdemeanor,
		100-200 gram	0-30 days/$250	—	no criminal record
Oregon	10-5-73	1 oz or less	$100	—	civil
		1 oz or more	0-10 yrs/$2500	—	

Source: Prepared by the National Organization for the Reform of Marijuana Laws and the Center for the Study of Non-Medical Drug Use.

Subsequently every state forbade its use. In recent years, however, there has been some modification of the legal approach to marijuana. By 1977, six states—Oregon, Alaska, Maine, Ohio, Colorado, and California—decriminalized marijuana for personal use, reducing penalties to a moderate fine for possession of small amounts of the drug, and making possession a misdemeanor or civil offense instead of a criminal act. Other states were considering similar legislation.

The recognition of a need for reform was due in part to the greatly widening marijuana constituency among students and numerous members of the middle and upper classes. When the dominent culture dismissed drug users as a troublesome minority, harsh penalties were legislated. But, when use by middle-class youth increased, and marijuana also became acceptable to many adults, modification of punitive laws became inevitable. In fact, data from various surveys suggest that more than 43 million Americans have tried marijuana at least once. For reasons such as these, even the federal government is deemphasizing its efforts to control marijuana use.

Cocaine Cocaine, the powdered derivative of the South American cocoa plant, is rapidly replacing other illegal drugs in popularity. An estimated 2 million Americans spend $20 billion to buy the 66,000 pounds of the substance that are imported each year.[57] The expense of the drug has contributed to its popularity, making it prized as much for its chic status as for the euphoria it produces. Despite its popularity, however, little is known about the effects of prolonged cocaine usage. Only recently has research begun to assess its full physiological and psychological impact.

The properties of *Erthyroxylon coca* (cocoa shrub) were first discovered by the Inca Indians of South America; the Spanish explorers of the sixteenth century noted that the Indians habitually chewed cocoa leaves. The effects— euphoria, decreased appetite, heightened tolerance to pain—allowed Indian laborers to work longer and harder, eat less food, and patiently endure misery and oppression.[58] It was almost three centuries before the drug was exported in quantity; however, chewing cocoa leaves never became popular in Europe or the United States. Although the pure form of the drug, alkaloid cocaine, was successfully extracted from the leaves in the nineteenth century, it was virtually ignored until the 1880s. One of the earliest appearances in the United States was in a drink advertised for its medicinal purposes—Coca-Cola. About the same time, experimenters in Europe began to explore the uses of pure cocaine. Freud, for example, recommended it as a cure for fatigue and depression; other physicians prescribed it for tuberculosis.[59] Although cocaine still has a legitimate medical use (chiefly as an anesthetic) the enthusiasm with which it was initially greeted has waned in fact, extended use of cocaine has several detrimental side-effects.

The positive effects of cocaine, which include greater strength and endurance and increased creative and intellectual power, result from its

[57]"The Colombia Connection," *Time*, January 29, 1979, pp. 22–29.
[58]George Andrews and David Solomon, eds., *The Coca Leaf and Cocaine Papers* (New York: Harcourt Brace Jovanovich, 1975).
[59]Oswaldo Tippo and William Louis Stern, *Humanistic Botany* (New York: Norton, 1977).

constricting effect on blood vessels and tissues. The pulse accelerates while blood pressure rises, much as it does when amphetamines are ingested. As with amphetamines, cocaine suppresses the appetite, so heavy users of the drug may experience weight loss or malnutrition. In a recent experiment, rhesus monkeys consistently selected cocaine over food; within a few days, the monkeys showed signs of behavioral toxicity as well as a 6-10 percent weight loss. Even when they suffered from the lack of food, the monkeys continued to favor the drug.[60] Cocaine is not physically addictive so the habitual user can stop taking the drug with relatively minor bodily discomfort. It is the psychological aspects of cocaine withdrawal—overwhelming depression and despair—that drives the user back to use of the drug.[61]

Besides its psychologically addicting characteristics, cocaine can produce other unpleasant side-effects. When taken in large quantities, it induces paranoid psychosis. A peculiar result of cocaine abuse is the phenomenon of *formication*—the illusion that bugs, ants, or snakes are crawling on or in the skin. In some cases, the hallucination is so intense that the user wounds himself in an attempt to kill the vermin. Those who have used cocaine regularly for several months report frequent instances of visual hallucination. One of the earliest attempts to study this aspect of cocaine use was made by Ronald K. Siegel of the University of California at Los Angeles. Working with 85 subjects who had taken one or more grams of the drug a day intranasally for the past year, he charted the frequency of hallucinatory experiences. Thirty-seven of the subjects claimed to experience altered visual perceptions, difficulty in focusing their attention and maintaining conversations, inability to concentrate on necessary details, and general preoccupation and introspection. Siegel discovered that many of these 37 subjects suffered from extreme pupil dilation (a result of cocaine use), while some reported multiple vision; 15 subjects reported hallucinatory experiences that involved not only sight but also taste, touch, smell, and hearing. In these cases, the hallucinations were first recorded after six months of cocaine use. Hallucinations involving other senses followed vivid and persistent visual hallucinations. The pattern Siegel discovered was a progression from relatively simple visual hallucinations (such as an increased sensitivity to light) to more complex ones (intricate zig-zag and herringbone designs) and the eventual involvement of other sensory perceptions.[62]

Nevertheless, current data seem to indicate that cocaine is relatively safer than other illegal drugs. While serious tissue damage to the nose can occur when large quantities of cocaine are consumed intranasally over a long period, few users die from cocaine abuse. In addition, since cocaine is so expensive (from $60 to $100 a gram on the street), it is used in very sparing quantities—quantities far too small to indicate the drug's true properties. Also, because the prime age group for all illicit drug consumption is relatively young (18-25 years of age), it is not yet possible to evaluate the long-range effects of cocaine or many other drugs. Cocaine remains, in the minds of many researchers, an unknown—and therefore potentially dangerous—quantity.

[60]Thomas G. Aigner and Robert L. Balster, "Choice Behavior in Rhesus Monkeys: Cocaine Versus Food," *Science*, vol. 201 (August 11, 1978), 534–535; "Monkeys Prefer Fix to Food," *Chemistry*, vol. 51, no. 8 (October 1978), 3.

[61]Andrews and Solomon, *The Coca Leaf.*

[62]Joel Greenberg, "The Lore of Cocaine," *Science News*, vol. 114, no. 11 (September 9, 1978), 187–191.

The Opiates

Opium has been known, and often esteemed, for centuries. It is derived from certain species of poppy and is the source of heroin, morphine, paragoric, and codeine, some of which are still widely used medically.

Early in the nineteenth century, physicians discovered that opium and morphine not only had therapeutic and pain-killing properties, but also caused physical and psychic dependency. It was observed that after taking the drug for a length of time, a user could no longer feel normal or content without it, and dosage had to be gradually increased. The user was addicted, or "hooked."

Heroin, a refined form of morphine, was introduced about 1898. At first it was hailed as a breakthrough, a drug with all the advantages of morphine and none of the addiction-producing characteristics. The medical profession soon recognized its mistake, but by then the illegal traffic in the drug had begun.

In the 1960s, most heroin reaching America was grown in Turkey and processed and distributed in Marseilles, France. A joint French-American campaign disrupted "The French Connection" in 1971, and an agreement between the United States and Turkey resulted in a ban on the growing of opium poppies in that country. The immediate result was a shortage of heroin, creating panic among addicts, many of whom enrolled in addiction treatment

Mainlining heroin brings the user a pervasive sense of well-being—a complete contrast to the agony and physical suffering an addict feels when deprived of the drug.
Al Kaplan/DPI

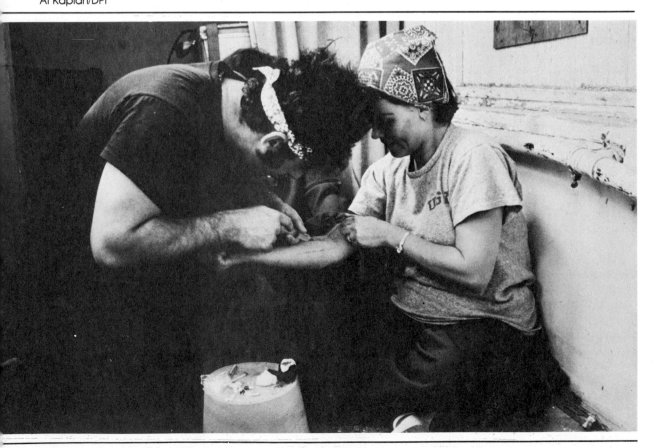

programs. The estimated number of heroin addicts dropped from about 600,000 in 1970 to 300,000 or less in early 1974, and officials were predicting that addiction rates would be permanently lowered. In 1975, however, heroin from Mexico and Southeast Asia became available on the New York market, and within a year, Mexico was supplying 90 percent of all heroin shipped to America. The Mexican government, prodded by the United States, took tough measures to stop the flow of illegal drugs across the border. Poppy fields were sprayed with powerful herbicides, which so limited the supply that the New York street price of heroin rose from $1.18 per milligram in 1975 to $1.75 per milligram in 1978.[63]

It is uncertain, however, if such measures effectively reduce addiction or even drug use. When Mexico began destroying its marijuana crops with the herbicide paraquat, the source of supply simply switched to another country. Today, Colombia is a prime supplier of both marijuana and cocaine. So far, the lesson seems to be that, as long as some Americans want to buy illegal drugs, someone, somewhere will supply them. It is important to note that there are many more heroin users than addicts. One recent study estimated that about 1.5 million people between the ages of 12 and 18 have tried heroin at least once.[64]

In contrast to marijuana, taking heroin is essentially an individual activity. Neophytes may need to be shown how to prepare and inject heroin, or how to "snort" it, but once they have learned, they seem to derive no particular benefit from the presence of others.

Heroin is usually injected into a vein, or "mainlined"; it can also be taken orally or sniffed, but its effect is more immediate and more powerful when injected. Contrary to popular belief, few addicts experience a sudden intense feeling of pleasure, or "rush," when using heroin. Instead, the user may feel esteem and composure. Because heroin slows the functioning parts of the brain, the addict's appetite and sex drive tend to be dulled; and after the initial euphoria he or she becomes lethargic and stuporous. Thus, addicts are responsible for few rapes or aggressive crimes not connected with theft.

The acknowledged relationship of crime to heroin addiction results not from the addict's state when influenced by the drug, but from the suffering caused by its absence. After an abstention of about 18 hours the withdrawal symptoms set in that usually entail acute physical agony—chills, nausea, heavy sweating, sharp abdominal and leg cramps, diarrhea, convulsions, rapid weight loss, and general exhaustion. Having had withdrawal symptoms once, the addict will do almost anything to avoid this repetition. Since addicts are seldom employable and a single day's supply of heroin may cost more than $100, most of an addict's day must usually be devoted to obtaining the necessary money. Their habits can rarely be supported without resorting to crime, usually crimes against property. (See Table 4-3.)

The typical addict is probably under 30, lives in an urban area, has serious health problems, and has a greatly shortened life expectancy. Besides hepatitis and other infections often caused by the intravenous injections, the heroin addict frequently suffers from malnutrition.

It has usually been thought that heroin use is most common at the lower socioeconomic levels; however, at least one recent study questions this point.

[63]"Mexican Connection," *Newsweek*, April 10, 1978.
[64]Selma Mushkin, "Politics and Economics of Government Response to Drug Abuse," *Annals of the American Academy of Political and Social Science*, 417 (January 1957).

Table 4-3
Sources of Funds for
Heroin

Shoplifting	22.5%
Burglary	19.0
Pickpocketing	5.4
Larceny	7.4
Robbery	3.4
Confidence games	4.7
Prostitution	30.7
Welfare	3.0
Other, legal sources	3.9
	100.0%

Source: S. Mushkin, "Politics and Economics of Government Response to Drug Abuse," *Annals of the American Academy of Political and Social Science* 417 (January 1975), 30.

In a survey of two neighborhoods in Brooklyn, New York, researchers found that

> heroin addiction is still concentrated in slum communities . . . but . . . the percentage of those with high school or college training who reported heroin use in their families was double that of those who had only grade-school education.
> Those with blue-collar occupations or annual incomes less than $6,000 had distinctly less heroin use in their families than those with white-collar occupations or incomes greater than $6,000.[65]

By 1975 it was estimated that there were 8,400 heroin addicts in Phoenix, Arizona, a predominately middle- and upper-middle class city where 80 percent of the population are Anglo whites; and in such middle-class, middle-American cities as Denver, Jackson, Omaha, and Des Moines opiate use was increasing rapidly. One survey indicated that one in every 12 high school seniors in Phoenix has used heroin, morphine, or cocaine. A local anti-addiction agency in that city had many teachers and lawyers among its clientele.[66]

The typical middle-class user is usually introduced to the narcotic at a party by a well-meaning friend, and a minority of users, estimated at perhaps 20 percent, are apparently able to use the drug without becoming addicted. Many of these are wealthy, and can support their habit without resorting to crime. Others are able, for long periods at least, to keep high-paying jobs. An observer of the drug scene in Phoenix says: "People in the middle class can function better on a dope habit than working-class people, even in their jobs. We've had some people function for 20 years in the community without being detected." This phenomenon, according to Martin Kasindorf, "raises a troubling question: Is narcotic addiction itself debilitating, or are only the poor debilitated by what they have to go through to pay for it?"[67]

[65]Dana Adams Smith, "Heroin-Use Study Refutes Beliefs," *New York Times*, July 23, 1972, p. 22.
[66]Martin Kasindorf, "By the Time It Gets to Phoenix," *New York Times Magazine*, October 26, 1975, pp. 18, 20, 26, 28.
[67]Other studies suggest that only 1 in 10 heroin users is an addict; see Nancy Hicks, "Drug Use Called Up among Youths," *New York Times*, October 2, 1975.

Hallucinogens, the popular psychedelic drugs of the late 1960s, distort the user's perceptions, creating sensory impressions of "sounds" and "sights" that do not actually exist. Although there are naturally occuring hallucinogens—such as mescaline, which is extracted from the peyote cactus—the most popular drug of this group is the synthetic aklaloid D-lysergic acid diethylamide (LSD). Ingestion of LSD causes the scrambling of nerve impulses, and the user becomes unusually sensitive to the environment. Colors seem unnaturally bright and shift kaleidoscopically; objects in the user's field of vision appear to expand and contract; and music can be confused with visual or olfactory perceptions. The focus of the LSD users' attention turns inward to the self and to the things they see—or believe they are seeing—around them. Perhaps for this reason, LSD has been used almost exclusively as a recreational drug among the middle and upper classes. In ghettos, where drugs are used as a form of escape, LSD has never gained acceptance.

Despite warnings about "bad trips" (in which the user feels panic and may injure himself or others) and possible brain and chromosome damage, evidence to verify these hazards remains inconclusive. Only rarely is the LSD user actually deluded into accepting his hallucinations as reality,[68] and some studies indicate that adverse reactions to the drug occur only when the user has preexisting mental problems.[69] There is no data to indicate that LSD can cause either physical or emotional dependency.

Drugs of the amphetamine family are popularly called "ups" or "uppers" because of their stimulating effect. They are usually safe when properly used and, unlike marijuana and heroin, are perfectly legal when prescribed by a physician. As a result, many people first become dependent on them through medical use. For example, truck drivers working on long-haul routes obtain prescriptions for a supply of amphetamines so that they can safely negotiate a long trip. They become accustomed to the lift, the energetic and spunky feeling, which the amphetamines provide and they become habitual users. Dieters seeking to lose weight are often given amphetamines by their doctors, and they soon find that the pills also help them to get through the day with more buoyancy and self-confidence. They, too, become users, continuing to take amphetamines long after they cease to be medically indicated.

A serious social problem is posed by extensive adolescent use of amphetamines. A study of colleges and other schools showed that amphetamines ranked among the most widely used drugs, following alcohol and marijuana.[70]

Amphetamines are usually taken orally, in tablet, capsule, or powder form, but they can also be "snorted" or injected. Injecting the drug intravenously, or "speeding," produces the most powerful impact and can cause the greatest harm. Although unlikely, an overdose may cause coma, with possible brain damage or even death. There are other dangers as well—the speeder may develop serum hepatitis, abscesses, long-term personality disorders, and psychotic states. This "amphetamine psychosis" is

---

[68]Nowlis, *Drugs on the College Campus*, p. 104.

[69]Richard Ashley, "The Other Side of LSD," *New York Times Magazine*, October 19, 1975, pp. 48–50, 59.

[70]Louis G. Richards, "Patterns and Extent of Abuse," in *Drugs and Youth*, ed. J. R. Wittenhorn, *et al.* (Springfield, Ill.: Charles C. Thomas, 1969), p. 142.

particularly likely to occur with long-term high-dose use. Secondary effects of continued use may include skin lesions, respiratory problems, and acute gastro-intestinal discomfort.

Chemically, the amphetamines are a family of stimulants including benzedrine, dexedrine, and methedrine. They are related to adrenalin, a hormone normally secreted by the adrenal gland, that stimulates the central nervous system. Organic effects of the amphetamines can be far-reaching: acceleration of metabolic action consumes the fat stored in the body tissues, there is a stepped-up heartbeat, respiratory stimulation, inability to sleep, and a reduced appetite. Other psychological and physical effects vary, depending on the user; among some users, for example, amphetamines are believed to have hallucinogenic effects. Most subjects feel stronger and euphoric with an enhanced ability to concentrate and express themselves verbally.[71]

Continued amphetamine use seems to create psychological dependence. Abrupt withdrawal may plunge the person accustomed to a heavy dosage into a suicidal depression. Even with lower levels of habituation, giving up the drug is extremely difficult because, to the person deprived of it, life becomes a dismal routine. Medical opinion used to hold that amphetamines were not addictive because withdrawal did not produce the syndrome familiar to withdrawal from other drugs. It is now recognized, however, that amphetamine withdrawal is accompanied by its own distinctive syndrome: apathy, decreased activity, and sleep disturbances. There is, then, some evidence of a physical dependence potential.[72]

Barbiturates   Barbiturates depress the central nervous system and are derived from barbituric acid. The first sleep-producing barbiturate was introduced in 1903; today there are some 2,500 known barbiturates. Of those ordinarily available on the legitimate market, over a dozen are widely used medications.

Barbiturates are drugs of enormous versatility. By themselves and in combination with other drugs, they are used to treat temporary insomnia, epilepsy, high blood pressure, and to relax patients before and after surgery. They are also useful for mental disorders. But, as with amphetamines, the potential for misuse is so great that mere possession without a prescription is unlawful.

Production statistics tell a lot about barbiturate use in the United States. Over 400 tons—3.6 billion average doses—of barbiturates are manufactured in the United States each year. According to Blum, "Enough barbiturates . . . are manufactured every year in the United States to provide thirty or forty doses for every man, woman, and child."[73]

Prolonged barbiturate use and high dosage can cause physical dependency with symptoms similar to those of heroin addiction. Indeed, many drug experts believe that barbiturate addiction is even more dangerous, and more resistant to treatment and cure, than heroin addiction. A barbiturate addict

---

[71]Lester Grinspoon and Peter Hedbloom, *The Speed Culture: Amphetamine Use and Abuse in America* (Cambridge, Mass.: Harvard University Press, 1975).

[72]National Clearinghouse for Drug Abuse Information, *Amphetamine* (Rockville, Md.: Alcohol, Drug Abuse, and Mental Health Administration, Report Series 28, No. 1, February 1974), pp. 9–10.

[73]Blum, *et al.*, *Society and Drugs*, p. 242.

deprived of the drug frequently experiences a range of symptoms which include cramps, nausea, delirium, and convulsions; abrupt withdrawal can be lethal.

Barbiturate overdose may also cause poisoning, convulsions, coma, and sometimes death. In fact, in the United States barbiturates are a leading cause of accidental deaths by poisoning, largely because they tend to heighten the effect of alcohol, sometimes with toxic results. Persons who take the drug to make them sleep may, if the first dose is not quickly effective, become confused as to how many pills they have taken, and then take an additional dose.

Taken in moderate doses, barbiturates, like alcohol, are mildly disinhibiting; however, reports of other personality changes show no consistent patterns. The barbiturate user may be calmed and relaxed—reactions normally associated with a depressant—or become convival and lively instead.

People frequently develop a habit of using both amphetamines and barbiturates, together or in alternation. Combined amphetamine-barbiturate use makes the normal rhythm of life, the alternation of rest and wakefulness, meaningless. It has been replaced by the chemical cycling of consciousness through "ups"—amphetamines—and "downs"—barbiturates. Such chemical regulation of activity, if prolonged, causes profound physical and psychological deterioration.

Social Problems Related to Drug Abuse

The drug problem traced to its very roots is essentially a "people problem." It centers on the people in the streets who use the drugs, and the people in government who make the laws and judgments affecting drug users.

A consideration of present attitudes and beliefs about drugs and drug control suggests several rather basic questions:

- Does society weigh the differences between drug users and abusers?

- Has sufficient thought been given to the fact that drug use and abuse have existed throughout human history? Is the desire to escape reality a legitimate human need?

- Can a society historically based upon individual initiative, productivity, moderation, self-restraint, and deferred pleasure deal rationally with behavior that is self-gratifying or escapist? Should we always consider a person who takes drugs without medical consultation to be either physically or psychologically ill?

- When does the government have the right to interfere in personal affairs and define permissible and proscribed behavior? And who is to judge what is "permissible"?

As these questions indicate, concern about drugs is integrally related to judgments about human nature and human behavior; the role of social institutions and the responsibilities of social control; the rights of individuals and their obligations to society; the definitions of danger, safety, risk, and abuse.

There is more than a suspicion that drugs can make people lose control over their lives—a possibility recognized by those who favor drug use and by those who oppose it. In the counterculture, this is known as "getting wasted," which produces "dead freaks," "zombies," useless to themselves, to society at large, and even to their own society. On the other hand, some drug users believe that a more widespread use of drugs, particularly marijuana, could reduce some of our social problems (such as war or aggression).

Most drug use does not aim to solve social problems; nor does it inevitably result in a "wasted" life. It is a fact, however, that in recent years young people have tended to use drugs more than adults and with increasing frequency. "Figures for alcohol, tobacco, and marijuana use show basically the same pattern: Use peaks at the 18-21 age bracket, levels off for a while and then falls off sharply. The fall-off for marijuana use comes at a younger age, the mid-30s, than for alcohol and tobacco use, the mid-40s, because it has not been widely used as long."[74] Young people also tend to experiment with several different substances. High school students are more likely than college students, only a few years older, "to have regular highs from psychedelics (LSD), barbiturates, cocaine, and even heroin as well as marijuana, several times a month at least. Further, young people do not try drugs *instead* of alcohol, but in addition to it."[75]

Drug use is also increasing among adults. The medico-pharmacological advances of the last half-century have made us a nation of drug takers and "pill poppers." We expect every ailment to be cured quickly with one prescription. In a strange perversion of our "inalienable right" to the "pursuit of happiness," we demand instant cures and instant gratification. Advertising, especially on television and in magazines, touts "immediate relief" for everything from mild headache to severe arthritis. And, as Kramer has pointed out, television itself is analogous to the drug experience: "Both depend on 'turning on' and passively waiting for something beautiful to happen."[76]

The escapist use of drugs throughout society may indicate that we cannot face and comprehend change, or even cope with minor problems. It may also indicate society's failure to provide its members with meaningful activities or values, a failure which for some necessitates the search for such values outside the mainstream of society.

Drugs and the Law

How effective is legal drug control? The answer is discouraging. Throughout the century drug laws have proliferated, the penalties have become harsher, and the number of drug users has steadily increased. Today, drug offenses severely tax an overburdened police and judicial system, and penal institutions are already unbearably overcrowded. In every federal and state jail, a large proportion of the inmates are drug offenders. In the most recent year for which statistics are available, there were about 630,000 arrests for drug-law violations. Some two-thirds of these were marijuana-related.[77]

[75]Yankelovich, "How Students Control Their Drug Crisis," pp. 39–41.
[76]E. H. Kramer, in F. Earle Bareus and Susan M. Jankowski, "Drugs and the Mass Media," *Annals of the American Academy of Political and Social Science* 417 (January 1975), 88.
[77]Richard S. Schroeder, "Marijuana and the Law," *Editorial Research Reports* (February 21, 1975), 124.

Often the punishment for drug offenses is unduly severe. As Nowlis states: "Drug legislation makes possession of a 'potentially dangerous' substance a crime with penalties in some cases equivalent to or in excess of those for such criminal acts as grand larceny and second degree murder."[78] In some states the penalties for selling or even giving a small quantity of marijuana to another person may be as high as 25 years, or even life, imprisonment for the first offense. Such disproportionate harshness is not only unjust for those sentenced, but tends to discredit the entire criminal justice system in the eyes of many who recognize the injustice, whether or not they themselves use illegal drugs.

The earliest attempt to control addictive drugs in the United States was the Harrison Act, passed by Congress in 1914, that strictly regulated the sale, use, and transfer of opium, coca, and coca products and made their possession unlawful except for "legitimate medical purposes." For the first time, narcotics distribution was strictly controlled by the government, specifically by the Narcotics Division of the Treasury Department, an agency vigilant and zealous in hunting down and prosecuting violators. The right of the government to control drug use was further reinforced by a series of Supreme Court decisions. Legitimate sources for procuring drugs vanished and addicts had to turn to illicit dealers. By 1925 the illicit drug trade had so increased that more legislation was considered necessary, and a series of measures designed to strengthen and expand the Harrison Act followed.

Penalties also were made stiffer. Twice in the 1950s, when increasing drug use became apparent, Congress reacted. In 1951, minimum federal prison sentences were established for all narcotics and marijuana violations, ranging from two years for first offenders to ten years for third offenders. In 1956, the growing magnitude of the drug problem spurred Congress to increase federal sentences for illegal sale or importation of drugs to a mandatory five years for the first offense and ten years for the second. Similar state laws followed.

More recently, the Comprehensive Drug Abuse Prevention and Control Act of 1970 established schedules of controlled substances in order of their potential abuse. Manufacturers and distributors of such substances must register annually with the Attorney General, who also determines annual production quotas for certain drugs. By decreasing the amount of drugs manufactured and in inventory, these provisions attempt to decrease the amount of legally produced drugs available for diversion into illegal channels.[79] The Drug Abuse Treatment Act of 1972 was primarily concerned with the health aspects of drug abuse; federal funds, for example, now support community treatment centers serving an estimated 300,000 addicts.[80] In 1973 a separate National Institute on Drug abuse was established within the newly organized Alcohol, Drug Abuse and Mental Health Administration of the Public Health Service. It is estimated that federal expenditures for all drug-abuse-related activities were $754 million in 1975, and that the total amount spent by the states may have been about the same.[81] Enforcement

[78]Nowlis, *Drugs on the College Campus*, p. 51.
[79]Oakley S. Ray, *Drugs, Society and Human Behavior* (St. Louis: C.V. Mosby, 1974), pp. 26–27.
[80]*U.S. News & World Report*, June 30, 1975, p. 29.
[81]Mushkin, "Politics and Economics," p. 28.

and treatment, however, are still largely under the aegis of the federal government.

Until recently, all this legislation has been punitive—the state's function is to punish, not to prevent or treat. Though campaign after campaign against drugs was being lost, the legislators seemed unable to try any other approach. General ignorance of the real physical and social effects of drugs, and the irrational fear of them which resulted, probably made any course other than uncompromising, severe punishment of offenders politically impossible.

Increasingly, however, punitive legislation is proving unworkable. It is now clear that punishing offenders does not affect the basic problem. Most of the present drug laws are based on an outdated and inadequate knowledge of the scientific and social aspects of drug abuse. When the Harrison Act was passed, legislators might have believed that penalties would have a deterrent effect, but not so today. If nothing else, we have the parallel example of Prohibition, which proved almost totally unworkable and fostered large-scale organized crime. Similarly laws prohibiting drugs have been responsible for the enormous growth of the illicit drug trade.

Our national inability to approach the problem of drug abuse except by repression stems in part from the ignorance of the real nature and effects of drugs, aided and abetted by a certain amount of media sensationalism. Perhaps more deeply, it stems from a vague feeling that the drug revolution may represent a basic challenge to our way of life and even our national existence. This may or may not be true, but so long as we believe it, we are probably going to react with irrational panic. Clearly, accurate knowledge and intelligent dissemination would seem to be prime necessities.

Of even greater importance to the workability of drug laws—or for that matter any law—is the support and compliance of the population. All across America, on college campuses and in industrial centers, in large and small communities, the beliefs, mores, and values incorporated in traditional drug laws are either being challenged or dramatically revised. This trend has been reflected with the liberalized laws passed by many states and in individual behavior.

Drug Use and Crime   If punishment is to deter illegal drug use, it must punish the major distributors—those operating at the highest levels of drug importation and manufacture. Drugs filter down through many levels and through many hands before they reach the neighborhood distributor. The pushers transacting business with junkies are more than likely to be addicts themselves and the lowest people in the hierarchy. The drug trade earns them the money or drugs to support their own habit. Top syndicate figures, however—the real money-makers in the business—are rarely arrested. At recent hearings of a Senate subcommittee, investigators testified that 90 percent of arrests by federal agents were of low-level pushers, instead of the drug traffic instigators. It was also charged that using undercover agents to buy drugs and arrest sellers fostered corruption and in fact often stimulated the illegal drug market.[82]

The nature of drug-related crimes varies with the drug involved. According to the National Commission on Marihuana and Drug Abuse, "The

[82]*U.S. News & World Report*, p. 29.

only crimes which can be directly attributed to marihuana-using behavior are those resulting from the use, possession or transfer of an illegal substance," and neither marijuana nor low to moderate doses of barbiturates are likely to promote violence, "although high dose use of [barbiturates] has been known to cause irritability and unpredictably violent behavior in some individuals." Amphetamine users, however, seem disproportionately involved in violent crimes such as robberies and assaults, and it was possible "that these crimes were directly attributable to acute reactions to the drug." Supporting evidence comes from Japan, where a limited period of amphetamine use during the mid-1950s was associated with a rise in violent crimes, which decreased markedly when amphetamine was diminished.

Heroin, however, is the drug most frequently associated with criminal behavior of various kinds. According to the National Commission on Marihuana and Drug Abuse:

> The available data indicate that most known opiate (primarily heroin) dependent persons had long histories of delinquent or criminal behavior prior to their being identified as drug users, that opiate use becomes a further expression of delinquent tendencies.

Thus, heroin users tend to have histories of illegal activity. Studies of the relationship to crime focus on the addict's necessity to resort to crime in order to support a heroin habit. Most note that the crimes committed for this purpose generally tend to be the nonviolent, money-making crimes such as shoplifting. More significant, perhaps, is the indirect evidence indicating "that when the drug users are active in a therapeutic program and presumably not using heroin, criminal activity decreases. That is, when heroin use decreases either by treatment or other means, criminal behavior is also said to decrease." In sum, heroin users tend to engage in money-acquisitive crimes, "most of which are directly related to supporting the drug habit," but that "the available evidence indicates that they are significantly less likely to commit homicide, rape, and assault than are users of alcohol, amphetamines, and barbiturates."[83]

Social Control

Efforts to rehabilitate narcotics addicts have been impeded by the attitude "once an addict, always an addict." Until very recently, statistical evidence supported the pessimists, and the prospects for returning detoxified addicts to normal living were bleak and discouraging. As we have already suggested, however, the social milieu in which addicts find themselves may contribute significantly to their label. One study of American soldiers in Vietnam who were addicted to heroin indicates that most were able to kick their habits rather easily when they returned home.[84] Drug use, as DuPont has noted, does not necessarily follow a predictable process from experimentation to addiction, but incorporates a wide range of behavior that includes "experimentation, occasional use, regular use, and heavy use."[85] The factors that

[83]National Commission on Marihuana and Drug Abuse, *Drug Use in America*, pp. 158–163.

[84]Kasindorf, "By the Time It Gets to Phoenix," p. 30.

[85]See Hicks, "Drug Use."

cause different individuals to fall into different categories of use are many and complex, and efforts to rehabilitate addicts have not always addressed themselves to the full range of problems which addicts may confront. Furthermore, different types of therapeutic programs may be more successful than others for different types of addicts. The various programs described here represent relatively recent attempts to address the problems of addicts more fully.

Rehabilitation Programs

Something similar to the community supervision idea has taken shape recently in the development of self-help addict communities, staffed by professionals and laypersons. The theoretical groundwork for the community treatment techniques was laid by Dr. Maxwell Jones, who borrowed the concept from Alcoholics Anonymous. Jones advocated group therapy and communal living for addicts so that all of the experiences of daily life would be shared in an atmosphere of constant supportive group interaction.

Halfway Houses.   Halfway houses are another means of attacking the high relapse rate of addicts who, detoxified and physically cured, are returned from institutional life to the community. Through the halfway house, individuals are able to re-enter the community gradually and at their own pace. This buffers the shock of moving from a protective, institutional environment to the much greater freedom of the outside world.

One of the most elaborate halfway house programs is that of Phoenix House. Here, in moving from the supervised environment to the open community, the former addict passes through a five-stage transitional program. The gradual reintegration into everyday life takes place in a Re-Entry House to which addicts who have completed their treatment are transferred. Educational facilities are part of the Re-Entry House program and include training in vocational skills and preparation for those who wish to undertake professional education.

This drug rehabilitation center offers professional supervision and support from former addicts. Relapses are less likely when the transition from a drug-dependent to a drug-free life is guided through a gradual re-integration program.
Paul Sequeira/Photo Researchers, Inc.

The Phoenix House community rests on two key precepts: that addicts, unless mentally impaired, must assume responsibility for their own actions; and that treatment should address itself to the addict's psychological difficulties as well as his physical dependency. Phoenix House relies upon ex-addicts in its rehabilitation program. Recovered drug-abusers are often more effective in breaking through the barriers of isolation and hostility that the addict feels. In addition, ex-addicts offer irrefutable proof that addiction is a curable disease. In operation since 1968, the Phoenix House program has helped many addicts to permanent recovery.

Methadone Maintenance.   Methadone, a synthetic narcotic, has been extensively tested as a treatment for heroin addiction, and is now in regular use in several programs. It is similar enough to heroin to satisfy the addict's physical craving, preventing the agony of withdrawal symptoms and the bleak depression of abstinence, but, unlike heroin, it does not induce a high. Consequently, an addict using methadone can continue to function more or less normally in the community. The drug, however, is unlikely to be acceptable to those addicts who seek a high, if heroin is available.[86]

Methadone is addictive, and it offers not a cure, but a "maintenance" treatment for addicts who do not respond to other types of therapy. Many, including those addicts enrolled in programs, believe that methadone keeps addicts dependent on drugs, and is therefore useful only as a short-term solution to wean them from heroin. Methadone treatment is also regarded, especially by both addict and non-addict minorities, as a form of social control imposed by the majority culture. These ambivalent attitudes toward methadone treatment apparently are not significant deterrents to potential clients. According to one survey, the major reasons cited by addicts for not entering treatment earlier were their inability to recognize their heroin addiction and the absence of treatment facilities in the immediate neighborhood. As Barry Brown, Gloria Benn, and Donald Jansen put it: "When the addict recognizes and is concerned about heroin dependence, his problems are too intense for ideological considerations. There is the clinic, the street, the jail, or the morgue. In that context the clinic becomes at least an acceptable alternative."[87]

Methadone is legally available only through approved programs, and in the early stages of such programs addicts are required to report to the treatment center for their daily dosage. Unfortunately, a black market in methadone has developed as some heroin addicts discovered that the drug could tide them over periods when they are unable to obtain heroin, and others perhaps attempted self-treatment outside of established programs. An overdose of methadone, as with heroin, can be fatal, and methadone-related deaths have been reported. Nevertheless, it has been estimated that at least 85,000 persons are now being treated with methadone, a substantial number of them under federally funded programs.

Narcotic Antagonists.   Narcotics users who are weaned from the physical addiction often have a psychological craving for drugs as soon as they return to their own environment. The need to overcome this problem led

[86]Richard Brotman and Fredric Suffet, "The Concept of Prevention and Its Limitations," *Annals of the American Academy of Political and Social Science* 417 (January 1974), 53–65.

[87]Barry S. Brown, Gloria J. Benn, and Donald R. Jansen, "Methadone Maintenance: Some Client Opinions," *American Journal of Psychiatry* 132 (June 1975), 623–628.

scientists to develop narcotic antagonists, substances which prevent the euphoria ordinarily produced by the opiates.

Two of the best-known opiate antagonists are Cyclazocine and Naloxone. The more widely tested rehabilitation technique is based on Cyclazocine, a synthetic analgesic which can be administered orally. Undesirable side effects were reported with Cyclazocine that stimulated the development of Naloxone. In several tests the latter has shown some therapeutic promise. By negating the positive sensations achieved by heroin, the narcotic antagonists help motivated addicts to overcome their psychological conditioning to the drug.

In addition, researchers at the University of Chicago studying heroin-saturated muscle cells have discovered an agent that could immunize against the effects of heroin. This substance stimulates the production of antibodies that specifically combat the effects of the drug. There are some problems involved in its use, including the most important question of selecting those to be immunized. Furthermore, those so immunized would also lose the ability to respond to common opium-based pain killers.[88]

The British System

From the beginning, the British approach to drugs as a social problem has contrasted sharply with the American. The British avoided branding drug addicts as criminals and treated their condition as a disease requiring therapy. From this difference in fundamental attitudes, there developed a totally different set of legal practices and government policies. As early as 1926, a British government advisory committee recommended: "With few exceptions, addiction to morphine and heroin should be regarded as a manifestation of a morbid state, and not as a mere form of vicious indulgence."[89]

The British system does not permit an addict access to an unlimited supply of narcotics; in fact, every precaution is taken to strictly regulate the possession and distribution of opiates and of several other drugs. Until recently such drugs could be prescribed by any licensed medical practitioner. Detailed records were required, and physicians found guilty of deliberate overprescribing or of diverting drugs to illegal use were liable to fine, imprisonment, and loss of license.

In the 1960s the rate of opiate addiction in Britain began to climb sharply. A government committee, the Brain Committee, concluded that overprescription and the activities of a few medical charlatans were largely, though not wholly, responsible for the spread of addiction. It recommended that a system of government-run clinics be established which alone would be authorized to prescribe heroin. Such a system was inaugurated in 1968.

The program, which requires physicians to notify the government of any patients suspected of being addicted, applies to narcotics—heroin, morphine, and cocaine—only, but does not affect marijuana, amphetamine, barbiturate, or hallucinogen users. British addiction peaked in 1968 with 1,476 new cases in the first year of compulsory notification. By 1970, it was clear that the upward spiral of heroin addiction had been curbed, with the first decrease in the annual addiction total in a decade. In 1974, the latest year for which figures are available, only 777 previously unknown, out of a total number of

[88]"Blocking the Effects of Heroin," *Science Digest* (April 1975), p. 27.
[89]Ministry of Health, Departmental Committee of Morphine and Heroin Addiction, *Report* (London: His Majesty's Stationery Office, 1926), p. 31.

1,769 cases, were reported; at the end of that year, 1,555 addicts were in treatment.[90]

No one believes that the clinics are the whole answer to Britain's heroin problem, but clearly they do help to contain it. Addicts who are registered with a clinic can obtain a supply of heroin or methadone legally and at reasonable prices; and because all known addicts are listed with one central authority (the Home Office), it is difficult for them to register with more than one clinic and obtain extra supplies for resale or excessive personal use.

The advent of methadone in Britain is partly responsible for the drop in heroin use. Unlike heroin, methadone is still available from private physicians, and methadone addiction is rising. While previously known addicts are given National Health Service prescriptions for heroin, new cases are being given methadone.[91] The increase in methadone use, however, is not sufficient to cancel out the reduction in heroin use. Barbiturates and amphetamines, as in the United States, also enter the picture, especially as most British addicts appear to be multi-drug users. Nevertheless, the total rate of addiction and of associated problems is evidently far lower than in the United States.

Granted that the British system has not succeeded in eradicating addiction and drug-related crime, certain facts are worth noting:

• The black market in hard drugs is far smaller and less lucrative in Britain than in the United States.

• British addicts have a lower rate of arrests for nondrug crimes than do their American counterparts. Since British addicts can buy cheap drugs, they have less need to steal to support their habit.

• More British than American addicts are able to keep jobs and live fairly normal lives. It is estimated that half of British addicts are employed.

If official statistics are any guide, the British drug problem is minuscule compared with the American. While it is not certain that the British system would work here—and considerable controversy has focused on this question—there is no doubt that it is worth studying. Its basic philosophy seems to have spared Britain many of the consequences traceable to a punitive approach, and for that reason alone it merits our respectful attention.

Educational Programs

Much drug education in the past has concentrated on scare tactics, and has painted a lurid picture of the terrible consequences of drug abuse. It was thought that emphasizing the demoralizing, sordid, and negative aspect of drugs would frighten people away from experimenting with their use. The alarmist approach, however, has a long record of failures, especially in dealing with the young. Emotional appeals of this type often discredit educators, destroying their credibility; and they have a reverse impact, arousing curiosity about the forbidden experience. They also conflict with the facts presented by friends or gained from firsthand experience, as well as with the present tendency among young people toward greater freedom and self-determination.

Perhaps the most damaging aspect of this approach is the tendency of the

[90]*The Prevention and Treatment of Drug Dependence in Britain* (New York: British Information Services, 1973), pp. 4–6.

[91]Kasindorf, "By the Time It Gets to Phoenix," p. 36.

The 1936 film, "Reefer Madness," seems a hilarious farce to many people from a contemporary vantage point. When it was released, however, it contributed to strong public polarization against marijuana. UPI

educator to exaggerate every possible ill effect and to ignore or deny the manifest positive features of drug taking, so that the student is in effect told not to understand but only to fear. When the National Coordinating Council on Drug Education evaluated 220 films on drug use, 84 percent of them were judged to be inaccurate, unscientific, and psychologically unsound. The basic concept of using education as an anti-drug tool assumes that informed people will usually not choose a destructive course of action; however, in practice, people often believe they are invulnerable to risk.[92]

A sound drug-education program requires an objective presentation of all the available information about the drugs under consideration. To a greater extent than many educators suspect, students today are knowledgeable and sophisticated about drugs and easily detect unbalanced or incorrect information.

While a rational approach to drug education is still in its infancy, some encouraging things are happening. Curriculum guides for teachers, texts, and audio-visual materials are now available; some states have added drug-education courses to the curriculum at various grade levels; and the federal government is helping to train teachers. The scare approach may be on its way out, and children may soon learn about drugs realistically.

Revision of Drug Laws

The drug problem can also be eased by revising drug laws, so that they deal with issues realistically and consistently. So far, the most insistent demands for reform have centered on marijuana. It is increasingly recognized that marijuana should not logically be classified with the far more dangerous hard drugs, and many, even those who do not favor its legalization, are tending to support reducing the penalties for its possession and sale.

In fact, some revision has taken place.[93] The 1972 report of the National Commission on Marihuana and Drug Abuse recommended changes in both federal and state laws. Under these recommendations, for instance, the private possession of marijuana for personal use would no longer be an offense, nor would the distribution of small amounts without profit to the distributor. Public use would be a criminal offense, but the maximum penalty would be a fine of $100; cultivation and distribution for profit would remain felonies. Persons would be held responsible for actions committed while under the influence of marijuana, and driving while under the influence of marijuana would be a misdemeanor subject to fine, imprisonment, and suspension of license.[94] While these recommendations still contain inconsistencies, they represent a considerable advance over previous government thinking; and, as mentioned earlier, similar laws have already been adopted by several states and are under consideration in others.

Even with regard to the hard drugs, in recent years there have been a number of advocates of law revision, though few have gone so far as to call for complete legalization of these drugs. One argument for legalization is that it would drive the price of heroin down, and addicts would no longer be forced into violent crime to support their habits; the British system is cited in

[92]Brotman and Suffet, "Concept of Prevention," p. 60.
[93]See, for example, "Marijuana: The Legal Question," *Consumer Reports* (April 1975), pp. 265–266.
[94]*Marihuana: A Signal of Misunderstanding*, pp. 190–195.

support of this position. On the other hand, easing the supply might tempt more people to experiment and perhaps become addicted.

Some cities are virtually bypassing the question of legality. Although free heroin, on the British pattern, is not yet provided to addicts, in many places treatment programs are widely available. Possession of heroin is still a crime, but an admitted addict can seek treatment without risking arrest or incarceration. While such programs are largely experimental, and not without problems of their own, their existence nevertheless suggests that in practice, if not in legal theory, there is a growing willingness to regard drug addiction as a sociomedical, not simply a criminal, problem. Richard Brotman and Fredric Suffet, for example, conclude that "because of the prevalence of recreational patterns of moderate drug use . . . the prevention of all illicit drug use is not an achieveable goal," and that we should "adjust our goals and focus our preventive efforts primarily on high-risk patterns of use—on those patterns, that is, where drug involvement demonstrably and significantly increases the chances of self-harm."[95]

The whole subject remains controversial and highly emotional, often with political overtones; we are far from a national consensus on it. Even if there were some generally accepted principles, the variety of causes and patterns of drug use make it likely that the drug problem, even if it can be alleviated, can never be completely solved.

Prospects

Although Prohibition has been repealed, the kind of thinking which engendered it is still highly in evidence. Chronic drinkers are still being thrown into the tank to "dry out"; people are still being arrested for possession of one marijuana cigarette; drug addicts are still receiving heavy jail sentences. Worse, in many places in the United States, treatment is still limited to the incarceration prescribed by law.

The scope of the problem is not small: even rough estimates count several hundred thousand narcotic addicts, from 2 to 2.5 million chronic users of barbiturates or other sedatives, perhaps as many as 5 million people taking oral amphetamines without prescription,[96] and some 14 million with severe alcohol-related problems. Obviously, previously attempted solutions have not worked, and reform is in order. Surveys have found no consistent relationship between excessive drinking in a given area and the rate of sale of alcoholic beverages or the number of liquor stores in the same area. Evidently whatever legal measures have been taken to control drug and alcohol abuse have little relationship to the extent and nature of abuse and addiction problems. Moral persuasion and scare tactics have likewise been unavailing. Our laws must, therefore, begin to operate as rehabilitative instruments. We can no longer ignore the fact that a punitive approach to social problems does not work—and this is especially true for drug- and alcohol-related problems. It is simply not realistic to treat a drug or alcohol abuser as a criminal. Unless the situation that created the problem is eliminated, and unless he or she receives extensive rehabilitative treatment, the addict cannot change.

[95]Brotman and Suffet, "Concept of Prevention," pp. 53, 64.
[96]Bertram S. Brown, "Drugs and Public Health: Issues and Answers," *Annals of the American Academy of Political and Social Science* 417 (January 1975), 110ff.

Suggested changes in federal and state drug laws have already been discussed. Analogous changes in the method of handling alcoholics have been proposed in a model program offered by the President's Commission on Law Enforcement and Administration of Justice. The commission recommends:

1.   Routine medical evaluation of all individuals suspected of intoxication and taken into custody by the police

2.   Routine training of police officers in handling public intoxication cases

3.   Repeal of drunkenness statutes

4.   Establishment of detoxification stations

5.   Development of effective referral systems from detoxification stations to other community resources for treating alcoholics, that is, outpatient clinics, domiciliaries, community houses, social centers

6.   Development or strengthening of treatment programs within correctional institutions

7.   Incorporation of special treatment for alcoholic offenders in parole and probation services

8.   Federal action in the area of alcoholism control.[97]

Programs of drug-abuse education and workshops in the field have been organized by the National Institute of Mental Health, and through the National Institute of Drug Abuse and the National Institute of Alcohol Abuse and Alcoholism. These should be expanded to better inform the public and to train workers in this area. Changes in health insurance coverage to recognize the definition of alcoholism—and drug abuse in general—as an illness would make various treatments more accessible. It would seem that our hopes for the future lie with preventive education and humane psychotherapy rather than with fear- and anger-arousing prohibitions and punishments. It is likely to be some time, however, before most citizens learn to regard alcohol and other drug abuses as primarily a sociomedical problem rather than a legal or a moral one.

[97]President's Commission, *Task Force Report: Drunkenness*, p. 17.

Summary

A *drug* is any chemical substance that affects bodily function, mood, perceptions, or consciousness. Which drugs are or are not legal in a particular society often depends on cultural bias, rather than on an objective analysis of the effects of each drug.

Drug abuse is the use of unacceptable drugs and the excessive or inappropriate use of acceptable drugs so that harm can result. Alcohol is an example of a legal drug that is widely and harmfully abused.

Problem drinking or alcoholism may be associated with a number of physiological, psychological, and ethnic factors. There has been a recent increase in the number of alcohol abusers among young people. Social problems related to alcohol abuse include the facts that alcoholics have a shortened life expectancy, alcohol is implicated in about half of all automobile accident fatalities and injuries, alcohol correlates highly with commission of serious crimes, and alcoholism often leads to broken families. Contrary to popular belief, only about 5 percent of alcoholics are of the "skid row" category.

Treatment for alcoholics has not been widely available, because of the traditional view of the alcoholic as an outcast. There are some indications that this attitude is beginning to change. The most successful treatment program for alcoholics thus far appears to be *Alcoholics Anonymous*, which combines a group therapy approach with an insistence on total abstinence from alcohol. Other therapeutic efforts include *Antabuse programs*, *community programs*, and *company programs*. Educational programs attempt to prevent alcohol-related problems from arising.

Physical dependence, or addiction, occurs when the body experiences withdrawal if use of a drug is discontinued. Psychological dependence, or habituation, occurs when the individual needs to use a drug for the feelings of well-being it engenders but is not physically addicted to it. There is considerable evidence that only a small portion of drug users are physically dependent on drugs.

Marijuana is generally smoked on social occasions, and causes an increased sensitivity to one's surroundings. There is little or no evidence that marijuana causes physical harm or leads to heroin use.

Unlike marijuana use, *heroin* use is largely an individual activity. It does not generally produce a euphoric "rush," but rather feelings of calm and well-being. Thus heroin addicts are not likely to commit aggressive crimes, but since heroin withdrawal is a painful process, addicts will steal to enable them to obtain the drug. There is evidence that heroin use among middle- and upper-class people has increased.

While some "bad trips" have been associated with the use of hallucinogens, particularly LSD, there is little evidence that they are physically harmful; in fact, they have some possible medical applications.

Amphetamines are widely abused stimulants. Heavy or prolonged use may cause extensive physical and psychological damage. The body quickly builds up a tolerance for the drug, and there is evidence that it is addictive. *Barbiturates* are depressants that can also cause addiction. Both barbiturate overdose and withdrawal can result in death. Barbiturates are particularly dangerous when used in conjunction with alcohol.

Despite the proliferation of drug laws, drug use among young people and adults is widespread and increasing. The criminal justice system and penal institutions have been severely overburdened. From the Harrison Act of 1914 to the Comprehensive Drug Abuse Prevention and Control Act of 1970, the emphasis of the government has been on punishment rather than on prevention and treatment of abuse.

Drug rehabilitation programs that have proved relatively effective include the Phoenix House—which focus on the psychological problems of addicts. The use of a synthetic narcotic, *methadone*, enables many addicts to function in society; however, it keeps the addict drug-dependent. *Narcotic antagonists*, which block the effects of heroin, are also available but are not widely used.

The British approach to the drug problem contrasts sharply with that of the United States; the British view the addict as ill rather than as a criminal. Under strict guidelines, addicts can obtain heroin or methadone at nominal cost. Though it is unclear how well the British system would work with the much more extensive drug problem in the United States, it has apparently reduced the illicit drug trade, the drug-related crime rate, and the number of unemployed addicts.

Bibliography

Bejerot, Nils. *Addiction and Society.* Springfield, Ill.: Charles C. Thomas, 1970.

Blum, Richard H., *et al. Society and Drugs.* San Francisco: Jossey-Bass, 1969.

Cahalan, Don. *Problem Drinkers: A National Survey.* San Francisco: Jossey-Bass, 1970.

Cortina, Rank M. *Stroke a Slain Warrior.* New York: Columbia University Press, 1971.

Duster, Troy S. *The Legislation of Morality: Law, Drugs, and Moral Judgment.* New York: Free Press, 1972.

Fort, Joel. *The Pleasure Seekers: The Drug Crisis, Youth and Society.* Indianapolis: Bobbs-Merrill, 1969.

Geller, Allen, and Boas, Maxwell. *The Drug Beat.* New York: Cowles, 1969.

Good, Erich. *The Marijuana Smoker.* New York: Basic Books, 1970.

Grinspoon, Lester. *Marijuana Reconsidered.* Cambridge, Mass.: Harvard University Press, 1971.

Houser, Norman W., and Richmond, Julius B. *Drugs: Facts on Their Use and Abuse.* New York: Lothrop, Lee, and Shepard, 1969.

McGrath, John H., and Scarpitti, Frank R. *Youth and Drugs: Perspectives on a Social Problem.* Glenview, Ill.: Scott, Foresman, 1970.

Marihuana: A Signal of Misunderstanding. First Report of the Commission on Marihuana and Drug Abuse. Washington, D.C.: U.S. Government Printing Office, 1972.

National Commission on Marihuana and Drug Abuse. *Drug Use in America: Problem in Perspective.* Washington, D.C.: U.S. Government Printing Office, 1973.

Nowlis, Helen H. *Drugs on the College Campus.* Garden City, N.Y.: Doubleday, 1969.

Ray, Oakley S. *Drugs, Society, and Human Behavior.* St. Louis: C. V. Mosby, 1972.

Russo, J. Robert, ed. *Amphetamine Abuse.* Springfield, Ill.: Charles C. Thomas, 1972.

U.S. Department of HEW. *Alcohol and Health.* Rockville, Md.: Public Health Service, 1974.

Westman, Wesley C. *The Drug Epidemic: What It Means and How to Combat It.* New York: Dial, 1970.

Whitney, Elizabeth D., ed. *World Dialogue on Alcohol and Drug Dependence.* Boston: Beacon, 1970.

Winich, Charles. *The Sociological Aspects of Drug Dependence.* Cleveland: CRC Press, 1974.

Wittenborn, J. R., Brill, Henry, Smith, Jean Paul, and Wittenborn, Sarah A. *Drugs and Youth: Proceedings of the Rutgers Symposium on Drug Abuse.* Springfield, Ill.: Charles C. Thomas, 1970.

Crime and Criminals

Facts about Crime and Criminals

- Over 10 million serious crimes were reported in 1977:
  - 463,000 robberies (taking property by force)
  - 3,232,000 burglaries (taking property from a home, unseen)
  - 5,855,000 larcenies (taking property in general)
  - 993,000 auto thefts

- In a recent year, 71 percent of all persons convicted of auto theft were imprisoned for an average of three years; however, only 16 percent of those convicted of securities fraud were sent to prison, and then only for an average of 19 months.

- White-collar crime by employees, suppliers, and competitors exceeds $40 billion a year.

- In one survey, 4 out of 7 people in business reported that they would violate a code of ethics if they could avoid detection.

- For every 100 reported crimes,
  - 20 persons are arrested
  - 14 persons are charged
  - 7 persons are referred to juvenile court
  - 2 persons are acquitted
  - 1 person is fined
  - 1 person is found guilty of a lesser offense
  - 3 persons are placed on probation
  - 3 persons are imprisoned

The issue of law and order has assumed tremendous importance in America today: crime is widely seen as one of our most pressing social problems. It is important to realize, however, that at least some crime has existed in almost all societies. As the French sociologist Emile Durkheim pointed out, wherever there are people and laws, there are crime and criminals:

> Crime is present . . . in all societies of all types. There is no society that is not confronted with the problem of criminality. Its form changes; the acts thus characterized are not the same everywhere; but, everywhere and always, there have been men who have behaved in such a way as to draw upon themselves penal repression. . . . What is normal, simply, is the existence of criminality.[1]

It is generally agreed that serious, violent crime has reached alarming proportions in the United States, but the extent of the increase is debated. One survey of five large American cities revealed that the actual rates for violent personal and property crime were several times higher than the official rates presented in the FBI's *Uniform Crime Reports (UCR)*, which are based on crimes reported to the police. Many victims do not report crimes to the police because they feel that nothing can be done or that the crime was unimportant.[2]

[1]Emile Durkheim, *Rules of Sociological Method*, 8th ed., trans. S. A. Solvay and J. H. Mueller, ed. G. E. G. Catlin (Glencoe, Ill.: Free Press, 1950), p. 65.

[2]Law Enforcement Assistance Administration (LEAA) study reported in UPI dispatch, April 15, 1974.

The official statistics are grim. Although the crime rate *fell* by 4 percent in 1977, it was still 50 percent higher than it was in 1968.[3] (See Table 5-1.) Official statistics, of course, do not tell the whole story. It has never been easy to assess, for example, the extent of organized and occupational crime with any substantial accuracy. Recent exposures of government and business scandals show that these types of crime are far more widespread and pervasive than had been realized.

Not only has crime itself increased, but the fear of crime, especially in large cities, significantly affects the lives of many people. As the President's Commission on Law Enforcement and the Administration of Justice observed in its 1967 report: "The existence of crime, the talk about crime, the reports of crime, and fear of crime have eroded the basic quality of life for many Americans."[4] Polls by the Law Enforcement Assistance Administration (LEAA), for example, found that 45 percent of the American population was afraid to walk alone at night near their own homes; 61 percent of the women felt unsafe in their own neighborhood at night; 47 percent owned guns, mostly for self-protection.[5]

Meanwhile, the crime rate remains alarmingly high, and youth gangs—relatively moribund in the 1960s—have reappeared in American cities. Some knowledgeable people in the field believe that the problem has reached crisis proportions, and the claim by the President's Commission that "America can control crime if it will" sometimes appears highly optimistic. At the very least, there are some serious questions to be asked about why crime occurs, why there is so much of it today, and what we can and should be doing about it.

[3] U.S. Department of Justice, *Uniform Crime Reports* (Washington, D.C.: U.S. Government Printing Office, October 18, 1978), pp. 35-37.

[4] The President's Commission on Law Enforcement and the Administration of Justice, *The Challenge of Crime in a Free Society* (Washington, D.C.: U.S. Government Printing Office, 1967), p. v.

[5] LEAA, *Sourcebook of Criminal Justice Statistics* (Washington, D.C.: U.S. Government Printing Office, 1977).

Table 5-1
Index of Crime,
United States,
1968-1977

Population	Crime Index total	Violent crime	Murder and non-negligent man-slaughter	Forcible rape	Robbery	Aggra-vated assault	Burglary	Larceny-theft	Motor vehicle theft
Rate per 100,000 inhabitants:									
1968	3,370.2	298.4	6.9	15.9	131.8	143.8	932.3	1,746.6	393.0
1969	3,680.0	328.7	7.3	18.5	148.4	154.5	984.1	1,930.9	436.2
1970	3,984.5	363.5	7.9	18.7	172.1	164.8	1,084.9	2,079.3	456.8
1971	4,164.7	396.0	8.6	20.5	188.0	178.8	1,163.5	2,145.5	459.8
1972	3,961.4	401.0	9.0	22.5	180.7	188.8	1,140.8	1,993.6	426.1
1973	4,154.4	417.4	9.4	24.5	183.1	200.5	1,222.5	2,071.9	442.6
1974	4,850.4	461.1	9.8	26.2	209.3	215.8	1,437.7	2,489.5	462.2
1975	5,281.7	481.5	9.6	26.3	218.2	227.4	1,525.9	2,804.8	409.4
1976	5,266.4	459.6	8.8	26.4	195.8	228.7	1,439.4	2,921.3	446.1
1977	5,055.1	466.6	8.8	29.1	187.1	241.5	1,410.9	2,729.9	447.6

Source: *Uniform Crime Reports* (Washington, D.C.: U.S. Government Printing Office, October, 1978), p. 37.

The Nature of Crime

Crime is defined as an act or omission of an act for which the state can apply sanctions. The criminal law, a subdivision of the rules governing society, prohibits certain acts and prescribes punishments to be meted out to violators. Confusion frequently arises because, although the criminal law prescribes certain rules for living in society, not all violations of social rules are violations of criminal laws. A swimmer's failure to come to the aid of a drowning person, for example, would not constitute a criminal act, although it might be considered a moral wrong. Many acts that are regarded as immoral are ignored in the criminal law but are considered civil offenses. Under civil law—those laws that deal with noncriminal acts of one individual injuring another—the state, representing society, arbitrates between the aggrieved party and the offender. For example, civil law is involved when a person whose car was destroyed in an accident sues the driver responsible for the accident in order to recover the cost of damages. The driver at fault is not considered a criminal unless he or she can be shown to have broken a criminal law, as, for instance, to have been driving while intoxicated. Further confusion results from changes in social attitudes, which usually precede changes in the criminal law. Old laws still "on the books" continue to make some acts criminal that are no longer considered wrong by society (See Chapter 3).

The legal definition of crime ignores the effect of social values in determining what laws are to be enforced. Although judges and prosecutors use criminal law to determine the criminality of certain acts, the very act of applying the law involves issues of class interest and political power: one group imposes its will on another by enforcing its definition of illegality on the powerless. For example, authorities are not nearly as anxious to enforce laws against consumer fraud as they are to enforce laws against the use of certain drugs, because consumer fraud is often perpetrated by powerful business interests with strong political influence. The drug user, on the other hand, usually lacks power and public support.

The history of vagrancy laws is another example of how groups in power create and enforce laws to protect their own interests:

> Vagrancy laws emerged in order to provide landowners with a supply of cheap labor. When this group no longer needed cheap labor and were no longer powerful, the laws fell into disuse. Similarly, when the interests of a new power class—e.g., the mercantile class—were threatened, the vagrancy statutes were reactivated and appropriately altered to reflect the desires and needs of this group. Finally, the use of vagrancy laws in contemporary society to keep bums and other undesirables off the streets, or at least out of respectable neighborhoods, suggests the influence of middle-class desires and power to shape criminal laws.[6]

In practice, the definition of criminality changes according to what the police believe criminal behavior to be. Given the thousands of laws on the books, the police have a wide power of discretion over which laws to ignore, which to enforce, and how strongly to enforce them. This discretionary power, in turn, offers the police many opportunities to exercise their own

---

[6]Clayton A. Hartjen, *Crime and Criminalization*, 2nd ed. (New York: Praeger, 1978), p. 33.

concept of lawful behavior in their decisions as to what citizen's complaint needs attention, who to arrest, and who to release.

In a two-year study of two groups of adolescents in the same high school, William Chambliss examined how the biases of the local police and community members affected their reactions to and treatment of middle- and lower-class delinquents, and how the behavior and appearance of the delinquents themselves determined the kind of treatment and response they received.[7] A group of middle- and upper-middle-class boys—the "Saints"— had been truant almost every day of the period that they were studied. They had vandalized houses and harassed citizens and the police; they drove recklessly, drank excessively, and openly cheated on exams. Yet only twice in the two years were members of the Saints stopped by a police officer; even then, nothing appeared on their school records. Many of them received school distinctions. Teachers and school officials ignored any acts that might be called delinquent and expected these boys to succeed in life.

The group called the "Roughnecks" on the other hand, were all from lower-class families. They could not afford to maintain the same kind of physical appearance as the Saints. While the Saints had cars and could "sow their wild oats" in parts of town where they were not known, the Roughnecks were confined to an area where they could be easily recognized, and therefore established a reputation for being delinquent. They did relatively poorly in school.

The demeanor of the two groups of boys differed markedly whenever they were apprehended by the police: the Saints, who were apologetic, penitent, and generally respectful of middle-class values, were treated as harmless pranksters. The Roughnecks, who were openly hostile and disdainful toward the police, were labeled by the police as "deviant." Chambliss found that the adult careers of the two groups followed the community's expectations. Almost all of the Saints went on to college and white-collar careers, while most of the Roughnecks either went on to low-status jobs or became criminals.

The study of the Saints and the Roughnecks demonstrates that factors such as low-income, high-unemployment, or minority-group status do not have an actual bearing on the commission of juvenile crimes. While such factors did account for a higher rate of detection and punishment, the rate of misbehavior was virtually the same for both groups. Differences in the official records of the two groups reflected a biased application of the disciplinary system. If such a bias can be observed to influence the accuracy of collected data on a limited scale, it is possible that a similar bias can undermine the accuracy of national crime statistics. Until recently, the standard index of criminal activity in the United States was the Federal Bureau of Investigation's annual *Uniform Crime Reports (UCR)*. This study supplies racial and economic profiles of those arrested for such common-law crimes as murder, rape, assault, and robbery. Recent data support the long-held assumption that minority-group members are more likely to be involved in crimes than are non-minority individuals.[8] Yet it must be remembered that *UCR* statistics cite

[7]William Chambliss, "The Saints and the Roughnecks," *Society*, vol. 2, no. 11 (November-December 1973), 24-31.

[8]1974-75 *UCR* statistics as cited by Michael J. Hindelang, "Race and Involvement in Common Law Personal Crimes," *American Sociological Review* 43 (February 1978), 93-109.

only those apprehended for their crimes. If, like the Saints of the Chambliss study, adult offenders belonging to non-minority and upper-class groups are rarely caught or punished, *UCR*-based data becomes inaccurate. Because it does not profile those who successfully evade prosecution, the *UCR* fails to reveal the whole range of criminal activity in America.

Acting on this hypothesis, researchers have attempted to find more reliable ways to track criminal activity. Self-report studies, which ask respondents to report their own criminal involvement through an anonymous questionnaire, have provided alternative data. In a study examining the correlation between racial factors and criminal activity, Michael Hindelang evaluated the results of various self-report studies. He found that data from such studies did not concur with *UCR* findings. While minority groups have a higher crime rate when judged by official data (such as juvenile or criminal court records or the *UCR* index), self-reporting techniques indicate that both whites and nonwhites have a similar rate of criminal activity. Thus, the preconception that race is a factor in criminality is disproven when different standards of measurement are used.

Another attempt to supplement *UCR* data has led to the development of victimization reports. These surveys, conducted by the United States Census Bureau, collect information from a representative sample of crime victims. Comparison of *UCR* and victimization indices show a discrepancy of data and, depending upon which standard is used, different conclusions can be drawn about the correlation between crime and socioeconomic status.[9] Neither index has been accepted as totally reliable in itself. While the drawbacks of the *UCR* method have already been pointed out, victimization surveys also present special problems. Data only reflects crimes that are reported, yet many victims—whether through fear, ignorance, or alienation from the system—do not file reports. Victimization surveys indicate that this is particularly true in low-income, high-crime areas, and this damages the accuracy of the statistics. Certain crimes are under-reported, so distortions occur because of selective reporting by victims.

The difficulty in finding a reliable index with which to measure the impact of socioeconomic status on criminal activity makes it necessary to consider many sources before forming a conclusion. By comparing thirty-five separate studies on the subject, one team of researchers has hypothesized that social class has no bearing on an individual's likelihood to be involved in criminal activity.[10] Those of the middle- and upper-classes have a delinquency rate proportionately equal to their lower-class neighbors. Again, it seems that poor, under-educated, and minorities have become the victims of selective law enforcement, stereotyping, and misleading statistics.

The rich and powerful, on the other hand, have been quite well insulated from such stigmata. They are so seldom sent to prison that when one of them is finally jailed for stealing—by fraud, embezzlement, or tax evasion—often a far greater amount of money than the most clever bank bandit has stolen, it makes nationwide headlines. Some sociologists, noting the difficulty of

[9]Alan Booth, David R. Johnson, and Harvey M. Choldin, "Correlates of City Crime Rates: Victimization Surveys Versus Official Statistics," *Social Problems*, vol. 25, no. 2 (December 1977), pp. 187-197.

[10]Charles R. Tittle, Wayne J. Villemez, and Douglas A. Smith, "The Myth of Social Class and Criminality: An Empirical Assessment of the Empirical Evidence," *American Sociological Review* 43 (October 1978), 643-656.

obtaining accurate information on the rate of such occupational crime, have contended that, since the upper classes constitute such a small proportion of the total population and the actual incidence of occupational crime is greater than official statistics reflect, the upper classes may actually have a higher rate of crime than the lower classes.[11] It will be helpful to bear these facts in mind in the following discussion on the various types of crime.

Types of Crime and Criminals

Most of us tend to think of crime in an overgeneralized way, and to have stereotyped notions about criminals. We usually speak of the "crime problem" without specifying which crimes we mean, and often label those who break laws as "criminals," without realizing that they are not law violators all the time. Professional thieves, for example, might behave quite conservatively outside their occupation, and juvenile delinquents might well become model adults. The very words "crime" and "criminal" are too broad to be useful in describing certain acts or persons. Actually, criminal acts and lawbreakers are almost as varied as non-criminal acts and law-abiders. No one term can encompass the wide range of behaviors that are illegal, nor can one term meaningfully describe people who are lawbreakers.

In this section we shall review nine major types of crime and criminals. Eight of these have been classified by sociologists Marshall B. Clinard and Richard Quinney, who categorized criminal behavior according to how great a part criminal activity plays in people's lives; that is, whether or not these people see themselves as criminals, and the extent to which they commit themselves to a life of crime. Such distinctions help sociologists understand why and how different law-breaking behaviors occur. The eight major categories of crime and lawbreakers as defined by Clinard and Quinney are (1) violent personal; (2) occasional property; (3) occupational (white-collar); (4) political; (5) public order; (6) conventional; (7) organized; and (8) professional.[12] We shall add a ninth category: juvenile delinquency. We shall look at each of these types and examine what kinds of activity they involve and where their perpetrators fit into the picture of criminality. Two kinds of activity—occupational and organized crime—will receive more extensive treatment because their social costs probably exceed the social costs of all the others combined.

Violent Personal Crime

This category of crime includes assault, robbery, and the various forms of homicide—acts in which physical injury is inflicted or implied. Although robbery occurs most often between strangers, murders are usually the result of a violent personal dispute between friends or relatives. Murders and aggravated assaults are, therefore, usually considered unpremeditated acts and not the result of criminal life styles or purposes. Violent behavior of this kind has usually been attributed more to cultural conditioning, and the offenders have been portrayed as normally law-abiding persons who are not

[11]Walter C. Reckless, *The Crime Problem*, 5th ed. (Englewood Cliffs, N.J.: Prentice-Hall, 1973).

[12]Marshall B. Clinard and Richard Quinney, *Criminal Behavior Systems: A Typology* (New York: Holt, Rinehart and Winston, 1973).

Double advantage: the cover of darkness and a city-wide police strike give young looters a perfect opportunity for this break-in.

UPI

likely to be engaged in other criminal activities. In recent years, however, there has been a disturbing increase in violent crimes between strangers: in 1977, for example, more than 40 percent of all murders were committed by an unknown assailant.[13] (The subject of violent crimes is discussed comprehensively in Chapter 6, "Violence.")

Occasional Property Crime

Crimes of this type include vandalism, check forgery, shoplifting, and some kinds of auto theft. Vandals, check forgers, shoplifters, and other such offenders are usually naive and unsophisticated in their operations, with no knowledge of professional criminal skills. Because occasional offenders commit their crimes only at irregular intervals, they are not apt to associate with habitual law-breakers. Non-professional shoplifters, for example, consider themselves to be respectable, law-abiders who steal articles from stores only for their own use. They excuse their behavior because what they steal has relatively little value and the "victim" is usually a large, impersonal organization such as a chain store, which can easily replace the stolen article.[14]

Neither non-professional shoplifters nor non-professional check forgers are likely to have a criminal record. They, together with vandals and car thieves, usually work alone and are not part of any criminal subculture; none of them seeks to earn a living from crime.

[13]Department of Justice, *UCR*, p. 12.
[14]Richard Quinney, *The Social Reality of Crime* (Boston: Little, Brown, 1970), pp. 252-253.

The phenomenon of occupational crime was defined and popularized by the sociologist Edwin H. Sutherland, first in a 1940 article, and then in his 1961 book *White Collar Crime*.[15] He analyzed the behavior of people who break the law as part of their normal business activities: corporation directors, who use their inside knowledge of the market to sell large blocks of stock at a tremendous profit; accountants, who juggle books to conceal the several hundred dollars of company money they have pocketed; stores that raise the list price of a $20 dress to $40, in order to offer it as a "sale" item at $28; firms that make false statements about their profits in order to avoid paying taxes. Such crime can also occur in the medical, legal, and other professions, as when a doctor submits a fraudulent accident report, or charges a patient for unnecessary and unrequested treatment. Such acts tend to be ignored by society: they rarely come to the criminal courts, and even then, they are rarely judged as severely as other criminal activities.

Since Sutherland described it, the category of occupational crime has also come to include such disparate acts as embezzlement, fraud in its various forms, false advertising, fee-splitting, labor violations, price-fixing, antitrust violations, and black-market activity. In this section we shall concentrate on embezzlement, fraud (mostly antitrust violations and consumer fraud), and the wide range of business and government crimes. Frequently, there is also a strong connection between organized crime and corrupt government officials; this will be discussed in the section on organized crime.

The occupational offender is far removed from the popular stereotype of a criminal. Few of us think that a conservatively dressed Wall Street lawyer or stockbroker living in an affluent suburb, with a well-paying, high-status job in the city, would be engaged in illegal activities. Because of their respectable appearances, it is difficult for most people to think of these offenders as criminals. In fact, occupational offenders often consider themselves to be respectable citizens and do everything possible to avoid being labeled as lawbreakers, even by themselves. Most embezzlers, for example, use elaborate rationalizations to explain their actions, seeing embezzling as a kind of secret "borrowing."[16]

Sutherland offered his own explanation of why people break the law. His theory of "differential association" asserts that occupational criminality, like other systematic criminality, is a behavior learned through frequent direct or indirect associations with those who already practice it, and lack of frequent contact with law-abiding behavior. (We discuss this theory later in this chapter.) Thus, those who become occupational criminals may do so simply by getting into businesses or occupations where their colleagues regard certain kinds of crime as the standard way of conducting business.

Embezzlement.   Embezzlement, or theft by an employee from his or her employer, is usually committed by otherwise law-abiding persons during their employment. Embezzlement occurs at all levels of business, from a clerk stealing from petty cash to a vice-president stealing large investment sums. Most cases are not detected, and companies are often unwilling to prosecute for fear of bad publicity. Even the federal government seems reluctant to

---

[15]Edwin H. Sutherland, "White-collar Criminality," *American Sociological Review* 5 (February 1940), 1-12; and *White Collar Crime* (New York: Holt, Rinehart and Winston, 1961).

[16]Quinney, *Social Reality of Crime*, pp. 253-256.

confront the issue. In 1978-1979, for example, the Justice Department allocated only 5.5 percent of its budget—$139 million out of $2.5 billion—to investigating and prosecuting white-collar crime. Yet conservative estimates by the Commerce Department, insurance companies, and the National Retail Merchants Association put embezzlement losses at almost $11 billion a day.[17]

A now-classic study of embezzlers was done by Donald Cressey, in his book *Other People's Money*.[18] Cressey interviewed convicted financial trust violators in prison, and found that three basic conditions were necessary before people turned to embezzlement. First, employees had to have a financial problem they were unable to share with others. Second, they had to have the opportunity to steal. Finally, and to Cressey this was the most crucial consideration, they had to be able to find a formula in words to rationalize the fact that they were not really committing a criminal act—such as "I'm just borrowing a little to tide me over." In this way embezzlers could feel that their actions would have society's understanding.

Fraud.   Fraud is obtaining money or property under false pretenses. It can occur at any level of business, and in any type of business relationship. A citizen defrauds the government by evading the payment of income tax; a butcher defrauds a customer by charging the pound-price for fifteen ounces of meat; an industry defrauds the public when members agree to keep prices artificially high. The cost of fraud may run from a few cents to millions of dollars, and the methods may be as crude as a butcher's thumb on the scales or as sophisticated as the coordinated efforts of dozens of lawyers, executives, and government officials.

Fraud has been a part of business life for so long that there is a standard Latin warning against it—*caveat emptor*, "Let the buyer beware." Some observers consider fraud especially prevalent in America today, and feel that the values most characteristic of American business—competition, selling, risk-taking, persuasion—tend to encourage it. (See Chapter 12.) It is perhaps worth noting in this regard that professional confidence men and women, whose livelihood depends on their ability to find respectable potential victims willing to take a chance on a dishonest deal, generally consider American businesspeople as their best "marks."[19]

It is impossible here to list all the kinds of fraud in our society, but we shall consider consumer fraud in some detail, and look briefly at business-government fraud.

Consumer Fraud.   The term "consumer fraud" is usually applied to cases of cheating in direct transactions between retail buyer and seller. Common examples are shortweighted food packages, failure to put required information on credit contracts, mislabeling of meat—so that a customer buys ground chuck for the price of sirloin—or unnecessary auto repairs. It has been estimated that $1 billion is spent annually on worthless goods and services,

---

[17]Representative John Conyers, Jr., "Rampant Crime in the Boardroom," *The Los Angeles Times* (January 3, 1979), p. 5, Part II; "Crimes Against Business Are Frequently Crimes by Business," *United Press International*, July 16, 1978.

[18]Donald R. Cressey, *Other People's Money: A Study in the Social Psychology of Embezzlement*, Reprint of 1953 ed. (Montclair, N.J.: Patterson Smith, 1973).

[19]Edwin M. Schur, *Our Criminal Society* (Englewood Cliffs, N.J.: Prentice-Hall, 1969), p. 171.

Appliance	Bureaucratic Sources			Traditional Sources	
	Discount House	Department Store	Chain Store	Neighborhood Dealer	Peddler
Television:					
Percent high price	8	22	31	53	67
Phonograph:					
Percent over $200	14	46	51	51	55
Washing machine:					
Percent over $230	30	50	29	54	87
Percent over $300	10	14	8	36	87

Source: Reprinted with permission of Macmillan Publishing Co., Inc. from *The Poor Pay More*, by David Caplowitz. Copyright © 1957 by the Free Press, a Division of Macmillan Publishing Co.

Table 5-2
Cost of Appliances According to Type of Source

and that consumer losses from fraudulent repair and other rackets amount to many more billions of dollars each year.[20]

Consumer fraud bears most heavily on the poor. For one thing, ghetto stores consistently charge higher prices for merchandise than do stores in more affluent neighborhoods, and often the merchandise is of poorer quality. Since the poor are often unaware of the possibility of comparative shopping or are unable to shop outside their own neighborhoods, they are trapped by these inflated prices. In addition, since many speak little or no English, and have no practical access to accurate information about their rights as citizens and consumers, it is difficult for them to complain effectively even when they know they are being cheated.

Many abuses to which the poor are particularly subject involve credit. By definition, the poor are poor credit risks and have a hard time getting credit from reputable firms. Consequently, they may be forced to borrow money from a neighborhood "loan shark" at highly inflated interest rates. Likewise, if they wish to buy furniture or appliances on the installment plan—and this is one of the biggest businesses in ghetto areas—they are apt to turn to a neighborhood store or door-to-door peddler offering "easy credit." The credit may be easy in the beginning, but the costs are usually excessive in the end. (See Table 5-2.)

Business-Government Crime. This can mean either the misuse of government funds by business organizations, with or without the collusion of government officials, or corporate bribes to legislators to further the corporation's interests. (See also Chapters 6 and 12.) There have also been cases of elected officials taking money from corporations in return for votes for legislation favorable to the corporation's interests. In some cases, the actions are clearly illegal, and when they come to light, scandal and prosecutions ensue; others occur in a gray area of irresponsibility, in which no one seems to have committed a crime, but something about the proceedings is felt to be wrong.

[20]"White Collar Crime: Huge Economic and Moral Drain," *Congressional Quarterly* (May 7, 1971), p. 1049.

Since the 1950s, an enormous amount of government money, particularly federal money, has been poured into numerous projects—housing, urban renewal, job training, education, and health. The money goes to states, municipalities, or business firms, through allotment or contract, and then presumably is spent for the designated purposes. Unfortunately, the availability of so much cash seems to offer an irresistible temptation to some of the people through whose hands it passes, and considerable sums are periodically siphoned off into private pockets. Given the amounts of money involved, and the far-flung nature of many government programs, it is hard to see how their administration can be adequately controlled. Nevertheless, some speculators have apparently profited from the public purse—at the expense of the needy—to a frightening degree.

The issue of corporate involvement in federal elections surfaced in the scandals surrounding the re-election of President Richard M. Nixon in 1972. Although it has been illegal since 1907 for corporations to give money in campaigns for federal office, at least seven large United States corporations admitted to having contributed amounts ranging from $30,000 to $100,000 to the 1972 Nixon re-election campaign. The money was funneled indirectly to the campaign committee through foreign branches or subsidiaries of the corporations, or by having company employees hand over special "bonuses" to several Nixon re-election committees.[21] Other business-government crimes involved American businesses and foreign governments: the Lockheed Corporation, for example, admitted in 1975 that it had spent at least $22 million in bribes in attempts to win sales of its products overseas.

Political Crime

Political offenses include such activities as "treason, sedition, and civil disobedience." In the eyes of the state, these activities threaten the existing social order and, if unchecked, could do the nation serious harm. The offenders, of course, believe that their law violations serve purposes and ideals higher than the state's.[22]

The best-known examples of this kind of offense occurred in the 1960s and early 1970s during the civil rights movement and the widespread opposition to American involvement in the Vietnam War. Protest groups defined the existing social structure and political institutions as illegitimate and engaged in sit-ins, draft-card burnings, draft evasions, and marches. Even when such actions are legal (such as a protest demonstration), they may be treated as illegal because of their political nature. The arrests of black and white protesters in the South during the early days of the civil rights movement, and the killing of students protesting the invasion of Cambodia at Kent State University in Ohio, were government responses to a perceived threat against the social order.[23]

Public Order Crime

In sheer numbers, public order offenders constitute the largest category of what society chooses to regard as criminals, their activities out-numbering by

[21]"Why It Was Better to Give Than . . . ," *Time* (November 26, 1973), p. 18.
[22]Quinney, *Social Reality of Crime*, pp. 256-259.
[23]See *The Report of the President's Commission on Campus Unrest* (Washington, D.C.: U.S. Government Printing Office, 1970), pp. 282, 449.

far all other types of reported crime. Public order offenses include prostitution, homosexuality, gambling, drug addiction, drunkenness, vagrancy, disorderly conduct, and traffic violations. Most of these are often called "victimless crimes" because they cause no physical harm to anyone but the offenders themselves. Society considers them crimes because they violate the order or customs of the community, but allows a certain measure of toleration to homosexuality, gambling, and prostitution.[24] (See Chapter 2.)

Public order offenders rarely consider themselves to be criminals or their actions to be crimes. The behavior and activities of prostitutes and drug users, however, tend to isolate and segregate them from others; and some, such as drug users, may find themselves drawn into criminal roles. The law defines certain drug use as illegal, and so users may come to see themselves as being outside the mainstream of society. They may also have to commit other criminal acts to pay for drugs. In this way, criminal laws can unintentionally expand and promote criminal behavior. (See Chapters 1, 3, and 4 for further discussion of this topic.)

[24]Quinney, *Social Reality of Crime*, pp. 259-264.

Three demonstrators attired as specters of Vietnam, Laos, and Cambodia march in a 1970 anti-war protest. Although their actions may be within the legal bounds of freedom of expression, political overtones and violent clashes with authorities often cause demonstrators to be treated as law-breakers.
UPI

Conventional Crime   Conventional offenders are most often young adults in their twenties who commit robbery, larceny, burglary, and gang theft as a way of life. Their criminal offenses usually begin in adolescence as members of juvenile gangs, where they join other truants from school to routinely vandalize property and fight in the streets. As juvenile offenders they are not organized or skillful enough to avoid arrest and conviction, and by young adulthood they have compiled a police record and may have spent time in prison.[25]

Conventional offenders could be called "semiprofessionals" since they are not as sophisticated in criminal techniques as organized and professional criminals, and move only by degrees into a criminal life. For this reason, the development of their self-concepts as criminals and their identification with crime are gradual. By the time they have built up a criminal record, they have usually made a fairly strong identification with criminality. The criminal record itself is society's way of permanently defining these offenders as criminals, and, once so defined, it is almost impossible for them to re-enter the mainstream of society and their criminal activities usually continue.

Since only a small percentage of known conventional crime results in arrest, most offenders of this type are convinced that crime *does* pay. Relative success in a criminal career leads the offender away from a conventional life. Moreover, the life of a successful criminal has a certain excitement. As James Q. Wilson puts it:

> One works at crime at one's convenience, enjoys the esteem of colleagues who think a "straight" job is stupid and skill at stealing is commendable, looks forward to the occasional "big score" that may make further work unnecessary for weeks, and relishes the risk and adventure associated with theft. The money value . . . of all these benefits is hard to estimate but is almost certainly far larger than what either public or private employers could offer to unskilled or semi-skilled young workers.[26]

Because offenders associate mostly with other criminals, they develop a camaraderie and outlook that scorns the benefits of law-abiding behavior.

Surprisingly, some conventional criminals give up crime in their late twenties and early thirties for reasons that are still not clear to criminologists. Perhaps they marry and have to support families, and find this more rewarding than crime. In the relatively low incidence of conventional criminality among older adults, family responsibility seems to be a more powerful factor than rehabilitation or coercion.

Organized Crime   The groups we usually think of as representing organized crime tend to be large and diversified regional, or even national, bodies. They may organize initially to carry on a particular crime, such as illicit drug traffic, extortion, prostitution, or gambling. Later they may seek to control this activity within a given city or neighborhood, destroying or absorbing the competition. Eventually they may expand into other types of crime, and seek to protect their members from arrest through intimidation or bribery of public officials.

Unlike other crime, organized crime is a system in which illegal activities

[25]Quinney, *Social Reality of Crime*, pp. 264-267.
[26]James Q. Wilson, "Lock 'em Up and Other Thoughts on Crime," *New York Times Magazine* (March 9, 1975), p. 20.

are carried out not haphazardly, but as part of a rational plan devised by a large organization which is seeking to maximize its overall profit. In order to operate most efficiently, organized crime relies on division of labor, and has numerous, diverse roles that must be performed. (However, there is some controversy over how structured organized crime is.[27])

A second major characteristic of organized crime, and one which it shares with some other types of crime, is that instead of being wholly predatory—like burglary, which involves only taking from victims—the syndicate supplies goods and services that a large segment of the public wants but cannot legally obtain. Without the public's desire for gambling, for money from loan sharks, or for drugs, for example, organized crime's base would collapse.

The Scope of the Problem.   Many people regard organized crime as almost a myth, belonging more to fiction and film than to everyday reality. This tendency is fostered by popular accounts of individual racketeers who are invariably referred to by their "in" names (for example, "Crazy Joe Gallo"). This makes it seem as if organized crime is simply a few television-style gangsters. The late Senator Robert F. Kennedy noted and deplored this tendency:

> The racketeer is not someone dressed in a black suit, white tie, and diamond stick pin, whose activities affect only a remote underworld circle. He is more likely to be outfitted in a gray flannel suit and his influence is more likely to be as far-reaching as that of an important industrialist. The American public may not see him, but that makes the racketeer's power for evil in our society even greater. Lacking the direct confrontation with the racketeer, the American citizen fails to see the reason for alarm. The reason, decidedly, exists.[28]

Organized crime gets its initial huge profits from supplying illegal goods and services to the American public. Its major source of profit, and in many cases the original activity of the syndicate or its parent gang, is its gambling operations—lotteries, "numbers," off-track betting, illegal casinos, and dice games. Some of these can be located anywhere—in a tenement, on business premises, in a restaurant or garage. Much illegal gambling in the United States today is controlled by organized crime, operating through elaborate hierarchies in which money is filtered from the small operator who takes the customer's bet through several other levels until it finally reaches the organization's headquarters. This complex system protects the leaders, whose identity remains concealed from those below. Centralized organization of gambling also increases efficiency, enlarges markets, provides a systematized method of paying graft to public officials, and makes it possible to avoid large losses by providing money to operators, so that they can "lay off" on bets (i.e., cover themselves against losses by making counterbalancing bets). It is estimated that syndicate profits from gambling amount to $6 or $7 billion a year.[29]

The second highest source of revenue for organized crime is loan-sharking, lending money at interest rates above the legal limit. These rates

---

[27]See Francis Ianni and Elizabeth Ianni, *A Family Business* (New York: Russell Sage Foundation, 1972).

[28]Donald R. Cressey, *Theft of the Nation: The Structure of Organized Crime in America* (New York: Harper & Row, 1969), p. xiii.

[29]President's Commission, *Challenge of Crime*, p. 189.

can go as high as 150 percent *a week*, and over 20 percent is standard. Through its profits from gambling operations, syndicated crime always has considerable cash to lend, and it can ensure repayment by the threat of violence. Most loans are to gamblers who need to repay debts, drug users, and small businesses unable to obtain credit from legitimate sources. Profits from loan-sharking are estimated in the multibillion-dollar range.

The narcotics trade is organized crime's third major source of revenue. Its direct dealings in narcotics are probably limited to importation from abroad and wholesale distribution in the United States. Lower-level operations are left to others, since that is considered too risky. Organized crime gets about $5 billion in profits each year from the narcotics trade.[30]

Organized crime uses some of its huge profits from its illegitimate activities to expand into legitimate businesses that serve as useful tax covers for syndicate members. They also confer a certain respectable status in the community. Finally, legitimate businesses serve as another source of profit—particularly since the syndicate, using its ready reserves of cash and threats of force, can temporarily lower prices to ruin competitors, employ strong-arm tactics to obtain customers, and generally conduct business outside of the law.

Direct investment is only one of several ways in which organized crime gets into legitimate businesses: It can accept business interests in lieu of money as payment for a loan or gambling debt; it can foreclose usurious loans in which businesses were put up as collateral; it can extort tribute from a legitimate business for the privilege of staying open. The tribute can be in the form of a demand that the business buy all its supplies from companies controlled by organized crime—thus assuring markets for those companies.[31]

Organized crime is also deeply involved in labor racketeering. By infiltrating labor unions, for example, it gains access to union funds; it may also make profitable deals with management by ensuring labor peace or by threatening a strike. A *New York Times* story of May 9, 1972 described investigations revealing that criminal infiltration into the New York City meat industry had inflated retail meat prices by as much as 15 percent. Possible collusion between key industry and union figures was suggested, but

> the daily operation is rather straightforward. Representatives of both the retail and wholesale outfits are approached by racketeers who make it clear that unless they inflate their prices and hand over the extra money, their companies will no longer be able to stay in business because of severe labor troubles.

The director of labor relations for one of the supermarket chains involved was described as an associate of at least one known syndicate figure.

Through its involvement in a wide range of businesses, both legal and illegal, syndicated crime inflicts major costs on our economy. These costs include higher prices for goods through the establishment of monopolies; lower-quality goods; the forced closing of businesses, with resulting unemployment; and manipulation of stock market prices. Through infiltration of labor unions, thousands of workers are defrauded and denied the benefits of true union representation. Through the narcotics trade, the drug problems of

[30]"The Losing Battle against Crime in America," *U.S. News and World Report* (December 16, 1974), p. 39.

[31]Charles Grutzner, "How to Lock Out the Mafia," *Harvard Business Review* (March-April 1970), 45-58.

cities are intensified and perpetuated. Finally, through corruption of public officials—a necessary adjunct to its other operations—syndicated crime helps to raise the general tax burden and evades overall law enforcement and the democratic process.

Organized Crime and Corruption.   Organized crime could not flourish without bribery. By corrupting officials—police, prosecutors, mayors, judges, legislators—organized crime seeks to ensure that laws that would hamper its enterprises are neither passed nor enforced.

As the report of the President's Commission on Law Enforcement and the Administration of Justice stressed, the harm from government corruption is greater today than ever before because government regulation affects most business and private activities. Thus the corrupter can control more matters that closely affect every citizen.[32]

There are various methods of corrupting officials: bribes can be given directly, or as a share of the profits from illegal operations; officials can be subverted by gifts or favors—a vacation, a campaign contribution, or the promise of voter support; threats can be made to support opponents in campaigns, or blackmail may be used. Sometimes officials are corrupted after taking office; sometimes people are placed in office who are already associated with the syndicate. The corruption occurs on all levels of government, from police officers to high elected-officials. It is especially effective to reach those in more powerful positions, since they can prevent overzealous lower-level personnel from enforcing the laws against syndicate activities. If the cooperation of the police chief can be obtained, for example, any police officer who tries to arrest gamblers may be shifted to another assignment or passed over for a promotion and/or salary raise. Other officers will quickly learn from this example.

The occasional exposé in the media or by a special investigative agency gives a vivid description of how the corruption process works and of the huge payoffs involved. In Brooklyn, New York, for example, some 37 plainclothesmen on the Public Morals Squad were indicted in 1972 after they were discovered to have taken payoffs amounting to a quarter of a million dollars annually from gambling establishments in four Brooklyn precincts. The group was so well organized that it even provided severance pay for members reassigned to other divisions and insurance to cover legal expenses if a member was caught.[33]

The ramifications of political corruption in a community's life are well illustrated in Gardiner's study of "Wincanton,"[34] a city that was long considered a wide-open center for gambling and vice. Under a local syndicate, bookmaking, numbers, pinball machines, and dice games flourished; bootleg whiskey was manufactured and sold; and brothels catered to men from all over the state. The head of the syndicate protected this empire through a well-organized system of corruption, based on two simple principles: "Pay top personnel as much as necessary to keep them happy (and quiet), and pay something to as many others as possible to implicate them in the system and

---

[32]President's Commission, *Challenge of Crime*, p. 191.

[33]*New York Times*, May 3, 1972.

[34]John A. Gardiner, with the assistance of David J. Olsen, "Gambling and Political Corruption," in President's Commission on Law Enforcement and the Administration of Justice, *Task Force Report—Organized Crime: Annotations and Consultants' Papers* (Washington, D.C.: U.S. Government Printing Office, 1967), pp. 61-79.

to keep them from talking." Payments totaling some $2,400 per week went to about fifteen key local and state officials, including the mayor, the police chief, some judges, state legislators, members of the city council, and a few others. Christmas gifts and political campaign contributions went to many more. The syndicate also bought the cooperation of some officials by helping them arrange corrupt activities of their own. Kickbacks on city contracts and equipment purchases became standard. Although the syndicate head went to jail on tax-evasion charges, the syndicate continued to function, and it was not until a year later, when the police chief was caught perjuring himself before a grand jury and hastily "blew the whistle" on his confederates, that the golden structure collapsed and an active reform administration was elected.

Professional Crime

Professional criminals are the ones we read about in detective novels or see on television: the expert safe-cracker with sensitive fingers, the sharp customer in a jewelry store who switches diamonds so quickly the clerk does not notice, or the counterfeiters working under bright lights in the basement of a respectable shop. This class of criminals also includes the less glamorous pickpockets, full-time shoplifters, check forgers, truck hijackers, sellers of stolen goods, and blackmailers.[35]

Professional criminals are dedicated to a life of crime; they live by it and pride themselves on their accomplishments. They are seldom caught and even if they are, they can usually manage to have the charges dropped or the sentence reduced to a comfortable term. Meyer Lansky, a particularly successful thief (who was also a top figure in a national crime syndicate hierarchy), spent only three months and sixteen days in jail out of a criminal career that spanned over fifty years.[36] These are the most highly evolved of all criminals, with the most sophisticated and skilled working methods. They rarely have to resort to physical violence.

Many professional criminals come from higher social strata than most people who get arrested for criminal activities. Frequently beginning as employees in offices, hotels, and restaurants, they keep their criminal life as a sideline. Eventually, their criminal careers develop to the point where they make their living almost entirely by illegal activities. This phase usually starts at an age when conventional criminals are giving up crime. As Quinney put it: "Unemployment occasioned by old age does not seem to be a problem of con men; age ripens their skills, insights, and wit, and it also increases the confidence they inspire in their victims."[37] Most professional criminals enjoy long, uninterrupted careers because experience makes them skilled at avoiding arrest. They often justify their activities by claiming that they are simply capitalizing on the fact that all people are dishonest and would most likely be full-time criminals if they had the chance and sufficient ability.

Juvenile Delinquency

According to official statistics, youths under 18 commit one-third of all crimes. There were more than 520,000 arrests of 18-year-olds in 1977. The statistics also show young people under 18 committing 10 percent of all murders and two-thirds of all robberies, rapes, and assaults.[38]

[35]Quinney, *Social Reality of Crime*, pp. 270-273.
[36]Thomas Plate, *Crime Pays!* (New York: Simon & Schuster, 1975).
[37]Quinney, *Social Reality of Crime*, p. 273.
[38]President's Commission, *UCR*, pp. 180-181.

There is, however, considerable variation in the types of crime committed by the different age groups, and these statistics must be examined closely. Most delinquent acts are *status offenses*—acts that would not be illegal if performed by adults. They include "running away from home, being incorrigible, ungovernable, and beyond the control of parents, being truant, and engaging in sexual relations."[39] Many juveniles, therefore, are considered delinquent for behavior and acts that would be legal if they were only a few years older.

Historically, children have been presumed to lack the "criminal intent" necessary to commit willful crimes; hence, juvenile law was designed primarily to protect and redirect young offenders, rather than to punish them. Judges are allowed a wide range in dealing with youthful offenders brought before them, so that an approach can be chosen that will be the most helpful, rather than impose a more or less predetermined sentence. In recent years, however, there has been increasing dissatisfaction with the practical workings of juvenile law. Some contend that authorities and law enforcers have too much latitude over how to construe juvenile behavior, and that standards differ too greatly between communities. Most juvenile officials continue to be concerned over such matters as "female sexuality, male braggadocio, and disrespect of adult authority," and capitalize on the ambiguity of terms such as "incorrigible" and "ungovernable" in order to jail any young person whom they think needs correction.[40] (See Chapter 11.)

Because of inadequate facilities and insufficiently trained judges and other personnel, the correctional action taken with regard to the young offender often amounts only to a trial and prison sentence, though the records may speak of "hearings" and a "training school." Moreover, these are frequently imposed without benefit of the elementary constitutional rights guaranteed to the adult offender—the right to counsel, the right to be confronted with witnesses and to cross-examine them, and the right to a trial

[39]Paul Lerman, "Delinquents without Crime," *Trans-action* (July-August 1971), p. 252.
[40]Lerman, "Delinquents without Crime," p. 253.

Much of juvenile law is based on the assumption that children lack true "criminal intent"; yet they commit two-thirds of all robberies, rapes, and assaults.

Edward Lettau/Photo Researchers, Inc.

by jury. In 1967 the issue reached the Supreme Court in the *Gault* case, in which a boy, who had participated in a lewd telephone call, was committed to a state "industrial school" for what could have been a maximum of six years. The court held that, in a case where commitment to a state institution and consequent curtailment of freedom is a possible result, the juvenile is entitled to the same rights of due process as an adult.[41]

Conditions and Causes of Crime

Criminologists and sociologists have offered a variety of sociocultural explanations to account for the prevalence of crime. For example, it has been said that countries that give their citizens a large degree of personal freedom have the greatest incidence of deviant or criminal behavior. Emile Durkheim, on the other hand, pointed out that a high crime rate is almost always the product of rapid economic development and social change. A sudden rise in prosperity and technology creates what he called "overweening ambition"—that is, people develop unreasonably high expectations for themselves. In their rush for material gain, some play by the rules while others ignore them; and it is true that our educational and economic systems promote an enthusiastic desire for wealth that can foster lawbreaking attitudes and an emphasis on personal attainment at the expense of others.

Other students of criminal behavior see this country's uniquely high crime rate as being fostered by its cultural heterogeneity. Countries with culturally homogeneous populations, such as England and Japan, have relatively low crime rates; London, for example, reported only 113 murders and 135 rapes in a recent year, while New York City had 1,690 murders and 3,735 rapes in the same period.[42] Generally, the low crime rates of homogeneous countries and communities are a result of social bonds and a sense of collectivity. The majority of citizens share the same cultural values and ethnic backgrounds. (This suggests why crime rates in the United States tend to be higher in cities than in more homogeneous rural communities.) The people share more or less the same idea of what a criminal act is and what is appropriate and law-abiding behavior. The police, as representatives of the citizens, will not be as ready to apply criminal sanctions in homogeneous communities as they would in heterogenous communities. Instead, they will tend to handle much law-violating behavior on an informal basis and make fewer arrests.[43]

Still other authorities believe that the high prevalence of crime in the United States is due to demographic, economic, and social factors. Demographic factors have swelled the numbers of youth in the 14-to-24 age group: in 1950 there were only 24 million persons in the United States in this age group; in 1960, 27 million; and by 1975 there were over 45 million. Seventy-seven percent of those arrested for property crime, which includes burglary, larceny, and auto theft, are under 25 years of age, and this same

[41]President's Commission on Law Enforcement and the Administration of Justice, *Task Force Report: Juvenile Delinquency and Youth Crime* (Washington, D.C.: U.S. Government Printing Office, 1967).

[42]Amedeo Odoni and Eleni Odoni, "Fundamental Wrongs," *The New York Times Magazine* (April 13, 1975), pp. 69-70.

[43]Quinney, *Social Reality of Crime*.

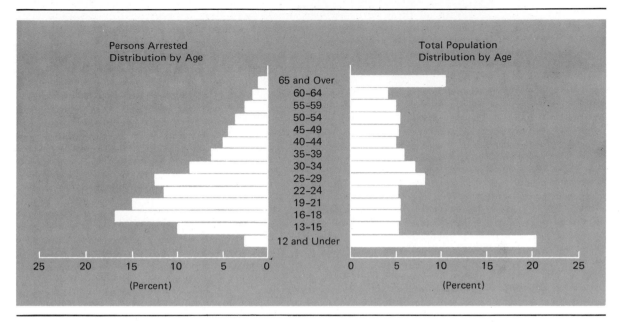

Figure   5-1

Source: *Uniform Crime Reports* (Washington, D.C.: U.S. Government Printing Office, October 1978), p. 171.

under-25 group accounts for almost 56 percent of all arrests. (See Figures 5-1 and 5-2.)

Social factors relative to crime are reflected in the much larger number of men than women who are charged with committing crimes. As women have begun to gain equal rights in industrialized countries, the ratio of male to female arrests has decreased, but men still lead in most categories (except prostitution and runaways). In the United States in 1977, although 84 percent

Figure   5-2

Source: *Uniform Crime Reports* (Washington, D.C.: U.S. Government Printing Office, October 1978), p. 170.

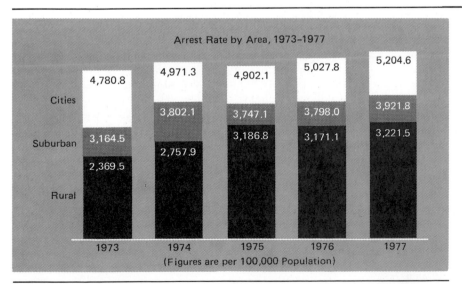

of all those arrested were men, more than 57 percent more women were arrested than in 1968.[44] The explanation for this seems to lie in the different patterns of socialization of men and women. Men in our society have traditionally been raised to be more aggressive, even more violent, than women, and they have therefore been more likely to commit certain kinds of crimes. Females, as a rule, have been regarded more protectively by both the police and the courts; thus they have been less likely to be arrested, and if arrested, less likely to be punished. It can be expected that both crime statistics and the attitudes of the criminal justice system will gradually reflect contemporary changes in the patterns of socialization for men and women.

All official statistics have shown a high incidence of crime among the lower socioeconomic classes, particularly among blacks, Puerto Ricans, and American Indians. We have already suggested, however, that the poor and minorities (particularly the nonwhite) have a much higher chance of coming into conflict with the established justice system than the more affluent. In fact, William J. Chambliss and Richard H. Nagasawa, in their study of delinquents, concluded that "official statistics are so misleading that they are virtually useless as indications of actual deviance in the population." These authors have suggested that the demeanor of different groups, the visibility of the offenses, and the bias of police and courts give rise to official rates of crime and delinquency that are "a complete distortion of the actual incidence."[45]

Others suggest that the higher official rates of property and personal violence crimes among minorities reflect the fact that unemployment among these groups, especially among their teenage members, is catastrophically high, ranging up to 40 percent. This point of view suggests that social and economic factors have intertwined to produce a great mass of people who feel they have no stake in society. As one journalist has written, there has developed "something like a permanent underclass, not so much exploited as left behind—an economic substratum unable to rise by unskilled labor that is no longer in demand, unable to compete in a highly organized technological society, heavily damaged by being in cities, . . . and embittered by evidence all around of its hopeless disadvantage."[46]

The continuing disintegration of family and community life and the relentless presentation of violence in the mass media have also been seen as reinforcing, if not causing, much present-day antisocial behavior. According to the director of the Fortune Society, an organization of ex-convicts, most convicts have a childhood history full of physical abuse and neglect, and many have spent their childhoods in homes, orphanages, and reformatories where physical punishment was a matter of course.[47] Physical abuse of children creates a personality structure marked by hostility, anger, and indifference to others. It alienates children from other people and the community and brutalizes them to the point where they have a diminished capacity to feel guilt.[48] (See Chapter 1.) The decline of traditional authority and the pervasive

---

[44]President's Commission, *UCR*, pp. 175, 183.

[45]William J. Chambliss and Richard H. Nagasawa, "On the Validity of Official Statistics: A Comparative Study of White, Black, and Japanese High-School Boys," *Social Forces* (Winter 1969), p. 71-77.

[46]Tom Wicker, *A Time To Die* (New York: Quadrangle, 1975).

[47]David Rothenberg, "Theoretical Contradictions," *New York Times Magazine* (April 13, 1975), p. 72.

[48]*Time* (June 30, 1975), p. 17.

presence of violence on television and in newspapers may also have reduced the forces that discourage criminal acts. (See Chapter 6.)

What are some of the social and economic factors that promote public toleration and outright acceptance of occupational crime? One key attitude, in crimes such as price-fixing and other instances of corporate collusion, is probably the feeling that government has no business regulating such matters in the first place. As one General Electric executive convicted of price-fixing maintained, "Sure, collusion was illegal, but it wasn't unethical."[49] Our nineteenth-century principles of rugged individualism and *laissez-faire*, however unsuitable to the vastly more intricate economic world of the twentieth century, remain precious to many people, and when conditions are favorable, they easily persuade themselves to act on them, whatever the law may require. It may also be that otherwise honest people will perform illegal acts they know are wrong, because of the pressures to which they are subjected in their lines of business.

Again, modern American society largely takes deception for granted. This is particularly apparent in advertising. We are so accustomed to advertisements which promise us heaven in some form or other for the price of a bottle of shampoo or a pack of cigarettes, and TV promotions of wonderful toys which turn out, after being paid for, to be cheap plastic junk, that we scarcely see anything improper about them. In fact, advertisements of an earlier day, giving only straight-forward information and ending with some such modest claim as, "The most economical one on the market," are reprinted on shopping bags and in catalogs as a nostalgic joke. Yet, as Edwin Schur points out, "modern mass advertising at its heart represents a kind of institutionalization of deception and misrepresentation."[50] Certainly we seem to assume that a certain amount of deception is to be expected in business and in government, and this expectation may well constitute a self-fulfilling prophecy—that is, by expecting people to try to deceive each other, we create an atmosphere which eventually encourages them to do so.

Another related element is that special American characteristic, the profit motive. Whether or not Americans are prepared, as is sometimes asserted, to "sell their souls for a buck," there is little doubt that many of us find profit hard to resist. We assume that it is natural for someone in business to want to increase their income, or for a company to make maximum profits; if this involves polluting a river or cooperating with a labor racketeer, our protests are muted and apologetic. The fact that a practice is profitable, increases sales, leads to growth, puts more products on the market, creates jobs, or otherwise adds something to a gross national product that must always be larger this year than it was last, seems to be enough justification to override moral, ecological, and even safety objections with extraordinary ease. This is not a case of conspiracy or of business barons plotting international destruction in the secrecy of their luxurious executive suites—as once people blamed the arms manufacturers for encouraging World War I—but rather a widespread assumption, seldom seriously examined by most people.

Organized crime is also strongly interrelated with American values, culture, and institutions. For one thing, it depends on the willingness of

---

[49]Ralph Nader and Mark Green, "Crime in the Suites," *The New Republic* (April 29, 1972), pp. 17-18.

[50]Schur, *Our Criminal Society*, p. 168.

millions of Americans—from those who place an occasional bet with a bookie to businesspeople who knowingly accept criminal loans—to buy illegal goods and services. Secondly, organized crime is furthered by the thousands of "respectable" people in business and professions who deal with it to make a personal profit—the corporation official who accepts the services of labor racketeers, the lawyers and accountants who offer their expertise to organized crime for the fees involved.

Moreover, many of the syndicate's recruits and workers, without whom the organization could not survive, have come from minority and immigrant groups living in the inner city. For these groups organized crime is the only evident means of social mobility—because society has failed to provide other, legitimate avenues of opportunity.[51] Ralph F. Salerno points out the effect of the "successful" criminal on ghetto youth:

> To them he has "made it"; he has "beat the system" by being associated with organized criminal activities. The dope peddler, the gambling operator, and the loan shark—without the benefit of education and without the demands of gainful employment—can drive the expensive auto, dress well, and manifest affluence. This is regarded by youth as perhaps the only opportunity for "breaking out" of the slums.[52]

As long as the more visible signs of organized crime—drug pushers and houses of prostitution—stay in the ghettos, "respectable" Americans who use some of the services of organized crime for their own profit seem to be willing to ignore the consequences of their dealings.

Organized crime also relies on the pliability of government officials, and their willingness to suspend law enforcement in exchange for campaign funds or private kickbacks. Such corruption is essential, in fact, for in one sense a crime syndicate is peculiarly vulnerable to honest law enforcement. Its activities continue over a long period; its places of business and at least its lower-level operatives have to be known to its customer; it acquires complicated lines of communication, supply, and distribution. It would be seriously hampered if it could not ensure that the police or the courts would stay out of its way.

In all these cases organized crime flourishes because it is compatible with the American ethos of personal profit, and because a substantial number of private citizens, businesspersons, professionals, and government officials place personal gain ahead of responsibility for the general welfare. In pursuing its own profits, organized crime is simply playing the same game, imbued with the very American value of making money.

Explanations of Crime (Sociological Theories)

Although partial explanations of the causes of crime have been advanced by researchers from many disciplines, no comprehensive theory can account for the wide range of crimes and criminals in today's society. Explanations that

[51]Stuart L. Hills, "Combatting Organized Crime in America," *Federal Probation* (March 1968), p. 25.

[52]Ralph F. Salerno, "Organized Crime and Criminal Justice," *Federal Probation* (June 1969), pp. 11-17.

seem workable for urban-gang crime may not apply to suburban delinquency or to burglary by an individual. Other approaches, that focus on individual criminals and delinquents, may fail completely to explain gangs and delinquent subcultures. An adequate, systematic, comprehensive explanation of the causes of crime and delinquency is a prerequisite for a meaningful program of control and prevention. In this section we will examine four major sociological approaches and evaluate them in light of recent research. (A fifth approach, control theory, is described in Chapter 6.)

This approach was first introduced by Sutherland in 1939 as *differential association*; with some later modifications, differential association still seems to explain the widest range of criminal acts. It may be considered a "genetic" or "historical" explanation, because it deals with the processes operative during the early experiences of the criminal, as differentiated from "mechanistic" or "situational" explanations, which are based on the processes operating at the moment the crime is committed.

Group-Supported Crime

Criminal behavior, according to this orientation, is the result of a learning process that occurs chiefly within small, intimate groups—family, friends, neighborhood peer groups, and so on. The lessons include both the techniques of committing crimes and, more importantly, the specific direction of motives and drives. This direction is formed as a person learns favorable and unfavorable definitions of the legal codes; that is, in some parts of society a person is surrounded by those who define the legal codes as rules to be followed, while in other parts of society another person may associate only with those who define the laws as hindrances to be avoided or overcome.

The basic principle of differential association, succinctly stated, is that "a person becomes delinquent because of the excess of definitions favorable to violation of law over definitions unfavorable to violation of law."[53] People internalize the values of the surrounding culture, and when their environment includes frequent contact with criminal elements and relative isolation from noncriminal elements, they are apt to become delinquent or criminal. The boy whose most admired model is another member of the gang or a successful neighborhood pimp, for example, will seek to emulate this model and will receive encouragement and approval from his peers when he does so successfully.

While the child usually encounters both criminal and noncriminal patterns, these associations vary in frequency, duration, priority, and intensity. The concepts of *frequency* and *duration* are self-explanatory. *Priority* means that attitudes learned early in life, whether lawful or criminal, tend to persist in later life, although this tendency has not been fully demonstrated. *Intensity* is a rather imprecise concept referring to the prestige of, and emotional ties with, the source of the criminal or anticriminal patterns.

Since Sutherland last modified his theory in 1947, it has been further adapted by other researchers. Robert L. Burgess and Ronald L. Akers, for example, have reformulated the approach in terms of reinforcement learning. They have translated Sutherland's principle, quoted earlier, to read as follows: "Criminal behavior is a function of norms which are discriminative for criminal behavior, the learning of which takes place when such behavior is

---

[53]Edwin H. Sutherland and Donald R. Cressey, *Principles of Criminology* (Philadelphia: Lippincott, 1966).

more highly reinforced than noncriminal behavior."[54] Burgess and Akers feel that this restatement has partially rectified their principal dissatisfaction with Sutherland's approach, which was the great difficulty of empirically demonstrating its validity.

Despite recent modifications, Sutherland's work has suggested many practical steps to reduce the incidence of crime. As summarized by Malcolm Klein in the *Encyclopedia of Social Work*, these range from group treatment of offenders in certain circumstances, reward systems, and prosocial role-playing to specific neighborhood programs such as the Chicago Area Project (to be discussed later in this chapter).[55]

Anomie Approach

This orientation, also known as the *goals and opportunities* approach, is held by many modern scholars, notably Robert K. Merton. Merton begins by arguing that a society has both approved goals and norms and approved ways of attaining them. When some members of the society accept the goals or norms but have insufficient access to the approved means of attaining them, their adherence to the approved standards of conduct is likely to be weakened, and they may try to reach the goals or norms by other, socially unacceptable, means.[56] In other words, criminal behavior occurs when socially sanctioned means are not available for the realization of highly desired goals or norms.

The disparity between goals or norms and means, or *anomie*, often varies with nationality, ethnic background, class, religion, and other social characteristics. Some nations emphasize adherence to behavioral norms—as in Japan, where even gigantic antigovernment student demonstrations are conducted according to an informal but rigid code—and for them the degree of anomie may be fairly low. Other nations place relatively more emphasis on attaining goals and less on achieving them through socially sanctioned norms. Merton maintains that the United States is such a society, and cites our status as the industrialized nation with the highest crime rate. Identifying anomie as a basic characteristic of American society, Merton lists several kinds of adaptations common in America. One of these, *innovation*, "refers to the rejection of institutional practices but the retention of cultural goals. This would seem to characterize a substantial part of the deviant behavior that has been accorded the greatest share of research attention—namely . . . 'crime' and 'delinquency.'" In particular, it seems to characterize the behavior of lower-class juvenile gang members who have adopted socially approved goals but abandoned socially approved methods of attaining them.

This kind of rejection occurs widely in groups with the greatest "disjuncture" between goals, norms, and opportunities. In this country, it is most often found among those who have the most difficulty obtaining a good education or training for well-paid jobs, and particularly in lower socioeconomic groups of blacks, Indians, and Spanish-speaking peoples. Higher crime rates among such groups are not axiomatic, but may be expected only when

[54]Robert L. Burgess and Ronald L. Akers, "A Differential Association-Reinforcement Theory of Criminal Behavior," *Social Problems* 14 (Fall 1966), 128-147.

[55]Malcolm Klein, "Crime and Delinquency," *Encyclopedia of Social Work*, ed. Robert Morris, (New York: National Association of Social Workers, 1971), p. 168.

[56]Robert K. Merton, *Social Theory and Social Structure* (New York: Free Press, 1968), p. 232.

the goals people internalize are dictated to them by a society which simultaneously erects barriers to their attainment through socially sanctioned means. If different goals were set for different socioeconomic classes, as under the caste system in India, for example, presumably there would be no connection between anomie and the poor. In Merton's words:

> It is when a system of cultural values extols, virtually above all else, certain *common* success-goals *for the population at large* while the social structure rigorously restricts or completely closes access to approved modes of reaching goals *for a considerable part of the same population*, that deviant behavior ensues on a large scale.

Since the first formulation of the anomie approach, subsequent research seems to have provided at least some support for its basic premise, although there are types of crime and delinquency that it fails to explain adequately— such as vandalism or assault when they are not for monetary gain.

This omission is related to the question most frequently raised about Merton's work: are financial success and material possessions only middle-class goals, with the lower classes holding different values and aspirations? A study by Wan Sang Han in Atlanta, Georgia, involving white Protestant high school seniors, seems to support Merton's theory in general, although not conclusively. The students were asked how much more schooling they would *wish* to have in a society with equal opportunity for all, and how much they *expected* to receive in view of their actual situations, including their own abilities and their parents' financial resources. The answers to the question involving their wishes supported Merton, but the answers regarding the students' expectations favored those who maintain that different classes have different goals.[57]

Many sociologists have come to believe that people in the lower classes tend to hold two sets of beliefs simultaneously. That is, they share the norms and values of the larger society, but are forced to develop standards and expectations of their own so they can deal realistically with their particular environment. (This idea is discussed more fully in Chapter 7, "Affluence and Poverty.") For example, people in the lower class share with the more affluent the view that crime is bad. It is not surprising, therefore, that other studies have supported Merton's view that anomie, rather than poverty itself, is a major cause of crime and delinquency.[58]

Delinquent Subcultures

After a decade of relative calm, there seems to be a resurgence in the activities of youth street gangs. The gangs have become more noticeably active in six of the nation's largest cities—New York, Chicago, Los Angeles, Philadelphia, Detroit, and San Francisco. In each of these cities, from 4,000 to 15,000 youths in the 10- to-30 age group belong to such gangs. The increase in the use of handguns by gang members and their habit of randomly choosing victims make them potentially more dangerous than they were in the past.[59]

---

[57]Wan Sang Han, "Two Conflicting Themes: Common Values versus Class Differential Values," *American Sociological Review*, 34 (October 1969), 679-690.

[58]See Marcia Guttentag, "The Relationship of Unemployment to Crime and Delinquency," *Journal of Social Issues* (January 1968), pp. 105-115.

[59]"Street Gangs Turn from 'Rumbles' to Wanton Crime," *U.S. News and World Report* (July 7, 1975), pp. 15-18.

Among the sociologists who explored the origin and character of delinquent groups was Albert K. Cohen in *Delinquent Boys*. Cohen views the formation of delinquent gangs as an action by members to alleviate the difficulties they face at the bottom of the status ladder. Gang members are typically children from working-class homes who find themselves measured, as Cohen puts it, with a "middle-class measuring rod" by those who control access to success in society at large, including teachers, the business community, police, religious leaders, and public bureaucrats. Untrained in such "middle-class virtues" as ambition, the ability to defer the gratification of immediate desires for the sake of long-term goals, self-discipline, and academic skills, and hence poorly prepared to compete in a middle-class world, they form subcultures whose status criteria they can meet.

This delinquent subculture, which Cohen characterizes as non-utilitarian, malicious, and negativistic,

> takes its norms from the larger culture, but turns them upside down. The delinquents consider something right, by the standards of their subculture, precisely *because* it is wrong by the norms of the larger culture.[60]

It is this assertion of Cohen's that has drawn the most fire from his critics. Paul Lerman, for example, tested adherence and non-adherence to social values in a group of 555 New York City boys and girls. Although he agreed with Cohen on the versatility of the subculture and the ambivalence of ghetto youngsters toward school and work, he found the non-utilitarian aspects of delinquency which Cohen emphasized only in the younger age ranges.[61]

Another major work on delinquent subcultures by Richard Cloward and Lloyd Ohlin also uses the works of Sutherland and/or Merton, but differs with Cohen by proposing three different kinds of delinquent subcultures.[62] The three subcultures—*criminalistic, conflict,* and *retreatist*—are based on the notion that delinquents perceive a lack of opportunity for attaining "success," measured in terms of working-class conceptions of "success." The *criminalistic* subculture is based on organized, predatory theft, and is most often associated with adult organized crime, into whose ranks delinquents may move as they become older and more adept. The *conflict* subculture is organized around battles with rival gangs, and is likely to arise when the youngsters involved have few if any contacts with the criminal world. The *retreatist* subculture is composed of those who have failed in normal society, are not able to compete in the theft subculture, or are cowardly or inept fighters. Those in this subculture might retreat from the dominant culture and the active subcultures through such devices as the use of narcotics.

Cloward and Ohlin differ from Cohen not only in proposing the three different subcultures, but also in maintaining that the boys who join delinquent gangs are those who have not only been unable to compete in the larger society, but who have also seen the cause of their failure as lying in the social order itself, rather than in any deficiency of their own. Once they have fixed the blame on society and communicated to each other the extent of their alienation, the creation of some sort of delinquent subculture—in this case, a

---

[60]Albert K. Cohen, *Delinquent Boys* (New York: Free Press, 1971).

[61]Paul Lerman, "Individual Values, Peer Values, and Subculture Delinquency," *American Sociological Review* 33 (April 1968), 219-236.

[62]Richard A. Cloward and Lloyd E. Ohlin, *Delinquency and Opportunity: A Theory of Delinquent Gangs* (New York: Free Press, 1960).

The gang subculture may offer a special status to a young person who does not have the opportunity to meet the success standards of middle-class society.

Jim Anderson/Woodfin Camp & Assoc.

gang—becomes likely. The authors maintain that the more socially disorganized the ghetto, the more likely it is that the subculture established will be of the conflict-retreatist types. Therefore, they see the decline of the old, ethnically organized ghettos and the increase in unstable social patterns in today's ghettos as fostering the violent gang subculture and hindering the theft-oriented subculture associated with organized crime.

Cloward and Ohlin have been criticized more frequently than Cohen, and often more vigorously. David J. Bordua charges that they have ignored the life history of the boys and their families, and he also maintains that "the system" is less to blame than the boys themselves, who have progressively cut off opportunities and destroyed their own abilities.[63] Bordua seems to be saying that delinquents, not working-class boys in general, have eliminated their own opportunities; in addition, he feels that the theory of delinquent subcultures might work for blacks, but not for whites, whom he sees as more or less equal regardless of class. He fails to substantiate, however, his claim that cut-off opportunities are an effect rather than a cause of delinquency.

In addition to these shortcomings in Cloward and Ohlin's theory, James F. Short and Fred L. Strodtbeck have found that outside of the very largest urban ghettos, delinquent subcultures tend to be somewhat more versatile. A

[63]David J. Bordua, "Delinquent Subcultures: Sociological Interpretations of Gang Delinquency," *Annals of the American Academy of Political and Social Science* 338 (November 1961), 134.

single gang may be engaged in all three kinds of delinquent behavior at different times.[64]

Some sociologists do not believe that delinquent subcultures are formed as frustrated reactions to the dominant culture. Instead, they see delinquency as generated by the lower-class culture itself. A study by Walter Miller, for example, based on his long experience with street gangs, identifies *trouble, toughness, smartness, excitement, fate,* and *autonomy* as the six "focal concerns" of lower-class culture that often lead to the violation of middle-class social and legal norms.[65] *Trouble* is important to the individual's status in the community, whether it is seen as something to be kept out of or something to be gotten into. Usually there is less worry over legal or moral questions than over possible complications resulting from the involvement of police, welfare investigators, and other agents of society. *Toughness* is the typical emphasis on masculinity, physical strength, and the ability to "take it," coupled with a rejection of art, literature, and anything else considered "feminine." This is partly a reaction to female-dominated households and the lack of male role figures to emulate, both at home and in school. *Smartness,* in the street sense of the term, denotes the ability to outwit, dupe, or "con" someone, rather than intellectual ability. A successful pimp, for example, would be considered "smarter" than a bank clerk. To relieve the crushing boredom of ghetto life, residents of lower-class communities often appear to seek out situations of danger or excitement, as gambling or high-speed joyrides in automobiles. *Fate* is an important concern because lower-class citizens frequently feel that important events in life are beyond their control, and they will often resort to semimagical resources such as "readers and advisors" on spiritual matters as a means to change their luck. Finally, *autonomy* is of major concern to this group, who are apt on the one hand to express strong resentment of any external controls or exercise of coercive authority over their behavior, yet frequently seem to seek out restrictive environments, perhaps even by obtaining commitment to mental hospitals or prisons.

After his analysis of the lower-class community, Miller turns to the specific values and attributes of lower-class adolescent street gangs. He notes several attributes common to almost all gangs: the prevalence of single-sex gangs, due to the difficulties and conflicts arising from double-sex interaction over a prolonged period of time; the psychological and educational stability, often lacking in the home, that is available through the gang; and the aid provided by gang membership in establishing and maintaining sex-role identity. Miller also points out that since the primary concerns of gang members are status and "belonging," they will commit gang-sanctioned illegal behavior rather than risk exclusion from the gang. In other words, gangs oriented toward these values will automatically violate middle-class legal norms against fighting, gambling, and disturbing the peace.

Miller's analysis has been criticized on the grounds that not all lower-class groups, all of which supposedly share the same focal concerns, are delinquent. And as we have already suggested, the assumption of a widespread "lower-class culture" untainted by middle-class values is open to question.

[64]James F. Short, Jr., and Fred L. Strodtbeck, *Group Process and Gang Delinquency* (Chicago: University of Chicago Press, 1965).

[65]Walter B. Miller, "Lower Class Culture as a Generating Milieu of Gang Delinquency," *Journal of Social Issues* 14 (1958), 5-19.

Social Control

Given the alarming extent of both conventional and occupational crime, a discussion of efforts that have been made toward the social control of crime is particularly significant. These efforts can be classified under four headings: *retribution-deterrence, rehabilitation, prevention,* and *criminal and juvenile justice reforms*. This last category includes efforts to control occupational, white-collar, and organized crime.

Retribution and deterrence—to "pay back" the guilty for their misdeeds and to dissuade them and others from repeating them—have historically been the primary objects in society's handling of lawbreakers. It is only relatively recently that rehabilitation of offenders—providing them with the ability and the motivation to build themselves a law-abiding and socially approved life—has gained wide acceptance; our correctional system, however, is still largely punitive. Retribution of the offender is no longer of the "eye for an eye, tooth for a tooth" formula, that demanded that slanderers have their tongues torn out, thieves have their hands amputated, and rapists be castrated, but the retributive orientation of our prison philosophy becomes abundantly clear when public outcry demands longer sentences for particularly ugly or infamous crimes such as murders or political assassinations. Punishment arises from the fear and rage experienced by the society that identifies with the victim of the crime.

Retribution-Deterrence

The punishments meted out to murderers, forgers, and others serve, or are meant to serve, several purposes. According to Jackson Toby, besides the more frequently discussed roles of preventing further crime and rehabilitating the offender, punishment serves to sustain the morale of those who do conform to societal rules. That is, those who identify the offender as one who willfully violates the law demand his or her punishment partly to reinforce their own ambivalent feelings about conformity. They feel that if they must sacrifice to obey the law, someone who does not should not be allowed to "get away with it." Others, seeing criminals as people who are not evil but sick and who commit their criminal acts because of an organic or psychological disorder, do not feel the desire for punishment but instead advocate the "treatment" of offenders to correct the disorders that caused them to become criminals. Even this, however, may conceal a retributive bias.[66]

Writers, such as James Q. Wilson, have suggested that society needs the firm moral authority derived from stigmatizing and punishing crime. While Wilson grants that prisoners must "pay their debts" without being deprived of their civil rights after release from prison and suffering the continued indignities of parole supervision and permanent unemployment, he reaffirms the moral value of stigmatizing crime and the person who commits it:

> To destigmatize crime would be to lift from it the weight of moral judgment and to make crime simply a particular occupation or avocation which society has chosen to reward less (or perhaps more) than other pursuits. If there is no stigma attached to an activity, then society has no business making it a crime.[67]

[66]Jackson Toby, "Is Punishment Necessary?" in *Combatting Social Problems,* ed. Harry Gold and Frank Scarpitti (New York: Holt, Rinehart and Winston, 1967), pp. 307-315.
[67]James Q. Wilson, *Thinking About Crime* (New York: Basic Books, 1975), p. 71.

The deterrent value of punishment is also stressed. This approach has been described by Robert Martinson:

> The goal is deterrence—individual and general deterrence—and the hardliners assert that punishment is the appropriate means to this goal. They demand that the threat [of punishment] contained in every penal statute be carried out promptly, so that everyone will be assured that it is a credible threat: to legally convict and then punish an offender will "deter" him from further offending; it will also "deter" potential offenders from committing crime.[68]

There is little proof that punishment effectively prevents crime. People are also kept from committing crime and other antisocial acts by their successful integration into society, although undoubtedly some people would not hesitate to engage in criminal acts if they were sure that there would be no retribution. The argument for punishment as a deterrent is most often the argument heard for capital punishment, since execution can hardly be called either humane or rehabilitative. Even in this case, there is little evidence of a relationship between murder rates and the use of capital punishment. Thorsten Sellin has concluded that "the presence of the death penalty—in law or practice—does not influence homicide death rates." Dogan D. Akman, in a survey of Canadian penal institutions, found no empirical justification for the argument that the policy of commuting death sentences to life imprisonment would result in additional safety hazards for prison staff and inmates. Walter C. Reckless has also found no evidence for the deterrent effect of capital punishment.[69]

Rehabilitation   The relatively recent development, during the last century and a half, of the idea of rehabilitating offenders rests on the concept of crime as a social aberration, and the offender as a social misfit whose aberrant behavior can be modified to conform to the social norm, or "cured." Unfortunately, there are as yet no definitive research theories specifying the form of rehabilitation which will be most effective with a particular kind of offender. The answers to the questions which James Robison and Gerald Smith asked in their study of the California penal system: "Will the clients act differently if we lock them up, or keep them locked up longer, or do something with them inside, or watch them more closely afterward, or cut them loose officially?"—seem so far to be no. Yet there is no conclusive evidence that certain alternatives, such as prison counseling programs or outright discharge, are more effective in reducing recidivism rates than other more punitive alternatives.[70] All that can be said is that some of the rehabilitation experiments undertaken to date have been more successful than others. Some of the programs have treated the offender in the society at large, while others have attempted to work within the present institutional system of correction.

[68]Robert Martinson, "Planning for Public Safety," *New Republic* (April 29, 1972), pp. 21-23.

[69]Thorsten Sellin, "Homicides in Retentionalist and Abolitionist States," *Capital Punishment*, ed. Thorsten Sellin (New York: Harper & Row, 1967), pp. 135-138; Dogan D. Akman, "Homicide and Assaults in Canadian Prisons," in Sellin, *Capital Punishment*, pp. 161-168; Walter C. Reckless, "Use of the Death Penalty," *Crime and Delinquency* 15 (January 1969), 43-61.

[70]James Robison and Gerald Smith, "The Effectiveness of Correctional Programs," *Crime and Delinquency* 17 (January 1971), 67-80.

One example of the latter, institutional projects, is worthy of mention. In California, the PICO (Pilot Intensive Counseling Organization) Project was established under the California Youth Authority to assess the effect of individual interview therapy on older delinquents. The young offenders were first divided into groups according to who were amenable and non-amenable to treatment, and each of these two groups was then divided into a treatment group and a control group. The amenables were those who, in the judgment of an examining group at the time of admission, were "bright, verbal, and anxious," and evidenced an "awareness of problems," "insight," a "desire to change," and "acceptance of treatment." All of the delinquents in the study underwent the ordinary treatment in the California correctional system for minors, except that the treated youths also received one or two weekly individual counseling sessions with psychiatrists or clinical psychologists and, in some cases, group therapy as well. The results indicated that the treated amenable delinquents had a much higher success rate, as measured by early favorable discharges and continued freedom from institutional control. The two control groups, amenable and non-amenable, had almost identical rates of return to custody; the treated non-amenables, surprisingly, had the highest return rate of all. The success achieved with the amenables is encouraging, but the failure with the treated non-amenables suggests the difficulty in establishing effective rehabilitative treatment for all delinquents. Stuart Adams, reporting on the project, points out that the problem could lie either with giving the wrong treatment to non-amenables or with giving them too little treatment.[71]

The very nature of our current prison system is a major hindrance to rehabilitative efforts. It removes offenders from practically all contact with the general society and its norms, and subjects them to almost continual contact with those who have committed crimes ranging from murder and petty larceny to homosexual rape and fraud. Within prison walls offenders are punished by a deprivation of liberty, autonomy, heterosexual contacts, goods and services, and the security that is normally obtained from participation in ordinary social institutions.[72] According to Lloyd N. McCorkle and Richard Korn, these deprivations, and especially the last, drive prisoners into a special social order within the prison. Adherence to this social order, which may be necessary for both mental and physical well-being, further separates inmates' goals and drives from those held by society at large, and makes it more difficult for them to relate to whatever retraining or rehabilitative measures are available from the institutional staff. The apparently inevitable conflict between custodial and therapeutic members of the institution's staff, with the former regarding the latter as enemies of discipline and the latter regarding the former as obstacles to treatment, further aggravates the problem.[73]

Rehabilitative treatment of prisoners in the existing penal system is further complicated because individual attention and treatment cannot be provided without sacrificing at least some institutional control. If a therapist were to give special treatment to prisoners who were particularly hard to handle, even if the treatment were central to the therapy the prisoners

[71]Stuart Adams, "Interaction between Individual Interview Therapy and Treatment Amenability in Older Youth Authority Wards," in *Inquiries Concerning Kinds of Treatments for Kinds of Delinquents* (Sacramento: California Board of Corrections, 1961), pp. 27-44.

[72]Toby, "Is Punishment Necessary?", pp. 307-315.

[73]Lloyd W. McCorkle and Richard Korn, "Resocialization within Walls," *Annals of the American Academy of Political and Social Sciences* 293 (May 1954), 88-89.

required, the other prisoners would see this special treatment as a direct result of the specially treated prisoners' deviant behavior and might well imitate it.[74]

The usual "rehabilitation" which prisoners receive consists of work training. Unfortunately, most prison work is generally of a menial and unsatisfying nature, such as kitchen helper and janitor. Daniel Glaser reports that only one convict in four obtains work related to the prison job after release. The reasons are various: most prisons have difficulty providing enough work to occupy all inmates; available incentives, such as slightly better pay and work conditions, are inadequate to attract prisoners to types of work that would be most beneficial upon their release; and records maintained by prison officials on prisoners' work programs are poor. Glaser did find, however, that although the percentages were low, those who had a prison job that was beneficial after release had lower rates of recidivism.[75]

[74]Donald Cressey, "Limitations of Treatment," in *The Sociology of Punishment and Correction*, 2nd ed., ed. N. Johnston, *et al.* (New York: Wiley, 1970), pp. 501-508.

[75]Daniel Glaser, *The Effectiveness of a Prison and Parole System* (Indianapolis: Bobbs-Merrill, 1964), pp. 10-11, 250-259.

Inmates of a Bermuda prison participate in a cooking class. Much confusion surrounds the effectiveness of such rehabilitative programs.
UPI

The difficulty of rehabilitating an offender within prison has led to varied attempts to reform the offender within, or partially within, society at large. This seems to have several benefits. Treating offenders without exposing them totally to the deficiencies apparent in the current prison system not only spares them the anti-social effects of prolonged exposure to a criminal society, but reduces the cost of custodial facilities and personnel. This makes treatment resources more available to those who seem to offer the best chance for rehabilitation, that is, those who are most amenable. Perhaps the oldest and most widely used system of this kind is the work-release program, under which prisoners are allowed to leave the institution for a certain period each day in order to work at productive outside jobs. Although this type of program is used throughout the world and has been known in the United States since it was first authorized in Wisconsin in 1913, it has only become widely used since the mid-1950s. Today at least 24 states and the federal government have authorized some form of work-release program.

Although the idea of releasing convicted felons into society, even for limited periods, has met with expected opposition, in general the programs seem to have worked well. Besides removing convicts from the criminal society within the prison, work-release programs reimburse the state, through the prisoners' wages, for some of the costs of their maintenance, and also allows the prisoners to support their dependents, helping to keep them off the welfare rolls.[76] In addition, the work-release program is a practical step toward reintegrating the offender back into society, since many of those who successfully complete the program retain their jobs after their release.[77]

The program is not applicable to all prisoners, especially those considered incorrigible, and is less successful in some areas of the country than in others. Elmer H. Johnson has noted the difficulty encountered by state agencies in finding jobs for work-releases, and the problem of finding suitable housing for those involved, since prisons are typically located in rural areas, far from the heavily populated centers where most jobs can be found.[78]

Even more innovative programs have been utilized in an attempt to rehabilitate younger delinquents. This is to be expected, since our society is less likely to consider minors fully responsible for their actions, and more likely to feel that they can still be saved from becoming lifetime criminals. In contrast to the California rehabilitation experiment described earlier, many of these programs were predicated on the concept of keeping the young offenders out of the conventional reformatory system that resembles an adult prison system in many ways. One such program, described by Susan Henderson, allowed delinquent girls to live at home but required them to attend special classes during the day at the San Mateo County (California) Juvenile Hall. The classes emphasized individual instruction in subjects needed for graduation from the local high school, combined with group discussions of common problems with the other girls in the program. The program involved weekly visits with the girl's probation officer and required close and reliable family supervision. From the commencement of the program in 1965, the county's rate of commitment of girls to institutions and

[76]Serapio R. Zalba, "Work-Release—A Two-Pronged Effort," *Crime and Delinquency* 13 (October 1967), 506-612.

[77]Stanley E. Grupp, "Work Release and the Misdemeanant," in Gold and Scarpitti, *Combatting Social Problems*, pp. 332-341.

[78]Elmer H. Johnson, "Report on an Innovation—State Work-Release Programs," *Crime and Delinquency* 16 (October 1970), 417-426.

foster homes was cut by about 25 percent. This reversed an almost 20 percent annual increase over the previous six years. This high rate of success, for which the program was largely responsible, has led the county to make plans for expanding the program.[79]

Rehabilitation as it is currently practiced has no single approach that guarantees success. Although several programs have been notably effective for particular situations, universal criteria have not been developed. Programs that are successful in one area or with a particular kind of offender often fail when moved to another part of the country or when applied to a different kind of offender. Walter C. Bailey analyzed 100 studies of correctional procedures and found that "evidence supporting the efficacy of correctional treatment is slight, inconsistent, and of questionable reliability."[80] Rehabilitative treatments may be ineffectual either inherently or due to the ambivalence of the "crime and punishment" setting within which they occur. Some forms of rehabilitation may be effective for certain criminals under certain conditions, but we have not yet adequately defined the conditions or identified the criminals. Many of the current reformative attempts may be based on incorrect theories of the causes of delinquency and criminality. Whatever the reason, there is as yet no conclusive demonstration of the validity of various rehabilitative practices.

Finally, prison rehabilitation programs have tended to make release contingent on participation in the programs. Inmates are forced into behavior modification procedures, individual and group therapy sessions, and vocational training whether they like it or not, and many find themselves having to act "rehabilitated" in order to qualify for parole. Those who refuse must usually serve longer terms and endure worse living conditions. A new program developed by the Just Community of Niantic, Connecticut, has made rehabilitation voluntary, and an inmate's participation does not necessarily shorten the term.[81]

Prevention   The concept of preventing crime and delinquency before they occur is an attractive one, but, as with rehabilitation, difficult to implement. Aside from the deterrent effect of harsh punishment and repression, crime prevention is customarily defined in three different ways: as the sum total of all influences and activities that contribute to the development of a nondeviant personality in children; as the attempt to deal with specific conditions within the person's environment that are believed to produce crime and delinquency; and as those specific services provided to individuals or groups that are designed to prevent further crime and delinquency. Prevention programs under the first definition include measures designed to improve the social environment of the children concerned, encompassing such things as improved housing for ghetto dwellers, equal job opportunities, and other attempts to improve the quality of life of those in the lower socioeconomic classes. Although programs with these aims do exist, and one of their goals may be the reduction of crime and delinquency in the target area, they are seldom undertaken with this goal uppermost. Moreover, studies of youths involved in antipoverty programs

[79]Susan Henderson, "Day Care for Juvenile Delinquents," *Judicature* (June-July 1969).
[80]Walter C. Bailey, "Correctional Outcome: An Evaluation of 100 Reports," *Journal of Criminal Law, Criminology, and Police Science* 57 (June 1966), 153-160.
[81]"The Crime Wave," *Time* (June 30, 1975), p. 22.

have not as yet found any positive correlation between such participation and reduced delinquency.[82]

The second definition covers programs and attempts based on Sutherland's theory of differential association, and includes efforts to reduce the exposure of children to the antisocial and/or illegal activities of those around them, to improve the child's family life, and to create a viable and conforming social structure within the community itself. Several projects of this sort have been attempted, and some, such as the famous Chicago Area Project, have been notable successes.

Programs that attempt to work within the third definition—prevention of further delinquency and crime—are still in the majority, however. They include such established programs as parole, probation, training schools, and other institutions, as well as freer, more experimental programs.[83] The difficulty of comparing the efforts under this and the other two definitions of delinquency prevention is apparent, since each deals with quite different sets of circumstances.

The Chicago Area Project, for example, was established in the mid-1930s in the Chicago slums, where the weakening social structure of the large immigrant population was no longer able to control its children. The project sought to develop youth welfare programs, using local youths for manpower, that would be viable and permanent additions to the community after the project leaders had left. It was reasoned—correctly, as it turned out—that the local youth, who were then involved with a large network of gangs, would have better success than outside workers in establishing recreation programs (including extensive summer camping), community improvement campaigns, and programs devoted to reaching and assisting delinquent youngsters and even some adults returning to the community after release from prison. The project not only demonstrated the feasibility of using untrained local youths to establish effective youth-welfare programs, but it also indicated, despite the difficulty of establishing empirical data, a possible decrease in the delinquency rate.[84] Most similar projects, however, that have since been attempted have had negligible impact on delinquency rates.[85]

Delinquency prevention projects aimed at specific individuals rather than groups have also had discouraging results. These studies typically contrast two groups of similar individuals, one of which receives intensive and extensive counseling from psychologists, guidance counselors, and social workers, while the other remains uncounseled, serving as a control. Edwin Power and Helen Witmer found, in a very detailed study of two groups of 325 "problem boys" who were considered to be "predelinquents," that the counseling the treatment group received was no more effective than the normal forces active in the community in preventing delinquent acts. They did find, however, that the control boys committed slightly more serious offenses than the treatment boys, although the difference was not statistically

[82]Gerald D. Robin, "Anti-Poverty Programs and Delinquency," *Journal of Criminal Law, Criminology, and Police Science* 60 (1969), 331.

[83]John M. Martin, "Three Approaches to Delinquency Prevention: A Critique," in Gold and Scarpitti, *Combatting Social Problems*, pp. 351-352.

[84]Solomon Kobrin, "The Chicago Area Project—A 25-Year Assessment," *Annals of the American Academy of Political and Social Sciences* 322 (March 1959), 20-29.

[85]Walter B. Miller, "The Impact of a 'Total-Community' Delinquency Control Project," *Social Problems* 10 (Fall 1962), 169-191.

significant. There seems to be an indication, though, that the control group may have a higher rate of recidivism as they grow older.[86]

Henry J. Meyer, Edgar F. Borgatta, and Wyatt C. Jones found similar results over a four-year period with a group of girls entering a New York City vocational high school. Measured by a wide range of criteria, both inside and outside the school system, the treatment girls, who were extensively counseled by a private, nonsectarian, voluntary social agency, failed to score significantly lower than the control group in undesirable and antisocial behavior. The conductors of the survey did find, however, that the differences between the two groups, although too small to be statistically significant, did favor the girls who had received counseling services.[87]

These cases indicate the enormous difficulty in proving the effectiveness of preventive measures. Although they seem to fail at least as often as they succeed, the difficulty may be more with the specific kind of counseling services offered than with the idea of prevention itself. When delinquency prevention seems to be a failure, there are often some signs that there may have been some beneficial effect, even if not of the magnitude desired. We must remember that most of the programs described here are experimental and have not been attempted on a large-scale basis. Further research and more governmental funding for programs of this sort are two of the main needs in this field.

Criminal and Juvenile Justice Reforms

There is little doubt that the problems of our criminal justice system have reached crisis proportions. Many critics have pointed out that criminal justice is too often based on political considerations and that the judicial system itself is overly complicated and burdened with too many laws and too wide a diversity of procedural methods. The result is that the administration of justice to conventional, juvenile, occupational, and organized criminals is unfair and inconsistent.

Conventional Crimes. In 1977, there were 11 million violent and property crimes committed in the United States. Of these only 21 percent were "cleared" by arrests, and less than 6 percent ended in convictions. This makes crime an attractive proposition for many.[88] Part of the reason for this state of affairs is that through the process of plea bargaining—whereby the offender agrees to plead guilty to a lesser charge and release the courts from having to conduct a time-consuming jury trial—most of those convicted for what are regarded as serious crimes receive shortened sentences. It has been estimated, however, that if the plea bargaining process were reduced to even 80 percent of the serious crimes, the number of trials would double and put an enormous strain on the court system.

A further problem with the current administration of justice is that up to now, sentencing has been haphazard and has often resulted in prisoners "serving wildly different sentences for the same offense. Sentencing is too

---

[86]Edwin Powers and Helen Witmer, *An Experiment in the Prevention of Delinquency* (New York: Columbia University Press, 1951), pp. vii-xi, 320-338.

[87]Henry J. Meyer, Edgar F. Borgatta, and Wyatt C. Jones, "An Experiment in Prevention through Social Work Intervention," in *Behavior Sciences for Social Workers*, ed. Edwin Thoman (New York: Free Press, 1967), pp. 363-383, 470-471.

[88]President's Commission, *UCR*, pp. 37, 160, 218.

often a projection of the value system of the judge."[89] A study of the sentencing of draft evaders revealed that the length of term often depended upon where the trial took place. In Oregon, for example, 33 violators were convicted and 18 were put on probation; in Texas 16 were convicted and none received probation. None of the Oregon violators' sentences exceed three years, but almost all the Texas violators were given the maximum sentence of five years.[90]

The disparity in sentencing is also connected to the social class of the defendant. Jack Newfield cites a 1973 case in which the director of a nursing-home corporation swindled $200 million out of the company's shareholders, making $14 million in profits for himself. He could have received at least a five-year prison sentence, but instead received a one-year sentence and was eligible for probation after four months. In a contrasting case the next day, a judge sentenced an 18-year-old Puerto Rican youth to five years in prison for stealing a car worth no more than $100, although the youth had not used a gun or committed any violent acts.[91] The current glaring disparity in sentencing obviously undermines every citizen's sense of justice, as Willard Gaylin suggests:

> When serious criminals go unpunished, when minor offenses are excessively punished, when a chosen group receives lesser punishment or a despised group more punishment, it threatens all of us in that society, even the law-abiders. It corrodes the basic structural prop of equity that supports our sense of justice. An excessive disparity in sentencing threatens that kind of breakdown.

Juvenile Justice and Public Order Reforms.   Compounding the criminal justice problem and greatly overloading the court calendars are the thousands of cases involving juvenile and public-order offenders. Many criminologists and legal authorities agree that there are far too many laws in force in most state codes that cover not just behavior that is illegal only for children—the so-called "juvenile status" crimes—but also nonviolent adult "victimless crimes," such as marijuana possession, adultery, homosexuality, prostitution, and drunkenness. Status and public order offenders constitute 40 percent of the case load in both juvenile and adult courts. Edwin M. Schur has, therefore, advocated a thorough reform of the concept of juvenile justice that would include a greater toleration for a broader range of behavior and would make only specific antisocial acts criminal; for these there would be "uniformly applied punishment not disguised as treatment."[92]

Occupational Offenses.   There are many facets to the legal reforms necessary to curb occupational crime. One would increase the penalties for occupational crime to create a more effective deterrent. Frequently today, a company worth hundreds of millions of dollars faces a fine of only $50,000 and its executives only $5,000 upon conviction for fraud or price-fixing. Large corporations can regard these penalties as an acceptable risk. One way to

---

[89]"The Crime Wave," p. 18.

[90]Willard Gaylin, *Partial Justice* (New York: Knopf, 1974), pp. 5-7.

[91]Jack Newfield, *Cruel and Unusual Justice* (New York: Holt, Rinehart and Winston, 1974), p. xiii.

[92]Edwin M. Schur, *Radical Nonintervention: Rethinking the Delinquency Problem* (Englewood Cliffs, N.J.: Prentice-Hall, 1973), p. 23.

increase fines, of course, is simply to raise the dollar amount of the allowable penalty for each crime, or to make penalties a fixed percentage of a company's profits.[93]

Some critics have felt that an extremely effective deterrent would be to increase the likelihood of jail terms for occupational offenders. In the past, those convicted of occupational crime have rarely gone to jail; for example, only forty executives have been jailed for antitrust violations in the last eighty-five years.[94] These criminals have much to lose in terms of status and community respect by going to jail. The threat of prison, even for a short term, might be more effective for them than increased fines.

There are other ways to increase the penalties for occupational crime. A regulatory agency such as the Federal Trade Commission could require a company convicted of fraudulent advertising to use a certain proportion of its advertising budget during the next few years to inform consumers that previous claims were misleading. This type of remedy is particularly applicable for consumer fraud, since its deterrent value depends on the company's fear of unfavorable consumer response.

Another aspect of legal reform involves changing laws to make them less easy or tempting to break. Complicated tax laws, for example, full of alternatives and loopholes, may invite cheating. Streamlining the laws might both discourage cheating and make it easier to detect when it does occur.[95] The law could also be reformed to make accomplices to occupational crimes, as well as principals, vulnerable to court action, so that for each such crime, many more corporate employees would face punishment.

Stronger enforcement, obviously, must accompany legal reform for it to be meaningful; and this means more money and more manpower for enforcement agencies. To detect more income tax cheating, for example, means that more auditors must be hired by the IRS. To detect collusion between corporations, the federal antitrust unit must have more investigators, with the expertise and time to gather evidence for a successful court case. Similarly, once a case against occupational offenders has been won in court, the judge must be willing to invoke the penalties that the law allows. If the law provides for a jail term, the judge must not hesitate to send the convicted person to jail merely because of a respectable appearance—a prison sentence seems inappropriate for a "respectable person."

These two approaches—legal reform, particularly tougher penalties, and enforcement—could probably effectively deter occupational crime. More than most other types of crime, occupational crime involves calculation, advance planning, and the weighing of gains against possible costs. Increasing the costs, as well as the risk of detection, might well force occupational criminals to conclude that honesty is more profitable.

Another approach focuses on public education—making people aware of the prevalence and the costs of occupational crime to them. As has already been pointed out, publicizing the names of firms convicted of such crime can be an effective tool. Public education can also lead to legal reform and tougher enforcement.

[93]"White Collar Crime: Huge Economic and Moral Drain," *Congressional Quarterly*, p. 1049.
[94]"More Punch for Antitrust—Moves You Can Expect," *U.S. News and World Report* (November 25, 1974), pp. 47-48.
[95]Schur, *Our Criminal Society*, p. 190.

Finally, perhaps the most active effort against occupational crime at present is being conducted on the consumer front. Consumer advocates have two means of correcting the disparity in knowledge and power between consumers and industry. The first is to make consumers less gullible and more sophisticated—for example, by teaching them to compare prices or to read contracts closely—so that they can do as well as possible under existing circumstances. The second is to increase the role of government, both local and national, in protecting the consumer. The oldest government function in this area has been to set standards for certain products. For example, the government has long regulated sanitary standards for meat wholesalers in order to protect the consumer, since it is clear that no individual consumer has the power to make sure that meat purchased has been prepared in a sanitary way. Consumer advocates would like to expand these laws— particularly those requiring safety features for products—and strengthen their enforcement.

Again, government can require that consumers be given true information about the products they buy—the real weight content of a package, the ingredients and nutritional value of a food product, the effective interest charges on a loan or an installment purchase. Unit Pricing and the Truth-in-Lending Law are recent attempts to gain some of these ends. The creation of a federal "consumer advocate" agency could also do much to decrease abuses (such as false advertising) by industry as a whole, and to ensure that consumers will pay fair prices for safe products.

Combating Organized Crime.   Organized crime is pervasive and costly. Authorities agree that, so far, efforts at combating it have been woefully inadequate. Only about 500 full-time employees at all levels of government, and minuscule financial and personnel resources, have been committed to fighting organized crime.[96] One reason for the paucity of resources has been the apparent public indifference to the problem—most people do not worry about organized crime as much as they worry about being mugged or burglarized. They fail to realize, however, that thieves may be drug users who need money to buy drugs—and that one reason they are drug users in the first place is that a crime syndicate imported heroin, supplied it to the pushers, and encouraged them to find customers. Because of public indifference to organized crime, there is usually little pressure on police departments to devote more people and money to combating the problem.

There are other reasons why it is particularly hard to fight organized crime. A major one is the difficulty of getting proof of syndicate activities that is acceptable in court. Witnesses rarely come forward—fearing retaliation, or they themselves are too deeply implicated. In any case, since top personnel are so well insulated from others in the syndicate, witnesses rarely can testify usefully about them and their plans. Documentary evidence is equally rare, since the transactions of syndicated crime are seldom written down. Sometimes, corruption hinders effective prosecution of organized crime. In a ten-year study of the New York State Court's disposition of individual Mafia heroin dealers, the Joint Legislative Committee on Crime discovered that 47.7 percent of the cases were either acquitted or dismissed.[97]

Beyond this, the basic approach of law-enforcement agencies and the

---

[96]President's Commission, *Challenge of Crime*, p. 197.
[97]Newfield, *Cruel and Unusual Justice*, pp. xii-xiii.

courts has been the short-term, well published prosecution of individual criminals. The crucial fact about organized crime is that since it is an organization, it can therefore endure regardless of the fate of individuals. In any case, again because of the insulation and protection of top members, the police are rarely able to arrest the most important leaders of syndicated crime.

It would seem that a different approach and more effective strategies are needed. Dwight C. Smith and Ralph F. Salerno, for example, suggest we need to weaken the organization as such, whether or not we jail individuals. They propose five strategies: *subvert* the organization by breeding or aggravating internal dissension; *alienate* current or prospective members by making membership unattractive; *disrupt* activities, reducing profit and increasing costs; *block* activities by alerting and educating the public; and *penetrate* the organization by infiltration or buying information, thereby gaining the means to subvert, alienate, and disrupt.[98] For all this to be effective, an adequate intelligence system is essential. Syndicate activities must be studied, patterns of action and communication learned, probably future moves anticipated, and law-enforcement agencies must somehow coordinate their efforts and share the resulting information. At present three or four different agencies may be investigating the same person without the other's knowledge, resulting in waste of resources, duplication of effort, and sometimes active interference in work.

The President's Commission on Law Enforcement and the Administration of Justice has also made several suggestions for dealing with organized crime.[99] The basic one, of course, is more money and more personnel for gathering evidence and prosecuting criminals. This means establishing special units to fight syndicated crime wherever it exists. Equally important are coordinated local, state, and federal efforts. This would increase personnel for any one investigation and improve efficiency. An important aspect would be the centralizing and computerizing of all data about syndicated crime collected by different enforcement agencies, so that any agency would have access to information from any source.

Other suggestions focus on methods of obtaining better, tighter proof. These include special investigative bodies set up to bypass local prosecutors or investigators who may appear incompetent or corrupt; broad statutes for witness immunity; adequate protection of witnesses, perhaps through the creation of federally administered residential facilities; and more workable rules for proving perjury. Clarifying the nature and permissible limits of electronic surveillance—wiretapping and bugging—is also urged.

Still another approach is to legalize gambling, prostitution, narcotics—all the currently illegal activities that provide syndicated crime with the bulk of its income. If buyers could obtain such commodities legally, the reasoning goes, sources of supply would multiply, the price would drop, "protection" would no longer be needed, and the syndicate would lose its monopoly and its profits. This is being tried with gambling: lotteries and off-track betting corporations have been established in a few states. Whether they will substantially affect the syndicates is not yet clear.

Political corruption has been made more risky by requiring candidates to

---

[98]Dwight C. Smith and Ralph F. Salerno, "The Use of Strategies in Organized Crime Control," *Journal of Criminal Law, Criminology, and Police Science* 61 (March 1970), 101-111.

[99]President's Commission, *Challenge of Crime*, pp. 200-209.

disclose the sources of their campaign funds. Syndicate figures, however, commonly use superficially legitimate channels to funnel money to candidates they support, so it remains to be seen if politics on at least the federal level can be made corruption-free.

Finally, it has been suggested that people in business could do more themselves to prevent syndicates from infiltrating legitimate businesses. In particular, they could be more alert to the signs of syndicated crime—such as merchandise offered at lower-than-wholesale prices—and then be more ready to report it, either to the police or to special business committees that would be set up for that purpose.[100] Many have already suggested that our criminal justice system is in crisis. A House subcommittee stated that the federal government's crime program set up under the Omnibus Crime Control Safe Streets Act of 1968 was characterized by "inefficiency, waste, maladministration, and in some cases, corruption." This program, under which nearly $1.5 billion had been sent to the states to improve law enforcement, was described by the subcommittee as having had "no visible impact on the incidence of crime in the United States."[101]

Nonetheless, efforts are being made: attempts to increase minority representation on police forces, to train police in techniques for handling some of the newer law-enforcement problems with a minimum of violence or coercion, and generally to improve relationships between the police and their communities have been made.

The persistent outbreak of prison disturbances across the nation points to some of the problems that exist within our corrections agencies. Some criminologists have urged a shift from prisons to halfway houses, graduated release and furlough programs, and expanded educational and vocational opportunity; yet, so far, very little has changed. The National Council on Crime and Delinquency has found that 80 percent of correctional expenditures go toward the operations of the institutions, and only 20 percent to such community-based services as juvenile aftercare, parole, and probation.[102] Considering that work-release, as described earlier, seems to be effective in rehabilitating the adult criminal, it is unfortunate that more funds are not allocated to it. The recent movement among prisoners themselves to organize and demand some recognition of their human and constitutional rights, even behind bars, together with public pressure, could produce some progress, but the prospect remains fairly bleak.

Because of the concern about crime, many criminologists, legislators, and officials at all levels of government are also advocating harsher and more specific penalties for every kind of crime, and they are studying criminal justice reforms that will increase the chances of offenders getting caught. Congress passed a law in 1975 to reduce recidivism by requiring speedy trials and strengthening the supervision of those out on bail. Although $3 billion has been spent since 1967 on the "war on crime," more than half of it has gone to police forces for innovations and modernizing; authorities generally agree that much more money will have to be spent on prisons and courts. In 1978

---

[100]Grutzner, "How to Lock Out the Mafia," pp. 45-58.

[101]"Crime Program Held Inefficient," *New York Times* (April 11, 1972).

[102]National Council on Crime and Delinquency, *Goals and Recommendations: A Response to "The Challenge of Crime in a Free Society." The Report of the President's Commission on Law Enforcement and the Administration of Justice* (Hackensack, N.J.: National Council on Crime and Delinquency, 1967).

Prisoners survey the damage of their overnight riot. Despite their criminal pasts, convicts are demanding attention for their human and civil rights.

UPI

Congress created 152 new federal judgeships, expanding the federal judiciary by a quarter, to reduce the backlog of cases before the courts.

Crowded court calendars, backlogs of cases, and long delays in trials are responsible for the fact that although the number of serious crimes—according to official statistics, at least—has increased by 63 percent since 1968, only recently has there been an increase in the number of offenders jailed. Many repeat offenders do not go to jail, and it is clear that the current forms of rehabilitation have neither decreased the crime rate, nor made released inmates any less committed to a criminal life. Wilson cites studies that estimate that the present rate of serious crime could be reduced by one-third if all serious offenders were jailed for a minimum of three years.[103] Though this emphasizes punishment rather than remedying the conditions that breed crime, it has many adherents. Prisons have begun to emphasize punishment instead of rehabilitation; and the head of the Federal Bureau of Prisons announced recently that future prison policies would concentrate on confining and isolating criminals. Authorities also see the obvious need to eliminate the disparity in sentences and make them the same for similar crimes, while also making them "more punitive, surer, more swiftly imposed, and more definite in length."[104] This will produce more prisoners and more prisons. Since rehabilitation programs will be strictly voluntary, they will have no bearing on when a prisoner is released; thus parole boards, which base their decision to parole prisoners on the somewhat arbitrary standard of how well they have been rehabilitated, may find their functions reduced or eliminated.

Reforms are also being proposed for the juvenile justice system. A national commission has recommended that sentences for juvenile offenders be based solely on the seriousness of the crime, and that juvenile court proceedings be opened to the public in order to make judges more accountable and to end disparity in juvenile sentences. Serious and violent juvenile cases would first be heard in juvenile courts and then tried in adult courts, which could then sentence juvenile-murderers to longer prison terms than most of them currently receive.[105] The great harm done by mixing juvenile status offenders with delinquents who commit serious crimes is beginning to be realized. For example, the President's Commission on Law Enforcement and the Administration of Justice proposed a radical plan similar to those adopted in some European countries: status offenders would be handled either by a Youth Services Bureau that would operate in neighborhoods or by the family and child welfare system.[106] The federal government has since undertaken some large-scale measures to counteract the juvenile problem. Congress allocated $384 million in 1974 under the Juvenile Delinquency Prevention Act, which established an Office of Juvenile Justice and Delinquency Prevention, created a National Advisory Committee on Juvenile Problems, and dispensed federal grants for youth programs. The act also requires that the federal Law Enforcement Assistance Administration develop programs to keep juvenile status offenders out of prison.

[103]Wilson, "Lock 'em Up," p. 69.
[104]"Big Change in Prisons: Punish—Not Reform," *U.S. News and World Report* (August 25, 1975), pp. 21-22.
[105]Marcia Chambers, "Radical Changes Urged in Dealing with Youth Crime," *New York Times* (November 30, 1975), p. 58.
[106]Lerman, "Delinquents without Crime," pp. 258-259.

As long as the public remains indifferent to occupational crime, and does not quite believe in the reality or menace of organized crime, it will be difficult to combat these crimes effectively. Another important point is that while both organized and occupational crime affect everyone, the poor in particular bear the brunt. Consumer frauds have a vicious impact on the poor, and syndicated crime milks the ghettos. In both cases the criminals are relatively strong and influential, while their victims are weak—the reverse of the situation for other crimes, where the criminals often lack influence as compared to their victims. This suggests why the latter crimes have received the greatest attention from law-enforcement agencies. Occupational criminals are often leading citizens, with influence on what laws are passed and how they are enforced. Organized crime buys its influence with payoffs and force. Consumer advocates are aware of this fundamental power relationship when they insist that consumers must be organized, with their own lobbyists and advocates.

Since the Watergate scandals and the recent exposure of widespread corporate bribery practices, Congress is now considering some of the following proposals: bringing misdemeanor charges against government and business officials who, in failing to properly supervise their organizations, allow criminal practices to go on; granting protection from any retaliation to informers who bring cases of illegal activities to the attention of authorities; suspending from interstate trade any organization that repeatedly fails to modify its illegal practices; making prison terms a certainty for offenses such as price-fixing and tax evasion; and fining corporations up to $500,000 for antitrust violations.[107] It remains to be seen how many of these proposals—if any—will be instituted.

In conclusion, we should remember that crime and delinquency are complex social problems. Situations of such complexity are not amenable to simple or total solutions. Certainly alleviating poverty, deprivation, hopelessness, and anomie would do much to reduce crime, but it is unlikely that conventional and occupational crime will be eliminated. One can only hope that further research and experimentation will lead to the development of successful approaches to the growing problems of crime and delinquency.

[107]"Losing Battle," *U.S. News and World Report*, p. 40.

Summary

The official crime statistics in the United States, which are based only on crimes known to the police, reveal only part of the true incidence of illegal activity, since much crime, particularly "white-collar" crime, goes unreported. Nevertheless, there has been a dramatic increase in the crime rate and the public has reacted with increased demands for stricter law enforcement.

Although crime in the legal sense is simply any act for which the state can apply sanctions, it can also be seen as the product of conflicting class interests and police ideology. People without influence are often put at a great disadvantage in their confrontations with the law.

Nine types of crime and criminals have been identified according to how large a role crime plays in an individual's life and the degree to which individuals define themselves as criminals. *Violent personal crime* includes such acts as robbery in which physical injury is inflicted or implied; these acts are often unpremeditated and, except in the case of murder and assault, generally occur between strangers. *Occasional property crime* includes such acts as vandalism and shoplifting; offenders can easily justify their actions and generally do not regard themselves as criminals. *Occupational (white-collar) crime* takes in a wide range of activities such as embezzlement, fraud, and business-government crime; it is committed by people who accept it as normal and who think of themselves as respectable citizens—most such crime is never detected. *Political crime* includes such acts as treason and civil disobedience, which are perceived as threats to the state; violators see themselves as acting idealistically. *Public order crime* includes such "victimless crimes" as drunkenness and prostitution; offenders rarely see themselves as criminals, though they may be driven into a criminal role by society's attitude toward them. *Conventional crime* includes theft, often committed by young adults; offenders generally see these crimes as a way of life, though many give up their criminal careers as they grow older. *Organized crime* controls a large network of gambling operations, loan-sharking, and narcotics rings; it exists largely because of corruption and the public demand for the services it provides. *Professional crime* involves illegal acts committed by those with highly developed criminal careers; offenders are rarely caught and are likely to continue their careers to a relatively late age. *Juvenile delinquency* is crime committed by young offenders; though juveniles commit a large percentage of violent crimes, the bulk of juvenile crimes are status offenses that would not be illegal were they committed by adults.

There are many explanations for the present high crime rates, such as the personal freedom, rapid technological change, and cultural heterogeneity within our society. Some observers emphasize demographic and economic factors such as the large number of crime-prone and disadvantaged youth. Still others point to family and community disorganization, physical abuse of children, and media violence to account for the high level of violent crime. Both occupational and organized crime flourish because of our cultural beliefs, such as individualism, *laissez-faire* government policies, and materialism.

The four major sociological explanations of crime are: (1) the *differntial association theory*, which views criminal behavior as the result of a learning process and the internalization of criminal values; (2) the *anomie theory* in which society holds out the goal of material success to all its members, but denies access and approved means of reaching it to large groups; (3) the *delinquent subcultures theory*, which suggests that those unable to compete in the larger society form their own groups that provide reachable goals and norms; and (4) the *lower-class culture theory*, which views specific lower-class values and codes of behavior as responsible for delinquency and crime.

Society's efforts to control crime can also be classified into four areas: *retribution-deterrence*, which has been the prevailing philosophy for handling criminals, is based on the principles of retribution and of providing an object lesson to others who may be tempted to commit similar crimes; *rehabilitation*, under which criminals are viewed as either victims of society or as sick people who must be led to conform to society's values or cured of their sickness; *preventive measures*, which are designed to either improve the general social environment of pre-delinquent children or to focus on specific crime-producing conditions; and *criminal and juvenile justice reforms*, which would reduce sentencing disparities, decriminalize certain victimless crimes and juvenile status offenses, increase penalties for occupational crime, redouble efforts to combat organized crime, and make our law-enforcement system more efficient.

Bibliography

Albini, Joseph L. *The American Mafia: Genesis of a Legend.* Englewood Cliffs, N.J.: Prentice-Hall, 1971.

Chambliss, William. *Criminal Law in Action.* Santa Barbara, Calif: Hamilton, 1975.

Cloward, Richard A., and Ohlin, Lloyd E. *Delinquency and Opportunity: A Theory of Delinquent Gangs.* New York: Free Press, 1967.

Cohen, Albert. *Delinquent Boys.* New York: Free Press, 1971.

Empey, LaMar T., and Lubeck, Stephen G. *Explaining Delinquency.* Lexington, Mass.: Heath Lexington Books, 1971.

Gardiner, John A. *The Politics of Corruption: Organized Crime in an American City.* New York: Russell Sage Foundation, 1970.

Gaylin, Willard. *Partial Justice.* New York: Knopf, 1974.

Gibbens, T.C.N., and Ahrenfeldt, R. *Cultural Factors in Delinquency.* Philadelphia: Lippincott, 1966.

Hartjen, Clayton A. *Crime and Criminalization,* 2nd ed. New York: Praeger, 1978.

Hunt, Morton. *The Mugging.* New York: Atheneum, 1972.

Newfield, Jack. *Cruel and Unusual Justice.* New York: Holt, Rinehart and Winston, 1974.

Quinney, Richard. *The Social Reality of Crime.* Boston: Little, Brown, 1970.

Reckless, Walter C. *The Crime Problem,* 5th ed. Englewood Cliffs, N.J.: Prentice-Hall, 1973.

Safa, Helen Icken, and Levitas, Gloria. *Social Problems in Corporate America.* New York: Harper & Row, 1975.

Schur, Edwin M. *Radical Nonintervention: Rethinking the Delinquency Problem.* Englewood Cliffs, N.J.: Prentice-Hall, 1973.

Violence

Facts about Violence

- There are as many homicides every year in Philadelphia (population 2 million) as in all of Great Britain (population 54 million).
- More Americans own guns than smoke cigarettes, drink alcohol, or own dishwashers or stereos.
- By the age of 15, the average child will have witnessed over 13,000 killings on television.
- Between 1820 and 1945, 59 million human beings were killed in wars, murders, quarrels, and skirmishes.
- About 14,000 Americans (one every 22 minutes) are murdered and over 63,000 women (one every 8 minutes) are raped each year.
- Between 25,000 and 60,000 Americans commit suicide each year.

In the view of many Americans, violence is a critical, contemporary social problem. We have noted, in the chapter on crime and criminals, that crime ranks high among the problems considered particularly serious at the present time. Kidnappings, terrorist bombings, political assassinations, and the threat of nuclear annihilation all serve to show how pervasive violence is in our culture. The stability of American institutions and, indeed, the fate of the nation itself may depend upon present and future efforts to reduce the level and types of violence in this nation and in the world.

Much of the violence in human history has not, until recently, been recognized as such. This is particularly true for violence associated with the rise or expansion of a political party or social movement; since violence is generally defined as wrong, most groups reflexively try to forget, justify, or disguise their use of it now as in the past. As Hugh Graham and Ted Gurr note: "Probably all nations are given to a kind of historical amnesia or selective recollection that masks unpleasant traumas of the past."[1] In this respect, America is probably no worse, and no better, than most nations. While such extralegal violence as murder, rape, or gangland activities have elicited general public condemnation, other forms of violence, often linked with the historical development of the nation, have been accepted or even praised—for example, the violence involved in most wars in which the nation has been engaged, whether for expansion or for self-defense. Likewise, in troubled times and on the frontiers, vigilante activities have often been approved by the local community as the only available means of maintaining order. In general, violence by constituted authority, or on behalf of the state, is less likely to be condemned than violence by private citizens or in defiance of authority. Probably the two most famous recent examples of this were the public reaction to the confrontation between the Ohio National Guard and student demonstrators and bystanders at Kent State University in May 1970 and the Attica prison uprising in New York State in September 1971. Although the guardsmen at Kent State fired indiscriminately in response to minimal provocation, killing 4 students and wounding 10 in this episode, the

[1]Hugh Davis Graham and Ted Robert Gurr, ed., *The History of Violence in America: A Report to the National Commission on the Causes and Prevention of Violence* (New York: Bantam, 1969), p. 792.

general public response supported the Guard and the authorities. Similarly, although the quelling of the Attica rebellion resulted in the death of 11 guard hostages and 32 convicts—almost all shot by state police when they stormed the prison—no police officer was ever indicted.

It is only recently, in the wake of a growing number of political assassinations, civil disorders, violent protests and demonstrations, and rising crime statistics, that a greater effort has been made to study the causes and effects of violence in American society. Such study was long overdue; despite the relative stability of its institutions, the United States has witnessed more violent behavior than other nations of comparable development. In one study of civil strife in 114 nations and colonies, for example, the United States ranked first among 17 Western democracies and twenty-fourth in the overall sample in the magnitude of strife.[2] This record does not include the recent statistics of individual crimes indicating that violent crimes in our society have increased 70 percent since 1968. According to official statistics, which grossly under report crime, over 14,000 Americans are murdered, over 63,000 are raped, over 522,000 are seriously assaulted, and over 404,000 are robbed annually. Whereas in the past such crimes occurred almost exclusively in cities, today's crime rates are increasing most rapidly in the suburbs.[3] Few, if any, areas in the nation remain unaffected by the problem of violence.

The significance of the problem of violence and the need to find means to control and prevent it are apparent. Before we can control violence, however, we must better understand its nature and origins. To find the origins of lawlessness, bloodshed, and gunplay, it is necessary to retrace the entire course of American history.

An Historical Perspective

The "myth of peaceful progress"[4] in American history, appealing though it may be to our self-esteem, cannot survive careful scrutiny. The dark shadow of violence has colored many of the highly celebrated events and movements in American history. Howard Zinn has written that the failure to recognize the role of violence in American social progress and to acknowledge how much our behavior toward other nationalities and peoples has been characterized by overt violence has resulted in a "double standard" in the American attitude toward violence:

> There is, on the one hand, a national tendency to absolutize the value of social change at the expense of human life when the violence required for this change is directed at other nations or other races; and on the other hand, a tendency to absolutize the value of peace at the expense of social change *within* the national framework.[5]

The United States was born in a violent struggle against British rule. Independence cost seven years of warfare and the lives of 25,000 soldiers of

---

[2]T. R. Gurr, "A Comparative Study of Civil Strife," in Graham and Gurr, *History of Violence*, pp. 572-632.

[3]Federal Bureau of Investigation (FBI), *Uniform Crime Reports (UCR)* (Washington, D.C.: U.S. Department of Justice, October 18, 1978), p. 35.

[4]Jerome H. Skolnick, *The Politics of Protest* (New York: Simon & Schuster, 1969), p. 9.

[5]Howard Zinn, "Violence and Social Change in American History," in *Violence in America*, ed. Thomas Rose (New York: Random House, 1969).

the Continental Army. This revolutionary struggle embedded in our national ideology the belief that violence is permissible in the service of a good cause. As Richard Maxwell Brown writes: "The meanest and most squalid sort of violence was from the very beginning to the very last put to the service of revolutionary ideals and objectives."[6]

Violence and aggression are woven deeply into the fabric of American history; repeatedly, the past shows that rewards went to the violent and the strong. For more than two centuries during the westward expansion, for

[6]Richard Maxwell Brown, "Historical Patterns of Violence in America," in Graham and Gurr, *History of Violence*, p. 63.

This portrayal of the Battle of Bunker Hill marks an important contribution to American ideology: that violence serving a "good cause" is viewed as acceptable and even honorable behavior.

Library of Congress

example, the Indians were systematically exterminated and their lands seized. Such a reign of genocide—which went hand-in-hand with democracy—has been described, in Zinn's words, as "the shadowed underside of the most cherished events in American history."[7]

The fate of the Indians is symptomatic of violence patterns throughout American history. Although democracy guarantees rights to everyone, it often fails to enforce them. In practice, the reality of power counts for more than the ideal of justice. The enslavement and suppression of blacks is another example of power; it is not surprising that the ultimate remedy to the slavery dispute was the Civil War—the democratic enactment of violence on a mass level. Such paradoxical applications of democracy have given rise to traditions of vigilantism and interpersonal violence, while the right to bear arms in the cause of liberty has become confused with the right to use them indiscriminately. The notion that acts of illegitimate violence can be remedied by further acts of illegitimate violence is a savage anachronism, yet vestiges of it can still be seen in contemporary culture.[8]

The effect of this violent history and the ambivalent American attitude toward it must be remembered when considering manifestations of violence today.

The Concepts of Violence

The word "violence" has a generally—and deservedly—negative connotation; it has been defined as "behavior designed to inflict physical injury to people or damage to property."[9] It may be considered legitimate or illegitimate, depending on who uses it, and why and how it is used. Some special uses of violence, particularly in athletics, are so socially accepted that they are usually perceived as not violent, but as healthy and even character-building activities.

Also not thought of as violence is what Johan Galtung calls "structural violence"—that is, "the dominance of one group over the other, with subsequent exploitative practices."[10] In such a situation, the threat of, or potential for, violence is usually sufficient to keep the dominated group "in its place," but the effect on social relationships and development is very much the same as that of overt violence. This aspect of violence will not be discussed at length, but it should be noted that the recognition by a dominated group of the structural violence that has been used against it may be a significant factor in the genesis of such overt group violence as civil disorders and rebellion.

Jerome Skolnick has pointed out that violence "is an ambiguous term whose meaning is established through political processes." What a society classifies as violent is apt to depend in considerable part on "who provides the definition and who has superior resources of disseminating and enforcing his definitions." War provides a classic example of this: the acts of one's own side are generally defended as honorable, while the other side is described as the

[7]Zinn, "Violence and Social Change," p. 71.

[8]Roger Lane, "Criminal Violence in America: The First Hundred Years," *Annals of the American Academy of Political and Social Science*, 423 (January 1976), 1-13.

[9]Graham and Gurr, *History of Violence*, p. xxx.

[10]Johan Galtung, "Peace Thinking," in *The Search for World Order*, ed. Albert Lepawsky, Edward H. Buehrig, and Harold D. Lasswell (Englewood Cliffs, N.J.: Prentice-Hall (ACC), 1971), p. 124.

aggressor and its violent acts are considered atrocities. Similarly, within a single nation, accusations of violent behavior are exchanged between the political authorities and their relatively powerless adversaries:

> Within a given society, political regimes often exaggerate the violence of those challenging established institutions. The term "violence" is frequently employed to discredit forms of behavior considered improper, reprehensible, or threatening by specific groups which, in turn, may mask their own violent response with the rhetoric of order or progress.[11]

Several writers have attempted to justify the use of violence by a colonized people against the colonial authorities, or the "have-nots" against the "haves." Anticolonial and revolutionary art is characterized by the impassioned defense of violence when the violence is used by those rebelling against established institutions. Frantz Fanon, the African psychiatrist whose experiences in the Algerian war made him a revolutionary, speaks of violence as a "cleansing force" that frees the spirit and restores self-esteem; it unifies the people and teaches them to assert themselves against any future attempt at tyranny, even by their own leaders.[12] Herbert Marcuse writes of the revolutionary potential of those who have been divorced from the participatory processes of advanced industrialized nations, "the substratum of the outcasts and outsiders, the exploited and persecuted of other races and other colors, the unemployed and the unemployable."[13]

There are, then, many dimensions and facets to be considered in discussing the concept of violence. A useful distinction to be made is between violence exercised on behalf of or under the protection of the state, or institutional violence, and the non-institutional violence of those opposed to established authority. While violence in both of these categories may be either constructive or destructive, institutional violence is usually presumed to be legitimate until proven otherwise, while those engaged in non-institutional violence are subject to reprimand and punishment. Thus, wars or violent police actions are usually considered legitimate because they are conducted under the aegis of the state; however, violent protests and demonstrations, revolutionary activity, civil disorders, and violent criminal activity are not given similar official sanction. Although this situation is in part a matter of the difference in power between the "ins" and the "outs," it is based also on the traditional idea that the state may, and even must, do some things that an individual citizen may not do in order to fulfill its responsibility for protecting the general welfare. It is when the state is seen as using its privilege of violence for ends contrary to the general welfare that the right of non-institutional violence—sabotage, terrorism, rebellion, revolution—is likely to be asserted.

Violence has obvious limitations as an instrument of social progress, the most evident being that its exercise entails the physical injury of other people. And although some advocates of revolution seem to develop almost a mystique of violence—for example, Jean-Paul Sartre's "violence, like Achilles' lance, can heal the wounds that it has inflicted"[14]—one of the principal

---

[11]Skolnick, *Politics of Protest*, p. 4.
[12]Frantz Fanon, *The Wretched of the Earth* (New York: Grove Press, 1968), p. 94.
[13]Herbert Marcuse, *One-Dimensional Man* (Boston: Beacon Press, 1964), p. 256.
[14]Jean-Paul Sartre, Preface to Fanon, *The Wretched of the Earth*, p. 30.

problems facing leaders of violent groups, both revolutionaries or military generals, is to stop the process of violence once it has achieved its desired purposes. When people have used violence to gain some common end, they are apt to continue to use violence to gain more particular ends, or even, sometimes, almost as an end in itself. Since war began, soldiers have been looting conquered towns; and more than one united revolution has ended in brutal factional strife.

Explanations for Violence

The Biological Viewpoint

Why do people behave violently? Is it simply their nature?

"No person living today can question the statement that man, *Homo sapiens*, self-proclaimed to represent the pinnacle of evolution, is the most dangerous living species."[15] According to R. Charles Boelkins and John F. Heiser, between 1820 and 1945, humans killed 59 million of their own kind in wars, murders, quarrels, and skirmishes, one person killing another every 68 seconds for 126 years. On a less dramatic scale, minor physical violence is commonplace in many American homes. As Steinmetz and Straus put it: "It would be hard to find a group or institution in American society in which violence is more of any everyday occurrence than it is within the American family."[16] Since violence is such a common occurrence among people, some social scientists have argued that humanity's aggressive tendencies are inherent or instinctual.

According to this view, only social organization keeps violent inclinations under control. Freud's death wish, Lorenz's conception of aggression as a survival enhancing instinct, and Ardrey's territorial imperative are all based on a form of this argument:

> Man is a predator whose natural instinct is to kill with a weapon. The sudden addition of the enlarged brain to the equipment of an armed, already successful, predatory animal created not only the human being but also the human predicament.[17]

Lord of the Flies, William Golding's disturbing novel of degeneration and violence among boys on a desert island, is one of many fictional presentations on the same theme.

Others argue that aggression is natural, but that violence is not. Boelkins and Heiser maintain that "aggression is a basic behavioral response that has multiple determinants whose precise effects vary with the sex, the age, and the species of the organism." Aggression in people and animals serves an adaptive purpose, while violence is a "short-term coping mechanism that enables adjustment but which in the long run will prove maladaptive to both the individual and the species."[18] Since, in the nature of things, there can be

---

[15]R. Charles Boelkins and John F. Heiser, "Biological Bases of Aggression," in *Violence and the Struggle for Existence*, ed. David N. Daniels, Marshall Gilula, and Frank Oehberg (Boston: Little, Brown, 1970), p. 15.

[16]Suzanne K. Steinmetz and Murray A. Straus, "The Family as Cradle for Violence," *Society*, vol. 10, no. 6 (September-October 1973), 69.

[17]Konrad Lorenz, *On Aggression* (New York: Bantam, 1967), p. 235; and Robert Ardrey, *The Territorial Imperative* (New York: Atheneum, 1967), p. 332.

[18]Boelkins and Heiser, "Biological Bases," p. 48.

no culture-free environment to test for the presence or absence of a human instinct of violence, there will probably never be a definitive answer. Evidence that we have does not seem to support the hypothesis of instinctive violent or destructive urges.

Frustration-Aggression and Control Theories

Others have argued that violence toward others, toward society, or toward oneself, in suicide, is a form of aggression resulting from individual frustration. An unfulfilled need produces the frustration, and the frustration is vented in aggression. The strength of the impulses, needs, or wishes obstructed determines the amount of frustration that determines the degree of aggression. Prejudice, lack of affection, and poverty are suggested as some of the common causes of frustration.[19] This frustration-aggression hypothesis has been described as "the easiest and by far the most popular explanation of social violence—whether political turmoil, the hot summers of riot and disorder, or robberies and juvenile delinquency."[20] The main problem with this theory is that it fails to explain why frustration leads to aggression in some instances and not in others, and that it can be defined so broadly as to include just about any conceivable situation.

Related to the frustration-aggression model is the control theory, according to which a person's ability to restrain or control impulsive behavior correlates with the existence of close relationships with significant-other persons. In this view, people whose relationships with others are inadequate or unsatisfactory may resort to violence when their attempts to relate to others in their fashion are frustrated. One study, for example, shows a lack of close relationships in a substantial proportion of teenage boys from different backgrounds who had a history of physically aggressive behavior.[21] The fact that violence is significantly more prevalent among ex-convicts, alcoholics, and others who are out of the mainstream of society, estranged from family and friends, is also cited as evidence for the control thesis. Murderers, accordingly, are likely to be "egocentric, impulsive, rebellious, or sadistic persons who cannot control their emotions."[22]

Of course, not all persons who fit this description become murderers, nor do all murderers fit this description. One study suggested that there were actually two specific personalities prevalent among murderers. One was undercontrolled—those who were unable to restrain aggressive impulses, who had "never developed internal taboos against lashing out when provoked, and had few inhibitions about satisfying their acquisitive or sexual desires aggressively." The second was the exact opposite—overcontrolled persons who inhibited their aggressive impulses almost completely and for whom "even socially acceptable outlets for aggression, such as swearing or pounding on a table, were off-limits." Such persons are said to repress their anger or hostility to the breaking point, until they suddenly and unpredictably explode.[23]

It is difficult to demonstrate how valid the control thesis is since most

[19]See John Dollard, *et al., Frustration and Aggression* (New Haven: Yale University Press, 1939).

[20]Leonard Berkowitz, "The Study of Urban Violence," in *When Men Revolt and Why*, ed. James C. Davies (New York: Free Press, 1971), p. 182.

[21]Travis Hirschi, *Causes of Delinquency* (Berkeley: University of California Press, 1969).

[22]Donald T. Lunde, "Our Murder Boom," *Psychology Today* (July 1975), p. 39.

[23]Study by Ed Magargee, in Lunde, "Murder Boom," p. 39.

murders and many other violent crimes are spontaneous and their causes are not always clear. The lack of close relationships could simply be one factor among many that lead to violent behavior. The control thesis, however, does suggest one clue to why violent crimes are increasing. In the past, there were various social factors—generally accepted moral standards, church membership, a highly favorable view of family life, and more intimate, smaller communities—that aided in the development of controlled personalities. The erosion of traditional authorities may have left more people feeling isolated and thus made them more likely to see violence as an acceptable form of behavior.

Subculture of Violence

It is also suggested—and this is the position of many sociologists—that violence is a learned behavior, acquired through the process of socialization. Accordingly, since members learn the norms of a particular society and behave in ways considered socially desirable, aggressive or violent actions are most likely to occur in a culture or subculture in which violence is accepted or encouraged. Members of such a subculture conform to group norms and peer pressure. This learned violent behavior can then be used to gain specific goals—"aggression by children and adolescents to secure attention, by adults to express dominance strivings, by groups in competition for scarce values, by military personnel in the service of national policy."[24] The learning approach assumes that there will be more violence if violent behavior is presented as a model to be emulated than if the society vigorously and uniformly deplores violent conduct.

Originally devised to explain juvenile gang behavior, subcultural theory in recent years has also been seen as the key to violence in general. In this model, members of violent subgroups have a low provocation threshold, perceiving threats to their integrity in situations that would not be so perceived by members of the dominant society. Normative behavior in such groups requires spontaneous combative response to provocation.[25] There are even those who claim that all American males share to some extent in a subculture of violence—the relatively low rate of commission of violent acts by women is cited as evidence. Eugene C. Bianchi, for example, sees professional football as a metaphor for America's "physical brutality, profit-maximizing commercialism, . . . authoritarian-military mentality and sexism." He notes that school and family join in forming "male children into competitors and achievers."[26]

If violence is a consequence of social learning, frustration is not a necessary prerequisite for its occurrence. Rather, violent habits are acquired through imitation, or as a result of rewarding destructive behavior. It has been shown, for instance, that physically aggressive parents tend to have physically aggressive offspring. Other laboratory studies have indicated that children who observe adults displaying physical aggression will in their later play activities be more aggressive than children not similarly exposed. On the basis of this and other research, Frederick Ilfeld concludes that:

[24]Ted Robert Gurr, *Why Men Rebel* (Princeton: Princeton University Press, 1970), p. 32.
[25]Marvin E. Wolfgang and Franco Ferracuti, *The Subculture of Violence* (London: Tavistock, 1967).
[26]Eugene C. Bianchi, "The Superbowl Culture of Male Violence," *Christian Century* (September 18, 1974), pp. 842-845.

Violence in a sport like hockey is accepted and even encouraged as an important part of the game. Would less violence occur in sports—and in society as a whole—if violent behavior were not rewarded but deplored?
Roberto Borea

physical punishment by parents does not inhibit violence and most likely encourages it. It both frustrates the child and gives him a model to imitate and learn from. The learning of violence through modeling applies to more than just parental behavior. It is also relevant to examples set by the mass media, one's peer or other reference groups, and local and national leaders.[27]

The subculture of violence theory asserts that aggression is the by-product of a culture that idealizes a tough, machismo image. This theory developed from the analysis of official statistics, which suggests that certain subcultural groups have a higher violent crime rate than do other segments of society. But, as suggested in Chapter 5, the stereotype that most acts of aggression are committed by young, minority-status males may well be erroneous—official statistics do not register the actual incidence of crime. Since statistics do not reflect the attitudes or ideologies of individual offenders, it is difficult to ascertain the motives for their crimes. Data collected for the President's Commission on the Causes and Prevention of Violence (1968) indicated that interpersonal violence received a uniformly low rate of approval by all socioeconomic groups. Another survey, comparing prison inmates who had committed violent crimes with those who had

[27]Frederick Ilfeld, "Environmental Theories of Violence," in Daniels, Gilula, and Ochberg, *Violence and the Struggle for Existence*, p. 81.

committed nonviolent ones, found that both groups adhered to a similar system of values. One recent study that interviewed male inmates of British prisons convicted for acts of hostile aggression cited that none of the men desired to protect their reputation or win peer-approval as a result of their crime. The highest percentage of crimes sprang from the aggressor's desire to inflict harm on his victim.[28] Those who commit acts of hostile aggression seem to share not an adherence to external or uniquely subcultural codes, but rather, a similarity of internal psychological factors, and this can affect anyone, in any social, economic, or ethnic group. Studies such as these and others have led Howard S. Erlanger to conclude that

> although the subculture of violence thesis has received a certain measure of acceptance in the field, a wide variety of evidence suggests that it is questionable. . . . More of available evidence is inconsistent with the thesis than consistent with it.[29]

One of the most disturbing questions in this debate is the pervasive role of the mass media in communicating or fostering violent attitudes. A *Christian Science Monitor* survey of television programming conducted six weeks after the assassination of Senator Robert Kennedy in 1968 found 84 killings in 85.5 hours of prime time evening and Saturday morning programming. The bloodiest evening hours were between 7:30 and 9:00, when the networks estimated that 26.7 million children between the ages of 2 and 17 were watching television.[30] Other studies reveal similar conditions. According to one estimate, an average American child will view over 13,000 television killings by the age of 15. So-called "action-adventure" programs in prime time that have increased threefold in the last twenty years proliferate because they are less expensive to produce (therefore more profitable), and because violence is an effective plot device for solving complications and gaining viewer attention.[31] It has also been shown that two-thirds of leading-hero characters are involved in violence. It is significant to note that there is twice as much violence in entertainment programs in the United States than in the United Kingdom.[32]

Since television became ubiquitous in the 1950s, its impact on young viewers has been the subject of considerable research. Leo Bogart, among others, believes that the "overwhelming weight of evidence from this research supports the thesis that exposure to filmed or televised violence tends to lead young children to a state of heightened excitability and to an increase in subsequent displays of aggression."[33] The Task Force on Mass Media and Violence of the National Commission on the Causes and Prevention of Violence expressed its concern that "exposure to mass media portrayals of

Media Influence

[28]Leonard Berkowitz, "Is Criminal Violence Normative Behavior?" *Journal of Research in Crime and Delinquency*, vol. 15, no. 2 (July 1978), 148-161.

[29]Howard S. Erlanger, "The Empirical Status of the Subculture of Violence Thesis," *Social Problems* 22 (December 1974), 282-283.

[30]Alberta E. Siegel, "Violence in the Mass Media," in Daniels, Gilula, and Ochberg, *Violence and the Struggle for Existence*, p. 226.

[31]"Drop that Gun, Captain Video," *Newsweek* (March 10, 1975), pp. 81-82.

[32]Leo Bogart, "Warning: The Surgeon General Has Determined That TV Violence is Moderately Dangerous to Your Child's Mental Health," *Public Opinion Quarterly* (Winter 1972-1973), 491-521.

[33]Bogart, "Warning," p. 499.

violence over a long period of time socializes audiences into the norms, attitudes, and values for violence contained in those portrayals."[34] The Task Force concluded that audiences that have learned violent behavior from the mass media are likely to perform violent acts in situations where they expect to be rewarded for such behavior, where they do not observe disapproval of the portrayed violence from a fellow viewer, or where they encounter a situation similar to that portrayed.

Another study suggests that the effects of television are more subtle. Timothy F. Hartnagel and his associates found that

> TV violence influences behavior in an indirect fashion, through its impact on learned values and attitudes or through a more general impression that is communicated about the nature of social reality. Values and attitudes or perceptions of the world may be substantially affected by television programming which may, in turn, influence behavior.[35]

This view suggests that young viewers may become calloused by overexposure to such programming and that, while they may not become violent themselves, they may more readily tolerate violence in others.

The influence of mass media, particularly television, in the reporting of protests, demonstrations, civil disorders, and other forms of potentially violent activity is another important issue. There are two questions here: Do the media distort the facts by stressing the violent aspects of news events; and does the presence of media reporters at such events tend to increase the possibility that violence will occur? Both charges have been made, and both appear likely in some instances. Distortion and provocation, however, are difficult qualities to measure, and the matter is far from settled. Gladys Engle Lang and Kurt Lang suggest that although the general practices of the media "both contribute to the appearance of increased frequency and accelerate the cycle of protest," the presence of television and other news media in specific situations of potential violence "probably acts more as a *deterrent of violence* at such events than as an instigator."[36] On the other hand, there is some fear that the extensive publicity given to "dramatic acts of deviant behavior," such as bomb scares, airplane hijackings, prison riots, and political assassinations, may be "contagious," inspiring large numbers of new attempts at similar behavior.[37] The rash of kidnappings, hijackings, and assassination attempts in recent years has been attributed in part to such media contagion.

It is an oversimplification, of course, to assume that any portrayal of violence will always tempt spectators to act out what they have just seen.[38] Both the context of the stimulus and the attitude of the viewer must also be considered. The wish to imitate what is seen on the TV or movie screen is likely to depend largely on how it is presented, although we still lack hard evidence as to what the relevant variables are. Similarly, the emotional

---

[34]*Mass Media and Violence: A Report to the National Commission on the Causes and Prevention of Violence* (Washington, D.C.: U.S. Government Printing Office, 1969), p. 367.

[35]Timothy F. Hartnagel, James J. Teevan, Jr., and Jennie M. McIntyre, "Television Violence and Violent Behavior," *Social Forces*, vol. 54, no. 2 (December 1975), 341-351.

[36]Gladys Engle Lang and Kurt Lang, "Some Pertinent Questions on Collective Violence and the News Media," *Journal of Social Issues* 28 (1972), 108-109.

[37]Brown, "Historical Patterns," p. 59.

[38]Lawrence Alloway, *Violent America: The Movies, 1946-1964* (New York: Museum of Modern Art, 1971), p. 66.

condition of individual viewers will predispose them to react to what they see in different ways. Scenes of a prison riot are likely to evoke quite distinct reactions from the high school dropout who feels oppressed and trapped by "the system," than from the ambitious and successful young executive.

In sum, although violence is certainly in part a consequence of social learning, we do not yet know enough about how people react to cultural symbols to say categorically that a violent culture breeds violence. The learning explanation assumes that people act more violently when they are involved in a culture that permits or encourages violence. It is perhaps just as plausible to reason, however, that where people are more violent, their cultural norms will reflect it. Thus, the causal relationship might more accurately be described as reciprocal.

The influence of media violence on young people has alarmed both parents and social scientists. Here the cruel and violent villain of an immensely popular film receives a hero's welcome from a crowd of school children.
UPI

Inter- and Intrapersonal Violence

Criminal Violence   Violent crime may not be the most common type of crime, but it is the most frightening. Those who return to a burglarized home often report a sense of revulsion at the thought of strangers' hands rifling through bureau drawers and handling prized personal possessions, the intrusion itself being seen as a defilement even beyond the sense of loss of property. But the defilement of one's own body, one's self, in a violent attack is a far more terrifying prospect; this, more than any other crime, threatens our lives and our personal integrity, and demonstrates that our destinies may not be in our own hands.

Statistically, however, violent crime is the least prevalent of all crimes. According to the Federal Bureau of Investigation's *Uniform Crime Reports (UCR)*, the violent crimes of murder, robbery, aggravated assault, and forcible rape make up less than 10 percent of all crimes reported; the remainder are crimes against property.[39] Further, nonviolent crimes are in general far more profitable than violent ones; the so-called white-collar crimes—tax evasion, price-fixing, embezzlement, swindling, fraud—involve billions of dollars annually. One particular corporate price-fixing conspiracy yielded more money each year it continued than all of the hundreds of thousands of burglaries, larcenies, and thefts in the nation during those same years.[40] (See Chapter 5.)

Crime statistics, as previously noted, must be interpreted with great caution. Because of changes in police practices and better recording procedures, many crimes that previously would have gone unrecorded are now reflected in official figures. Even allowing for this, it is still apparent that violent crime is increasing rapidly, although not as quickly as crime in general. (See Table 6-1.) If we consider the forms of violent crime, we shall see some interesting similarities and differences in the patterns of their occurrence.

Criminal Homicide.   Criminal homicide takes two forms. *Murder* can be defined as "the unlawful killing of a human being with malice aforethought." Malice aforethought requires a "guilty mind" but not necessarily premeditation and planning.[41] *Manslaughter* is unlawful homicide without

[39]*UCR*, p. 307.
[40]Ramsey Clark, *Crime in America* (New York: Simon & Schuster, 1970), p. 38.
[41]Marshall B. Clinard and Richard Quinney, *Criminal Behavior Systems: A Typology* (New York: Holt, Rinehart and Winston, 1967), p. 21.

Table 6-1
Index of Violent
Crime

	Violent Crimes	Homicide	Forcible Rape	Robbery	Aggravated Assault
Total Number	1,009,500	19,120	63,020	404,850	522,510
Rate (per 100,000 inhabitants)	466.6	8.8	29.1	187.1	241.5
Percent change since 1968	+56.4	+27.5	+83.0	+42.0	+67.9

Source: U.S. Department of Justice, *UCR*, October 18, 1978, p. 35.

malice aforethought. In practice, the distinction between manslaughter and murder is often very narrow. Someone may attack another person without intending to kill, but death may be the accidental outcome. Depending on circumstances, one case might be judged to be murder, another manslaughter. Often the deciding factor is the degree of provocation the victim offered the assailant.

Paradoxically, most murderers do not have criminal records. There are, of course, those who use actual or threatened violence in the form of both assault and homicide as tools in criminal careers, but these are exceptions; professional criminals, as a rule, try to keep violence to a "necessary" minimum, and in particular to avoid killing because of the "heat" it will bring on them from the law. Most murderers do not see themselves as real criminals and, until the murder, neither does society.[42] Murderers do not conform to any criminal stereotype, and murder is not the final step on a ladder of criminal behavior.

There are, however, certain social and geographical patterns. First, known murders occur most often in cities; in the United States, for example, homicide is more likely to take place in large cities—but not all that much more likely. The murder rate for large metropolitan areas is about 10 per 100,000 population, compared to 5 per 100,000 in smaller cities; the murder rate, however, in rural areas is a surprisingly high 8 per 100,000.[43] The incidence of murder is unevenly distributed throughout large cities; Donald T. Lunde points out: "Most city neighborhoods are just as safe as the suburbs."[44] There are also regional differences; for instance, murder is more likely to occur in the South, even though this is one of the more rural parts of the country. This seems to be due to Southern culture that tends to legitimatize personal violence and the use of weapons.

Most murderers are men, socialized to be more violent and to use guns for recreation or for military purposes; guns are the most common cause of fatal injuries. More than 70 percent of all murderers are under 35, the average age is close to 20. Most victims are young, too, generally between 20 and 30. Victims are also likely to be members of minorities: the rate of homicide victimization for blacks and other minorities is about nine times the total national rate. (In actual numbers, about half of all murder victims are members of minorities.) More than 90 percent of the time, killer and victim are of the same race, and, Lunde observes, "in the few instances where racial lines are crossed, it's more often whites murdering blacks than the reverse."

More significant than the demographic status of murderers and their victims is the relationship between them. Several studies have indicated that this relationship is generally close, often one of family or intimate friendship. Usually the precipitating event is a quarrel: a Philadelphia study found that approximately one-third of 588 murders resulted from general quarrels, while family and domestic altercations accounted for 14 percent, jealousy 12 percent, disagreements over money 11 percent, and robbery only 7 percent. In 59 percent of all homicides, the victims were close friends and relatives; in only one out of every eight murders was the victim a stranger.[45]

[42]Clinard and Quinney, *Criminal Behavior Systems*, p. 22.
[43]*UCR*, p. 36.
[44]Lunde, "Our Murder Boom," p. 38.
[45]Marvin Wolfgang, *Patterns in Criminal Homicide* (Philadelphia: University of Pennsylvania Press, 1958), p. 191.

Other studies have found that one-fourth of all murderers are close relatives of their victims, and half of these are husbands or wives killing their spouses. Lunde reports that

> More than 40 percent of murder victims are killed in residences. . . . More women die in their own bedrooms than anywhere else. One in every five murder victims is a woman who has been killed there by her spouse or lover. Husbands are most vulnerable in the kitchen; that's where wives are apt to pick up knives to finish family arguments.
>
> The other half of murders involving close relatives include parents killing children, children killing parents, or other close relatives killing each other. These victims usually die in the living room from gunshot wounds. Another six percent of murders [are] between more distant relatives.[46]

Even though almost 45 percent of homicides today are related to another crime (the rate was 10 percent twenty years ago), these killings, too, are usually unpremeditated—a thief surprised by a night watchman, a bank robber confronted by an armed guard, and so on. But most murders occur in the heat of the moment during a quarrel between two people who know each other well. Murderer and victim both may have been drinking, perhaps together, before the fatal event; half of all homicides are alcohol-related. (See Chapter 4.)

The mentally ill commit murder at the same rate as the general population, as Lunde points out, but multiple murderers, such as the "Son of Sam" are almost always psychotic, being either paranoids or sexual sadists.[47] These murderers may hear voices "commanding" them to kill, believe they are superhuman or "chosen" for a "special mission," and/or kill to avert imagined persecution by "others." Sadists may torture before killing and/or mutilate their victims afterward. Unlike most murderers, these psychotic killers are seldom personally acquainted with their victims, who are often representatives of a type or class—rich businessmen or "establishment" women. Assassins may sometimes act out of strictly political motivation and as part of a group conspiracy with roots in a more or less realistic appraisal of a national cause or political situation. In the United States, however, assassinations have rarely been in response to realistic situations but have been committed or attempted by emotionally disturbed or highly irrational individuals.

Assault and Robbery.   Murder and assault are similar. Assault is an attempt to injure or kill. Murder is therefore a form of aggravated assault, except that the victim dies. Often it is purely accidental whether an extreme case of assault becomes murder; it may depend on the weapon used or on the speed with which the injured receives medical attention.

Since murder and assault are similar kinds of crime, most observations concerning murder also apply to assault. A person who commits assault is, perhaps, somewhat more likely to have a criminal record than one who commits murder, but it is still uncommon.[48]

Robbery may be defined as taking another person's property by intimidation—a robbery in which violence was actually used is recorded as an

[46]Lunde, "Our Murder Boom," pp. 35-36.
[47]Lunde, "Our Murder Boom," p. 39.
[48]Clinard and Quinney, *Criminal Behavior Systems*, p. 22.

assault—and accounts for 40 percent of all reported crimes of violence. Unlike murder or assault, robbery usually occurs between strangers; it is also the one major violent-crime with a high interracial and interclass rate. For example, in one survey undertaken by the National Commission on the Causes and Prevention of Violence, it was found that blacks robbed whites in 45 percent of robberies surveyed. Robbery is obviously a criminal attempt to obtain money or other property, and whites are more likely than blacks to be perceived as affluent. It is also likely that blacks will be over-represented in official crime statistics. (See Chapters 5, 7, and 8.) Nevertheless, many robberies occur within the same race: the commission found that 38 percent of robberies involved black offenders and victims.[49] Blacks were also twice as likely to be robbed as whites.

Rape.   Until recently, forcible rape was defined as the act of forcing sexual intercourse upon a woman against her will. The laws for statutory rape, a form of this crime bearing lesser penalties, prohibit men from having sexual relations with females who are less than the legal age as established by state law. Although most arrests are for statutory rape, it is forcible rape that attracts the most attention.

Because of misconceptions about the nature of forcible rape and the sex-role stereotyping that has long flourished in American society, traditional methods of dealing with this crime have proven inadequate. Although the penalties for forcible rape are harsher than for other violent crimes, the conviction rate is negligible. Forcible rape represents only about one-sixteenth of all violent crimes.[50] Of the forcible rapes reported, only 11 percent result in conviction[51]—lower than for any other type of violent crime except robbery; moreover, an estimated 80 percent of all rapes are never reported.

There are many reasons why conviction and report rates are so low. It has been suggested that juries, inhibited by severe or mandatory penalties, may find the defendant not guilty of rape while convicting him of charges that incur less stringent punishments. In the past, forcible rape was an extremely difficult crime to prove. Evidence requirements—the presence of bruises or torn clothing, corroborating eyewitnesses, or medical proof of intercourse—were unrealistic. Relatively few rapes have witnesses; new findings conclude that many rapists experience sexual dysfunction—thus decreasing the likelihood that rape can be verified by the presence of semen in the victim. Difficulties such as these have discouraged victims from reporting the crime, and many women who did press charges often encountered further problems. Defending attorneys sought to discredit the plaintiff's testimony by suggesting that she had provoked or cooperated with her assailant. In some cases, the victim's previous sexual behavior was used to imply that she was promiscuous, and therefore not a reliable witness. Women who suffered the initial trauma of rape all too often found themselves the further victims of unresponsive and even hostile court proceedings. Many rape victims also fear the revenge of the rapist.

These conditions persisted as long as rape was viewed as an exclusively

[49]*Violent Crime: The Report of the National Commission on the Causes and Prevention of Violence* (New York: Braziller, 1969), p. 43.

[50]*UCR*, p. 37.

[51]*UCR*, p. 218; Frances S. Coles, "Social Scorn and the Rape Victim," *Human Behavior*, vol. 7, no. 5 (May, 1978), 70.

sexual crime. The perpetrator of the "crime of passion" was thought to be driven by overwhelming and uncontrollable desires. Rapists were believed to be different from others who committed violent crimes. This is only partially true; unlike murderers and those who commit assault, rapists often have a long history of criminal offenses. These offenses, however, tend to be for crimes other than rape.[52] This relatively high rate of criminal involvement suggests that the rapist's motivation may be violent, not sexual. A team of Massachusetts researchers found that rapists reported that feelings of anger, the need for power, and the wish to control their victim were factors in their act; sex itself does not seem to motivate the crime of forcible rape. Rather, sex becomes the means through which the assailant expresses his hostility.[53]

Defining forcible rape as a crime of violence rather than passion helps place it in the proper perspective and invalidates the idea that the rape victim can initiate the crime by arousing the desires of the rapist. It also suggests that women are not the only victims of this crime—men can also be raped, either by other men or by women. The old stereotypes of men as masters and women as objects of desire and domination worked to the disadvantage of both male and female rape victims. The 1970s women's movement and the changing attitudes of society have brought the public to a new understanding of this crime. Although rape laws still vary from state to state, the nation-wide trend is to revise existing statutes in favor of the victims. Corroboration of a witness is no longer necessary, and the plaintiff's sexual history is admissible only if it involves a previous contact with the accused; and—though women are still the most likely victims of rape—men are now entitled to press charges against their attackers. The rape victim today is treated with more consideration and sensitivity than before.[54] Round-the-clock medical and counseling services are available, and police units staffed with specially trained personnel (often women) help the victim overcome the trauma of the experience. As a result of these measures, more victims are willing to seek justice; between 1968 and 1978 the number of reported rapes rose nearly 99 percent.[55]

The media's attention to the subject of rape has also helped to reform public thinking. Researchers, law-enforcement groups, and women's organizations have addressed the problem of rape prevention. One study suggests that when a weapon is not used, the victim's best strategy is to subvert the assailant's desire for control by resisting the attack.[56] A show of fear will only feed the rapist's desire to dominate the victim.

The United States is the leader among modern, stable nations in the reported rate of murder, assault, robbery, and rape, although both crime and violence are increasing in Western Europe. The fear of violent crime has directly affected the lives of many citizens.

> In some urban neighborhoods, nearly one-third of the residents wish to move because of high rates of crime. . . . Bus drivers in many cities do not carry

[52]*Violent Crime*, p. 44; and James Selkin, "Rape," *Psychology Today* (January 1975), p. 72.

[53]"Impotent Rape: The Evidence Can Be Misleading," *Human Behavior*, vol. 7, no. 6 (June 1978).

[54]Frank R. Scarpitti and Ellen C. Scarpitti, "Victims of Rape," *Society*, vol. 14, no. 5 (July/August 1977), 29-32.

[55]*UCR*, p. 218.

[56]Selkin, "Rape," p. 71.

change, cab drivers in some areas are in scarce supply, and some merchants are closing their businesses.[57]

Clearly, unless this trend is reversed, the quality of American life may soon be dramatically changed. And if it is to be reversed, we need to do more than strengthen our police forces. Violent crime cannot be understood or controlled unless we examine the social conditions that breed it—a fact that the civil disturbances during the last decade forced on our attention.

Social Action and Domestic Violence

Although we are unlikely ever to achieve a society completely free from strife, there are several general steps that might help to reduce the level of internal violence. Most of these measures come under one of two headings.

Gun Control.   In recent years there has been an increasing demand for **Regulation** stricter supervision, probably by federal legislation, of the purchase and sale of firearms, particularly cheap handguns, or the "Saturday night specials," that are readily available in many areas. Opponents of gun-control legislation, represented primarily by the National Rifle Association (NRA), constitute one of the most powerful interest groups in the nation. They argue that it is the constitutional right of Americans to bear arms in order to protect themselves and their families from danger, and therefore gun control is unconstitutional. Nonetheless, it must be noted that the statistics on violence by means of guns are alarming. In 1977, 83 of the 93 local, state, and federal police officers slain on duty were killed by guns. About 63 percent of all homicides in the nation were committed through the use of firearms; 48 percent of homicides involved handguns. (See Figure 6-1.) More than 41 percent of all robberies and 23 percent of all cases of assault involved the use of a firearm.[58] Overall, more than 301,000 crimes involve the use of a gun. Although these figures represent a slight decrease since 1974, the United States still leads all other Western nations in the number of homicides by guns, both in absolute terms and in terms of the rate per 100,000 population. The United States also leads in the rates of both suicide by gun and accident by gun.

Opponents of gun control claim that the decision to commit murder has nothing to do with the possession of a gun; a killer can stab, strangle, poison, or batter a victim to death. Gun control would therefore make little difference. Although this argument sounds logical, it ignores the lethal potential of guns that are about five times more likely to kill than are knives, the next most commonly used murder weapon. One study found that for every 100 reported knife attacks, an average of 2.4 victims died, while for every 100 gun attacks, an average of 12.2 victims died.[59] And since, as we have noted, most murders are the spontaneous results of passion rather than planned in cold blood, it follows that the easy availability of guns is likely to increase the death rate in criminal assaults. In most cases, murders are the

[57]*Violent Crime*, p. 34.
[58]*UCR*, pp. 10, 19, 21, 290, 292.
[59]Christian Gillin and Frank Ochberg, "Firearms Control and Violence," in Daniels, Gilula, and Ochberg, *Violence and the Struggle for Existence*, pp. 249-250.

Figure 6-1
Homicide by Type of
Weapon Used
Note: Due to rounding,
figures do not total 100
percent.
Source: U.S. Department of
Justice, *Uniform Crime
Reports* (Washington, D.C.:
U.S. Government Printing
Office, October 18, 1978),
pp. 290, 292.

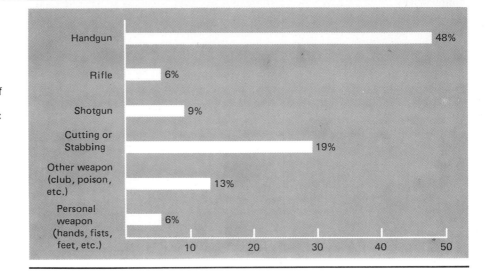

result of three factors: impulse, the lethal capacity of the weapon, and the availability of the weapon. Strict gun control would eliminate or at least reduce the last two.

Recent polls have shown that more than 72 percent of Americans would approve of gun control legislation, but their will is being frustrated by the NRA, whose members can churn out as many as 500,000 letters on request.[60] The vast damage caused by guns is directly traceable to the fact that at least 40 million handguns and from 90 million to 200 million guns of all types are owned by Americans, and that another 5.25 million are manufactured each year. Following the 1968 Federal Gun-Control Act, which restricted the import of inexpensive handguns, the level of imports dropped; however, because of a loophole permitting the assembly of guns in this country from imported parts, there was little, if any, effective lessening of gun availability. Proponents of gun control argue that a strong federal law applying uniformly to all parts of the country is needed, and cite countries such as Japan and England that have such regulations and have very low gun-murder rates.[61] In a study on the effects of gun control laws throughout the United States on the rate of violence, Douglas R. Murray found that such laws were ineffective. They did not lower rates of violence or even lower rates of gun ownership.[62] This suggests that gun control laws will have to be made much more stringent, and enforced much more rigidly—as they are abroad—in order to reduce the rate and severity of violent crime.

Media Violence.   Deemphasizing violence in the media is another suggested step toward reducing violence in society. We cannot prove

[60]U.S. Department of Justice, L.E.A.A., *Sourcebook of Criminal Justice Statistics, 1977.*
[61]"Big New Drive for Gun Controls," *U.S. News and World Report* (February 10, 1976), p. 25; and James D. Wright and Linda L. Marston, "The Ownership of the Means of Destruction: Weapons in the United States," *Social Problems* 23 (October 1975), p. 93.
[62]Douglas R. Murray, "Handguns, Gun Control Laws, and Firearm Violence," *Social Problems* 23 (October 1975), 81-93.

conclusively a causal relationship between the two, but "the weight of social science stands in opposition to the conclusion that mass media portrayals of violence have no effect upon individuals, groups, and society."[63] Richard E. Goranson concluded that the "burden of proof was not upon the critics to prove that violence was harmful, but upon the broadcasters to demonstrate that it was not."[64] In 1972, the United States Surgeon General's Study of Television and Social Behavior was concerned with how children are affected by televised violence, and commissioned more than forty new research projects to examine the issue. Although controversy surrounded the committee membership, its findings, and research (because of the large number of industry representatives on the panel), Surgeon General Jesse L. Steinfeld stated that

> it is clear to me that the causal relationship between televised violence and antisocial behavior is sufficient to warrant appropriate and immediate remedial action. The data on social phenomena such as television and violence and/or aggressive behavior will never be clear enough for all social scientists to agree on the formulation of a succinct statement of causality. But there comes a time when the data are sufficient to justify action. That time has come.[65]

Either by legislation or by voluntary regulation within the industry, it should be possible to reduce the incidence of killings and the reliance on shoot-and-slug formulas, especially in movie and television programming. The problem here is that the media have not, so far, been notably imaginative about devising ways to present more constructive approaches to social relations. One small step has been the "family hour," in which the first hour of prime time television—from 8 P.M. to 9 P.M.—is devoted to programming considered suitable for family viewing, with the more violent programs being shown at later hours, when they are accompanied by warnings that their content might be disturbing to some members of the audience. Clearly, much remains to be done to substantially reduce the level of violence on television and in the other media.

Social Reforms

Any attempt to deal with crime and violence without recognizing the basic social conditions underlying them is likely to fail. We have already noted the high correlation between crime and poverty and social deprivation. Former Attorney General Ramsey Clark has summed up the situation well:

> In every major city in the United States you will find that two-thirds of the arrests take place among about two percent of the population. Where is that area in every city? Well, it's in the same place where infant mortality is four times higher than in the city as a whole; where the death rate is 25 percent higher; where life expectancy is ten years shorter; where common communicable diseases with the potential of physical and mental damage are six and eight and ten times more frequent; where alcoholism and drug addiction are prevalent to a degree far transcending that of the rest of the city; where education is poorest—the oldest school buildings, the most crowded and turbulent schoolrooms, the fewest

[63]*Mass Media and Violence*, p. 375.
[64]Richard E. Goranson, in Bogart, "Warning," p. 495.
[65]Bogart, "Warning," p. 521.

certified teachers, the highest rate of dropouts, where the average formal schooling is four to six years less for the city as a whole.[66]

The official reaction to the rise in violence in this country has been basically to accompany reform with control, presumably on the theory that the needed reforms will inevitably take time, and that meanwhile violence must not be allowed to disrupt society entirely. The danger in this dualism is that too much emphasis may be placed on the immediate need for control, while reform is neglected. Skolnick has pointed out some of the resulting problems:

We may suggest as a general rule that a society which must contemplate massive expenditures for social control is one which, virtually by definition, has not grappled with the necessity of massive social reform. There are various possible levels of social reform, ranging from merely token and symbolic amelioration of fundamental problems to significant changes in the allocation of resources—including political power. We feel that contemporary efforts at reform remain largely at the first level. Precisely because society leaves untouched the basic problems, the cycle of hostility spirals: there is protest, violence, and increased commitment to social control. As we spiral in this direction, the "need" for massive social control outstrips the capacity of democratic institutions to maintain both social order and democratic values.[67]

[66]Clark, *Crime in America*, p. 11.
[67]Skolnick, *Politics of Protest*, p. 9.

In a drive to control crime on Chicago's rapid transit lines, police canine units have begun patrolling subway routes with a concentrated effort in high crime areas.

UPI

In effect, Skolnick is saying that society can afford to spend only so much; if it chooses to spend most of that amount on control, it will not be able to spend enough on reform. And the chronic shortage of funds that has hampered many reform programs would seem to bear him out.

Nonetheless, some things are being done. Community mental health centers in some states are providing substantial help to people in need. Drug and alcohol rehabilitation programs are multiplying; educational and job-training assistance are becoming more common, and more job areas are gradually being opened to minorities, though unemployment still remains much higher among minorities than among non-minorities (see Chapter 8); efforts are being made to improve police-community relations, and to recruit minority members into police forces; a variety of black groups have been formed in a number of cities—such as Chicago, Philadelphia, and New Orleans—to fight crime in inner city areas;[68] and some residential facilities have been created for teenagers with troubled home lives who might turn to violent behavior.

When people who cannot get funds for a day-care center that will free welfare mothers to work, or see the police force expanded and equipped with new weaponry, or watch while the government allocates huge sums for military expenditures, or see that corporate officials involved in multimillion dollar crimes are merely fined, or government officials convicted of subverting justice receive minimum sentences and are soon released, while a poor teenager who shoplifts a coat gets sentenced to 6 years' imprisonment, they may understandably feel that society has a warped sense of priorities. One of the most interesting recent developments is the political organization of poor people and other groups to press for a reordering of priorities. This may significantly affect what is done, and how it is done, to eliminate the causes of violence in our society in the coming decades.

Terrorism: Undeclared Warfare

Aside from its most obvious drawback—the loss of human life—war engenders a whole family of tragedies. It wastes both money and human energy; it destabilizes economies, impedes social progress, and disrupts millions of lives. By providing an overwhelming and violent alternative to social problems, it prevents nations from solving oppression, injustice, and poverty. Warfare, however, has always existed. As the weapons race has grown more sophisticated, and the means to annihilation more accessible, the prospects for total holocaust have paradoxically decreased. Nuclear war would ultimately defeat both "victor" and "vanquished" and, as this grim fact is absorbed by world leaders, nations are careful to preserve at least the illusion of peaceful relations. Major powers of the nuclear age prefer to wage their disputes in a lesser arena or by proxy—the cold war, the ground wars in Southeast Asia, and United States and Soviet support of opposing factions throughout the world are all examples of limited aggression.

Recent years, however, have seen a revival of an unhappy variation on the ancient theme of war. Terrorism has become one of the most dangerous threats to world order. In its effects, and sometimes in its causes, terrorism is

---

[68]Charlayne Hunter, "Blacks Organizing in Cities to Combat Crimes by Blacks," *New York Times* (February 22, 1976), p. 1.

comparable to the more traditional forms of war. It destabilizes governments, preys upon innocent victims, and taps vast monetary and human resources. Yet unlike war, which openly pits opponents against each other in a recognized trial of strength, terrorism is covert. It seeks to control the masses, by intimidating its victims through fear and coercion.

Although isolated random acts of terrorism have occured throughout history, modern terrorism began in the early nineteenth century, when it was used to promote various revolutionary causes throughout Europe.[69] Within the past decade, however, the incidence of terrorist attacks has risen alarmingly. The kidnapping of politicians and business leaders, bombings, hijackings, blackmail, and the taking of hostages are now common perils. Robert H. Kupperman, a noted authority on terrorism, estimated that between 1968 and 1978, more than 1,000 lives were lost as the direct result of terrorist acts.[70] This estimate does not attempt to assess the additional grief, suffering, and financial burdens inflicted on those unwillingly involved in such actions. In March 1977, the National Advisory Committee on Criminal Justice Standards and Goals published a special report examining the United States' vulnerability to terrorist attack. The report found that, although America has thus far been spared the violence evident in such countries as Italy and West Germany, it is not invulnerable. Because of the proliferation of densely populated urban and industrial areas, the strategic use of nuclear or biological weapons—both well within the technological means of many terrorists—could cripple the country and effectively blackmail the American government. The study warns that:

> The relative peace of recent months is a false calm, and we must see in the current social situation an accumulation of trouble for the future. There will surely come a time when once again socioeconomic conditions will generate violent reactions.[71]

Almost simultaneously with the report, early in 1977, a dozen Hanafi Muslims invaded three federal buildings in Washington and held 132 hostages for 38 hours. None of the hostages were involved in the Hanafi cause or with the cause of the Black Muslims, whom the Hanafi opposed.[72] Such incidents have prompted the development of hostage negotiating teams in almost all major American cities and inspired further research on the causes, casualties, and ultimate control of terrorist aggression.

Terrorism can be perpetrated inside as well as outside of the established system, and state terrorism is well known in this century. Adolph Hitler and Josef Stalin were prime practitioners of state terrorism, in which, power, fear, and legalized murder on an overwhelming scale are used to subjugate the masses by the millions. While the victim of illegitimate terrorism may hope to be rescued by government or police forces, the victim of state terrorism can have no such expectations. Instead, the extreme nature of state terrorism—the death camps of Auschwitz or the penal colonies in Siberia—have led many to argue that counterterrorism is a justifiable reaction to it.

[69]Louis Heren, "Curbing Terrorism," *Atlas World Press Review*, vol. 25, no. 1 (January 1978) pp. 31-33.
[70]"Terrorism: Why the U.S. Is Vulnerable," *U.S. News & World Report* (March 6, 1978), pp. 66-68.
[71]Quoted in *U.S. News & World Report* (March 14, 1977), p. 69.
[72]"The 38 Hours: Trial by Terror," *Time* (March 21, 1977), pp. 16-20.

In dealing with terrorism that exists outside the established order, it is necessary to make some distinctions. A 1977 study divided terrorism into two types: the terrorism of perpetrators affiliated with a recognized government and the terrorism of independent agents who are essentially autonomous. The report stated that while the first type of terrorism has remained stable, the second has shown a marked increase since 1967.[73] It is this second form of terrorism, labeled transnational terrorism, that has become more common.

More and more countries have been affected by transnational terrorism, and the number of perpetrator groups is rapidly expanding. Because of the underground nature of terrorist organizations, it is difficult to completely understand their methods of operation. Even the beliefs and specific goals of a terrorist group are often obscure, and their dogmas are frequently romanticized blends of older ideologies. Terrorist groups differ from one another in their adherence to various forms of separatism, nationalism, anarchism, Leninism, and Maoism. The one point that they do agree upon is the radical-Marxist theory on the necessity of armed revolution.[74] As one researcher puts it, terrorists are members of "disgruntled minorities who do not shrink from violence in their ambition to remake the world."[75] Yet terrorist groups are by no means isolated factions operating without benefit of financial or technological resources. Members of groups engage in bank robbery, forgery, kidnapping and ransom, and other illegal activities to bring in massive incomes. These incomes in turn finance complex and sophisticated strategies. Despite their ideological differences, there is reasonable evidence to suggest a high degree of mutual protection and cooperation among divergent terrorist groups. As Claire Sterling points out, groups are bound together by such mutual concerns as the transport of stolen arms, forgery and theft of documents, cadet training camps, and refuge for members wanted by the law; and these concerns tie them to a vast underground network that—due to its complex organization and strict secrecy—continues to flourish beyond the reach of national and international law.

The terrorist recruit is often well educated, young, of upper-middle or middle-class background. As individuals, terrorists wish to save the world, although their concept of salvation is tailored to their own inflexible beliefs. The terrorist believes that the purity of motives justifies whatever methods employed. In this detachment from reality, this fanaticism, and this total willingness to surrender life itself for the cause, the terrorist true believers bring about their own dehumanization—they see themselves as the catalyst, worthless in itself, through which social change can be wrought.[76]

In this process, not only is the perpetrator dehumanized, but the victim, who in the terrorist's mind is merely a pawn in the struggle for societal reform, is also stripped of his or her human rights and identity. The terrorist wishes to punish society for its wrongs, to intimidate it into accepting his or her demands. The terrorist preys upon both known and unknown victims, assured that—as representatives of an abhorrent society—the victim is responsible for society's wrongs and unworthy of compassion or remorse.

[73]Heren, "Curbing Terrorism," p. 31.
[74]Claire Sterling, "The Terrorist Network," *The Atlantic*, vol. 242, no. 5 (November 1978), 37-47.
[75]"International Terrorism," *America*, vol. 138, no. 17 (May 6, 1978), 356-357.
[76]Conrad V. Hassel, "Terror: The Crime of the Privileged—An Examination and Prognosis," *Terrorism*, vol. 1, no. 1 (1977), 128.

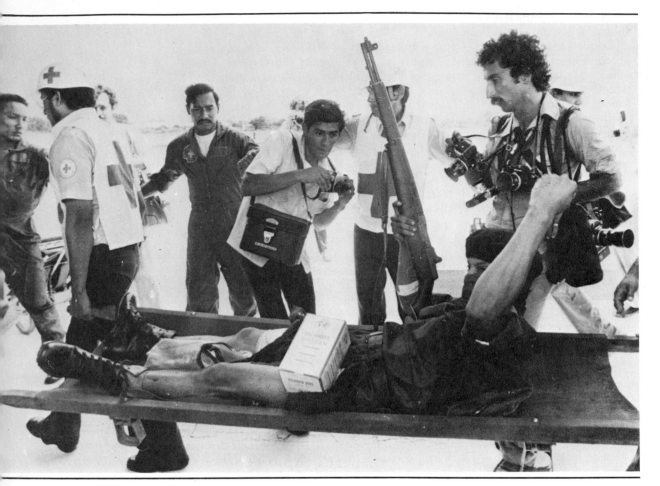

An injured terrorist raises a defiant fist. No truly democratic and free society can be completely defended from a well-organized terrorist movement.

UPI

Because any society is the combined achievement of thousands of individuals and many generations, the injustice of terrorist thinking is obvious. Terrorist victims are innocent people whose lives are subverted and destroyed by the fanatical intolerance of renegade groups.

Those who suffer from terrorists can be divided into two groups.[77] The first are random victims, people who find themselves in the wrong place at the wrong time. Bombings, hijackings, and the spontaneous seizing of hostages victimize those who are merely available. Other members of society are intimidated by the very casualness of this type of terror and—so the terrorist hopes—will pressure their government to meet the terrorist's demands. Anthony Cooper has written: "It is no accident that it is the lamb, rather than the tiger, that is chosen for this kind of ritual slaughter." The other category of victims includes individuals who are singled out because of their public

[77]H. H. Anthony Cooper, "The Terrorist and the Victim," *Victimology: An International Journal,* vol. 1, no. 2 (Summer 1978), 229-239.

prominence. These victims, too, become dehumanized symbols: all politicians shoulder the burden for whatever political injustices the terrorist perceives; all businesspeople are held personally responsible for commercial waste and greed. Perhaps the most tragic example of this way of thinking was the kidnapping and murder by a radical group of Palestinians, of the Israeli athletes during the 1972 Munich Olympic Games. More recent examples are the 1978 kidnapping and murder of former Italian Prime Minister Aldo Moro by the Italian Red Brigades, and the murder of West German industrialist Hans-Martin Schleyer by the Baader-Meinhof gang. In both of these instances, well-organized terrorist groups kidnapped carefully selected victims—men and women who were both symbolic and powerful—in hopes of winning concessions from the Italian and West German governments. When they failed in this objective, the "execution" of their hostages was carried out as threatened. Despite their belief that all victims are in some way culpable, terrorists also hope to capitalize on their victims' innocence in the eyes of the world.

Various measures have been recommended to cope with terrorist aggression. Some governments have rigidly rejected terrorist's demands in hopes of discouraging future attacks. The advisability of this posture, however, is questionable. The Italian government's policy that led to the murder of Aldo Moro should theoretically have inhibited further incidents. Yet terrorist aggression has continued to flourish in Italy.[78] H. H. Antony Cooper states that such "no negotiations" policies only assist in dehumanizing the victim. Inversely, an official show of compassion and humane concern may be a vital defense against terrorism. The National Advisory Committee report of 1977 proposed defensive measures (including legislation to provide for information-gathering activities and emergency privileges for state and federal authorities) and recommended their immediate implementation. Efforts to deter terrorism, according to Dr. Robert Kupperman, should concentrate on three areas: efficient crisis response and management, improved physical defenses (such as better security systems, well-trained police, and sophisticated hostage teams), and wider intelligence networks. Yet ultimately—and ironically—in an open and democratic society there is no certain defense against the terrorist menace.

Prospects

Our history has been violent, and studies of crime, civil disorders, and terrorism provide little indication that the development of effective means of reducing or controlling our violent inclinations is at hand. It is significant, however, that the vital nature and magnitude of the problem are now being recognized. Much further research is needed, particularly on the origins of violence, the development of peaceful means of settling disputes, and the encouragement of alternatives to violent behavior, such as negotiation and non-violent protest. Efforts should be made to reduce the frustrations caused by relative deprivation, and to provide more adequate mechanisms for the expression of social and political grievances. Also, societal condemnation of violent behavior should be uniform, and not based on a double standard

[78]"Coping with 'Terrorists'," *The Progressive*, vol. 42, no. 7 (July 1978), p. 11.

condoning some forms of violence while at the same time denouncing others.[79]

In the words of Irving L. Horowitz: "It is untrue that violence settles nothing. It would be closer to the mark to assert that violence has settled all historical issues so far, and most of them in the wrong way."[80] The most immediate consequence of violence is usually not change but further violence, and this escalation must be reversed if we are ever to live at peace with ourselves.

[79]Alan J. Rosenthal and Frederic W. Ilfeld, Jr., "Summary of Recommendation," in Daniels, Gilula, and Ochberg, *Violence and the Struggle for Existence*, pp. 392-394.

[80]Irving L. Horowitz, "The Struggle Is the Message," in *The Troubled Conscience*, ed. Irving L. Horowitz (Palo Alto, Calif.: James E. Freel And Associates, 1971), p. 35.

Summary

The incidence of violence in the United States has increased considerably over the past few decades, and concern over violence has become wide-spread. America has a history of violence, from the Revolutionary War, through the extermination of the Indians and the Civil War, to the costly conflicts in the twentieth century. Violence may be viewed as legitimate or illegitimate, depending on who uses it and the purpose for which it is used.

Among explanations for violence are (1) people are innately aggressive; (2) individual frustration leads to aggression; (3) the lack of development of internal controls leads to violence (*control theory*); (4) norms of a subcultural group with a low provocation threshold make violence acceptable (*subcultural theory*); and (5) external influences, such as media presentation of violence, inspire additional violence. It is likely that all of these factors are responsible to some extent, and equally likely that no one explanation will suffice for all instances.

Crimes of violence against a person are the most frightening of all crimes, although they are the least frequent of crimes. Homicides are somewhat more likely to be urban than non-urban crimes; most murderers are men, although the number and proportion of women killers are increasing. Murderers are likely to be related to or acquainted with their victims, and to be of the same race as their victims. Most murders are not premeditated, but take place during quarrels.

Murder and assault are similar crimes, and often it is a matter of chance whether a cause of assault becomes murder. Unlike murder and assault, robbery usually occurs between strangers. Although there is a high interracial component to robbery, blacks are twice as likely to be robbed as whites.

Rape is the least reported of violent crimes; women traditionally have been intimidated in various ways when they do report that they have been raped. Rapists are the least often convicted of all violent criminals, because traditional evidentiary requirements are unrealistic and penalties excessively harsh. Activism from the women's movement is encouraging women to resist the attacker and report rapes, and is stimulating legal changes in order to make conviction more likely.

The proliferation of firearms in this country has had a direct impact on the number of murders, since firearms are more likely to be used in the heat of a quarrel and are more likely than any other weapon to cause death. Thus the reduction of domestic violence would require the passage and stringent enforcement of gun control legislation. Reducing the level of violence in the media would also be desirable, since there is substantial evidence that media violence influences antisocial behavior. Finally, social reforms to correct the deprived conditions that breed violence are essential.

The threat of mass annihilation in a nuclear war seems, for the present, to have diminished. Yet the new surge of terrorism threatens the stability of governments as well as the rights and safety of individuals. Terrorism—intimidation through tactics of fear and coercion—preys upon victims who tend to be either randomly selected or chosen because they represent whatever the terrorist wishes to destroy. Terrorists suffer from confused and misguided impulses; they believe their goals justify any means, and in their fanaticism they sacrifice innocent lives for obscure and often purposeless objectives. Terrorism can be combatted, but special methods must be developed for this new form of aggression. These include tightening security and intelligence networks and training special forces in how to handle hostage situations.

Bibliography

Arendt, Hannah. *On Violence*. New York: Harcourt Brace Jovanovich, 1970.

Campbell, James S., Sahid, Joseph R., and Stang, David P. *Law and Order Reconsidered: Report on the Task Force of Law and Law Enforcement to the National Commission on the Causes and Prevention of Violence*. New York: Bantam, 1970.

Daniels, David N., Gilula, Marshall, and Ochberg, Frank, eds. *Violence and the Struggle for Existence*. Boston: Little, Brown, 1970.

Davies, James C. *When Men Revolt and Why.* New York: Free Press, 1971.

Fogelson, Robert M. *Violence as Protest: A Study of Riots and Ghettos*. Garden City, N.Y.: Doubleday, 1971.

Graham, Hugh D., and Gurr, Ted R., eds. *The History of Violence in America: A Report to the National Commission on the Causes and Prevention of Violence*. New York: Bantam, 1969.

Graham, Hugh D., et al. *Violence: The Crisis in American Confidence*. Baltimore: Johns Hopkins University Press, 1972.

Gurr, Ted R., *Why Men Rebel*. Princeton: Princeton University Press, 1970.

Gurr, Ted R., et al. *Anger, Violence and Politics: Theories and Research*. Englewood Cliffs, N.J.: Prentice-Hall, 1972.

Kennett, Lee, and LaVerne, James. *The Gun in America*. Westport, Conn.: Greenwood, 1975.

Lorenz, Konrad, *On Aggression*. New York: Bantam, 1967.

7

Affluence and
Poverty

Facts about Affluence and Poverty

- More than 20 percent of American families earn more than $25,000 a year.
- In a recent year, almost 250 people with annual incomes of over $200,000—including five people with annual incomes of over $1 million—paid no taxes.
- The wealthiest 1 percent in our society own 56.5 percent of all corporate stock.
- Almost 25 million people—11.6 percent of the nation's population—are below the government-defined poverty level.
- 31.3 percent of blacks and 22.4 percent of Hispanics are below the poverty line, compared with 8.9 percent of whites.
- Only about 1 percent of those on welfare are unemployed males.

At home and abroad, America is considered a wealthy nation. This image is fostered by the media, commercial advertising, and politicians who proudly proclaim that "this is the richest country in the world." As we contemplate our industrial output, agricultural abundance, and personal possessions—even in an inflationary period—we concur. And there is, indeed, objective evidence for this image: the median annual American family income of $18,264 and gross national product of $1,889 billion are the highest in the world.

Unfortunately, these figures distort the nature of American affluence, for in our society enormous wealth is concentrated in the hands of a relatively small number of people. Most Americans can either barely make ends meet or live in dire poverty. For example, 9.3 percent of America's 57 million families receive annual incomes *below* $5,000. (See Table 7-1.) Another 18 percent earn between $5,000 and $10,000 annually, and about 18.5 percent earn between $10,000 and $15,000. Only 22 percent of American families have yearly incomes of $25,000 or more.[1] This income distribution pattern has not changed significantly since the Depression,[2] when Franklin Roosevelt found "one-third of our nation ill-housed, ill-clad, ill-nourished."[3]

Equality is central to the ideology of American society; middle-class values and standards are the norm. But this semi-official image ignores both the handful of extremely rich Americans and the tens of millions who share only minimally in the national affluence. This chapter describes this income discrepancy in greater detail and indicates how the American economic structure contributes to it. Also suggested is how both gross inequality and poverty can be reduced.

[1]U.S. Bureau of the Census, "Consumer Income," *Current Population Reports*, Series P-60, no. 116 (Washington, D.C.: U.S. Government Printing Office, July 1978).

[2]Lester C. Thurow and Robert Lucas, "The American Distribution of Income: A Structural Problem," in *Social Problems and Public Policy: Inequality and Justice*, ed. Lee Rainwater (Chicago: Aldine, 1974), p. 77.

[3]Franklin D. Roosevelt's Second Inaugural Address.

Total Money Income	Families Number (thousands)	Percent Distribution
Total	57,215	100.0
Under $2,000	1,134	2.0
$2,000 to $2,999	920	1.6
$3,000 to $3,999	1,533	2.7
$4,000 to $4,999	1,756	3.1
$5,000 to $5,999	2,031	3.5
$6,000 to $6,999	2,116	3.7
$7,000 to $7,999	2,094	3.7
$8,000 to $8,999	2,117	3.7
$9,000 to $9,999	2,026	3.5
$10,000 to $10,999	2,132	3.7
$11,000 to $11,999	1,966	3.4
$12,000 to $12,999	2,313	4.0
$13,000 to $13,999	2,038	3.6
$14,000 to $14,999	2,103	3.7
$15,000 to $15,999	2,310	4.0
$16,000 to $16,999	2,053	3.6
$17,000 to $17,999	1,948	3.4
$18,000 to $19,999	3,855	6.7
$20,000 to $24,999	7,962	13.9
$25,000 to $49,999	11,326	19.8
$50,000 and over	1,482	2.6

Note: Median Income was $16,009.

Source: U.S. Bureau of the Census, "Consumer Income," *Current Population Reports,* Series P-60, no. 116 (Washington, D.C.: U.S. Government Printing Office, July, 1978), p. 2.

Table 7-1
Annual Income Distribution of American Families—1978

The Affluent Few

Those very few who, either through inheritance or personal effort, have acquired great fortunes are able to live in a manner hardly comprehensible to those of lesser means. Consider Ferdinand Lundberg's description of the residential pattern of the Rockefeller family:

> A prime example . . . is the Rockefeller estate, *Kykuit,* of 4,180 acres . . . . Such land in the region sells at $5 or $10 thousand per acre and higher . . . . The place has many scores of buildings, for the maintenance and the housing of a large staff, and includes a $1 million playhouse (at cost many years ago) that holds bowling alleys, tennis courts, swimming pool and squash court.
>
> The Rockefeller brothers also have New York City residences. John III and his wife share a large duplex apartment on the upper East Side and in 1950 built a house for guests near fashionable Beekman Place. Nelson and his family occupy a triplex penthouse in Millionaire's Row on Fifth Avenue facing Central Park. . . .

Nelson owns a large ranch in the highlands of Venezuela on which he sojourns at intervals. Laurance has a plantation in Hawaii and Winthrop has a palatial working plantation in Arkansas.

When Rockefeller I died the *New York Times* (May 24, 1937) said the single granite house had cost $2 million to build, while the estate took $500,000 a year at Depression prices to maintain. The entire affair required a staff then of 350. Standard equipment throughout are elevators, air conditioning and just about anything in the way of appurtenances, comforts and conveniences one cares to name. The domicile of no potentate is any better equipped.[4]

Today there are about 155 American families worth $100 million, and 66 worth between $100 and $500 million.[5] These are the super-rich, and they can afford to live super-luxuriously. One such family flies flowers daily to its Florida mansion from its New Jersey greenhouses. Another lives for part of the year in a 115-room mansion equipped with three secretaries, three chefs (one each for meat, pastries, and candy), and numerous servants who are on duty in three shifts around the clock.[6] A Christmas catalogue from a Houston department store typically offers the super-rich such gifts as ten private swimming lessons from Olympic champion Mark Spitz, at a cost of $115,000.[7] Olympic Towers, on New York's Fifth Avenue, has its own indoor block-long park, three-story waterfall, two floors of shops, a private wine cellar, and a health club, among other amenities. A nine-room duplex with wood-burning fireplace and circular staircase, with a private elevator and sauna, costs $650,000 and a monthly maintenance cost of $946. Somewhat more modest is the one-bedroom suite that sells for $122,000. Only 8 percent of the building's 230 apartments were financed; the remaining 92 percent were simply paid for in cash.[8]

Affluence of this kind is not necessarily wrong. Ease, pleasure, and beauty in life are indeed worthy and desirable goals. Throughout history they have been considered the hallmark of a civilized life. Affluence on this scale, however, is far from essential; the cost of only one of the items previously mentioned would have fed, clothed, housed, and educated several poor families for an entire year. It is when super-affluence exists alongside the real, not to mention the relative, deprivation suffered by a much larger group at the other end of the socioeconomic spectrum that it becomes excessive. More importantly, the wealth of the super-affluent gives them undue influence in American society, which perpetuates the already unfair status quo.

The Rich Get Richer . . .

The United States has a graduated income tax, ranging from zero percent for individuals making below about $3,300 annually to 70 percent for those making over $100,000 a year. This higher tax rate for upper income levels is justified largely for three reasons: the well-to-do get more out of the economic system, and can afford to pay more taxes; they have a greater investment in the economic system, and should pay more to maintain it; and, finally,

[4]Ferdinand Lundberg, *The Rich and the Super-Rich* (New York: Bantam, 1968), pp. 849-851.

[5]Arthur Lewis, "The New Rich of the Seventies," *Fortune* (September 1973), p. 170.

[6]Ruth West, "The Care and Feeding of the Very Rich," *McCall's* (August 1969), p. 56.

[7]"Mail Order Magi," *Time* (November 15, 1974), p. 99.

[8]Associated Press dispatch.

redistributing at least some income from the rich to the poor is fair and just in a democratic society. In practice, however, many of the rich avoid paying their fair share of taxes. The American economic system is their old and trusted friend; they are legally able to extract more from it than they put in.

Skillful use of the labyrinth of deliberately complicated and arcane provisions of the tax laws can entirely erase the nominally very high taxes owed by those with large incomes. A 1976 Internal Revenue Service (IRS) report, for example, found that there were many rich people who paid little or nothing to the government. Almost 250 people with annual incomes of over $200,000 paid no taxes at all. Included in this group were five people with annual incomes of over $1 million.[9] In fact, although the tax rate for the highest tax bracket is 70 percent, individuals in this bracket pay, on the average, only about 42 percent of their income in taxes.[10]

Tax evasion? Not at all—at least not so as to draw any unwelcome attention from the IRS. It is simply that United States tax laws favor the rich, so that a person in the upper income brackets has many quite legal ways to dodge paying taxes. Best known of these is the capital gains tax, in which profits from the sale of investments are taxed at only one-half their true value. But there are any number of loopholes—fast depreciation on buildings and machinery, deductible expenses on farms and citrus groves, tax-free interest on state and municipal bonds, and deductions for gifts to charitable institutions (which may often be family foundations). Moreover, the super-affluent can make tax-free investments that are not available to the less wealthy. The income from state bonds—often sold in denominations of $1 million—does not have to be reported on tax returns.

It is true that the middle and upper-middle classes take advantage, of the same loopholes whenever possible; but the benefit to the very rich is excessive. For example, a $100 deduction reduces by about $70 the taxes of someone in the highest tax bracket, but only by about $14 the taxes of someone in the lowest bracket. If we look at the country as a whole, these differences become even more apparent. In 1974, for instance, the wealthiest 1.2 percent of all taxpayers received nearly one-fourth of the $58 billion in deductions, credits, and other tax-reducing advantages taken by all taxpayers. Another study found that in one year the country's 6 million poorest families received only about $90 million in tax credits; about 24 times that amount— over $2 billion—went to the richest 3,000 families, the super-affluent making over $1 million annually.[11] The 1978 tax reforms did little to change this situation. Although individual taxpayers still receive the largest portion of the tax savings, the majority goes to operators of unincorporated businesses, professional and farm enterprises, and to investors. High level executives and self-employed people receive a sizable reduction on "personal-service income" and the tax on long-term capital gains has been reduced. The 1978 tax bill gave more than 25 percent of the overall reduction (over $20 billion) to the 1.4 percent of taxpayers who earn more than $50,000 a year,[12] the

[9]"Latest Figures Show 244 People with Incomes of $200,000 or More Paid No '74 U.S. Income Taxes," *New York Times*, May 6, 1976, p. 19.

[10]"How the Rich Escape Taxes," *U.S. News & World Report*, June 3, 1974, p. 49.

[11]Brookings Institution study, in Philip M. Stern, "Uncle Sam's Welfare Program—for the Rich," *New York Times Magazine*, April 16, 1972, p. 28 ff.

[12]S. M. Miller, "Can the Poor Solve America's Problem?" *Society*, vol. 15, no. 6 (September/October 1978), 7.

rationale being that this minority contributes a large share of the country's taxes. Although the graduated income tax is supposed to be a great equalizer, the special laws and provisions over the years have done little to achieve that equality.

. . . at the Expense of the Poor

The minimum income for which a federal income tax return must be filed was raised in 1978 to $3,300 (up from $2,930) for single persons, and $5,400 (up from $4,700) for married couples. Despite this measure, poor people still bear a sizable tax burden. Within the past twenty years, such levies as payroll and sales taxes have increased substantially. For example, in 1960, payroll taxes accounted for 16 percent of the total federal taxes; by 1976, the percentage had risen to 31. These levies are regressive, in that they disproportionately burden lower- and middle-income earners. For example, someone who earns $3,000 a year and who pays $60 sales tax is being taxed at an effective rate of 2 percent for purchases alone; the same $60 sales tax represents a tax rate of .06 percent to someone with a $100,000 income. Furthermore, the effects of inflation and unemployment fall hardest on the poorest families. As a consequence, upper-income people are actually paying proportionately less into the nation's coffers than they did 20 years ago, while lower- and middle-income people are now paying more.[13] To compound the inequality, the lower-bracket person's income since it is almost certainly entirely derived from wages, has *already* been subject to withholding taxes, while the wealthier person's income is at least partially tax-exempt, since in all

[13]Cambridge Institute Study of 1972, cited in John D. Rockefeller II, *The Second American Revolution* (New York: Harper & Row, 1973), p. 81.

This couple can enjoy carefree retirement living aboard a 46-foot houseboat. For people born into wealth or able to achieve it, conspicuous consumption is the normal way of life.
UPI

likelihood it is derived from a variety of sources, many of which are less highly taxed. As Upton and Lyons point out:

> The reality of the American capitalist system is that tax legislation, whatever its progressive intent or the country's need for revenue, is designed to protect and encourage private investment. Thus earned income (wages and salaries), which most families depend on, is subject to much higher effective tax rates than property income (dividends, interest, rent, etc.).[14]

At any time, available capital and assets are finite, and because some people have more, other people will, inevitably, have less. It has been estimated that if the nation's wealth were evenly distributed, every adult would have a net worth of about $25,000. In fact, the wealthiest 4.4 percent of the population have an average net worth of more than $200,000, while close to half the population have an average net worth of about $3,000.[15]

What are the sources of this great wealth? A recent study found that 1 percent of families and individuals with the largest incomes own 56.5 percent of all corporate stock. The richest one-half of one percent own 49.3 percent of all corporate stock. The richest 1 percent also owns 10 percent of all privately owned real estate, more than 52 percent of all federal, state, and local bonds, 8.5 percent of the nation's cash supply, and almost 81 percent of all trust assets (the income from which is largely untaxed). In contrast, the poorest 20 percent of Americans have about 5 percent of total national income and almost no assets.[16]

Again, it must be emphasized that these proportions have remained essentially unchanged for many years. Whatever measure or standard is used, the implications are the same: the rich own more, earn more, and use more—much, much more—and they have been doing so for a long time. We shall see that this is largely because the competition for resources unfairly and heavily favors the rich.

The Nature of Affluence

The Perpetuation of Wealth

Today wealth has largely accumulated in the hands of descendants of wealthy families. While there are still "self-made" *nouveaux riches,* opportunities for achieving wealth in this era of scarce resources are limited. The new fortunes are fewer, and smaller, than the "old money." It takes many years, plus favorable conditions, to amass a large fortune. For example, only a substantial amount of capital will produce an adequate return on investments. Barring a rare and unexpected windfall—building a very much better mousetrap, winning a state lottery, or writing a best seller—the lower- to middle-income person is not likely to have substantial sums available for really profitable investment. Thus those who make money generally start out by having—that is, inheriting—money. Large fortunes accumulated with the aid of the income tax laws (which, as we have seen, protect capital in preference to salaried income) can be given, more or less undiminished, to one's children, aided by loopholes in the inheritance tax laws.

[14]Letitia Upton and Nancy Lyons, *Basic Facts: Distribution of Personal Income and Wealth in the United States* (pamphlet) (Cambridge, Mass.: The Cambridge Institute, 1972), p. 4.

[15]"The Super-Rich," *The Progressive,* August 1974, p. 41.

[16]"Consumer Income," *Current Population Reports,* p. 775.

A quarter-century ago, it was noted that thirteen families, including the Du Ponts, Mellons, and Rockefellers, owned more than 8 percent of the stock of the 200 largest nonfinancial (i.e., nonbanking, non-insurance, non-investment) corporations. Half of the large share-holdings in those 200 corporations were directly owned; the rest were in the form of trusts, estates, and family holding companies. One family, or a few families, effectively controlled the voting stock in about 40 percent of these corporations, while these corporations in turn controlled half of the remaining corporations. Thus, only 30 percent of the 200 largest non-financial corporations were not controlled by a small group. A more recent study suggests that this situation remains substantially unchanged. Lundberg states that one person or a single family was in control of approximately 150 of the 500 biggest companies, while each of the other 350 companies was controlled by a small number of owners. Most of these controlling assets were either inherited or purchased with funds obtained through inheritance. As Lundberg notes: "The only dropouts from the upper strata of ownership have been produced by ending of a family line."[17]

Just how is an individual or family able to control a corporation, even by assuming a small portion of the stock? What is the impact of this type of control? Corporations are controlled by their investors—the stockholders—and those investors who own the largest blocks of stock have the most power in the corporation. Thus a person who owns only 5 percent of the corporation's stock but is the largest stockholder, in effect, controls the corporation; his or her real power is equal to the corporation's total value. A large corporation has a great influence on society—through the advertising it purchases in the media, through the institutions and foundations it supports, through its control of prices of the goods or services it offers, and so on. By and large, the power of those who control the major corporations is not directed toward redistributing wealth fairly but toward increasing their own income and their corporation's profits. (See Chapter 12.)

Inequality is perpetuated and exacerbated by several factors: inheritance taxes concentrate wealth in the hands of the already wealthy; investments, a major source of income, generally require large sums of money to be profitable; the tax laws favor both investors and the rich (who are generally the same people); and the rich, as major investors, control corporations through which they exert enormous political and economic power.

Who Are the Affluent?   According to a Census Bureau study, fewer than 0.4 percent of all households are worth $500,000 or more. Of these, only 39 percent have no inherited assets.[18] One out of every thousand Americans, or 218,000, are millionaires.[19] As previously mentioned, about 153 men and women are worth $100 million or more. Hunt (oil), Mellon (banking), Du Pont (chemicals), Rockefeller (oil and banking), and Ford (automobiles) are among the family names (and "occupations") appearing more than once in the $200-million-and-up section of the list.

[17]Lundberg, *The Rich and the Super-Rich*, pp. 211, 213, 292.

[18]Board of Governors, Federal Reserve System, *Survey of Financial Characteristics of Consumers* (Washington, D.C.: U.S. Government Printing Office, August 1966).

[19]*Statistical Abstract of the United States, 1978* (Washington, D.C.: U.S. Government Printing Office, 1978), p. 475.

This pattern of family-oriented financial control exists only with the collaboration of the laws on inheritance. Inheritance taxes somewhat diminish the wealth passed on by the merely well-to-do, but through such devices as trusts and family foundations, the wealthy can preserve and transmit large fortunes relatively intact. Thus the economic standing of children is likely to duplicate that of their parents; earning ability depends directly on inherited access to capital for investment.

The Wealthiest Class.   It has been said that the rich are the least studied and least understood class in the United States.[20] Most rich people prefer to remain inaccessible, and can afford various aides to handle their public responsibilities and guard their privacy. An extreme case was Howard Hughes, a billionaire who spent millions on lawyers, private detectives, and guards in order to maintain total privacy.

The wealthy are also most likely to marry others of the same class. Such intermarriage occurs naturally, since they socialize together in exclusive neighborhoods and private clubs. As children, they meet their peers in private boarding schools, often in New England. As adults, they share social and business connections and similar religious background—usually Protestant.[21] Jews and Catholics are less likely to be accepted in the schools, clubs, neighborhoods, and board rooms of the wealthiest people. For example, Jews comprise about 3 percent of the population in the United States and 8 percent of its college-educated population, but less than .5 percent of the total executive personnel in leading American industrial companies.[22]

Corporation Executives.   In 1978, each of the three top executives at Ford received more than $1,000,000 in salary and bonuses. Their weekly salary alone was greater than the annual salary of over 70 percent of our population. Other top executives also receive more than adequate renumerations, though not only in outright wages. Bonuses, director's fees, and deferred compensation raised the average annual earnings of the nation's thirty top corporate officers to more than $500,000.[23]

Besides very generous salaries, corporation executives often receive numerous perquisities or fringe benefits—profit-sharing plans and stock options, expense account dining and travel, hotels or the use of an apartment maintained by the company, taxis or transportation in a company car or airplane, life insurance, medical plans, and much more. Most of these benefits are designed to provide additional, tax-exempt or tax-reduced compensation for key executives. The expense accounts even of lower-echelon executives can easily add the equivalent of several hundred dollars a month, in lunches, cocktails, dinners, and taxis—tax-free to the executives as well as the corporations. Over the years, only negligible changes have been made in the tax laws governing expense accounts; these chiefly require more thorough documentation of expenses. Though it may be inconvenient to jot down every tip and taxi fare, the benefits are still clearly worth it as was revealed by the outcry when President Jimmy Carter vainly proposed to curtail them in 1978.

[20]"Secrets of the Very Rich," *Newsweek,* October 7, 1974, p. 78.
[21]E. Digby Baltzell, *The Protestant Establishment* (New York: Random House, 1964).
[22]Lundberg, *The Rich and the Super-Rich,* p. 363.
[23]"Annual Survey of Executive Compensation: The Year Stock Options Came Back," *Business Week* (May 10, 1976), p. 117.

The Significance of Affluence and Poverty

The affluent live longer and better, can afford the best medical care in the world, the finest education, the very best materials and workmanship in all their possessions. Less publicly, by purchasing the usually unacknowledged services of politicians, police officers, and other public officials to forward or defend their interests, they can buy social preference and influence government policy. This capacity for both conspicuous and inconspicuous consumption gives the extremely wealthy a potential power grossly out of proportion to their numbers in American society.

For the poor the situation is reversed. Although America's poor seldom die of starvation and they generally have more than do the hopelessly poor of the third world, they lead lives of serious deprivation by comparison not only with the wealthy, but with generally accepted middle-class standards. Poverty, as Ben Bagdikian has pointed out,

> is measured by the standards of a man's own community. If most of America is well-fed, the man who can't find three meals a day for his family is poor. If most of America has modern weather-proof housing, the man whose home is leaky and has no piped water is poor. If most of America has enough medical care to stay alive until age seventy, the man who can't afford to live beyond age fifty-five is poor.[24]

This relative deprivation profoundly affects the style and quality of the lives of the poor. It extends beyond mere distribution of income, and includes inequality in education, health care, police protection, job opportunity, legal justice, housing, and many other areas. The poor are more frequently subject to mental illness than are other Americans. They require more medical treatment and have longer and more serious illnesses. Their children are more likely to die than are those of the more affluent, and their life expectancy is below the national average. They are more likely to become criminals or juvenile delinquents. Also, the poor contribute more than their share of illegitimacy, alcoholism, divorce, and violence to American society. (See Chapters 2, 4, and 5.)

Not only do the poor have less money, but their money buys less. The poor must often purchase necessities as soon as they have cash—for example, with the arrival of their welfare checks; they cannot "shop around" for sales or bargains and are often victimized by shopkeepers who raise their prices on the day welfare checks are delivered. They seldom have enough money at one time to save by buying in bulk. When they buy on credit, the poor get higher interest rates because they must take longer to pay and are considered poor credit risks. Inflationary price rises affect the poor first, and more severely. The cost of essential consumer goods, ranging from rice and sugar to toilet paper and soap, rises almost monthly, but the wages of the lowest paid or marginally employed persons, and various government income assistance stipends, rise slowly if at all.

Furthermore, the poor cannot begin to approach the level of consumption portrayed as adequate by business and advertising. The harmful effects of

---

[24]Ben Bagdikian, *In the Midst of Plenty* (New York: New American Library, 1964), p. 8.

affluence-oriented advertising on the poor have been described by Herman Miller:

> Far from being a symptom of affluence, the ownership of the automobile or the television set may be a cause of poverty because it is purchased in lieu of a good diet, medical care, education, or other goods that would yield a much greater return in terms of increasing productivity.[25]

These inequalities reflect the ambivalent American attitude toward poverty: "On the one hand, we believe achievement is related primarily to self-reliance and self-help; on the other hand, we have been forced to concede that failure cannot always be laid at the door of the individual."[26] Those who, for one reason or another, must turn to public assitance are often pictured as lazy, shiftless, or dishonest. Their private lives are scrutinized and the procession of social workers and welfare investigators through their homes denies them their basic right of privacy. The poor who are on welfare cannot spend the money they receive as they see fit, but are treated "like children who have to account to parents for the wise use of their pocket money . . . . The very granting of relief, the very assignment of the person to the category of the poor, is forthcoming only at the price of a degradation of the person so assigned."[27]

The problems of the poor are further compounded by the attitudes of those whose economic position is not much better than their own. Recent statistics indicate that an income of about $15,000 is necessary for a decent living standard for a family of four. Almost half the families in America, including many white-collar as well as blue-collar workers, have incomes below this level, although above the level of poverty. This group has been the source of the greatest opposition to social welfare programs for the poor. Faced with an increasing tax burden, the rising cost of living, and a feeling that they have been overlooked by a government preoccupied with the less fortunate, people of the lower-middle class tend to view the poor in very negative terms.[28]

It is said that "money talks," and in America the voice of the rich is, if not always loud and clear, usually quite persuasive. Despite their numbers, the poor have remained largely silent, their lives constricted by deprivation. The questions of how the poor are viewed by the more affluent, how they look at themselves, and how they might escape their predicament touch on the fundamental nature and purpose of the American system.

The Nature of Poverty

Poverty is a deceptively simple term to define. For most people, poverty means not having enough money to buy things considered necessary and desirable. Various more formal definitions, however, have been offered. John

---

[25]Herman Miller, "The Dimensions of Poverty," in *Poverty as a Public Issue*, ed. Ben B. Seligman (New York: Free Press, 1965), p. 27.

[26]Paul Jacobs, "America's Schizophrenic View of the Poor," in *The State of the Nation*, ed. David Boroff (Englewood Cliffs, N.J.: Prentice-Hall, 1965).

[27]Lewis A. Coser, "The Sociology of Poverty," *Social Problems* 13 (Fall 1965), 145, 146.

[28]Robert E. Lane, *Ideology: Why the American Common Man Believes What He Does* (Glencoe, Ill.: Free Press, 1962).

Kenneth Galbraith stresses the sense of degradation felt by the poor, and concludes that "people are poverty stricken when their income, even if adequate for survival, falls markedly behind that of the community."[29] Another study regards "minimum levels not only of income, assets, and basic services, but also of self-respect and opportunities for social mobility and participation in many forms of decision-making"[30] as important. Poverty may mean a condition of near starvation, bare subsistence (the minimum necessary to maintain life), or it may mean any standard of living measurably beneath the national average. To deal more effectively with poverty as a social problem, a generally agreed-upon, scientifically based, and more specific definition is needed.

Many experts have tried to determine a minimum income level, or poverty line, below which a family or individual could be officially termed poor. President Johnson's Council of Economic Advisers considered only cash income in its evaluations of what determines poverty. Others, such as the Bureau of the Census, excluded capital gains but included all other money income.

S.M. Miller *et al.* noted that these formulas entirely ignore several important areas, including capital gains.[31] Among them are non-income compensation or fringe benefits: free lunches, stock options, company-financed vacations, medical services, cars, subsidized education, and deferred compensation plans. Many more of these kinds of benefits are available to those at higher money-income levels, which tends to increase the contrast between the effective incomes of some groups of workers and the poor.

Unfortunately, to consider all these factors would require figures that are unavailable, and therefore monetary income is used to measure poverty. There are two basic approaches: the fixed income line and the relative income line.

The Fixed Income Approach

Earlier attempts to establish a dividing line between poverty and non-poverty were usually couched in terms of a specific cash income. Leon Keyserling, in 1962, for example, suggested a level of $4,000 for a family of four, which at that time qualified 23 percent of the population as poor. In addition, he regarded those with an income of between $4,000 and $6,000 as "deprived." On this basis, in the early 1960s, the poor and the deprived together constituted 46 percent of the population.[32]

Oscar Ornati suggested distinguishing among various degrees of poverty: minimum subsistence, minimum adequacy, and minimum comfort and assigned income levels for each category.[33] A similar attempt was made by Herman Miller, who suggested that local welfare standards be used, so that poverty would be relative to the specific expectations.[34]

[29]John Kenneth Galbraith, *The Affluent Society* (Boston: Houghton Mifflin, 1958).

[30]S. M. Miller, Martin Rein, Pamela Roby, and Bertram M. Gross, "Poverty, Inequality, and Conflict," *Annals of the American Academy of Political and Social Science* (September 1967), 18-52.

[31]Miller, *et al.*, "Poverty, Inequality, and Conflict," pp. 52-118.

[32]Leon Keyserling, *et al.*, *Poverty and Deprivation in the United States*, Conference on Economic Progress (Washington, D.C.: U.S. Government Printing Office, 1962), pp. 19ff.

[33]Oscar Ornati, *Poverty Amid Affluence* (New York: Twentieth Century Fund, 1966), p. 13.

[34]Herman P. Miller, *Rich Man, Poor Man* (New York: Crowell, 1964), p. 81.

Because of the subjective manner in which poverty levels were being formulated, Mollie Orshansky of the Social Security Administration attempted to develop a more rigorous standard. She pointed out that the only acceptable measure of adequacy for the essentials of living is food. Standard criteria for acceptable nutrition have been established by the National Research Council, and the Department of Agriculture regularly prepares cost estimates on average food prices to achieve this nutritional minimum. Concluding that an average family spends one-third of its total income on food, Orshansky multiplied the food budget by 3 to arrive at a poverty income level. According to this standard, 34 million persons, or between 15 and 20 percent of the population, did not earn enough to pay for simple nutritional needs.[35]

With 1963 as the base year, annual adjustments were made to take into consideration the cost of the items in the economy food budget. Because of growing differences between the rise in cost of the economy food budget and the greater rise of the overall cost of living, in 1969 the Social Security Administration definiton was amended to reflect changes in the Consumer Price Index (CPI). Thus, in 1978 the official poverty line, adjusted to reflect inflation and based on the CPI, was $6,200 for a nonfarm family of four. (Farm families are assigned a lower figure because it is assumed they supply some of their own food.) According to Bureau of Census figures for that year, 25 million people or 11.5 percent of the nation's population were poor.[36]

The Relative Income Approach

A prime defect of the fixed income approach is that it ignores the phenomenon of relative poverty, the comparative deprivation of one category of people when measured against another. Victor Fuchs therefore proposed that any family be classified as poor if its income were less than half of the median family income.[37] The poverty line in 1974, by this definition, was $6,420, which meant that about 20 percent of the population would be considered poor.

Contrary to the Orshansky formula or any arbitrary income standard, the use of such a relative standard implied that poverty could not be eliminated as long as income distribution remained unequal. And, in fact, the number of poor in America has tended to remain stable when measured by the Fuchs formula, while it has decreased measurably by the absolute standard of fixed income.

Fuchs recognized the shortcomings of his proposal. He admitted that using one-half rather another fraction of median income as the measure of poverty was somewhat arbitrary. However, he contended that this liability was compensated for by the fact that his standard was politically neutral and not subject to manipulation by special interest groups. Further, he believed that it could keep pace with changing contemporary standards, whereas fixed minimum budgets are soon out of date; and that it constituted a first step toward a national policy with regard to income distribution.

[35]Mollie Orshansky, "Consumption, Work and Poverty," in Seligman, *Poverty as a Public Issue*, p. 62.

[36]"Consumer Income." *Current Population Reports*, p. 1.

[37]Victor Fuchs, "Toward a Theory of Poverty," Task Force on Economic Growth and Opportunity, *The Concept of Poverty* (Washington, D.C.: U.S. Chamber of Commerce, 1956).

No universally accepted definition of poverty has yet been formulated. Interested groups have utilized the most convenient or appropriate formula, usually either the "official" fixed income definition or one of the other types discussed.

Who Are the Poor?

Poverty and Family Structure
At present, over 36 percent of all poor families are headed by women. This segment of the poor is of special concern since it is growing rapidly and because children in these families are continually exposed to the circumstances of poverty.

1.   Among poor white families, the proportion of female-headed families increased from 37 to 48 percent between 1973 and 1978.

2.   Among poor black families, the proportion of female-headed families increased from 33 to 56 percent during the same period.

3.   Thirty-seven percent of all poor children live in female-headed households.

4.   Forty-two percent of female-headed households live in poverty, compared to only 20 percent of households headed by males.[38]

Without aid from an income maintenance program, additional millions of Americans would be poor. Public transfers of funds through social programs in 1974 alone lifted 5.3 million households—roughly one-third of the nation's poor—above the poverty line. In 1976, social insurance and welfare programs increased the income of the poorest 20 percent of the population by $50 billion and lifted 9 million—nearly half of the pre-transfer poor—out of poverty.[39] These figures appear optimistic, but millions of Americans stay mired in poverty, and many observers argue that it is the fault of the welfare system. Current laws in many states provide more aid to female-headed households than to those headed by males, even though the incomes of both families are the same. Food stamps are available to all low-income families, but Aid to Familes with Dependent Children (AFDC) is a program that primarily benefits female-headed families. Medicaid excludes male-headed families altogether.[40] Much of the inequality of the system is due to the severe restrictions placed on female heads of families with regard to employment, primarily because of the need to care for the children. Child care is either unavailable or too expensive, and typically the jobs that are available pay too little to make the effort worthwhile. Consequently, over 60 percent of female heads of households do not even seek employment.[41] Moreover, Cox notes that fewer "than 10 percent of all female family heads, and only about 25

[38]*Statistical Abstract of the United States, 1978*, p. 764.
[39]See poverty status of families under "Alternative Definitions of Income", Background Paper no. 17 (Washington, D.C., Congressional Budget Office, 1977), p. 24.
[40]Irwin Garfinkel, "What's Wrong with Welfare?" *Social Work* (May 1978), pp. 185-186.
[41]*Manpower Report of the President* (Washington, D.C.: U.S. Government Printing Office, 1975).

percent of those (women) who are employed at all, hold a full-time, year-round job."[42]

Some women require public assistance until the time their children are old enough to attend school. Others, lacking skills or education, are forced to depend on welfare as a way of life. Although a large number of welfare mothers would like to work, the lack of facilities for job training and child care confronts them with a double obstacle.

There are some 10 million children living in poverty, about 16 percent of all children in America. The contrast between these children of poverty and other youth has been pointed out by Ben B. Seligman:

> Little progress has been made in more than three decades—and this is a long time. Caloric and nutritive deficiencies in their diet are serious enough to make poor children doze off in school, look fatigued, or suck their thumbs; it is difficult to pay attention when one is hungry. Poor children receive . . . less medical attention than those from more prosperous families; they are hospitalized less often and stay longer when they are admitted; and most poor children never get to see a dentist. And it is clear that poor children are much less likely to receive psychiatric attention for emotional disturbances than those from upper-income groups. The consequence is a tendency to equate emotional upset with a lack of intelligence, and this works to weaken the educational opportunities of poor kids.[43]

Poverty and Minorities

It should be noted that while whites are the largest group among welfare families, blacks and other racial minorities are proportionately overrepresented. For example, 31.3 percent of the black population and 22.4 percent of the Hispanic population have incomes below the established poverty level, compared with only about 8.9 percent of the white population.[44] Furthermore, according to one study, black families own less than 1 percent of the equity in American farms and business enterprises.[45]

Overall, the median income of whites is $17,285, while that of blacks is $10,174. Only 17 percent of all black family heads, and a little over 40 percent of all employed blacks, work at full-time, year-round jobs. Several factors are considered responsible for the lower earning power of blacks and other minority workers. They are less likely to be well educated; for example, the high school dropout rate for blacks aged 14 to 24 is about 16.5 percent, as opposed to 11 percent for whites. Among blacks over age 25, only 2 percent have attended college, and 72 percent have not graduated from high school.[46] Racial discrimination still closes employment opportunities to minorities. Even among college students, blacks earn only 80 percent as much as whites; and blacks and whites do not receive equal pay for similar work requiring the same experience and education. The higher percentage of female-headed families among blacks is another factor, which we have already considered.

[42]Steven R. Cox, "Why Eradicating Urban Poverty Requires a Long-Term Multi-Program War," *American Journal of Economics and Sociology* 34 (1975), 249-265.

[43]Ben B. Seligman, *Permanent Poverty* (Chicago: Quadrangle, 1968), p. 88.

[44]*Statistical Abstract of the United States, 1978*, p. 472.

[45]Henry S. Terrel, "The Wealth Accumulation of White and Black Families," *Proceedings of the American Economic Association*, May 1971.

[46]*Statistical Abstract of the United States, 1978*, p. 143.

Figure 7-1
Households Living in Units
Lacking Some or All
Plumbing Facilities, by
Race and Income

Source: U.S. Department of
Commerce, Bureau of the
Census, *Social Indicators
1976* (Washington: D.C.: U.S.
Government Printing Office,
1977), p. 82.

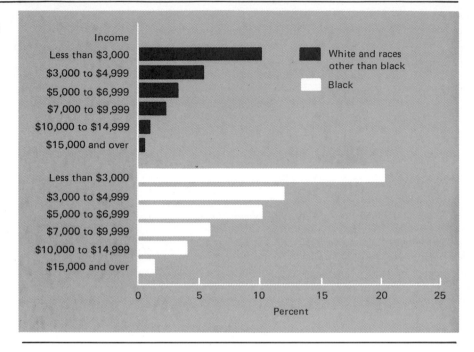

The discrimination to which blacks, Chicanos, Puerto Ricans, and other minorities are subject in matters of housing, education, and health care both exacerbates the effects and increases the likelihood of lower income. In housing, minority members are often forced to choose from a smaller supply, pay higher rents, and live in dilapidated or deteriorating dwellings. (See Figure 7-1.) In education, the quality of predominantly minority schools is often inferior to that of predominantly white schools. Concerning health care:

> There may be public facilities for poor Negroes in the cities, but they serve to humiliate rather than heal . . . . Clinics may be downtown, in neighborhoods inaccessible to a poor mother. If she is working . . . a trip means lost wages. There are long embarassing waiting periods to see several clinic bureaucrats before she gets to see the doctor, who most likely has never looked at her before nor will see her after that visit. The medical records are likely to have been mislaid, without which no diagnosis will be made or treatment prescribed. The poor are easily discouraged and then labeled as "careless" about their health or unwilling to "cooperate."[47]

In these and other areas, the disparity between black and white opportunity and treatment is both evident and disturbing. (See Chapter 8 for a more comprehensive discussion of these problems.)

**Poverty and
Geography**

Although urban poverty is probably best known today, almost half of all poor people live in rural or suburban areas, despite the fact that only 29 percent of the total American population live in rural areas. Rural poverty is not as

---

[47]Seligman, *Permanent Poverty*, pp. 48-49.

visible as urban poverty. Separated from the mainstream of urban life, it has remained largely hidden on farms, on reservations, in open country, and in small towns and villages. Unemployment in rural areas is far above the national average, particularly in Appalachia, the Ozarks, and certain Great Lakes regions. With jobs scarce and most work seasonal, the technological revolution in agriculture and other occupations has left poorly educated, unskilled rural workers without means of support.

The majority of the rural poor are white, but a high percentage of Southern blacks, Indians, and Mexican-Americans are poor as well. The general situation has been described by the President's Commission on Rural Poverty:

> Hunger, even among children, does exist among the rural poor, as a group of physicians discovered recently in a visit to the rural South. They found Negro children not getting enough food to sustain life, and so disease-ridden as to be beyond cure. Malnutrition is even more widespread. The evidence appears in bad diets and in diseases which often are a product of bad diets.
>
> Disease and premature death are startlingly high among the rural poor. Infant mortality, for instance, is far higher among rural poor than among the least privileged group in urban areas. Chronic diseases also are common among both young and old. And medical and dental care is conspicuously absent.[48]

Further, the commission found the quality of education to be so inferior that 3 million rural adults are classified as illiterate. It also found one in every thirteen rural houses unfit for habitation.

[48]President's Advisory Commission on Rural Poverty, "The People Left Behind," *Employment Service Review* (April 1968), pp. 17-19.

The rural poor are the migrant workers who, following the harvest, live in tar-paper shacks, with few possessions and less hope. They are the Indians on reservations, leading lives of destitution and regimentation, their decisions made for them by faraway bureaucrats, their children sent to federal boarding schools. They are the out-of-work coal miners. They are the small farmers and farm workers who cannot compete with modern, automated production techniques. Attempting to escape poverty, many of the rural poor migrate to urban areas, where they discover that the problems of the countryside are magnified in the cities, and that their shacks have been replaced by tenements.

In the cities, the lack of money is aggravated by higher living costs, overcrowded and inadequate housing, bad nutrition, insufficient medical care, unsanitary health conditions, and the other major problems that beset both the recently arrived and the entrenched urban poor. The hoped-for jobs are unobtainable since the demand for unskilled labor has evaporated in the wake of expanding technology. As more and more businesses move to the suburbs, transportation to work becomes either unavailable or too expensive for the poor. Frequently, rural immigrants swell the urban welfare rolls. (See Chapter 14.)

Poverty also varies according to region. In the United States, the greatest geographical concentration of the poor is in the South; about 41 percent of all poor families live in the Southern states.[49] Because the South is the most rural area of the country, it possesses the most prominent rural problems—low educational achievement, seasonal employment, low salaries, and few opportunities for unskilled workers—and these largely explain the region's high percentage of poor people.

As these factors indicate, some people appear to be more vulnerable to poverty than others. As Michael Harrington puts it, the poor made the simple mistake of

> being born to the wrong parents, in the wrong section of the country, in the wrong industry, or in the wrong racial or ethnic group. Once that mistake has been made, they could have been paragons of will and morality, but most of them would never even have had a chance to get out of the other America.[50]

Concomitants of Poverty

"Poverty," said George Bernard Shaw, "does not produce unhappiness; it produces degradation." Most Americans take for granted a decent standard of living—especially good health care, decent education and housing, and fair treatment under the law. We will examine the inequalities of treatment accorded to the poor in each of these areas, and the resulting degradation in the quality of their lives.

[49]U.S. Bureau of the Census, "Characteristics of the Low-Income Population," *Current Population Reports,* Series P-60, no. 115 (Washington, D.C.: U.S. Government Printing Office, 1976), p. 5.

[50]Michael Harrington, *The Other America: Poverty in the United States* (Baltimore: Penguin, 1963), p. 21.

Compared with the rest of us, the poor are less healthy by almost every standard (see Figure 7-2). For example, mortality rates for poor infants are almost double those of the affluent, and poor women are four times as likely to die in childbirth.[51] They are also more than five times as likely to give birth to

Health Care

[51]Robert L. Eichhorn and Edward G. Ludwig, "Poverty and Health," in *Poverty in the Affluent Society*, ed. Hanna H. Meissner (New York: Harper & Row, 1973), p. 173.

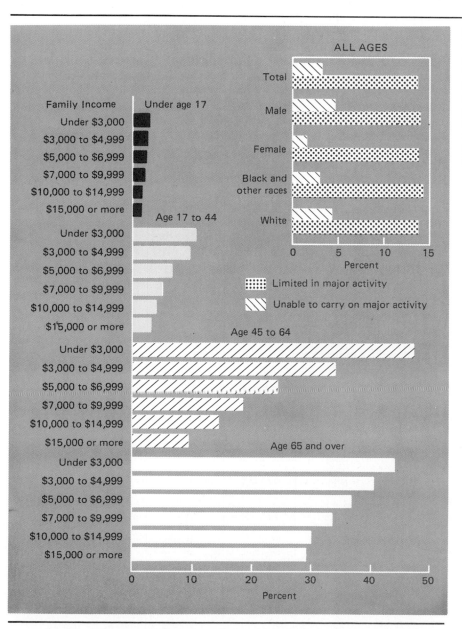

Figure 7-2
Persons Limited in Major Activity Due to Chronic Conditions, by Selected Characteristics

Source: U.S. Department of Commerce, Bureau of the Census, *Social Indicators 1976* (Washington, D.C.: U.S. Government Printing Office, 1977), p. 165.

their children in a municipal hospital or on the ward of a voluntary hospital.[52] Inadequately housed, fed, and clothed, the poor can expect to be ill more often with acute and chronic disorders—and to receive less adequate treatment. The poor visit doctors infrequently, compared to the more affluent, and are admitted to the hospital less often; but when they do need hospitalization, it is likely to involve repeated visits for longer stays. Until recently they were less likely to have insurance for hospitalization or surgery and consequently less likely to have elective surgery.[53] Little wonder that the life span of the poor is up to six years shorter, on the average, than the life span of the more affluent.

Discrimination against the poor is not limited to physical ailments. There is a greater proportion of diagnosed psychosis among the poor, and they are more likely than the middle class to be institutionalized and receive shock treatment or chemotherapy—temporary relief of symptoms—in place of psychotherapy. Even if they visit clinics for psychiatric treatment, elements of the system itself—long waiting periods, selection of "motivated" patients, endless paper work, lack of empathy due to cultural differences on the part of the therapists—combine to deprive the poor of individualized treatment.[54] (See Chapter 2.)

Not only do the poor have unequal access to health services, and receive less adequate treatment, but there is evidence that they often view sickness and health differently. The poor are less likely to identify symptoms for a variety of physical and mental illnesses, causing significant delay in seeking treatment. When they see a doctor, treatment may be cursory because the physician, knowing their financial distress, is less likely to suggest that the patient stay away from work until completely recovered.[55]

Since the inception of Medicare and Medicaid in 1965, the poor have had somewhat better access to various medical resources.[56] But there are problems with almost all insurance programs: coverage is often inadequate; coverage begins only after a specified "deductible" expense level has been reached; many people are not aware of what their insurance covers. Accustomed to medical treatment in a clinic, the poor continue to visit clinics even though Medicaid would cover private health services.[57] And clinical attention, by a team or changing cast of practitioners, is inevitably less individual and less thorough than private care. Many doctors will not treat Medicaid patients; others have treated them so "thoroughly" that they have abused the program outrageously.

Other federal programs have established health care centers in impoverished communities. But these are still not adequate to solve the health care problems of the poor. Because most such programs allocate federal funds to

[52]Frederick S. Jaffe, "Family Planning and Poverty," in Meissner, *Poverty in the Affluent Society*, p. 195.

[53]Eichhorn and Ludwig, "Poverty and Health," pp. 174, 175, 177; see Office of Management and Budget, *Social Indicators, 1973* (Washington, D.C.: U.S. Government Printing Office, 1973), p. 41.

[54]William Ryan, *Blaming the Victim* (New York: Random House, 1971), pp. 145, 158.

[55]Eichhorn and Ludwig, "Poverty and Health," pp. 178-180.

[56]Gregory L. Weiss and Robert L. Eichhorn, "Medical Care Programs for the Poor," in Meissner, *Poverty in the Affluent Society*, pp. 271–272.

[57]Emil Berkanovic and Leo G. Reeder, "Ethnic, Economic, and Social Psychological Factors in the Source of Medical Care," *Social Problems* 21 (1973), 246, 249.

match those provided by a state, county, or city, they are frequently underfunded precisely where they are the most needed: those localities with many poor residents are hard pressed to be able to afford these as well as all other necessary services.[58] Furthermore, each program and agency has different requirements, deadlines, and purposes, resulting in a mass of regulations, red tape, traveling, and interminable waiting periods before services are obtained.[59] Finally, these programs do little to solve the overall health problems of the poor, who are victims of malnutrition, air pollution, poor education, higher rates of disease, inadequate housing, inadequate sanitation, inadequate rodent control, and even inadequate clothing, as well as less satisfactory medical treatment.[60]

Education

In every respect the poor get less education than the nonpoor. Their children are in school for fewer years, have less of a chance of graduating from high school, and are much less likely than middle-class children to go to college. They are likely to be taught in overcrowded classrooms by often inexperienced teachers[61] and to receive little if any individual attention. Even if experienced, most teachers are of middle-class origin, and have had little or no training in working with disadvantaged children. They bring to their jobs preconceived and pejorative notions that poor children will read, speak, test, and behave poorly, and that their parents and home life do not encourage academic achievement. It is not surprising that these expectations are converted into self-fulfilling prophecies. One study showed that in the early grades, there was virtually no difference in reading performance between white and black children, but that differences appeared, increasing significantly and dramatically, from about the fifth grade on.[62] For such reasons, Kenneth Clark, the prominent black educator, has charged that "American public schools have become significant instruments in the blocking of economic mobility and in the intensification of class distinctions."[63]

Perhaps the ultimate tragedy of the inferior education the poor receive is that it perpetuates the cycle of poverty. In general, those less educated in our society receive less income and status and have greater difficulty in improving their economic condition. What is worse, children of parents with less than a high school education generally do not do as well in school as children whose parents completed high school. Thus the cycle in which poverty and education are inextricably linked is perpetuated from generation to generation.

Housing

The poor are likely to live in substandard housing—overcrowded, vermin-infested, needing major repairs, lacking basic plumbing facilities, and inadequately heated. In the United States, almost 75 percent of substandard

[58]Eichhorn and Ludwig, "Poverty and Health," p. 176.
[59]Weiss and Eichhorn, "Medical Care Programs," p. 277.
[60]Pete Isaacson, "Poverty and Health," *The New Republic*, December 14, 1974, pp. 15-17.
[61]Paul Lauter and Florence Howe, *The Conspiracy of the Young* (New York: New American Library, 1970).
[62]Ryan, *Blaming the Victim*, p. 44.
[63]Lauter and Howe, *The Conspiracy of the Young*, pp. 210-211.

housing is occupied by the poor. Some 3 million families with incomes under $5,000 occupy such housing, more than half of which is in rural areas.[64]

The poor also live in cities, particularly in "urban ghettos" or the "inner city." The urban poor have been described as "block dwellers," unable to get about and utilize the city's resources.[65] They are isolated and segregated both economically and racially.

Racial segregation increased when middle- and upper-income families left the city, and mainly white, lower-income families who could afford them moved into the newly vacated residences. When their more prosperous citizens leave, cities also lose businesses, and consequently their tax base, leaving poor residents with fewer jobs and less adequate services from increasingly hard-pressed city governments. Such suburban zoning requirements as minimum lot size are designed to attract newcomers who will add more to tax rolls than they require in services. Restrictions on multiple-dwelling structures have the same purpose: to prevent low-income housing from being erected in such communities, and to keep low-income and

Urban "block dwellers" are victims of the economic and racial restrictions of their own neighborhoods. Neither rehabilitation nor urban renewal offer total solutions to inner city problems.

Jan Lukas/Photo Researchers, Inc.

[64]U.S. Office of Management and Budget, Statistical Policy Division, *Social Indicators, 1973* (Washington, D.C.: U.S. Government Printing Office, 1973).

[65]Alvin L. Schoor, "Housing Policies and Poverty," in Meissner, *Poverty in the Affluent Society*, pp. 151-152.

minority families out of the suburbs. As William Ryan points out, tax credits available to homeowners amount to a substantial government subsidy to the nonpoor, and hasten the exodus of the middle and upper classes from the city.[66]

Rehabilitation of existing structures has been advocated as one solution to the housing problem, through which the poor "block dweller" need not be uprooted from familiar surroundings. But the cost of rehabilitating antiquated structures in deteriorating neighborhoods is too high, and the potential return on the investment is too low, to appeal to private builders. Because poor families cannot afford rentals or purchase prices that would be profitable to owners and builders, there is a serious problem of how to encourage private industry to provide low-income housing. Costs, in fact, have risen to such an extent in the last decade that not even middle-income metropolitan area housing is an attractive investment. Each year, there is an additional deficit of hundreds of thousands of housing units for the poor.

Urban renewal is the rehabilitation of a neighborhood by razing and replacing dilapidated structures. Under such programs, however, the displaced poor, and especially poor blacks, have simply been moved from one slum to another.[67] In one study of urban renewal in 26 cities where little or no relocation assistance was provided, 70 percent of displaced families entered substandard housing in the same neighborhood; in 15 cities that provided relocation aid, about a third of the families nevertheless ended up in substandard housing.[68] Another survey found that from 1949 to 1967, as many as 383,000 existing housing units were demolished—to be replaced by only 107,000 new and 75,000 rehabilitated housing units. This was a net loss of 200,000 units. Furthermore, although blacks were less than a third of the population in the cities being studied, 60 percent of the families displaced by urban renewal were black.[69] (It is small wonder that urban renewal has often been referred to as "Negro removal.") Whatever their intent, these programs have left the poor with the very worst housing. (See Chapter 14.)

Justice

By definition, justice should be even-handed; in practice, it is not. As described in Chapter 5, poor people are more likely than members of the middle and upper classes to be arrested, indicted, convicted, imprisoned, and given longer sentences for the same offense. Conversely, they are less likely to receive probation, parole, or suspended sentences. Also, poor adolescents are more likely to be labeled juvenile delinquents. Well-to-do youngsters who commit crimes are likely to be sent to a psychiatrist and left in their parents' custody; poor youngsters are likely to be sent to a correctional institution.[70]

The crimes poor people are likely to commit, because of their position in society—property theft and assault—tend to be those most disapproved of by those who make the laws—the middle and upper classes. These personal crimes tend also to be the most visible and widely publicized. The middle and upper-middle classes tend to commit so-called "white-collar" crimes— embezzlement, price-fixing, tax evasion, bribery, and so on. Though crimes

[66]Ryan, *Blaming the Victim,* pp. 182-183.
[67]Joseph Epstein, "The Row Over Urban Renewal," *Harper's* (February 1965), pp. 55-61.
[68]Schoor, "Housing Policies and Poverty," p. 154.
[69]U.S. Department of H.E.W., *Toward a Social Report* (Washington, D.C.: U.S. Government Printing Office, 1969); see Morton J. Schussheim, "Housing in Perspective," *The Public Interest* (Spring 1970), pp. 27-34.
[70]See Ryan, *Blaming the Victim.*

such as these involve much more money than street crime or property thefts, and may even pose a greater threat to social institutions, they tend not to be regarded as serious by our criminal justice system. Furthermore, white-collar crimes rarely become visible.

Even if arrested, prosperous citizens are more likely to be able to afford bail, to know their rights, to be skillfully, or at least competently, defended, and to receive a brief sentence. But the indigent defendant, unable to post bond, may be retained in jail for months. One plan to reduce the number of those held without bail was the Manhattan Bail Project, under which defendants considered good risks were paroled on their own recognizance. However, the rigid and unrealistic criteria used to determine who were good risks eliminated the most impoverished from consideration.[71]

Under the law, every accused person has the right to be represented by counsel; some cities, counties, and states provide public defenders. But there are many large cities and thirty-four states without defender services, and in federal courts there are neither paid defenders nor funds to compensate court-appointed counsel, who serve voluntarily. Where public defenders and court-appointed lawyers are provided, they are usually not the most skillful, nor have they financial resources or time for extended investigation.[72]

Inadequate defense is another of several reasons why the poor are more likely to be convicted and, if so, to receive more severe sentences than those who are better off. And those who have been arrested and convicted are likely to be sentenced to a jail that is over-crowded, where very few inmates can be truly rehabilitated. Released, they are stigmatized, unlikely to be able to get and/or hold a job. They often return to impoverished urban ghettos where the hopelessness of life increases their chances of becoming involved once again with the inequities of the judicial system.

Explanations of Poverty

Explanations of the causes and nature of poverty are plentiful; however, two approaches have predominated—the cultural and the situational. The proponents of the first argue that a "culture of poverty" arises after periods of extended economic deprivation. To achieve goals within this depressed state, new norms, values, and aspirations are developed. These eventually become independent of the situations that produced them, so that eliminating the problem does not eliminate the behavior developed to deal with it. The result is a self-sustaining system of values and behavior handed down from generation to generation.

The situational approach interprets the behavior of the poor as an adaptation to their environment. Patterns of behavior develop as a response to problems associated with low income and the accompanying economic and social deprivation. The poor have to forego middle-class values and aspirations because these simply do not apply to their circumstances. Children react similarly because they must make the same adjustments to the same problems their parents faced.

[71]Junius L. Allison, "Poverty and the Administration of Justice in the Criminal Courts," in Meissner, *Poverty in the Affluent Society*, p. 167.

[72]Allison, "Poverty and the Administration of Justice," pp. 169-171.

Oscar Lewis is one of the chief proponents of the cultural explanation. He argues that poverty is a subculture of society, transcending regional differences and showing "remarkable cross-national similarities in family structure, interpersonal relations, time orientation, value systems, and spending patterns."[73] According to Lewis, the roots of this culture form in societies where certain conditions exist, such as:

The Cultural Explanation

1. a cash economy, wage labor, and production for profit;

2. a persistently high rate of unemployment and underemployment for unskilled labor, and low wages for those employed;

3. the failure to provide social, political, and economic organization, either on a voluntary basis or by government imposition for the low-income population;

4. a set of values in the dominant class that stresses the accumulation of wealth and property, and that explains low economic status as a result of personal inadequacy or inferiority.[74]

The culture of poverty is thus an "adaptation and a reaction of the poor to their marginal position in a class-stratified, highly individuated capitalistic society." Through this need to cope, the poor develop a "design for living" or a set of solutions to their problems that tend to be passed down from generation to generation. Lewis argues that a "crucial characteristic" of the subculture is "the lack of effective participation and integration of the poor in the major institutions of the larger society." The poor pawn their goods, borrow from local money-lenders, use secondhand clothing and household items, abstain from labor unions or political parties, avoid banks, hospitals, or museums, hate the police, mistrust politicians, and have a low level of literacy and education. Thus deprived of leverage in the larger society, the poor have a low potential for protest.

Within the poor community itself, Lewis cites as typical "poor housing conditions, crowding, gregariousness, but above all a minimum of organization beyond the level of the nuclear family." This low level of organization contrasts sharply with the highly organized character of middle-class society. A stable and ethnically homogeneous slum population, however, may have a certain sense of local community, often similar to that of a village. Even without this, there may be a sense of territoriality, a setting-off of slum neighborhoods from the city without.

The family in the poverty subculture is often female-centered and authoritarian. There is little sheltering and protection in childhood, very little privacy, and early sexual initiation. Competition among siblings for limited goods and maternal affection tends to counteract a strong verbal emphasis on family solidarity.

Persons in this culture are apt to feel marginal, helpless, dependent, and inferior; they frequently have a weak ego structure, a lack of impulse control, and an inability to plan or save for the future. A sense of resignation and fatalism is common.

[73]Oscar Lewis, *The Study of Slum Cultures—Backgrounds for La Vida* (New York: Random House, 1968).

[74]Oscar Lewis, *La Vida: A Puerto Rican Family in the Culture of Poverty—San Juan and New York* (New York: Random House, 1966).

These characteristics, Lewis argues, tend to develop in any poverty culture, and are found in both rural and urban locations throughout the world. They enable the poor to cope with the special strains of their condition, but also prevent their escaping that condition. The poor can only eliminate the culture of poverty, according to Lewis, through organizational unity. Only by achieving solidarity within a larger group can they transcend their psychological and social traits.

The Situational Approach

Charles A. Valentine is one of the main critics of Lewis's explanation. In his view, many of the "class-distinctive traits" do not indicate cultural patterns at all. Instead, Valentine contends, "many of these features seem more likely externally imposed conditions or unavoidable matters of situational expediency, rather than cultural creations internal to the subsociety in question."

Valentine divides Lewis's list of poverty-culture traits into three categories. The first of these he calls "gross indicators or correlates of poverty": unemployment, underemployment, unskilled work, low-status jobs, meager wages, crowded and deteriorated housing, and lack of education. Valentine regards these as "conditions or symptoms" of poverty, rather than as ingrained patterns of social response:

> Lack of work, lack of income, and the rest pose conditions to which the poor must adapt through whatever sociocultural resources they control. That is, these conditions are phenomena of the environment in which the lower class lives, determined not so much by behaviors and values of the poor as by the structure of the total social system.[75]

"Behavioral patterns and relationships," the second category of traits, include a harsh childhood, authoritarianism, and little community organization. Rather than a "distinctive subcultural pattern," Valentine sees these traits as indicating a definite lack of a patterned existence, and concludes that it is uncertain whether they are "sanctioned and perpetuated by subcultural values and beliefs that are communicated through socialization" or whether they stem from "motivations that are consistent with the value orientations common to the total culture but capable of only distorted or incomplete expression within the limits of a poverty environment."

"Values and attitudes," Valentine's third set of traits, include hostility toward institutions of the dominant society, negative feelings about one's place in society, and low levels of expectation and aspiration. With regard to these, Valentine writes: "All these orientations are so strikingly consistent with objective situational facts that it seems hardly necessary to interpret them as ingrained subcultural values. Indeed, for modern Western people these would seem to be almost the inevitable emotional responses to the actual conditions of poverty."

Valentine concludes that Lewis's list of traits does not constitute a separate subsystem of values for the poor. He outlines his own point of view about the relationship between poverty, culture, and society in the following model, which takes a markedly activist view of how poverty and its associated cultural manifestations can be altered:

[75]Reprinted from *Culture and Poverty: Critique and Counterproposals* by Charles A. Valentine by permission of The University of Chicago Press (Chicago: University of Chicago Press, 1968), pp. 114-120.

Heterogeneous Subsociety with Variable, Adaptive Subcultures

a.   The lower-class poor possess some distinct subcultural patterns, *even though they also subscribe to norms of the middle class* or the total system in some of the same areas of life and are quite non-distinctive in other areas; there is variation in each of these dimensions from one ethnic group to another.

b.   The distinctive patterns of the poverty subcultures, like those of earlier subsocieties, include not only pathogenic traits *but also healthy and positive aspects*, elements of creative adaptation to conditions of deprivation.

c.   The structural position and subcultural patterns of the poor stem from historical and contemporary sources that vary from one ethnic or regional group to another but generally involve a *multicausal combination of factors*.

d.   *Innovation serving the interests of the lower class to an optimal degree will therefore require more or less simultaneous mutually reinforcing changes in three areas:* increases in the resources actually available to the poor; alterations of the total social structure; and changes in some subcultural patterns.

e.   The most likely source for these changes is one or more *social movements for cultural revitalization*, drawing original strength necessarily from the poor, but succeeding only if the whole society is affected directly or indirectly.[76]

Herbert J. Gans is critical of both the cultural and the situational approaches. He finds the situational explanation, the idea that people alter their behavior according to the situations and opportunities available to them, too simplistic. People are not "automatons," all reacting in the same manner to a common stimulus. On the contrary, he stresses the heterogeneous character of the poor:

The Cultural-Situational Approach

> Some have been poor for generations, others are poor only periodically; some are downwardly mobile; others are upwardly mobile. Many share middle-class values, others embrace working-class values; some have become so used to the defense mechanisms they have learned for coping with deprivation that they have difficulty in adapting to new opportunities; and some are beset by physical and emotional illness, poverty having created pathologies that now block the ability to adapt to non-pathological situations.[77]

Gans also rejects the cultural approach, with its implication that people react to change in terms of prior behavior patterns and values and accept only those changes that comply with their culture. He criticizes the idea that culture is "holistic," that no element of it can be changed unless the entire culture is altered, and argues that behavior results from a combination of cultural and situational influences: "Culture . . . is that mix of behavioral norms and aspirations that causes behavior, maintains present behavior, or encourages future behavior, independently of situational incentives and restraints."

[76]Valentine, *Culture and Poverty*, pp. 142-144.
[77]Herbert J. Gans, *People and Plans: Essays on Urban Problems and Solutions* (New York: Basic Books, 1968), pp. 321-346.

Gans maintains that the ultimate solution to poverty lies in the discovery of what restraints poor people are subject to in reacting to new opportunities even when they conflict with their present cultural values. He believes that we must examine the kinds of change needed in our economic system, social order, and power structure, and in the norms and aspirations of the affluent majority that permit a poor class to exist.

The Adaptation Approach

Lee Rainwater, a sociologist studying poverty, offers another explanation. While he admits that a lower-class pattern of behavior and belief exists, he characterizes it differently from other theorists. He feels that conventional society has somehow imposed its norms on the lower class even though the members of this class cannot achieve these norms. Lower-class culture therefore contains some elements unique to its group and shares others with the larger culture. Thus the distinctive lower-class subculture has only "limited functional autonomy."[78]

Rainwater argues that policy should be based on the concept that "lower-class culture is an adaptation not to an absolute deprivation of living below some minimum standard, but to the relative deprivation of being so far removed from the average American standard that the lower-class individual cannot feel himself part of the society." He advocates "resource equalization strategy"; that is, giving the poor enough resources to eliminate this relative deprivation and to ensure that "there is no class of people below the 'average man' in terms of prestige, income and other advantages."

The Value-Stretch Approach

Proponents of the culture of poverty explanation attribute to the poor a value system characterized by a lack of desire to participate in the institutions of the larger society, and acceptance of behavior considered antisocial by the more favored classes. Critics argue that the behavioral differences between the classes are not values but coping mechanisms by which the poor adjust to the realities preventing them from conforming to more socially desirable behavior. Hyman Rodman agrees that all classes share the general values of society, but claims that the lower class has an additional set of values representing realistic levels of attainment. Not that the lower class rejects majority values, or desires less; rather, for the lower class two sets of values exist simultaneously, in a hierarchy in which the more desirable, those values shared with the overall society, are the least attainable. He therefore argues that the lower class has a wider range of values than the other classes, and he calls this the "lower class value stretch." He describes how this double-value system works:

> Lower-class persons . . . do not maintain a strong commitment to middle-class values that they cannot attain, and they do not continue to respond to others in a rewarding or punishing way simply on the basis of whether these others are living up to the middle-class values. A change takes place. They come to tolerate and eventually to evaluate favorably certain deviations from the middle-class values. In this way they need not be continually frustrated by their failure to live up to unattainable values. The resultant is a stretched value system.[79]

[78]Lee Rainwater, "The Problem of Lower-Class Culture and Poverty-War Strategy," in *On Understanding Poverty*, ed. Daniel P. Moynihan (New York: Basic Books, 1969), pp. 229-259.

[79]Hyman Rodman, "The Lower Class Value Stretch," *Social Forces* 42 (December 1963), 205-215.

L. Richard Della Fave introduces the terms *preference*, the ideal of preferred value; *expectation*, the level that a person expects to be able to achieve; and *tolerance*, the least a person will accept or settle for. He notes that the value-stretch mechanism is set in motion when the *reconciliation gap* between preference and expectation becomes too great. "The values of the poor do resemble those of the middle class, but only in terms of . . . preference. [They] differ most . . . in terms of expectation and tolerance."[80] As a result of realistic adaptation to reality, say both Rodman and Della Fave, the poor expect less and are satisfied with less.

Employment, Unemployment, and Welfare

As noted earlier, many people feel that the poor are largely to blame for their own poverty. The general argument is as follows: "The poor class consists of the unemployed who are responsible for their condition because they will not work. If they could be persuaded to work for a living, or if they were forced to take jobs, poverty could then be eliminated. What we have now is a group of 'freeloaders' who are getting by on welfare." The inaccuracy of this argument is evident when one examines the data on poverty, work, and welfare.

Work and the Poor

A study based on the latest available census data reveals some interesting facts about the poor and unemployment. According to these figures, the composition of the poor is as follows:

Children under age 14	32.8%
Elderly, 65 and over	14.6
Ill and disabled, 14–64	5.5
In school, 14–64	8.0
Total	60.9%

This means that over 60 percent of the poor are essentially unable to seek or to hold jobs because of their age, state of health, or educational commitments. Of the remaining 39.1 percent:

Did not work, age 14–64	13.2%
Worked, age 14–64	25.9

Therefore, only about 13 percent of the poor could have been employed but were not. A breakdown of this group by sex is even more revealing:

Male unemployed	1.0%
Female unemployed	12.0[81]

[80]L. Richard Della Fave, "The Culture of Poverty Revisited: A Strategy for Research," *Social Problems* 21 (1974), 609-621.

[81]"Characteristics of the Low-Income Population," *Current Population Reports*, Series P-23, no. 57 (Washington, D.C.: U.S. Government Printing Office, 1975). Figures are approximations.

Contrary to the widespread myth that welfare recipients are lazy, a pragmatic acceptance of welfare as a reality of unemployment crowds welfare offices such as this one.

Freer/Photo Researchers, Inc.

Of the high proportion of women in this group, the vast majority cannot work because they have to care for small children. This leaves only a tiny proportion of poor who might have secured employment but did not. This total does not compare unfavorably with the over 10 percent of the nonpoor who did not work or go to school and were not ill, aged, or disabled.

If so many of the poor are employed, why do they stay poor? Low-paying jobs and underemployment are primarily responsible. Almost 25 percent of the employed poor work full-time, yet still receive an income below the poverty line. The highly publicized and lucrative contracts obtained by labor unions in certain industries have obscured the plight of many other workers.[82] In addition, certain industries and groups of workers are not covered by minimum wage laws.

Of the poor who do work, about three-fourths are employed in less than full-time, year-round positions. Many, particularly the unskilled, suffer because of seasonal layoffs, bankruptcies, and automation and cutbacks in certain industries. Economic recessions and depressions also contribute to

[82]Gus Tyler, "Marginal Industries, Low Wages, and Higher Risks," *Dissent* (Summer 1961).

unemployment. By the end of 1978, for example, the official unemployment rate was about 6 percent (involving well over 6 million people)—and official statistics generally account for only two-thirds of those actually unemployed. (See Chapter 13.) Even official statistics, however, indicate that unemployment hits some groups harder than others. The black unemployment rate of 13.5 percent, for instance, is twice the white unemployment rate. And one study has shown that each 1 percent increase in national unemployment means a 4 percent increase in unemployment among low-level groups.[83]

For several reasons, most unemployed poor who do not seek employment are convinced that they will not find any work. They believe that employers will consider them too old or too young; they lack skills, education, training, or experience; they are black or Indian; they cannot speak English; and finally, many cannot find work for more than subsistence pay.

As was pointed out earlier, the welfare poor have been the victims of many misconceptions. Among the most common are:

The Poor on Welfare

1. Welfare families are loaded with kids—and have more children just to get more money.
2. Most welfare families are black.
3. Why work, when you can live it up on welfare?
4. Give them more money and they'll spend it on drink and big cars.
5. Most welfare children are illegitimate.
6. Once on welfare, always on welfare.
7. Welfare people are cheats.
8. Welfare's just a dole, a money handout.
9. The welfare rolls are full of able-bodied loafers.[84]

The facts, however, contradict these widely held misconceptions. In corresponding order, HEW found that:

1. Over half—54.2 percent—of welfare families have either one or two children. The usual payment for an additional child is $35 a month, insufficient to cover the cost of rearing another child.
2. Whites comprise the largest racial group among welfare families, with 48.3 percent of the total. Blacks represent 43.3 percent. American Indians, Orientals, and other racial minorities make up the remaining 8.4 percent.
3. Payments for basic needs to a welfare family of four with no other income vary from a low of $197 per month in Mississippi to a high of $463 per month in Alaska. Welfare payments in all but three states, excluding payments for special needs, are below the established poverty level.
4. Most welfare families say that if they received any extra money, it would be used for essentials. Among welfare mothers, almost half said they would spend their money on extra food.

[83]"Inflation and Inequality," *New York Times*, October 13, 1975, p. 39.
[84]U.S. Department of H.E.W., *Welfare Myths vs. Facts* (pamphlet) (Washington, D.C.: U.S. Government Printing Office, 1972).

5. Of the more than 7 million children in welfare families, 68.8 percent are legitimate. Only in recent years has the government made family planning services available to welfare families.

6. Half the families on welfare have been receiving assistance for 20 months or less, and two-thirds for less than 3 years.

7. Only about 5.6 percent of welfare families are found to be ineligible, and less than one-half of 1 percent of welfare cases are referred for prosecution for fraud. Most errors involve honest mistakes by state and local welfare agencies or by recipients. (Conversely, studies have found that in many areas over half of those eligible for welfare do not receive it.[85])

8. Most welfare families are provided with other social services besides financial aid. Among these are health care advice and referrals (including Medicaid), counseling on financial and home management, employment counseling, and services to improve housing conditions and to enable children to continue in school.

9. Less than 1 percent of welfare recipients are able-bodied unemployed males. These men are required by law to sign up for work or work training in order to remain eligible for benefits. The largest group of working-age adults on welfare are 2.5 million mothers, most of them heads of families.[86]

But perhaps the most pernicious myth is that the poor do not share the "work ethic" of the middle class—that the poor are "lazy" or "shiftless" and would much rather be on welfare than work. Many studies have shown that the poor strongly share the work ethic of our society and regret being on welfare. As Leonard Goodwin notes, there are "no differences between poor and unpoor when it comes to life goals and wanting to work"; the differences are that the poor lack confidence in their ability to succeed and accept welfare as a necessity due to chronic un- or underemployment.[87] Despite all evidence, these "welfare myths" are still widely accepted in America and constitute a major obstacle to attempts to improve the present welfare system.

Social Action

The need for government intervention in the basic economic life of Americans first became apparent in the 1930s with the unemployment and financial distress of the Great Depression. Since then, many new economic programs have been developed, and more were proposed. Yet, despite programs designed to ensure adequate income or to supply the means to achieve this goal, poverty continues at about the same rate as over forty years ago. Before examining some of the new proposals that sociologists and economists have

[85]In Patrick Moran and Patricia Lee Austin, "The Social Bases of the Welfare Stigma," *Social Problems* 21 (1974), 648.

[86]Moran and Austin, "The Social Bases of the Welfare Stigma;" see Subcommittee on Fiscal Policy, Joint Economic Committee, Congress of the United States, *Income Security for Americans* (Washington, D.C.: U.S. Government Printing Office, 1974).

[87]Leonard Goodwin, *Do the Poor Want Work?* (Washington, D.C.: The Brookings Institution, 1973); see Charles Davidson and Charles M. Goetz, "Are the Poor Different?" *Social Problems* 22 (1974), 229; and Moran and Austin, "The Social Bases of the Welfare Stigma."

advanced to alleviate or eradicate poverty, it would be useful to review what already is in operation.

Current government programs can be divided into four basic categories: human resource development, social insurance, cash income support programs, and programs providing income-in-kind. Human resource development programs are geared toward increasing the employability of the poor by raising their educational and skill levels; they include both formal educational programs in classroom settings and on-the-job training programs. One of these is the Job Corps, a residential program that provides remedial education, training in job skills, and guidance and counseling to those between the ages of 14 and 21. Another is the Neighborhood Youth Corps, which provides part-time work for youths in school during the school year and in the summer, consisting largely of work around the school. There is also an out-of-school program for high school dropouts, with work generally in hospitals, parks, and other public institutions. By far the most ambitious program is the $12 billion Comprehensive Employment and Training Act (CETA) passed by Congress in 1973, and renewed in August 1978. CETA's primary beneficiaries are the disadvantaged, the poor, the long-term unemployed, and, especially, welfare recipients. The program's aim is to make employable the hardcore unemployed, and places strong emphasis on training skills, with incentives for employment within the private sector. CETA has always favored communities with exceptionally high jobless rates.

Social insurance programs are intended to compensate for loss of income, regardless of income level or need. Through unemployment insurance, for example, cash benefits are paid for short periods to insured workers who are involuntarily unemployed. Workmen's compensation programs provide wage replacements to insured workers who suffer occupational injuries. Veterans' compensation plans issue benefits to disabled veterans to make up for their loss of earning potential. Social Security payments to the elderly also fall within this category.

Cash income support programs are provided for unemployable persons, those not covered by any form of social insurance, and those with special needs. Veterans' pensions fall into this category, as do direct subsidies to families and individuals in the form of public assistance, or welfare. Americans do not like welfare programs. Those who receive benefits complain of the humiliation involved in declaring oneself poor in order to qualify for aid; those who do not receive benefits complain that welfare recipients end up with higher incomes and better medical attention than they do. Recent reforms in the welfare system have sought to solve these problems with improved programs such as aid to the blind, old age assistance, aid to families with dependent children (AFDC), and aid to the permanently and totally disabled, all of which are specifically aimed at the poor.

Income-in-kind programs provide goods and services such as food, housing, and medical care to the poor. These programs include public housing and urban renewal; health plans such as Medicare and Medicaid (see Chapter 2); and food supplements such as the commodity distribution program, which distributes surplus farm products to poor households, and food stamps, which in effect subsidize discounts on food purchases.

Although the major economic and social disruptions of the Depression are today only a memory, the less drastic but nonetheless real economic problems of the 1970s—inflation, stagnating productive output, and high rates of unemployment in all sectors of the economy—are still very much with us. Government programs, some of which have been expanded to deal with current problems, have proved insufficient to free the poor from their poverty. In general, these programs fail to deal directly with the problem, to help all the needy, and to restore dignity and incentives to the poor. A more equal distribution of wealth would seem to be an absolute necessity, and several plans have been proposed to achieve it. They can be divided into two general types: plans for employment and economic growth, and income maintenance programs.

Employment and Economic Growth

The 1970s were a period of generally high unemployment. During those years, the nation's productive capacity outran private and public consumption of goods, as lack of income resulted in a curtailment of spending. Presumably, if spending could be increased, it would stimulate business activity and create more jobs. Several suggestions for accomplishing this goal were offered, all of them requiring governmental participation: stimulating the private sector, extending economic legislation, and providing public employment.

Stimulating the Private Economy.   Tax cuts have been proposed, and periodically attempted, as a means of putting more money into the hands of the public. Presumably, this would increase public spending; and if, simultaneously, the level of government spending were maintained, the expected result would be more production, more jobs, and more income. An adjunct proposal was for tax cuts for corporations; by allowing corporations to keep a larger portion of their profits, it was hoped to encourage industrial expansion and investment, again resulting in more jobs, more consumer income, and more spending.

Lowering interest rates was also considered. Expanding the supply of credit might encourage industry to borrow in order to build, expand, modernize, or develop, and thus increase production. This would then lead to increased employment.

Garth L. Mangum has suggested still another method by which the government might stimulate employment for low-income groups. He suggested that reluctance to hire less qualified workers be counteracted by reimbursing employers for a portion of the workers' salaries. Such a government subsidy of the unskilled worker would reduce what Mangum calls the "worker's competitive disadvantage," the gap between his or her potential earnings on the open market and his or her desired income. This money would be considered a reimbursement to employers for training costs.[88]

Extending Economic Legislation.   Over 1 million persons are employed in occupations not regulated by the minimum wage law. If this coverage were extended to include all workers, such as agricultural laborers, a significant increase in income, and therefore in purchasing power, would be gained by a portion of the population presently unable to secure even subsistence wages.

Government as Employer.   In addition to manipulating the private sector to create employment situations, the government itself might serve as

[88]Garth L. Mangum, "Guaranteeing Employment Opportunities," in *Social Policies for America in the Seventies: Nine Divergent Views,* ed. Robert Theobald (Garden City, N.Y.: Doubleday, 1969), pp. 47-50.

the "employer of last resort," providing permanent employment in new or expanded social services or temporary jobs in major projects of shorter duration. This proposal has several advantages. It would reduce the number of people on welfare; it would provide training and experience which would ultimately qualify its participants for private employment; and it might offer a psychological incentive, by giving people the chance to earn a living rather than relying indefinitely on public assistance.

Government programs such as welfare, Social Security, and old-age assistance are intended to redistribute income to the poor. As already indicated, however, these programs are both inadequate and unjust. It has been charged that some of these programs are a response to threats of civil disorder, and that others restrict aid so that unskilled workers are virtually required to take extremely low-paying jobs.[89] Furthermore, the various income maintenance programs are a patchwork of requirements, standards, and benefits that differ from state to state and therefore often work at cross-purposes. The details of these programs, moreover, are enmeshed in so many regulations and directives that many potential recipients are unaware of their rights or are hindered from claiming them because of bureaucratic red tape. Some maintenance programs reduce benefits as outside income increases. Because many of the needy qualify for benefits under more than one program—food stamps and AFDC, for example—they may receive more in benefits than they could earn at work (especially since earnings would be subject to taxes and work expenses). Finally, the AFDC program, which has the largest share of state and federal welfare budgets, actually encourages the breaking-up of families because families can get a higher income with the husband absent than if he is at home and working in a low-paying job.

Income Maintenance Programs

Robert A. Levine has suggested how an income maintenance program might correct the deficiencies of the present system:

1. It should, from the very beginning, provide a decent level of support for all recipients across the country.

2. Need, rather than "deservedness," should be the sole requirement for eligibility. Such need should be defined simply in terms of the family income and should be based on a simple affidavit testifying to it. Enforcement would be by simple spot-check, as it is in the federal income tax system, rather than by detailed, dehumanizing investigation.

3. To preserve the incentive to work and leave the welfare rolls, the recipients should be allowed to retain much of their income maintenance payments even when their earnings increase, up to some break-even level.

4. To keep families together, payments should be made on the same basis to intact families as to broken families. They should be made to families with employed as well as unemployed male heads.

5. The income maintenance system should be separated from the services provided by social workers. Family receipt of such services should be voluntary and should not be a condition of eligibility for income maintenance.

[89]Frances Fox Piven and Richard A. Cloward, *Regulating the Poor: The Functions of Public Welfare* (New York: Pantheon, 1971).

6. The application of the system as well as its basic rules should be national and not determined by states or localities.[90]

Although many recommendations for reform have been made along these lines, one specific proposal, the negative income tax, has received widespread support. While the mechanics of its implementation have not yet been resolved, its merits make it worthy of discussion here.

The negative income tax would use the income tax system to equalize income distribution. Families earning less than a designated minimum would receive payments, or "negative taxes," to bring their incomes up to the minimum level. Families at the minimum level would receive no benefits, and families earning more than the minimum would be taxed, as is now the case. Thus the surplus of the more fortunate would be redistributed to compensate the poor.

To maintain the incentive to work under this plan, negative tax payments would not be decreased as fast as earned income rose. That is, if a worker's annual income increased by $1,000, his or her negative tax payment might be cut by, say, $500. Thus the worker would still have a total income of $500 more than if he or she had not worked.

The negative income tax plan has several important advantages. It would support the needy with cash, and would guarantee a respectable income to everyone. Since it would apply to all the needy, it might allow consolidation of the various specialized programs now in operation. It would shift more of the costs of the system to the federal government. Finally, it would motivate workers to increase their earnings.

The plan has its opponents, however. It has been criticized as not providing for temporal or regional variations in the cost of living, and for not meeting the special needs of certain families. Nevertheless, it is one attractive alternative to current programs.

Prospects

It is clear than eradicating poverty would involve not only income supports for the poor but a moderate restructuring of our economic system to achieve greater equality in income distribution. In Lee Rainwater's words: "Many of the social problems associated with poverty would not be more than moderately reduced"[91] if the poor were simply raised to a minimum standard of living. The poor must also be given the means to break the self-perpetuating cycle of poverty. A national health insurance program to assure adequate health care delivery to the less affluent, a public housing program that provides adequate living quarters for those who need them, a system of education that allows people to fulfill their capabilities, a job training program that teaches useful skills, an end to discrimination in housing and justice—these are the programs which, besides income support, would help to alleviate poverty.

[90]Robert A. Levine, *The Poor Ye Need Not Have With You: Lessons from the War on Poverty* (Cambridge, Mass.: M.I.T. Press, 1970), pp. 201-202.

[91]Lee Rainwater, "Poverty in the United States," in Rainwater, *Social Problems and Public Policy* (Chicago: Aldine, 1974), p. 74; see Herbert Gans, "More Equality: Income and Taxes," *Society* (January-February 1974), pp. 62-69.

Unfortunately, the condition of the poor is likely to remain the same, at least for the immediate future, since there is no indication that funds for the necessary programs will be forthcoming. The lower and middle classes are already overtaxed, and the affluent are unlikely to surrender their advantages willingly. Tax loopholes will not be closed, corporate power will not be lessened, and military spending will not be reduced as long as those in power reflect the interests of the wealthy. As Randall Bartlett stated:

> The greater the concentration of wealth held by any agent, the greater the political power. Gigantic corporations not only possess excessive control over their markets, but they also possess excessive control over government decisions. The same applies to extremely wealthy individuals . . . . In either the political or the market operations of a society . . . the wishes of the agents with the greatest wealth will carry the greatest weight. It is not a new "conspiracy" that makes it so. It is merely the action of self-interested rational men.[92]

How, then, is economic reform to be effected? Ultimately, the poor must become a potent political force. Traditionally, this has been difficult since feeling that they have little stake in the system, the poor have generally stayed aloof from politics. Additionally, conflicts, particularly along racial lines, have divided the poor, weakening their political impact. The creation of the National Welfare Rights Organization in the late 1960s was a first step in the right direction. This organization has effectively lobbied to improve the poor's access to public aid. Further organizational efforts, however, must be made by the poor if they are to become effective on a larger scale. As Gunnar Myrdal put it: "No privileged class in history has ever climbed down from its privileges and opened its monopolies out of good will. I believe very much in idealism. But it plays the role only when there is pressure from below."[93]

Without a rethinking of national goals and a greater commitment to domestic rather than military spending, progress in equalizing income in our society will be slow and incremental, partially determined by the ability of the poor themselves to organize and make their demands heard. The poor, then, are likely to remain with us for a long while, expected to be content with only crumbs from the abundant national table. They continue to serve as living reminders of the gap between the rhetoric and the reality of the American experience.

[92]Randall Bartlett, *Economic Foundations of Political Power* (New York: Macmillan, 1973), p. 156.
[93]Interview appearing in *The Boston Globe*, May 26, 1968.

Summary

Though equality and affluence are believed by many Americans to be integral parts of our society, in fact poverty and gross inequities in income distribution are widespread. Affluence exists in America, but for relatively few, and often at the expense of the poor.

Affluence—and inequality—have been protected by tax laws that encourage large fortunes to be handed down from one generation to the next and that subject earned income to a much higher effective tax rate than investment income. Moreover, the control of many corporations by rich investors gives those investors economic and political power out of proportion to their actual number.

The poor are deprived not only by the standards of the affluent but also by middle-class standards. They pay more of their limited income for essentials and are further subjected to the social stigma of poverty. Experts differ as to the definition of poverty: some use the *fixed income approach*, which sets a fixed annual income as the poverty line; others use the *relative income approach*, which measures poverty as a fraction of median income to include the relative deprivation of the poor.

Some factors associated with poverty are advanced age, households headed by women, membership in a minority group, and rural residence. Compared to the more fortunate, the poor die earlier, and are more likely to be ill and receive inadequate treatment. Their education is often inferior, thereby perpetuating the cycle of poverty. They are more likely to be segregated economically and socially; and are more likely to be arrested, poorly defended, convicted, and given long sentences for the same crime than the more affluent.

Several explanations of poverty have been offered. The *cultural explanation*, proposed by Oscar Lewis, suggests that people create a subculture of their own as an adaptation to poverty. This subculture enables the poor to cope but also limits their effectiveness in the larger culture. It is passed on to the next generation, perpetuating the poverty cycle. Charles Valentine disagrees with this and instead offers the *situational approach:* The traits Lewis observed are not all creations of a subculture but, rather, often represent behavioral responses to existing conditions. If the poor had more money available, their behavior would change. Herbert Gans combines these two approaches, suggesting that poor people cannot be easily categorized and that their behavior results from both cultural and situational influences. Lee Rainwater believes that the lives of the poor are even more complex than Gans suggested; not only do the poor have a particular subculture and situation, but they also have absorbed some of the beliefs of the larger culture. Thus they do not feel deprived in isolation but relative to the rest of society. The *value-stretch concept* articulated by Hyman Rodman and L. Richard Della Fave extends this idea to suggest that the poor have two simultaneous sets of values— those of the larger society, which are preferred, if unattainable, values, and those values they realistically expect to achieve.

There exist common misconceptions about the poor. For example, they are assumed to be lazy; in fact, very few of the employable poor do not work. There are also many misconceptions about the poor on welfare. For example, it is believed that the welfare poor are mostly black; in fact, most welfare recipients are white.

Current government antipoverty programs fall into one of four categories: human resource development, social insurance, cash income support, and providing income-in-kind. Other suggestions to increase the government role include stimulating the private economy (through tax cuts, for example), extending economic legislation (by expanding the minimum wage law), and having the government serve as the "employer of last resort." Present maintenance programs can be improved by increasing benefits to a decent level, eliminating red tape and unnecessary requirements, allowing benefits to continue up to a certain point even if earnings increase, and eliminating state or local control over benefits. A *negative income tax,* which would use the income tax system to equalize the distribution of income, has also been proposed. It is unlikely that these proposals will be realized unless the poor organize politically.

Bibliography

Baltzell, E. Digby. *The Protestant Establishment.* New York: Random House, 1964.

Ficker, Victor, and Graves, Herbert S. *Deprivation in America.* Beverly Hills, Calif.: Glencoe Press, 1971.

Harrington, Michael. *The Other American: Poverty in the United States.* New York: Macmillan, 1970.

Haveman, Robert H. *A Decade of Federal Antipoverty Programs.* New York: Academic, 1977.

Levitan, Sar A. *Programs in Aid of the Poor in the 1970s.* Rev. ed. Baltimore: Johns Hopkins Press, 1973.

Messiner, Hanna H., ed. *Poverty in the Affluent Society.* New York: Harper & Row, 1973.

Miller, S. M., and Roby, Pamela A. *The Future of Inequality.* New York: Basic Books, 1970.

Pilisuk, Marc, ed. *Poor Americans: How the White Poor Live.* 2nd ed. Chicago: Aldine, 1973.

Piven, Frances Fox, and Cloward, Richard. *Regulating the Poor: The Functions of Public Welfare.* New York: Pantheon, 1971.

————. *Poor People's Movements: Why They Succeed, How They Fail.* New York: Pantheon, 1977.

Rainwater, Lee, ed. *Social Problems and Public Policy: Inequality and Justice.* Chicago: Aldine, 1974.

Ryan, William. *Blaming the Victim.* New York: Random House, 1971.

Stein, Bruno. *On Relief: The Economics of Poverty and Public Welfare.* New York: Basic Books, 1971.

Prejudice and
Discrimination

Facts about Minorities

- The median income for blacks and Hispanics is about two-thirds that of whites.
- Over 24 percent of Hispanics, and about 31 percent of blacks, are below the poverty line.
- About 85 percent of whites aged 25 or older have completed high school, compared with about 71 percent of blacks and 40 percent of Hispanics.
- Unemployment among blacks is twice that of whites; unemployment among Hispanics is a third higher than that of whites.
- About 1 percent of elected officials in this country are black.

Inequality is almost as old as humanity. Indeed, much of recorded history is an account of constantly shifting power relations as some groups have sought first to achieve dominance over others and then to maintain it.

Inequality is not peculiar to any geographical area. Within the last four decades we have seen dramatic evidence of it in many parts of the world: the repression of blacks by whites in South Africa; the repression of the Bengalis of Bangladesh by the ruling groups of Pakistan; discrimination against Catholics in Northern Ireland and against Jews in the Soviet Union; and many other cases.

The United States, too, has a long history of inequality. In our case, however, it directly contradicts the fundamental principles on which the nation's existence is said to be based. Belief in the essential equality of people has always been at the core of the American self-concept. Our national anthem describes our country as "the land of the free"; we have praised it as the refuge of the world's oppressed. But many of us are reluctant to accept that the reality falls considerably short of the ideal.

The first black slaves were brought to what is now the United States in 1619, and by the time of American independence from England in 1776, they numbered about three-quarters of a million. Meanwhile, the original inhabitants of the continent, the American Indians, were being progressively driven from their homes as white settlers pushed westward. As the Industrial Revolution gathered momentum in the nineteenth century, wave after wave of immigrants arrived to find themselves relegated to the most menial labor and the poorest living conditions. The earlier arrivals fought their way upward in a bitterly competitive society, and the descendants of those who had come earliest defended their position at the top:

> We are a nation of immigrants, but one in which the original dominant immigrant group, the so-called Anglo-Saxons, effectively preempted the crucial levers of economic and political power in government, commerce, and the professions. This elite group has tenaciously resisted the upward strivings of successive "ethnic" immigrant waves . . . . The Anglo-Americans have used their access to the levers of power to maintain their dominance, using legal force surrounded by an aura of legitimacy for such ends as economic exploitation; the restriction of immigration by a national-origin quota system which clearly branded later immigrants as culturally undesirable; the confinement of the original Indian

inhabitants largely to barren reservations; and the restriction of blacks to a degraded caste.[1]

Achieving the promise of American equality has been easiest for those whose ancestors were English Protestant; more difficult if they were non-English Protestant, Catholics, or Jews; very difficult if they were Japanese or Chinese; and nearly impossible for blacks, American Indians, Puerto Ricans and other Hispanic Americans.

This discrepancy between American ideals and American realities was the subject of a classic study in the late 1930s and early 1940s by the Swedish economist and social scientist Gunnar Myrdal. Myrdal focused on black Americans, whose position as a "poor and suppressed minority" in the land of freedom and opportunity seemed to him to create for their white counterparts

[1]Hugh Davis Graham and Ted Robert Gurr, *Violence in America: Historical and Comparative Perspectives, A Report to the National Commission on the Causes and Prevention of Violence* (Washington, D.C.: U.S. Government Printing Office, 1969), vol. 2, 625.

Georgia in 1956: the "Intrastate" sign shows passive compliance to an Interstate Commerce Commission order desegregating interstate travel.

UPI

what he called the "American dilemma." The dilemma was specifically a white person's problem because, as Myrdal put it, "practically all the economic, social, and political power is held by whites."

Myrdal saw reason to hope that white Americans would eventually resolve the problem on the side of the "American Creed." He believed that after a long period of relative stagnation, fundamental changes were occurring that would lead to full and real equality for black Americans.[2]

While the constitutional bases for black equality were laid in the 1860s and 1870s with the Thirteenth, Fourteenth, and Fifteenth Amendments, it was not until the mid-twentieth century that the rights guaranteed by these amendments began to be effectively claimed. Starting with Supreme Court decisions that affected specific, small areas of life, black Americans began to work their way toward equality. The major legal breakthrough came in 1954, in the historic *Brown v. Board of Education* decision that "separate educational facilities are inherently unequal."[3] The Supreme Court later applied this "separate cannot be equal" doctrine to a wide range of public facilities.

The Civil Rights Act of 1964 was another important step. Unlike the Civil Rights Acts of 1957 and 1960, the 1964 act provided a means to fight discrimination in employment and public accomodations, and ways to deny federal money to local governmental units that allowed discrimination. There followed a comprehensive Voting Rights Act in 1965, and a federal prohibition against housing discrimination in the Civil Rights Act of 1968. Subsequent "affirmative action" orders by President Lyndon B. Johnson aided the enforcement of these new laws; in addition, he set up new programs, such as the Head Start program, to counter the effects of discrimination.

But still the discrepancy remained between the legal equality of black Americans and their factual inequality. The impatience of at least some American blacks was turning to anger, and in August 1964 a riot erupted in Watts, a black section of Los Angeles. Before the wave of violent protest that began in Watts subsided, it had struck almost every major urban center in the country. In 1967, following particularly destructive riots in Newark and Detroit, President Johnson appointed a National Advisory Commission on Civil Disorders to investigate the origins of the disturbances and to recommend ways to forestall or control them in the future. The commission's findings suggested that there had been very little study since the work of Myrdal. Describing the basic causes of the disorders, the commission said:

> The first is surely the continuing exclusion of great numbers of Negroes from the benefits of economic progress through discrimination in employment and education, and their enforced confinement in segregated housing and schools. The corrosive and degrading effects of this condition and the attitudes that underlie it are the source of the deepest bitterness and at the center of the problem of racial disorder.[4]

The commission's basic conclusion was that "our nation is moving toward two societies, one black, one white—separate and unequal."[5]

[2]Gunnar Myrdal, *The American Dilemma* (New York: Harper & Row, 1962).
[3]347 U.S. 483 (1954).
[4]*Report of the National Advisory Commission on Civil Disorders* (Washington, D.C.: U.S. Government Printing Office, 1968), p. 203.
[5]*Report of the National Advisory Commission,* p. 1.

The situation of other minorities—American Indians, Chicanos (Mexican-Americans), Puerto Ricans, Asians, some white ethnic groups, and others—while less intensively studied, is similar. One form of discrimination to which these groups are particularly vulnerable is harassment at, or exclusion from, the voting booth, largely due to an inadequate command of the English language. The 1975 extension of the Voting Rights Act attempted to alleviate this particular inequity by requiring cities with sizable "language minority" populations to hold bilingual elections; it also permanently banned literacy tests as a voting prerequisite.[6]

Despite such legal aids, inequality and oppression remain facts of American life that are increasingly difficult to hide. But before we can describe these inequities, and suggest measures to correct them, we must first understand how inequality arises.

The Meaning of "Minority"

Categories of people who are treated less equally than other categories in the same society are referred to as minorities. But what is a minority? How does a minority situation come about? Why are some categories of people accorded unequal treatment?

Wagley and Harris suggest five characteristics of a minority:

1.   Minorities are subordinate segments of a complex society.

2.   Minorities tend to have special physical or cultural traits that are seen as undesirable by the dominant segments of the society.

3.   Minorities develop a group conscious or "we-feeling."

4.   Membership in a minority is transmitted by a rule of descent—one is born into it—which can impose the minority status on future generations, even if by then the special physical or cultural traits of the minority have disappeared.

5.   Members of a minority, whether by choice or by necessity, tend to practice endogamy—that is, to marry within the group.[7]

The characteristics singled out by Wagley and Harris seem most apt for the racial or ethnic minority, especially one that is just beginning, or has not yet begun, to be assimilated. As assimilation proceeds, some of the minority characteristics will fade—group consciousness may wane, marriage outside the group may increase, distinctive cultural traits may be abandoned. That is, there is no sharp break between totally dominant and totally minority groups, but, rather, what might be called a "continuum of minorityness." Various immigrant groups in the United States have moved along this continuum, edging progressively closer to equality and shedding some or all of their distinctive minority characteristics. It should be emphasized, however, that the physical distinctiveness of racial minorities has made assimilation much more difficult for them than for other immigrant groups, who are defined

[6] "'75 Voting Act—Help for Those Who Don't Read English,'" *U.S. News & World Report* (August 11, 1975), p. 28.

[7] Charles Wagley and Marvin Harris, *Minorities in the New World* (New York: Columbia University Press, 1958), p. 10.

largely by cultural rather than physical traits. Thus, racial minorities have tended to remain minorities for much longer.

Wagley and Harris's definition is somewhat less accurate for non-racial and non-ethnic minorities. The aged, for example, constitute a minority both in absolute numbers and in the treatment they receive from society, yet they are not born into a minority. Women do not marry within the group; membership in the homosexual minority is not transmitted from one generation to another. Nevertheless, these minorities do share in the major characteristics—subordinate status, special traits, and, increasingly, a group self-awareness.

Dominance and Subordination

Subordinate status is the principal characteristic of a minority. In almost any society, the desire for some goods, tangible or intangible, exceeds the supply, and groups within the society are likely to compete for these goods and for the power to control them. The group or groups that attain the most power dominate the other groups, controlling their access to the desired goods and often, ultimately, to other goods—social, economic, political, and personal—as well. The dominant group need not be the most numerous; it must merely be able to prevent effective challenge to its power by the subordinate group.

Once established, however, the dominant-subordinate relationship is not thereby fixed for all time. Either by the efforts of the subordinate group itself, or as a result of changing legal or economic conditions that erode the power base of the dominant group, power relationships can be altered. We can see in our own society that women today are not as subordinated as they were even a few years ago. Most of the former colonial areas of Africa, Asia, and elsewhere are now independent nations, and some formerly less influential nations, such as Japan and China, are now world powers. In a few counties in Mississippi, where blacks considerably outnumber whites, extensive voter registration has enabled these once-subordinate blacks to become politically significant.

Dominance can also vary with place. Before the Italian, Japanese, or Chinese left their native lands to come to America, they belonged to the dominant ethnic group. On the other hand, the first emigrants from England to Massachusetts left a subordinate status, as members of a persecuted nonconformist religious group, to become the dominant group in the new colonial society. And today the Soviet Jew who emigrates to Israel moves likewise from subordinate- to dominant-group status.

Except for such geographical migrations, however, it is usually very difficult for members of a subordinate group to attain a share of dominance, for the dominant group naturally wants to protect its privileged position. And among its principal weapons are prejudice and discrimination.

Prejudice and Discrimination Defined

Discrimination is "the differential treatment of individuals considered to belong to a particular social group."[8] To treat a member of a subordinate group as inferior is to discriminate against that person. Members of the

---

[8]Robin M. Williams, Jr., *The Reduction of Intergroup Tensions* (New York: Social Science Research Council, 1947), p. 39.

dominant group tend to use one standard of behavior among themselves and a different, less than equal, standard for any member of the subordinate group.

Discrimination is overt behavior. But to justify and explain their behavior to themselves, people tend to adopt new values and beliefs or to adapt old ones. Additionally, people generally tend to be ethnocentric—to see their own behavioral patterns and belief structures as desirable and natural and those of others as less natural and less desirable. These two tendencies usually result in prejudice against the subordinate group—"an emotional, rigid attitude (a predisposition to respond to a certain stimulus in a certain way) toward a group of people."[9]

But while prejudices are attitudes, not all attitudes are prejudices. Both share the element of *pre*judgment—the tendency to decide in advance how to think about a situation or an event. But unlike other attitudes, prejudice involves a strong emotional investment that strongly resists change. Prejudiced persons tend to be so committed to their prejudgments about a category of people, that even if presented with rational evidence showing that prejudgment to be wrong, they will maintain their prejudice, and probably even defend it strongly, denouncing the new evidence. For whatever reason, they will not or cannot adapt to the facts.

Gordon Allport believes that: "Prejudgments become prejudices only if they are not reversible when exposed to new knowledge." He defines prejudice directed against a category of people as

> an antipathy based upon a faulty and inflexible generalization. It may be felt or expressed. It may be directed toward a group as a whole, or toward an individual because he is a member of that group.[10]

It should be pointed out, however, that prejudice need not always be an antipathy. One may well be prejudiced in favor of a person or group of people, with a similar disregard for the objective evidence.

Thus, prejudice is based on one's attitude; it is a tendency to think about people in a categorical, predetermined way. Discrimination, on the other hand, is behavioral: the overt less-than-equal treatment of people because they belong to a subordinate group. Prejudice and discrimination are closely related, and both are often present in the same situation.

Robert Merton outlines four possible relationships between prejudice and discrimination: unprejudiced and nondiscriminatory, unprejudiced and discriminatory, prejudiced and nondiscriminatory, and prejudiced and discriminatory.[11] While it is possible to be both completely free of prejudice and completely nondiscriminatory, or to be a bigot, most people fall somewhere between these two extremes. It is possible to be prejudiced against a particular group, but not discriminate against it; it is also possible to discriminate against a particular group, but not be prejudiced against it.

For example, the builders of a new, expensive cooperative-apartment house may not be personally prejudiced against Jews, but they may refuse to sell an apartment to a Jewish family—that is, they may discriminate against

[9]George E. Simpson and J. M. Yinger, *Racial and Cultural Minorities: An Analysis of Prejudice and Discrimination* (New York: Harper & Row, 1965), pp. 10, 82.

[10]Gordon Allport, *The Nature of Prejudice* (New York: Doubleday, 1958), pp. 9, 10.

[11]Robert K. Merton, "Discrimination and the American Creed," in *Discrimination and National Welfare*, ed. R.H. MacIver (New York: Harper & Row, 1949), pp. 99-126

them—out of fear, founded or unfounded, that Jewish owners would make it more difficult to sell the remaining apartments. Or the reverse may occur; in a corporation working under government contract, and thus subject to federal Equal Employment Opportunity regulations, the employment director may be very prejudiced personally against both blacks and women, but may hire a black woman as a management trainee—that is, not discriminate against her—in order to comply with the law.

Suppose the builders were confronted with a different situation—a black rather than Jewish family attempting to buy one of their apartments. The builders might very well discriminate from both personal prejudice and concern for profits. And suppose the employment director were in a different situation, one affecting his or her own exclusive community. He or she might lead the fight to keep black families from buying houses and integrating the community. This points up two facts: that, at least to some extent, prejudice and discrimination depend on which minorities and what situations are involved. It is very difficult to keep personal prejudice from leading, sooner or later, to some form of discrimination, particularly if a significant number of people share the same prejudice.

Origins of Prejudice and Discrimination

We have said that prejudice and discrimination are weapons used by the dominant group to maintain its dominance. It would be a mistake, however, to see them as always, or even usually, conscious weapons. Unless and until the subordinate group mounts a serious challenge to the existing power, prejudice and discrimination are apt to seem very much a part of the natural order of things. Their origins are many and complex, and it is necessary to consider both the felt needs of individual persons and the structural organization of society to explain them. To blame them wholly on warped personalities, or wholly on oppressive social structures, as has sometimes been done, is to oversimplify the situation. Each of these approaches has its value, and they complement one another.

Psychological Factors

Frustration-Aggression.   At one time or another most human beings feel frustrated. They want something, but because of reasons, events or other people, they cannot get it. This can lead to feelings of anger and aggression, that they may express in any of several ways. The most obvious way would be to strike back at the source of the frustration. But often this is impossible, either because it is unknown, because people are subjectively unable to recognize the source, or, finally, because they are in such a position, usually a dependent one, that they cannot risk striking back. Whatever the reason, the results are the same. They are unable to vent their anger and aggression on the real source of their frustration.

Instead, the aggression is often directed at a safer and more convenient target, usually one that somewhat resembles the real source of frustration. That is, the aggression is displaced onto a *scapegoat*. When the scapegoat is not limited to one particular person, but is extended to include all similar people, it may produce a more or less settled prejudice.

For example, suppose that a middle-aged man, who has been working for

twenty years at the same job, is told by his young supervisor that his job will soon be eliminated by automation. The man is understandably angry, and frightened. But were he to vent his aggression on the supervisor, he knows he would then almost certainly be fired. Later that night, he is telling his woes to friends at the local bar, when a long-haired young man comes in for a beer. Our man accuses the youth, and "all you lazy kids," of being good for nothing and ruining the country, and only the intervention of the bartender prevents him from assaulting the young man.

It is fairly clear that this man has displaced his aggression toward his young supervisor onto the "kids." Rather than deal with the supervisor and the whole range of factors that led to the prospect of his job being eliminated, he finds it much easier and more comprehensible to blame the problems of the country on all young people. (Further discussion of frustration-aggression theory can be found in Chapter 6.)

Projection.   Another source of prejudice and discrimination is projection. Many people have traits that they perceive as undesirable. They have an understandable wish to rid themselves of these traits, but they cannot always do it directly—either because they find the effort too difficult or because they are unable to admit to themselves that they possess these traits. In this case, they may relieve themselves by attributing the unwanted traits to someone else, often to some other group in society. This makes it possible for them to

Despite some progress toward equality, the need for the National March against Racism in 1974 pointed out that the oppression of minorities in this country is still very much a reality.

Marilyn Schwartz/Photo Researchers, Inc.

reject and condemn the traits without rejecting and condemning themselves, for now it is the other person or group who is guilty of them. Since the emotional pressures behind projection can be very intense, it is difficult to under-cut it by rational argument.

An often-cited example of projection is the view that whites have held of black sexuality. Many whites saw blacks as inordinately sexual, as being totally promiscuous and unfettered in their sexual relations, and there was much concern about protecting white women from sexual attacks by black men. Historically, it was white men who enjoyed virtually free sexual rein with black women, particularly slaves. White society, however, regarded overt sexuality as unacceptable, and it is likely that white men felt some guilt or anxiety about their sexual desires and adventures. In order to exorcise that guilt, white men projected their own lust and sexuality onto the black man—a much easier course than admitting the discrepancy between their own behavior and their values.

Socialization and Social Structure

While the emotional needs of insecure persons account for some prejudice and discrimination, they do not explain why certain groups become and remain objects of prejudice and discrimination. To understand this, we need to look at some larger social processes.

Competition and Exploitation.   As noted earlier, the demand for more than the available supply of certain goods gives rise in many societies to a competitive struggle for possession that usually results in dominance for one group and subordination for others.[12] Even if the initial objects of competition are economic goods, it is ultimately a struggle for power and hence a political process. Once established, this political dominance is likely to be reinforced by the more specifically economic process of exploitation, where the dominant group uses the labor of the subordinate group for a less than equitable return. Slavery and serfdom are the most obvious forms of such exploitation, but nominally "free" workers may also be exploited, and frequently are—for example, migrant farm workers, sweatshop factory laborers, illegal aliens, and unorganized clerical and service workers.

Economic exploitation is one form of discrimination practiced by the dominant against the subordinate group. Historically, the subordinate group has been the work force of unskilled labor. Before the 1940s, unskilled jobs were plentiful and more easily available to blacks as exploitable labor. With the development of protective labor legislation, however, employers could no longer use the subordinate group for "cheap labor." Blacks were then systematically denied jobs as white-dominated unions maintained a strong-hold on the skilled jobs, and employers sought cheaper unskilled labor by transferring basic manufacturing operations abroad, to South Korea, Taiwan, or Hong Kong, for example.[13]

Discrimination can take many other forms. Some of these are practical—members of the subordinate group may be legally prevented from owning

---

[12]See Donald L. Noel, "A Theory of the Origin of Ethnic Stratification," *Social Problems* 16 (Fall 1968), 157-172; and Simpson and Yinger, *Racial and Cultural Minorities*, pp. 81-82.

[13]Edna Bonacich, "Advanced Capitalism and Black/White Race Relations in the United States: A Split Labor Market Interpretation," *American Sociological Review*, vol. 41 (February 1976), 34-51.

property or voting, or they may be extralegally terrorized into submission, as often happened to strikers in the early labor movement. Some are symbolic, as when a black person is refused service in a restaurant. All are aimed, consciously and unconsciously, at keeping the subordinate people "in their place."

Since members of the dominant group know that they are treating subordinate group members as inferiors, they need to justify this behavior. A typical human tendency to rationalize one's own behavior is aided by the ethnocentric tendency to see one's own group as right and worthy and other groups as therefore wrong and unworthy.

Members of the dominant group tend to tell themselves that it is right and proper that they have more—that they are smarter, more clever, and racially superior—and they come to believe that they deserve what they have. The subordinate group, as they see it, is lazy, stupid, heathen, biologically inferior, or otherwise unworthy and therefore deserves less (or perhaps needs less). Thus those groups in a society who are different from the dominant group, who have less power, and who are economically useful to the dominant group tend to become the targets of prejudice and discrimination.

Social Norms.   A social norm, in essence, is a social standard that specifies what kind of behavior is correct and appropriate in a given situation. It is relevant to our discussion because, while it does not tell us why prejudice and discrimination begin, it does help to explain how and why they are perpetuated.

Social norms are learned in a process that begins almost at birth. Small children soon learn what kind of behavior brings the approval of their parents and what is apt to be rebuked. The same process continues as they encounter other significant figures. Gradually children internalize the accepted values and mores of society. They receive approval from parents, from other adults, and later from peers, when they behave in socially acceptable ways; they experience disapproval when they do not.

Through this process, most children are socialized about the prevailing norms of the society into which they were born. If the society is prejudiced against certain minorities and engages in discriminatory behavior, the children will generally learn those prejudices and behaviors and will think they are correct and natural. The original reasons for prejudice and discrimination remain deeply embedded in the folkways and mores of the society, in the cultural heritage passed on from generation to generation. Prejudice and discrimination thus acquire a life of their own quite apart from their origins.

The human tendency to social conformity is also likely to support prejudice and discrimination. Even if some members of a dominant group are ambivalent toward the subordinate group and personally feel no special prejudice, nevertheless, if most people around them are prejudiced and engage in discriminatory behavior, the ambivalent and indifferent people will usually go along. It is easier for them to conform to the group norms than to deviate and perhaps bring hostility upon themselves.

Stereotyping.   Still another source of prejudice and discrimination is stereotyping, attributing a fixed and usually unfavorable or inaccurate conception to a category of people. Whereas social norms are concerned primarily with behavior and only indirectly with attitudes, stereotyping is basically a matter of attitude, affecting, and affected by, discriminatory behavior.

Usually a stereotype contains some truth, but it is exaggerated, distorted, or somehow taken out of context. Stereotyping has much to do with how humans normally think because we tend to perceive and understand things in categories.

Naturally, we apply this same mental process to people. We build up mental pictures of minorities, pictures made from overgeneralized and highly selected impressions and bits of information, and we use these pictures to define all members of a minority regardless of their individual differences. Thus we come to assume that all Indians are drunks, all blacks are lazy, all Puerto Ricans are short, all Italians are gangsters, all Jews are shrewd, all Englishmen are reserved, all Swedes are blond, all Frenchmen are lovers, all long-haired young people are drug addicts, all old people are senile, all working women are secretaries. None of these generalizations will stand even perfunctory analysis. Yet many people habitually use such notions when thinking about minorities.

Institutionalized Discrimination

If discrimination is a socially learned behavior of dominant group members, designed to support and justify their continued dominance, it is reasonable to expect that such discrimination will, often unwittingly, be built into the very structure and form of society. To members of a society who are socialized to accept and believe that members of certain minorities "just are" to be treated as inferiors, it would be perfectly natural to formulate public policy and build public institutions that would discriminate against those minorities.

To some extent this is exactly what has happened in the United States. If many blacks, Chicanos, American Indians, Puerto Ricans, women, aged, and members of other minorities do not have "equal protection of the laws" in their dealings with public institutions and public policy, it is not necessarily because of the conscious prejudice of public officials. More fundamentally this discrimination is the unconscious result of the structure and functioning of public institutions and policies themselves. It is almost as if the discrimination were part of the very definition of the society.

As an example, people living near Indian reservations often see the Indians as lazy and incompetent, unable to exercise any initiative or do anything to improve their often deplorable condition of life. What such people fail to realize is the degree to which apparent Indian incompetence is a result of the way in which the Indians are governed by society. As Robert Thomas points out in discussing the Sioux of the Pine Ridge reservation in South Dakota:

> The Sioux tribal government is, in effect, without power. Most of the day to day decisions about Sioux life, about roads, schools, relief, are made by Bureau [of Indian Affairs] personnel . . . . Further, what decisions the tribal council makes are subject to approval by the Secretary of the Interior . . . . The Bureau of Indian Affairs is *the* economic and political force in Pine Ridge reservation . . . . Bureau personnel attend most public meetings and usually call them to get the Sioux to agree to some program or other, *and* direct them as well . . . . Tribal

projects are supervised by Bureau officials . . . . The Pine Ridge reservation is, as are most American Indian reservations, an example of a very complete colonial system.[14]

In short, the Indians have been made unable to handle their own affairs by an administrative structure that has denied them any opportunity to learn new ways of doing things while simultaneously rendering old tribal ways useless and ineffective.

Health care provides another example. From conception to old age, minorities suffer from poor nutrition, lack of disease prevention, and generally inadequate medical treatment. Studies show that minorities suffer a shorter life expectancy, greater infant and maternal mortality, and two to five times more instances of death from infectious, preventable diseases than do non-minority Americans. (See Chapters 2 and 7 for fuller discussions of this topic.) Does this mean that the dominant culture has deliberately chosen to keep minorities sick and undernourished as a form of oppression? The answer is "no." But the American health care systems, housing codes, and social welfare arrangements are structured to the advantage of the white middle and upper classes simply because it did not occur to the lawmakers that such a structure was not in the best interests of all concerned.

As it would be difficult to discuss all categories of institutional discrimination against all minorities, we will, therefore, focus on four major categories: education, employment, housing, and social justice. We will also limit our examples to four minorities: blacks, Chicanos, American Indians, and Puerto Ricans. But the patterns we will describe apply in general to other categories as well, such as health care and consumer issues, and to other minorities, including women and the aged. (See Chapters 9 and 10.)

Education

In the United States, education probably generates more emotion than any other issue, particularly the question of whether black, Puerto Rican, Chicano, and American Indian children attend the same schools as white children. The question is sometimes put in terms of busing to achieve racial balance, of quality education for all, and of public tax support for private schools. Families have been known to move repeatedly to find better public schools for their children; parents in the inner cities, primarily minority parents, are demanding greater local community control over city schools. Increasingly, political campaigns involve educational issues.

Americans take public school systems very seriously. Undoubtedly one reason is that in this country education has generally been seen as the way to social and economic advancement. It is almost an article of faith that American children should get more education than their parents and achieve higher social and economic status.

We have long assumed that higher education leads to a higher income. Whether or not this is true (and new data have begun to call it into question), there is no doubt that among those working at this time, the more highly educated usually receive substantially higher salaries.[15] Evidence further

[14]Robert K. Thomas, "Powerless Politics," *New University Thought* 4 (Winter 1966-1967), 44-53.

[15]National Center for Education Statistics, *The Condition of Education* (Washington, D.C.: U.S. Government Printing Office, 1975).

suggests that even better than a sheepskin (diploma) is a white skin, for minorities at all levels of education earn less than their non-minority counterparts.

Minorities have less chance of finishing high school or attending college than do whites. In 1977, 85 percent of whites 25 years of age or older had completed four years of high school or more, while only 71 percent of the blacks and 40 percent of the Puerto Ricans and Chicanos in the same age group had gone this far.[16]

By the same token, blacks are about twice as likely as whites to be high school dropouts. In 1977, 29 percent of blacks age 25 to 34 had not completed high school, as compared with 15 percent of whites in this age group. While blacks represent 11 percent of the total United States population, they comprised only 7 percent of the total college enrollment. This figure

Demonstrators in California protest a court decision favoring Allan Bakke, a rejected medical school applicant. The Supreme Court found that the school's affirmative action admissions policies discriminated against white students.
UPI

[16]U.S. Bureau of the Census, "Population Profile of the United States: 1977," *Current Population Reports,* Series P-20, no. 324 (Washington, D.C.: U.S. Government Printing Office, 1978), p. 11; and Reynolds Farley, "Trends in Racial Inequalities: Have the Gains of the 1960s Disappeared in the 1970s?" *American Sociological Review,* vol. 42, no. 1 (April 1977), pp. 189-208.

represents a tremendous numerical increase during the past several years. Of all college-age blacks, only 11 percent were in college, compared to 25 percent of whites of that age group. Black students were most likely to be attending public four-year colleges, while their white counterparts were equally likely to be enrolled in both public or private four-year colleges.[17]

Insofar as it is built-in factors of society that cause minorities to be less well prepared for schooling at any given level, less able to pay the "hidden" costs of "free" education (books, supplies, transportation, clothing, and class trips), and less likely to finish, minorities are the objects of institutional discrimination in American education. But they are also the objects of another kind of discrimination: the manner in which they are portrayed in American textbooks.

Lately there has been increasing recognition of the existence and seriousness of this form of discrimination. Paraphrasing a report prepared by the Indian Historical Society after evaluating forty-three textbooks on American history used in the fourth, fifth, and eighth grades in California, Jeannette Henry asks:

> What is the effect upon the student, when he learns from his textbooks that one race, and one alone, is the most, the best, the greatest; when he learns that Indians were mere parts of the landscape and wilderness which had to be cleared out, to make way for the great "movement" of white population across the land; and when he learns that Indians were killed and forcibly removed from their ancient homelands to make way for adventurers (usually called "pioneering goldminers"), for land grabbers (usually called "settlers"), and for illegal squatters on Indian-owned land (usually called "frontiersmen")? What is the effect upon the young Indian child himself, who is also a student in the school system, when he is told that Columbus discovered America, that Coronado "brought civilization" to the Indian people, and that the Spanish missionaries provided havens of refuge for the Indians? Is it reasonable to assume that the student, of whatever race, will not discover at some time in his life that Indians discovered America thousands of years before Columbus set out upon his voyage; that Coronado brought death and destruction to the native peoples; and that the Spanish missionaries, in all too many cases, forcibly dragged Indians to the missions?[18]

Discrimination and Busing.   The most prominent issue with respect to minority education is school desegregation. Desegregation has been a long time in coming. In 1972, eighteen years after the Supreme Court decision that disallowed the "separate but equal" doctrine, and seventeen years after the 1955 decision that mandated integration "with all deliberate speed," nearly a third of minority students attended public schools with 80 percent or more minority enrollment; some 60 percent attended schools with 50 percent or more minority enrollment; and only 39.6 percent of minority students attended public schools with less than 50 percent minority enrollment.[19] The school population of 35 major cities was 75 percent or more black.[20]

De jure segregation—segregation required by law, once standard in the Southern states—is now a thing of the past, but *de facto* segregation, a result of housing patterns, economic patterns, gerrymandered school districts, and

[17]"U.S. Bureau of the Census, "Population Profile of the United States: 1977," p. 12.
[18]Jeannette Henry, *The Indian Historian* 1 (December 1967), 22.
[19]National Center for Education Statistics, *The Condition of Education*, p. 70.
[20]"Busing: Why Tide Is Turning," *U.S. News & World Report* (August 11, 1975), pp. 24-26.

sometimes intimidation, is harder to eradicate. The principal remedy suggested thus far is busing—transporting pupils from their local schools to other schools in order to achieve a reasonable racial balance in all the schools within a particular area. Predictably, busing has become one of the most emotional political issues of our day.

The basic argument for busing is that:

1. Minority children, or perhaps all children, will receive a better education in racially balanced rather than in racially segregated schools.

2. Busing effectively achieves a racial balance.

Unfortunately, both facets of the argument have turned out to be somewhat weaker in practice than they were in theory. Attendance at racially balanced schools has been accompanied by some increase in minority achievement; and a good many school districts that had undertaken extensive busing programs to create integrated schools have found that their schools remain about as segregated as before, if not more so. Because American parents usually regard their children's education as particularly important, and because white parents fear that integration will lower standards in the schools, they may be inclined to leave heavily integrated districts, to send their children to private schools, or to protest vehemently against busing, even though they may not be notably prejudiced or inclined to discriminate in any other respect.

Washington, D.C. is commonly cited as an example. After busing was instituted, so many white residents moved to the suburbs that in 1970 the school system was 94 percent black.[21] As William Raspberry, a *Washington Post* columnist, commented early in 1970: "We find ourselves busing children from all-black neighborhoods all the way across town to schools that are rapidly becoming all-black."[22] Other cities have had similar experiences. In Inglewood, California, for example, combined minorities constituted 38 percent of the public school enrollment when court-ordered busing was put into effect in 1970; by 1975, minority enrollment was 80 percent, and the busing order was rescinded by the same judge who had ordered it.

James Coleman, in 1966, implied that integration, by exposing minority students to the higher achievements of the middle-class majority, would improve the performance of the former without diminishing that of the latter.[23] Nine years later Coleman seems to have reversed himself: "Desegregation through the courts probably will have served in the long run to separate whites and blacks more severely than before."[24] Recognizing the complexities involved in the phenomenon of "white flight," Coleman added that "it's not entirely lower-class blacks that middle-class whites are fleeing. They are fleeing a school system that they see as too large, as unmanageable, as unresponsive, to find a smaller, more responsive system."[25] In this regard, it

---

[21]"The Turn from 'Integration'," *U.S. News and World Report* (March 9, 1970), p. 30.

[22]*Washington Post*, February 20, 1970.

[23]James S. Coleman, *et al.*, *Equality of Educational Opportunity* (Washington, D.C.: U.S. Government Printing Office, 1966), pp. 3-7.

[24]"Busing: Why Tide Is Turning," p. 25. The data upon which Coleman based his conclusion have since been questioned; see the April 1976 issue of *Harvard Educational Review*.

[25]Maurice deG. Ford, "School Integration and Bussing: Courts, Bussing and White Flight," *The Nation* (July 5, 1975), p. 13.

STOP FORCE BUSI

CHILDRE BELON: TO TH FAMIL' NOT T STATE

THE GLOBE IS GOOD FOR WRAPPING FISH

BUS GARRITY

MARSHFIELD

THE WHITES HAVE RIGHTS TOO!

HELL No! Bussing must go

has been pointed out that busing children over long distances costs money that might otherwise by used to improve instruction. And busing tends to weaken local control and interest in the schools. It is difficult for parents to take an active part in school affairs when the school is not easily accessible.

Busing may also provoke racial tensions within a community, especially when community cooperation is not sought prior to a busing program. Lower-class urban whites, who cannot afford the suburbs, often see attempts to integrate their neighborhood schools as threats to their way of life. For example, in 1975 a federal judge ordered the exchange of some 24,000 students between the black and southern sections of Boston, in order to counter the segregating effects of gerrymandered school districts. (The better-quality middle-class suburban schools, however, were not involved in the busing program.) In effect, blacks were being bused from schools that were overcrowded and inadequate. The Irish and Polish of South Boston, who saw themselves as oppressed ethnic minorities and felt that their community, power, and cultural identities were being threatened, opposed the busing violently, and it was months before the school system achieved any semblance of order.[26]

As previously suggested, there is also considerable controversy about

Busing, an emotionally volatile issue, provoked this Boston rally; 8,000 peaceful protesters gathered in 1974 to voice their complaints against forced integration.
UPI

[26]John Buell and Tom deLuca, "On Busing," *Progressive* (April 1975), pp. 26-27.

whether or not school integration, even if achieved, will result in better education. Coleman found that the most important predictors of children's success in school were their backgrounds and social environments; schools were of relatively little importance in affecting achievement. In a more recent study, Sar Levitan, William Johnston, and Robert Taggart found that "there is no proof that integration, increased outlays per pupil, more relevant curricula, or any changes have had, or will have, a rapid and significant impact"[27] on improving the school performance of black slum children. On the other hand, a state-wide survey of Michigan's school system suggested that there was a positive relationship between school services and student achievement.[28] A study of ten communities across the United States by the United States Commission on Civil Rights found large improvements in the quality of education in all communities studied as a result of school desegregation.[29] Despite the efforts of a host of experts, the evidence about the effects of desegregation on academic achievement is thus far inconclusive.

It should be noted, however, that improving educational equality is *not* the only purpose of desegregating schools. Many observers see desegregation as a way for whites and minority group members to learn to live with each other on a personal basis. According to this viewpoint, stereotyping and racism are much less likely to occur when people get to know each other as individuals. As David Cohen points out, desegregation "seems a necessary step toward equality because it is an obvious way to break down racist ideas and institutional arrangements."[30] For example, while the *idea* of busing remains unpopular, cities like Boston have not only learned to live with it, but even to overlook it in a concern for improved education that would benefit both blacks and whites. Others say that it is difficult to accurately test the educational progress of students who are bused when busing and desegregation are accompanied by disruption, hostility, or violence. In Maurice Ford's words:

> Very few civil rights leaders are surprised that test scores do not substantially improve, or racial attitudes markedly change, during an initial period of desegregation . . . . Indeed, given the level of violence and tension in [newly desegregated] schools, it would be a miracle if test scores did not go down and stereotyped attitudes did not become more fixed in these initial stages. The hope is not so much for the present. . . . The hope is that . . . when the present turmoil has subsided, black and white . . . children . . . will begin to go to school together in peace and begin to learn to love and respect each other and to appreciate each other's diverse talents and contributions.[31]

There is considerable evidence that in certain situations, busing *can* be an effective method of desegregating schools. For example, school officials in a few smaller communities were able to ease fears about the effects of busing by

[27]In Juan Cameron, "Black America: Still Waiting for Full Membership," *Fortune* (April 1975), p. 172; and Sar Levitan, *et al.*, *Still a Dream* (Cambridge, Mass.: Harvard University Press, 1975).

[28]James W. Guthrie, *et al.*, *Schools and Inequality* (Cambridge: M.I.T. Press, 1971).

[29]U.S. Commission on Civil Rights, *School Desegregation in Ten Communities* (Washington, D.C.: U.S. Government Printing Office, 1973).

[30]David K. Cohen, "Segregation, Desegregation, and Brown: A Twenty-Year Retrospective," *Society* (November–December 1975), p. 37.

[31]Howard Husock, "No More Mileage in Bussing," *The Nation*, vol. 325, no. 23 (December 21, 1977), 712; Ford, "School Integration and Bussing," p. 13.

calling a series of parents' meetings before the school term began. Black and white parents discussed and planned the busing program together, and racial hostilities were prevented. In the ten communities studied by the Civil Rights Commission, the busing program worked because funds were provided to improve the quality of all the schools involved.[32] School officials in some other communities (such as Goldsboro, North Carolina) created highly desirable special programs in black schools that white children could not participate in unless they were bused.[33] In other areas, compromise busing plans were developed to prevent white flight. For example, in Louisville, Kentucky, children attend their neighborhood schools two days a week and are bused to integrated schools in another county the other three days.[34] In cases such as these, desegregation was accompanied by a marked increase in educational quality for black children.

Perhaps the best way to make busing effective would be to bus children between town or city schools to much higher-quality suburban schools. Not only would disadvantaged minority children obtain the best possible education, but white flight would no longer be possible. In 1974 the Supreme Court ruled in a Detroit case that stated that while the Constitution required desegregation within a city, it did not require it between city schools and suburban schools usually in another county.[35] (In fact, where city and suburban schools are combined in a one-county system—such as Charlotte, North Carolina, and Nashville, Tennessee—well-to-do whites could not leave the school system and busing has been successful.)[36] Despite some successful busing programs, most communities have either instituted busing programs in ways that provoke racial antagonisms—such as in Boston—or have been forced to abandon busing because a sufficient number of white students were no longer available within the community.[37]

Clearly busing is a complex question, and all the evidence is not yet available. In common justice, and in conformity with the meaning of the Constitution, the nation is bound to do all it can to provide equality of educational opportunity—not only in law but in fact—for all children. The question is, how? Most Americans still seem to believe that integration is a necessary and desirable part of the solution. A 1975 Harris survey found 56 percent of adults in favor and 35 percent opposed to desegregation of public schools. These percentages did not vary significantly in any region of the country. On the question of busing, however, opinions were sharply reversed: 20 percent favored busing and 75 percent were opposed to it.[38] A recent Gallup poll found that among blacks, only 40 percent were in favor of busing, and 47 percent were opposed.[39] How, then, are we to achieve equal educational opportunity for all children? And, if by integration, how are we to manage this without compulsory busing? One possible approach is through the desegregation of housing.

[32]U.S. Commission on Civil Rights, *School Desegration in Ten Communities.*
[33]Diane Ravitch, "The Solution That Has Failed to Solve," *New York Times,* December 21, 1975, Section 4, p. 3.
[34]Ford, "School Integration and Bussing."
[35]Cohen, "Segregation, Desegregation, and Brown," p. 34.
[36]"Busing: Why Tide Is Turning," p. 26.
[37]Sandra Stencel, "Educational Equality," *Editorial Research Reports* (August 24, 1973), p. 659.
[38]Louis Harris, *The Harris Survey* (New York: Chicago Tribune, N.Y. News Syndicate, October 2, 1975), p. 1.
[39]Ravitch, "The Solution That Has Failed to Solve," p. 3.

Housing   Housing segregation, the separation and isolation of minorities into regions, cities, neighborhoods, blocks, and even individual buildings, has become increasingly solidified during the last several decades. The major demarcation has been between the whites in the suburbs and the blacks and other minorities in the cities.

A look at some recent census findings will indicate the growth of white out-migration from cities to surrounding suburbs. In the 1960s, the white population of the central cities in the Northeast declined by 10 percent. During the same period, the white population of the suburban areas of the these same cities increased by 15 percent.[40]

While whites were moving to the suburbs, blacks were moving to the cities at an even faster rate. During this decade, the black population of New York City increased by 38.2 percent. Other cities with black populations of 50,000 or more experienced similar gains. Dallas, Los Angeles, Boston, and Detroit showed net increases of over 20 percent; only Birmingham, Alabama, had a decline in black population due to out-migration.[41] Though this rate of white migration to the suburbs and black migration to the cities declined during the 1970s, a segregated pattern of housing had already become firmly established.

Within cities, minorities are segregated into specific, usually less affluent neighborhoods. A *New York Times* analysis of the 1970 census figures showed that more than two-thirds of New York City's 2,159 census tracts were either 90 percent white or 90 percent black. There remain, according to the *Times*, only a few integrated neighborhoods in New York, but the trend is clearly toward minority-dominated areas. This usually also means the expansion of poverty and the spread of "urban-blight." Dr. Abraham C. Burstein of New York's Human Resources Administration estimated that over 80 percent of the black population in New York live in the city's twenty-six officially designated poverty areas.[42] More recent statistics indicate that blacks make up only 5 percent of the nation's suburban population; three-fourths of all blacks live in urban areas and 60 percent live in the central cities.[43] (See Chapter 14.)

Most of today's housing crisis began after World War II, when the population began to grow rapidly, accompanied by widespread migration to the cities. At that time the government, primarily by means of the mortgage programs of the Federal Housing Administration (FHA) and the Veterans Administration (VA), joined with private builders to encourage private development of the suburbs as a way to solve the housing shortage.[44] This seemed a reasonable approach, in view of the American free-enterprise tradition, and in terms of number of dwelling units provided, it worked spectacularly well. Unfortunately, the free-enterprise market created housing

---

[40]"Trends in Social and Economic Conditions: Population Change by Region for Central Cities and Suburban Rings," *Current Population Reports*, Series P-23, no. 33 (September 3, 1970).

[41]Negro Population in Selected Places and Selected Counties," *1970 Census of the Population* (Washington, D.C.: U.S. Government Printing Office, June 1971).

[42]Edward C. Burks, "Blacks and Puerto Ricans Up Million Here in Decade," *New York Times*, March 6, 1972, pp. 1, 22.

[43]"The Social and Economic Status of Black Population," *Current Population Reports*, Series P-23, no. 5, July 1975, (Washington, D.C.: U.S. Government Printing Office, 1976), p. 1; and Cameron, "Black America," pp. 168-169.

[44]See Bernard Weissbourd, *Segregation, Subsidies and Megalopolis* (Santa Barbara, Calif.: Center for the Study of Democratic Institutions, 1964).

for those who could pay for it, which many minority people could not. Even for those who could, the FHA and VA guidelines for mortgage guarantees, designed to maintain the stability of neighborhoods and to encourage home ownership by young families with reasonably dependable earning prospects, presented obstacles and discouragement.[45] According to one study:

> From 1935 to 1950—a period in which about 15 million new dwellings were constructed—the power of the national government was explicitly used to prevent integrated housing. Federal policies were based on the premise that economic and social stability could best be achieved through keeping neighborhood populations as homogeneous as possible. Thus, the *Underwriting Manual* of the Federal Housing Administration . . . warned that "if a neighborhood is to retain stability, it is necessary that properties shall continue to be occupied by the same social and racial group." It advised appraisers to lower their valuation of properties in mixed neighborhoods, "often to the point of rejection." FHA actually drove out of business some developers who insisted upon open policies.[46]

It was not until 1962, when President John F. Kennedy signed a limited anti-discrimination executive order, that the federal government housing program became at all integrationist. Although it would be inaccurate to cite federal housing policy as the only cause of housing discrimination—other factors such as the refusal of some whites to sell their houses to blacks, the suburban zoning patterns that tended to keep out poorer families, and the ties within minority communities themselves all contributed—it must be said that the officially sanctioned practices and policies of the federal housing agencies from the mid-1930s until 1962 are among the major reasons why American housing is segregated. It has also been pointed out that although since 1965 federal law has prohibited discrimination in the rental, sale, or financing of suburban housing, this law has remained largely unenforced.[47]

Housing available to minorities is often overpriced, primarily as a result of "blockbusting." In this too common practice, real estate agents use warnings of a minority "invasion" and of lowered property values to frighten white homeowners into selling their houses to the agent at reduced prices. The agent then resells the houses at inflated prices to members of minorities. Today, blacks occupy about one-tenth of all housing units in the country, but more than twice as many black households as white households lack some or all plumbing facilities.[48] (For a further discussion of housing and poverty, see Chapters 6 and 14.)

Statistics, of course, do not tell the whole story. Robert Burnette in *The Tortured Americans* describes the housing problems of another American minority:

> Until 1961 Indians were excluded from plans for public housing projects. They lived, as many still do, in tarpaper shacks, rickety log houses, ragged tents, abandoned automobile bodies, and hillside caves. When public housing did become available to the Indians, the inevitable corruption that attaches itself like a leech to such projects made a mockery of the program's intentions.

[45]Eunice Grier and George Grier, "Equality and Beyond: Housing Segregation in the Great Society," *Daedalus* 95 (Winter 1966), 77-87.
[46]Grier and Grier, "Equality and Beyond," p. 82.
[47]See Cameron, "Black America."
[48]"Social and Economic Status of Black Population," p. 134.

Burnette reports how things went for his tribe, the Rosebud Sioux, after the inception of a federal housing program in 1967:

> By the end of 1969 the program was a complete failure—except to those who made criminal profits from the construction of the homes. Today there are 375 cheap, defective houses made of ⅜-inch plywood on the reservation. Ceilings are caving in, roofs leak, walls are crooked, and floor joists show through the tiles. Over three hundred of the houses do not have back or frontsteps. Over a fourth of the houses are uncompleted; they have no toilets, no plumbing or bathtubs, no cupboards or cabinets or sinks.[49]

Moreover there can be no doubt that the "housing problem" which minorities suffer is the direct result of the prejudice directed against them as minorities. As Karl Taeuber puts it:

> Negroes took over housing formerly occupied by whites. . . . Racial residential segregation came about through deliberate discrimination and related social factors. A peculiarly distorted housing market evolved, based not on the color of a man's money but the color of his skin.[50]

Furthermore, as Cameron points out,

> blacks who aspire to be homeowners have also been hit by a cruel economic trend; just as their incomes began rising rapidly, the cost of housing shot up rapidly, too. To make matters worse, industry has followed the move of middle-income whites to the suburbs. Effectively barred from living near the relocated businesses, blacks have found themselves shut out of jobs.[51]

One feature of the growing political awareness of American minorities has been a demand for effective action on the housing front. Most of the government-sponsored low-income housing programs of the past have floundered on corruption, poor planning, or community resistance. Somehow, in the next few years, the nation must find a way to provide decent housing for all its people.

Employment

The idea of work as the way to better oneself is deeply ingrained in the American ethos. Although probably no longer as pervasive as it once was, the American work ethic still holds that if you really want a job, you can find one, and if you work hard, you will make money. The corollary to this is the notion that if you are wealthy, you deserve your wealth because you worked for it; and if you are poor, it is because you are lazy. (See Chapter 13.)

Thus one hears the argument that if only blacks and Puerto Ricans and Indians would make the effort to find jobs and stick to them, they could improve their lot. Unfortunately, discrimination is no less prevalent in employment than it is in education and housing.

In some ways, discrimination in employment is a direct result of discrimination in education. We have already noted the relationship between

[49]Robert Burnette, *The Tortured Americans* (Englewood Cliffs, N.J.: Prentice-Hall, 1971), pp. 22, 145-146.

[50]Karl E. Taeuber, "The Effect of Income Redistribution on Racial Residential Segregation," *Urban Affairs Quarterly*, vol. 4, no. 1 (September 1968), 13.

[51]Cameron, "Black America," p. 169.

income level and education level. Since today the chances of finding even an entry-level job without a high school diploma are slim, this lack of education means that many minority persons will spend their lives underemployed or unemployed. This, in turn, means a low income, resulting in inferior housing, with the likelihood of a poor education for the next generation, and so on—a cycle of discrimination built into the system.

Is there any escape from this cycle? What of those jobs that inherently do not require much formal education, that one learns mostly through apprenticeship—the kind of jobs represented by many labor unions?

Historically, labor unions especially at the higher levels, have been in the forefront of civil rights battles, but union locals have often resisted minority demands for membership. William Gould points out a basic conflict between the rhetoric of union leadership and established union policies and practices. Unions, like other institutions, are resistant to internal change or economic sacrifice for the purpose of accommodating the demands of minority workers.[52] There are only so many jobs to go around, and those who have them want to keep them.

This means that union-sponsored job-training programs are generally closed to minority workers. Progress in opening apprenticeship and training programs has been slow. As the national economic and general employment picture has worsened in recent years, the opening of these programs has been marked by growing bitterness and resistance. The New York City Commission on Human Rights reported that "a pattern of exclusion exists in a substantial portion of the building construction industry, effectively barring non-whites from participation in this area."[53] With the exception of the carpenters' and electricians' unions, trade unions in New York City have fought every attempt to open their programs to nonwhites. One local went so far as to reject the results of court-ordered competitive tests when twenty-nine of the top sixty scores were achieved by blacks, claiming that to score so high, the blacks must have cheated.[54]

Nationally, there has been some improvement in this situation. By 1975 blacks comprised a third of all new members in trade unions and 12 percent of total union membership. In some unions, notably those of steel and auto workers and state and municipal employees, blacks accounted for a third of the membership.[55] These newly unionized black workers, however, are among the first to be laid off (because of union seniority systems) during a recession.

The overall employment picture is not bright. Current statistics indicate that minority members hold a disproportionate number of the lower-level, lower-paying jobs. Even when they do secure better jobs, they are frequently paid less than white workers in comparable jobs. Latest figures from the Census Bureau show that blacks and Hispanics are more likely than whites to be service workers and laborers and less likely to be salespeople and white-collar workers; while 6.7 percent of the white labor force work as salespeople, only 2.5 percent of the black and 3.9 percent of the Hispanic labor force have such jobs. By contrast, less than 33 percent of whites are

[52]William B. Gould, "Discrimination and the Unions," in *Poverty: Views from the Left*, eds. Jeremy Larner and Irving Howe (New York: William Morrow, 1968), pp. 168-183.

[53]In Julius Jacobson, "Union Conservatism: A Barrier to Racial Equality," in *The Negro and the American Labor Movement*,ed. Julius Jacobson (Garden City, N.Y.: Doubleday, 1968).

[54]Jacobson, "Union Conservatism."

[55]Cameron, "Black America," pp. 162-165.

Figure 8-1

Percent of Persons below the Poverty Level by Race and Spanish Origin

Source: Bureau of the Census, "Characteristics of the Population below the Poverty Level, *Current Population Reports,* Series P-60, no. 115 (Washington, D.C.: U.S. Government Printing Office, July, 1978), p. 3.

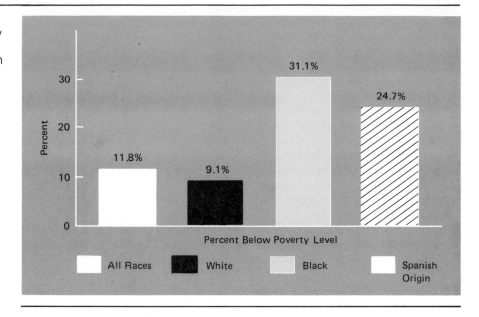

blue-collar workers as opposed to more than 40 percent of blacks and almost half of Hispanics. Blacks and Hispanics, moreover, are apt to have the lowest level blue-collar jobs.[56] Of course, the situation has improved somewhat since 1964, when fewer than one in five blacks had white-collar occupations; today approximately one in three blacks have white-collar jobs. At the opposite end, more than 50 percent of whites are white-collar workers.[57] Furthermore, the unskilled worker is not only badly paid but can lose his or her job through technological change.

Sharp differences still distinguish the average incomes of black and white workers. In 1951 the median income of black workers was about 57 percent of that for white workers. Today the gap is not much narrower. For example, in 1978 the median income for white families was estimated to be $16,430, for blacks it was $9,560, and for families headed by a person of Spanish origin it was $11,420.[58] About 35 percent of black families earned more than $10,000 a year, but about a third of all blacks families (8 million people) were below the poverty level, a figure that has remained constant for years.[59] (See Figures 8-1 and 8-2.) Unemployment among minorities is also much higher than among whites. In early 1979 the unemployment rate for whites was about 5 percent, for blacks 11.2 percent, and for Spanish-speaking

[56]Philip L. Roner and Carol Leon, "Employment and Unemployment During 1978: An Analysis," *Monthly Labor Review,* vol. 102 (February 1979), 10.

[57]*Manpower Report of the President* (Washington, D.C.: U.S. Government Printing Office, April 1975), pp. 34-35.

[58]Bureau of the Census, "Money Income and Poverty Status of Families and Persons in the U.S.: 1977," *Current Population Reports,* Series P-60, no. 116 (Washington, D.C.: U.S. Government Printing Office, 1978), p. 1.

[59]Cameron, "Black America," p. 162.

workers 8.2 percent.[60] For more than two decades the unemployment ratio of blacks to whites has been approximately 2 to 1, except for a temporary narrowing of the gap in 1970–1971. For teenagers the gap is even greater: in 1978, the unemployment rate for black teenagers was 36.3 percent, compared to 13.9 percent for their white peers.[61] (See Figure 8-3 and Chapter 13.)

The employment plight of blacks and other minorities is well summed up by Rashi Fein:

> What is recession for the white (say, an unemployment rate of 6 percent) is prosperity for the non-white . . . . Therefore, perhaps it is appropriate to say that whites fluctuate between prosperity and recession but Negroes fluctuate between depression and great depression.[62]

Social Justice

Justice is the final area we will examine in our attempt to highlight the pervasive nature of institutionalized discrimination. Two basic assumptions in American law have always been, first, that justice is blind—that racial, ethnic, economic, or social considerations are irrelevant to one's guilt or innocence under law—and, second, that any accused is considered innocent until proven

[60]Roner and Leon, "Employment and Unemployment," p. 44.

[61]John Herbers, "Changes in Society Holding Black Youth in Jobless Web," *New York Times,* March 11, 1979, p. 44.

[62]Rashi Fein, "An Economic and Social Profile of the Negro American," in *The Negro American,* eds. Talcott Parsons and Kenneth B. Clark (Boston: Beacon Press, 1966), pp. 114-115.

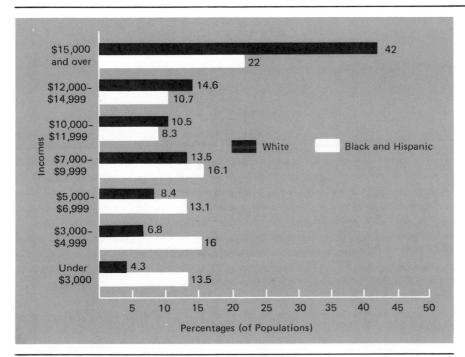

Figure 8-2
White and Minority Family Incomes

Source: Bureau of the Census, *Current Population Reports,* Series P-60, no. 101 (Washington, D.C.: U.S. Government Printing Office, 1976).

Figure 8-3

Unemployment among Various Labor Force Groups

Source: U.S. Government Statistics.

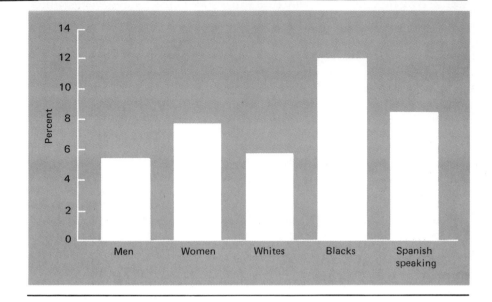

guilty in a court of law. But do these assumptions apply equally to everyone?

As noted in Chapter 5, minorities are overrepresented in official arrest records, and it seems probable that, in general, they are more likely to be arrested and charged with a crime, whether or not they are guilty. Following arrest, there is the hurdle of the bail system. It is here that the American social justice system is perhaps most inherently discriminatory against minorities. To begin with, bail involves money: those who have it can usually secure their release after their arrest, to await trial in freedom, subject only to the limitations of the bail agreement. Those who do not are punished, in effect, because of the long delay in many jurisdictions (particularly in big cities) between arrest and trial that condemns them to wait in jail—often for months, sometimes for more than a year—until their case comes up. This borders on punishment before conviction, and certainly runs counter to the American legal precept of presumed innocence.

One of the few systematic studies of the entire bail system, the Manhattan Bail Project, found that abuses of the bail system produced even more inequality than this. Theoretically bail prevents punishment before conviction and ensures that the accused will attend the trial. Most judges, however, use bail punitively—they set excessively high bail simply to make it more likely that defendants will be detained. Unfortunately, defendants who cannot raise bail and therefore stay in jail are more likely to fare badly in court.[63] As Paul Wice points out:

> Numerous studies clearly show that detained defendants are far more likely to be found guilty and receive more severe sentences than those released prior to trial. Limited visiting hours, locations remote from the counsel's office, inadequate

[63]Charles E. Ares, Anne Rankin, and Herbert Sturtz, "The Manhattan Bail Project," *New York University Law Review* 38 (1963), 67-92.

conference facilities, and censored mail all serve to impede an effective lawyer-client relationship.[64]

In effect, then, under the current bail system, minority defendants are often presumed guilty because they are poor. Subsequent studies have since confirmed the widespread misuse of the bail system. For example, the United States Commission on Civil Rights found similar practices with regard to Chicanos in the Southwest:

> The system of bail in the Southwest frequently is used more severely against Mexican-Americans than against Anglos as a form of discrimination. In certain cases, Mexican-American defendants are faced with excessively high bail. Defendants in other cases are held without any opportunity to put up bail or are purposely confused by local officials about the bail hearing so that they unknowingly forfeit their bail. In one area local farmers put up bail or pay fines for migrant workers and make them work off the amount in a situation resembling peonage or involuntary servitude.[65]

In his survey, Wice found a nationwide problem of bail being used punitively. The most significant factor affecting the amount of bail set was the seriousness of the crime charged, despite evidence that this is not directly related to whether or not the defendant will appear for trial. The criterion least frequently considered by judges was, paradoxically, the one with the greatest influence on defendant's ability to post bond—namely, their financial status.[66]

From this evidence it is easy to see why more minority defendants are convicted than are acquitted. Even those who can pay bail can rarely afford a costly defense, and those who are detained have little opportunity to prepare a defense.

This inequality in the administration of justice extends even to the sentencing process itself. Though blacks are only about 11 percent of the population, they comprise 42 percent of the jail population; whites are much more likely to be released on their own recognizance or given suspended sentences. In prison, sentences for blacks tend to be longer than sentences for whites, particularly for serious offenses. (See Table 8-1.) In a recent year, for example, the average prison sentence for murder or kidnapping was *ten times* longer for blacks than for whites (for those sentences not being appealed). Fully half of all those sentenced to death were black.[67]

Such discrimination was not in the original intention of American justice, though the perversion of that justice by the authorities has sometimes been deliberate. Now that various organizations concerned with constitutional law and civil liberties are becoming increasingly aware of the dangers of discriminatory justice one may hope that some abuses will eventually be eliminated. But given what seems to be a common human propensity to oppress the weak, we can never take social justice for granted. Here, if anywhere, eternal vigilance is truly the price of liberty.

[64]Paul Bernard Wice, *Bail and Its Reform: A National Survey* (Washington, D.C.: U.S. Government Printing Office, 1973), p. 23.

[65]Report of the United States Commission on Civil Rights, *Mexican Americans and the Administration of Justice in the Southwest* (Washington, D.C.: U.S. Government Printing Office, 1970), p. 52.

[66]Wice, *Bail and Its Reform*, pp. 4-5, 13-14.

[67]"Social and Economic Status of Black Population," pp. 6, 162, 170-171.

Table 8-1
Length of Sentences
for Selected Crimes,
by Race

Appeal Status and Type of Crime	Median Number of Months Sentenced	
NOT ON APPEAL	Black	White
Murder or kidnapping	66.1	5.8
Rape	10.7	5.9
Robbery	52.9	11.5
Burglary	10.5	10.8
Assault: Aggravated	13.3	11.1
Simple	6.0	2.6
Larceny: Grand	10.0	10.2
Petty	2.9	2.8
Auto theft	5.6	4.7
Drugs: Sale	9.3	5.0
Possession or use	11.2	5.4
ON APPEAL		
Murder or kidnapping	598.9	439.7
Rape	498.9	598.9
Robbery	236.1	166.8
Burglary	37.4	86.8

Source: "The Social and Economic Status of the Black Population in the United States." *Current Population Reports*, Series P-23, no. 54, (Washington, D.C.: U.S. Government Printing Office, July 1975), p. 174.

Some Consequences of Prejudice and Discrimination

The harmful effects of prejudice and discrimination are not limited to minorities. The lives of members of the dominant group itself are also nearly always stunted by the artificial barriers and warped perceptions that such social divisions entail. (See Chapter 9.) Here, however, we will consider principally the effects on the subordinate group, for these are usually more demonstrably serious.

What happens to people who must live with institutionalized discrimination and its accompanying prejudice? There are, of course, effects on the individual personalities of minority members. And both individuals and groups develop protective reactions against this prejudice and discrimination.

First, let us consider the effects of discrimination on individual personalities. In his ground-breaking work, *Children of Crisis*, psychologist Robert Coles documents some of the personality effects among the first black children to attend desegregated schools in the South. These children were subjected to blatant discrimination and bitter prejudice, including outright mob action against them and their parents. For several months, Coles observed the children and particularly how they depicted their world and themselves through drawings. His account of the drawings of one black girl, Ruby, during this time is particularly fascinating. For months she would never use brown or black except to indicate the ground. However, she distinguished between white and black people.

> She drew white people larger and more lifelike. Negroes were smaller, their bodies less intact. A white girl we both knew to be her own size appeared several times taller. While Ruby's own face lacked an eye in one drawing, an ear in another, the white girl never lacked any features. Moreover, Ruby drew the white girl's hands and legs carefully, always making sure that they had the proper number of fingers and toes. Not so with her own limbs, or those of any other Negro children she chose (or was asked) to picture. A thumb or forefinger might be missing, or a whole set of toes. The arms were shorter, even absent or truncated.

At the same time Jimmy, a white classmate of Ruby, always depicted blacks as somehow related to animals or at least extremely dirty and dangerous. After about two years of contact with Ruby and other black children in his desegregated school in New Orleans, Jimmy grew less fearful of blacks, and the change was reflected in his drawings. Coles concludes that children of each race were conditioned to fear and distrust members of the other race, but that with continuing friendly contact these prejudices were broken down and that the children eventually helped to change their parents' attitudes as well.[68]

Kenneth Clark describes the destructive effect of discrimination as he perceived it in some black adults:

> Human beings who are forced to live under ghetto conditions and whose daily experience tells them that almost nowhere in society are they respected and granted the ordinary dignity and courtesy accorded to others will, as a matter of course, begin to doubt their own worth. Since every human being depends upon his cumulative experiences with others for clues as to how he should view and value himself, children who are consistently rejected understandably begin to question and doubt whether they, their family, and their group really deserve no more respect from the larger society than they receive. These doubts become the seeds of pernicious self- and group-hatred, the Negro's complex and debilitating prejudice against himself . . . . Negroes have come to believe in their own inferiority.[69]

Black separatism is another reaction to the discrimination and prejudice of the dominant whites. In the 1920s, Marcus Garvey espoused another, more extreme form of separatism. His plan was to seize control of Africa from European colonial powers and build a free United Black Africa to be peopled by New World blacks and like-minded Africans. But the most common reaction against inequality during the last decades has been public protest. Following the success of the Montgomery bus boycott of 1955 and 1956 (when blacks avoided riding buses until discriminatory seating rules were eliminated), a broad social movement for desegregation emerged. Initially under the leadership of Dr. Martin Luther King, Jr., protests were directed against laws unequally enforced, or that created a statutory inequality—that is, against obstructions maintained to deny minorities rights and privileges enjoyed by other Americans.

[68]Robert Coles, *Children of Crisis* (New York: Dell, 1968), pp. 47, 53, 60.
[69]Kenneth B. Clark, *Dark Ghetto* (New York: Harper & Row, 1965).

In the 1960s, however, as perceptible progress slowed, and resistance and backlash increased with growing economic pressures and political uncertainty, minority protest sometimes took more violent forms. Feelings of anger, frustration, and rage provoked urban riots across the country. Often, the last straw that led to a riot was the arrest of blacks by white police officers.[70] The police served as visible symbols of the attitude of the entire white majority: white power, white discrimination, white repression. It is no wonder that when blacks felt themselves to be the victims of bitter discrimination, the police often sparked a violent response. At no time, however, did a majority of blacks approve of the violent protests that took place, whether or not they felt that these helped the black cause.[71] By the mid-1970s race riots had ceased to be a significant form of protest by blacks. The recession during this period saw both whites and blacks suffering from high unemployment rates and inflation (though not, as we have seen, in the same proportions), and expectations of progress were reduced. Furthermore, the end of both the Vietnam War and the draft caused a general decline in protest movements that also may have affected blacks. There may have also been a sense that riots had reached the limits of their effectiveness, and that more deliberate, organized efforts had become necessary. There is also the possibility, as Frances Piven and Richard Cloward have theorized, that

[70]*Report of the National Advisory Commission,* p. 206.
[71]Peter Godman, *Report from Black America* (New York: Simon & Schuster, 1970), pp. 229-270.

Leaders of the American Indian Movement, such as Dennis Banks and Russell Means, who occupied Wounded Knee, and Cesar Chavez, who organized Chicano migrant workers, represent minorities which are no longer willing to be passive objects of prejudice and discrimination.

UPI

welfare rolls were increased in response to the riots and that this had the effect of mollifying blacks.[72] (See Chapter 6.)

In any event, blacks apparently still felt that institutions were not responsive to their needs and problems. Whereas in 1963, the federal government was seen as a positive force by 83 percent of blacks, by 1972 black confidence in government was down to a low 16 percent. (This paralleled a similar, but not as dramatic, trend among whites.) Along with reduced confidence was a sense that much still remained to be done: for example, 79 percent of blacks favored an increase of federal assistance to the poor.[73] Another survey found that four out of ten blacks considered the American system no longer viable and advocated radical alternatives to end discrimination.[74] Though the majority of American blacks still hope for peaceful change, they are also aware that discrimination is still rampant in our society, and that it will require major efforts on a legal, political, and economic front to eliminate it completely.

[72]Frances Fox Piven and Richard A. Cloward, *Regulating the Poor: The Functions of Public Welfare* (New York: Random House, 1971). For further discussion of this thesis see Michael Betz, "Riots and Welfare: Are They Related?" *Social Problems,* vol. 21, no. 3 (1974); "Correspondence," *Social Problems,* vol. 22, no. 2 (1974); and William A. Muraskin's review in *Contemporary Sociology* (November 1975).

[73]Louis Harris, *The Harris Poll* (New York: Chicago Tribune, N.Y. News Syndicate, November 22, 1972).

[74]"Black Americans, 1963-1973," *Editorial Research Reports* (August 15, 1973), p. 624.

Bob Fitch/Black Star

Recent years have also seen a growing activism on the part of Chicanos and American Indians. Cesar Chavez, the head of the United Farm Worker's Union, has led strikes and instigated nationwide boycotts of grapes, lettuce and bananas to improve conditions for his migrant Chicano workers. American Indians protested against their economic and social powerlessness in places such as Wounded Knee, Phoenix, and Alcatraz prison in California. These skirmishes were less visible because they usually occurred in isolated or sparsely settled areas and are comparatively nonviolent. But the growth of "red power" movements and new efforts to organize Chicano workers clearly heralded a reawakened American Indian and Chicano consciousness.

Social Action

With the rise in consciousness of blacks and other minorities and the demands of minorities for a more equal share in the benefits of the American way of life, various programs have been instituted to alleviate the effects of prejudice and discrimination. In this section we shall examine some of the approaches, goals, and effectiveness of these programs.

Manpower Training Programs

Before the "War on Poverty" in 1964, the principal concern of national manpower policy had been with manpower as a national economic resource, and particularly with the scientific and technical manpower needed to support an expanding technology. In the mid-1960s the focus shifted to the worker— to helping those who had difficulty finding employment because of inadequate training and/or a lack of available jobs. The concurrent economic recession has made this an especially difficult task, since obviously no amount of training can guarantee a job if an employer is not hiring. Consequently, there has been considerable pressure on the government to provide jobs—to act as the "employer of last resort"—as well as to train workers. (See Chapter 7 for a discussion of government employment programs.)

The training effort itself has been hampered by poor coordination among the various programs. There is no federal manpower policy as such. Programs have been established under the Manpower Training and Development Act, the Vocational Education Act of 1963, the Vocational Rehabilitation Program, manpower components of the Economic Opportunity Act, and the Comprehensive Employment Training Act of 1973. Each of these legislative efforts was drafted to meet a current crisis, without much thought to its relation to the others. In addition, they are underfunded and too small in scale for the size of the problem. For example, the average enrollment at any given time in all training programs for the disadvantaged is under 300,000; yet in a recent year 1.3 million people were unemployed for fifteen weeks or longer, and the total number of jobless exceeded 6 million.[75] The fifteen-week unemployment figure alone is more than four times the average number of trainees.

The manpower programs that began in the late 1960s did, however, make some positive contributions. Besides those persons who received job training and consequently secured higher-paying jobs, many more improved their

[75]*Manpower Report of the President*, pp. 29, 82, 114.

skills in other ways. Some entered counseling programs and went to school, and were thus better able to keep their jobs; others qualified for high school equivalency diplomas, improving their chances of finding employment. Motivation, for example, is an important factor if job training is to be effective, and actual on-the-job experience is often necessary for those unaccustomed to the discipline of holding a job.

Thus there are two major problems involving these manpower programs that remain to be solved. First, a way must be found to relate the training programs to the marketplace, so that, after training, there will be a reasonable likelihood of obtaining an actual, paying job. At present, only about 62 percent of the enrollees in these programs find employment.[76] Second, the underfinancing of these programs must be ended. Only a massively expanded manpower training program could make a significant impact on the lack of job training among minority groups.

Head Start

Head Start is a blanket term covering most federally funded preschool programs aimed at preparing disadvantaged youngsters for school. They were once the most popular programs among parents, administrators, and activists, although their principles and effectiveness have been attacked.

At its inception in the 1960s and during its early operation, Head Start performed several roles. It was a showcase program whose immediate effects became political capital to its supporters. Early research found improvements of 8 to 10 points in the IQs of 480 children in a summer Head Start program in Baltimore in 1965.[77] These immediate, measurable gains in cognitive achievement heralded an enormous expansion of Head Start operations and a push for year-long programs throughout the country. From small beginnings, Head Start grew to cost several hundred million dollars a year, serving over a half-million children, and supported by everyone from Congress to parents, but especially by educators and their lobbyists.

The initial goals of Head Start and its early popularity obscured some basic flaws. For one thing, while the concept of early intervention was popular among child development researchers, and while their research did in fact suggest that there is a real potential for intellectual improvement through early childhood training, there remain to this day few unchallenged guidelines as to exactly what is to be taught, how, when, and by whom.[78]

As with most massive social action programs, Head Start eventually suffered severe internal and external criticism. It has been criticized primarily on two points: first, that it has not done its job and, second, that it has done the wrong job. Most who feel that it has not done its job argue that the early gains in cognitive achievement by Head Start participants were deceptive. Results of an evaluation study by the Westinghouse Learning Corporation and Ohio University indicated that gains in cognitive skill disappeared by the third grade, and that disadvantaged students who had not participated in Head

[76]*Manpower Report of the President*, p. 115.

[77]Sar A. Levitan, "Head Start: It Is Never Too Early to Fight Poverty," *Federal Programs for the Development of Human Resources* (Washington, D.C.: Joint Economic Committee, Subcommittee on Economic Progress, 1968), pp. 425-428.

[78]Walter Williams and John W. Evans, "The Politics of Evaluation: The Case of Head Start," *Annals of the American Academy of Political and Social Science* 385 (September 1969), 122.

Start performed at equivalent levels.[79] These results were the main reason federal funding for Head Start was eventually reduced.

Other critics argued that Head Start did too little and did it too late to be effective. According to this view, the most important period for a child's emotional, social, and intellectual development is the first three years of life, when the child begins to acquire language and learn to manipulate the surrounding world. Parents, not teachers, are therefore the most important educators, and for intervention to be effective, it must begin during infancy in the child's own home. An experimental program in Brookline, Massachusetts, is attempting to test the effectiveness of this very early intervention approach by supplementing the parents' role with trained teacher-counselors who visit each young child regularly.[80]

Defenders of Head Start argue that cost-effectiveness analysis is inappropriate in this type of program, and that many of the gains do not show up on IQ tests. They emphasize improved motivation and psychological adjustments among Head Start students and suggest that these students have pulled the non-Head Start disadvantaged up to their level rather than regressing themselves.[81]

Radical critics of childhood intervention policy suggest that the whole thrust of the program is wrong. Stephen and Joan Baratz question the logic of intervention and its theory, which they say equates difference with inferiority. In fact, they believe, the inability of many minority children to learn in the standard educational environment may be a consequence not of their fundamental unpreparedness for learning, but of the school's unwillingness to teach them on the basis of the often considerable linguistic and cognitive skills they have already acquired in their own culture. Rather than destroy the disadvantaged preschoolers' culture, by eradicating their natural linguistic and logical methods, they recommend teaching the white middle-class majority's social *modus operandi* only in addition to the minority's ways. To brand children as incompetent in the school system and at the same time strip away the skills they have developed in order to survive in their subculture is a double punishment.[82]

Ray Rist expands on this criticism, suggesting that Head Start programs are based on the assumption that "what poor children needed was an initial boost of socialization to acquaint them with the values, behaviors, and ideas of non-poor middle-class Anglo conformity so that they would . . . pull themselves out of poverty." According to Rist, this approach ignores the institutional, economic, and social barriers minorities face even after they leave school. It also ignores the fact that "each minority and ethnic culture has within it valuable and positive attributes that could be of contribution to the fabric of American society." What is needed, Rist believes, are educational settings "where those values and cultural forms valued by the minority group would be retained, but also where minority members would be equipped to partake of the dominant culture as they desire." All such programs are bound to fail, however, as long as prejudice and discrimination continue to exist in the rest of society.[83]

[79]Williams and Evans, "Politics of Evaluation."

[80]Maya Pines, "Head Head Start," *New York Times Magazine* (October 26, 1975), p. 14.

[81]"How Head a Head Start?" *New Republic* (April 25, 1969), pp. 8-9.

[82]Stephen S. Baratz and Joan C. Baratz, "Early Childhood Intervention: The Social Science Base of Institutional Racism," *Harvard Educational Review* 40 (Winter 1970), 29-50.

[83]Ray C. Rist, "Race, Policy, and Schooling," *Society* (November–December 1975), 59-63.

Some good may have come from early childhood intervention and enrichment programs, but they are hardly a panacea. The educational deficiencies of disadvantaged minorities, like all poverty-related problems, are not susceptible to simple, one-shot solutions. However, since education will almost certainly continue to reflect the majority culture, it will be necessary to provide minority children with a fair chance to learn those terms—simply as a necessary entree into society. On the other hand, for the benefit of *all* students, the cultural values and insights of the minorities must be allowed into our school systems, as they are beginning to be in the form of ethnic studies and women's studies programs at various levels; and all of the other forms of discrimination that we have discussed—in housing, unemployment, health care, legal justice, and the rest—must be corrected if minority children are to be as free to learn and to grow as their white classmates.

Prospects

We have seen that prejudice and discrimination harm both individuals and society as a whole, and we have considered some of their effects that are evident today and some of the efforts being made, by government agencies and by minorities themselves, to improve the situation. Some things are better today than in the past, and it is unlikely that America's minorities will ever again accept uncomplainingly the subordinate status to which they were long condemned. But it is not yet certain whether improvement can achieve real, practical equality.

It is clear that designing effective busing programs will depend on changes in attitudes toward minorities or, at the very least, changes in the laws that now deny high-quality suburban schools to inner city students. It is unlikely, however, that such changes will occur soon, and recent new efforts have sought to improve the quality of minority education without busing. Progress has been sketchy but some state courts have declared the inequalities in school financing unconstitutional. These inequities may arise because city schools are poorly financed from public funds while suburban schools are well-financed by local property taxes. Suburban resistance to change in school funding has been fierce, however, and in related cases the Supreme Court has shown itself reluctant to reform school funding practices. It therefore remains to be seen how true educational quality for all students can be achieved.

Attacks on exclusionary zoning ordinances that put the cost of suburban housing beyond the reach of the poor have been hampered by a Supreme Court decision that non-residents of a community have no right to contest its zoning regulations. A recent decision by the United States Court of Appeals in New York did give nonresidents the right to challenge federal Housing and Urban Development grants to a community with discriminatory zoning practices. If this decision is upheld, communities who wish to qualify for federal funds will have to modify their zoning rules.[84] However, the decision leaves unaffected those communities that do not wish to receive grants. A more positive development was the Supreme Court's 1976 decision that the Department of Housing and Urban Development would have to provide low-cost housing for minorities in suburbs if its public funding programs contributed to segregation within the city. It is likely, however, that most

---

[84]"Another Crack in the Suburban Zoning Wall," *Business Week* (July 21, 1975), p. 11.

suburbs will remain off limits to those who desperately need decent low-income housing, and that public funds will have to be used to supply or subsidize adequate housing in poorer communities.

Large-scale improvement of minority employment opportunities will depend, of course, on improvements in education, expansion of manpower training programs, the ending of discriminatory wage and hiring practices, and a renewed dedication to a full-employment economy. Meanwhile, the "last hired, first fired" policies of many companies must be ended if minorities are to preserve their gains of the past fifteen years. A recent district court decision addressed this very situation when it held that a company must keep three separate seniority lists—for white males, women, and minority members—so that layoffs would not change the proportions of these groups in the work force.[85]

Equality of justice ultimately depends on the eradication of conditions that breed crime and of prejudices that lead to overrepresentation of minorities in arrest rates. Much can be done in the meantime, however, to reduce the discriminatory effects of the criminal justice system itself. For example, bail reform projects in many towns and cities have ensured pretrial release of those defendants who are good risks but who are otherwise likely to be detained because they cannot raise high bail. The method they generally used was to set a moderate bail, notify the defendants repeatedly of their scheduled court appearances, and supervise them casually throughout the pretrial period. Wice found that these programs were significantly more effective in assuring appearance at trial than traditional bail practices.[86] Inequities in sentencing can be reduced by limiting the judge's role in the setting of penalties. For example, mandatory minimum and maximum penalties can be established for each crime, thus reducing the effects of a judge's personal prejudices in sentencing.

[85]"Affirmative Action and Layoffs," *Monthly Labor Review* (February 1975), pp. 77-78.
[86]Wice, "Bail and Its Reform."

Summary

Social inequality has a long history in the United States, but contradicts the egalitarian principles on which the nation was established. All minorities, ethnic as well as racial, have been subordinate to the dominant White Anglo-Saxon Protestant majority culture, but in particular blacks, Hispanics, and American Indians have been and continue to be exploited. The constitutional bases for equality were buttressed by Supreme Court decisions, several Civil Rights acts, and various other acts and presidential orders. But realities have not caught up with principles or laws.

Minorities have been defined as categories of people who receive treatment less equal than that accorded other categories. The principal characteristic of a minority is its subordinate status; the principal weapons the dominant group uses to maintain the status of the subordinate group are prejudice (irreversible prejudgment) and discrimination (overtly unequal treatment).

Psychologically, prejudice and discrimination can result from projection and from feelings of frustration that lead to scapegoating. Sociologically, they can result from the competition of groups for economic goods, which can lead to political dominance of one group and the exploitation of the other. Eventually prejudicial attitudes become stereotypes and discriminatory practices become social norms.

Institutional discrimination exists in many areas, particularly education, housing, employment, and social justice. The effort to compensate for the effects of educational discrimination through busing has run into opposition. There is doubt as to whether or not integration has led to gains in learning or achievement, but considerable agreement that the turmoil that usually accompanies it can be detrimental to learning. Movements for reform of school financing to more nearly equalize per pupil expenditures and to improve education where the children are instead of busing them are gaining adherents.

Housing segregation has resulted in the clustering of minorities in substandard dwellings, usually in inner cities. Discrimination in employment results in minorities having lower-paying jobs and higher rates of unemployment. Arrest, bail, and sentencing practices also are more likely to fall with discriminatory harshness upon minority groups. Some reforms and improvements are beginning to be felt in these and related areas, including affirmative action plans in hiring and job training; early intervention in education; challenges of federal grants to communities with discriminatory zoning laws; and bail reform projects.

Prejudice and discrimination have resulted in feelings of personal and group inferiority; in movements for separatism; in general hostility toward members of the dominant culture; and, in the mid-1960s, in civil disturbances. The majority of blacks still hope for peaceful change, although younger people are less patient. And the majority of whites favor integration, although they strongly disapprove of such measures as busing to achieve it. The effects of discrimination may yet be eliminated if the majority is willing to share its privileges, if the working classes of all races can cooperate for mutual benefit, and if all Americans would act on their belief that all persons are created equal.

Bibliography

Bahr, Howard M., Chadwick, Bruce A., and Day, Robert C. *Native Americans Today: Sociological Perspectives.* New York: Harper & Row, 1972.

Blauner, Robert. *Racial Oppression in America.* New York: Harper & Row, 1972.

Greeley, Andrew M. *Ethnicity in the United States.* New York: Wiley, 1974.

Greenspan, C.L., and Hirsh, L.M. *All Those Voices: The Minority Experience.* New York: Macmillan, 1971.

Howard, John R., ed. *Awakening Minorities: American Indians, Mexican Americans, and Puerto Ricans.* Chicago: Aldine, 1970.

Kitano, Harry H. *Race Relations.* Englewood Cliffs, N.J.: Prentice-Hall, 1974.

Morre, Joan W., and Cuellar, Alfredo. *Mexican Americans.* Englewood Cliffs, N.J.: Prentice-Hall, 1970.

Pettigrew, Thomas. *Racially Separate or Together?* New York: McGraw-Hill, 1971.

Rainwater, Lee. *Behind Ghetto Walls: Black Families in a Federal Slum.* Chicago: Aldine, 1970.

9

Sex Roles and Inequality

Facts about Sex Roles and Inequality

- The proportion of women of working age in the labor force has increased by one-third since 1950, to about 45 percent; however, women's median annual earnings as a percentage of men's have declined since 1950, from about 65 to less than 59 percent.

- Women are concentrated in service occupations, making up, for example, 99 percent of the nation's secretaries but less than 1 percent of the nation's engineers.

- Of families headed by women 33 percent are below the poverty line, compared to 6 percent of families headed by men.

- Surveys of school textbooks consistently find that females are under-represented; when females do appear, they are generally pictured in passive or dependent roles.

- Women who do not conform to traditional stereotypes of femininity, and men who do not conform to traditional stereotypes of masculinity, are more likely than other men and women to be labeled as mentally ill.

"You've come a long way, baby" is the advertising slogan for a brand of cigarettes that seeks to project an image of the independent but glamorous woman. "The woman who smokes our cigarettes," the ad seems to say, "is professional but sexy." Another brand has literally ridden to success with ads in which rugged, leathery cowboys gallop off into the sunset. The message: "Our smokers are all-American males, tough, laconic, unemotional." Both of these ads, of course, are simplistic. But it is precisely because they portray stereotypes of behavior defined by sex that they also symbolize many of the problems of sexism in America today. For example, women have undoubtedly progressed toward equality in our society. Many careers that were once effectively closed to them are now wide open. Women today have more independence and a wider choice of life styles than ever before. Yet, many barriers still exist, not the least of which is the widespread belief that an important—and perhaps central—part of a woman's role is to be sexually appealing to men. How she appeals may change with fashion, but the necessity for sex-appeal stays constant.

Men, on the other hand, have traditionally been portrayed as naturally strong, dominant, and self-reliant. Evidently this image appeals to men themselves, but it has inhibited their ability to be individuals, to be in touch with their own and others' emotions. Too often, men have forgotten that sexism, which for so long constricted the options open to women, has oppressed men as well. Although this chapter will focus primarily on the adverse effects of sexism on women, we shall also discuss how men suffer from it.

Over the past several decades women have made many notable gains. In 1940, less than 17 percent of women in the labor force were married. Today over 55 percent of women in the labor force are married.[1] The proportion of

[1] U.S. Department of Labor, *Manpower Report of the President* (Washington, D.C.: U.S. Government Printing Office, 1975); and U.S. Bureau of the Census, *Statistical Abstract of the United States, 1978* (Washington, D.C.: U.S. Government Printing Office, 1978).

women in law, medical, and engineering schools, though still low, is rising steadily.[2] More women are even entering such traditionally male fields as business and the military; and at the same time, more men are entering such traditionally female occupations as nursing, librarianship, and elementary-school teaching. The attitudes of the American public toward women's advancement have also undergone a marked change: whereas in 1970 a Harris poll indicated that only 42 percent of Americans approved of "efforts to strengthen and change women's status in society," a 1975 Harris poll indicated that 63 percent of Americans approved such efforts, including more than half of American men.[3]

Despite some gains achieved by women, sharp disparities exist in the treatment accorded men and women in our society. In some ways women are actually worse off today than they were before. Whereas in 1956 women's full-time, year-round median wages were 63 percent of men's, in 1977 they were less than 59 percent. Women are still shunted into the "girl's ghetto": housekeeping, retail trades, insurance, real estate, and such service positions as secretaries, receptionists, telephone operators, and clerks. About 75 percent of the working women in America are employed in these kinds of jobs.[4] Women today account for a lesser percentage of college faculties than 100 years ago, and a smaller proportion of graduate students than in 1930.[5] Despite the progress made in many areas, women today still make up only 5 percent of elected officials in the United States, only 10 percent of the nation's physicians, and only 7 percent of the nation's lawyers and judges.[6] Even where women are in the same professions or occupations as men, their salaries are lower. Statutes that discriminate against women are still "on the books"; subtle and persistent discrimination in employment and salaries is still widespread. In the meantime, efforts are being made to have the Equal Rights Amendment (ERA)—which would help combat these inequities—added to the Constitution.

Clearly, the position of women in our society—and, as we shall see, in many other contemporary societies—is a subordinate one. Women are still kept from full and equal participation in society. Conversely, men are being kept from less stressful, rigid, and aggressive roles and occupations.

Traditional Sex Roles

In Chapter 8 we suggested that prejudice—a predisposition to regard a certain group in a certain way—often becomes the justification for discriminatory behavior. That is, if we believe that a certain group is "inferior" or "different," we can easily defend our treating that group as less than equal. We also suggested that the norms of society are an important source of prejudice and discrimination. If an entire society is prejudiced against a certain group and discriminates against it, such prejudice and discrimination will be accepted by most members of that society as natural and right.

[2]J.B. Parrish, "Women in Professional Training," *Monthly Labor Review* (May 1974), pp. 40–43.
[3]"Women of the Year," *Time* (January 5, 1976), pp. 6–16.
[4]"Working Women: Joys and Sorrows," *U.S. News & World Report* (January 15, 1979), p. 64.
[5]Warren Farrell, *The Liberated Man* (New York: Random House, 1975), p. 150.
[6]"Women of the Year," p. 8.

Until recently, it was widely accepted that the only desirable role for a woman was that of wife, mother, and housekeeper and that a woman should revolve her entire life around these roles. A man, on the other hand, was required to be the leader and provider. Betty Friedan was among the first contemporary feminists to identify and criticize this traditional view of female-male roles, and she labeled it the "feminine mystique":

> The feminine mystique says that the highest value and the only commitment for women is the fulfillment of their own femininity. It says that the great mistake of Western culture, through most of its history, has been the undervaluation of this femininity. It says this femininity is so mysterious and intuitive and close to the creation and origin of life that man-made science may never be able to understand it. But however special and different, it is in no way inferior to the nature of man; it may even in certain respects be superior. The mistake, says the mystique, the root of women's troubles in the past, is that women envied men, women tried to be like men, instead of accepting their own nature, which can find fulfillment only in sexual passivity, male domination, and nurturing maternal love. . . . The new mystique makes the housewife-mothers, who never had a chance to be anything else, the model for all women . . . a pattern by which all women must now live or deny their femininity.[7]

So pervasive was this view, and so internalized by men and women, that Friedan called the dissatisfaction of the women she studied with their traditional roles "the problem that has no name."

Many of us now think of the traditional roles of women and men as being somewhat outdated or at least as representing only some of many roles that people today can adopt. At the time Friedan wrote her book, and to a large extent even today, such a view was the basis for social behavior. Women, for example, were considered too delicate to do "men's work," and so were legally denied many career and job opportunities. Males were supposed to "act like a man," to be dominant and unemotional. For women chastity and fidelity were major virtues; for men promiscuity was considered "natural," at worst a venial fault. Women and men were considered "different," and so were treated differently by our social institutions—including our government and its legal system. The way we socialize and educate our children—in fact, the entire range of the norms and values of our society—in some measure have reflected and continue to reflect the different standards of behavior we have for men and women. Nevertheless, few people questioned whether these different standards were justified. As John Stuart Mill wrote,

> Everything which is usual appears natural. The subjugation of women to men being a universal custom, any departure from it quite naturally appears unnatural.[8]

This double standard of behavior is hardly unique to our own society. In many contemporary Latin American and Moslem countries the status of women is far more subordinate than in our own. Comparatively few women in these societies have the freedom that men have or have careers outside the home. And though, ostensibly, women in the Communist countries of

[7]Betty Friedan, *The Feminine Mystique* (New York: Dell, 1963), p. 43.
[8]John Stuart Mill, "The Subjugation of Women," in *Three Essays by John Stuart Mill* (London: World's Classic Series, 1966), p. 441.

The role indicated by this woman's traditional Moslem dress presents a strange contrast to her modern career role.
UPI

Eastern Europe have greater equality with men—most of the physicians in the Soviet Union, for example, are women—in fact disparities exist in these countries as well. Women still do most of the housework; and they are underrepresented in political parties, those countries' most powerful groups.[9] This traditional hierarchy is extremely resistant to change. For both women and men are shaped by the culture they grow up in, so that most adults are thoroughly indoctrinated or socialized into the roles their culture has prescribed for them. As a result, they often tend to judge their own worth by how well they fill these traditional roles. Change is suspect because it threatens their self-worth and identity. Thus many women strongly oppose attempts to give them equal status with men. Thus, in the Iranian revolution of 1978–1979, for example many Iranian women—though by no means all—resumed wearing the chador, the traditional garment that veiled their faces and bodies from the eyes of men. In America a women's organization—Stop-ERA, led by Phyllis Schlafly—has been in the forefront of the battle to prevent ratification of the Equal Rights Amendment.[10]

[9]See Robert R. Bell, *Marriage and Family Interaction*, 4th ed. (Homewood, Ill.: Dorsey Press, 1975), pp. 368-369; Hilda Scott, *Does Socialism Liberate Women?* (Boston: Beacon Press, 1974).

[10]See *The New York Times*, February 4, 1979, p. 4 and February 15, 1979, p. 60. For the effect of the traditional sexual ideology on women, see Sandra L. Bern and Daryl J. Bern, "Training the Woman to Know Her Place: The Power of a Nonconscious Ideology," in *Roles Women Play: Readings Towards Women's Liberation*, ed. Michelle H. Garskof (Monterey, Calif.: Wordsworth, 1971).

Nevertheless, it seems clear that there is considerable variation in the types of behavior considered appropriate for men and women, and that to a large extent these behaviors reflect the values of a particular society more than any innate or natural qualities. Whereas it was once supposed—by Freud, for example—that behavioral differences between men and women were innate,[11] today we know that these differences are largely learned by individuals as they are socialized into their culture. (See Chapter 3.) And though it was once believed that there were universal standards of "masculine" or "feminine" behavior, in fact other societies have standards far different than our own.

In the 1950s, for example, sex researcher John Money and his colleagues found that the best predictor of a person's sex role was not his or her physiological sex but the sex he or she had been assigned at birth. Specifically, male children who had been raised as females, or female children who had been raised as males, identified as members of the other sex even after their physical sex became known to them.[12] For reasons such as this, many researchers use the term *gender identity* to refer to a person's sexual self-image and to distinguish it from physiological gender.[13]

Several studies have been done that show how boys and girls in our society are socialized into their traditional sex roles. Lisa Serbin and Daniel O'Leary, for example, found that nursery-school teachers responded much more to a boy's behavior than to a girl's, tending to reinforce aggression among boys and passivity among girls. (Interestingly enough, the teachers were unaware that they were doing this.[14]) Ruth Hartley found that small boys were taught that they should not be "sissies" and that girls were weak and unimportant.[15] When women are not socialized into a conventional pattern— as fewer and fewer women today are—their behaviors begin to resemble those of men. For example, our study found that today's women are far stronger and more athletic than their counterparts of thirty years ago and that they are meeting male standards of physical performance. This suggests that even a woman's "weakness" is largely a reflection of traditional social expectation.[16]

While the values of our own society have, until recently, reinforced traditional sex roles, it is becoming increasingly apparent that these values conflict with freedom, perhaps our society's highest value. Robin Williams points out that

> the American conception of freedom is clearly that . . . of the protection of particular liberties and the tolerance of disagreement rather than the homogenization of private groups and individuals into an omnipotent general will. . . . So long as American society safeguards the right of the individual to a wide range of moral autonomy in decision making, so long as the representative character

[11]Clara Thompson, "'Penis Envy' in Women," in *Psychoanalysis and Women,* ed. Jean B. Miller (New York: Penguin Books, 1973).

[12]John Money, *et al.,* "An Examination of Some Basic Sexual Concepts: The Evidence of Human Hermaphroditism," *Bulletin of the Johns Hopkins Hospital* 97 (1955), 301-319.

[13]Clarice S. Stoll, ed., *Sexism: Scientific Debates* (Reading, Mass.: Addison-Wesley, 1973), p. 7.

[14]Lisa A. Serbin and K. Daniel O'Leary, "How Nursery Schools Teach Girls to Shut Up," *Psychology Today* (December 1975), p. 57.

[15]Ruth E. Hartley, "Sex Role Pressures and the Socialization of the Male Child," in *Men and Masculinity,* ed. Joseph H. Pleck and Jack Sawyer (Englewood Cliffs, N.J.: Prentice-Hall, 1974), pp. 7-13.

[16]Stoll, *Sexism,* p. 107.

structure of the culture retains a conscience that is more than simple group conformity—so long will freedom be a major value.[17]

George Owen suggests that traditional sex roles limit human freedom because they prevent women and men from fulfilling their own full potential. Men in our society, for example, frequently feel that they must deny the satisfactions they feel as husbands or fathers in order to pursue their careers single-mindedly; women feel they must make their roles as wives and mothers paramount and deny their abilities in other areas. Moreover, women's and men's career choices frequently reflect cultural expectations rather than their inner needs and desires. To Owen, the breaking down of traditional sex roles will open up the possibility of freedom to many women and men—people will be free to do what is best for them.[18] As one observer put it:

> The present models of neither men nor women furnish adequate opportunities for human development. That one half of the human race should be dominant and the other half submissive is incompatible with a notion of freedom. Freedom requires that there not be dominance and submission, but that all individuals be free to determine their own lives.[19]

The Nature of Sexism

Sexism is the counterpart of racism and ageism, discussed in Chapters 8 and 10, respectively. It may be defined as the "entire range of attitudes, beliefs, policies, laws, and behaviors discriminating against women (or against men) on the basis of their gender."[20] In this section we will describe some of the attitudes and practices that are a part of sexism in our society.

Stereotyping

As we stated in Chapter 8, a source of prejudice and discrimination is stereotyping, defined as the attributing of a fixed and usually unfavorable and inaccurate conception to a category of people. Stereotypes often make it easier to justify unequal treatment of the stereotyped person or group.

Among the popular, traditional stereotypes about women are that they are naturally passive, domestic, and envious. It was this catalogue of stereotypes that Friedan lumped together and labeled the "feminine mystique." However, as Marc Fasteau points out, there is a "masculine mystique" as well—a set of stereotypes about men that limits their ability to function fully and effectively.[21] The masculine stereotype is that all men are tough, unemotional, and dominant; and however unrealistic and inaccurate this stereotype is, many men (and women) believe it. Many men avoid performing traditionally female tasks (such as washing dishes or working as a secretary) for fear that

[17]Robin H. Williams, Jr., *American Society*, 3rd ed. (New York: Knopf, 1970), pp. 482-483.

[18]George C. Owen, "Sexual Equality and Human Freedom," in *Dialogue on Women*, ed. Robert Theobald (Indianapolis: Bobbs-Merrill, 1967), pp. 88-94.

[19]Jack Sawyer, quoted in *Marriage and the Family*, ed. Carolyn C. Perucci and Deno A. Targ (New York: McKay, 1974), p. 9.

[20]Constantina Safilios-Rothschild, *Women and Social Policy* (Englewood Cliffs, N.J.: Prentice-Hall, 1974), p. 1.

[21]Marc F. Fasteau, *The Male Machine* (New York: McGraw-Hill, 1974).

through such performance their masculinity will somehow be threatened. And undoubtedly many men who would prefer the role of homemaker nevertheless feel compelled to seek careers in business or sports because they have been socialized to believe that domestic work is not masculine. Not only does the masculine stereotype limit the freedom that men have to engage in any activity or occupation they desire, it also limits their personal relationships. Many men feel that they cannot discuss their feelings with other men, lest they be ridiculed. Instead, they may tend to be extremely competitive (or, collectively, even violent) toward other men. They also feel compelled to try to dominate women, instead of relating to them as equals.[22] (See Chapter 5 for a discussion of the effects of male socialization on crime patterns.)

One of the unfortunate effects of stereotypes is that even people who are victimized by them tend to believe that they are true. Thus many women share attitudes that are prejudicial to women; this causes them to undervalue the work of other women and sets up psychological barriers to their own achievement. Goldberg, for example, found that women valued professional work that they thought was done by a man more highly than they valued the same work if they thought it was done by a woman. This held true even if the professional field was traditionally reserved for women (such as nursing).[23]

[22]Robert E. Gould, "Measuring Masculinity by the Size of the Paycheck," in Pleck and Sawyer, *Men and Masculinity*, p. 96; and Sandra L. Bem "Androgyny vs. the Tight Little Lives of Fluffy Women and Chesty Men," *Psychology Today* (September 1975), pp. 58-62.

[23]Philip Goldberg, "Are Women Prejudiced Against Women?" in *Toward a Sociology of Women*, ed. Constantina Safilios-Rothschild (New York: Wiley, 1972).

As a result of learned sexual stereotyping, many men and women have accepted and perpetuated a view of women as sex objects.

UPI

Matina Horner found that many women were motivated to avoid success, fearing that the more ambitious and successful they became, the less feminine they would be. Thus, in certain competitive situations, many women became anxious about the prospect of doing well and performed poorly when compared to their performance in noncompetitive situations. Horner suggests that the stereotype that women need to be wives and mothers is preventing many able women from achieving their full potential.[24] More recent data indicates that these attitudes are changing. Aghop Der-Karabetian and Anthony Smith note that "women have become more accepting of feminine characteristics not previously considered desirable,"[25] implying that women are beginning to view their socially deemed "weaknesses" as strengths. In another study, Daniel Bar-Tal and Irene Frieze suggest that the level of success-orientation relates more to one's belief in one's own ability, than to any one gender's lack of motivation.[26]

It is probably the stereotypic notions that men have about women, however, that most impede women's achieving equality with men, since men still hold most positions of authority in our society. One survey of 1,500 managers (almost all male) found that in making personnel decisions, managers unconsciously relied on traditional stereotypes about men and women. Thus managers were much more supportive of men than of women, assuming that men would give their careers the top priority that women would reserve for their family responsibilities. Managers tried harder to retain male employees than female employees, and in general favored the advancement of men more than of women. After analyzing these data, the authors of the survey concluded:

> When the results are extrapolated to the entire population of American managers, even a small bias against women could represent a great many unintentional discriminatory acts, which potentially affect thousands of career women. The end result of these various forms of bias might be great personal damage for individuals and costly underutilization of human resources.[27]

Job Opportunities and Salaries

Women are overwhelmingly concentrated in the lower-status jobs at the low end of the pay scale. They make up, for example, 85 percent of all file clerks, 96 percent of all typists, and 99 percent of all secretaries. Conversely, men make up over 80 percent of all white-collar administrators, over 95 percent of all blue-collar supervisors, and an even higher percentage of corporate directors. Women, who receive almost the same amount of education in the United States as men, comprise close to 45 percent of college enrollments.[28] Yet, after graduation, men get the better jobs and the higher incomes. Indeed, the average *male high school dropout* earns $1,064 more per year

[24]Matina S. Horner, "Femininity and Successful Achievement: A Basic Inconsistency," in *Feminine Personality and Conflict*, ed. Judith M. Bardwick (Belmont, Calif.: Brooks/Cole, 1970).

[25]Aghop Der-Karabetian and Anthony J. Smith, "Sex-Role Stereotyping in the U.S. Is it Changing?" *Sex Roles: A Journal of Research*, vol. 3, no. 2 (1977), 197.

[26]Daniel Bar-Tal and Irene Hanson Frieze, "Achievement Motivation for Males and Females as a Determinant of Attributions for Success and Failure," *Sex Roles: A Journal of Research*, vol 3, no. 3 (1977), 301-313.

[27]Benson Rosen and Thomas H. Jerdee, "Sex Stereotyping in the Executive Suite," *Harvard Business Review* (March–April 1974), pp. 45-58.

[28]See "Educational Attainment in the United States," *Current Population Reports*, Series P-20, no. 274 (December 1974).

Figure 9-1
Median Income in 1980 and 1970 for Males and Females.

Source: U.S. Bureau of the Census, Current Population Reports, Series P-20, No. 524 (Washington, D.C.: U.S. Government Printing Office, 1978).

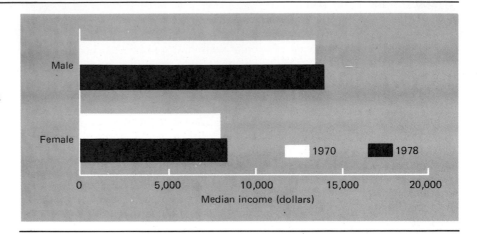

than the average *female college graduate*.[29] Although about the same proportion of women and men are professional or technical workers, women are concentrated in lower-paying fields such as nursing or teaching, while men are in such higher-paying professions as law and medicine.

This kind of sex differentiation—the distinctions made in the types of jobs men and women are permitted to perform—helps account for the fact that women's median annual salary is less than 59 percent that of men ($8,618 for women versus $14,626 for men).[30] (See Figure 9-1.) This salary differential becomes apparent as soon as people enter the labor market. Of the 1977 college graduates, for example, 20 percent of men but only 9 percent of women earn more than $10,000 a year.[31] Even when their jobs are the same, men and women earn vastly disparate salaries. (See Table 9-1.) For instance, on the average, female salespersons earn 55 percent of what male salespersons earn; female professionals earn about 65 percent of what their male counterparts earn.[32] Additionally, men who work jobs considered "female-identified," because of the high percentage of women occupying them, earn considerably less than men filling the more traditional "male-identified" positions.[33] Women are also more likely than men to be laid off, because it is assumed women need jobs less than men, who are assumed to have family responsibilities. Unfortunately, it is those women who are at the low end of the wage scale who suffer the effects of wage and job discrimination the most: 33 percent of families headed by a woman are below the poverty line, compared with 6 percent of those headed by a man.[34]

Wage and job discrimination are illegal according to the Equal Pay Act of 1963 and the Civil Rights Act of 1964, yet they continue to exist. Each year, for example, the Equal Employment Opportunity Commission receives about

[29]"Working Women," p. 64.
[30]"Working Women," p. 64.
[31]*Statistical Abstract of the United States, 1978*, p. 452.
[32]"Working Women," p. 67.
[33]Steven McLaughlin, "Occupational Sex Identification," *American Sociological Review*, vol. 43 (December 1978).
[34]"Characteristics of the Population Below the Poverty Level," *Current Population Reports*, P-60, no. 102 (January 1976), p. 2.

20,000 charges of sex discrimination.[35] One way such discrimination works was demonstrated by Levinson in a study of job inquiries.[36] Levinson and his co-researchers selected several classified advertisements in newspapers and defined the jobs advertised as "male" or "female," depending on their present sex composition. Male researchers inquired by telephone about the traditionally female jobs (such as secretary) and female researchers inquired about traditionally male jobs (such as auto mechanic). Afterward, this procedure was reversed, and researchers of each sex called to inquire about jobs considered appropriate for them. Levinson found that in 35 percent of all cases there was clear-cut sex discrimination. Male inquirers for a secretarial job, for example, were told the job was filled, while subsequent female callers were encouraged to apply. Sometimes the discrimination was more blunt: for example, women callers were told directly that "we don't hire girls as fuel attendants." Frequently, men inquirers for "sex-inappropriate" jobs were encouraged to apply for higher-level managerial positions, while women callers were told to apply for lower-level jobs.

Clearly, sex-typing of jobs is a major part of sex discrimination. Victor Fuchs, in a study of wage differentials by sex, concludes that sex discrimination is much more broadly based and

can be explained by the different roles assigned to men and women. Role differentiation, which begins in the cradle, affects the choice of occupation, labor force attachment, location of work, hours of work, and other variables that influence earnings.[37]

Fuchs concludes that a change in "role discrimination" is necessary before wage and job discrimination can be reduced.

[35]Citizens' Advisory Council on the Status of Women, *Women in 1975* (Washington, D.C.: U.S. Government Printing Office, 1976).

[36]Richard M. Levinson, "Sex Discrimination and Employment Practices: An Experiment with Unconventional Job Inquiries," *Social Problems*, vol. 22, no. 4 (April 1975), 533-543.

[37]Victor R. Fuchs, "Differences in Hourly Earnings Between Men and Women," *Monthly Labor Review* (May 1971), pp. 9-15.

	Women	Men
Professional, technical workers	$11,072	$16,939
Managers and administrators	9,804	16,674
Sales workers	6,272	14,586
Retail-sales workers	5,584	10,265
Clerical workers	8,128	12,843
Craft workers	7,765	13,638
Operatives	6,649	11,688
Service workers	5,840	10,036
Nonfarm laborers	7,613	10,104
Household domestics	2,570	N.A.

Table 9-1
Female and Male Annual Median Incomes by Occupation (in Dollars per Year).

Source: Reprinted from *U.S. News and World Report*, January 15, 1979. Copyright 1979 U.S. News and World Report, Inc.

Solomon Polachek considers consistent labor force participation the key factor in wage differential.[38] Traditionally, women have been seen as inconsistent members of the work force, withdrawing for stretches of time, thus depreciating their earnings potential. The lengthening of women's lifetime labor force participation signals progress, mostly for younger women now entering the market.

Legal, Civil, and Economic Rights

Many of our current laws and statutes discriminate against women and reinforce prejudice against them. (See Chapter 3 for a discussion of discriminatory rape laws.) Some states, for example, still require that women be given longer sentences than men for the same crime, on the assumption that female criminals require more rehabilitation. (Conversely, many states treat women offenders more leniently than men, on the assumption that women require the state's protection—a type of reverse discrimination.) In Alabama, women were excluded from jury duty until a federal court ruled in 1966 that this was unconstitutional.[39] However, the Supreme Court has upheld the right of states to keep women from being automatically selected for jury duty—in many states women must volunteer for jury duty or else they are not called, while men are selected automatically. The justification for this was stated in the Supreme Court decision, which clearly expresses a stereotypic view of a woman's role:

> Despite the enlightened emancipation of women from the restrictions and protections of bygone years, and their entry into many parts of community life formerly considered to be reserved to men, woman is still regarded as the center of home and family life. We cannot say that it is constitutionally impermissible for a State, acting in pursuit of the general welfare, to conclude that a woman should be relieved from the civic duty of jury service unless she herself determines that such service is consistent with her own special responsibilities.[40]

Diane Schulder points out other examples of legal discrimination of women. For instance, a 1966 Supreme Court decision upheld a Texas law stating that a married woman could not enter into a binding contract on her own. In most states, it is illegal to be a prostitute but not illegal to frequent one; thus, prostitutes are routinely arrested while their customers remain free. In New York, where prostitutes and their customers are considered to be in equal violation of the law, male customers are still rarely prosecuted. Also, some states quasi-officially permit the "passion shooting" by a husband of a wife caught in an infidelity; the reverse, as Schulder puts it, "is known as homicide."[41]

It is the economic discrimination legally directed at women, however, that has perhaps most reinforced their subordinate status. A wide variety of laws and statutes are based on the idea that males are the breadwinners of a family and that women are dependents. This concept causes the work that

---

[38]Solomon W. Polachek. "Discontinuous Labor Force Participation," in *Sex, Discrimination, and the Division of Labor*, ed. Cynthia Lloyd (New York: Columbia University Press, 1975).

[39]Judith Hole and Ellen Levine, *Rebirth of Feminism* (New York: Quadrangle, 1971), pp. 59-60.

[40]*Hoyt v. Florida*, 368 U.S. 57 (1961).

[41]Diane B. Schulder, "Does the Law Oppress Women?" in *Sisterhood Is Powerful*, ed. Robin Morgan (New York: Random House, 1970).

women (and men) do in the home—and even the work that women do outside the home—to be consistently undervalued. Thus, for example, a woman automatically gets Social Security benefits if her husband dies, because her dependence on his wages is assumed. For a man to collect benefits if his wife dies, however, he must prove that he was financially dependent on her. (Even then, his benefits were lower than a widow's would be—until 1975, when the Supreme Court ruled that benefits must be equal.) While this provision of the Social Security Act discriminates against men, it also perpetuates the antiquated idea that women are not wage-earners.[42] At the end of 1975 the Supreme Court revoked another long-standing statute that discriminated against woman, when it ruled that pregnant women could receive unemployment benefits during the last three months of pregnancy. Previously, statutes in many states had assumed that unemployed women in the final stage of pregnancy were unable to work and therefore were not entitled to unemployment benefits.

Homemakers, who are still mostly women, suffer the greatest form of legal economic discrimination. No federal, state, or insurance agency takes the economic value of a homemaker into account.[43] Thus, homemakers cannot obtain private disability insurance, even though their spouses would have to hire help if they were disabled. Disability-insurance policies are written for those who earn wages—even though the work homemakers perform represents a clear economic contribution. In fact, at present, homemakers cannot be enrolled in the Social Security system in order to qualify for disability benefits, even if they were to pay the required taxes.

The undervaluation of the work of homemakers—the services performed by them are not even included in the gross national product—results in a number of other inequities. For example, homemakers do not receive full tax credit for the expenses of running a home, even though businesspersons can write off everything from telephone bills to lunches as business expenses. They are also ineligible for Workmen's Compensation. Perhaps most important, the monetary undervaluation of the work of homemakers results in the undervaluation of the homemaker *role*. Lekachman suggests, in fact, that redefining the household as an economic unit is a prerequisite for sexual equality. If this is done, he suggests,

> running an efficient home enterprise will confer respectability on the woman *or* the man who freely chooses this occupational alternative. Both sexes will be encouraged to make rational comparisons between home and outside employment . . . . Liberalization of household-expense deductions will facilitate, as a third choice, outside employment for husband and wife and engagement of child- and home-management specialists—male or female.[44]

Juanita Kreps suggests that flexibility of work-hours is one way to equalize home work. The rearrangement of work-hours for both men and women could encourage more male participation in home-making.[45]

[42]Women's Rights Project, *Social Security and Sex Discrimination* (New York: American Civil Liberties Union, July 17, 1974).

[43]"Economic Value of a Housewife," *Research and Statistics Note*, U.S. Department of Health, Education, and Welfare (August 28, 1975).

[44]Robert Lekachman, "On Economic Equality," *Signs—Journal of Women in Culture and Society*, vol. 1, no. 1 (Autumn 1975), 100.

[45]Juanita Kreps, "The Future of Working Women," *Ms.* (March, 1977).

Sexism, Social Class, and Race

The position of women of different social classes and races in our society can be succinctly described with a baseball metaphor: if you are a female, that's one strike against you; if you are a poor female or a nonwhite female, that's two strikes against you; if you are a poor, non-white female, you have struck out. (See Chapter 7 for further information on women and poverty, and Chapter 10 for information on elderly women.)

We have already mentioned that one-third of families headed by a woman are below the poverty line. Women in general are restricted in their employment opportunities, but women with children are even more restricted than their childless counterparts. In practical terms, the presence of children in the house limits the kinds of jobs female heads of families can have, because they cannot travel far from home or work the longer hours that higher-paying jobs often require. Moreover, because day-care centers are often not readily available few mothers can work. Those who do must use part of their salaries to pay someone to stay with their children while they are at work. Because only low-status, low-paying jobs are available to these women, and because of the lack of child-care facilities, over 60 percent of female heads of households do not seek employment. Unfortunately, the proportion of female heads of families has approximately doubled since 1970 and is continuing to increase. The problem of poverty among this group is therefore a constantly growing one.[46]

Female members of minorities tend to suffer double discrimination, both on the basis of sex and of race or ethnicity. Thus nonwhite females have even higher rates of unemployment than their white sisters, and are also even more likely to be working in blue-collar jobs. Unemployment among Spanish-speaking women, for example, is about 10 percent, a higher rate than among white women; and only 6 percent of Spanish-speaking women are in professional jobs, compared to 16 percent of all employed women.[47] Besides job and wage discrimination, however, nonwhite women also suffer several other additional stresses and strains caused by the difficult roles they must play and the stereotypes that exist about them. Some of these stereotypes are detailed below.

Black Women

According to available statistics, the black woman suffers the most from race and sex discrimination. Though a larger proportion of black women than white women work, black women are even more concentrated in the low-status jobs at the bottom of the pay scale. For example, more than three-fourths of working black women are in service jobs; nearly half work in occupations (such as domestics) not covered by the federal minimum wage. The average black woman's wage is lower than the average salary of a white man, of a black man, and of a white woman—even for the same work.[48]

To William Blakey, the economic discrimination against black women is,

[46]"Characteristics of the Low-Income Population," *Current Population Reports*, Series P-60, no. 98 (Washington, D.C.: U.S. Government Printing Office, 1975).

[47]"Spanish-U.S. Women Assayed by Census," *New York Times*, May 2, 1976.

[48]Virginia E. Prendergass, *et al.*, "Sex Discrimination Counseling," *American Psychologist* (January 1976), 44.

Victims of dual discrimination, black women may be the most exploited minority in our society.

Paul Sequeira/Photo Researchers, Inc.

however, only one facet of the double discrimination they suffer. As he put it:

It should not be necessary to cite the . . . lack of child care for working women, the failure to receive equal pay for equal work, the raping of black women by white and black men, the increasing number of forced sterilizations of black women, and the miserable treatment black women receive in prison in order to make the point that however bad a black man has had it, black women have it worse.[49]

[49]William A. Blakey, "Everybody Makes the Revolution," *Civil Rights Digest*, vol. 6, no. 3 (Spring 1974), 19.

Frances Beal echoes this point of view, suggesting that black women have been among the most exploited groups in our society. She cites the fact that unions with membership made up predominantly of nonwhite women (such as the International Ladies Garment Workers Union) usually have white males as their leaders, and suggests that these men have generally been insensitive to the needs of their union members. Beal also points out that in several states black women on welfare have been pressured to undergo sterilization procedures in order to continue to qualify for welfare benefits.[50]

Other researchers have explored the stereotypes that exist about black (and other nonwhite) women and the special psychological stresses to which black women are subjected. For example, black women have traditionally been believed to be more sexually promiscuous than white women; and, as we suggested in Chapter 8, this myth is one reason white men have exploited black women sexually, particularly during the time of slavery. The myth persists to this day, however: it is a popular stereotype that black women on welfare have many more children than white women on welfare, when, in fact, they have approximately the same number. (See Chapters 7 and 8.)

The special pressures that black women experience include the fact that black men have tended to adopt the prejudicial attitudes toward women in our society. As Virginia Prendergrass and her colleagues have described, black men may try to dominate their wives in order to compensate for their frustrations in dealing with a society that discriminates against them. Scanzoni, however, points out the higher the education is among black men, the less likely they are to be oppressive to their wives. He also suggests that due to the long-standing existence of black women in the labor market, there is possibly a greater sex-role egalitarianism among blacks.[51]

Puertoriqueñas Some of the problems that Puerto Rican women face in our society are faced by Puerto Ricans in general: difficulties with the English language, different cultural background and customs, and a lack of preparedness for the racial inequality of our society. (Puerto Rico is a racially mixed society in which members of different groups are generally treated as equals.) Like other minorities, Puerto Ricans suffer from discrimination in housing, education, employment, and wages that keeps them in a severely deprived condition.

Here again, however, Puerto Rican women are in many ways even more deprived than their male counterparts. The median income of Puerto Rican women is about half that of Puerto Rican men (which, in turn, is only about two-thirds of the white median income). And unemployment among Puerto Rican women is twice as high as among Puerto Rican men. Like other minorities, Puerto Rican women, even more than Puerto Rican men, are concentrated in the lower-paying occupations.

It is Puerto Rican women who are heads of families who suffer from discrimination the most. Because Puerto Rican children have special language and cultural needs, the shortage of child-care facilities prevents Puerto Rican

[50]Frances M. Beal, "Double Jeopardy: To Be Black and Female," in Morgan, *Sisterhood Is Powerful*, pp. 340-353.

[51]John H. Scanzoni. *The Black Family in Modern Society—Patterns of Stability and Security* (Chicago: University of Chicago Press, 1971); and John H. Scanzoni, *Sex Roles, Life Styles, and Childbearing: Changing Patterns in Marriage and the Family* (New York: Free Press, 1975).

women from seeking employment. Only about 13 percent of female heads of Puerto Rican families are able to work full time; an astonishing 60 percent of Puerto Rican families headed by a woman live below the poverty line.[52]

Like black women, Puerto Rican women in the United States suffer from popular stereotypes: for example, they are seen as docile, pampered, and inordinately sexual. However, it is the prejudice they face as women—both in their own culture and in the larger American society—that has, in addition to the prejudice they face as Puerto Ricans, most prevented their advancement. As Lourdes King put it,

> The Puerto Rican woman in the United States is caught between two forces. On the one hand, she is entrapped between the bleak economic and political powerlessness affecting the Puerto Rican population in general. On the other hand, she suffers from the socialization of sex roles which causes her to have guilt feelings about the fulfillment of her potential and its expression in a society which looks down . . . at her and her people.[53]

Like many black women, however, Puerto Rican women have been generally reluctant to affiliate themselves with the women's movement, because they stereotypically perceive it as being anti-male or anti-family.

Native Women

We have many fewer stereotypes for native, or American Indian, women than for native men. Most of the native women who lived and died on this continent passed silently through our history, with hardly a heroine or a colorful epithet to confer some distinction upon them. There are a few exceptions; the names of Sacajawea, Pocahontas, and Malinche stand out, but primarily as the women who were responsible for encouraging contact with white settlers or for sacrificing themselves for them. One derogatory stereotype is that of the stolid "squaw," an Algonquin word that originally meant "woman" later degenerated into "drudge."[54]

Despite the militant stands taken at Alcatraz and Wounded Knee, native people are still a barely visible minority (see Chapter 8), and native women are totally invisible. The facts available about the condition of American Indians largely refer to Indians as a people because few statistical agencies bother to keep separate records by sex. What statistics are available indicate that native peoples are a marginal group economically who are extremely dependent on federal funds for basic survival. The average length of education for Indians under federal supervision is about five years of school. Only one out of thirty graduates from college, compared to a national figure of one out of three. Winter unemployment rates reach 90 percent on some reservations; the birth and infant mortality rates are high; life expectancy is low. In fact, the health level of the American Indian was once described by President Lyndon Johnson as "the lowest of any major population group in the United States."[55] The Bureau of Indian Affairs (BIA), the federal agency responsible for native Americans, has few native men (and fewer native women) in mid-level or

[52]Lourdes M. King, "Puertoriqueñas in the United States: The Impact of Double Discrimination," *Civil Rights Digest* (Spring 1974), pp. 20-27.
[53]King, "Puertoriqueñas," p. 25.
[54]Shirley Witt, "Native Women Today: Sexism and the Indian Woman," *Civil Rights Digest* (Spring 1974), pp. 29-35.
[55]Witt, "Native Women Today," p. 34.

top-level administrative positions. Even in states in which Indians comprise a majority of BIA employees, a disproportionate number are in lower-level jobs.

The education of native Americans is also a BIA responsibility, and it is in this area where discrimination against Indian women is most visible. In Indian boarding schools, girls may study only domestic or secretarial work, while boys study such things as farmwork or crafts. Unfortunately, Indian women can rarely use even the domestic skills they have learned:

> Reservation life . . . cannot support the picture of the average American homemaker. The starched and relatively expensive advertised clothes are out of place and unobtainable. The polished floors and picture windows are so removed from the hogan or log cabin as to become unreal. The many convenient appliances are too expensive and would not run without electricity. The clean and smiling children require more water than the Navajo family can afford the time to haul. Parent Teacher Association meetings, of which she may have read, are the product of tax-supported schools with the parent in the ultimate role of employer. On the reservation the government-appointed teacher is viewed more as an authority figure than a public servant.[56]

Trapped by their education in low-level service jobs and by the condition of their race in extremely deprived circumstances, native women are among the greatest victims of racial and sex discrimination.

Chicanas

The Chicana, or Mexican-American woman, has traditionally been closely identified with family life. She has been bound by customs that stress her importance as a wife and mother and the need to obey her husband. This has created, as Consuelo Nieto put it, a double dilemma for the Chicana:

> On the one hand, she struggles to maintain her identity as a Chicana. On the other hand, her demands for equity as a woman involve fundamental cultural change. . . . Many Chicanas support the women's movement as it relates to equity and pay opportunities, for instance, yet for some . . . the closer the movement comes to their personal lives, the more difficult it becomes to tear themselves away from the kinds of roles they have filled.[57]

According to Nieto, the Chicana's task to achieve equality is made more difficult by the fact that she is often competing with Chicanos (rather than whites) for the same low-level job. Trapped by racial discrimination at the lower stratum of society, she is often unable to compete with men even at this low level because of her culture's norms about the role she should play.

Asian Women

Asian-American women are subjected to a number of different stereotypes and stresses. Most Asian cultures have stressed the subordinate role of women, and Western culture has vulgarized this by portraying Asian woman as pliant, eager to please, and exotically sexual. On the other hand, many Asian-American women come from upwardly mobile families who place heavy

[56]Witt, "Native Women Today," p. 31.
[57]Consuelo Nieto, "The Chicana and Women's Rights Movement," *Civil Rights Digest* (Spring 1974), pp. 36-42.

emphasis on education and assimilation into the predominant culture. Thus, while Asian-Americans do suffer from a racism based on appearance, like blacks, most of them have not grown up in dead-end slums with little hope for future advancement. For this reason many Asian-American women have identified with the Women's Liberation Movement and have formed groups to press for sexual, as well as racial and ethnic, equality.[58]

Sources of Sexism

We have described some of the causes of women's subordination from a historical point of view and have indicated some of the major inequities women face in our society and in other countries. In this section we will discuss in some detail the processes by which institutions in our society perpetrate, reinforce, and perpetuate sexism.

Socialization

Socialization refers to the process by which individuals develop into social beings. Janet Chafetz has suggested that

> through the socialization process humans came to more or less internalize the roles, norms, and values appropriate to the culture and subculture within which they function. Cultural definitions become personal definitions of propriety, normality, and worthiness.[59]

Most socialization takes place during interaction with other people—how they react to what we do will eventually influence how we will behave. We are also socialized through popular culture—films and books, for example. Socialization may be consciously imposed—for instance, compulsory education—or it may be as subtle and unconscious as the nuances we take for granted in our language. Eleanor Maccoby and Carol Jacklin suggest that the common belief in myths about sex differences, such as "girls are more suggestible than boys," "boys excel in mathematical abilities," "boys are more analytical than girls," etc. reinforce the socialization of sex-roles.[60]

A primary agent of socialization in our culture is the family—specifically parents. A number of studies have sought to determine how parents socialize their children into traditional sex roles. The broad and traditional outlines of how parents raise their children to be men and women in our society do not need to be documented by researchers, for they are self-evident. Long before a child is born, parents are deciding how they will treat it if it is a boy or a girl, what name the child will have and whether the nursery will be painted blue or pink. Later, when the child is born, the socialization process takes a number of obvious forms: little boys will be given toy trucks, while little girls will be given dolls; boys are encouraged to play ball, while girls are told to play house.

It is the more subtle forms of socialization that have interested

[58]Dwinelle Hall, *Asian Women* (Berkeley: University of California Press, 1971).

[59]Janet S. Chafetz, *Masculine, Feminine, or Human?: An Overview of the Sociology of Sex Roles* (Itasca, Ill.: Peacock, 1974), p. 69.

[60]Eleanor Emmons Maccoby and Carol Nagy Jacklin, "What We Should Know and Don't Know about Sex Differences," in *Human Sexuality, Contemporary Perspectives,* ed. Eleanor S. Morrison and Vera Borsage (Palo Alto, Calif.: Mayfield, 1977).

researchers. Michael Lewis, for example, found that parental influences cause differences in the behavior of boys and girls within the first two years of their lives:

> From the earliest age, girl infants are looked at and talked to more than boy infants. For the first six months or so, boy infants have more physical contact than girl infants, but by the time boys are six months old, this reverses and girls get more physical contact and more nontouching contact . . . . The motive appears to be cultural; mothers believe that boys should be more independent than girls and that they should be encouraged to explore and master their world.[61]

Lewis theorizes that this tendency of mothers to talk more to their daughters accounts in part for the greater linguistic skills that women demonstrate. The lack of physical contact experienced by boys after the age of six months, suggests Lewis, may account for the fact that they tend to be more independent as adults—and also more restricted in their expression of feeling.

David Lynn suggests that one cause of male-female differences is the fact that, traditionally, children have been raised by their mothers while the father was at work, absent from the home. The effect on little girls who are raised in this way, Lynn theorizes, is that they can easily identify with their mothers who are always there; however, they will tend to regard the absent father—and by extension, males in general—as more powerful and prestigious. Since boys, on the other hand, will have few male models available with whom to identify, their concepts of maleness will be based on an unrealistic cultural definition of masculinity, rather than on human models. They will have to learn what is expected of them from their peers and from whatever guidance they can derive from the media. Lynn suggests that the more critical identity problem with which boys are confronted accounts both for their greater problem-solving ability in adulthood and their constant anxiety about their masculinity.[62]

Education   Education represents a more formal type of socialization. Considering how much time children spend in school, the socialization they receive there inevitably affects how they behave. Several studies have indicated that by and large schools reinforce traditional sex-role stereotypes and socialize children into traditional sex roles.

A study Maye and McMillan conducted found that some female elementary-school teachers—disproportionately represented in elementary schools—shared traditional prejudices about women. One in four of those teachers studied believed women functioned best as wives and mothers and that women were less reliable workers than men.[63] It is likely that such attitudes cause teachers to set different standards of behavior for boys and girls. Florence Howe found, for example, that boys were permitted to be far more active and boisterous in the classroom.[64]

[61]Michael Lewis, "There's No Unisex in the Nursery," *Psychology Today* (May 1972), p. 56.

[62]David B. Lynn, *Parental and Sex Role Identification: A Theoretical Formulation* (Berkeley: McCutchan, 1969).

[63]Chafetz, *Masculine, Feminine, or Human?* p. 86-90.

[64]Florence Howe, "Sexual Stereotypes Start Early," *Saturday Review* (October 16, 1971), p. 81.

Even if teachers are informed and well intentioned, other parts of the educational system still stymie attempts to eradicate sexist training. For one thing, many school texts perpetuate stereotypes, myths, and half truths. In a survey of elementary-school reading-textbooks, researchers found that boy stories predominated (in a 5:2 ratio), that boys outnumbered girls in illustrations, and that there were more stories about smart boys who exercised initiative and achieved their goals than there were about girls.[65] The same stereotypes were found in a study of prize-winning preschool texts: females were underrepresented; they were pictured as passive and dependent, and were seen as playing traditional domestic roles. Boys were pictured as being much more decisive and adventurous. It is little wonder that by the age of four the relative advantages of each sex role are recognized by children: fully half of girls prefer the male role, while only a fourth of boys prefer the female role.[66]

The separate treatment generally accorded boys and girls in school further segregates the sexes and reinforces traditional roles. Boys and girls are generally lined up separately, for example, and in many schools are given different courses—girls take typing, boys take shop. It is the sex segregation that occurs during career counseling that is the most insidious, however, for it locks children into lifetime careers on the basis of sex rather than ability. Too often, counselors advocate only traditional female occupations to young women who are qualified and eager to enter so-called male preserves. A young girl who is a good math student may be told to go into teaching, while a young boy with equal skills may be directed toward engineering. Chafetz described it this way:

> Counselors defend such practices on the basis of what youngsters may "realistically" expect to face in the future: marriage, child care, and a lack of opportunity in a number of career fields for females, and the need to support a family at the highest income and status levels possible for males. "Realism," however, has always been an excuse for maintaining the status quo, and it is no different in the case of sex role stereotypes. If, for instance, females do not prepare to enter previously masculine fields, such fields will remain male-dominated, allowing another generation of counselors to assure girls that females can't work in them. In addition, it is questionable whether counselors' notions of more "reality" in fact keep pace with reality. There is undoubtedly a lag between expanding opportunities and changing sex role definitions on the one hand, and counselors' awareness of these phenomena on the other.[67]

Family

The traditional view of women is that a woman's primary role is that of homemaker. Women who do adopt this view of themselves and accept their traditional role do not always find that they achieve equal status even within the home. The very role of homemaker, as it is designed and regarded, often seems to perpetuate a woman's subordinate status, limit her freedom, and leave her feeling unfulfilled. As Robert Bell put it:

> It has been observed that women are often caught in a vicious circle because of their economic dependence on their husbands and their lack of contact with the

[65]Chafetz, *Masculine, Feminine, or Human?* p. 83.

[66]Lenore Weitzman, *et al.*, "Sex Role Socialization in Picture Books for Preschool Children," *American Journal of Sociology* (May 1972), p. 1125-1150; Farrell, *The Liberated Man*, p. 36.

[67]Chafetz, *Masculine, Feminine, or Human?* p. 88.

Men are increasingly sharing the traditional household chores such as cooking and finding them satisfying.

Mimi Forsyth/Monkmeyer

work world; and their being tied down to the house restricts, to a great extent, the kind of decisions over which they can claim expertise and, ultimately, control.[68]

Even in many nontraditional marriages in which there is a great degree of equality between husband and wife, the husband often has a more privileged position. One study of husband and wife psychologists, for example, found that even when both members of a couple are professionals, the woman often is forced into a somewhat subordinate position because it is assumed that the man's career is more important or more likely to be successful than the woman's. As a result, wives in professional pairs are less likely than their husbands to be satisfied with their careers.[69]

Many studies of different types of marriages tend to confirm that husbands are generally more satisfied with marriage than their wives who have to make more concessions. Among unhappy marriages, wives tend to feel more frustrated than their husbands: women go for marriage counseling

[68]Bell, *Marriage and Family Interaction*, pp. 370-371.

more often than men and initiate most divorce proceedings. Even among happy marriages, however, women report higher rates of dissatisfaction and depression than men, and women must make most of the adjustments to make the marriage work. In Jessie Bernard's words:

> Because women have to put so many more eggs in the one basket of marriage they have more of a stake in its stability. Because their happiness is more dependent on marriage than men's they have to pay more for it.[70]

The psychological consequences of overidentifying with a woman's domestic role were described by Pauline Bart in her study of depression in middle-aged women. Bart found that, contrary to popular opinion, women did not become depressed in middle age because of hormonal changes caused by menopause but rather because they found themselves left without any important function. She found that the lowest rates of depression occurred among middle-aged working women, who had their jobs to keep them occupied and provide satisfaction. Higher rates of depression were found among housewives whose children had grown up and left home; the housewife had fewer people dependent on her domestic role, and her sense of identity suffered. Bart found the highest depression rates were among housewives who had overinvolved or overprotective relationships with their children. For these women, the departure of their children from the household destroyed both their purpose in life and much of their self-esteem.[71]

Alice Rossi has pointed out that the development of technological tools to do human work has eliminated many of the traditional tasks of the homemaker—laundry is done largely by machine instead of by hand, cooking takes less time because of ovens and "instant foods," and so on. But this has not produced more free time for homemakers; instead, the other aspects of the traditional role—particularly motherhood—have, until recently, assumed greater importance. Women have been expected to devote full time to the task of rearing children; motherhood has become a "full-time occupation."[72]

This overemphasis on the importance of motherhood inevitably causes guilt feelings in women who are unfulfilled by the mother role and undoubtedly contributes to the depression Pauline Bart described. Moreover, the emphasis on motherhood devalues the importance of the father's role in a child's upbringing. Warren Farrell cites several studies that indicate that problems between children and fathers caused more delinquency and maladjustment than problems between children and mothers.[73] Nevertheless, the myth that a woman is best suited for the task of raising a child persists, preventing many women from exercising their capability outside the home and preventing many men from exercising their capabilities inside the home. The result is a sex differentiation that keeps women in a subordinate role and prevents members of both sexes from sharing in their family and work responsibilities.

[69]Rebecca B. Bryson, *et al.*, "The Professional Pair," *American Psychologist* (January 1976), pp. 10-17.

[70]Jessie Bernard, "The Paradox of the Happy Marriage," in *Woman in Sexist Society*, ed. Vivian Gornick and Barbara K. Moran (New York: Basic Books, 1974), p. 149.

[71]Pauline B. Bart, "Depression in Middle-Aged Women," in Gornick and Moran, *Women in Sexist Society*, pp. 163-186.

[72]Alice Rossi, "Equality Between the Sexes: An Immodest Proposal," *Daedalus*, Spring 1964.

[73]Farrell, *The Liberated Man*, p. 117.

Abortion   Abortion is one of the most controversial issues in America today, and many persons view it as the right to reproductive control, tied to the issues of birth-control, health care, and education.

Historically, anti-abortion laws did not come into full play until the mid-nineteenth century, when "certain governments and religious groups desired continued population growth to fill growing industries and new farmable territories."[74] Literally, governments sought control of the means of production by controlling reproduction. Ironically, in light of today's debates, another reason given for the passage of these laws was to protect women against the danger of crude operations. Yet history has shown that in fact the reverse happened: women still had abortions, legal or otherwise, and many deaths and injuries resulted. Those who could afford the services of expensive doctors stood a better chance of survival than poorer women who had to risk highly unsanitary and often degrading "back-street" conditions.

In the mid-1950s, agitation against the existing laws caused a few states to permit abortions in limited circumstances. Women could apply for abortions, but the decision was made by doctors and hospitals. As a result of medical red tape and high costs, patients who could afford private physicians were able to benefit most from the reformed laws, while many poorer women continued to have few alternatives but illegal abortions.

In 1970, New York State allowed abortion almost on demand, followed within the next two years by Alaska, Hawaii, and Washington State. Many women took advantage of this situation, and mortality and injury rates, as well as the number of illegal abortions, began to drop.[75] With the proven success and safety of legal abortions and continued pressure for federal legalization, the Supreme Court legalized abortion in 1973.

Abortion, however, has remained highly controversial, and many oppose it adamantly. An organized group who support the "Right-to-Life" or anti-abortion stand, are striving to repeal all pro-abortion laws with the vigorous support of the Catholic Church. They oppose abortion on moral grounds and raise fundamental questions about the nature of human life and the rights of unborn children. Their arguments certainly deserve serious consideration.

Related to reproductive control is the availability of education, health care, and birth control. Clearly, the need for abortion decreases with the increase of education, health care, and contraceptive alternatives. Many pregnancies among young women could be prevented by earlier education about birth control. Furstenberg suggests that schools for the most part "go ignored as sites for pregnancy prevention programs."[76] Although sexual attitudes have changed considerably, there is still a societal stigma about pre-marital sex, especially among adolescents, resulting, on the institutional level, in vague or haphazard sex education. (See Chapter 3.) For many poor women, access to education, good health care, and contraception remain lower than for other women, although strides are being made in the establishment of more social programs. In the final analysis, as more family

[74]Wendy Coppedge Sanford, *et al.* "Abortion," in *Our Bodies, Ourselves,* ed. The Boston Women's Health Book Collective (New York: Simon and Schuster, 1976), p. 217.

[75]Sanford, *et al.,* "Abortion," p. 218.

[76]Frank F. Furstenberg, Jr., "The Social Consequences of Teenage Parenthood," in *Human Sexuality in a Changing Society,* ed. Graham B. Spanier (Minneapolis: Burgess, 1979), p. 157.

planning centers and educational and counselling channels open to women, women can educate themselves about contraception and make the choice in reproductive control on their own.

Psychiatric Medicine

There can be little doubt that psychologists and psychiatrists—who are predominantly male—have stereotypic notions about women. Bruno Bettelheim once said that "as much as women want to be good scientists and engineers, they want first and foremost to be womanly companions of men and to be mothers." Erik Erikson wrote that a woman has "an 'inner space' destined to bear the offspring of chosen men, and with it, a biological, psychological, and ethical commitment to take care of human infancy."[77] A major survey of women psychologists who had been in psychotherapy found that therapists tended to foster traditional sex roles and were biased in their evaluations of their women patients. Some of the biases found in the survey include:

1. "The therapist lacks awareness and sensitivity to the woman client's career, work, and role diversity."

2. "The female client's attitude toward childbearing and child rearing is viewed as a necessary index of her emotional maturity."

3. "The therapist defers to the husband's needs in the conduct of the wife's treatment."

4. "The therapist . . . fosters concepts of women as passive and dependent."

5. "The therapist has a double standard for male and female sexual activities."[78]

As we discussed in Chapter 2, mental health clinicians have different standards of mental health for men and women: they believe that healthy *women* are passive and dependent, while at the same time they believe that healthy *adults* are active and independent.[79] The net effect of this bias is to reinforce traditional roles in women patients and to identify those women who do not fit the traditional mold as maladjusted or ill. Bell put it more generally:

> The psychiatric influence has been such that any problem is seen as individually based rather than socially determined. As a result, many women who have felt miserable and unhappy as housewives have defined themselves at fault or inadequate rather than recognizing that in many cases they are victims of social situations that cause their problems.[80]

Language and the Media

One of the dominant features of our society is the explosive growth of the communications industry over the past two decades. More books are

[77]Bettleheim and Erikson, quoted in Naomi Weisstein, "Psychology Constructs the Female," in Gornick and Moran, *Women in Sexist Society*, pp. 364-365.

[78]Report of the Task Force on Sex Bias and Sex-Role Stereotyping in Psychotherapeutic Practice," *American Psychologist* (December 1975), pp. 1169-1175.

[79]Phyllis Chesler, *Women and Madness* (New York: Avon, 1972), p. 68; see Mary B. Parlee, "Psychology," *Signs—Journal of Women in Culture and Society* (Autumn 1975), pp. 119-138.

[80]Bell, *Marriage and Family Interaction*, p. 377.

published every year and people spend more time watching television. How these and other media treat sex roles is therefore likely to have a considerable impact on attitudes and behaviors.

Language in the media (and in textbooks) often reinforces traditional sex-role stereotypes by its overreliance on male terms and its tendency to describe men and women with outmoded clichés. Stereotypic phrases might be "the future of man" instead of "the future of humanity"; "Bill and his attractive wife" instead of "handsome Bill and attractive Joan" or "Bill and Joan"; and "scatterbrained female," "clumsy male," and so on. The use of male pronouns when neutral subjects are referred to also implies that women are excluded from active life: for example, "the typical doctor enjoys *his* leisure time" instead of "typically doctors enjoy *their* leisure time."

While sexism in everyday language is subtle and unconscious, in advertising it is often blatant. One analysis of commercials for children's programs showed that almost all narrators were male, more females than males were involved in domestic activities, ten times as many boys as girls were physically active, and every child shown as economically dependent was a girl.[81] Researchers who analyzed the roles portrayed by women in print advertisements found that

> the advertisements presented the following cliches about women's role: (1) a woman's place is in the home, (2) women do not make important decisions or do important things, (3) women are dependent and need men's protection, and (4) men regard women primarily as sexual objects; they are not interested in women as people.[82]

Far fewer women than men were portrayed as employed, although almost half of all women do work outside the home. No women were shown in executive positions; instead, they tended to play largely decorative roles in these advertisements. Finally the vast majority of the buying decisions were shown to be made by men, particularly those involving major purchases, such as cars. In addition, as Lucy Komisar suggests, the woman in advertisements seems to be totally preoccupied with her domestic role or with attracting a man.[83] Such stereotypes tend to negate the changes that are already occuring in our society. Furthermore, they serve to reinforce traditional sex roles and make it difficult for men and women to see broader possibilities in their roles and their relationships.

Organized Religion

Women attend church more frequently than men
- pray more often than men
- hold firmer beliefs than men
- cooperate more in church programs than men

Yet organized religion is dominated by men.[84]

[81]Chafetz, *Masculine, Feminine, or Human?* pp. 82-83.

[82]Ahmed Belkaoui and Janice M. Belkaoui, "A Comparative Analysis of the Roles Played by Women in Print Advertisements: 1958, 1970, 1972," *Journal of Marketing Research* (May 1976), p. 168.

[83]Lucy Komisar, "The Image of Woman in Advertising," in Gornick and Moran, *Women in Sexist Society*, p. 306.

[84]Joseph H. Fichter, in Virginia R. Mills, "The Status of Women in American Churches," *Church and Society* (September-October 1972), p. 50.

In their theological doctrine and religious hierarchies, churches and synagogues tend to reinforce women's subordinate role. Organized religion has, historically, reinforced many secular traditions and norms. As such, it has tended toward the traditional view that men are primary and women secondary, and that a woman's most important role is procreative. In Judaism, women are required to obey fewer religious precepts than men because less is expected of them. Devout Jewish males recite a prayer each morning thanking God that they are not women. The Catholic Church still assumes overall authority over a woman's sexual behavior, forbidding birth control devices because they prevent reproduction. In all churches, God is referred to as "He"; most churches bar women from performing the most sacred rituals or attaining the highest administrative posts. The consequences of this are summed up well by Mary Daly:

> As long as qualified persons are excluded from any ministry by reason of their sex alone, it cannot be said that there is genuine equality of men and women in the church . . . . By this exclusion the church is saying that the sexual differentiation is—for one sex—a crippling defect which no personal qualities of intelligence, character, or leadership can overcome. In fact, by this policy it is effectively teaching that women are not fully human and conditioning people to accept this as unchangeable fact.[85]

Government

The federal government has a long history of discrimination against women.[86] A study in 1919 by the Women's Bureau (a federal agency created by Congress) found that women were barred from applying to 60 percent of all civil service positions, notably those involving scientific or other professional work. Women were considered in a separate employment category, and their salaries were limited. The professionals in the Women's Bureau, for example, were condemned by an act of Congress to receiving half the salaries males received for doing the same work in other federal agencies.

During World War II, the pattern of official discrimination continued. Despite the shortage of men, women were kept from most administrative and professional positions. The situation, if anything, was worse in the armed forces. Although the Army had a severe shortage of medical personnel, for example, it refused to commission women doctors. Only an act of Congress in 1943 forced the Army to change its hiring policies. In the domestic labor force, women were of necessity permitted to enter fields that had been previously closed to them. But although the National War Labor Board insisted on a uniform pay scale for both sexes, it permitted loopholes that effectively discriminated against women: for example, the equal pay provisions did not apply to traditionally female jobs, and industries were permitted to assign different job titles for men and women, even for the same work.

While discrimination against women has had less overt support by the government in recent years, patterns of discrimination still exist at the federal level. The 1964 Civil Rights Act, which prohibited discrimination on the basis

---

[85]Mary Daly, "Women and the Catholic Church," in Morgan, *Sisterhood Is Powerful*, p. 134.

[86]The following discussion is based on William H. Chafe, *The American Woman: Her Changing Social, Economic, and Political Roles, 1920–1970* (New York: Oxford University Press, 1972).

Jane Byrne's election to become Chicago's first woman mayor is a small victory against the discrimination women have suffered from government employers.
UPI

of (among other things) sex, specifically excluded federal, state, and local governments from its provisions. Thus, women who work for the government are overwhelmingly concentrated in lower-level clerical or service-type jobs, while administrative posts are largely held by men. Federal policy toward day-care funding has also discriminated against women. One New York survey found that seven out of eight mothers who utilized day-care centers could not earn a living wage without them. Nevertheless, federal funding for day-care centers has remained low.

The Legal System

We have already mentioned some of the laws that discriminate against women, such as those relating to jury duty. These laws, however, represent a small part of an entire legal structure that is based on the idea that men are the wage-earners in the family, while women are the homemakers.

Judith Hole and Ellen Levine have outlined many of the legal barriers to sexual equality.[87] For example, many state labor laws passed during the late nineteenth and early twentieth centuries set work standards that were designed to protect all workers—the maximum hours that people were required to work, the maximum weights that they were required to lift, and so on. The Supreme Court found, however, that such labor restrictions were unconstitutional in regard to men, since they violated constitutional liberties. Women, on the other hand, could still be required to obey these restrictions.

[87]Hole and Levine, *Rebirth of Feminism*, pp. 18-67.

In its 1908 decision, which upheld a state law limiting the hours women factory employees could work, the Court stated:

> History discloses the fact that woman has always been dependent on man. He has established his control at the outset by superior physical strength, and this control in various forms, with diminishing intensity, has continued to the present . . . . Differentiated by these matters from the other sex, she is properly placed in a class by herself, and legislation designed for her protection may be sustained, even when like legislation is not necessary for men, and could not be sustained.[88]

This decision in effect legalized and perpetuated those state laws that differentiated between men and women. As late as 1965, the Equal Employment Opportunity Commission (EEOC), which was empowered to enforce the 1964 Civil Rights Act, stated that state laws designed to "protect" women were not discriminatory.

The problem of legal differentiation between men and women also exists in other areas besides employment. Some state educational institutions are permitted to exclude women, either from their student bodies or their faculties. Many technical high schools admit only boys; many high schools prohibit pregnant or married girls from attending, but permit unmarried fathers or married boys to attend.

Hole and Levine also note that in most states, statutes applicable to married adults are dominated by the common-law tradition that recognized the husband as head of the family and guardian of his wife. As soon as she was married, therefore, a woman's legal identity became subordinate to that of her husband. Most states still require a woman to adopt her husband's name and place of residence. The family's property is usually in the husband's name, and thus the wife has no legal property rights. Women who are single or widowed often have difficulty obtaining credit, because it is assumed that they have no earning potential.

Men also suffer from inequities in family law. Husbands in most states are legally obligated to support their wives, regardless of the wives' financial status. Alimony is most frequently awarded to wives, only rarely to husbands, even if the wife can support herself. Until recently a father in a child-custody battle bore a heavier burden of proof that he was a more fit parent than the child's mother; child custody was routinely given by the courts to the mother, and only in cases where the mother was demonstrably negligent would the father's claim be seriously considered.

Social Action

Suggestions for reducing and eventually eliminating sexism in our society generally focus on two broad areas: changes in the socialization process and changes in the legal system. Altering the socialization process is necessary, because it is through socialization that norms and values are transmitted from one generation to the next. If children are to learn that men and women are equal, and that no attitude, aptitude, behavior, or role is limited to one sex alone, then parents, schools, and the media will have to change the substance

[88]Hole and Levine, *Rebirth of Feminism*, p. 32.

of what they are now conveying to children. Changes in the legal system are necessary, because many laws now codify traditional attitudes about sex roles and permit discrimination on the basis of sex.

Changes in Child-Rearing Practices

Perhaps the major obstacle to women's equality has been the "motherhood ethic"—the idea that women are most fulfilled as mothers and that children, particularly young children, require a mother's constant attention if they are to grow up to be healthy and adjusted.

It is evident that children do need loving, consistent care and attention, and the chance to build up a relationship with one or two regularly present adults. However, there is no evidence that these adults must be female. In fact, as we have already suggested, the absence of male figures can hurt the growing child. By the age of 3 or 4, children no longer seem to need the constant one-to-one relationship; rather, they need to be able to explore, to test their surroundings and themselves, in an atmosphere of security. This relative independence tends to increase as children grow, and while they continue to need adults to whom they can go for guidance, comfort, and role models, it is not evident that they need them to be constantly available.

One of the first steps to be taken toward achieving sexual equality is to have fathers share equally in the process of child raising (and homemaking in general). This does not mean that all fathers or all mothers will have to do exactly half the work that raising children (or keeping house) involves. But our society should encourage men to contribute as much to family life as women, and members of every family should be free to decide for themselves how best to allocate family responsibilities. It is obvious, however, that unless a sufficient number of women are freed from their family and household responsibilities, they will be unable to compete with men as equals. Conversely, unless the status of the homemaker role is raised and more men participate in it, many men who would be excellent homemakers will be forced by social pressure to pursue outside careers.

Aside from officially recognizing the economic contribution made by homemakers, as discussed earlier, several other steps could make it easier for men and women to share domestic tasks. For example, many companies already permit maternity leaves for their female employees who wish to take time off to care for their children. What is needed is for *parental* leaves to become institutionalized, so that men or women who want to take some time to raise a child will be free to do so without losing their jobs. Such a system is already in effect in Sweden, where parents are given a six-month leave upon the birth of their child; the six months can be divided equally between father and mother.[89]

Another idea is to upgrade the importance of part-time work, particularly by institutionalizing many of the benefits of full-time work—fringe benefits, unemployment insurance if fired, seniority, and so on. Thus, men and women will be freer to share the responsibilities of both supporting the family and taking care of the home and children. Finally, men and women must decide on an individual basis to assign household tasks equitably. Sharing such tasks will not only give many women more time for self-fulfillment, it will also enable men and women to begin to relate to each other as equals and will help

[89]Safilios-Rothschild, *Women and Social Policy*, p. 21.

prevent children from developing stereotypic notions about the role of each sex.

In many instances, however, even such reforms will not go far enough. For those men and women who do not wish to or cannot afford to stop working for a long period, and most important, for those women who are heads of families, provision for child day-care must be made. At present, there are over 9 million children with working mothers, yet there are less than a million places for them in day-care centers all over the country.[90] This means that many children of working mothers are without any care at all. Furthermore, many more mothers who would work if they could find proper day-care remain unemployed.

There is some controversy over institutional day-care for young children. It is well known, for example, that babies and children in large, impersonal residential institutions are often noticeably retarded in many aspects of their growth. It has also been noted that communally raised children, such as those of the Israeli kibbutz, while they usually grow up to be well-adjusted adults, tend to be somewhat lacking in qualities of imagination and ambition. There can be little doubt, however, that a well-staffed (a five-to-one ratio of children to teachers), well-organized day-care center can offer children opportunities and stimuli for exploration and discovery that may be considerably greater than those at home. Since the physical plant would be designed for children, most of the "don't touch" and "be careful" admonitions that might be necessary at home could be eliminated. Well-trained teachers would be alert to budding interests and abilities and would know how to encourage them; and there would be more space and a greater variety of play equipment than in most private homes.

It is obvious, however, that changes in the way children in our society are socialized should, ultimately, occur on an individual, day-to-day level if real sexual equality is to occur. Parents and teachers should learn to relate to each child as an individual rather than as male or female. For example, children should have a wide range of toys available (not just dolls for girls and trucks for boys) so that they can determine for themselves which interest them. They should also be taught at an early age that any occupation is open to them. Only if children are permitted to develop their own capacities can they become free of stereotypes that might otherwise hinder them.

Changes in the Educational Process

As with changes in child-rearing practices, changes in educational practices will involve the numerous social interactions that pupils and teachers have on a daily basis. Teachers and school administrators must become more sensitive to their own stereotypes about boys and girls (or men and women) and begin to treat students of both sexes equally—for example, by paying equal attention to male and female students and by not assigning tasks according to traditional sex-role stereotypes.

Rossi has suggested that one way to help break down the idea that only women take care of children (while men "work") is to attract more male teachers in the lower grades.[91] There is also a clear need to end hiring discrimination at the predominantly male school administrative level. Not

---

[90]Allyson S. Grossman, "Children of Working Mothers," *Monthly Labor Review*, vol. 101 (January 1978), 31.

[91]Rossi, "Equality Between the Sexes."

only would qualified women be able to obtain jobs previously closed to them, but students would see that women attain top positions as well as men. Changes in the standard curriculum and in vocational guidance would also be required to prevent traditional occupational and role stereotypes from arising. Boys and girls should be free (or required) to take both cooking and shop classes, for example, and both sexes should participate in whatever sports activities are available. Similarly, students should be able to determine for themselves in what field or occupation they are interested. Teachers or guidance counselors should help students make these choices based on their abilities, not gender.

Major publishers have become more sensitive to sexism in textbooks, and have issued guidelines to their editors on how to avoid it. Most books published today, however, still reflect traditional sex-role stereotypes: boys are still shown in active roles in illustrations, while girls are shown in passive subordinate roles; and male pronouns (such as "he" or "him") still predominate in the language of the text. Publishers need to show females and males in a variety of occupations and roles—women and men working in the professions, for example, as well as men and women performing domestic tasks.

Changes in the Legal System

Title VII of the Civil Rights Act of 1964 forbids discrimination on the basis of sex. However, as we have seen, wage and job discrimination against women remains widespread. Red tape that interferes with filing discrimination complaints; the backlog of cases that already exist; less than total enthusiasm on the part of the EEOC to enforce its provision of the act; and loopholes in the act itself, such as those exempting local, state, and federal governments, have all hindered its effective operation. Similarly, the Equal Pay Act of 1963 (as amended by the Education Amendments of 1972), prohibiting discrimination in salaries, has not solved the problem of wage discrimination. Such discrimination is difficult to prove—even in those relatively few instances when a woman is angry enough to sue—and the act does not cover hiring and promotion policies.

The ERA was passed by Congress in 1972; it was designed to fill loopholes in previous anti-sex-discrimination acts and to forbid sex discrimination in the private sector as well as at every level of government. Its provisions are:

Section 1. Equality of rights under the law should not be denied or abridged by the United States or by any State on account of sex.

Section 2. The Congress shall have the power to enforce by appropriate legislation the provisions of this article.

Section 3. The amendment shall take effect two years after the date of ratification.

There are several other aspects of the legal system, not covered by the antidiscrimination measures we have discussed, that nevertheless impede women's equality. For example, tax laws need to be changed to permit larger tax deductions for day-care; in this way many more parents could afford to work.

Prospects

Although temporary setbacks may occur, it is unlikely that the progress women have already made toward achieving equality will be significantly hindered in the near future. There are many indications that progress will continue to be made. Only a decade ago, for example, less than 6 percent of women entering college planned careers in traditional male fields such as business, medicine, law, or engineering; today approximately 17 percent of women in their first year of college plan to enter such fields.[92] Several companies have begun "management awareness programs" to make managers more sensitive to their attitudes toward hiring and promoting women employees.[93] Some churches (such as the American Lutheran Church and the Episcopal Church) have begun to ordain women clergy for the first time.

Under pressure from concerned women and men, antidiscrimination laws already in existence are being somewhat more stringently enforced, and new laws to increase sexual equality are constantly being proposed. In a landmark 1973 settlement American Telephone and Telegraph was forced to pay $15 million in back pay to its female employees because it had been giving its female employees less pay than men for the same work (a violation of the Equal Pay Act). The Equal Credit Opportunity Act, signed into law at the end of 1974, makes it unlawful for any creditor to discriminate against anyone on the basis of sex or marital status. And new legislation introduced into the House of Representatives would provide Social Security coverage for homemakers as if they were self-employed workers, thereby allowing disabled homemakers to collect disability benefits and making widows or widowers eligible for survivor's benefits to help pay for substitute homemaker services.

Continuing demographic changes, indicating changes in attitudes, also make it more likely that pressures toward women's equality will increase. The growing belief in shared childcare and homework, continued employment during pregnancy, the growing acceptance of childless marriages, the postponing of marriage and child-rearing until education and careers are well under way, as well as the right to choose to remain unmarried—all point to the freeing of both men and women for mutually satisfying employment. As the number of educated women continues to grow, dissatisfaction with lower-status and lower-paying jobs will also increase, forcing employers to change their hiring and promotion policies. Finally, the growing availability of birth control devices, and increases in the life span, make it likely that women will spend less time raising children and more time in work and leisure activities.

The issues of the women's movement for equality have often eclipsed the need for men to examine and change their own sexual roles. Inspired by the successes and discoveries of women, however, many men are exploring the roles that have also bound them, and are discovering new-found freedom in a move toward sex-role egalitarianism. Although the shift in male attitudes appears "mainly among younger, educated men in their 20s and 30s, the group usually quickest to respond to new social currents,"[94] there is reason to

[92]*New York Times*, January 25, 1976. p. 8.
[93]Farrell, *The Liberated Man*, p. 141.
[94]David Gelman, "How Are Men Changing?" *Newsweek* (January 16, 1978), p. 52.

Sexual equality can bring new supplies of talent to the work force: qualified men to former female-dominated fields such as elementary education.

Mark Godfrey/Magnum

believe that sex-role stereotyping among men is continuing to change. At work and at home there is more room for equal participation. The growing presence of women in the work force is making way for a new egalitarianism as women become "bread winners" as well, and men more freely participate in child rearing and home work. Many men are now asserting their parental rights in cases of divorce. There is hope for a continual lessening of society's rigid requirements of "masculinity," freeing many men to open themselves to emotional expression and participation in previously "feminine" activities and occupations.

What would some of the probable effects of sexual equality be? One obvious answer is that society's supply of talent in every segment of the work force would increase. More men would participate in traditional female fields, such as elementary-school teaching and nursing, and more women would participate in such traditional male fields as science or engineering. The opening up of these fields to both sexes would be likely to increase the number of people participating in them; thus the talent and creativity available in our society would grow. Breaking down the occupational barriers that now separate women and men would also help women and men to relate to each other as equals. Also, because fewer men would be providing sole support for their families, there would be more flexibility in working life: men and women would be freer to leave their jobs if they were unhappy in them, and in general there would be a greater sharing of economic and homemaking responsibilities. This would reduce the pressures that exist today for men to "succeed" and for women to remain "dependent." The most important result of true sexual equality, then, may be simply that people would be free to be themselves.

Summary

Though traditional sex roles have been changing in recent years, they are far from gone. Progress has been hampered by the prejudicial attitude that women are best suited for the roles of wife, mother, and housekeeper and that men should be dominant.

Studies of the wide variety of sex roles in other societies suggest that differences in sex roles between men and women are not innate but are learned by individuals as they are socialized into their culture. In our own society, traditional sex roles are being increasingly seen as limits to individual freedom.

Sexism is the range of attitudes and behaviors that discriminate against women and men on the basis of gender. Inaccurate and unrealistic stereotypes about men and women are a part of sexism: many of those who are victimized by these stereotypes believe them, limiting their own freedom of action; more important, these stereotypes are used by those in authority to justify discriminatory behavior. Thus, jobs and wages have become sex-typed: women have been concentrated in lower-status, lower-paying jobs, and receive lower wages even when they perform the same work as men. The legal system also codifies traditional stereotypes about the kinds of things men and women do.

Black women, Puertoriqueñas, native women, Chicanas, and Asian women typically suffer double discrimination—on the basis of sex and of race. Even more than their male counterparts, they are concentrated in the lower stratum of society.

Socialization is a primary source of sexism. Parents begin to reinforce traditionally masculine behavior in boys and feminine behavior in girls as soon as their children are born. Schoolteachers, guidance counselors, and textbooks also differentiate between boys and girls along stereotypic lines. Traditional family roles also perpetuate sexism, because they require that women give up more of their freedom than men. Psychiatry perpetuates sexism, because it tries to force women into traditional patterns of behavior. Language and the media reinforce sexism, because they take male dominance and female subordination for granted. Finally, organized religion, government, and the legal system make it difficult to end sexism, because they give legitimacy to traditional views of women and men.

Suggestions for eliminating sexism in our society involve changing the socialization process and the legal system. Despite occasional setbacks, such changes are likely to take place as more women become educated and enter the labor force and as more women and men come to understand the benefits that sexual equality would bring.

Bibliography

Bell, Robert R. *Marriage and Family Interaction,* 4th ed. Homewood, Ill.: Dorsey Press, 1975.

The Boston Women's Health Book Collective, ed. *Our Bodies, Ourselves.* New York: Simon & Schuster, 1976.

Chafetz, Janet S. *Masculine, Feminine, or Human?: An Overview of the Sociology of Sex Roles.* Itasca, Ill.: Peacock, 1974.

David, Deborah S., and Brannon, Robert, eds. *The Forty-nine Percent Majority.* Reading, Penn.: Addison-Wesley, 1976.

Farrell, Warren. *The Liberated Man.* New York: Random House, 1975.

Friedan, Betty. *The Feminine Mystique.* New York: Dell, 1963.

Gornick, Vivian, and Moran, Barbara K., eds. *Woman in Sexist Society.* New York: Basic Books, 1974.

Lloyd, Cynthia R., ed. *Discrimination and the Division of Labor.* New York: Columbia University Press, 1975.

Miller, Jean B. *Psychoanalysis and Women.* New York: Penguin, 1973.

Morrison, Eleanor S., and Borsage, Vera, eds. *Human Sexuality, Contemporary Perspectives.* Palo Alto, Calif.: Mayfield, 1977.

Pleck, Joseph H., and Sawyer, Jack, eds. *Men and Masculinity.* Englewood Cliffs, N.J.: Prentice-Hall, 1974.

Rossi, Alice S., ed. *The Feminist Papers.* New York: Bantam, 1974.

Safilios-Rothschild, Constantina. *Women and Social Policy.* Englewood Cliffs, N.J.: Prentice-Hall, 1974.

Scarzoni, John H. *The Black Family in Modern Society.* Chicago: University of Chicago Press, 1971.

Spanier, Graham B., ed. *Human Sexuality in a Changing Society.* Minneapolis: Burgess, 1979.

10

Aging

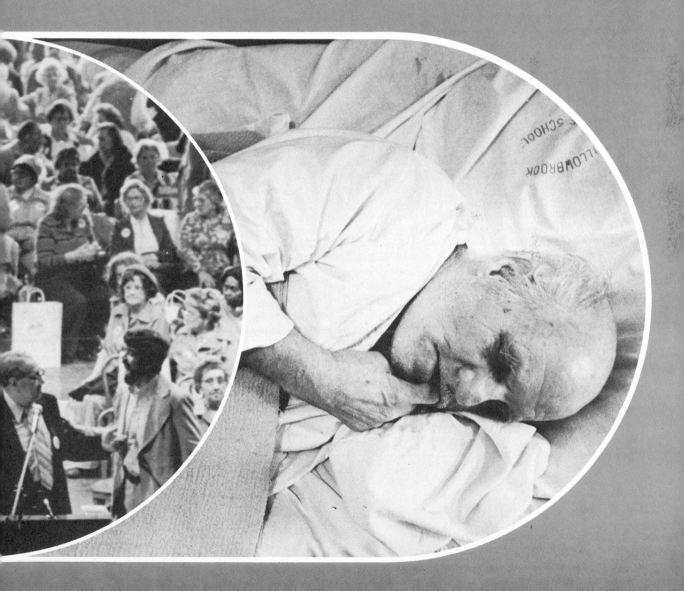

Facts
about the
Elderly

- In 1900, the life expectancy in the United States was 47.3 years. Today it is approximately 73 years.
- In 1970 there were more than 20 million people 65 and older in the United States—representing almost 10 percent of the total population.
- Nearly 60 percent of all elderly women are widows.
- About 30 percent of Americans over age 65 have incomes below the poverty line; only 10 percent have incomes of at least $10,000, and less than 1 percent have incomes of $25,000 or more.
- Most older people live in cities; by the year 2000 almost 85 percent of them will live there.
- About 25 percent of the old in America live with one of their children.

Aging is a natural and universal process. It begins with out first breath, goes on now, and will continue until we die. The concept of the continuing, lifelong process of aging is not widely accepted in our youth-oriented culture, so most Americans tend to regard aging as a negative experience that signals the approach of death. The concept of aging carries such a stigma, in fact, that we mask it with euphemisms like "developing" or "growing" when we describe the process in young people.

Aging is a biological, social, and psychological process. In almost every society age is one of the major characteristics that determines groupings and role assignments. How old people are plays a large part in affecting how they feel about themselves and whom they identify and what society expects of them. As S. N. Eisenstadt put it:

> Every human being passes through various ages, and at each one he attains and uses different biological and intellectual capacities . . . . This gradual unfolding of power and capacity is not entirely a universal, biologically conditioned, inescapable fact . . . . Their cultural definition varies from society to society. In all societies, age serves as a basis for defining the cultural and social characteristics of human beings, for the formation of some of their natural relations and common activities, and for the differential allocation of social roles.[1]

In our culture, role assignments tend to be based on arbitrarily established ages. One must attend school from 6 to 16. One cannot vote until age 18. The law dictates when a person can marry, sign a lease, run for office—all on the basis of age alone. At age 65, people are designated as "old" and encouraged to retire from the mainstream of life—despite their mental capabilities, motivations, or health. The new role assigned to those who are designated old is a "roleless" one, involving no power, no responsibility, and few rewards.[2]

[1] S. N. Eisenstadt, "Archetypal Patterns of Youth," in *Youth: Change and Challenge.* ed. Erik H. Erikson (New York: Basic Books, 1963).

[2] Vivian Wood, "Age Appropriate Behavior for Older People," *The Gerontologist* (Winter 1971), Part II, p. 74.

Sociological Perspectives

Matilda White Riley and Joan Waring have provided one interpretation of the problem of aging. According to their theory, society is composed of two shifting structures—one made up of people, the other of the roles assigned to them. Age dynamics and societal dynamics are the sources of these often conflicting structures.[3]

Age dynamics are essentially a biological phenomenon, but they also have a social impact. Age dynamics mean the movement of groups of people, born in the same period, through the various stages of life. These groups form age-cohorts. Different age-cohorts experience the process of aging differently because of the spirit of the times in which they live. The age-cohort born in 1900, an era in which most children left school by age 10 and went to work, had a very different kind of childhood than did the age-cohort born in the affluent 1950s—these people raised in the 1960s and 70s, could remain dependent until their mid-twenties. The age-cohort who matured in the Depression years of the 1930s had very different career experiences from those who entered the labor market during the expansive economy of the early 1960s.

Societal dynamics, in turn, govern the structure of the social roles the age-cohorts fill. Societal dynamics affect the number and kinds of constantly changing roles available to people at a time. A boy growing up in the largely agricultural economy of the late nineteenth century might have expected to hold the life-long role of farmer, but the economic and political events of the 1920s might have forced him to assume a role in industry. An economic recession can cause the unexpected retirement of workers; a war may bring housewives into the labor market; increasing affluence may mean that young people can remain students for a longer period. All these involve changes in roles and expectations.

Aging means a constant flow of cohort groups through a sequence of socially controlled roles. The experience is different for each group. And according to Riley and Waring, age dynamics and societal dynamics are in constant interplay.

> Their frequent disjunctures give rise to many of the social problems associated with aging . . . . Roles and people are continually pressing upon one another for change. The differing life course patterns in successive cohorts are not only changed by, but in turn change, the role structure of society.[4]

Some of the most common problems are the so-called generation gap and the confusion that arises when roles and role expectations change. These changes are especially difficult for the elderly to comprehend. A woman born before World War I and raised in an extended family may feel abandoned when her married children place her in a nursing or old-age home. Her children, however, born and raised in an era of nuclear families, may feel that the nursing home will help to preserve her feeling of independence—an important concept to them—and provide her with needed peer companions.

---

[3]Matilda White Riley and Joan Waring, "Age and Aging," in *Contemporary Social Problems*, 4th ed., ed. Robert K. Merton and Robert Nisbet (New York: Harcourt Brace Jovanovich, 1976), pp. 357-407.

[4]Riley and Waring, "Age and Aging," pp. 364-365.

According to Robert C. Atchely, the social problems of the aged are aggravated by three factors that all have an impact on the role assigned to the elderly. They are *labeling*, the defining of the old as weak and incapable, and the application of that definition arbitrarily to everyone 65 or older: the concept of *work as the basis of personal value*, the prevailing theory inherited from our Puritan forebears that links personal worth to one's job and characterizes nonworkers as useless and parasitic; and the *economic deprivation* that usually comes with mandatory retirement.[5] (See Chapter 7.)

These three factors are inextricably linked, and each reinforces the others. Labeling leads to discrimination against older workers, reducing their responsibility while still on the job, and forcing their retirement. Characterized as weak and incompetent, older people often lose their self-confidence and begin to conform to the stereotype assigned to them. Retirement often removes people from the mainstream of life, diminishes their status and social contacts, and places them in what has been called a "roleless" role. This roleless role consigns still vital people to a vaguely defined position on the fringe of society. In a world where one's job is the basis for one's worth and acceptance, the retired are relegated to a position of low esteem. People who once described themselves as accountants, salespersons, or secretaries are suddenly and arbitrarily considered noncontributors to the world's activities. It is a role that reduces both their income and their responsibility.

[5]Robert C. Atchley, "Aging as a Social Problem: An Overview," in *Social Problems of the Aging*, ed. Mildred M. Seltzer, Sherry L. Corbett, and Robert C. Atchley (Belmont, Calif.: Wadsworth, 1978), pp. 4-21

Too many of the elderly live in isolated rooms, with no access to food, medical care, and other essentials of life.
Bruce Davidson/Magnum

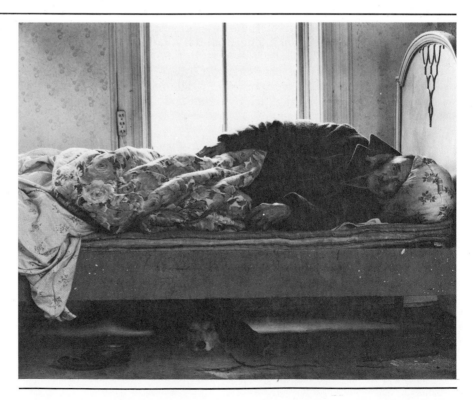

Poverty is a major contributor to the mental and physical deterioration associated with old age. Reduced income affects every area of the retiree's life: mobility, diet, entertainment, housing, interests, health, and appearance. Even though Medicare has relieved some of the problems of health care, many elderly people still suffer medical problems simply because they cannot get to the sources of care or because of the inequitable distribution of Medicare. (See Chapter 2.)

Poverty among the elderly is widespread. More than 55 percent of all Americans over 65 have annual incomes of less than $5,000. Social Security is the sole source of support for 80 percent of all retired Americans.[6] Private pensions are far less common than is generally believed, and, like other assets, such as property or investments, they are concentrated among people who held high-paying jobs during their working years. Even these people may face poverty in the future as inflation reduces the buying power of their fixed incomes. Those who held low-paying or semi-skilled jobs before retirement are the poorest of the elderly poor.

In tribal and agrarian communities, old people play an active role in the work force, the family, and the community. Their status increases with the passing years. In many African and Asian nations, for example, land tenure, kinship, and ceremonial affairs continue to be the province of the aged. In the United States and most Western countries, the dominant productive and cultural roles of the aged have been disrupted by industrialization and the migration of at least some family members to cities. (See Chapter 14.) In this sense, the problems of the aged can thus be seen as part of the larger complex of social changes called "modernization" (not to be confused with "progress"). Modernization has been identified as the cause of the rise in life expectancy as well as the source of the problems that result from it. Donald O. Cogwill has described modernization as

The Effects of Modernization

> the transformation of a total society from a relatively rural way of life based on animate power, limited technology, relatively undifferentiated institutions, parochial and traditional outlook and values, toward a predominantly urban way of life based on inanimate sources of power, highly developed scientific technology, highly individual roles and a cosmoplitan outlook which emphasizes efficiency and progress.[7]

In other words, many of the problems which the aged face in America today are social problems that arise from the particular nature of modern Western society. With the number and proportion of the elderly increasing, the problems of aging are attracting more attention. Technological and scientific advances have succeeded in reducing the infant mortality rate and eliminating or curing many once-fatal diseases. Since many of these advances occurred within a short period of time, record numbers of people began living to old age. If the birth rate of a nation continues to increase along with the rate of longer life expectancy, overpopulation and shortages can occur. (See Chapter 16.) Today's tight job-market is linked in part to this phenomenon.

[6]Neal E. Cutler and Robert A. Harootyan, "Demography of the Aged," in *Aging: Scientific Perspectives and Social Issues,* ed. Diana S. Woodruff and James E. Birren (New York: Van Nostrand, 1975), pp. 59-62.

[7]Donald O. Cogwill, "The Aging of Populations and Societies," *The Annals of the American Academy of Political and Social Science,* vol. 415 (September 1974), 11.

The children born during the post-war baby boom—a true example of the population explosion—are reaching maturity at the same time that a record number of still vital people are arriving at old age. Both of these groups are competing for a limited (and sometimes declining) number of jobs. The young are looking for work, the old are trying to retain it. At present the usual way of coping with this problem is forced retirement.

> As the lives of workers are prolonged, death no longer creates openings in the labor force as rapidly as it once did. Thus competitive pressures are generated between the generations in the labor force. Eventually a social substitute for death as a means of exit is instituted in the form of the practice of retirement.[8]

Forced retirement means that many active, capable older people must be denied the psychological and economic rewards of work and confront a new and unwanted role. Fortunately, modern technology has created more effective means of contraception that will eventually reduce the rate of population growth and mitigate the competition for jobs and the displacement of older workers. (See Chapter 15.)

Two other aspects of modernization—education and urbanization—have also affected the present older generations. Advanced technologies have created thousands of new jobs that require skill and education, but they have also made certain skills obsolete and eliminated entirely or reduced the need for thousands of low-skill jobs. Older workers tend to be less educated, and their skills may be unnecessary in modern industry. They are often forced out of the labor market as a result.

Urbanization, like technology, has created new jobs for mobile workers who are willing to relocate from rural areas or small towns to the cities or from the older industrial cities of the North and Midwest to the new urban centers of the "Sunbelt." These mobile workers tend to be young; older workers are more likely to remain in the communities where they grew up and raised their families.

Age Stratification.   Riley and Waring, who described the process of age dynamics and societal dynamics, have also detailed the process of age stratification. Age, they point out, operates like race or class in segregating people into different groups or strata. Like the class system, age stratification limits the kinds of roles its members can hold. Some degree of age stratification seems acceptable and inevitable. People are attracted to their peers and to those with whom they share common experiences and concerns. Certain activities seem to draw certain age groups. But says Riley:

> Many of these age-related differences in access to the good things in life are violations of societal ideas of equity or harmony. They inhibit communication and understanding between generations. They can create a sense of relative deprivation or inadequacy and feelings of hostility with reference to other age strata.[9]

Age stratification may produce some of the disengagement and retreat that is so common among the elderly in America. Denied jobs and opportunities to play rewarding roles, the young often express deviant

[8]Cogwill, "The Aging of Populations and Societies," p. 11.
[9]Riley and Waring, "Age and Aging," p. 363.

reactions in the form of crime. Old persons express deviancy by becoming dependent, uninvolved, or by manifesting behavior associated with senility.

Age stratification leads to age segregation and age conflict. From childhood we are segregated by age in play groups, classes, and clubs; the retirement community, restricted to persons of a specified age, continues this process. In the wake of age stratification comes suspicion, mistrust, and hostility. The young lack confidence in their elders. The old often fear the young. Isolation of age groups and inter-generational conflicts prevail.

Role Expectations and the Elderly. We have already seen how retirement assigns the elderly to a roleless role that is lacking in definition and status. Retirement has also been described as the state in which people must adjust to the loss of a valued role and search for a new one. Old people find it especially difficult to play this new role because they are given very little information about how they should act and what is expected of them.

During the long period of adulthood, people are required to conform to behavioral standards that are based on achievement: one expects certain conduct from a doctor; a mother is expected to act in a specific fashion; we demand certain kinds of behavior from public officials. When people retire, however, they lose their achieved roles and the behavioral standards that accompany them. They are left with a set of expectations based on age alone: they are expected to "act their age."

This is particularly difficult because the old lack a code of age-appropriate behavior and a clear-cut description of their new role. At best, they are confronted by a set of "don'ts": don't get in the way, don't interfere, don't be sexual, don't do anything unconventional.

Who Are the Elderly?

It is common practice to term anyone over age 65 as old. Recently social scientists have begun to identify groups within this growing population. The group between 65 and 75, who are still inclined to be healthy and active, are called the "young-old." Those over 75, a group more likely to require support services, are the "old-old." Another group, "the frail elderly," has also been identified as those over 65 who, because of health or economic problems, cannot perform the basic activities of life without help. Assistance may range from full-time nursing care, and the delivery of a hot meal each day, to help with shopping or cleaning.

The number of the aged in America is increasing along with the rate of life expectancy.[10] In recent times this increase has risen dramatically. Three thousand years ago a newborn child could expect to live only to age 18; in 1970, a newborn American could expect to reach 70.9 years. Although it took more than 3000 years to achieve this increased life-span, the greatest increase came during this century. From 1900 to 1970, life expectancy in the United States climbed by 26.3 years—from 47.3 to 73.6.

Thus, the proportion of the aged in the American population grows larger with each decade. (See Table 10-1.)In 1900 there were 3.1 million Americans over 65; in 1970 there were 20.2 million. More important, their proportion of the total population has more than doubled, from 4.1 percent in 1900 to 9.9 percent in 1970. More than half—14.6 million—of the elderly live in urban

---

[10]Throughout this discussion, demographic data on the aged draws largely on Cutler and Harootyan, "Demography of the Aged," pp. 31-69.

Table 10-1
Population Age 65 and Older in the United States 1900–2020

Year	Number in Thousands	Percent of Population
1900	3,099	4.1
1910	3,986	4.3
1920	4,929	4.7
1930	6,705	5.4
1940	9,031	6.8
1950	12,391	8.2
1960	16,679	9.2
1970	20,177	9.9
1980	24,051	10.6
1990 (projection)	27,768	11.0
2020 (projection)	40,261	13.1

Source: From *Aging: Scientific Perspectives and Social Issues,* edited by Diana S. Woodruff and James E. Birren © 1975 by Litton Educational Publishing, Inc. Reprinted by permission of D. Van Nostrand Company.

areas. Fifty-five percent of these are concentrated in heavily-urbanized areas, with 6.8 million old people in the central cities. For many, then, the problems of aging are complicated by the problems of the urban environment: crime, decaying neighborhoods, the shortage of affordable housing, and congestion. (See Chapter 14.) The suburbs contain the smallest population of the elderly—only 4.3 million. High property taxes, high cost of home maintenance, and transportation problems have been identified as the causes of this pattern.

Although most of the elderly live in urban areas, they also represent the highest proportion of the populations of small towns. This phenomenon is the result of the patterns of migration that have occurred since World War II, when many people moved from farms to small towns. Many of these people are now elderly. In turn, their children have relocated from small towns to suburbs or cities. Another migration is the recent movement of retired people to the West and South.

The greatest proportion of the elderly population is white and female. Sixty-seven percent of the elderly live with family members. A little more than 27 percent live alone and only about 6 percent live in institutions.

Although 39 percent of males between the ages of 65 and 69 are in the labor force, there is a sharp drop in employment—34 percent—after age 64. Still many elderly people both work and seek work. According to the 1970 Census, for example, 10 percent of those 85 or older are still in the labor force.

With a decline in work comes a decline in income. The median income for families headed by a male 65 to 69 years old was $3,037 in 1970. Nineteen percent of the families headed by over-65-year-old males live below the poverty line, compared with 11 percent of the families in the population as a whole.[11]

[11]Hanns G. Pieper, "Aged Americans: A Profile of a Growing Minority," in *Let's Learn About Aging,* ed. John R. Barry and C. Ray Wingrove (New York: Wiley, 1977), pp. 14-20.

The Aging Process: Biological Aspects

Chronological Aging

Chronological aging is the accumulation of years. It is an automatic process over which the individual has no control. We know from our own observations that not everyone ages at the same rate. Not all 60-year-olds manifest the same qualities of age. Some people look and act middle-aged before they leave their twenties, while some 50-year-olds radiate the kind of vitality and good looks associated with youth.

The dramatic increase in the life expectancy rate and the growing population of the old in America has spurred new interest in the aging process and its causes. A new field of study and practice—gerontology—has emerged. Gerontologists are attempting to identify the physical causes and effects of the aging process and to control the factors that diminish the rewards of a long life.

Primary Aging and Secondary Aging

There are two categories within the aging process: primary aging and secondary aging. Primary aging is the result of molecular and cellular changes. Its effects are seen in all the characteristics that we associate with advancing years: gray hair, wrinkles, susceptibility to disease. As the body ages, its systems degenerate. The brain, for example, loses thousands of cells daily from birth onward. Some of the body's systems, like the skin, are able to regenerate their cells, although less effectively with each passing year. Others, like the kidneys, lack regenerative powers and eventually wear out.

The decline of the body is not the result of primary aging alone. People age at different rates. Some researchers are convinced that each of us carries a personal "timetable" within our cells, a timetable controlled by our genes. Others believe that secondary aging factors are also involved. Secondary aging is "an accelerated version of normal aging."[12] It is caused by environmental factors: deconditioning or lack of exercise, stress, trauma, diet, disease.

The role of stress is particularly important in aging. One of the most salient age-related changes is the decline in the homeostatic capacity—the ability to tolerate stress. This makes older people more susceptible to stress, and it takes them longer to return to normal after exposure to a stressful situation.

The reduced capacity to cope with stress is the result of primary aging, while stress itself is an agent of secondary aging. Together they may be responsible for many of the illnesses that plague the elderly. Older people are confronted by numerous stress-producing situations in the form of life changes. Widowhood, the death of friends and family members, loss of status and productivity are all stressful changes. Studies have demonstrated that illnesses such as leukemia, cancer and heart disease often strike the elderly in the wake of stress-producing changes.

The role of secondary aging factors has been demonstrated in several studies involving societies where people live to an advanced, but vital, old age. One of these is the much publicized Georgian Soviet Republic, whose inhabitants survive well into their second century in good mental and physical health. Like most vigorous old people, the Soviet Georgians participate fully

---

[12]Joan Arehart-Triechel, "It's Never Too Late to Start Living Longer," *New York Magazine* (April 11, 1977), p. 38.

in society, retirement is unknown, and aging is honored. Life is simple, family ties close, and there is little of the stress that characterizes American culture. In addition, these people, who are physically active throughout life, use no tobacco, drink little, and eat low-calorie, low-fat foods.[13]

Physiological Dimensions of Aging

Aging is a gradual process; not all of the body's systems age at the same rate. The process of decline, however, usually starts relatively early in life. By the mid-twenties the skin loses its elasticity and starts to dry and wrinkle; by 30 the muscles have begun to shrink and diminish in strength. As times passes, the capacity of the lungs is reduced and less and less air is drawn into the body, circulation slows and the blood supply diminishes, bones become brittle and thin, hormonal activity ebbs, and the reflexes become slower.

Aging is not a disease itself, but it does increase the susceptibility to disease caused by a decline in the functioning of the immunological system. Disease in old age, therefore, becomes chronic rather than episodic. Some gerontologists believe that were we able to maintain a fully functioning immunological system, we might live for centuries. Dr. Alex Comfort writes in *Aging: The Biology of Senescence:*

> If we kept throughout life the same resistance to disease, stress, injury which we had at the age of 10, about half of us here today might expect to survive 700 years.[14]

Throughout history, humanity has sought to banish the effects of aging. Western folklore is filled with stories of how people schemed, fought and bargained for eternal youth. Today we stand on the verge of finding, if not the mythical fountain of youth, at least some effective ways of delaying the debilitations of age. There is growing evidence indicating that many of the effects of aging are neither inevitable nor irreversible. Exercise has been found to be one of the most promising methods of reversing the aging process or holding it in abeyance. Reduced oxygen intake, diminished lung capacity, and slow circulation—and all their related mental and physical problems—are the result not just of age, but of the inactivity that comes with it. In one study, a group of 70-year-old men proved how the aging process can be reversed. They participated in a daily exercise program and at the end of a year they had regained the physical fitness levels of 40-year-olds.[15] Other researchers, studying the effects of vitamin therapy, diet and hormones on the aging process, are demonstrating that the debilitating conditions associated with age are caused by more than the mere accumulation of years.

Aging determines the number of years we live and the quality of our lives. By controlling the aging process and by eliminating or delaying some of the conditions that we now accept as the fate of the elderly, we may reduce some of our negative feelings about growing old and about the old themselves.

[13]Ruth B. Weg, "Changing Physiology of Aging: Normal and Pathological," in Woodruff and Birren, *Aging: Scientific Perspectives,* p. 249.

[14]Alex Comfort, *Aging: The Biology of Senescence* (New York: Holt, Rinehart, and Winston, 1964), p. 1.

[15]Arehart-Triechel, "It's Never Too Late," p. 38.

Psychological Dimensions of Aging

The aging process produces psychological as well as physical effects. Social factors, too, influence the psychological consequences of age. Self-concepts and roles are particularly important as aging occurs. One theory views older people as trapped in a contracting social situation—their world grows smaller and smaller as they leave work, as their friends and family die, and as their own mobility decreases. Their social role has changed too and they become less influential and less important.

New roles always require some adjustment, but for the elderly this adjustment is complicated because their new roles are poorly defined; there are few role models or reference groups on which they can pattern their behavior. Because of the nebulous quality of their new role and the absence of models, old people become dependent on labels and on the opinions of others for their self-definition. In our society, labels applied to the old are systematically negative because they are based on an ethic that equates personal worth with economic productivity.[16] (See Chapter 8.)

This negative labeling is one of the causes of the psychological difficulties experienced by the aged. Everyone needs role definitions, but other age groups can find theirs by studying role models and by following reference groups. The old lack such models and thus tend to rely on the image, even though it is negative, that is imposed on them. They internalize it and eventually their self-image and behavior correspond to the weak, incompetent, useless image that has been forced on them. (See Table 10-2.)

Age and Personality

Although many of our basic attitudes and character traits are formed in early childhood, our personalities continue to grow and develop throughout life. The personality changes we perceive in the elderly are the result of this developmental process. Several explanations have been advanced about the causes of personality changes in the old.

[16]J. A. Kuypers and V. L. Bengston, "Social Breakdown and Competence," *Human Development*, vol. 16 (1973), 199.

Table 10-2
Self-Image of Public Age 65 and over Compared with Total Public's Image of "Most People over 65"

	Self-Image of Public 65 and over	Total Public's Image of "Most People over 65"	Net Difference
Very friendly and warm	72%	74%	+ 2%
Very wise from experience	69	64	– 5
Very bright and alert	68	29	–39
Very open-minded and adaptable	63	21	–42
Very good at getting things done	55	35	–20
Very physically active	48	41	– 7
Very sexually active	11	5	– 6

Source: *The Myth and Reality of Aging in America.* A study for the National Council on the Aging, Inc. by Louis Harris and Associates, Inc. (Washington, D.C.: The National Council on the Aging, 1975), p. 53.

Two renowned musicians, Arthur Fiedler, conductor of the Boston Pops and Eubie Blake, composer, defy traditional expectations of age-based roles.

UPI

The Kansas City Study of Adult Life, a six-year program involving a large sample population, produced new insights into age and personality development. One of the goals of this study was to define the psychological dynamics of "successful" aging—what caused some people to enjoy a happy, satisfying old age. Two popular theories—the activity theory and the disengagement theory—about the personality dynamics of aging were explored.

The activity theory states that old people have the same needs that they had in middle age and in order to remain happy and content they must continue to satisfy those needs. The key to satisfaction is activity and involvement. It may appear that old people want to withdraw from the world, but when this happens it is usually the world that has withdrawn from the old person.

The disengagement theory, on the other hand, holds that some withdrawal by the elderly is necessary and natural. The elderly have different needs than the middle-aged. As aging occurs, interests shift from the outer world of activity to the inner world, and energies are turned toward the self.

One of the findings that emerged from the Kansas City Study was that by themselves neither of these theories sufficiently explained the psychological dynamics of aging, but that both play some role.

> As men and women move beyond age 70 in a modern, industrialized community they regret the drop in role activity that occurs in their lives; at the same time, most people accept this drop as an inevitable accompaniment of growing old, and they succeed in maintaining a sense of self-worth and a sense of satisfaction with past and present life as a whole. Other older persons are less successful in resolving these conflicting elements—not only do they have a strong negative affect regarding losses in activity but the present losses weigh heavily and are accompanied by a dissatisfaction with past and present life.[17]

Individual personality plays a significant role in successful aging, the study found. In fact, the research suggests the patterns of personality change in old age can be predicted while a person is still in the middle years. Personality changes like physical aging do not follow a universal pattern: "Aging is not a leveler of individual differences, except perhaps at the very end."[18]

One of the reasons why our personalities change with the passage of time may be the shift in our perceptions of ourselves and the world. A 30-year-old is likely to view the world as a challenging arena where rewards await the daring and aggressive. At 60, one's environment is apt to be seen as a more dangerous and complicated place.

Age also influences our expectations about our roles and rewards. "Each person interprets his present situation in terms of what his expectations have been. Expectations are an important factor in understanding levels of psychological well-being."

> Individuals whether or not they can easily verbalize it, develop a view of the "normal expectable life cycle." They form expectations based upon the

[17]Robert J. Havighurst, "Personality and Patterns of the Aging," *The Gerontologist*, vol. 8, no. 1 (Spring 1968), 12.

[18]Bernice L. Neugarten, "Personality and the Aging Process," *The Gerontologist*, vol. 12, no. 1 (Spring 1972), 12.

consensually-validated sequences of life events: what these events should be, when they should occur. They make plans, set goals, and reassess those goals along a timeline shaped by those expectations.[19]

Research indicates that people have a well-defined time-table for the earlier years of life: when one should attend school, establish a career, achieve success, marry, start a family, and so on. These time-related expectations form a system of social controls and standards of behavior. Age deviancy—being out-of-synchronization with this system of major life events—almost always brings negative consequences. People may experience psychological stress when they do not conform to age expectations and psychological problems may develop. Problems with age-related expectations increase in the latter years when there are fewer expectations about time-related events and roles but increased need for and acceptance of them.

It is a widespread belief that intellectual ability declines with age. Many people are, therefore, reluctant to place older people in positions of authority or to attempt to retrain or re-educate them. Research has shown, however, that this belief is incorrect. Reflexes and responses slow, but intellectual capacity, barring organic problems, remains unchanged until very late in life:

Intellectual Functioning and Age

> The average person growing in our society need not expect to show a typical deterioration of mental functioning in the later years. Rather, limitation of mental functions occurs precipitously in individuals over the age of 65 or 70 and is closely related to health status. Expectations of mental performance must be based upon the elderly individual's characteristics rather than on assumptions about the population at large. The expectation is therefore given good health and freedom from cerebral vascular disease and senile dementia, individuals can expect high levels of mental competence beyond the age of 80.[20]

Sociological Dimensions

In all societies age helps determine role assignments. Every culture has its rites of passage that mark a member's progress through life and indicate new status weaning, coming of age, acceptance as an elder. In simpler cultures, for example, a warrior may become a tribal elder when he can no longer endure the rugged pursuit of game or the rigors of warfare, or when he has proven his wisdom and strength in some fashion. Chronological age plays a part in the process, but it is not the sole criterion for role assignment.

In Western industrialized societies, however, the criterion for these passages is an arbitrarily selected, chronological age that alone often determines the role. And that role in turn determines what society expects. Sometimes these age-based role assignments are reasonable and related to the abilities of a certain age level: pre-school children cannot be expected to be other than dependent on their parents; a teenager does not have the experience to manage a large corporation or a town government. As people

[19]Neugarten, "Personality and Aging," p. 13.
[20]James E. Birren, "Psychological Aspects of Aging and Intellectual Functioning," *The Gerontologist*, vol. 8, no. 1, Part II (1968), p. 19.

grow older, however, age-based roles can cause confusion. One can vote at age 18, yet most people at age 18 are not accorded full status as adults.[21]

We have seen how age-stratification can result in age discrimination and deviance. Riley has suggested that any of the age-related problems in our society could be corrected by changing our educational system to altering our concept of retirement.

The Aged as a Minority

Social gerontologists frequently refer to the aged as a minority pointing out that the elderly exhibit many characteristics of other minorities. (See Chapter 8.) Like racial and ethnic groups, the elderly are the victims of prejudice, stereotyping, and discrimination. They are thought to be inflexible, a burden on the young, or incompetent workers. These prejudicial concepts are proved wrong when the elderly are given opportunities.

Like racial and ethnic minorities, the elderly are often allowed those opportunities in times of national emergency. During World War II, for example, many old people, blacks, women, and other groups formerly thought to be unemployable were brought into the labor force and performed in a way to prove the stereotypes wrong.

The aged exhibit typical minority reactions to prejudice against them including self-consciousness, sensitivity, and defensiveness about their social and cultural role, along with self-hatred.[22]

Some social scientists, like Milton L. Barron, argue that while the elderly do indeed share many of the characteristics of minorities, they are not a true minority group. Unlike traditional minorities—blacks, Indians, Jews, specific nationalities—the elderly do not exist as an independent sub-group. Everyone has the potential for becoming old. The old have belonged to the majority in the past and they still live within the families of the majority. Barron suggests that it would be more accurate to describe the elderly as a "quasi-minority." This term, he argues, is a better reflection of the unique position of the elderly in our society.[23]

The potential political power of this quasi-minority is enormous. Not only are the elderly increasing in actual number and proportion of the population but they themselves are changing significantly. Most of the elderly are poorly educated by today's standards—50 percent never went beyond elementary school and only 5 percent are college graduates. Twenty percent are foreign-born, and therefore unfamiliar with American laws and political process. The coming generation of elderly will be mostly native-born, well-educated, well-informed, and politically conscious.[24]

Myths and Stereotypes about the Elderly

Popular culture characterizes all old people as senile, lacking individuality, tranquil, unproductive, conservative, and resistant to change. These beliefs persist despite abundant evidence to the contrary. Many of the myths about

[21]Riley and Waring, "Age and Aging," p. 365.
[22]Milton L. Barron, "The Aged as a Quasi-Minority Group, in *The Other Minorities*, ed. Edward Sagarin, (Lexington, Mass.: Ginn and Company, 1971), p. 149.
[23]Birren "Psychological Aspects of Aging," p. 148.
[24]Pieper, "Aged Americans," pp. 7-23; and J. T. Willis, "Aging, Politics and Political Attitudes," in Barry and Wingrove, *Let's Learn About Aging*, pp. 197-206

older workers, for example, were disproved when they were drawn into the labor force during World War II. Other studies have demonstrated that the elderly are no more difficult to train than the young, in addition, they have a lower than average absentee rate, and compare favorably with younger workers on accident rates and productivity.

Some of the most pernicious myths about the elderly are directed against older women. In our society women become devalued much sooner than do men, therefore in old-age women tend to have a more negative image than their male counterparts. (See Chapter 9.) Barbara Payne and Frank Whittington collected and analyzed several major studies about the sexual stereotypes of old age. They found most to be untrue or based on cultural expectations of sexual roles and social conditioning rather than sex itself.[25] Some of the topics they considered were:

1. *Health*. Older women are portrayed as being hypochondriacs and having more health problems than older men. A number of investigations, including the noted Duke (University) Longitudinal Study of Aging, show that there is neither "objective or subjective physical health differences between the sexes." Women who, in the past particularly, have been rewarded for being "delicate," acted slightly more pessimistic about their health, while men, who are rewarded for being robust and tough, expressed more optimistic feelings about their physical state. Medically, there was no difference.

2. *Marriage*. In a society in which women have traditionally achieved worth only through marriage, widowhood or remaining single are viewed in an extremely negative light. Older women, in particular, are characterized as "mateless." Fifty-three percent of women over 65 are widowed, 38 percent are married, and only 9 percent are divorced or never married. Seventy-seven percent of men over 65 are married, however. This reflects cultural trends such as that females tend to outlive males, and that older men who want to remarry after the death of a spouse have a greater choice of partners in their own and younger age groups. Marriage between older men and younger women is usually socially accepted, while the reverse almost never is.

3. *Widowhood*. According to a popular stereotype, widows continue to base their identity on that of their dead husband. This is generally untrue; older women, though many of them are widows, demonstrate a strong sense of personal identity. One study, cited by Payne and Whittington, shows that their reactions are not functions of age but of class and education, with well-educated and working-class women experiencing less crisis when confronted with widowhood.

4. *The Rocking-Chair Image*. Older women, in particular, are characterized as grandmotherly types who confine their interests to knitting and rocking by the fireside. A number of studies, including the vast National Recreation Survey, show that there is little difference between the leisure activities of older men and women, and little difference between the kinds of leisure activities that people have in their middle- and later-years. There is a frequent crisis of leisure, however, occurring when people suddenly face the

---

[25]Barbara Payne and Frank Whittington, "Older Women: An Examination of Popular Stereotypes and Research Evidence, *Social Problems*, vol. 23, no. 4 (April 1976), 488-501.

prospect of more free time—for women this usually occurs around meno-pause, and for men at retirement from a career.

The most widely accepted stereotype about the old is that they are sexually inactive because of both lack of desire and lack of ability. A number of studies have proved that this is incorrect. Eric Pfeiffer, Adrain Verwoerdt, and Glenn Davis collected data on the sexual activities of older people (one of their samples included subjects as old as 94) and found that:

> While there was an overall pattern of declining interest and activity with advancing age, it was also clear that sex still continued to play an important role in the lives of the vast majority of the subjects studied.[26]

Like the studies reported by Payne and Whittington, the investigation by Pfeiffer, *et al.* revealed that elderly men enjoyed more sexual interest and activity than elderly women. The principal reason for this distinction, all the studies show, is that elderly men are more likely to have a readily available,

Love after 70: contrary to popular myth, sex is an important part of the lives of most elderly people.
Geoffrey Gove/Photo Researchers, Inc.

[26]Eric Pfeiffer, Adrain Verwoedt, and Glenn Davis, "Sexual Behavior in Middle Life," *American Journal of Psychiatry*, vol. 128, no. 10 (April 1972), 82.

socially sanctioned, sexually capable partner. Many of the age-related changes in sexual behavior, Pfeiffer's study notes, have their antecedents in middle age and in a person's sexual history. Women who have been sexually active throughout their adult lives continue to enjoy sexual activity in old age. Those who have had a less than satisfactory sex life tend to use age as an excuse for avoiding sex.

Recently, the image of the old as victims has been given great prominence. This image has been considerably portrayed and reinforced by the media in both news reports and dramatic presentations. While this kind of reporting may alert the elderly to potential dangers, such as confidence schemes or attacks by physically violent criminals, it also serves to reinforce their image to others as weak, incompetent, and targets of calculated persecution.

Victimization of the Elderly

Reporting of "crime waves" against the elderly has had such a profound effect that a recent Louis Harris poll among the elderly showed fear of crime to be their major concern. The majority of the respondents ranked this above sickness, poverty, loneliness, isolation, and any of the other problems commonly associated with old age.[27]

A systematic survey of the statistics, however, reveals that so-called crime waves against the elderly are usually media-created phenomena. Mark Fishman analyzed one heavily reported crime wave against the elderly that filled the newspapers and airwaves of New York City in late 1976 and found no statistical evidence for such an event at all. During the period in question the murder rate in that city had actually declined slightly and crimes involving elderly victims were running no higher than usual for other age groups. Fishman concluded that the media, always anxious for themes around which to report news, had simply focused on one aspect of street crime in the city and in so doing created the impression that elderly people were in more danger than ever before.[28]

Because many elderly people do live in high-crime areas of cities, they run a risk, as do many of their neighbors, of being victimized. (See Chapters 5 and 6.) When this does happen, the elderly as individuals suffer more than do victims of other age groups. Less physically robust, the old are more likely to sustain serious injury during a physical assault and to recover more slowly from that injury. Often alone and isolated, old people may lack the friends and family who can provide the emotional support that helps to dispel the fear and depression that follows victimization.

Health Care and the Aged

Since health declines as people get older, the aged have a greater tendency toward chronic illness. To complicate matters further, older people are less able to pay for medical care or to travel to clinics, hospitals, or doctors' offices where they can receive care.

Many assumed that with the passage of Medicare and Medicaid, the

[27]Steven Schack and Robert S. Frank, "Police Service Delivery to the Elderly," *The Annals of the American Academy of Political and Social Science*, No. 438 (July 1978), 83.

[28]Mark Fishman, "Crime Waves as Ideology," *Social Problems*, vol. 25 no. 5 (June 1978), 531-543.

problem of health care for the elderly would be eliminated. While these programs have alleviated some of their health-related problems, they are by no means completely successful. As discussed in Chapter 2, Medicaid and Medicare services are inequitably distributed and are more accessible to the middle class. Still, their cost is staggering and thousands of the elderly lack adequate care.

Although the problem of medical care for the aged is inextricably linked to the national crisis in health services, there are some aspects of this problem that are unique to the aged. One major geriatric health issue involves institutionalization. There are one million elderly people in long-term care facilities—between 17 and 25 percent of them are there, not because they require constant attention, but because no alternative services are available. Unnecessary institutionalization of the elderly is a costly proposition, both in terms of public spending and in the negative psychological effects on the occupants. Representative Claude Pepper of Florida, a vociferous proponent for the rights of the elderly, and chairman of the House Committee on Aging, made these comments on a recent General Accounting Office (GAO) report recommending home health care:

> The Government has adopted a costly, counter-productive institutional bias toward the nation's elderly citizens who need health care . . . . It is tragic that home health care is considered the alternative to institutionalization . . . . This institutional bias is both callous and costly.
> Until older people become greatly or extremely impaired, the cost of nursing home care exceeds the cost of home care including the value of the general support services provided by family and friends.[29]

Numerous studies on inappropriate placement of elderly patients in institutions and data revealing that this has accelerated their deterioration have caused health agencies and legislators to give serious consideration to home health services. These services include visiting nurse programs, various forms of therapy, home health aides, and personal care services. Such programs would require new and increased interaction between physicians, patients, and social service agencies, and would shift the traditional emphasis of medicine from treating sickness to maintaining health. Comprehensive health care for the elderly will also involve dealing with problems such as housing and transportation that are not now considered a part of health services.[30]

Housing and the Elderly

"What does housing mean to the elderly? Aside from his spouse, housing is probably the single most important element in the life of an older person." This was the finding of the 1971 White House Conference on Aging. Today, a decade later, while there is a growing commitment to provide adequate housing for the elderly, the problem remains a vast and complicated one. Housing means more than just a roof over one's head; it is a combination of social and environmental factors, as well as physical ones. As Francis Carp

[29]Faye G. Abdellah, "Long-Term Care Policy Issues: Alternatives to Institutional Care," *Annals of the American Academy of Political and Social Science*, 438 (July 1978), 31.

[30]Stanley Brody, "Comprehensive Health Care for the Elderly: An Analysis," in Seltzer, *et al., Social Problems of the Aging*, p. 197.

puts it: "Successful housing must occur within a matrix of transportation, shopping, recreation, medical services and other social opportunities. . . . the value of the matrix may well overshadow the value of the individual dwelling itself."[31]

Housing is of even greater importance to older people because they spend so much time at home and their reduced mobility demands that their housing be located near services and transportation. The housing problems of the elderly are complicated by the pressures of reduced income; typically, a retirement income is about half of a working income—often it is even less than that. This limited income means that the old have to spend a larger percentage of their earnings on housing or live in a sub-standard dwelling.

One in every five elderly persons lives in sub-standard housing; more than half live in housing built before 1939. Most live in urban areas and many of these are in decaying inner-city neighborhoods. These neighborhoods typically offer few services and inadequate, outmoded rental units. Although cities abound with services, the elderly, because of reduced mobility and income and the inaccessibility of their neighborhoods, take advantage of few of them. Carp remarks: "The old are no more citizens of the city than was the kitchen maid of former generations a citizen of her mistress' house." (See Chapter 14.)

At present only about 7.8 percent of the elderly reside in the suburbs, but this is expected to change. Many suburbanites are expected to retain their residences in these communities after retirement, and there is even some movement of the more affluent old to suburbs. Although housing and environmental conditions tend to be better in the suburbs, a new problem may emerge with this trend: the stranding of elderly people in secluded suburban homes and the problems experienced in driving and maintaining a car, especially as gasoline becomes more expensive and less available.

The rural elderly are the poorest and the most ill-housed of all. The average old person in a rural community or small town has $400 to $700 less annual income than have the elderly in the city. Rural housing frequently lacks the basic amenities we take for granted: electricity, indoor plumbing, central heating, telephone. Moreover, rural isolation confines the person to a limited and lonely life.[32]

Housing for the Elderly.   In 1956—quite late in comparison with other industrialized nations—the United States began to construct special housing for the elderly. The Department of Housing and Urban Development (HUD), has found housing for some 750,000 old people, about 600,000 of them in special projects for the elderly. But this figure represents only 3 percent of all older Americans; and it is estimated that for every elderly urban household in public housing there are 40 others in need of it. In numbers that means 4 million elderly people or 20 percent of the elderly population still require housing.

It is doubtful that those needs will even come close to being met in the near future; however, planners and designers are studying better ways of creating housing for the elderly. The most recognizable trends in housing for

[31]Frances M. Carp, "Housing and Living Environments of Older People," in *Handbook of Aging and the Social Sciences*, ed. Robert H. Binstock and Ethel Shanas (New York: Van Nostrand-Reinhold, 1976), pp. 244-271.

[32]For these and the following statistics on housing for the elderly, see Carp, "Housing and Living Environments of Older People," pp. 250, ff.

the old are the high-rise, low-rent public housing projects and special retirement communities for more affluent retirees. Both of these types of communities are age-segregated, and researchers have recently begun to investigate the effects of this phenomenon.

In other countries, Great Britain, France, and Sweden, for example, public housing projects integrate different age groups, with generally positive results; however, one classic American study of age-segregated housing conducted by I. Rosow in 1967 has suggested a definite benefit to age-segregation.[33] The persons in this study, all apartment dwellers, expressed a need and desire for a living situation in which most of their neighbors were their peers. Later studies have shown that Rosow's conclusions may have been influenced by a number of variables. His respondents, for example were all long-time residents of an older neighborhood. Subsequent studies show that most elderly apartment dwellers do tend to like age-segregated housing, while people who live in homes in age-integrated neighborhoods and who are active in their community are less anxious to live exclusively among people their own age.[34]

Further study of this issue will have to be done in the future; at present we are confronted by conflicting opinions. There is evidence to indicate that age-segregated communities can be useful and positive because they provide needed models and group experiences in which the retired can learn their new roles. Others argue that this "subculture of aging" isolates the elderly and reinforces stereotypes about them.

Nursing Homes.   One recommendation that constantly recurs when planners discuss housing for the elderly is the inclusion of accessible aides and therapists. Availability of such personnel and services would reduce the number of elderly who must be consigned to nursing homes.

Although many nursing home scandals have been reported, scant legislative attention is focused on the problem. Part of the reason for this is the effective job done by lobbyists representing the nursing-home owners, and that the government and the public vastly underestimate the number of elderly Americans in nursing homes.

According to the "five percent fallacy," only that small proportion of older Americans live in quality, high-standard extended-care facilities. Two important studies—one by Kastenbaum and Candy in Detroit, the other by Gari Lesnoff-Caravaglia in Springfield, Illinois—show otherwise. Both of these furnished data that show that more than three-fourths of all old people die in nursing homes. Writes Caravaglia:

> The five percent figure is comforting and helps to ensure our denial of both death and aging. Also the image of the five percent fallacy draws our attention away from the fact that *where* many of these older people spend their days provides little by way of "nursing" and virtually nothing by way of a "home."[35]

These studies illustrate the real magnitude of the nursing home problem: it is a problem in both human and economic terms. Older patients are not only sick, but indigent, and the concern of no one but the Federal government.

[33]I. Rosow, *Social Integration of the Aged* (New York: Free Press, 1967).
[34]Carp, "Housing and Living Environments," p. 258-260.
[35]Gari Lesnoff-Caravaglia, "The Five Percent Fallacy," *International Journal of Aging and Human Development*, vol. 9, no. 2 (1978-79), 192.

A 90-year-old blind man enjoys a spin on the dance floor. Unlike many nursing homes which do not address the humanistic problems of institutionalized aging, this facility provides organized social activities.

UPI

The nursing home industry, by virtue of its almost total dependence on Medicaid funds, is a government industry. It is an industry in which an absence of standards, an absence of effective means of enforcing those standards, and an absence of punishment for violators invites corruption and fraud.

Medicaid reimburses nursing-home operators on the basis of services that they *claim* to have rendered; however, there is almost no actual inspection of those claims. Payment is made on a flat per-patient basis; until 1972, inspection records that did exist were not available to public scrutiny. As a result, the nursing home industry mushroomed into the kind of activity that prompted one Wall Street expert to say was fail-proof in terms of profits.

Doctors are able to charge for examining up to 100 patients, when in fact they merely remain in the home's office for a few hours or confine their ministrations to a few acute cases. Operators can charge the government $14 per day per patient for food and spend only 78 cents as did one Chicago facility. The chances of being audited are minimal, and even if violations are detected, the usual penalty is only the reimbursement of fraudulently obtained funds.[36]

Why do failures at reform, such as the Nixon Administration's 1971 crackdown, usually fail? Mary Adelaide Mendelson and David Hapgood offer this explanation:

> Lack of effective public pressure is . . . the most basic reason for the failure of nursing home regulation. The primary victims—the patients—are unable to make effective protest against their lot. . . . The financial victims—the taxpayers—are no more effectively organized to combat this form of waste than they are any other. Older people—strong lobbyists on some issues—have not had much impact on nursing home policy. One possible reason is that older people have more reason than most to fear an institution in which they may soon find themselves. Most of all, the lack of public pressure for nursing home reform may simply be another expression of our turning away from the realities of old age.[37]

Job Discrimination and Economics

Older workers are frequent targets of job discrimination. The most common practice of discrimination at work is mandatory retirement, a life-altering experience with social, economic, and emotional effects. Some observers predict that the mandatory retirement age will decline in coming decades and that by the year 2000, workers will be forced off the job at age 55.[38] The accepted practice of mandatory retirement gives companies a convenient tool for cutting labor costs. In a tight economy, or slow-growth period, a company can simply retire its high-salaried older employees and put low-salaried younger workers in their places.

Older workers also encounter job discrimination when seeking new employment. The 1967 Age Discrimination in Employment Act, designed to protect workers between 40 and 65, has still not succeeded in eradicating

[36]Mary Adelaide Mendelson and David Hapgood, "The Political Economy of Nursing Homes," in Seltzer, *et al.*, *Social Problems of the Aging*, pp. 258-264.

[37]Mendelson and Hapgood, "Political Economy of Nursing Homes," p. 264.

[38]*The New York Times*, December 21, 1975, Section 4, p. 14.

discrimination against the elderly. Prospective employers can no longer advertise for applicants "under 30," but another less blatant line like "1 to 3 years experience" accomplishes the same goal—attracting only young people. When they do obtain interviews, older workers often complain that they are rejected on the basis of overqualification—another euphemism for "too old." For these reasons, older unemployed workers remain jobless longer than do their younger counterparts.

Forced retirement of older workers wreaks havoc on income. Secretary of Commerce Juanita Kreps pointed out that the economic situation among retired persons worsens with every year, and that the older, over-75 group is the poorest of all.[39] Her economic model reveals the difficulties of saving for retirement—most people are not even able to begin such a program until age 50. And economic growth—as it now is defined in the United States—has no effect upon the retired person whose wages are not tied to the general rise in spending power. Kreps notes that it is false to attribute a worker's rise in income to productivity, since rise in income is really a function of technological progress. She suggests that an alternative method of distributing the rewards of technical progress should be considered:

> Rising real incomes can accrue to all persons in the society through a gradual reduction in prices. Everyone who is a consumer shares the benefits of growth; money wages remain essentially unchanged, while the purchasing power of these wages rises as the prices of goods decline.

Social Security

The Social Security system was never designed to be the main source of income for the elderly. It was originally intended as a form of insurance against unexpected income reduction: retirement, disability, or the death of a wage-earning spouse. In reality, the system has become a kind of government-administered public pension plan—with two-thirds of all retired married couples and five-sixths of all retired single people relying exclusively on Social Security for their incomes. Most people do not have pensions, investments, or savings sufficient to support them in retirement, and this, coupled with the prevailing practice of mandatory retirement, has made Social Security the major source of income for the elderly. So the inequities that are built into the Social Security system add enormously to the burdens of the aged.

Perhaps the greatest flaw in the Social Security system is that its benefits are too small for the purpose they must now do. Maximum payment per individual worker were allowed to rise to $6,600 in 1979, and some cost-of-living increases have been permitted since then, but 80 percent of retirees must live on less than half of their pre-retirement annual incomes, with a sizable portion still below the poverty line despite this assistance.[40]

Social Security is financed by fixed wage and payroll taxes based on the first $25,900 of annual income. Income above this amount is not taxed for Social Security. This means that lower paid workers pay a higher proportion of their income in Social Security tax than do higher paid workers. Social Security benefits, however, depend on the amount of tax paid, not on a

---

[39]Juanita M. Kreps, "Economic Growth and Income Through the Life Cycle," in Seltzer, *et al.*, *Social Problems of the Aging*, pp. 182-95.

[40]Barbara Koeppel, "The Big Social Security Ripoff," *Progressive* (August 1975), pp. 13-14.

percentage of total income. Thus, the poorest workers will remain the poorest after retiring, because their benefits will be lower.

Additional Earnings.   Those who wish to supplement their Social Security by continuing to work find they are confronted with the heaviest tax burden of any age- or income-group. Until age 72, a person cannot earn more than $230 per month without incurring a reduction in Social Security benefits. For every dollar earned in excess of that, 50 cents in Social Security is deducted—in effect, a 50 percent tax rate. The earned income is fully liable to both income tax and Social Security tax. Thus individuals over 65 who work are not only deprived of a pension they have already paid for, but they are compelled to continue paying for this benefit even though they are not permitted to receive it. This inequity is compounded by the fact that nonwage income—such as capital gains or interest on savings—may be earned in any amount without affecting Social Security benefits. The well-to-do, who are likely to have these kinds of non-wage incomes, can therefore receive their Social Security in full, while less affluent workers who try to supplement their small Social Security income are penalized.

Women.   The Social Security system also discriminates against retired women. At age 65, a woman is entitled to benefits equal to half of those her husband receives, even if she has never worked. She can either receive benefits on her own account—because she has paid Social Security taxes—or benefits through her husband. But she cannot do both. Since most husbands work longer than their wives, most women can collect higher Social Security payments by drawing from their husband's account. Thus the woman who may have worked all her adult life often collects none of the money she paid in Social Security taxes.

One of the problems that will confront the Social Security system in the future is the continuing growth in the dependency ratio. The dependency ratio expresses the relationship between the number of working people in the population and the number of non-working ones. As mandatory retirement ages drop, as the birth rate declines, and as the population of older people rises—all these are occurring simultaneously—the number of non-workers will come to represent a greater and greater burden on the workers, whose Social Security taxes will have to become greater.

Projections indicate that by 1985, the United States will require only one-half of its present labor force to maintain the Gross National Product. Unless society wants to increase that level of production, the labor force will have to be balanced. This might be done by reducing the work week or work year, but the more traditional solution would be to drop the mandatory retirement age. Some experts say this could go as low as 38![41] If this occurs, the effect on the dependency ratio would be devastating. Even without such a drastic occurrence, the dependency ratio between those who work and those they support can be expected to grow.

Multiple Jeopardy   If all of us will meet with discrimination in old age, then what is the situation of those, who because of race, nationality, or sex, have already been the victims of prejudice? Some sociologists believe it is a state of multiple

[41]Frances M. Carp, "The Retirement Process," in Barry and Wingrove, *Let's Learn About Aging*, pp. 269-288.

jeopardy. To be old, black (or Hispanic or American Indian), and female, in American society, for example, implies a state of greater hardship than to be in just one or two of those categories.

Those who have met racial, ethnic, or sex discrimination can expect to find additional indignities in old age. The rural poor—who are already discriminated against because of where they live—have lower incomes, worse housing, and fewer social and medical services, for example, than do old people in favored suburban areas.

Seventy percent of the 1.6 million elderly blacks in this country live below the poverty line. Their health is poorer than that of whites, and they have fewer contacts with social service workers. Their old age is a bitter culmination of the discrimination they have suffered all their lives. Most are ineligible for Social Security since, although they may have worked all of their lives, their jobs were usually menial ones not covered by the program. Their health is poor because of inadequate diet and the effects of stressful jobs. In addition, a high rate of black women live alone—a result of welfare regulations that encourage men to desert their families. There are 130 women for every 100 men in the elderly black population. Although many of these women continue to play their traditional matriarchal role, others are condemned to a bleak old-age in state homes or hospitals.

Women, no matter what their race, are disadvantaged in old age. As they move away from the nubile ideal of female attractiveness established by our youth-oriented society, they become more and more devalued. (See Chapter 9.) There are 13.5 million elderly women in America and many of them have financial problems. Because their salaries were lower than those of men, their pensions and social security benefits are also lower. The Social Security system gives no credit for child care and labor in the home, the principal occupation of most women in the recent past. In addition, we have seen how married women who did work outside the home are prevented from collecting benefits on the Social Security contributions they made before retirement. Older women, who want to work, suffer the double burdens of ageism and sexism. (See Chapter 9.)

Retirement

Retirement is a fairly recent concept. Before the advent of modern technology, the economy demanded a larger labor force, and as a result, people worked into old age, often modifying the nature of their work to accommodate their diminished strength.

Since the 1930s, however, the practice of mandatory retirement has grown increasingly popular. It is a highly controversial issue and is quickly becoming more so. While some observers argue that the mandatory retirement age will be eventually lowered to meet the demands of an increasingly automated economy, others insist that it will be abolished altogether. In 1978, Congress seemed to favor the middle ground between those opposing views by modifying the Age Discrimination and Employment Act to raise the minimum age at which workers can retire, solely on the basis of age, to 70. In federal government jobs, age can no longer be considered a criterion for forced retirement. Only a few jobs—at high executive levels or in very small companies—are exempted from this new regulation.

Mandatory retirement is a complicated issue that touches not just the elderly, but everyone in our society. It is a question that involves demographics, economics, health, and civil rights. Proponents of mandatory retirement argue that it is a humane system that gives workers, who may be loosing enthusiasm and energy, an easy exit; it allows workers to plan for the future by giving them a sure cut-off date; it opens new avenues of promotion and hiring for younger workers; and it gives companies a better opportunity to meet affirmative-action standards for hiring minorities.

Its opponents stress the fact that it is discriminatory. They point to a wealth of statistical data that show that working ability—especially in white-collar jobs—does not decline until a very advanced age. They argue that it strains the Social Security system and those who must contribute to it. And, they point out, mandatory retirement is physically detrimental and frequently condemns people to inescapable poverty.

Finally we are confronted by the question of whether people really want to retire. If private pension plans and public benefits could be improved, if a guaranteed minimum income were enacted, if inflation were brought under control, would people be more anxious to have leisure in their old age? Frances Carp explains that retirement means different things to different people:

> Retirement has many meanings to those undergoing it: the end of individual worth and social contact, a haven of rest, relief from an unpleasant, overtaxing, or health-draining job, or completion of commitment to society and initiation of self-realization. It may be a ceremony between one career and another; it may represent the opportunity to start one's "real" lifework or to draw two paychecks.[42]

The Dilemma of Retirement

We have mentioned earlier how the concept of retirement is generated by the forces of modernization. Technology, urbanization, education, and scientific advances have all fostered a society in which life is prolonged, but grows less valuable with age. Many of the problems facing retired people stem from their inability to adjust to a life without work. This is perhaps more difficult for the present generation of the old who grew up embracing the traditional Puritan ethic than it will be for future generations. Most of today's elderly had few leisure activities in youth and middle life and place little value on the ones they did have.

Although many older people have retired from jobs they disliked, they face difficulty in adjusting to a new role that offers an unprecedented amount of leisure:

> While some gerontologists refer to retirement as a role, it seems more useful to view retirement as a state in which the individual has to make an adjustment to the loss of a major role. Finding substitutes for occupational role is often seen as part of this adjustment. Creation of new roles for retirees is sometimes seen as a societal responsibility[43]

[42]Carp, "The Retirement Process," p. 273.
[43]Wood, "Age Appropriate Behavior," p. 75.

Adjustment to the new role of retiree is often difficult. Part of this difficulty lies in the lack of role models and reference groups. This is a problem all older people must cope with, even the fortunate few who have financial security and good health:

Problems of Adjustment

> Persons successful in adapting to old age have dropped their pursuit of the primary values of American society and picked up workable substitutes: conservation instead of acquisition and exploitation; self-acceptance instead of continuous struggles for self-advancement; being rather than doing; congeniality, cooperation, love and concern for others instead of control of others.[44]

As with any other life experience, the adjustment to retirement varies for different people. One study indicates that about one-third of the retired population has difficulty with the adjustment.[45] The most common cause of this difficulty is a reduced income. Forty percent of those interviewed cited this reason; another 22 percent mentioned missing their former jobs as the chief problem; 38 percent cited age-related factors such as fears about health or loss of a spouse. The persons who had the most difficulty were those who were inflexible and those who found their primary source of satisfaction and self-image in work. The happiest retirees were typically those who were able to develop a new hierarchy of values: one that stressed personal relationships, self-development, and leisure activities rather than economic status, power, or position within a company.

The notion of retirement as "the golden years" of leisure following a lifetime of work may be just another of the euphemistic visions our society has imposed on old age. For today's elderly, the notion of leisure may, in fact, be threatening.

Retirement and Leisure

One study conducted by M. Powell Lawton shows that the later years are more likely to be sedentary rather than leisure ones.[46] His research indicates that sleep and TV-watching out-ranked traditional leisure activities such as sports, gardening, clubs, and other recreational pastimes. The reason for this, Lawton suggests, is the past experience of today's older people. This elderly age-cohort was born in an era when the average work week was 50 hours long. Their own lives began in the period of the 48-hour week when vacations were rare and holidays were few. Housewives cared for larger homes and larger families and had few labor-saving devices or products. These people had little opportunity to develop an understanding or appreciation of leisure. Moreover, many people in this generation are poorly educated—a factor that makes them less likely to enjoy reading or activities that focus on new knowledge or self-improvement. The gross reduction in income, fear of crime, lack of transportation, and reduction in physical mobility also contribute to the sedentary life of the old.

Future generations of retirees will probably be different. Those who have

[44]Wood, "Age Appropriate Behavior," p. 75.

[45]Robert C. Atchley, "Adjustment to Loss of Job at Retirement," in Seltzer, *et al.*, *Social Problems of the Aging*, pp. 52-59.

[46]M. Powell Lawton, "Leisure Activities for the Aged," *Annals of the American Academy of Political and Social Science*, vol. 438 (July 1978), pp. 71-79.

A group of retirees spend
their leisure hours at
shuffleboard. Too many
people over 65 let their
lives become sedentary
rather than actively
relaxed.

Rollie McKenna/Photo
Researchers, Inc.

enjoyed affluence, travel, and education are more likely to enjoy retirement.
This trend is already surfacing in the form of retirement communities that
offer golf, swimming, and recreational centers. The cohorts that follow these
younger retirees, the people who came of age in the 60s and after, to whom
leisure and self-growth are as desirable as social status and work, will probably
come to retirement with even more interest in and awareness of the uses of
free time.

Ageism

As we mentioned earlier in this chapter, modernization with its urbanization,
technological progress, and emphasis on education is one of the primary
causes of the devaluation of the aged. So extreme and unremitting is this bias
that it has been termed "ageism" by many experts including Dr. Robert
Butler, director of the National Institute on Aging.

Many attitudes prevalent in modern society contribute to ageism. One of
these is a desire to end "aesthetic pollution."[47] Older adults do not meet the

[47]Rochelle Jones, *The Other Generation: The New Power of Older Americans* (Englewood
Cliffs, N.J.: Prentice-Hall, 1977), p. 79.

national standard of youthful beauty, and many people may simply be affronted by the appearance of the old. Another source of ageism is the attitude that the old are useless—people feel that since they do not work and cannot reproduce, they serve no purpose. Those who *do* hold jobs are resented for taking a position a young person probably needs.

Because the roots of ageism go so deeply into the social and psychological fabric of our culture, this phenomenon will be extremely difficult to eliminate, perhaps more difficult than racism or sexism.

Ageism is a prevailing force in industry and government. The HEW Administration on Aging has low status and limited access to decision-makers. When Congress makes budget cuts, programs for the aged are a frequent target. When state and local government participate in revenue sharing, they rarely use any of the funds to help the aged. One analysis of the spending of 219 local governments revealed that only 28 of them spent any of their money specifically on older adults. Old people are underrepresented in antipoverty programs, job-training courses, and social service programs. Former HEW Secretary Robert H. Finch provided a telling reason for this. Programs for the elderly, he said, result in very little "payoff."[48]

The old fare no better in business and industry. "Age discrimination," reports the Senate Special Committee on Aging, "is the only form of discrimination that enjoys widespread social approval within corporate life." Being young, concludes the report, is "an underlying corporate value."

Although the Age Discrimination in Employment Act of 1967 prohibits discrimination against workers ages 40 to 65, little is done to enforce it. After 10 years of existence, a total of only 265 complaints were filed, and the office responsible for investigating violations did not have even one employee assigned full-time to age discrimination cases. Critics have pointed out that the law itself exhibits blatant ageism, since it protects workers up to age 65, but does nothing for those above that age—who probably need protection even more.

Ageism promotes mandatory retirement based on age. The result takes a heavy toll on the health, self-respect, social status, and economic security of older people. Mandatory retirement is the most serious and the most pervasive form of ageism in this country.

Although the number of older Americans grows each year, the health professions are doing little to anticipate or cope with the problems of the elderly. Ageism is present in both the medical and scientific communities. Less than a third of the medical schools in America offer courses in gerontology and of 20,000 medical school professors, only 15 are involved full-time in the field of aging.

Just as women and minorities have had to contend with negative images in the media, so do old people. Television, which does so much to shape and maintain attitudes, persists in portraying old people as "doddering old fools who cause problems for their relatives or as wise old ancients who are always ready with a pithy saying or a piece of warm gingerbread."[49]

Newspapers and magazines are not much better. In an analysis of 265 articles on aging that appeared in a large Midwestern newspaper, it was found that a negative image of both the old and the aging process was promoted. Instead of featuring older people active in their communities, the paper

[48]Jones, *The Other Generation*, pp. 85-86.
[49]Jones, *The Other Generation*, pp. 89-93.

stressed stories about "well-preserved physical culture addicts and 'old timers' reminiscing about the good old days." Despite the growing number of older people, the paper carried less than 2 articles a day on the elderly or on aging, and half of these were human interest features with no information on the realities of aging.[50]

Social Consequences of Ageism

Ageism has been highly successful in isolating the old from the mainstream of American life. It forces people out of jobs and into retirement, which for many means isolation. The daily social contacts of the working world are gone, and reduced income may bring reduced mobility or prevent participation in social activities.

Retirement, as we have seen before, also causes the loss of an important role, that of a productive worker. The new role imposed on the older person has a lowly status and a negative image. Soon the elderly conform to society's expectations and feel weak, incompetent, and unproductive. Although this does not happen to every retired person, it is far from uncommon.

The difficulties of the old in our society are mirrored by their higher-than-average suicide rate. The aged comprise approximately 10 percent of the population, they are responsible for about 25 percent of reported suicides. Studies have indicated that the isolation of old age, the absence of external social restraints—friendships, spouse, family, and co-workers—are contributing factors.[51]

Though declining health, loss of status, and reduced income play a part in the suicides of the elderly, lack of relationships seems to exert the most consistent influence. One analysis of nine years of suicides of the elderly in Pinellas County, Florida, suggests some of the social factors that cause old people to end their own lives. This study indicated that widowed males were more likely to commit suicide than any other group of old people. Widowhood is more difficult for men, it is suspected, because it not only robs men of an important relationship, but because it forces them into the unfamiliar role of housekeeper. Widowhood for women involves a less drastic role change. The study shows that elderly women are more likely to have extended family ties, friends, and club memberships that provide them with social restraints against suicide. Elderly men who enjoyed these kinds of contact were less likely to commit suicide. The highest suicide rate in the entire sample was that of the lowest-class level. Besides being poor, these people were less likely to be married, to be in touch with relatives, or to be involved in social organizations.[52]

Other research has focused on the high suicide rate among elderly married men who have social ties only to their spouses. This seems to indicate that the loneliness and isolation of old age can often be stronger than the social restraint against suicide usually provided by marriage.

Family Problems of the Aged

One of the most pervasive myths about the aged is that they are abandoned by their children. In this myth, the past is portrayed as a "golden age" in which

---

[50]Jones, *The Other Generation*, p. 94.

[51]E. Wilbur Bock, "Aging and Suicide: The Significance of Marital Kinship and Alternative Relations," *The Family Co-Ordinator* (January, 1972), pp. 71-78.

[52]Bock, "Aging and Suicide."

Americans lived in extended families; however, history, research, and clinical studies have shown that this is incorrect. America has never been a society of extended families. Elaine M. Brody estimates that the overwhelming majority of today's old people who live alone do so voluntarily. Almost universally, they wish to live near their children but not with them; however, about 25 percent of America's old *do* live with one of their children. Those who don't, see their children frequently—as often as several times a week.[53]

The institutionalized old are not typical. They represent a special population of the elderly who are, on the average, a decade older than the rest of the old population, largely female, and suffering from a severe chronic physical or mental ailment. Most of them have outlived their relatives, only half have surviving children and only 10 percent have a spouse. For these family members, to place an aged relative in an institution is usually a difficult experience. As Brody puts it:

> Prior to the institutionalization most families have endured severe personal, social, and economic stress in attempting to avoid admission; it is typically the last, not the first resort; and the decision is made reluctantly. The "well" spouse usually is in advanced old age. The adult children often are approaching or engaged in the aging phase of life with attendant age-related stresses and often are subjected to competing demands from ill spouses or their own children.[54]

Opinions about how many of these old people could remain at home if support services were available range from 60 to only 12 percent. It is a complex problem; for one thing, as more people live to an extremely old age, the total family unit ages. People of 65 may have to provide 24-hour care for their parents of 90 and may be experiencing economic and health problems of their own. In short, there may be several generations of elderly people in one family—all requiring different degrees of care. Moreover, the increasing mobility of Americans may leave parents and adult children separated by thousands of miles, making home care impossible.

The rising rate of divorce, the emergence of single parent families, and the trend toward smaller families will also affect the future possibilities of home care for the aged. Future generations of old people may have few or no relatives to care for them, or they may have weak family ties.

The changing role of women also affects how the old are treated. Historically, tending the elderly has been the task of the daughter or daughter-in-law, who were full-time housewives. As women continue to work outside the home, they will be less able to care for aged parents.

Future social programs for the elderly will have to reflect these sociological trends to be successful. The American family of the late twentieth century will have fewer children, but the same number of grandparents and great-grandparents. In addition, there will be multiple patterns of kinship created by divorce and remarriage. The focus of tension may be broadened to include not just parent and growing child, but adult and aging parent. The "young-old" years are becoming, perhaps for the first time in the history of the family, a period of parent-child stress. (See Chapter 11.)

[53]Elaine M. Brody, "The Aging of the Family," *Annals of the American Academy of Political and Social Science*, vol. 438 (July 1978), 18-21.

[54]Brody, "The Aging of the Family," p. 21.

Death

Dying, like aging, is a continuous process. It is a simple fact, but one that most Americans have difficulty accepting. Perhaps the most fundamental cause of our anti-age attitude is our overwhelming fear of death. In modern society, age and death are closely linked in symbol and reality:

> To exorcise the fear of death, we make those who are about to die redundant and irrelevant while they are still alive. By rendering the about-to-die trivial in life, we lessen the fear that death holds for us. If the about-to-die do not matter, we reason, death may be meaningless also, and we need not be afraid of it.[55]

A double standard of death prevails in our society. When a child or a young person dies, people grieve openly, lamenting the unrealized potential and undeveloped talent. While this is fitting, there is also another reason for this style of mourning—the death of a child holds no personal threat for those who have already survived childhood.

The death of an older person elicits very different reactions. The family views it as natural and right, and there is a lessened sense of loss and anger. This attitude acts as a defense against the personal threat that the death of an old person carries. It is the ultimate expression of old age.

This double standard of death, it should be noted, is by no means universal. In some societies, where children are not considered fully human, the death of the young is not mourned. When infant mortality was high, little attention was given to the passing of children, but then the old were fully mourned. Until we come to terms with the reality of death as a natural process, we cannot come to terms with age.

In ancient times, death was viewed as a mode of transition from one state of being to another. Today, more complex and varied meanings are assigned to it. According to Richard A. Kalish:

> Death is a biological event, a rite of passage, an inevitability, a natural occurrence, a punishment, extinction, the enforcement of God's will, absurd, separation, reunion, and time for judgment. It is a reasonable cause for anger, depression, denial, repression, guilt, frustration, relief, absolution of self, increased religiousness . . . . It has one set of meanings for the dying person, another for those who love him, yet another for those responsible for his health care, and still another set of meanings for those involved with funerals, legal documents, insurance, estates, and trusts, public health statistics, wars and executions.[56]

Death and age have always been closely associated, but today death is, in the public mind, almost exclusively the fate of the old. As Kalish writes, some significant consequences flow from this association:

> Although the old have always died, the dying have not always been old. It is only in very recent decades that death has become primarily the province of the elderly, rather than an event scattered erratically across the life span . . . . Because of the close association between old age and death in modern industrial

---

[55]Jones, *The Other Generation*, p. 79.

[56]Richard A. Kalish, "Death and Dying in a Social Context," in Binstock and Shanas, *Aging and the Social Sciences*, p. 483.

societies, the individual and social issues relating to death are in many ways individual and social issues of aging . . . . One of the significant reasons that the old are avoided and isolated is their proximity to death.[57]

In recent times, there has been renewed interest in the meaning of death. In the past, the church encouraged a consciousness of death as man's fate and instructed its adherents in its consequences—judgment and reward or punishment. Today, social scientists study death in terms of its psychological and social impact. Their efforts, it is felt, are helping to remove some of the taboos that make this difficult experience even more trying.

Learning to Die

Research indicates that the old, perhaps because of a natural process of disengagement, have less fear of death than do the young. There are also indications that during the process of dying, a distinct pattern of feelings and behavior emerges, called the "dying trajectory." This trajectory, of course, differs from person to person and from situation to situation.

The best-known description of the trajectory of dying was proposed by Elisabeth Kübler-Ross. She feels that the dying process is characterized by (1) denial and isolation, (2) anger and resentment, (3) bargaining and an attempt to postpone death, (4) depression and sense of loss, and (5) acceptance. By understanding the dying process, caretakers, physicians, friends, and family members can make the experience easier and more meaningful. Being informed of one's true condition has been identified as being very important to the terminally ill.[58]

A number of recent studies suggest that current practices in hospitals and nursing homes—where most old people die—offer almost no possibility of a good and meaningful death. Critically ill patients, it has been observed, are usually treated as though they were already dead. Their autopsies are planned, they are often stashed in hallways or supply closets; their relatives may even be approached regarding donation of the person's organs. If the patient is comatose, he fares even worse.

Hospices.   The recent hospice movement promises to bring reform to the American way of dying. Hospices are special institutions designed for the terminally ill. They are as comfortable and as homelike as possible and are staffed by personnel specially trained in working with the dying. The hospice places primary emphasis on the use of home-health services for the dying including visiting nurse services, on-call physicians, and counselors. The home-health care program enables many people to live their final days in familiar surroundings, as close as possible to their loved ones.[59]

Surveys indicate that most people would prefer to die at home. Being at home with one's family seems to provide a greater chance for "death with dignity"; being institutionalized implies loss of control and individuality.

"Death with dignity" has become a popular phrase as people confront the issues of relegating the old and terminally ill to institutions and a life provided by extraordinary means through machines. Dr. Melvin J. Krant, testifying before the Senate's Special Committee on Aging, pointed out that we can never be guaranteed death with dignity until we are better informed about

[57]Kalish, "Death and Dying," p. 494.

[58]Elizabeth Kübler-Ross, *On Death and Dying* (New York: Macmillan, 1969), and *Death, the Final Stage of Growth* (Englewood Cliffs, N.J.: Prentice-Hall, 1975).

[59]Abdellah, "Long-Term Care," p. 35.

death, and have stopped institutionalizing the old and dying. Death, he insists, must be accepted once again as a natural consequence, not as a failure.[60]

Funerals   One of the most effective ways a person can insure death with dignity is through a "living will." This legal document allows people—while they are still in good mental and physical health—to set down some guidelines for their death and its aftermath. People use living wills to prevent themselves from being placed on respirators for extraordinarily long periods of time, for donating their organs to science, and for mandating their funeral arrangements and mode of burial.

It should be noted that funeral services and ceremonies are important parts of the event of death. The mourning process—wakes, mourning attire, "sitting shiva," eulogies, gravemarkers—serves a dual purpose. As Kalish points out, they are the last rite of passage for the dead and the means by which the survivors cope with their own loss.

> One major function of the funeral and related rituals is to provide the support of the extended family and the community for those who have suffered the loss . . . . "The wake and the funeral reaffirm the group identity of the survivors, often with the help of the religious collective representations, extending all members into afterlife."

These rituals are in a state of transition today as many people request charitable donations in lieu of flowers and request cremation and subsequent scattering of their ashes instead of burial. Social scientists point out that these new approaches to the funeral ritual represent not a secularization, but the rise of a new kind of spiritual symbolism.[61]

Social Policy and Prospects

A demographic analysis by Erdman Palmore projects that future generations of aged Americans will be healthier than the present aged because of better lifelong nutritional habits and medical care. The health of the elderly as a group is already improving because of Medicare and Medicaid.

As occupational and educational levels continue to rise, the income gap between the young and the old may be lessened in the future. "Higher occupations and more education mean more and better pensions, Social Security benefits, savings and earnings."

According to Palmore:

> That the relative status of the aged in health, income, and education is rising and probably will continue to rise for the rest of this century contradicts the theories that the status of the aged continues to decline in modernized societies, that age stratification is becoming more important in the USA, and that the aged are becoming more like a disadvantaged minority group . . . . It supports the

---

[60]Melvin J. Krant, *"Death With Dignity,"* in Seltzer, *et al., Social Problems of the Aging,* pp. 94-107.
[61]Kalish, "Death and Dying," p. 503.

opposite theories that in most modernized societies such as the USA the relative status of the aged "bottoms-out" and begins to rise; that we are moving in the direction of an "age-irrelevant" society."[62]

Political Action Groups

Older Americans are fast becoming one of the most politically organized and influential groups in America. Their power lies not just in their numbers, but more importantly in that they tend to be more active voters than the young. Older Americans are also forming pressure groups to increase their power. Some are local, or grassroots movements, but there are already three national groups with Washington headquarters and state affiliates. During the early 1970s the National Council on Senior Citizens demonstrated the emerging power of the old by mounting an extensive lobbying effort for an increase in Social Security benefits.

The effects of senior power are being felt all across America. Forty-eight states, for example, have granted some form of property tax relief to elderly home owners. But at the same time, this activism is inspiring a backlash from the young and middle-aged who feel that their taxes subsidize reduced fares, tax breaks, and other benefits for the elderly. Older adults argue that their exemptions are justified since they use fewer tax-supported services, such as schools, than do younger families.[63]

Others claim that the political clout of older Americans is exaggerated. Robert Binstock, former Director of the White House Task Force on Aging, insists that the aged are not as cohesive as many politicians think. They do not, he says, vote as a single block, but on a variety of individual principles and interests prejudices. Many people in the senior age group do not identify with the elderly, but with the middle-aged. Lobbying groups and special interest organizations are giving the aged greater access to legislators and more visibility, but when it comes to an election these are "electoral bluffs."[64]

The growing numbers and the growing voice—whether perceived as a voting bloc or recognized as a special interest group—of the elderly is affecting government policies and programs. The last fifteen years have seen some significant strides toward securing a better life for the aged: Medicare and Medicaid, food stamps, increased Social Security payments, nutritional programs, homemaker services, housing. Though none of these has succeeded in reaching their goals, each one represents an indication of an increasing responsiveness on the part of government to the needs of the aged.

Many of these programs are not as successful as they could be since they do not reach most of the people who need them, often a result of inequitable distribution, such as lack of Medicare clinics in decaying neighborhoods. In other instances, elderly people simply refuse the services offered to them. Several studies have investigated the causes of this unwillingness on the part of the elderly to take advantage of the programs and services offered to them and all point to similar conclusions. The elderly often simply do not understand what the program can do for them, they may be confused by

---

[62]Erdman Palmore, "The Future Status of the Aged," *The Gerontologist*, vol. 16, no. 4 (1976), 301.

[63]Jones, *The Other Generation*, p. 229.

[64]Robert H. Binstock, "Aging and the Future of American Politics," *The Annals of the American Academy of Political and Social Science*, vol. 415 (September 1974), 199-211.

regulations, may hesitate to travel to a government office, or to sign required papers. More often they decline assistance because government programs carry a stigma especially

> to the older elderly who have had a most difficult life, and have been socialized to a culture and ideology which stressed individualism and promised rewards to anyone who worked hard. They worked under exploitative circumstances and yet believed that anyone who asked for assistance or refused to work under such circumstances was a chisler. This was the beauty of the Protestant ethic. And now, even, when they are old, sick, disabled, and poor, often as a result of their work history, they feel ashamed of accepting help. "I've never asked for anything in my life," "I always made my way through," were frequent comments.[65]

Both rural and urban people from working class backgrounds revealed the same negative attitude toward public assistance.

The younger generation of elderly—those between 65 and 75—are more willing to use the programs and services offered to them. Their attitude may represent a new trend among the old. Studies also suggest that state programs can reach more old people if they are sensitive to this attitude. Older people find it hard to accept a service or benefit that demands a declaration of poverty or involves the outright payment of money. It is easier to accept meals, visits from a social worker, rent subsidies, free transportation or reduced fares.

[65]Elizabeth Moen, "The Reluctance of the Elderly to Accept Help," *Social Problems*, vol. 25, no. 3 (February 1978), 299.

Summary

Age is one of society's bases for designating role assignments. In our industrialized society, arbitrarily determined age levels dictate the progress of our lives and the roles we play. The old are allotted a "roleless" role, and this is one of the major problems of aging. It is only in recent times that aging has represented a social problem. In the past, one's status often increased with age, but never diminished. People continued to perform their usual roles as long as they were physically capable.

Rapid advances in health technology have meant that a record number of people are surviving to an advanced age. At the same time, modernization has diminished the status of the old, making their knowledge outmoded and their skills obsolete.

Mandatory retirement places older people in a role that our work-oriented society regards as worthless and parasitic. These labels frequently alter an old person's self-image and cause severe psychological stress. The most serious consequence of mandatory retirement, however, is economic. Social Security benefits do not cover many of today's old, and those who do receive benefits receive very little. The old are poorer than any other economic or minority group, many of them live in substandard housing, and because of the ideals of their particular generation, refuse to accept government assistance. Those who are both old and minority group members are in a position of multiple jeopardy. Although the aged exhibit many of the characteristics of a minority, they are more accurately termed a quasi-minority. The aged, unlike ethnic minorities, are not a separate group. Many belong to the families of the dominant group. Ageism is the most accepted form of discrimination in America: it keeps old people out of jobs and out of the mainstream of life. It creates a feeling of alienation and it may contribute to the higher-than-average suicide rate among the elderly. Like sexism, ageism is based on popular, but false, stereotypes.

The growing number and proportion of old people is having a profound effect on American society and that effect will grow more pronounced in the future. Already social scientists are identifying different age groups among the aged. Those from 65 to 75 are the young-old; those above 75 are the old-old.

By the year 2000, ours will be an "old" nation. This will mean possible changes in the Social Security system, since dependents will be fast outnumbering workers. The coming generations of older Americans will be better educated, more politically aware, and healthier than the present group. They will also have different attitudes about the work ethic and the concept of leisure.

One source of ageism is the fear of death. With the decline in the infant mortality rate and the conquest of a number of many fatal diseases, death has become almost the exclusive province of the old. By denying the existence of the old, by ignoring them and isolating them, people can also deny the inevitability of death.

Bibliography

Barry, John R., and Wingrove, C. Ray, eds., *Let's Learn About Aging.* New York: Wiley, 1977.

Binstock, Robert H. and Shanas, Ethel, eds., *Aging and the Social Sciences.* New York: Van Nostrand-Reinhold, 1976.

Comfort, Alex. *Aging: The Biology of Senescence.* New York: Holt, Rinehart, and Winston, 1964.

Downs, Hugh. *Thirty Dirty Lies About Old.* New York: Argus, 1979.

Jones, Rochelle. *The Other Generation: The New Power of Older Americans.* Englewood Cliffs, N.J.: Prentice-Hall, 1977.

Kübler-Ross, Elizabeth. *Death: the Final Stage of Growth.* Englewood Cliffs, N.J.: Pentice-Hall, 1975.

————. *On Death and Dying.* New York: Macmillan, 1969.

Riley, Matilda W. et al., *Aging & Society.,* volumes 1 and 2. New York: Russell Sage, 1969, 1972.

Seltzer, Mildred M., Corbett, Sherry L., and Atchley, Robert C. *Social Problems of the Aging.* Belmont Calif.: Wadsworth, 1978.

Woodruff, Diana S., and Birren, James E. *Aging: Scientific Perspectives and Social Issues.* New York: Van Nostrand, 1975.

11

Family Stress

Facts about Family Stress

- More than half of all married women currently work outisde the home.
- Almost 70 percent of all parents believe that the children of working mothers are not as well cared for as the children of non-working mothers.
- More than 1 million children are the victims of child abuse each year.
- It is estimated that some 300,000 children between the ages of 3 and 15 have been used in the production of pornography.
- Nearly 2 million wives are beaten by their husbands each year.
- Currently there is one divorce for every two marriages.

The American family is sometimes said to be on the verge of collapse; however, since similar warnings have been issued in numerous societies throughout history, there is probably no need for panic, especially since the reported threats to family life always seem to be similar: breakdown of parental authority, strife between husbands and wives, and increasing disregard of sexual morality. It seems that virtually every society has an ideal of what family life and organization should be, and feels threatened by any deviation.

In a rapidly changing society, family problems may be regarded partly as the result of new social conditions. These problems need not constitute simply a breakdown; they may also be part of a general movement toward constructive reorganization of the family. Like other institutions, the family is affected by social change and adopts new forms that are more compatible with new societal patterns.

It is, however, important to distinguish between the problems of individual families and changes in the overall family system in a given society. Many marriages may end in divorce; many children may be raised by one parent or by other relatives; but a societal system may presume that these situations will occur and continue to regard the nuclear family as the norm. In another society, an extended family system might remain the norm despite frequent breakup into nuclear units. A social problem arises only when the pressure for change can no longer be accommodated within the limits of the existing societal structures, or when those who wish to maintain these structures fear that they cannot.

This chapter, therefore, will examine various types of problems related to family structure today and alternative family structures that have become common.

Kinship Units

A kinship unit is a group of individuals related to one another either by bloodlines or by some convention equivalent to marriage. Within the group there is usually a division of authority, privilege, responsibility, and economic and sex roles.

Definitions of kinship may differ from one society to another, resulting in differing behavioral standards. The unit may consist of a *nuclear family*—father, mother, and their children living apart from other kin—or an *extended family*—parents, children, grandparents, aunts, uncles, and all others living together. In the latter instance, parents may retain authority over their married sons and daughters, and marriage between first or even second cousins may be forbidden; in the former case, the nuclear family unit will probably be independent, and marriage between second, if not first, cousins may be considered perfectly normal.

The nuclear family is the predominant type of family in industrial societies, whereas the extended family is more likely to be found in agrarian cultures. The emergence of industrial centers seems to favor the development of smaller family units that are geographically and socially more mobile, although extensive ties with relatives may still exist.

The further change from a more or less classical industrial society to an increasingly affluent technological one may be expected to cause additional changes in the structure and functions of the family. Economic pressures for family stability may be reduced; more women may be able to raise their children without reliance on the children's fathers. Indeed, some sociologists believe that the transition of societies from agrarian to industrial to technological has steadily reduced the economically useful size of the family; whereas the farming family may have needed many "hands," families in industrialized societies—at least where child labor is outlawed—are better able to manage in smaller sizes.

But whether extended, nuclear, or as yet undefined, all family types are characterized by an organization of roles. If the family is to function adequately, its members must perform these roles in ways compatible both with the expectations of other family members and with society's standards.

Five criteria of adequate functioning have been suggested by Paul Glasser and Lois Glasser:

Adequate Family Functioning

1. *Internal role consistency among family members.* In order for family members to contribute to the proper functioning of the family, they must understand what is expected of them and of other family members.

2. *Consistency of family roles and norms and actual role performance.* The requirements each family member is expected to fulfill do not suddenly change, nor is there a severe change in the way family members fulfill their required roles.

3. *Compatibility of family roles and norms with societal norms.* For adequate family functioning, the "internal organization of the family must be carried out in behavior acceptable to the external system of environment surrounding it." The limits of society's tolerance of non-conformity to its norms vary, as might be expected, from society to society.

4. *Meeting the psychological needs of family members.* A family does not function adequately if it is unable to meet the long-run emotional and psychological needs of its members.

5. *The ability of the family group to respond to change.* To maintain itself over a long period of time, the family must be able to respond to

demands for change, whether these demands originate inside or outside the family unit.[1]

Failure to perform any one of these functions could lead to problems within the family. Such failure is usually involuntary, as a result of either external or internal crises.

External crises are those imposed from outside the family, for example, the death of a parent. This event disrupts role relationships, since the role of the deceased parent, such as child care, housekeeping, or financial support, must be shifted, and adjustments must be made. Similarly, role relationships may be disrupted by wars and economic depressions. Absence of a parent during military service changes both his or her roles and those of the other parent, while unemployment of a parent who works can be psychologically unsettling to the entire family. The parent suffers a loss of self-esteem and/or of authority, and all members of the family are likely to be frightened and anxious over the unexpected economic insecurity.[2]

Internal crises are those imposed from within the family, such as a serious physical or mental disorder of a child or parent. Many families adjust to these problems and are able to assume the roles of the handicapped member and to accept the helping responsibility. This burden, however, may cause tension and strain between family members. Marital infidelity can be another source of internal crisis, particularly if one or both of the partners perceives it as a threat to the family. A major change in family role may also provoke an internal crisis. For example, the parent who suddenly decides to work, instead of taking care of the children, or the parent who stops working, may cause other family members to feel threatened or confused. Often, the very factor that keeps families functioning well—the consistency of roles and behaviors—may threaten the family's functioning when flexibility becomes more important.

These stresses and other interpersonal problems may reduce the family to an "empty shell," kept together not so much by feelings of warmth and attraction among the members as by outside pressures. Within the shell, members of the family feel no strong attachments for each other; they neglect mutual obligations and in general keep communication to a minimum.

Carolyn Cline has distinguished three types of empty-shell marriages. The first she refers to as the *conflict-habituated relationship* characterized by considerable tension and conflict. The husband and wife may quarrel frequently in private, yet appear compatible in public. The atmosphere in such a home is usually tense and bitter.

A second type is the *devitalized relationship*, in which interaction between husband and wife lacks any real interest or excitement. Apathy and boredom constitute the main elements of the marriage, but serious or violent arguments are rare.

The third type is the *passive-congenial relationship* where both partners

---

[1] Paul H. Glasser and Lois N. Glasser, "Adequate Family Functioning," in *Family Structure Dynamics and Therapy, Psychiatric Research Report*, No. 20, ed. Irvin M. Cohen (Washington, D.C.: American Psychiatric Association, 1966), pp. 8-17.

[2] Robert F. Winch and Rae Lesser Blumber, "Societal Complexity and Familial Organization," in *Selected Studies in Marriage and the Family*, 3rd ed., ed. Robert F. Winch and Robert McGinnis (New York: Holt, Rinehart and Winston, 1953), pp. 70-92.

are content with their lives and feel adequate but not actually happy. There is little overt conflict, and the partners may have interests in common. These interests, however, tend to be somewhat insignificant, and there is little evidence that the spouses contribute in any meaningful way to each other's real satisfactions.[3]

In a sense, it is surprising how often these empty-shell marriages manage to continue. Habit and fear of change may explain some of it. There is also the economic factor—one spouse may doubt his or her ability to manage alone, and knows it would cost more to support oneself and/or pay alimony than to maintain a single-family household. More positively, husband and wife may feel strongly that divorce or separation would be wrong or would harm the children. There is also usually a social pressure to stay together: in many places, particularly the suburbs, social life for adults more or less presupposes married couples. Also, some marriage counselors assume that their job is to preserve the marriage, although their clients might be happier unmarried. Unhappiness within families is unfortunate, but it is not usually seen as a threat to society; divorce or separation, on the other hand, are often regarded as social "evils" or "problems" since many marriages stay together even after they have ceased to function well.

Family Happiness and Working Wives

In the traditional concept of the American family, the husband worked in the paid labor force while the wife worked—unpaid—at home. In 1960, 62 percent of American families still conformed to this model. Today, such households account for less than 47 percent of all family units.[4] Quite simply, what had been accepted as the norm for generations has become an exception. Whether in the conventional two-partner family or the female-headed household, the wife or mother who is employed in the paid labor force is now increasingly the rule. (See Chapter 9 and Figure 11-1.)

Recent research indicates that a wife's job may often help, not hinder, family well-being. Susan Orden and Norman Bradburn, in a 1970 study, investigated the relationship between perceived marriage happiness and the work-status of the wife, and concluded that where the wife worked as a matter of choice, the marriage was as happy or happier than if she chose to remain at home; whereas if she worked out of necessity, marriage happiness suffered. The relative values of work by choice and remaining at home varied at different stages of the family life cycle: when there were pre-school children, happiness was rated as higher if the wife remained at home; when the children were in grade school, work by choice seemed to make for greater happiness; after the children entered high school the two choices seemed about equal. Only when the wife worked as a matter of necessity was marriage happiness in all cases lowered.[5]

Yet, in fact, attitudes about working mothers have not changed as fast as statistics have. A recent study conducted for General Mills revealed that:

[3]Carolyn Cline, "Five Variations on the Marriage Theme: Types of Marriage Formation," *Bulletin on Family Development* 3 (Spring 1962), 10-13.

[4]Murray S. Weitzman, "Finally the Family," *Annals of the American Academy of Political and Social Science,* vol. 435 (January 1979), p. 64.

[5]Susan R. Orden and Norman M. Bradburn, "Working Wives and Marriage Happiness," *American Journal of Sociology* 57 (1970), 392-407.

Figure 11-1
Types of Families,
1950–1990

Source: Murray S. Weltzman,
"Finally the Family," *Annals
of the American Academy
of Political and Social
Science,* vol. 435 (January
1979), p. 76.

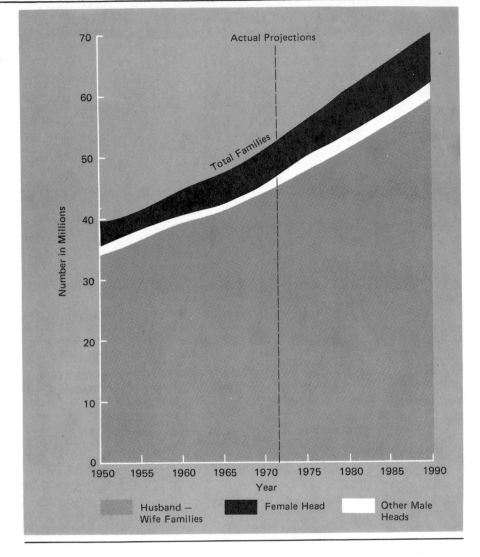

Even the women's movement has not resolved the question of working mothers. The great majority of parents, both mothers and fathers, believe that a mother of young children should not work unless the money is needed. Consistent with this view, most of the parents do not agree that the children of working mothers are more independent, more responsible, or better off. Among all parents, 69% believe that the children are worse off. Only working mothers split evenly on the question, with 49% saying the children are better off and 48% believing they are not as well off.[6]

[6]Yankelovich, Skelly, and White, Inc., *The General Mills American Family Report 1976–77: Raising Children in a Changing Society* (Minneapolis: General Mills, 1979), p. 128.

Children are commonly believed to bring joy to any household, and the desire to have them is certainly one of the major reasons why couples marry. In a study of the degrees of satisfaction and emotional well-being, researchers have discovered that over 2,000 people expressed at different stages of their lives, that young, married, childless couples were the happiest of all groups considered. (Single people were the least happy.) When married couples began to have children, their reported happiness decreased and feelings of stress rose markedly. Some dissatisfaction was due to the financial burden and sacrifices involved in bearing and raising children; some of it was due to the fact that most young parents suddenly found that they had much less time to spend together. It was not until after the children had left home that married couples regained a state of satisfaction comparable to what they had experienced as childless newlyweds.

Many young couples in this country have decided that children are not necessary for marital happiness, as evidenced by the large decline in the United States birthrate—1978 registered the second lowest annual fertility rate in American history.[7] Some sociologists believe that childless marriages

[7]Robert Reinhold, "U.S. Reports Modest Revival for Marriages," *New York Times*, April 5, 1979, p. 67.

Family Happiness and Children

Although children bring a certain joy to families, researchers have found that overall happiness may actually decrease when couples have children.
Ray Ellis/Photo Researchers, Inc.

are less stressful and more emotionally satisfying. The survey also revealed that childless couples over age 30—particularly the husbands—were the most satisfied with their lives, probably because they experience less financial anxiety than same-aged fathers. Childless wives over age 30 reported almost the same degree of satisfaction in their lives as same-aged mothers, an indication that many young wives today do not regard childbearing as necessary to a woman's role.[8] Furthermore, unlike in the past when children contributed to the family's earnings by working in the family business or farm, or even in a factory, children today represent a considerable financial liability that many couples prefer to defer or avoid altogether.[9]

The Black Family

There has been considerable interest in recent years in the distinctive character of the black family in America. It has been hypothesized that the poverty and discrimination consistently experienced by black people may have led to special adaptations in family life. Since family life is basic to personality development, these adaptations may be helping to perpetuate some of the conditions that contribute to poverty and discrimination. Such is the implication of the so-called Moynihan Report, which identifies the problem of black poverty as being rooted in a "tangle of pathology" and the weaknesses of the matriarchal family structure characteristic of the lower-class black community. The report established the stereotype of the black family as female-headed or female-dominated, a situation that is said to emasculate the male and to lead to patterns of low education, low achievement, unemployment, crime, and poverty.[10]

Undoubtedly, there is a high percentage of female-headed families among the black poor, as well as a high rate of illegitimacy. It should be remembered, however, that these characteristics tend to be more common at the lower socioeconomic levels of any ethnic group, so that poverty is as likely to be the cause as it is to be the effect of black family structure. It is too easily forgotten that the majority of black families, as well as white, are stable and male-headed. As lower-class blacks move up the socioeconomic ladder into the middle class, instability decreases, as it does among whites.[11] It should also be remembered that statistics about deviant behavior tend to be unreliable, and to exaggerate the amount of deviance among both the black and the poor. In fact, the data and the conclusions of the Moynihan Report have been challenged by researchers in the Chicago area. Alan Berger and William Simon compared the juvenile delinquency rates, at all socioeconomic levels, in a large sample of black and white families in Illinois and concluded that there is little difference in how these families treat their children and that the black female-headed family is not the primary cause of antisocial behavior patterns.[12]

Nevertheless, there are certain fairly consistent differences between

[8]Angus Campbell, "The American Way of Mating: Marriage Sí, Children Only Maybe," *Psychology Today* (May 1975), pp. 38-43.

[9]Kenneth Keniston, *All Our Children: The American Family under Pressure* (New York: Harcourt Brace Jovanovich, 1977), p. 19.

[10]Daniel Moynihan, *The Negro Family: The Case for National Action* (Washington, D.C.: U.S. Department of Labor, Office of Policy Planning and Research, 1965).

[11]John H. Scanzoni, *The Black Family in Modern Society* (Boston: Allyn & Bacon, 1971).

[12]Alan S. Berger and William Simon, "Black Families and the Moynihan Report: A Research Evaluation," *Social Problems* 22 (December 1974), 160-61.

black and white families. Instability among lower-class black families seems to be somewhat greater than among similar white families, and the illegitimacy rates of blacks are higher. The female-headed family is also more common among black than among white poor. (See Chapter 7.)

Probably, poverty and discrimination account for most of these differences. In our culture, as in most, it is still expected that the man will be the principal breadwinner of the family, yet the black man finds this much more difficult than his white counterpart, particularly if he has had little education and/or job training. In some ways, the welfare system, set up to counteract the effects of poverty, has also contributed to the instability of the black family. Because the most common welfare grants, Aid to Families with Dependent Children (AFDC), are given only to the mother, the system encourages the father to abandon his family and so establish the woman as head of the household.[13] It has also been suggested that the welfare system encourages black men to "abandon" their families because abandonment will enable the families to receive both welfare benefits and the husband's job earnings, each of which alone would be inadequate as a sole source of family support. In any event, women may come to regard men as unreliable providers and see little reason to marry. Instead, they may prefer a less formal arrangement that allows them to leave or to send the men away when they choose, while retaining full rights to any children of the union.[14]

In brief, insofar as the black family is distinctive, this is probably a consequence, for the most part, of the special intensity and duration of the poverty and discrimination suffered by black Americans. (See Chapters 7 and 8.) In effect, the black family is not so much a social problem as it is a current sociological issue; hence we shall not undertake a detailed study of the black family as such, but consider the evidence and possible causes of problems among families in general, bearing in mind that some of these may occur with particular frequency among the black poor.

Family Problems

The purpose of social organization, whether in society as a whole or in a small group such as the family, is collective action to achieve mutual goals. Since the most clearly necessary function of the family is the rearing of children, it is natural to judge the condition of a family by how well it appears to be doing this. Only recently have the emotional health and happiness of the adult members of the family come to be regarded as perhaps equal in importance to the welfare of the children; and even now, when the two appear to conflict, society usually takes the children's side. There is good reason for this, since children, especially young children, need care and protection if they are to survive in a world where death by starvation, exposure, disease, or physical abuse is quite possible. They also need proper education if they are to survive as assets and not as liabilities to society. Adults, having more strength, knowledge, and experience, are expected to be better able to fend for themselves and adjust to unfavorable circumstances.

In this section we shall consider a number of types of family problems

[13]Elliot Liebow, *Tally's Corner* (Boston: Little, Brown, 1967), p. 86.

[14]Hallowell Pope, "Unwed Mothers and Their Sex Partners," in *The Black Family: Essays and Studies*, ed. Robert Staples (Belmont, Calif.: Wadsworth, 1971), p. 365.

prevalent today. Two of these, illegitimacy and divorce, appear to be of particular concern to society. Both seem to threaten the institution of marriage, which is considered to be a vital part of American society. (In fact, as we shall see, there is some evidence that the high expectations people in our society have of marriage contribute to the incidence of divorce.) In addition, both family problems generally result in children who are being cared for by only one parent. This is not only widely considered to be bad for the child's development, but it might result in an additional economic burden to the rest of society. A third problem—abuse—whether of children or between spouses has existed for ages, but has only recently been regarded as a serious and widespread social problem.

Child Abuse   Child abuse is an ancient phenomenon. Until quite recently, the concept of "children's rights" was relatively unknown, and parents, teachers, and guardians were allowed virtually total authority over the children in their care. Severe treatment of the child was often justified by "the belief that severe physical punishment was necessary either to maintain discipline, to transmit educational ideas, to please certain gods, or to expel evil spirits."[15] Today, child abuse is a serious problem in the United States. According to the results of a national study of child abuse, over 1 million children in the United States are the victims of neglect or physical mistreatment each year; one in five, or 200,000, die from causes and "circumstances associated with abuse and neglect." Douglas Besharov, Director of the National Center on Child Abuse and Neglect, states: "If you have a communicable disease that struck as great a rate of children, you'd say you had an epidemic on your hands."[16] Only in the last few years has any attempt been made to deal with the problem on a national scale. The Child Abuse Prevention and Treatment Act, or the Mondale Law, was passed by Congress in January, 1974 to help states and communities organize programs for parents who abuse their children.[17] Also in 1974, the National Institute of Mental Health established a national center in Denver to study the problem more thoroughly and set up a national commission to resolve the complicated legal problems and to change federal and state laws involving child abuse.[18] Grant programs have also been funded under the new law to identify the causes of child abuse and to provide treatment through self-help programs and lay therapy.

Despite this, why has the general public shown so little concern until now? Several years ago, an authority on the subject noted:

> Our ignorance regarding the problems of child abuse and child neglect is . . . not quite total, but is severe enough to be inexcusable. We do not know what the incidence or prevalence of these conditions are. We do not know how to go about casefinding and/or identification of these conditions. We have little knowledge of how to discriminate levels of severity, and are poor at prognosticating future course, with or without available treatments, in many instances. Finally, we do not know how to "treat" either of these social conditions in the

---

[15]Samuel Radbill, "A History of Child Abuse and Infanticide," in *The Battered Child,* 2nd ed., ed. R. Helfer and C. Henry Kempe (Chicago: University of Chicago Press, 1974).

[16]"Child Abuse Rate Called 'Epidemic'," *New York Times,* November 30, 1975, p. 44.

[17]Celeste MacLeod, "Legacy of Battering," *The Nation,* June 8, 1974, p. 719.

[18]*National Conference on Child Abuse: A Summary Report* (Rockville, Md.: National Institute of Mental Health, 1974), p. 6.

sense of bringing about enduring change in the parents involved with much consistency, and with any efficiency. Other than that, we are scientifically in an excellent position.[19]

The reasons for this passivity to the problem of child abuse are many. One is the difficulty of definition. How are we to define child abuse? And how are we to establish that abuse has actually occurred in a particular case? Is the degree of injury to the child the only criterion, or must the parent's intention be considered as well? Elizabeth Elmer reports one study of 33 hospitalized children whose injuries (multiple bone injuries over a period of time) appeared to be unequivocal evidence of abuse; yet in 11 cases, or one-third of the total, the researchers concluded, after fuller investigation, either that the child had not been abused, or that it was impossible to tell whether he or she had been abused or not.[20] In a more recent study, Marc Marsden and David Wrench proposed the following definition of child abuse: "A deliberate attack against a child resulting in physical injury perpetrated by any person exercising his responsibility as a caretaker."[21]

As David Gil noted in 1970, this type of definition is unsatisfactory because in real-life situations "it may not always be possible to differentiate between intentional and accidental behavior."[22] In most cases the parents are the ones to testify, and a claim that the child's injury was "accidental" is hard to disprove. Although clinical advances have enabled physicians frequently to identify a specific "battered child syndrome," the problem of differentiation remains a serious one.

A second obstacle to research is a concern for the traditional rights of the parent and, unfortunately, one of these rights involves physical violence. As Suzanne Steinmetz and Murray Straus put it: "The most universal type of physical violence is corporal punishment by parents. Studies in England and the United States show that between 84 and 97 percent of all parents use physical punishment at some point in their child's life."[23] If parents are to be responsible for raising and training children, they need to exercise a certain degree of authority, including the right to punish. Our culture has traditionally approved of corporal punishment ("Spare the rod and spoil the child"), and has strongly defended the right of individual parents to govern their children as they think right. Ironically, one of the first court cases in which an outside agency successfully intervened to protect an abused child was the Mary Ellen case in New York City, in 1866, in which the plaintiff was the Society for the Prevention of Cruelty to Animals.[24]

The recent concern with "children's rights" has somewhat changed this picture. Child labor laws, actions of the Society for the Prevention of Cruelty to Children, and the changes in handling juvenile delinquents that have

[19]Norman Polansky, "The Current Status on Child Abuse and Child Neglect in This Country," *Report to the Joint Commission on Mental Health for Children*, February, 1968.

[20]Elizabeth Elmer, "Hazards in Determining Child Abuse," *Child Welfare* 45 (January 1966), 28-33.

[21]Marc F. Marsden and David F. Wrench, "Significant Findings in Child Abuse Research," in Emilio C. Viano, ed., "Child Abuse and Neglect," *Victimology Special Issue*, vol. 2, no. 2, (Summer 1977), 201.

[22]David Gil, *Violence Against Children* (Cambridge, Mass.: Harvard University Press, 1970).

[23]Suzanne K. Steinmetz and Murray A. Straus, "The Family as Cradle of Violence," *Society,* vol. 10, no. 6 (September/October 1973), 109.

[24]Serapio R. Zalba, "Battered Children," *Trans-Action* 8 (July–August 1971), 60.

resulted from the Gault decision of the Supreme Court (see Chapter 5) have helped to reinforce these rights. The rights of parents and the preservation of the family unit, however, are still regarded as of primary concern, even when the nature of the injury would, in any other situation, warrant criminal investigation and possible prosecution. Indeed, even in some of the worst cases, the traditional autonomy of the family unit keeps the authorities from intervening or even learning about the problem. Some researchers estimate that only one case in three is ever discovered.[25]

The belief that children are better off in their own homes is reinforced by the recognized inadequacy of facilities in many child-care institutions. When we consider that in one year in California alone some 20,000 children were found to need protective services,[26] the possibly disastrous effects of a wholesale removal of such children from their homes can be imagined. Partly for this reason, there has been an increasing movement toward alternative solutions that seek to treat rather than punish parents, in an effort to eliminate the causes of abuse without breaking up the family.

Some authorities feel that the definition of child abuse should be broadened to include psychological violence, malnutrition, inadequate medical care, poor education, and poverty. While these obviously harm the child, they are not usually as direct an effect of family interactions as are assault or neglect by parents or other home caretakers.[27] Hence, and for reasons of space, we shall restrict ourselves in this chapter to the narrower definition.

A number of recent studies have attempted to identify the significant social and cultural factors related to child abuse. Since the first nationwide study was undertaken only as recently as 1965, the findings of these studies must be regarded as preliminary.

Physical Abuse.   According to a study by David Gil, the victims of child abuse appear to be fairly evenly distributed over all age groups and between the two sexes, although there are some changes in sex distribution during different stages of childhood and adolescence. At least half of the victims had been abused prior to the reported incidence. A significant proportion of children seem to invite abuse through provocative behavior, although this plays a much smaller role in explaining attacks on children than the manner in which "American culture encourages subtle, and at times not so subtle, ways the use of 'a certain measure' of physical force in rearing children in order to modify their inherently nonsocial inclination." Of all cases of abuse, almost 90 percent were committed by the children's parents, and among these, 14 percent of the mothers had themselves been victims of abuse as children.[28]

The family in which there is child abuse typically manifests one or more of the following characteristics:

1.   There is only one parent with a very low level of educational attainment and low socioeconomic status.

[25]Laurie Beckleman, "Why the Cry of the Beaten Child Goes Unheard," *New York Times Magazine,* April 16, 1978, p. 85.

[26]Zalba, "Battered Children," p. 59.

[27]Marsden and Wrench, pp. 201–205.

[28]David Gil, "Child Abuse—A Nationwide Study of Child Abuse and Its Connection with Accident Research," in *Childhood Accidental Injury Symposium Proceedings,* ed. Roger J. Meyers (Charlottesville, Va.: University of Virginia School of Medicine, April 1966), pp. 19-26.

2. The family is likely to have received some kind of public assistance aid within a year of the abuse incident and has four or more children in it.

3. The family changes its place of residence frequently and the parents are highly authoritarian.

While this profile matches in many ways the one usually associated with families living in poverty, we must point out that any correlation is inherently biased by the fact that "the poor and nonwhites are more likely to be reported for anything they do or fail to do." There are, however, specific problems that are unique to poverty-striken families:

> The poor are subject to the same psychological conditions which may cause violent behavior toward children as the nonpoor; but, in addition to this, they are subject to the special environmental stresses and strains associated with socio-economic deprivation. Moreover, they have fewer alternatives and escapes than the nonpoor for dealing with aggressive impulses toward their children.[29]

Because studies based on official statistics tend toward an inherent bias against the poor, it is of interest to consider a study by Brandt Steele and Carl Pollock. For five and a half years the authors, both psychiatrists, studied 60 families in which significant child abuse had occurred. These families were not chosen by any valid sampling technique and therefore cannot be regarded as statistically representative; they were merely those who happened to come to the authors' attention. They did, however, span a wide range of socioeconomic and educational levels, and they included urban, rural, and suburban residents. The information obtained from them led the authors to conclude that poverty, alcoholism, unemployment, broken marriages, and similar social and demographic factors were less significant than previous studies had seemed to suggest. Rather, they found a typical personality pattern among abusive parents: the parent demands a high level of performance from the child, at an age when the child is clearly unable to understand what is wanted and unable to comply; and the parent expects to receive from the child a degree of comfort, reassurance, and loving response such as the child would ordinarily receive from the parent. The authors, quoting an earlier study, refer to this situation as "a reversal of the dependency role, in which parents turn to their infants and small children for nurturing and protection." When the expected performance and nurturing are not forthcoming, the parent retaliates as a small child might, with violence; but in this case, unfortunately, the violence is not by the weak against the strong, but by the strong parent against the weak and defenseless child.[30]

It is important to note that in *every case studied*, Steele and Pollock found that the abusive parents had themselves been subject in childhood to similar unreasonable demands, and that in a few cases they found evidence of the same experience among the grandparents. It would seem, therefore, that child abuse could well be part of a behavior pattern transmitted through the

---

[29]David Gil, "Physical Abuse of Children: Findings and Implications of a Nationwide Survey," *Pediatrics Supplement* 44 (November 1969), 862; and Gil, *Violence Against Our Children*, p. 92-138.

[30]Brandt F. Steele and Carl B. Pollock, "A Psychiatric Study of Parents Who Abuse Infants and Small Children," in Helfer and Kempe, *The Battered Child*, pp. 103-113.

An intolerable cycle of abuse is transmitted like other family patterns; child abuse is often perpetuated when abused children become abusive parents.
David R. White/Woodfin Camp & Assoc.

generations among some families, and that it might be found to correlate with other factors in family organization.

In order to break this cycle of abuse, some therapy groups have attempted to teach "parenting" techniques to mothers and fathers who themselves were abused children. The clinic workers try to supply these parents with substitute satisfactions and encourage them to call for help whenever they feel tempted to strike their children. Parents are also encouraged to seek meaningful relationships with other adults and not to invest their children's behavior with so much significance. Dr. C. Henry Kempe, who initiated the first treatment programs for parents at the Denver Child Abuse Center, found that 80 percent of the children could be returned to their parents "without risk of further injury, if their parents received intensive help during that period [when the child lived in a temporary foster home], and if there was a follow-up program after the child went home." For those parents who resist the "therapeutic approach" because of past unfortunate experiences with social workers, there is Parents Anonymous, established in 1970 and organized in ways similar to Alcoholics Anonymous. Regular meetings are held during which parents help each other to stop mistreating their children. There are now more than 100 chapters in the United States, and many other groups have begun to use the same technique.[31]

[31]MacLeod, "Legacy of Battering," pp. 719-20.

Some recent studies attribute the growing incidence of child abuse—a more than 35 percent increase since 1972—to wider social factors, such as economic recession and the typical isolation of the nuclear family. According to Vincent Fontana, head of New York City's Task Force on Child Abuse, the rising rate of abuse has been caused in large part by the economic frustrations of high unemployment and the deteriorating quality of life in the United States. In this view, child abuse now frequently occurs in more stable middle-class families because the recent recession has caused so many parents to be out of work. Unemployed fathers, unaccustomed to spending so much time at home, suffer from a loss of self-esteem and "unfocused rage" that they often take out on their children.[32]

Others see the lack of an extended family and friendly neighbors as being partially responsible for the high incidence of child abuse.

> There has probably never been a country where the nuclear family is as totally responsible for child raising, or where so many people live in isolation. . . . In other time and places, parents in stress could send their children to a sister or neighbor for a while. An abused child might run to such homes for refuge, until mom or dad calmed down. Infant battering was hard to hide when the rest of the family lived close by and neighbors knew one another well.[33]

Some social workers believe that an adequate number of day-care centers for abused children could provide the kind of refuge needed, and eliminate by half the number of placements of abused children in foster homes.

Psychological Abuse.   A less direct but no less damaging form of child abuse involves the growing pornographic exploitation of children. (For incest and child rape within the family, see Chapter 3.) Authorities estimate that some 300,000 children from the ages of 3 to 15 have been used in the production of pornographic films and magazines, having been photographed "in every imaginable sex act with each other and with adults."[34] In Los Angeles alone, police estimate that more than 3,000 children under age 14 are used in child pornography each year. Some of these children are runaways; others have been hired out by their parents or are filmed having incest with them.[35]

Researchers have found that some of these children "voluntarily" participate in pornography, by consenting to display themselves or to have sex with adults before the camera. Yet psychologists believe that most children are, nonetheless, victimized by the experience. Studies beginning in the 1930s have found that sexually exploited children have persistent difficulties coping with the problems of day-to-day life and a severely reduced ability to interact naturally with other children or adults.[36] As Dr. Judianne Densen-Gerber puts it: "They are emotionally and spiritually murdered."[37]

In conclusion, child abuse constitutes a serious and growing national problem. Although efforts have been made to identify its causes, the nature of

[32]"Hard Times for Kids, Too," *Time,* March 18, 1975, p. 88.
[33]MacLeod, "Legacy of Battering," pp. 719-20.
[34]"Child's Garden of Perversity," *Time,* April 4, 1977, p. 55; "Child Pornography: Outrage Starts to Stir Some Action," *U.S. News and World Report,* June 13, 1977, p. 66.
[35]Viano, "Child Abuse and Neglect," p. 176.
[36]Alvin A. Rosenfeld, "Sexual Misuse and the Family," *Victimology,* vol. 2, no. 2 (Summer 1977), 228-229.
[37]"Child Pornography," p. 66.

the problem and its solution indicate the need for expanded social services and legal protection, so that a wider-based attack on sources of environmental and psychological stress and a careful reconsideration of rights of children can be found. Some observers, such as David Gil, believe that violence between adults is directly traceable to the violence they received as children. Fontana emphasizes this same point: "The probable future tendency of abused children is to become murderers, robbers, rapists, and perpetrators of violence in society."[38]

Spouse Abuse   Instances of violence between spouses have long been acknowledged and even, to a degree, been tolerated as a part of domestic life. Wives are the most frequent victims (although instances of battered husbands are by no means unknown[39].) As with violence directed against children, the traditional autonomy of the family and the subordinate role of women within it have usually made the authorities reluctant to intervene.[40] Only recently has spouse abuse become an issue of social concern, and it is still difficult to assess its frequency and impact on American family life.

Many researchers believe that spouse abuse is directly related to the high incidence of violence in American family life. As Straus puts it: "There seems to be an implicit, taken-for-granted cultural norm which makes it legitimate for family members to hit each other. In respect to husbands and wives, in effect, this means that the marriage license is also a hitting license."[41] A recent survey found that 28 percent of the married couples interviewed had been involved at some time in physical violence against some member of their own family.[42] A subsequent study of more than 2,100 couples found that 3.8 percent of the husbands had physically assaulted their wives within the previous twelve months. "Applying this incidence rate to the approximately 47 million couples in the United States means that in any one year approximately 1.8 million wives are beaten by their husbands."[43]

Moreover, these attacks were seldom isolated instances. According to Straus, the typical pattern is between two and three serious assaults a year. During a five-year marriage, one woman had been repeatedly beaten—by hand and with a baseball bat—slashed with a knife, and had had her face pushed into a hill of red ants.[44]

A surprising number of these women make no attempt to leave their abusers. Lenore Walker suggests that this passivity is fatalism. A pattern of dependency, of "learned helplessness," is established early in many women's lives:

> It seems highly probable that girls, through their socialization in learning the traditional woman's role, also learn that they have little direct control over their

---

[38]MacLeod, "Legacy of Battering," p. 722.

[39]Suzanne K. Steinmetz, "The Battered Husband Syndrome," *Victimology*, vol. 2, no. 3–4 (Fall/Winter 1977), 499-509.

[40]Wayne King, "Right of Women to Self-Defense Gaining in 'Battered Wife' Cases," *The New York Times* May 7, 1979, p. A18.

[41]Murray A. Straus, "Wife Beating: How Common and Why?" *Victimology*, vol. 2, no. 3–4 (Fall/Winter 1977), 443-458.

[42]Steinmetz and Straus, "Family as Cradle of Violence," p. 109.

[43]Straus, "Battered Wives," p. 445.

[44]King, "Right of Women to Self-Defense," p. A18.

lives no matter what they do . . . . They learn that their voluntary responses really don't make that much difference in what happens to them. Thus, it becomes extremely difficult for such women to believe their cognitive actions can change their life situation.[45]

It has been traditionally argued that spouse abuse (and other types of family violence) are more common in lower-class than in upper- or middle-class families. William J. Goode, thus, theorized that lower-class children were socialized by their early experiences to regard violence as an acceptable solution to conflict situations, behavior that as adults they carried over to their own marriages.[46] Police statistics often seemed to bear this out. Crime and altercations involving the poor or minorities are far more apt to become police matters than similar situations among upper- or middle-class persons. (See Chapter 5.) And, in fact, a recent study found that per capita, the police were called upon to intervene in domestic situations as often in Norwalk, Connecticut, a largely white, middle-class suburb, as in Harlem, a predominantly black, lower-class section of New York City.[47]

Illegitimacy

Anthropologist Bronislaw Malinowski has suggested that in most primitive societies there is a social dogma stating that "every family must have a father; a woman must marry before she may have children; there must be a male in every household."[48] In other words, every child born is expected to be provided with a legitimate father who will act as protector and guardian. When this principle is violated, the violators are punished in some way.

Actually, there are societies in which marriage is not always a social prerequisite for parenthood. In parts of West Africa, for instance, a woman may bear a child out of wedlock, and no stigma will be attached either to her or to her child as long as there is reasonable certainty as to the father's identity. It is not sexual activity out of wedlock that is frowned upon, but rather promiscuity.

In our society many of the social stigmas traditionally associated with premarital pregnancy and illegitimacy have been reduced. Compared to a few years ago, relatively few illegitimate children today are given up for adoption. Nevertheless, premarital pregnancy is still frowned upon, generally because it indicates that sexual behavior out of wedlock has occurred; it is considered redeemable only if the couple is willing to marry before the child is born. Society still expects children to be provided with two recognized parents in at least a minimally stable and recognized situation, and the failure (or indifference) of parents in this respect may meet with various degrees of social condemnation. One form of such condemnation is the legal classification of the child as illegitimate.

It is important to bear in mind this legal aspect when considering the social problem of illegitimacy. Granted that the one-parent family faces

[45]Lenore Walker, "Battered Women and Learned Helplessness," *Victimology*, vol. 2, no. 3-4 (Fall/Winter 1977), 528-529.

[46]William J. Goode, "Violence Among Intimates," in *Crimes of Violence*, ed. D. Mulvihill and M. Tumin (Washington, D.C.: U.S. Government Printing Office, 1969).

[47]Morton Bard and Joseph Zacker, "The Prevention of Family Violence: Dilemmas of Community Intervention," *Journal of Marriage and the Family*, vol. 33 (1971), 677-682.

[48]Bronislaw Malinowski, *The Sexual Life of Savages in North-Western Melanesia* (New York: Halcyon House, 1941), p. 202.

special problems—and especially so in a society where the nuclear family is the norm—these problems are in themselves no different whether the single parent be unmarried, widowed, or divorced. Many of the distinctive difficulties of the unwed mother and her child, at least in the United States, are a matter of legal status.

The legal consequences of illegitimacy vary greatly from country to country and, in the United States, from one state to another. In many Communist countries, there are no legal sanctions against illegitimacy. In Sweden, Norway, and Denmark, for example, illegitimate children are given substantially the same rights as legitimate ones; however, in many countries, including the United States, the laws concerning illegitimacy are very old, and discriminate to some degree against the illegitimate child.

Usually, the major legal discrimination involves the child's right to inherit the father's property. For example, the New York State Court of Appeals has upheld a state law that prevents a child from inheriting from his or her father unless paternity has been established in court within two years of the child's birth and while the father is still living.[49] Other legal discriminations include the ineligibility of the mother to collect various forms of welfare support for the child, and the child's inability to use the father's name under certain circumstances. Historically, the "bastard" was legally *filius nullius*, no one's son. Gradually legislation was enacted that obligated the parents to provide support and to relieve the public of responsibility. Since that time—the sixteenth century—there has evolved a patchwork of laws on the subject, many of which are now common in the United States.

In 1964 the United States Supreme Court struck down as unconstitutional some laws that discriminate against the illegitimate child. In *Levy v. Louisiana,* the state of Louisiana had argued that greater rights should be granted to legitimate offspring than to illegitimate ones, primarily in order to safeguard the institution of marriage. But the Supreme Court decided that such discrimination was not justified, regardless of marriage, because it amounted to punishing one individual for another's behavior.[50] The Supreme Court has since further declared unconstitutional sections of the Social Security Act that prohibit illegitimate children of a disabled worker from receiving benefits if they were born after the worker became disabled. According to the Court:

> Illegitimacy is a characteristic determined solely by the accident of birth, . . . is a condition beyond control of the children, and is a status that subjects the children to stigma of inferiority and a badge of opprobrium.[51]

As a result of such decisions and others, it can be anticipated that the legal position of the child born out of wedlock will be substantially improved in the next few years. Already a number of states have discontinued the practice of noting illegitimate status on birth certificates, and at least two—Arizona and Oregon—have abolished the concept of illegitimacy

[49]"Supreme Court Roundup: Children of the Unwed," *New York Times*, December 12, 1978, p. B17.

[50]Harry D. Krause, "Why Bastard, Wherefore Base?" *Annals of the American Academy of Political and Social Science*, vol. 383 (May 1969), 65-67.

[51]"Illegitimates as Dependents," *Monthly Labor Review* (October 1974), pp. 68-69.

altogether.[52] This is a hopeful development, for, granted that legal disabilities hardly constitute the whole problem, their removal makes it much more likely that we shall be able to deal effectively with that part of the problem that remains.

Social Trends in Illegitimacy.   In the late 1950s, only about 5 percent of all births were to unmarried women; by the 1970s, more than 10 percent were.[53] This rise has occurred despite the fact that the overall birthrate—legitimate as well as illegitimate—is declining among women aged 25 and above.[54] The availability of more reliable contraceptives, the legalization of abortion, and declining peer group pressure to have children have all contributed to this general decline.

For women under 25 (and especially for those under 20), the statistics are quite different, however:

> More than one million adolescent girls get pregnant every year . . . . Of these about 60 percent have babies. About 600,000 of these babies are born every year—21 percent of all births in the country—and their mothers range in age from 12 to 19. Some 94 percent do not give up their babies for adoption. They decide instead to keep the infants, even though about half are still unmarried by the time of birth.[55]

Another researcher points out: "During the early 1970s, children born to unmarried 14- and 15-year-old girls increased by 75 percent."[56]

Women between the ages of 15 and 24 constitute roughly 40 percent of the total population of childbearing age, yet in a recent year they accounted for 80 percent of the illegitimate births.[57] Many of these women in this age group are not knowledgeable about the reproductive process and tend not to use contraceptives. For example, one study revealed that while 26 percent of unmarried, sexually active women under age 25 had never used contraceptives, 84 percent, nevertheless, strongly wanted to avoid becoming pregnant.[58] The relatively young age of these women suggests one reason why illegitimacy is a serious problem: the great majority of illegitimate children are born to girls and women who are simply not yet prepared, by education, experience, or maturity, to undertake the dual responsibility of parenthood and economic support. Unless some way can be found to overcome these disadvantages, society inevitably has to provide a good part of the family's support, usually through some form of welfare payments; and society has not shown itself notably generous about doing so.

The Problems of Illegitimacy.   Recent evidence suggests a growing acceptance of illegitimacy on the part of society. For example, in her study of unwed mothers, Prudence Rains found that "the most striking feature of the girls' accounts of their first experiences in finding themselves pregnant is the

[52]Krause, "Why Bastard, Wherefore Base?" p. 70.

[53]Keniston, *All Our Children*, p. 5.

[54]Reinhold, "Modest Revival for Marriage," p. C7.

[55]Lacey Fosburgh, "The Make-Believe World of Teenage Maternity," *The New York Times Magazine*, August 7, 1977, p. 7.

[56]John C. Kelly, "Epidemic: Teenage Pregnancy," *Family Health* (February 1978), p. 6.

[57]U.S. Bureau of the Census, *Statistical Abstract of the United States, 1975*, pp. 31, 56.

[58]Cynthia P. Green and Kate Poteteiger, "Major Problems for Minors," *Society* (May/June 1978), p. 8.

extent to which they expect far more severe reactions from others than they typically experience."[59] Similarly, Catherine Breidis found that "in spite of girls' anxiety about telling their parents of illegitimate conception, moral repercussions are seldom forthcoming."[60] The relaxation of sexual mores, the widespread increase in sexual activity, and the growing independence of women have resulted in the present situation, in which more unmarried women are having and keeping their children rather than obtaining abortions or giving their children up.[61] (See Chapter 9.)

In fact, when we speak of the social problems of illegitimacy today, we nearly always mean primarily the problems created by the presence in society of numbers of one-parent families headed by women unable to earn an adequate living for themselves and their children. The mother who gives up her child for adoption is absorbed back into the general population and ceases to be regarded as a problem—or at least as this kind of problem; and her child, if adopted, rarely becomes one. Likewise, the unwed mother who is able to support herself and her child, or the married woman who raises her illegitimately conceived child as a member of her legitimate family, arouses little concern.

Thus the problem of illegitimacy results from the fact that the lower-class unwed mother who decides to keep her child is likely to be ill equipped to support and care for it. Clark Vincent, in a study of white women attended at two California maternity homes, found that those who chose to keep their children scored lower, as a group, on a personality profile than did those who released their children for adoption. Those who kept their children were slightly older than those who did not, but had less education, and came from families of lower socioeconomic status. They were more likely to have experienced broken or mother-dominated homes, and showed more negative attitudes concerning sex. These findings corroborate the opinions of many counselors and caseworkers that "many of the unwed mothers who are most insistent on keeping their child appear the least likely, because of personality and family-life experiences, to become adequate mothers."[62]

In this sense, the social problem of illegitimacy is part of the problem of poverty, for middle- and upper-class unwed mothers who keep and raise their children are generally no less financially adequate as parents than their married counterparts. In one study of unwed mothers who kept their children, almost 42 percent reported incomes near or below the poverty line.[63] If this kind of situation is to be avoided, provision must be made to enable these women to complete their education and to obtain and hold adequate jobs. Counseling services must also be made available. Perhaps more important, in a preventive sense, the poor must be given greater access to birth control and abortion facilities. As it is, the unwed mother who is forced to rely on AFDC or other forms of public assistance is almost assured thereby of poverty and social disapproval. Our policy seems to be to provide enough help to keep people from freezing or starving, but not enough to enable them to become self-sufficient. For families with illegitimate children,

Bruce Roberts/Photo Researchers, Inc.

[59]Prudence Rains, *Becoming an Unwed Mother* (Chicago: Aldine, 1971).

[60]Catherine Briedis, "Marginal Deviants: Teenage Girls Experience Community Response to Premarital Sex and Pregnancy," *Social Problems* 22 (April 1975), 489.

[61]Fosburgh, "Make-Believe World of Teenage Maternity," p. 7.

[62]Clark E. Vincent, *Unmarried Mothers* (New York: Free Press, 1961), p. 191.

[63]Mignon Sauber and Eileen Corrigan, *The Six-Year Experience of Unwed Mothers as Parents* (New York: Community Council of Greater New York, 1970), p. 38.

adequate financial assistance, aid in all necessary aspects, and refusal to stigmatize are necessary. With these, many more of our illegitimate children and their mothers might be enabled to become accepted, contributing members of society, instead of being resented as burdens on the taxpayer.

All but unheard of in the nineteenth century and still rare before World War I, divorce has only recently come to be regarded as a relatively commonplace phenomenon. From the early 1930s until the late 1950s, divorce rates in the United States remained fairly constant—about 1.3 per 1,000 population.[64] As late as 1966, the divorce rate was still only 2.5. Today, about half as many couples get divorced each year as marry—1,122,000 divorces as opposed to 2,243,000 marriages—representing a divorce rate of 5.1 per thousand population.[65] Since the mid-1960s, in other words, the divorce rate has doubled. (See Table 11-1.)

This marked rise has affected almost all segments of society. The traditional correlations between socioeconomic and educational levels and frequency of divorce are no longer as true as they once were. For example,

Divorce

[64]William J. Goode, "Family Disorganization," in *Contemporary Social Problems*, ed. Robert K. Merton and Robert Nisbet (New York: Harcourt Brace Jovanovich, 1976), pp. 514-515.

[65]National Center for Health Statistics, *Births, Marriages, Divorces, and Deaths for 1978* (Washington, D.C.: U.S. Government Printing Office, 1979).

Table 11-1
Divorce Rates, 1960–1978

Year	Number of Divorces	Rate per 1,000 population
1960	393,000	2.2
1961	414,000	2.3
1962	413,000	2.2
1963	428,000	2.3
1964	450,000	2.4
1965	479,000	2.5
1966	499,000	2.5
1967	523,000	2.6
1968	584,000	2.9
1969	639,000	3.2
1970	708,000	3.5
1971	768,000	3.7
1972	845,000	4.1
1973	913,000	4.4
1974	977,000	4.6
1975	1,036,000	4.9
1976	1,077,000	5.0
1977	1,097,000	5.1
1978	1,122,000	5.1

Source: U.S. Department of Commerce, Bureau of the Census, *Statistical Abstract of the United States, 1978* (Washington, D.C.: U.S. Government Printing Office, 1978).

divorce used to be much more likely among those with only a high school education than among those who had completed college, and among the poor than the middle- and upper-middle classes. But in the last few years, the divorce rate has been rising among college-educated couples and among those in the higher socioeconomic groups.[66]

Divorce rate figures tell us relatively little, beyond suggesting a rough correlation with large-scale socioeconomic happenings—for example, low divorce and drastic economic recession, high divorce and the massive readjustment demanded by the end of an all-out war. A study by Abbott L. Ferriss of divorce rates, based on marriage cohorts—persons whose marriages took place in the same year—gives a somewhat more refined picture.[67] While it confirms the common belief that a marriage is most vulnerable in its early years—about one-third of divorces take place within the first three years of marriage and 65 percent within the first nine years—it also showed that in most cases the divorce rate for a given length of marriage remained fairly stable. There was a slight decline in the divorce rate for those marriages of six to seven years' duration or more. This analysis by cohort makes it possible to see more clearly where the strains are most likely to occur. It also suggests that the causes are to be sought not only in dramatic social changes but also in continuing basic conditions that may be somewhat aggravated by the special pressures of our time.

Some Explanations for Divorce Trends.   The institution of marriage is experiencing severe pressures today, and one of the results is the sharp increase in the frequency of divorce. To examine all of these pressures would be beyond the scope of this chapter, but we can point out some of the more easily recognizable ones. Most commonly cited, perhaps, is the change from the extended family to the nuclear family system. Another is the degree to which functions once performed by the family have now been assumed by outside agencies. Other factors are the relaxation of attitudes regarding divorce, the reformation of divorce laws so that divorces are more easily obtainable, and the growing number of educated women who can earn a living independently of their husbands. (The general change in role expectations, particularly among women, is fully discussed in Chapter 9.)

The change to a smaller family unit, coupled with the high mobility of many modern families, lays more complete responsibility on husband and wife for the satisfaction of one another's emotional needs. Where once there were plenty of relatives or long-term neighbors at hand, so that the marriage partners had others to go to when they needed companionship, today they must more often count on receiving it mainly from each other.

The decrease in family size has been accompanied by a decrease in family function. Food production, education, entertainment, and other activities once centered in the home are now performed by outside agencies. As Kenneth Keniston describes it:

> In earlier times, the collapse of a marriage was far more likely to deprive both spouses of a great deal more than the pleasure of each other's company. Since

[66]Paul C. Glick, "Some Recent Changes in American Families," in U.S. Bureau of the Census, *Current Population Reports*, Series P-23, no. 52 (Washington, D.C.: U.S. Government Printing Office, 1975), pp. 7-8.

[67]Abbott L. Ferriss, "An Indicator of Marriage Dissolution by Marriage Cohort," *Social Forces* (March 1970), p. 357.

family members performed so many functions for one another, divorce in the past meant a farmer without a wife to churn the cream into butter or care for him when he was sick, and a mother without a husband to plow the fields and bring her the food to feed their children. Today, when emotional satisfaction is the bond that holds marriages together, the waning of love or the emergence of real incompatibilities and conflicts between husband and wife leave fewer reasons for a marriage to continue. Schools and doctors and counselors and social workers provide their supports whether the family is intact or not. One loses less by divorce today than in earlier times, because marriage provides fewer kinds of sustenance and satisfaction.[68]

That is, the inducements—social and personal—to preserve the family are not as strong as they used to be.

Another probable cause of family tensions is the whole complex of difficulties that arise out of cross-class marriages. Scanzoni considers some of these in detail in a study based on interviews with wives in both continuing and dissolved marriages. He found that marriages were much more likely to be dissolved between persons of significantly different occupational or educational backgrounds. Thus 43 percent of divorced women in the study came from white-collar backgrounds and had married sons of manual or skilled workers; 18 percent came from families of skilled workers and had married sons of manual workers. A further 19 percent came from backgrounds of lower class than their husbands. By contrast, the largest percentage of women in existing marriages came from the same general occupational backgrounds as their husbands. Similar figures appear for educational level. This implies that persons of different backgrounds are apt to hold different expectations of achievement and behavior in marriage, and that these differences may create significant strains between the partners.

Further differences noted by Scanzoni may or may not be class-related. Partners in the dissolved marriages were less likely to share the same friends than partners in the existing marriages; conflict was more frequent in the dissolved marriages, and (at least as the wives perceived it) the husband was more likely to be the final decision-maker, with or without his wife's counsel. In most existing marriages, decisions were made together.[69]

Somewhat surprisingly, Scanzoni did not find very much difference between the dissolved-marriage and the existing-marriage groups with regard to their attitude toward divorce. Both groups apparently tended to believe both that marriage should be permanent and that divorce might sometimes be preferable. This led him to hypothesize that most people keep both beliefs "in readiness," as it were, and employ whichever is called for by their particular situation. The rise in divorce rates, he suggests, results from the increase in need for divorce and from the change in overall social arrangements that puts a greater strain on marriage.

Another study of marital stress suggests a more refined picture of the effect of class on marriage. Leonard Pearlin found that inequality in status was not in and of itself a significant cause of stress in marriage. A more important factor was the desire of a partner to improve his or her status. Those for whom status improvement was not important, or who married a partner of higher status, were relatively undisturbed by the different status of their partners.

[68]Keniston, *All Our Children*, p. 21.
[69]John Scanzoni, "A Social System Analysis of Dissolved and Existing Marriages," *Journal of Marriage and the Family* 30 (August 1968), 452-461.

Those who wished to improve their status, however, were more likely to experience marital stress if they had married a partner of lower status. In Pearlin's words:

> Status inequality by itself is of little or no consequence. The importance of such inequality to marital problems . . . depends on the meaning and value that are attached to it.[70]

Because of an increased tolerance for divorce, it can be presumed that partners who might once have resigned themselves to an unhappy marriage, or fought constantly but stayed together, may now feel more inclined to seek their freedom. Women—at least educated women—are better able than they once were to earn an adequate living, and the increasing tolerance of sexual activity outside of marriage liberates them in another aspect. In addition, the child of divorced parents is no longer likely to suffer embarrassment, pity, or discrimination in school. And the chances for remarriage of divorced persons, at least of men, appear to be fairly high.

There are still many problems associated with divorce, and these problems have not been reduced simply because divorce has become common. The process of divorce, even when it is desired by both partners, almost inevitably brings with it considerable emotional and financial burden. These stresses fall particularly hard on women, who may have to work and care for children without adequate economic and psychological help from their partners.[71] Well-educated women, because of the increased job opportunities available to them, are better able to cope and in fact may voluntarily choose not to remarry. Other women have more restricted options. Most husbands, for example, do not continue supporting their families after a divorce, although they are often legally required to pay at least child support. Divorced mothers are therefore frequently forced into poverty and have to accept welfare. They are also more intensely stigmatized by divorce than their husbands and are often refused credit in banks and department stores. Our society assumes that divorced people will soon remarry, and so adequate supports are not provided to single parents. In fact, because of their restricted social and economic opportunities, women are far less likely to remarry than men.[72]

Thus it is clear that divorce still creates problems both for the individuals involved and for society as a whole—particularly with the recent unprecedented increase in divorce. Many of the social and economic barriers to divorce that have been lowered undoubtedly created more severe problems now than in the past. It can be said, in fact, that most people have come to regard divorce as, if not always a good, at least a lesser evil in their own cases. These social and economic changes have been accompanied—sometimes with more than a little delay—by changes in divorce laws, the means by which society formally legitimizes the ending of a marriage contract.

[70]Leonard I. Pearlin, "Status Inequality and Stress in Marriage," *American Sociological Review* 40 (June 1975), 356.

[71]Campbell, "The American Way of Mating," p. 43.

[72]R. A. Brandwein, C. A. Brown, and E. M. Fox, "Women and Children Last: The Social Situation of Divorced Mothers and their Families," *Journal of Marriage and the Family* (August 1974), pp. 498, 501.

Divorce Laws.   American divorce law has its roots in medieval English ecclesiastical law. Under this law, absolute divorce was theoretically impossible, but legal separation was permitted, as was annulment if it could be shown that the marriage was invalid. These provisions, together with various informal arrangements, stretched the formal rigidity of the marriage law enough to make something equivalent to divorce available to a fair proportion of those who wished it.

A further provision, that of parlimentary divorce, was instituted during the period of the Restoration. By this means, a special statute could be obtained, decreeing divorce in a particular case. Since legislative divorce was extremely expensive, it was in practice available only to the very wealthy.

Ecclesiastical law was never introduced into the American colonies, but legislative divorce was, and it flourished, with considerable abuse, until constitutionally prohibited in the mid-nineteenth century. Judicial divorce—that is, the granting of divorce by the courts—developed in the eighteenth century. By the mid-nineteenth century, most states allowed divorce on several grounds, the most common being adultery, physical cruelty, and desertion. New York allowed only adultery as grounds for divorce, and South Carolina permitted no divorce at all until 1949.

In the first decade of the twentieth century, it became known that divorces could easily be obtained in Nevada, and it soon became common for persons from states with strict divorce laws to migrate to Nevada, establish residence for the necessary period (at first 6 months, later reduced to 6 weeks), obtain a divorce, and return home. Such "migratory divorce" was neither a new nor particularly American phenomenon, and after a number of court tests in the 1940s and 1950s, its validity was established, provided the granting state had jurisdiction over at least one of the parties at the time the decree was granted. This, of course, undermined the position of the states with stricter laws, and was probably one reason for the gradual addition of further grounds for divorce in most jurisdictions. New York, for instance, in its Divorce Reform Law of 1966, added abandonment, cruel and inhumane treatment, and imprisonment to its former sole grounds of adultery, and—perhaps more important—created new "no-fault" grounds whereby divorce became possible after a two-year separation agreement or decree.[73] A number of other states have made similar changes, and cruelty is now frequently construed to include "mental cruelty" or "mental suffering," which can almost always be alleged by the plaintiff if no more tangible grounds are available.

Nevertheless, many lawyers and others concerned with marriage and divorce are convinced that present laws need drastic reform. Their basic contention is that the very concept of "fault" in divorce proceedings is not only erroneous but harmful. Not only does it force the court to assign blame for a marital breakdown that is in reality the result of a whole complex of factors, but it makes the process of getting the divorce unnecessarily painful and damaging to everyone concerned. Intensely private and personal matters may have to be publicly discussed and even fought over, children may have to testify about their parents' behavior, and whatever bitterness and resentment are present are likely to be heightened and rendered more permanent. The

[73]Henry Foster, Jr., "Reforming a Divorce Law," *The Humanist* 30 (May-June 1970), 16-17.

consequences for the children, who are bound to be caught in the middle of such affairs, are especially bad.

Even when the divorce is uncontested—as the great majority are—the fault concept is dangerous, according to its critics. As David Cantor explains:

> Because the defendant can always delay a divorce, and often defeat it, the divorce itself becomes an object of trade . . . . The defendant . . . negotiates by offering the plaintiff an uncontested hearing—for a price. The price will normally be agreement to terms of alimony, support, custody, visitation or division of joint assets which the plaintiff, if not under duress, would not accept. These issues then become determined not on the basis of objective fairness, but rather on the basis of the plaintiff's desperation.[74]

Cantor's proposed solution is simple but drastic—anyone who asks for a divorce should be thereby entitled to it. He or she should not have to prove anything, nor should any defense or delay be permitted. This, Cantor feels, would free the discussion of arrangements regarding money and children from undue pressure, so that there would be a chance of a reasonably fair settlement. It would also minimize the emotional damage to both the parties and their children.

There is much to be said for this approach. It would amount to legal recognition of the fact that a dead marriage cannot be held together in any but the most superficial sense by court action, and of the parallel fact that the parties themselves are best qualified to know when the marriage is dead. As Joseph Goldstein and Max Gitter point out: "The state . . . has no way to implement a denial of divorce; it cannot force people to establish a meaningful relationship."[75]

Goldstein and Gitter's proposed divorce status differs significantly from Cantor's only in that it provides for a statutory waiting period between the initial application and the granting of the divorce. The state would be responsible for ensuring a fair settlement with regard to assets and children, but it would not be permitted to inquire into the reasons behind the divorce. The decision, by either party, to divorce would itself be taken as sufficient proof of marital breakdown.

> This policy—that no marriage must be *maintained* without the full and free consent of husband and wife—is but a concomitant of the state's policy that no marriage can be *established* without the full and free consent of the parties.[76]

Despite the misgivings on the part of those committed to the fault concept, or of those who fear that easy divorce will endanger marriage and the family, the trend seems to be in this direction. California was the first to eliminate most of the traditional grounds and replace them with one: "irreconcilable differences." Texas, while retaining the old grounds, has added the new one that divorce may be granted if the marriage has become "insupportable" to either party.[77] Since 1970 it has been possible to receive a divorce "on demand" in thirteen states; eleven more states have included a

---

[74]David J. Cantor, "A Matter of Right," *The Humanist* 30 (May–June 1970), 10.

[75]Joseph Goldstein and Max Gitter, "Divorce without Blame," *The Humanist* 30 (May-June 1970), 13.

[76]Goldstein and Gitter, "Divorce without Blame," p. 15.

[77]James B. Brady, "Introduction," *The Humanist* 30 (May-June 1970), 9.

no-fault provision along with the traditional fault grounds,[78] and by 1974 almost all state legislatures were planning to do the same. However, it would be misleading to conclude that no-fault divorce laws have won the day entirely, as Paul C. Glick points out:

> In states where no-fault is only one of several grounds for divorce, one spouse may threaten to charge the other "with fault" but settle for a no-fault divorce in return for a more favorable property or support settlement. For this reason, the number of no-fault divorces in those states may not indicate the true number of couples who obtained divorces without negotiations involving fault and the adversary concept.[79]

One woman in this group has adapted the structure of her family to the requirements of her profession. Her daughter has been sitting in on editorial conferences since she was five weeks old.
UPI

Alimony—the money one marriage partner pays for the support of the other, usually the husband to the wife—has been closely tied to the concept of fault and guilt in divorce proceedings. Until the no-fault provisions were adopted in most states, the main purpose of a divorce trial was to fix blame on one party or the other and to make the guilty party, usually the husband, pay a certain amount over and above what he would have paid ordinarily; if the fault rested with the wife, she would have received less than the ordinary amount. Now that a decree of divorce can be granted without the need to punish either partner, alimony can be awarded on the more realistic basis of financial need and ability to provide. Theoretically, this means that it would no longer be unusual for a man to receive some form of alimony payment from his ex-wife, if she has the greater earning power; and that a woman with no children will not necessarily be granted alimony from her husband, or, if at all, the alimony she receives would be only temporary to give her time to become self-supporting.

The no-fault reforms and reduced alimony settlements have, however, sometimes resulted in unfair treatment of women. The great increase in the number of divorces has released many women into an employment market that cannot absorb them. They have therefore been forced to seek welfare since the courts have had little power to compel so many ex-husbands to contribute to their ex-wives' support. Another injustice involves the rights to property held in common between husband and wife. Several states retain common-law property rulings that permit the holder of the title to the property to keep it. In this way, a woman may have allowed her husband to hold in his name assets belonging to both; if she divorces him, she loses any claim to this property and is not compensated for her loss by higher alimony payments.[80]

Another tendency in divorce reform has been for the courts to urge or to require some form of family counseling and therapy. In theory this is a good practice—reconciliation may sometimes be possible if the partners are helped to gain a better understanding of themselves and their problems, and if social agencies can do something to alleviate unfavorable external conditions (such as by locating a more adequate apartment or finding a spouse a job). The danger lies in the fact that such a system requires highly competent personnel and considerable understanding and sensitivity on the part of all the officials

[78]Steve McDonald, "The Alimony Blues: Now Women Sing Them, Too," *New York Times Magazine*, March 16, 1975, p. 20.
[79]Glick, "Recent Changes in American Families," pp. 8-9.
[80]McDonald, "Alimony Blues."

involved. In the hands of an unimaginative bureaucracy it could become a Kafkaesque monster, forcing on people useless "help" without understanding or sympathy. Until our family courts can be better financed and better staffed than they often are, compulsory reconciliation procedures seem risky. Optional services, provided by the exceptional official or provided in the unusually favorable personal situation, could, however, be of real value.

In conclusion, it can be said that while divorce represents the failure of a social institution—marriage—to provide the intended physical, emotional, and other satisfaction to its members, it also offers freedom to the parties, once such a failure has occurred, to start over on their own or to try marriage again. Divorce will probably never be a pleasant experience, but it can be made considerably less painful and harmful than it has generally been in the past. Divorce law reform is an important and necessary step toward that end.

Prospects

The family, as we have seen, is a dynamic institution, changing its shape in accordance with the needs of society. Possible indications of future change are evident in the symptoms of family problems that we have explored—illegitimacy, child abuse, the high divorce rate, and the plight of the aged. Clearly the family is in a state of flux, but the form it will ultimately take remains uncertain.

One important trend that has not been discussed so far but is symptomatic of the changing status of the family is the large increase in the number of those who remain single in the United States. Throughout the 1940s, single people accounted for only 1 out of every 10 households; now they account for 1 in every 5. Furthermore, young men and women at what have been considered the most marriageable ages—20 to 24 years—are choosing to remain single. In 1960, 28 percent of the women and 53 percent of the men in this age group chose to remain single; today, more than 40 percent of the women and 57 percent of the men had chosen to do so.[81] It is impossible to say whether this trend will continue indefinitely or how it will affect traditional living arrangements, but it does indicate a fundamental change in basic attitudes toward marriage and the desirability of family life. It would seem that young persons of marriageable age are more interested in experimenting with other life styles and developing their own potential than in conforming to traditional marriage patterns.

Today's low marriage and high divorce rates are not necessarily signs that family life is less valued today than in the past. Instead, the figures may mean that people are forming more realistic attitudes about what they expect from marriage; and with the easing of divorce and alimony laws, they are not hesitating to end unhappy relationships. Another factor in this trend is that women are finding more roles open to them than ever before in the employment market, are apparently enjoying their independence, and are discovering more satisfying alternatives to marriage. (See Chapter 9.)

The problems of child and spouse abuse have already begun to receive the prominent attention they deserve, and thus behavioral and social causes have started to emerge. We can hope, therefore, that they will be alleviated as public awareness grows.

[81]Glick, "Recent Changes in American Families," pp. 3, 12-13.

Summary

Kinship units consist of individuals related to one another through bloodlines or marriage, and usually take the form of *nuclear* or *extended families*. The small nuclear family is a product of industrial society; the new technological society that is now evolving from it has made some roles and functions of the nuclear family unnecessary.

The family is subject to many kinds of internal and external pressures that may cause tension and strain between family members and lead to various types of "empty-shell" marriages. Wives are increasingly finding outside employment, a trend that has been found to help family stability; they are having fewer children or none at all, a trend that indicates that many young wives do not regard childbearing as necessary to a woman's role. The female-headed family and its relationship to the welfare system have become a problematic issue.

The most prevalent symptoms of family problems today are child abuse, spouse abuse, illegitimacy, and divorce. The incidence of child abuse has risen drastically in the last few years, and several organizations are now dealing with the problem on a national scale. Spouse abuse is a serious problem and much more common than is generally supposed. Until abortion was legalized, the illegitimacy rate was on its way to an all-time high; even so, illegitimacy is still a serious social problem because of the legal sanctions against illegitimate children and the economic burden they may place on society. The divorce rate is now at its highest in history, and its incidence is not confined to any particular social class; the most common reasons for divorce include the increased tension within the isolated nuclear family, the taking over of family functions by outside agencies, the increasing independence of women, and the availability and acceptance of divorce. The no-fault divorce and alimony laws that have made divorce so easily available have also made divorced mothers a new deprived social group.

Bibliography

Adams, Bert N. *The Family: A Sociological Interpretation.*, 2nd ed. Chicago: Rand McNally, 1975.

Bernard, Jessie. *The Future of Marriage.* New York: Random, 1973.

Cooper, David. *The Death of the Family.* New York: Pantheon, 1970.

de Beauvoir, Simone. *The Coming of Age.* New York: Putnam, 1972.

Goode, William J., *et al. Social Systems and Family Patterns.* New York: Bobbs-Merrill, 1971.

Hartley, Shirley F. *Illegitimacy.* Berkeley: University of California Press, 1975.

Kephart, William. *The Family, Society and the Individual*, 3rd ed. Boston: Houghton, Mifflin, 1972.

Sussman, Marvin. *Sourcebook in Marriage and the Family*, 4th ed. Boston: Houghton Mifflin, 1974.

12

Corporate Power

Facts about Corporate Power

- The top 500 U.S. corporations account for 66 percent of all sales and 72 percent of all profits.
- Less than 1 percent of all corporations employ 75 percent of the total labor force.
- Since 1930, the number of workers employed by the federal government has increased by 350 percent.
- About 75 percent of all defense contracts are awarded to the nation's 100 largest corporations.
- In a recent year, more than 2,000 former high-ranking military officers were employed by the top 100 defense contractors.
- The annual sales of the largest companies often exceed the Gross National Products of many nations.

The child born in 1900 would, then, be born into a new world which would not be a unity but a multiple . . . . He could not deny that the law of the new multiverse explained much that had been most obscure, especially the persistently fiendish treatment of man by man; the perpetual effort of society to establish law, and the perpetual revolt of society against the law it had established; the perpetual building up of authority for force, and the perpetual appeal to force to overthrow it; the perpetual symbolism of a higher law, and the perpetual relapse to a lower one; the perpetual victory of the principles of freedom, and their perpetual conversion into principles of power . . . .[1]

When Henry Adams wrote his autobiography in 1906, he foresaw many of the problems of the latter half of the twentieth century. Born in 1838, Adams was the grandson of one president and the great-grandson of another. He was in a unique position to observe the problematic and far-reaching effects that the Industrial Revolution would have upon America. The pattern that he identified at the turn of the century is even more evident today. As the population of America grew from the 4 million of his great-grandfather's time to the 220 million of today, some erosion of individual independence has taken place. On a basic level, more people means that the significance of each person's opinion must count for less. More significantly, as society and its problems have become more complex, the individual citizen finds society's problems increasingly difficult to understand. We find ourselves baffled by a situation that often seems beyond the ability of anyone to control.

In the last quarter of the twentieth century, the United States remains the greatest democracy on earth. Yet the individual American is increasingly dwarfed by the sheer size and power of the government and economic system that exist to serve the common good. Theoretically, we exert our political influence at the polls and our economic influence by buying or refusing to buy in the marketplace. As Judge Learned Hand wrote, "Our democracy presupposes a multiplicity of tongues."[2]

[1]Henry Adams, *The Education of Henry Adams* (New York: The Modern Library, 1931), pp. 457-458.
[2]Quote reproduced in *The New York Times*, April 17, 1979, p. A19.

Today, however, the efficacy and validity of this system have been questioned. Many feel that, once elected, officials are subject to so many pressures that it becomes difficult, often impossible, for them to fairly represent their constituents. Yet the government's policies affect all Americans, not only the political leaders and civil servants who make them.

In the business sector, the picture is similar. The day of the small businessman, the self-employed entrepreneur, the family-run farm is rapidly fading, or perhaps is already gone. With the growth of national and multinational corporations, both workers and consumers seem to be components in a vast chain. Employees, of course, are directly affected by depending on the company not only for their salaries, but for a wide variety of benefits and services ranging from medical and pension plans to psychological satisfaction. But beyond the obviously dependent employees there are many others: the shareholder whose savings are invested in the company; the consumer who relies upon the company's product; the worker in a related industry whose job depends on the company's decisions; and the general public whose welfare is affected by the company's interest in maintaining environmental standards.[3]

The free-enterprise system, so fundamental to American history, has often been perceived as a self-regulating network.[4] Yet many economists argue that some restrictions are necessary just to counterbalance the natural advantages that corporations, by their very size and power, enjoy.[5] When a business dominates the production or marketing of a particular product, for example, the theoretical checks and balances of the free-enterprise system lose most of their meaning. As the effectiveness of market-imposed guidelines decreases, those decisions made within the corporation become more significant—in some cases, the oil industry, for example, affecting the welfare of the entire nation. Traditionally, the government and the American people have been reluctant to interfere with business activities. Increasingly, however, we have looked to the federal government to protect our welfare through legislation and a host of regulatory agencies. In effect, two bureaucracies—big business and big government—now deal with each other. This equation places new emphasis on their internal structure. Thus, before discussing the nature and relationship of a big business and big government, we must first understand the nature of bureaucracy.

Bureaucracy

Bureaucracies are seldom popular, but it would be naive to conclude that they have been thrust upon the majority by the self-serving minority. The formation of bureaucracies, both corporate and political, seems not only a natural evolution of society but a necessary one. Max Weber, who wrote the classic sociological study of bureaucracy, argued that bureaucratic organizations have recurred periodically throughout history because they are the most

---

[3]Ralph Nader, Mark Green, and Joel Seligman, *Taming the Giant Corporation* (New York: Norton, 1976), pp. 16-20.

[4]See Walter Adams, "Competition, Monopoly, and Planning," in *American Society, Inc.*, ed. Maurice Zeitlin (Chicago: Rand McNally, 1973), p. 245.

[5]John Kenneth Galbraith, *The Affluent Society* (Boston: Houghton Mifflin, 1976), p. 253.

efficient means of planning and executing complex, large-scale projects.[6] To provide mass goods or services to a vast population it is more expedient to create one large organization than several small ones. Both human and financial resources are conserved, and it is easier to standardize the quality and delivery of the finished product.

Weber contends that the efficiency of the bureaucracy is directly attributable to characteristics inherent in its structure. He defined these characteristics as

1.   fixed rules that apportion work systematically to each office or department;

2.   a hierarchical order in which work done by employees at one level is reviewed by other employees at a higher level;

3.   the maintenance of rules and regulations, in writing, that serve as a continuing blueprint for the organization;

4.   the accretion of skills by the employee while moving up in the structure to ensure that positions will be filled only by those possessing the necessary expertise;

5.   the freedom of the organization to achieve optimum use of the talents and abilities of those in its employ, in exchange for the assurance that office-holding is a secure, full-time pursuit;

6.   the standardization of procedures that can be both taught and learned, to guarantee maximum objectivity and efficiency in carrying out assigned tasks.

Weber's analysis applies both to corporate and governmental bureaucracies, for both are essentially alike in structure, operations, and decision-making procedures. When an organization expands, whether business or government department, not only its size, but its nature is transformed. Large organizations function differently than small ones *because* of their very size and complexity. For example, as many observers have pointed out, the larger the organization, the greater the gap between those who make decisions and those responsible for their execution.[7] When a business is relatively small, the company president can make, implement, and oversee policy. As the company grows, however, these tasks must be increasingly delegated to subordinates. In very large corporations those who make decisions are many times removed from those who implement them; and those who oversee the decisions—for example, plant managers and inspectors—are even lower on the chain of command. Often there is very little contact between these separate agents, often no consensus about goals, and no way for those outside the power echelon to share in making the decisions that they must ultimately oversee.[8]

Similar drawbacks affect the political bureaucracy. As departments expand and multiply, as elected officials rise from local to state levels and

[6]Max Weber, "Formal Characteristics of Bureaucracy," in *Readings in Introductory Sociology*, ed. Dennis H. Wrong and Henry L. Gracey (New York: Macmillan, 1967), pp. 380-381.

[7]Nader, *et al.*, *Taming the Corporate Giant*, p. 17; G. William Domhoff, *Who Rules America?* (Englewood Cliffs, N.J.: Prentice-Hall, 1967), p. 39.

[8]James S. Coleman, *Power and the Structure of Society* (New York: Norton, 1974), pp. 97-98.

from state to federal levels, their contact with the public often becomes increasingly remote.[9] The result is that, for the individual both to deal with and to work in, bureaucracies can become highly impersonal and frustrating structures. Bureaucracies, however, tend to relate well to other bureaucracies, particularly in their highest echelons.[10] As we shall see, the interlocking of corporate and political bureaucracies has engendered considerable concern. But before discussing this relationship, we must first assess certain aspects of the corporate and governmental bureaucracies.

Big Business

The United States' shift from an agrarian economy to an industrial one has been accompanied by a concentration of economic power in a relatively few large corporations. In their modern form, corporations are a relatively recent development in American history, arising from the burst of commercial and industrial activity on a national scale that occurred after the Civil War. At first, these new companies were dominated by the business magnates who created or controlled them, the so-called "robber barons," men like Andrew Carnegie, John D. Rockefeller, and J. P. Morgan. By the first decade of the twentieth century, the already large corporations were becoming still larger through expansion and merger with other companies. Real dominance by any one individual or even family became impossible. Instead, increasingly complex and sophisticated organizations developed in which effective control of the corporations' operations passed to salaried managers—bureaucrats, in effect—and legal ownership of the corporation was dispersed among thousands or even millions of shareholders.

This pattern is still in effect today, and its effects have become more intense as the sheer size and seeming all-pervasiveness of the modern giant corporation have grown through diversification and concentration of resources. Thus, American Telephone and Telegraph has more than 3,000,000 stockholders and as many employees as the state governments of California, Illinois, Michigan, Ohio, Pennsylvania, and Florida combined. ITT (the International Telephone and Telegraph Corporation) has absorbed companies ranging from hotel and car-rental chains to bakeries and publishing firms. Much the same could be said of any number of other huge corporations. While it has been argued that this is a necessary and beneficial development for a highly complex, industrialized society,[11] it also involves problems that will become apparent in our discussion.

The Shrinking Marketplace

To the American who is bombarded at every turn with advertisements, inducements to buy, and a staggering array of goods and services from which to choose, the concept of a shrinking marketplace is difficult to grasp. Yet while the number and variety of products seem to increase, their sources of production, in fact, diminish. Another prime example of this pattern is provided by the automobile industry. In 1904, there were some 35 manufacturers of American automobiles. With the founding of General Motors (GM) in 1908, this began to change. Although new companies continued to appear

[9]Domhoff, *Who Rules America?*, pp. 84-85.
[10]Gabriel Kolko, *Wealth and Power in America* (New York: Praeger, 1971), p. 57.
[11]John Kenneth Galbraith, "The Technostructure and the Corporation in the New Industrial State," in Zeitlin, *American Society, Inc.*, p. 225.

(there were 88 automobile and automobile-related concerns in 1921), large corporations like Ford and GM gradually acquired the smaller companies. While some independents survived until the late 1940s, the trend toward centralization accelerated. Today the automotive industry, perhaps the single most important industry in the country, is dominated by four key corporations that manufacture more than 90 percent of all automobiles produced in the United States.[12] From these parent corporations have sprung subsidiaries controlling everything from the raw materials used in production to automobile insurance, financing, and maintenance.

This pattern is called *oligopolization*—the division of wealth and power among fewer and fewer competitors. The acceleration of this trend since World War II, and particularly during the 1960s, has left the United States with a marketplace in which a relatively small number of producers control the consumer demands of buyers. As Ben B. Seligman has written:

> Indeed, the 500 largest industrial firms had sales in 1969 equivalent to almost half the gross national product, a gain of some 8 percent over 1962. Of all the active enterprises in the United States, only about 2,500 could be counted as economically significant, and these were controlled by no more than one-tenth of a percent of the recorded stockholders. More and more, the major economic activity of the nation was being sustained by the large corporations.[13]

Nor has this trend been reversed. Although there are about 200,000 manufacturing corporations in the United States, the top 500 corporations account for about 66 percent of the sales and 72 percent of the profits of all American industrial products.[14]

This concentration of economic power is not unique to the industrial section—it affects every sector of the economy. For example, Daniel Zwerdling has pointed out, the food industry became highly centralized in the 1970s. The Safeway Corporation, for instance, owns not only grocery stores (2,400 throughout the nation), but food manufacturing plants (109), bakeries (16), beverage bottlers (4), meat processing plants (3), coffee plants (3), warehouses (60), their own trucking fleet (2,100 tractor-trailers), and interests in such diverse operations as a fast food chain and plants that manufacture soap, peanut butter, and salad oil.[15]

Effect on the Workers. For the American worker, oligopolization means that a steadily decreasing number of employers have come to dominate the labor market. Of those workers employed in manufacturing in 1955, 44.5 percent worked for the top 500 firms; in 1977, more than 75 percent did.[16] This has had several effects: it has encouraged the development of another bureaucracy—that of big labor; it has narrowed the competition for workers' skills and services; and it has increased the likelihood that in the negotiations between big labor and big business, the public interest will rank third, if at all.

---

[12]Department of Commerce, *Annual Survey of Manufacturers, 1976: Value of Shipment, Concentration Ratios* (Washington, D.C.: U.S. Government Printing Office, 1978).

[13]Ben B. Seligman, *The Potentates* (New York: The Dial Press, 1971), pp. 325-326.

[14]Bureau of the Census, *Statistical Abstract of the United States, 1978* (Washington, D.C.: U.S. Government Printing Office, 1978), p. 578.

[15]Daniel Zwerdling, "The Food Monopolies," *The Progressive* (January 1976), p. 14.

[16]*Statistical Abstract of the United States, 1978*, p. 573.

AFL-CIO president George Meany addresses a rally in support of striking teachers. In many respects, big labor has come to resemble the giant government and corporate bureaucracies.
UPI

Effect on the Consumer.   For the American consumer, the outlook is no brighter, for oligopolization also means a less competitive marketplace. A direct result of decreasing competition can be seen in *parallel pricing*, sometimes called *price leadership*. Under this system, corporations within a given industry tend to maintain certain price levels. When U.S. Steel raises its price per ton, for example, Bethlehem Steel does the same; when one automotive concern announces a price increase, others follow suit. There is little incentive for a corporation to retain a low price. It is more advantageous for all companies concerned to raise their prices and share in the increased revenues. Prices can thus be artificially inflated, and the consumer can no longer choose from a large number of products whose prices are determined by competition. Instead, fewer products are offered, more or less similar, whose prices may only vary by pennies, if at all. Even a decrease in demand fails to lower prices, for parallel pricing is not responsive to ordinary economic principles. As Ralph Nader and others have concluded:

> Thus, in much of American industry, a few giant firms jointly act as would a monopolist or cartel. There are higher prices: the Federal Trade Commission has estimated that car and camera consumers overpay, respectively, nine and eleven percent for their products due to the concentrated structure of their industries.[17]

Advertising

When products are virtually indistinguishable in price and quality, manufacturers mount intense advertising campaigns to create the illusion of product differentiation. Advertising rarely makes consumers better-informed purchasers. Rather, it leads them to believe that romantic success depends upon a certain toothpaste; that the successful executive drives a certain kind of car; or

[17]Nader *et al., Taming the Giant Corporation,* p. 27.

that the housewife failing to clean her carpet with a certain product will incur the gossipy criticism of her guests. In a recent year, the top 100 national advertisers spent more than $3.6 billion to influence consumers—a bill which, ultimately, is paid by consumers in the form of increased retail prices.[18]

Even when faced with little or no competition, advertising campaigns continue. For example, the telephone industry, a virtual monopoly, spends millions of dollars annually to create a wider market for its products. It is not enough to subscribe to the service; consumers are cajoled to use their phones more frequently, to "keep in touch by long distance," to equip their homes with an abundance of telephones that are not merely utilitarian but elaborately—and expensively—decorative.

Conglomerates

"No Frills" household items offer one alternative for the consumer who wants to save money and escape the constant bombardment of product advertising.
UPI

There is a strong rationale for the monopoly of the telephone industry, which is sanctioned and protected by the government: service is most effectively provided by a single company. Separate companies, each with its own power network, would increase the number of telephone poles and feet of wire without necessarily guaranteeing subscribers the ability to contact the customers of competing companies.

Other near-monopolistic corporations, however, are less easy to justify. Certainly, mergers (the combining of separate businesses into a single enterprise) have contributed to corporate oligopolization. While America experienced previous waves of mergers (in 1898–1904, 1919–1921, and 1926, for example) no movement was as far-reaching as that of the late 1960s. Three thousand mergers occurred in 1967 alone, a rate 25 percent above that of 1966. This practice of achieving corporate power through an endless series of mergers has been attributed to the impotence of federal anti-trust laws.[19] Other advocates point out that, while legislation like the Cello-Kefauver Act of 1950 can control certain types of mergers, it has done little to regulate the formation of conglomerates.

The conglomerate, a combination of firms operating in greatly diversified fields, is a special phenomenon of the 1960s. Among the potential dangers of unsupervised conglomerate mergers are the loss of competition (through acquisition of competitors), reciprocity (in which a parent company buys and sells exclusively among its subsidiaries), entrenchment of leading firms when acquired by a strong parent company, tacit agreements by conglomerates to respect each other's spheres of monopolization, and greater corporate secrecy (as, for example, when subsidiaries do not issue separate financial statements but are grouped under the data of the conglomerate).

Many of these conglomerates launch intensive public relations campaigns to affirm the virtues of free enterprise and reinforce the concept of individualistic American free enterprise. The Mobil Oil Company, for example, one of the world's largest conglomerates, with assets in the billions of dollars, consistently sponsors cultural events and advertises in newspapers to promote its image as a benevolent force in the economy and even national security of the United States.[20]

[18]*Statistical Abstract of the United States, 1978*, p. 855.
[19]Seligman, *The Potentates*, p. 329.
[20]See, for example, Mobil Oil Company advertisment, *The New York Times*, May 24, 1979,

Despite the image conglomerates seek to project, they often appear impersonal and are only rarely associated with individuals. As Seligman has stated, "By the nineteen-sixties, the personal touch was no longer the dominant motif in American business. It was the impersonal corporate entity that was to set the tone of the economic environment."[21] At its most beneficial, this trend helps guard against the ascendancy of individual dictators.[22] Yet it can also produce a remote leadership. As Robert Heilbroner put it, "we are left with a largely faceless group known as 'management' whose names the public neither knows nor cares about."[23]

Some economists and sociologists ascribe this development to the growing power of technicians. In the early 1920s, Thorstein Veblen argued that technologists, through their unique ability to control the apparatus of production, had, in fact, become the dominant economic force in society.[24] More recently John Kenneth Galbraith has used the term "technostructure" to denote what he considers the key group within the corporation:

> It extends from the most senior officials of the corporation to where it meets, at the outer perimeter, the white and blue collar workers whose function is to conform more or less mechanically to instruction or routine. It embraces all who bring specialized knowledge, talent or experience to group decision-making. This, not the management, is the guiding intelligence—the brain—of the enterprise. There is no name for all who participate in group decision-making or the organization which they form. I propose to call this organization the Technostructure.[25]

Other sociologists dispute this thesis. For example, Leonard Silk and David Vogel argue that technologists only achieve decisive power within a corporation by transforming themselves into "profit-oriented businessmen."[26] What seems indisputable, however, is the gulf between top corporate management and the general public.

The Federal Bureaucracy

Like big business, the federal government has vastly expanded since World War II. In 1929, the federal budget was equivalent to about 1 percent of the entire gross national product (GNP); today, it is almost 20 percent of the GNP.[27] And, as might be expected, an ever-increasing number of workers is being diverted from private industry into the services of the governmental bureaucracy. As the government produces no product—and, indeed, often

[21]Seligman, *The Potentates*, p. 327.

[22]Leonard Silk and David Vogel, *Ethics and Profits* (New York: Simon & Schuster, 1976), p. 206.

[23]Robert Heilbroner, *The Limits of American Capitalism* (New York: Harper & Row, 1966), p. 25.

[24]Thorstein Veblen, *The Engineers and the Price System* (New York: Augustus Kelly, 1963), p. 16. (Originally published in 1921.)

[25]John Kenneth Galbraith, *The New Industrial State*, 2nd ed. (Boston: Houghton Mifflin, 1971), p. 71.

[26]Silk and Vogel, *Ethics and Profits*, p. 207.

[27]U.S. Office of Management and Budget, *The Budget of the United States Government* (Washington, D.C.: U.S. Government Printing Office, 1977), p. 278.

The invocation of the House of Representatives: the increasing growth and centralization of the federal government has accompanied the increased size and power of corporations.
UPI

succeeds only in creating inefficient, self-perpetuating agencies—this trend is of dubious advantage for the national economy. Yet, since 1930, the number of workers employed by the federal government (excluding military personnel) has risen by about 350 percent.[28]

This expansion has accompanied and encouraged a transference of power from the states and municipalities to the federal government. The centralization of power within the government bureaucracy has paralleled a similar trend in the corporate bureaucracy, and with similar dangers—the control of resources by a relatively small group and a decline in the ability of the majority to influence the decision-making minority.[29] Yet, this has not been thrust upon the American citizen unaware. It is ironic that the American public, always suspicious of big business, has itself encouraged the centralization of the federal bureaucracy by its strident requests for governmental

[28]Department of Commerce, Bureau of the Census, *Historical Statistics of the United States* (Washington, D.C.: U.S. Government Printing Office, 1975), p. 1102; *Statistical Abstract of the United States, 1978*, p. 278.

[29]Advisory Commission on Intergovernmental Relations, *Improving Urban America: A Challenge to Federalism* (Washington, D.C.: U.S. Government Printing Office, 1976).

protection and intervention. The outcry against big government has grown even louder since the Watergate scandals, yet we continue to look toward Washington to solve any number of problems. If the federal government is expected to plan, provide, and administer an ever-increasing variety of services (services formerly in the private sector or performed by states or municipalities), then its continued bureaucratic growth is inevitable.

Unfortunately, mere bureaucratic growth does not guarantee each citizen an increased share of the benefits. As with the corporate bureaucracy, there is a tendency for resources to be trapped within the structure. Not infrequently, federal programs fail because of sheer bureaucratic inefficiency—the allocated resources having been either consumed by mismanagement and the misappropriation of funds or rendered virtually inaccessible by thickets of red tape. Other programs seem to be administered not to solve the current social problems or meet the national needs for which they were ostensibly enacted, but to benefit a particular business or industry. The classic example is the relationship between the Pentagon and the defense industry, the so-called military-industrial complex. But other instances are furnished by federal health and housing policies. (See Chapters 2 and 14.)

Big Business and Big Government

This is not to deny that governmental involvement in the economy cannot provide both direct and indirect benefits to individuals. For example, government-guaranteed mortgage and educational loans have simultaneously allowed many to enjoy a higher standard of living and helped to boost the overall economic outlook.[30] Students who receive a better education will be more employable and their life-long contributions to society—in work as well as in increased tax revenues—will more than repay the government's initial investment. With mortgage loans, the increased demand for houses serves to stimulate the housing industry that employs thousands of American workers. Just as these measures help individuals, they also benefit the industries whose products the consumer can now afford to buy.

The ultimate efficacy of these programs, however, depends upon the willingness of business to make similar investments; otherwise the government merely succeeds in creating a cycle in which taxpayers repeatedly overpay for the "benefits" they receive because the bureaucracies must be paid to keep the system in operation.

The federal government offers other incentives to big business in the form of tax subsidies, favorable legislation, and a climate that is generally sensitive to the needs of large corporations. These measures also help individuals by stimulating economic growth; it would be naive to dismiss all government-to-business assistance programs as harmful. What is attractive to big business, however, is not necessarily in the public's interest. Some method of regulation must be found to keep business from pressing an unfair advantage. Corporations can exert political influence by making campaign contributions to legislators sympathetic to their interests, by maintaining personal friendships with those highly placed in the government, by the interchange of executives on the topmost administrative levels, and by employing professional lobbyists to represent their interests in Washington.[31]

[30]Ben B. Seligman, *Economics of Dissent* (Chicago: Quadrangle Books, 1968), p. 275.

[31]John S. Lang, "Drive to Curb Kickbacks and Bribes by Business," *U.S. News & World Report*, September 4, 1978, pp. 41-44.

The individual consumer, the common stockholder, and the middle-income worker do not enjoy these advantages to the same degree.

> When a major corporation from a state wants to discuss something with its political representatives, Senator Philip Hart has said, "you can be sure it will be heard. When that same company operates in 30 states, it will be heard by 30 times as many representatives."[32]

Yet despite literally thousands of regulations, attempts by the government to neutralize the power of the corporate bureaucracy and protect the interests of the individual have, to date, not proven wholly effective.

The Problems of Government Regulation

The Regulating Agencies.   To understand the failure of governmental intervention, it is necessary to know something of the regulatory agencies themselves. These bureaus are semi-autonomous federal agencies whose members are appointed by the President for a set term to oversee either a particular industry (the Food and Drug Administration, for example), or some aspect of the whole economy (the Occupational Safety and Health Administration, for example). The upper echelons are not composed of consumer advocates; rather, they are largely staffed by former business executives. It is not at all unlikely, for example, to find the former president of one of the big four automobile producers presiding over a commission on automotive safety. The limitations of such a system are self-evident: although the chairpersons thus elected have an indisputable knowledge of the field, their interests are so vested that, even in their most conscientious efforts, they have difficulty being impartial.[33] Those who appear before them are often old friends; makes and models nominated for recall may be the very projects they helped create. Moreover, there is nothing to guarantee that those appointed to watch-dog agencies have severed their ties with the industry they are asked to regulate. As we shall see, there is a revolving-door rate of exchange between the corporate bureaucracy and the governmental one, with top executives moving easily from one sector to another and back again. As C. Wright Mills has pointed out:

> Since government regulation of business has become important, a government job has become important as one link in a business or legal career in the private corporate world. One serves a term in the agency which has to do with the industry one is going to enter. In the regulatory agencies especially, public offices are often stepping stones in a corporate career, and as organizations the agencies are outposts of the private corporate world.[34]

The Fitzgerald Case.   Under these conditions, the interests of government and those of corporate America frequently converge. The emphasis is on the "team player," and the person who blows the whistle is looked upon as a troublesome outsider. A classic example of the inefficacy of the regulatory

[32]Ralph Nader and Mark Green, "2 + 2 = 3," *The New York Times*, April 17, 1979, p. 19.
[33]Lester B. Salamon and Gary L. Wamsley, "The Federal Bureaucracy: Responsive to Whom?" in *People vs. the Government*, ed. Leroy N. Reeselbach (Bloomington, Ind.: Indiana University Press, 1975), pp. 151-152.
[34]C. Wright Mills, *The Power Elite* (New York: Oxford University Press, 1956), p. 240.

procedure can be found in the case of A. Ernest Fitzgerald. In November 1968, Senator William Proxmire, chairman of the Senate's Joint Economic Subcommittee, investigated the cost of the C-5A cargo plane, built for the Air Force by the Lockheed Aircraft Corporation. Fitzgerald was himself a member of the Air Force—deputy for management systems in the Office of the Assistant Secretary of Defense for Financial Management—and his particular specialty was cost control. When Fitzgerald appeared before the Proxmire subcommittee, he testified that production of the C-5A involved a $2 billion overrun. This was not news to Air Force analysts, who had detected the overrun at least two years before. Yet the Air Force presented a team front; plans for the C-5A went forward, and the possibility of spending more than $2 billion over the initial figure was never disclosed. The boondoggle came to light only because of Fitzgerald's personal initiative and sense of responsibility—for which he was dismissed by the Department of Defense.[35]

On the surface, the C-5A incident involved the efforts of one arm of the federal government (the Senate) to regulate another (the military). Yet this is deceptively simplistic. Big business was a prominent figure in the issue in the form of Lockheed, the corporation in possession of the $2 billion overrun contract. The fate of A. Ernest Fitzgerald underscores a basic flaw in the existing regulatory system: when a person's livelihood is intricately connected with the industry he or she is asked to oversee, it can be difficult to place the public welfare ahead of one's own. For example, when young executives from Detroit are recruited to evaluate automobile safety, is it reasonable to expect them to regulate their own industry and possibly thwart their own careers? Because watchdog agencies have hitherto failed to take this into account, they have, as John Kenneth Galbraith has stated, "become, with some exceptions, either an arm of the industry they are regulating or servile."[36] In the final analysis, regulatory programs implemented by the government seem to have failed to represent the private citizen.

The Military-Industrial Complex.   The case of A. Ernest Fitgzerald and the efforts of Senator Proxmire's committee to make the Pentagon accountable for its expenditures bring us to another facet of government-corporate relations—military spending. The military, of course, is indisputably a part of the federal government. And since most military spending is awarded to large corporations, the government has become virtually a partner of big business in the allocation of wealth. Today a substantial percentage of annual corporate profits derive from defense contracts.[37] As President Eisenhower wrote: "This conjunction of an immense military establishment and a large arms industry is new in the American experience . . . . In the councils of government we must guard against the acquisition of unwarranted influence whether sought or unsought, by the military-industrial complex. The potential for the disastrous rise of misplaced power exists and will persist."[38]

Because military spending is done in industries that employ civilian workers, the immediate effect benefits the economy. Increased spending

[35]Ralph Nader, *et al.*, *Whistle Blowing: The Report of the Conference on Professional Responsibility* (New York: Grossman, 1972), pp. 39-40.

[36]John Kenneth Galbraith, *The Great Crash* (Boston: Houghton Mifflin, 1972), p. 171.

[37]Charles H. Anderson, *The Political Economy of Social Class* (Englewood Cliffs, N.J.: Prentice-Hall, 1974), p. 220.

[38]President Dwight D. Eisenhower, *Farewell Radio and Television Address to the American People*, January 17, 1961.

during World War II finally ended the Depression and opened a new era of American prosperity. Wartime spending during the Korean War, the Cold War, and the war in Vietnam similarly stimulated the economy. Conversely, when military spending decreased as, for example, by $10 billion in 1953–54 following the Korean War, the economy declined sharply. Despite the positive effects, it can be argued that America has become dangerously dependent upon military spending to stimulate economic growth.[39] Indeed, the present economic structure is so reliant upon massive defense spending that budgetary curtailment is almost impossible. As Seligman has pointed out, a substantial—50 percent—cut in the military budget would be economically unfeasible:

> It is clear that a decrease in military spending in the kind of economy we now have would depress the level of GNP and, in human terms, create no little amount of unemployment. A successful disarmament program would be of great concern not only to those industries involved in research and development, electronics, aircraft, and the like, but to all the peripheral industries which service them.[40]

While military spending has stimulated the economy in the short run, its long-term effects can be far less desirable. "The suspicion grows," Seligman warns, "that business investment may have been displaced by governmental spending, especially for war purposes, as the prime mover in the American economy." When government spending displaces private investment, an artificial element is built into the economic structure. Because it is the taxpayer who is the ultimate source of all federal funds, it is his direct cash outlay—not that of industry—that supports the economy. As investment from the private sector decreases, a proportionate increase in federal spending is required to keep the economy from faltering; and as federal spending increases, so, of course, do taxes. In effect, taxpayers are paying both to keep themselves and other taxpayers in defense-related industries and to provide those industries with profits.

The military-industrial complex is firmly entrenched in the American economy, and the largest and most influential corporations benefit most from it.[41] Of the billions of dollars' worth of defense contracts awarded annually, about three-quarters have gone to the nation's 100 largest corporations.[42] As Charles H. Anderson has written:

> Many firms are largely or virtually entirely military contractors, and many others depend upon defense spending for their profit margins. From 1961 to 1967 [for example] Lockheed received $11 billion in defense contracts, constituting 88 percent of its total sales; General Dynamics received $9 billion for 67 percent of its sales; McDonnel-Douglas $7.6 billion for 75 percent; Boeing $7.1 billion for 54 percent; and Ling-Temco-Voight $8 billion for 70 percent. Other firms represent themselves as civilian producers but are big military contractors as well: General

[39]See Harry Magdoff, "Problems of U.S. Capitalism," in Zeitlin, *American Society, Inc.*, pp. 295-296.

[40]Seligman, *Economics of Dissent*, p. 277.

[41]See David Baulton, *The Grease Machine: The Inside Story of Lockheed's Dollar Diplomacy* (New York: Harper & Row, 1979).

[42]Marc Pilisuk and Tom Hayden, "Is There a Military-Industrial Complex That Prevents Peace?" *Journal of Social Issues*, vol. 21, no. 3 (July, 1965), 77.

Electric received $7 billion during this period, AT&T $4.1 billion, General Motors $2.1 billion . . . .[43]

Moreover, military spending is characterized by an absence of competitive bidding and, as we have seen, by the government's acquiesence in huge cost overruns.[44] The Proxmire subcommittee's investigation into the Air Force C-5A overrun was only one example. Lockheed had in fact filed overrun claims on four previous contracts. The government's offers of settlement were rejected by Lockheed, who seemed willing to take the matter to court. Meanwhile, the aircraft corporation insisted, the government should continue to underwrite the massive overrun costs of the C-5A program. As Senator Proxmire wrote at the time:

> The reason for the claims, simply stated, is that Lockheed is spending far more on the contracts than the government originally agreed to pay. The question is, who picks up the tab for the cost overruns, the contractor who entered into binding commitments with the government, or the taxpayer? . . . Naturally, this corporation has the right to demand anything it wants to demand. But is it necessary, is it even legal or proper, for the Pentagon to accede to all of its demands?[45]

The full extent of the advantages enjoyed by major defense contractors is best illustrated by the practice of subcontracting that occurs when the corporation in possession of a government contract hires a smaller, secondary firm to manufacture the stipulated product. This secondary firm can produce cheaper and more efficiently than the contract-holding corporation; yet the government, because of the Defense Department's commitment to a select few corporations, is seldom even aware of the secondary firm's role. Instead, it is the large corporation that reaps the reward, subcontracting to obtain the product at a low price and selling it to the government at a substantial profit. The waste of this practice is obvious, even to military personnel themselves who have pointed out that "millions could be saved if the Army could . . . 'break out' subcontracted elements of the system, that is, buy them directly from the manufacturer rather than through one or two middlemen."[46]

The interests of corporations within the military-industrial complex are represented in Washington by professional lobbyists. There is also a less formal, purely personal alliance that exists between the Pentagon and its major contractors. The Proxmire subcommittee found that a disproportionately high number of ex-military personnel were employed within the defense industry. More than 2,072 former officers (ranking colonel, Navy captain, or higher) were employed by the top 100 contractors, and their positions within the corporations tended to be influential ones. Though Senator Proxmire was careful to emphasize that there was no indication of collusion or wrong-doing, and that this practice did not violate any existing laws, he warned against such alliances:

[43]Anderson, *The Political Economy of Social Class*, p. 255.

[44]Donald C. Baron, "Federal Waste: The $50 Billion Rathole," *U.S. News & World Report,* September 18, 1978, p. 29.

[45]William Proxmire, "The Whistle Blower as Civil Servant," in Nader, *et al., Whistle Blowing: The Report of the Conference of Professional Responsibility,* pp. 17-18.

[46]Joseph Goulden and Marshall Singer, "AT&T and the IBM," in *The Military-Industrial Complex,* ed. Carroll W. Pursell, Jr. (New York: Harper & Row, 1972), p. 240.

But what can be said, and should properly be said, is that there is a continuing community of interest between the military, on the one hand, and these industries on the other.

What we have here is almost a classic example of how the military-industrial complex works.

It is not a question of wrongdoing. It is a question of what can be called the "old boy network" or the "old school tie."

This is a most dangerous and shocking situation. It indicates the increasing influence of the big contractors with the military and the military with the big contractors. It shows an intensification of the problem and the growing community of interest which exists between the two.[47]

The Power Elite   The strong alliances formed between the government, the corporate world, and the military have led some to suggest that there is, in fact, a single power elite that controls the wealth of the American economy. C. Wright Mills, one of the earliest proponents of this theory, argues that:

> There is no longer, on the one hand, an economy, and, on the other, a political order, containing a military establishment unimportant to politics and to money-making. There is a political economy numerously linked with military order and decision. This triangle of power is now a structural fact, and it is the key to any understanding of the higher circles in America today. For as each of these domains have coincided with the others, as decisions in each have become broader, the leading men of each—the high military, the corporation executives, the political directorate—have tended to come together to form the power elite of America.[48]

In *The Power Elite*, Mills sites several factors in contemporary American society that promote the formation and maintenance of a ruling class:

1.   the shared interests of the industrial, military, and political institutions;

2.   the similar backgrounds, objectives, and perspectives of men in the upper levels of these institutions, and their high rate of interchangeability;

3.   the filling of key positions with men who, "by training and bent, are professional organizers of considerable force and who are unrestrained by democratic party training."[49]

The ascendance of the power elite has, according to Mills, produced several negative effects. These include the decline in the power of elected officials; the semi-organized stalemate of legislative activity; the creation of a civil service responsive to the power structure; and the increased transference of the decision-making process from the public (or public-audited) to the private sector.

[47]Speech by Senator William Proxmire, "Over 2,000 Retired High-Ranking Military Officers Now Employed by 100 Largest Military Contractors," *Congressional Record*, 91st Congress, 1st session, March 24, 1969.
[48]C. Wright Mills, *The Collected Essays of C. Wright Mills*, ed. Irving Louis Horowitz (New York: Oxford University Press, 1963), p. 27.
[49]Mills, *The Power Elite*, p. 296.

Mills is the classic proponent of the existence of an elite power-holding class, but he is not alone in his conclusions. As recently as 1976 Leonard Silk and David Vogel noted that "the displeasure of businessmen increases as government becomes more responsive to nonbusiness pressures."[50] Silk and Vogel were referring specifically to the lethargy big business has shown in acceding to environmental standards and product safety codes, and its disinterest in tempering profit-motive with social conscience. (See Chapters 13 and 16.) The inequality on which industrial efficiency rests can have far-reaching and detrimental repercussions. As Silk and Vogel put it, "The pattern of authority and reward within the firm becomes, for businessmen, the desirable model against which to compare political and economic relationships in the rest of the society." Nader has taken a similarly pessimistic view, predicting the need for far more stringent regulatory measures than any that now exist:

> Undue corporate power is incompatible with democracy for two reasons. First, democracy assumes the clash of many voices in the political marketplace, a clash big business can dominate by its size and resources. And second, though corporate executives decry the rise in government bureaucracy, their own actions may make it inevitable. Unless business comes to completely control government—a flash point we have not yet reached—a democratic government must eventually attempt to impose some form of public authority over private power.[51]

Multinational Corporations

Few aspects of the discussion of corporate power are more controversial than the operations and even the existence of multinational corporations. The definition of a multinational corporation is extremely broad. David Blake and Robert Walters define it as "those economic enterprises that are headquartered in one country and that pursue business activities in one or more foreign countries."[52] In this sense multinationals have existed at least since the international banking houses of the Italian Renaissance.[53] American firms like Singer, United Fruit, and Firestone have had extensive foreign operations— and political influence—since the late nineteenth century.[54]

For the most part, however, these were national companies with secondary foreign operations. The sharp rise in foreign investments and the concentration of financial resources that followed World War II have led to the development of *supra*-national corporations. These companies are international organizations that operate across national boundaries, whatever their country of origin may be. The size, wealth, influence, and diversity of operations of these corporations have grown enormously. The United States Chamber of Commerce estimates that by the year 2000, 54 percent of the

---

[50]Silk and Vogel, *Ethics and Profits*, p. 191.

[51]Nader, *et al.*, *Taming the Giant Corporation*, p. 224.

[52]David H. Blake and Robert S. Walters, *The Politics of Global Economic Relations* (Englewood Cliffs, N.J.: Prentice-Hall, 1976), pp. 80-81. Much of the discussion that follows is based on the account of multinationals in Chapter 4, "The Multinational Corporation: Challenge to the International System?"

[53]A. W. Clauson, "The International Corporation: An Executive's View," *The Annals of the American Academy of Political and Social Science*, vol. 403 (September 1972), 21.

[54]Richard J. Barnet and Ronald E. Muller, *Global Reach: The Power of the Multinational Corporations* (New York: Simon & Schuster, 1974), pp. 41, 87.

Despite the picketers, stockholders of the multinational Eastman Kodak Company overwhelmingly rejected a proposal to withdraw its South African operations. Protesters saw a conflict between Kodak's interest in South Africa and United States human rights policy.
UPI

world's projected wealth—some $4 trillion in assets—will be controlled by a few hundred multinational firms.[55] Already, for example, the annual sales of companies like GM, International Telephone and Telegraph (ITT), and the Seven Sisters of the petroleum industry exceed the GNP of many nations—not just those of the poorer countries of the Third World, but of highly industrialized countries like Switzerland and South Africa.[56]

Critics have charged that these companies are, in effect, autonomous states with their own interests and foreign policies, which they place above any national allegiance.[57] But because most of the multinationals are American in origin with headquarters in this country, Americans and others tend to see them as American companies. As a result, their operations affect both the economic and foreign policies of the United States more than those of other countries. The United States government has traditionally and legitimately protected the foreign investments of American companies. Critics of the multinationals, however, argue that the interests are put before those of the nation and, indeed, often conflict with them. They see the close relations that exist between the upper echelons of business and government as responsible for inducing government to intervene to protect the interests of United States-based multinationals.[58] The complicity of the Central Intelligence Agency (CIA) and the Nixon Administration in the overthrow of the Allende regime in Chile is the most famous example of this type of action.[59] (Allende had confiscated various American-based commercial holdings, particularly those of ITT and mining companies.) Other United States-based multinationals have regularly used bribery and kickbacks to secure foreign orders.[60] Critics of the multinationals emphasize that because the world rightly or wrongly associates such multinationals with the United States, the actions of these companies can often discredit the United States in the eyes of foreign opinion.

At home, labor leaders have charged that by investing so heavily abroad (in a recent year, United States-based multinationals had foreign investments in excess of $107 billion[61]), these companies have been responsible for the United States' losing more than 900,000 jobs between 1965 and 1971 alone.[62]

Supporters of multinationals, on the other hand, consider these firms both necessary and beneficial. The increasing interdependence of the world's economy, they argue, is itself a positive development and requires companies to operate as widely as possible.[63] Moreover, they point out that most countries, from highly industrialized countries like Britain to developing states like Kenya, encourage foreign investment. Problems between multinationals and host governments undoubtedly can arise, but, as Blake and

[55]Nader, et al., Taming the Corporate Giant, p. 28.

[56]Louis Turner, Invisible Empires (New York: Harcourt Brace Jovanovich, 1971), pp. 135-136.

[57]See Anthony Sampson, The Sovereign State of ITT (New York: Fawcett, 1974).

[58]Blake and Walters, Politics of Global Economic Relations, pp. 199-205.

[59]Barnet and Muller, Global Reach, p. 83.

[60]See Boulton, The Grease Machine.

[61]U.S. Department of Commerce, Special Survey of U.S. Multinational Companies (Springfield, Va.: National Technical Information Service, 1972), p. 3.

[62]Blake and Walters, Politics of Global Economic Relations, p. 101.

[63]Jack N. Behrman, National Interests and the Multinational Enterprise (Englewood Cliffs, N.J.: Prentice-Hall, 1970).

Walters put it: "If multinational firms were purely exploitative in their activities, they would be denied access to most countries."[64]

Supporters of multinationals also argue that far from hurting the economy, these companies generate exports and thereby create jobs for American workers and markets for American goods. In 1970, for example, commerce between American headquarters and their foreign subsidiaries accounted for almost a third of all American exports.[65]

As with large corporations in the United States, the problems with multinationals seem to arise not from their existence but from their regulation.

Prospects

It might appear that the simplest way to safeguard the individual American citizen lies in strict regulations limiting the size of corporations. Yet this conclusion would be extremely short-sighted. Smaller is not necessarily better, and corporate size can be beneficial. Many large businesses make contributions to the American standard of living that small operations could not match. For example, technology is greatly furthered by the "shared effort" aspect of the corporate bureaucracy, in which large companies can afford to employ the most gifted teams of researchers and engineers available. Moreover, large corporations provide the consumer with reasonably priced, mass-produced goods. When a corporation acquires a subsidiary to manufacture parts used in the assembly of its finished product, for example, the consumer ultimately profits. Because the subsidiary company supplies the necessary parts to the parent corporation at a cheaper rate than would an independent manufacturer, the saving is reflected in the retail price. America, home of the world's largest corporations, also offers its citizens perhaps the greatest access to goods and services. The very richness and complexity of American life must also be reflected in its government. The federal government has grown in size and power because in the twentieth century the American people felt that they needed it. As with the corporate bureaucracy, the government does not need to be made smaller, but more responsive to the needs of individual Americans.

How this responsibility is to be effected is still uncertain. Abuses by the bureaucracy, either within the corporate structure or the governmental one, are the result of two factors: the inadequacy of existing regulations and the willingness of any bureaucracy to take advantage of them. But bureaucracies are composed of individuals. Still strong in our national ideology is the concept of the individual American by whom and for whom the country was founded and is run. And it is still primarily the individual American who must make the system work. Willingness to blow the whistle on government policies and corporate actions that take unfair advantage of the ordinary citizen will succeed not only in bringing specific incidents to light but in creating a climate that demands high levels of government and corporate accountability.

[64]Blake and Walters, *Politics of Global Economic Relations*, p. 100.

[65]U.S. Congress, Senate Committee on Finance, *Implications of Multinational Firms for World Trade and Investment and for U.S. Trade and Labor*, 93rd Congress, 1st session (1973), p. 180.

Mere citizen vigilance, however, is not enough. As we saw, the cost overrun of the C-5A was exposed, but who approved the project in the first place? Some form of official review must, it seems, be implemented at the decision-making level. Official regulatory measures fall into two categories: those which are self-regulatory and are implemented within the corporation or governmental branch, and those which are initiated outside the structure and mandated by law. Christopher D. Stone suggests that one way of eliciting responsibility from within the corporation is by altering the traditional structure of the board of directors. For example, he proposes that 10 percent of the membership of any board be composed of persons with no financial interest in the corporation.[66] The president of Harvard University, Derek C. Bok, has suggested reforms in the education of corporate executives to emphasize the ethical and public responsibilities of businesses and "the proper division of power between government and the corporation."[67]

Internal methods of regulation and review can also be brought to bear upon the governmental bureaucracy. Several steps have already been taken. For example, the General Accounting Office, an independent agency that reports directly to Congress, can now audit the efficiency of all departments of the executive branch of the federal government. Another step was the passage of the Freedom of Information Act in 1974, which forbids the government from denying access to all information not deemed vital to the national security.

One reform currently being tried out by several cities and states is the originally Scandinavian institution of the Ombudsman. The Ombudsman is an officer of Parliament who investigates citizens' complaints against the bureacracy and recommends remedies when they are justified. Ombudsmen on a national scale already exist in Sweden, Finland, Denmark, Norway, New Zealand, Canada, Ireland, and the Netherlands. A federal Ombudsman might be an effective ally for the rights of individual citizens.

[66]Christopher D. Stone, *Where the Law Ends* (New York: Harper & Row, 1975), pp. 139-150.

[67]"President of Harvard Seeks a Restructuring in the Business School," *New York Times*, April 30, 1979, p. 14.

Summary

As America has grown in size, wealth, and power, the role of the individual citizen has been gradually eroded. This has partly been the result of the growth of political and corporate bureaucracies. The government and corporate bureaucracies are similar in structure and are likely to relate well to each other. The decision-making minority have more contact with each other than with the masses whose lives they affect. The tendency of government to form alliances with big business and *vice-versa* has led many to argue that new systems of regulation and review must be designed to protect the ordinary citizen.

The trend in modern American business is toward centralization, in which fewer and fewer companies assume more and more power. The practice of merging (the combining of separate companies into a single enterprise) has contributed to this trend. Recent mergers have produced conglomerates (combinations of companies operating in separate industries) that further reduce competition in the marketplace. This pattern is repeated within the government bureaucracy, which steadily expands.

While the intermingling of government and corporate concerns can sometimes help the economy, it can also prove detrimental. Efforts by the government to establish supervisory agencies have, to date, been largely ineffective largely because these agencies are staffed with executives whose careers are rooted in the corporate world.

The military-industrial complex is another example of the strong alliances that bind the corporate bureaucracy to the political one. The intermingling of high-ranking corporate, political, and military personnel have led some to speculate that there exists, in America, a power elite—a small group that controls inordinate amounts of wealth and power.

More evidence of the corporate takeover can be seen in the emergence of multinational corporations that operate across national boundaries. To make government and big business accountable for their actions, individuals must become more alert, and new methods of regulation and review must be developed and implemented such as the Scandinavian office of the Ombudsman, an official of Parliament who investigates complaints against the bureaucracy.

Bibliography

Barnet, Richard J., and Muller, Ronald S., *Global Reach: The Power of the Multinational Corporation*. New York: Simon and Schuster, 1974.

Coleman, James S., *Power and the Structure of Society*. New York: Norton, 1974.

Galbraith, John Kenneth, *The New Industrial State*, 2nd ed. Boston: Houghton Mifflin, 1971.

Mills, C. Wright, *The Power Elite*. New York: Oxford University Press, 1956.

Nader, Ralph, Green, Mark, and Seligman, Joel, *Taming the Giant Corporation*. New York: Norton, 1976.

Nader, Ralph, Petkas, Peter J., and Blackwell, Kate, *Whistle Blowing*. New York: Grossman, 1972.

Stone, Christopher D., *Where the Law Ends: The Social Control of Corporate Behavior*. New York: Harper and Row, 1975.

Zeitlin, Maurice, ed., *American Society, Inc.*, 2nd ed. Chicago: Rand McNally, 1977.

13

Work

Facts about Work

- 30 years ago, 1 married woman in 5 was in the labor force; today the ratio is almost 1 out of every 2.
- Since World War II, the average work week has decreased from almost 60 hours to 36.2 hours.
- Over 100 studies in the last 20 years have demonstrated that almost all workers want responsibility in their jobs as well as the feeling that the work they do has significance.
- Each year more than 390,000 cases of job-related illnesses occur and more than 100,000 Americans die of such illnesses.
- Every working day 14 million workers may be exposed to toxic substances as part of their job.
- In a recent year, occupational maladies cost industry $11 billion dollars in compensation and 25 million lost workdays.

"What do you want to be when you grow up?" is a question first asked of little children. The question becomes more pressing, and by the time of high school graduation, at least a tentative vocation is chosen. Thus we are introduced to the great importance of work in our society.

A division of labor exists in all societies, if for no other reason than to provide food and shelter for all the members. Our society requires some form of employment if a person is to stay in the mainstream of life; it is scarcely an exaggeration to say that we are largely defined by our work. Ostensibly, everyone has an opportunity to work; and one of the major responsibilities of our entire educational system is to train people to work in the occupations and professions that keep society functioning. While unemployment compensation and welfare payments are available to those who are temporarily out of work or unable to support themselves, such compensation is designed for maintenance at a subsistence level.

It would seem, therefore, that work is more than a means to provide the worker with the essentials of life and society with goods and services. In our society, great emphasis is placed on the "work ethic"; we believe in the value of work. Because work is considered useful, productive, and honorable, most people feel that to consider themselves worthwhile and to be so considered by others, they must work. Thus, when a representative sample of people was asked: "If by some chance you inherited enough money to live comfortably without working, do you think that you would work anyway, or not?" 80 percent said that they would prefer to keep on working.[1] Another study, limited to manual and service workers, replicated this finding: 83 percent of these workers said that they would continue working even if they had enough money to stop.[2]

The importance of work in our society is also indicated by the extent to which it determines a person's place in the social structure. In the past, birth

[1]Nancy C. Morse and Robert S. Weiss, "The Function and Meaning of Work," *American Sociological Review* (April 1955), p. 191-198.

[2]Curt Tausky, "Meaning of Work Among Blue-Collar Men," *Pacific Sociological Review* 12 (Spring 1969).

largely determined social position, and vocational choices available. Today the situation has changed somewhat. Self-determined vocational choice largely defines our social position. We value jobs differently, but we nearly always accord status on the basis of occupation. This partly explains the reluctance of many older persons to retire; employment gives them a place in society, and permits them to participate in and contribute to community life. (See Chapter 10.)

Work has not always been so esteemed; the ancient Greeks considered it a curse imposed on humanity by the gods.[3] Except for large-scale agriculture, the birthright of aristocrats, work was believed to brutalize the mind and leave it too coarse or too fatigued to contemplate truth or practice virtue. As Aristotle remarks in his *Politics:* "No man can practice virtue who is living the life of a mechanic or laborer," and "We call those arts vulgar which tend to deform the body, and likewise all paid employments, for they absorb and degrade the mind."[4] Although the Romans regarded commercial banking as acceptable employment, in general they too considered work vulgar and demeaning.

The Hebrews' attitude toward it was somewhat ambivalent. Like the Greeks, they regarded work as drudgery; but they also believed that it was penance for original sin. Herzberg has discussed this attitude toward work as the difference between an "Adam" view of human nature and an "Abraham" view.[5] Adam, expelled from the Garden of Eden, is forced to work for his daily bread. For Abraham, God's chosen man, however, work is less an act of the body than a means of spiritual fulfillment.

The early Christians inherited this more complex concept of work and elaborated upon it. They accepted the idea of work as a punishment for original sin, but they also believed that people worked both to make their own living and to help those in need. Thus work became important to physical and spiritual well-being. But, as Adriano Tilgher notes, it still had no intrinsic worth in itself.[6]

With the advent of Protestantism and the rise of capitalism, work became an acknowledged basis of society. Martin Luther believed that labor was a service to God, and thereby endowed work with a certain religious significance that it has not lost even today. It was John Calvin's teachings, however, that transformed the religious view of work into a wellspring of modern capitalism. Calvin preached that work is the will of God, but that people should renounce the fruits of their labors and use their profits to launch new ventures, which in turn would provide more profits for investment, and so on. Humanity must discipline itself to work ceaselessly to make the Kingdom of God manifest on earth. Calvin also believed that no one should be bound to an occupation by the accident of birth. Instead, he argued, people should do the work that brings the greatest success to self and society. These religious ideas and the development of a more democratic society helped to destroy the ancient aristocratic disdain for labor that became the roots of our modern-day ethic of work for work's sake, stripped of its religious connotations.

Because people work for so much of their lives, it is important to try to

[3]Adriano Tilgher, "Work Through the Ages," in *Man, Work, and Society,* ed. Sigmund Nosow and William H. Form (New York: Basic Books, 1962), pp. 11-12.

[4]Aristotle, *Politics,* Book 3, section V; Book 8, section 11 (Jowett translation).

[5]Frederick Herzberg, *Work and the Nature of Man* (New York: World, 1966), pp. 15-16.

[6]Tilgher, "Work Through the Ages," pp. 13-20.

understand the social problems related to work. In this chapter, we shall discuss five of these: unemployment, occupational health, automation, the need for job satisfaction, and leisure time. Each affects a significant number of people. The economic recession of the late 1970s created a serious and growing unemployment problem in our society, with serious personal and social implications.

Increasing automation, while it may provide many benefits, also causes problems. Many consider it a threat to job security, but, in fact, the social implications of automation are much more complex. It is widely feared that increased automation may subordinate people to the machine, resulting in more depersonalized tasks that offer the worker very little satisfaction. The use of leisure time may not seem at first to be a problem at all since we would all like more free time. Yet the use of the increasing leisure time available to most employed Americans poses special problems that could change the work ethic itself.

The physical toll exacted by work has always been a serious problem. But modern industrial conditions have aggravated the possibility of grave and permanent damage from both job related accidents and pollution.

Trends

Work, like other important aspects of our society, has been changing significantly. Before discussing the problems in detail, we want to explore four patterns of change, or trends, which seem significant: the increase in the number of white-collar workers; specialization; the emergence of an "employee society"; and changes in the age and sex composition of the labor force.

The Increase in White-Collar Workers

The greatest change in America's occupational structure has been the transition from an agricultural economy to an industrial distributive one, dominated by large corporations and government organizations. The magnitude of the resulting change in the labor force can be gauged from a few figures. In 1900, 27 percent of the total labor force were farm workers and 18 percent were white-collar workers. In 1978, just over 3 percent of the total labor force were farm workers, whereas nearly 48 percent were white-collar workers.[7]

White-collar workers—professional, managerial, clerical, and sales personnel—now comprise the largest occupational category in the nation, surpassing the blue-collar group in 1956. Most of the new white-collar jobs are professional and clerical. Clerical personnel have increased by more than 500 percent since 1900 and include about 17.8 percent of all employed persons. Clerical workers now vie with skilled and seimiskilled workers as the largest occupational group in the labor force.

The decline in farm employment since the turn of the century has been as dramatic as the rise in white-collar employment. Farm workers—farmers, managers, and farmhands—once the largest occupational category in the United States, are now the smallest.

While the total proportion of blue-collar workers in the labor force has

[7]*Statistical Abstract of the United States, 1978* (Washington, D.C.: U.S. Government Printing Office, 1979), p. 481.

remained stable since about 1900, their composition has undergone some important changes. Semiskilled and skilled operatives and craftsmen have increased proportionately, while the proportion of unskilled labor has decreased.

Similarly, the slight overall net gain shown by service occupations masks some important changes within that category. People employed as private household workers are now only 1.4 percent of the total labor force; in 1900 they were 5 percent of the total. Other service personnel—hotel workers, guards, waiters, and barbers—have increased their proportion by 200 percent. They now comprise 13.7 percent of all employed persons, as compared to 4 percent in 1900.[8]

Specialization

Our discussion of the shift to a white-collar economy involved only four broad categories of employment (white-collar, blue-collar, service, and farm workers). Within these categories, of course, there are literally thousands of jobs. The *Dictionary of Occupational Titles*, published by the Department of Labor, lists 21,741 different jobs—a total that contrasts sharply with the 325 occupations recorded by the 1850 census.[9] The vast difference indicates the increasing specialization of labor and the complexity of its divisions. Wilbert Moore emphasizes that this increase in specialization has been so great that it may now be more appropriate to speak not of the division but of the diversification of labor.[10] He noted some of the unusual jobs one might choose—tea taster, water smeller, clock winder, and the like.

Specialization of labor: an elephant pedicurist.
UPI

Specialization has several important implications. First, lower-echelon workers who were trained only for a single, narrow job, and who lose that job, may have difficulty finding another like it. Second, these workers often feel that they are merely adjuncts to a machine or a process, with little chance to develop and use more than minor skills or abilities. This feeling often prompts dissatisfaction with work. Finally, the increase in specialization has created problems of worker coordination and cooperation that present the managers of organizations with some of their greatest challenges.[11]

An Employee Society

It is not uncommon, upon asking people what they do for a living, for them to respond with the name of the organization for which they work. Increasingly, the modern American worker is an "employee." After 1950 the proportion of working people classified as self-employed dropped to less than 10 percent of the work force. Small business owners, independent shopkeepers, and some family-owned and family-managed companies survive, of course, but their number diminishes every year, and each year they employ less of the labor force. Self-employment is disappearing because small business owners find it increasingly difficult to compete against the large corporations in industry, farming, and the professions. In addition, many prefer the job security of

[8]*Statistical Abstract of the United States, 1978*, p. 418.
[9]Seymour Wolfbein, *Work in American Society* (Glenview, Ill.: Scott, Foresman, 1971), p. 45.
[10]Wilbert E. Moore, "The Attributes of an Industrial Order," in Nosow and Form, *Man, Work, and Society*, p. 46.
[11]Harry Braverman, *Labor and Monopoly Capital: The Degradation of Work in the Twentieth Century* (New York: Monthly Review Press, 1974), pp. 31-32.

working for a large organization to the high risks of entrepreneurship. As self-employment and small-business opportunities dwindle, more people work for government, large corporations, unions, public school systems, universities, hospitals, and most other private and public institutions. (See Chapter 12.)

Age and Sex Composition of the Labor Force

The labor force, as defined by the government, consists of all persons, 16 years of age or over, not in institutions, who worked one hour for pay during one survey week (the employed) and those who did not work during the survey week, do not have a job, and are actively seeking work (the unemployed).[12] In this group, the most significant trend is toward the inclusion of married women and the exclusion of older men.

Older men are being eliminated from the labor force primarily because of educational and occupational obsolescence. As discussed in Chapter 10, employers hesitate to keep or hire older men when younger and better-trained people are available, usually at lower salaries. Middle-aged women have displaced older men in many clerical and professional jobs, and young high school and college graduates are starting to replace them in all fields. Whereas 40 percent of males over 65 were in the labor force in 1954, by 1964 only 28 percent were still in the work force;[13] by 1977 they had declined to 19.3 percent. Meanwhile, more women aged 20 to 64 have entered the labor market, with the first great increase appearing in the 45-to-54 age-group. Forty-one percent of these women participated in 1953-1954; by 1977 their rate of participation had risen to 55.5 percent. The second great increase occurred between 1965 and 1975, as young women in the 20-to-34 age-group joined the labor force; this younger generation of women was much better educated, many of them having gone to college. Nevertheless, most of them had to become secretaries, waitresses, bookkeepers, teachers, retail clerks, and typists—traditional female jobs. Although women are now being employed in greater numbers than ever before, the economic recession of the mid-1970s has caused a general decline in their employment, particularly among those who are heads of households;[14] and while many women are highly motivated to work, outside employment has not released most working married women from their household and family tasks. The married woman typically works many hours at home besides having an outside job. (See Chapter 9.)

Problem Aspects of Work

Among the work-related problems that arise in our society, the alienation of workers from their daily jobs would seem to be of major social importance. Marx and other nineteenth-century social critics attacked the assignment of people to activities that had no inner meaning for them. Factory workers, they claimed, were simply part of a productive process, losing control of both the

[12]R. A. Nixon, "An Appreciative and Critical Look at Official Unemployment Data," in *Work, Young and Unemployment*, ed. Melvin Herman, Stanley Sadofsky, and Bernard Rosenberg (New York: Crowell, 1968), p. 31.

[13]Susan S. Baker, "The Growth and Structure of the Labor Force," *The Conference Board Record* (October 1965), p. 45-54.

[14]*Statistical Abstract of the United States, 1978*, pp. 398, 483.

process and the product. Alienation, as Marx conceived it, is a process that takes away people's capacity to express themselves in their work.[15]

In modern work situations, several elements combine to produce a sense of alienation. But the essential source is the clash between a person's self-image and the kind of person work forces him or her to be. Those who see themselves as needing the companionship of others may feel that a job that prohibits socialization with fellow workers is stifling. Another may be alienated by a job that offers little opportunity for personal judgment. Other people may see themselves as independent and decisive, but find that in their jobs their bosses are constantly and closely supervising them.

A common assumption is that alienation resulting from work has serious social consequences beyond the immediate experience of the worker. Melvin Seeman has summed up this "generalization" idea of alienation:

> Alienated work is troublesome because its effects generalize out of the work sphere into other areas of social life; the lack of control in work leads to a sense of low control in political and social affairs; the hostility bred in the work situation overflows into intergroup antagonism; the disagreement at work encourages loose commitment to the normative order in general.[16]

In a study conducted in Sweden, however, Seeman found that work alienation did not in fact generalize in this way. He had predicted that the correlates of work-induced alienation would be a sense of powerlessness, prejudice toward minority groups, distrust of the larger society, and avoidance of political activity, coupled with ignorance about political affairs. But the data, based on a random sampling of 558 working men aged 20 to 79, did not support his predictions. These workers may simply have come to terms more easily than might be imagined with work life offered by their society. They may not have felt a need to convert their work into a source of deep satisfaction, and may have been content simply to tolerate it, usually by creating situations, however minor, of humor, sociability, competitiveness, or argument.

Studies more recent than Seeman's tend to contradict his findings. Several researchers have found that many of those in boring, monotonous jobs are angry, sometimes resulting in severe psychological depression or escape into fantasies and/or drugs.[17] Harold Sheppard and Neal Herrick found that alienation occurs when work is unsatisfying, and that alienated workers often feel politically powerless, do not vote regularly, and favor extremist and authoritarian candidates.[18]

The symptoms of alienation are not necessarily confined to blue-collar workers. Alienation seems to be inescapable in any pyramidal hierarchy that limits autonomy and chances to use individual skills. Increasingly, white-collar workers feel estranged from their employers and the long-term interests of their companies. Turnover rates for white-collar workers are high, and white-collar union membership has increased substantially over the past two decades. Management, in turn, reinforces white-collar employees' sense of

---

[15]Daniel Bill, *The End of Ideology* (Glencoe, Ill.: Free Press, 1960), p. 338.

[16]Melvin Seeman, "On the Personal Consequences of Alienation in Work," *American Sociological Review* (April 1967), p. 274.

[17]Report of the Special Task Force to the Secretary of the Department of Health, Education and Welfare, *Work in America* (Cambridge, Mass.: M.I.T. Press, 1973), pp. 22-23.

[18]Harold L. Sheppard and Neal Herrick, *Where Have All the Robots Gone?* (New York: Free Press, 1972).

powerlessness, estrangement, and insecurity by viewing them as "expendable." Unlike many blue-collar workers who have union protection, white-collar workers have little job security and are often the first to be fired when a company's business goes bad.[19]

Unemployment

Until recently, to be unemployed in America was to be out of the cultural and social mainstream. The economic recession of the 1970s, however, has made unemployment commonplace. It is no longer unusual to find holders of advanced college degrees lining up at state unemployment offices or taking menial jobs. (The desire to work becomes much stronger when a person's very subsistence is threatened; for this reason, millions of workers are keeping jobs they do not like, rather than leaving to find better ones.[20]) Prolonged joblessness causes serious psychological and social damage. A significant part of today's work force has been denied not only the financial benefits of a regular and sufficient income from their work efforts, but also the secondary emotional rewards of a steady job; the sense of self-worth that comes from

Being without a job means more than standing on line in unemployment offices. The unemployed are cut off from an important focus of social contacts, as well as from a major source of self-respect.
Ray Ellis/Photo Researchers

[19]Braverman, *Labor and Monopoly Capital*, pp. 31-32.
[20]"Staying Put: What Recession Is Doing to Job Hopping," *U.S. News and World Report* (April 14, 1975), pp. 65-66.

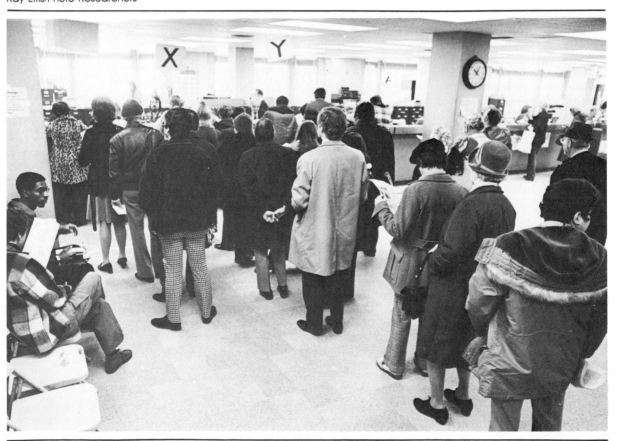

doing a job well and having others value that performance; the sense of community fostered by daily association with colleagues; in sum, the feeling that one is participating in society and contributing to it. The unemployed person, whether older and involuntarily retired, partially or intermittently out of work, or chronically unemployed, is denied many of these rewards. And each of these groups is growing. (For problems of the involuntarily retired see Chapter 10.)

The Intermittently and Chronically Unemployed.   In a competitive society, job insecurity is common. Even when the national unemployment rate was low, many people were unemployed for part of the year. Part-time work is another constant factor. For some people, such as semi-retired doctors or lawyers, students or homemakers with spare-time jobs, or "moon-lighters" who take part-time work as a second job, part-time work is a matter of choice. For others it means an adequate living.

Most serious, however, has been the recent sharp rise in intermittent and long-term unemployment. The national jobless rate jumped from 5.2 percent in 1974 to over 9 percent in 1975, the highest it had been since the Depression. By 1978 it had declined, but still exceeded 6 percent—some 7 million persons.[21] The 1970s recession affected not only the chronically unemployed—women, minorities, teenagers, the unskilled and the semiskilled—but highly specialized white-collar employees such as middle-level managers and engineers. Particularly hard hit were academics, especially recent Ph.D.s in the liberal arts and social sciences. Declining enrollments, increased interest in technical or professional training, a decrease in government grants and private donations, and the tax revolt, as well as rising costs, all contributed to a decline in the number of faculty positions. Some found part-time teaching jobs, others were forced to make a career switch. The recession also hurt the employment of skilled workers in construction, manufacturing, and trade. Most of these trained but jobless workers in business, academia, and in skilled blue-collar work are adult males and heads of households.

Many of the unemployed are young and/or nonwhite. In 1954, for example, 16.5 percent of black teenagers were unemployed as opposed to 12.1 percent of whites. In 1978 this figure had risen to 36.3 percent for blacks and 13.9 percent for whites. Blacks age 20 to 24 have an unemployment rate of more than 20 percent against only 9.5 percent for whites of the same age. In fact, the unemployment rate for blacks is twice as high today as in 1968, the worst year for the destructive urban riots of the 1960s.[22] Unfortunately, the chronically unemployed and their children rarely acquire the capacity to break out of the unemployment pattern without some state or federal help. Many of them are high school dropouts, and their low educational level equips them only for those low-skill jobs that are rapidly disappearing from the occupational structure. These young men and women may not yet have family obligations, but they often have the pride and sense of self associated with youth; consequently, they are reluctant to take dead-end jobs as domestics, or kitchenworkers. (See Chapters 7, 8, and 9 for fuller discussions of unemployment, poverty, and discrimination.)

[21]U.S. Bureau of Labor Statistics, *Employment and Earnings* (Washington, D.C.: U.S. Government Printing Office, April 1978), p. 487.

[22]John Herberts, "Changes in Society Holding Black Youth in Jobless Web," *New York Times*, March 11, 1979, p. 44.

The "Invisible" Unemployed and the "Discouraged" Worker.   As stated earlier, the labor force is made up of those persons, age 16 or over, not in institutions, who worked one hour for pay during the survey week (the employed) and those persons who did not work during the survey week, do not have a job, and are actively seeking work (the unemployed). By definition, all other persons over the age of 16 are not in the labor force and are therefore not included in government unemployment reports. This definition, as R.A. Nixon and others point out, persistently underestimates the size of the labor force and the volume of unemployment. For one thing, it excludes those unemployed persons who, though able and willing to work, did not, for whatever reason, actively seek work during the one survey week. A second factor is the failure of the official data to reflect adequately the underemployment of those who would like to work full-time but can find only part-time jobs. Citing several research studies directed at uncovering the magnitude of such "hidden" unemployment, Nixon concludes that "an accurate measure of currently available, unutilized manpower resources requires an increase of at least 50 percent in the official estimates."[23] Thus, if, as in 1979, the officially derived unemployment rate is about 6 percent, the actual rate, according to Nixon's estimates, would be 12 percent or more.

The problem of "invisible" unemployment became more serious with the recent recession. The average duration of unemployment increased from a low of 9.3 weeks in 1973 to 14.3 weeks in 1977. Furthermore, 14.8 percent of the unemployed, or over 1 million people, had been jobless for up to 6 months or more; and over a million had stopped looking for work altogether because they thought it would be impossible to find. These became known as "discouraged" workers, people who were out of work not because of personal disadvantages such as being too old or too young, untrained or overeducated, but because industries and manufacturers had cut back production and had eliminated a large number of jobs.[24]

What happens to people without work? A 1960 study of 105 unemployed able-bodied men in Detroit showed that the outstanding common characteristic was extreme personal isolation.[25] Half of the men could name no close friends, half never visited neighbors, and few belonged to organizations or engaged in organized activities. These findings were in sharp contrast to the social life of an equal-size sample of employed men. Such data tend to substantiate the thesis that work is necessary if one is to be, in any full sense, "among the living." When work ties are cut, participation in community life declines and a sense of isolation grows. Thus those with the most tenuous work connections—the retired, the elderly, those who have been squeezed out of the labor market, and those who seldom get into it—are often isolated from their communities and American society.

Further studies on the emotional and social effects of long-term unemployment were conducted by D. D. Braginsky and B. M. Braginsky in 1975.[26] The Braginskys confined their research to high-status unemployed men who had been thrown out of work in the mid-1970s recession, a steadily increasing group in the United States. The subjects consisted of two groups,

[23]Nixon, "An Appreciative and Critical Look at Official Unemployment Data," pp. 35-36.

[24]Bureau of Labor Statistics, *Employment and Earnings,* p. 408.

[25]Harold L. Wilensky, "Work as a Social Problem," in *Social Problems,* ed. Howard Becker (New York: Wiley, 1966), p. 129.

[26]D. D. Braginsky and B. M. Braginsky, "Surplus People: Their Lost Faith in Self and System," *Psychology Today* (August 1975), p. 70.

one a control group of employed white-collar men and the other a group of 46 jobless men age 23 to 59. Almost half of the jobless men were college graduates, many had been engineers and company managers, and 80 percent had become unemployed for the first time in 50 years.

According to the study, these men undergo a "social transformation"; the trauma of unemployment causes a permanent change of attitude that persists even after they are re-employed. Loss of a job is commonly interpreted as a judgment of incompetence and worthlessness. In the Braginsky study, the unemployed men, facing a drop in salary and lack of real work, expressed these feelings. Their self-esteem was lowered and they felt alienated from society. They experienced depression, a common reaction to loss. Most of the men spent their days writing resumés and looking for work; but many others slept late and watched television. Most suffered deep shame and avoided their friends. Their low self-esteem made them feel insignificant and obscure, that they were no more than a statistic, and that they could be easily replaced in their families. Many of those who did find new jobs still did not fully recover their self-esteem.

In his study of mental hospitalization and economic downturns and upturns in New York State, Harvey Brenner demonstrated a high inverse correlation between mental hospital admission and the index of employment. Admissions to mental hospitals, he hypothesized, increase during economic downturns and decrease during upturns. Brenner further notes other studies that show suicides climb when the economy changes.[27]

Perhaps the most disturbing effect of prolonged unemployment is the loss of faith in the social order. Men in the Braginsky study revealed a deep cynicism toward established institutions and toward other people—an attitude that intensified when they returned to work. Their political beliefs were radicalized: each man was forced to question how much confidence he should place in institutions and how much responsibility the political system had for his unfair treatment.

Yet another consequence of chronic unemployment was highlighted by the National Advisory Commission on Civil Disorders in 1967. Noting that grievances concerned with unemployment and underemployment were second in intensity only to complaints about police practices, the Commission reported that

> employment problems have drastic social impact in the ghetto. Men who are chronically unemployed or employed in the lowest status jobs are often unable or unwilling to remain with their families. The handicap imposed on children growing up without fathers in an atmosphere of poverty and deprivation is increased as mothers are forced to work to provide support.

> The culture of poverty that results from unemployment and family breakup generates a system of ruthless exploitative relationships within the ghetto . . . . Children growing up under such conditions are likely participants in civil disorder.[28]

---

[27]Harvey Brenner, *Mental Illness and the Economy* (Cambridge, Mass.: Harvard University Press, 1973).

[28]*Report of the National Advisory Commission on Civil Disorders* (New York: Bantam, 1968), pp. 13-14.

Thus it becomes clear that work plays a fundamental social role in our society. The lack of it is felt as a serious deprivation. At best, a person without work is a lonely, second-class citizen; at worst, he or she is a hopeless reject who may readily vent a sense of alienation and frustration in antisocial activity, perhaps in violence.

Automation   In the next few decades, automation may fundamentally change the character of work in America. Many people fear—not unrealistically—that the principal change will be a reduction in the number of jobs.

Areas of Automation.   There have been three major developments in the computer-controlled production methods called automation. The first consisted of linking together into a continuous process several production operations previously performed separately. In such an integrated system—first developed for the oil refining and chemical industries, which need a high degree of control—the product moves from start to finish completely automatically.

Electronic data processing (EDP), which records, stores, and processes information, was the second development in automation. The most familiar example of this is the office computer that handles bookkeeping, accounting, billing, and countless other clerical operations. EDP permits a bank teller to take the dates and sums from a savings passbook and to give the waiting customer an instant report on compounded interest. On more than half of all long-distance telephone calls, EDP eliminates the need for an operator by doing the routine work—recording the numbers of caller and receiver, checking the time and charges—while managing the information more quickly and accurately than the operator could.

The third development was that of feedback control computers, or servo-mechanisms, which compare the work actually being done with what should be done, and automatically adjust the work process when necessary. A simple and familiar example is the living-room thermostat, which automatically controls the heating system of a household to maintain a specified temperature. The same principles are employed in a Great Lakes steel mill computer that keeps track of over 1,000 variables, and controls mill operations with a speed and accuracy far beyond any human ability. If the computer finds an error in a product line, it can make the necessary adjustments to correct the error on the next item in a fraction of a second.[29]

Impact on Organizational Structures.   What are the effects of such technology? Marshall Meyer, among others, points out that computer control not only affects workers but also alters the administrative structure of the bureaucratic organization.[30] For one thing, most automated operations require a separate data-processing staff. Such computer specialists are different from many of the other people in a factory. They have skills that the others do not understand, and their job is not actually to produce the product but to provide efficient means of producing it. Automation, therefore, creates a new interdependence between the workers directly concerned with the end

[29]Ben B. Seligman, "Automation and the Work Force," in *The Guaranteed Income*, ed. Robert Theobald (Garden City, N.Y.: Doubleday, 1966), p. 143.

[30]Marshall W. Meyer, "Automation and Bureaucratic Structure," *American Journal of Sociology* (November 1968), p. 256-264.

One of the consequences of automation has been a concentration of monotonous jobs at the low end of the salary scale. Note that almost all the keypunch operators in this office are women.
Leo Choplin/Black Star

product and the data-processing staff which helps to accomplish the others' goal. People with high status in the organization but no technical expertise must deal cooperatively with technical experts, such as programmers or systems analysts, who have no supervisory authority at all—a relationship unique to modern organization. Such cooperation is not easy. Because of their lack of computer expertise, managers may insist on a technically unreasonable request, and may use the authority of their position to force the data-processing staff to comply. Conversely, data-processing specialists may use the authority of their expertise to deny even a reasonable request that is inconvenient. Such line-staff conflicts are also an administration problem. Meyer speculates that as automation increases, the interdependence between the high-status non-experts and the low-status experts will force organizations to alter their basic structure.

Effect on Workers.   When automatic processes become more widespread, as is likely to happen, they will affect every type of worker—white- and blue-collar, supervisor and manager, semiprofessional and professional—in factories, in laboratories, offices or stores. We still do not know precisely how; therefore, almost all current predictions about the effects of automation are educated guesses.

In fact, studies of how automation affects workers produce contradictory findings. For example, Meyer's study showed that computerization so decreased job satisfaction that many workers wanted to quit. Yet the same study reports that eventually the faster working pace of the new job gave most workers an increased sense of satisfaction. Automation impacts differently on each individual industry. In printing, for example, linotype machine operators have been replaced by phototypesetters. Some workers, like carpenters, complain that the advent of mass-produced prefabricated buildings has robbed their jobs of interest and craftsmanship. Yet other jobs have been enriched and made more demanding.

For people of the working class—that is, those performing manual work and services—one trend is the shift to a different kind of work performance. Future jobs will probably require less physical ability and greater mental ability and concentration. Instead of operating one machine on a production line, the new worker may have many tasks and responsibilities—monitoring several machines, for example, and keeping the entire system functioning smoothly.

Among office workers—clerks, salespeople, supervisors, bookkeepers—automation is likely to reduce the skills that their jobs require. Since the object of automation is to replace human fallibility—with machines that control other machines, measure electronically, record, self-correct, and make decisions faster than a person can react—only low-skilled jobs probably remain for people. When automation reaches most offices, the heavy job concentration will probably be at the low end of the salary scale—for instance, in key-punching, which is simple, monotonous, precise, and high-speed work.

It is on the higher levels that automation may change work most dramatically. New hierarchical patterns are already emerging, and certain traditional roles of top and middle management are diminishing. Ida Hoos discovered that as computers run more operations, EDP executives wield more power, and top people in other departments find their functions and authority being undercut. Even vice-presidents find themselves·bypassed when the computer takes over business operations relating to procurement, production, sales, and similar functions. "Vice presidents in charge of," writes Hoos, "find their official functions atrophying; there is not much for them to be in charge of."[31]

It seems that automation may exacerbate conditions that produce job discontent. Work will probably become more demanding and precise, making it perhaps less appealing. Simultaneously, workers may become more alienated from their jobs since they will be less involved in making a product. Also, opportunities for human interaction may decline.[32]

Yet there is another side. Money and job security for workers will probably be greater. Because machines will run automatically, workers may have more free time available on the job. It is also possible that workers will establish freer relationships with those higher up in the organizational hierarchy because they will be working closely with planners and programmers. In any event, while we cannot know precisely how future generations of workers will react to large-scale automation, it seems safe to say that ways will be found to keep work at least tolerably satisfying.

Job Satisfaction   When people go to work they sacrifice some personal freedom and assume some risk. A job demands that a person put his or her time at another's disposal. It may also mean spending money and time for commuting and enduring physical hazards and discomforts, psychological traumas, boredom, and frustration. In return workers can expect in varying degrees pay and fringe benefits, job security, meaningful work, opportunity for advancement,

[31]Ida Russakoff Hoos, "When the Computer Takes Over the Office," *Harvard Business Review* 79 (July–August 1960), 102-112.
[32]Willis W. Harmon, "Chronic Unemployment: An Emerging Problem of Post-Industrial Society," *The Futurist* (August 1978), p. 210.

flexibility in worktime, decent surroundings, and good working spirit among peers and supervisors.[33] Each of these factors affects workers' satisfaction.

As previously stated, there are contradictions in the research on job satisfaction. We have already cited two studies in which most workers said they would continue to work even if it were not necessary financially. Yet Table 13-1 presents the results of another study in which the majority of workers in every category—white-collar, blue-collar, and unskilled—said that if given the chance, they would not choose the same kind of work again.[34]

In the last decade, there have been many changes in the factors that contribute to job satisfaction. A new generation of workers, raised in the affluence of the 1950s and 1960s and well educated, has brought new ideals to their jobs. Daniel Yankelovich calls them the "New Breed."[35] New Breed workers, while still interested in the traditional concerns of benefits and salary, also place great emphasis on individuality and independence. They are less loyal to their employers and identify less closely with their jobs than did their parents. One of their most cherished values is leisure time, those hours that they can devote to their own self-growth and personal interests undisturbed by family or job responsibilities. Because of these attitudes, New Breed workers seek jobs that will provide them with opportunities to use their skills fully and still allow time for leisure. The concept of flexitime and staggered hours is very appealing to these workers—so appealing, in fact, that one survey showed that many workers were willing to remain in jobs they disliked because of flexible schedules.[36]

[33]Herbert C. Morton, "A Look at Factors Affecting the Quality of Working Life," *Monthly Labor Review* (October 1977), p. 64.

[34]H.E.W., *Work in America*, p. 15; and Robert Blauner, "Work Satisfaction and Industrial Trends in Modern Society," in *Class, Status, and Power*, ed. Reinard Bendix and S. M. Lipset, (New York: Free Press, 1966), p. 476.

[35]Daniel Yankelovich, "The New Psychological Contracts at Work," Psychology Today (May 1978), p. 46.

[36]Patricia A. Renwick and Edward E. Lawler, "What You Really Want From Your Job," *Psychology Today* (July 1978), p. 79.

Professional and Lower White-Collar Occupations		Working-Class Occupations	
Urban university professors	93%	Skilled printers	52%
Mathematicians	91	Paper workers	42
Physicists	89	Skilled autoworkers	41
Biologists	89	Skilled steelworkers	41
Chemists	86	Textile workers	31
Firm lawyers	85	Blue-collar workers, cross section	24
Lawyers	83	Unskilled steelworkers	21
Journalists (Washington correspondents)	82	Unskilled autoworkers	16
Church university professors	77		
Solo lawyers	75		
White-collar workers, cross section	43		

Table 13-1 Percentages in Occupational Groups Who Would Choose Similar Work Again

Source: U.S. Department of Health, Education and Welfare, *Work in America* (Washington, D.C.: U.S. Government Printing Office, 1973), p. 16.

To the New Breed woman, a job holds great symbolic significance. It is a "badge of membership in society and an indispensable symbol of self worth."[37] Although most women work primarily for money—either to support a family or a style of living—the influence of the feminist movement has changed their attitudes about the meaning of a paying job.

The search for psychological satisfactions from work—not just material ones—characterizes the New Breed. In one survey a group of mostly young workers revealed that they wanted to feel a sense of accomplishment from their jobs, using their knowledge, participating to some extent in decisions, and learning new skills.[38]

Education is one of the factors that helped create the New Breed. Because the number of these educated people far exceeds the number of jobs suited to their expectations—one out of every four Americans in 1980 is a college graduate—there is a good chance that many workers will be underemployed and dissatisfied. Employers of the next decade will face a new challenge in this critical area of job satisfaction. Since they will not be able to relieve underemployment by higher salaries or benefits, they will have to find other methods of improvement.

Job enrichment—combining several functions to make a job more challenging—is one possibility. But Robert Schrank, a former assembly-line worker and union organizer, has suggested that the only way to reduce worker dissatisfaction with jobs that are intrinsically dull, unchallenging, or beneath their abilities, is to allow some of the privileges that already sweeten management and professional positions: flexible schedules, an opportunity to socialize more freely during the work day, more breaks, or a chance to "escape" for a brief time with a telephone call.[39]

Job Satisfaction and Dissatisfaction. Numerous studies have found certain common causes of job satisfaction and dissatisfaction. The sources of job satisfaction seem to be:

- Monetary Compensation (including fringe benefits). Satisfied workers feel they are paid fairly for their services.

- Psychological Satisfaction. These involve the nature of the job itself. A satisfactory job provides an opportunity to learn, is closely matched to a worker's ability and preferences, and provides a sense of accomplishment. A job may also satisfy by providing an opportunity to work with interesting or congenial people.

- Control. Workers feel more satisfied in jobs that allow some decision-making, especially over their own schedules. This is why flexitime is so appealing and why punching time-clocks is so universally disliked.

- Physical Factors. Workers find more job satisfaction in an environment that is pleasant and free from hazards. Availability of transportation and commuting time are also important.

- Institutional Aspects. These include both physical amenities—cafeterias, lounges, gyms, and the like—and promotion-from-within policies,

[37]Yankelovich, "The New Psychological Contracts," p. 49.

[38]Emma Rothschild, "Auto Production Lordstown," *Transaction* (Winter 1979), pp. 330-342.

[39]Robert Schrank, "How to Relieve Worker Boredom," *Psychology Today* (July 1978), p. 79.

training programs, and good personnel policy that assures equal opportunity for advancement and education.

- Political, Economic, and Social Aspects. Workers are also affected by the prevailing national mood. A general spirit of prosperity is mirrored in job satisfaction.[40]

Stanley Parker found that dissatisfaction does not always spring from the absence of one of these sources of satisfaction. There are additional factors that seem to cause discontent. Some workers complained of repetitive work, where one boring task followed another, or the same task went on forever. They also disliked making only a small part of a product, or doing fragmented tasks, making them feel like onlookers rather than participants in the work process. Dissatisfaction also arose from jobs that made many workers superfluous. A final cause seemed to be excessively close supervision.[41]

Are the causes of job satisfaction and dissatisfaction different for different classes or workers? Are white-collar workers, like accountants or engineers, affected by the same factors as blue-collar workers, like assemblers or welders? A recent study compared a wide variety of workers drawn from these two separate categories. Each subject was asked about the things that he or she liked and disliked about work and was then asked to describe a good day on the job. A number of common characteristics were then extracted from these descriptions and analyzed. These included amount of work, enjoyment of the tasks, smoothness of the work flow, achievement, promotion, responsibility, recognition, money, interpersonal atmosphere, and working conditions. The results indicated that satisfaction or dissatisfaction for both blue- and white-collar workers depended on the same intrinsic characteristics of the job.[42]

Income and Satisfaction.   It is becoming increasingly apparent that the chance to do meaningful work is of primary importance. Many jobs, however, are simply dull. For workers who already earn enough to live adequately, additional income cannot always offset the increasingly common meaninglessness of work. This applies particularly to younger workers, who are apt to be better educated and less concerned than their predecessors about such problems as job security. They particularly resent work they consider trivial and boring, and they want to control the circumstances of their labor. In one instance, over 85 percent of the eligible workers at the newly automated automobile assembly plant in Lordstown, Ohio, turned out for a strike vote in early 1972; 97 percent voted in favor of the strike.[43] At the heart of the workers' protest was their dissatisfaction with the assembly-line process and their demand for a greater voice in decisions affecting their immediate working lives.[44]

Attempts to Make Work More Satisfying.   Organizations have tried to enhance employee job satisfaction. This has occasionally been done out of a belief that satisfying and rewarding work is important to those who have to

[40]Morton, "A Look at Factors Affecting the Quality of Work Life," p. 64.

[41]Stanley Parker, *The Future of Work and Leisure* (New York: Praeger, 1971), pp. 44-45.

[42]Edwin A. Locke, "Satisfiers and Dissatisfiers Among White-Collar and Blue-Collar Employees," *Journal of Applied Psychology*, vol. 58, no. 1 (August 1973), 67.

[43]Barbara Garson, "Luddites in Lordstown," *Harper's Magazine* (June 1972), pp. 68-73.

[44]Rothschild, "Auto Production Lordstown," p. 340.

work. For the most part, however, such programs seek to raise productivity, improve quality, or reduce various personnel and operating costs. There have been two basic approaches to improving employee job satisfaction. One, centered on "human relations," focuses on the social context of work and seeks to improve communications in the organizational hierarchy. Several American corporations have recently instituted "climate surveys" in which employees are asked to complain and criticize their jobs. Even when problems cannot feasibly be corrected, tensions seem to be temporarily relieved by allowing employees to let off steam.[45]

A few European companies have gone a step further and given their employees an opportunity to participate actively in management decisions and company policies. In America, workers are being allowed to make some decisions about work schedules. The increasingly popular concept of flexitime or sliding work hours allows employees to arrive and depart from the job when they choose, so long as they work during specific core hours and for a certain amount of time per week. Flexitime seems to affect job satisfaction considerably.[46]

Job Satisfaction and Life Satisfaction.   Few studies have related job satisfaction to other areas of life. The Seeman study, cited earlier, failed to find a correlation between alienation at work and certain anticipated social effects. On the other hand, a study by Arthur Kornhauser, which assessed the mental health of factory workers in large and medium-sized automobile factories, found that approximately half of such highly skilled workers as printers showed "good" mental health, as against about one-third of the "ordinary" semiskilled workers and an even lower proportion of the "repetitive, machine-paced" semiskilled workers.[47] Good mental health included absence of anxiety and emotional tension; trust in and acceptance of people rather than hostility toward them; sociability and friendship rather than withdrawal; self-esteem; and overall satisfaction with life. The results of this study of people with very different personalities and backgrounds suggest that if job satisfaction and life satisfaction are inseparable, the picture of the American worker as "contented" is a distorted one.

In his classic study of automobile factory workers, Ely Chinoy cited the "coming to terms" that Seeman hypothesized as the worker's "solution" to the problem of alienation:

> Men cannot spend eight hours per day, forty hours each week, in activity which lacks all but instrumental meaning. They therefore try to find some significance in the work they must do. Workers may take pride, for example, in executing skillfully even the routine tasks to which they are assigned . . . . They may derive a moral satisfaction from doing "an honest day's work." . . . They may try to squeeze out some sense of personal significance by identifying themselves with the product, standardized though it may be, and with the impersonal corporation in which they are anonymous, replaceable entities.[48]

[45]"A Productive Way to Vent Employee Gripes," *Business Week* (October 16, 1978), pp. 168-71.

[46]Fred Best, "Preferences on Worklife Scheduling and Work-Leisure Tradeoffs," *Monthly Labor Review* (June 1978), pp. 31-37.

[47]Arthur Kornhauser, "Toward an Assessment of the Mental Health of Factory Workers," *Human Organization* (Spring 1962), pp. 43-46.

[48]Ely Chinoy, *Automobile Workers and the American Dream* (Boston: Beacon 1955), pp. 130–131.

At this point it is difficult to draw conclusions from the research on job satisfaction. It does seem likely that there is more deep dissatisfaction with work than most research indicates, and that various work and career situations greatly affect job satisfaction. But there is still much to be learned about why or why not we like our work.

More Leisure Time

The problem of what to do with free time may seem to be a false issue to the many millions of un- or underemployed, whose problem is how to fill months of unwanted "leisure" with some form of productive activity. Their plight illustrates the difficulty of discussing leisure activity apart from work, for leisure is meaningful only when it is just that, a regular break in the work cycle and a reward for time spent in the job—that for most people means doing something not necessarily enjoyable. Despite the recent economic slowdown, however, most workers today have almost 1,200 more hours of leisure time per year than their counterparts had at the turn of the century; they also start working later and retire earlier, giving them an average of nine more years of life in which they do not work.[49]

If leisure were a separated sphere from work, new nonworking time could be occupied by building more theaters and resorts, starting education for leisure activities in grammar schools, and offering adult classes in retirement. But leisure is related to work. Americans want to earn what they enjoy, what they feel they need and want—a house, a car, a trip, a sailboat.

[49]Juanita Kreps and Joseph Spengler, "Future Options for More Free Time," in *The Future of Work*, ed. Fred Best (Englewood Cliffs, N.J.: Prentice-Hall, 1973), pp. 87–88.

The concept of leisure time could not exist without the contrast of work. These tourists would probably find their sightseeing less enjoyable if it were not a vacation—an anticipated part of the work cycle.

F.B. Grunzweig

For most people, the question is still not one of work *or* leisure. It is work *and* leisure.

How are people using their leisure? What is its meaning and function? Are people, caught in stultifying jobs, turning to leisure to give their lives significance and satisfaction, even challenge? Is our society, built on the industrial system, shifting its ideological center from work to leisure? Are the lines between work and leisure blurring—somewhat as they were in preindustrial days—with interpersonal relations becoming more important in each? The social effect of leisure is becoming a serious concern for possibly the first time since industrialization and the Protestant ethic made work the primary business of living. In the early days of industrialization, Adam Smith considered factory life so degrading that only the hours away from work could restore human qualities and values. He, and later Marx, saw the factory as completely dehumanizing. But both were comparing the new industrial life to a somewhat romanticized nostalgia for a pre-industrial age, with which they were still in touch; and Smith especially overlooked the passive and boring elements that had always existed in that pastoral world. They also missed the touches of creativity—the tricks of the trade or the imaginative employee "sabotage"—that were a feature of the factories of their times, and indeed still exist. Yet it is fair to say that industrialization developed so rapidly, and forced people of a rural tradition into factories with so little preparation, that merriment was pushed to the periphery of daily life. The "fringe benefits" of both hard factory work and the Protestant ethic occurred during whatever was left of the night and on Sundays, in the taverns and churches, as well as during occasional "seasons" of unemployment and on the increasingly rare holidays.

The Use of Leisure Time.   Leisure in many ways reflects work; while most workers use their leisure time and working time in a seemingly different manner, their approaches to work and leisure are often similar, in structure if not in content. A package tour of Florida or Africa is activity organized in much the same way as most offices and factories. There are other lesiure activities that involve behavior similar to that of work—that may gain relief from the monotony of work without making the return to work a difficult adjustment.[50] Stanley Parker cites bingo as an example of this use of leisure. Bingo has several features that imitate the work experience of the many people who enjoy it—concentration, limited movement patterns, supervision, and intervals for refreshments.[51]

Another example occurs in the research of Fred Blum, who studied the specific leisure pursuits of packing-house workers, most of whom carried their work attitudes into the weekend, even though they were tired and wanted to escape from work and everything it represented. Often they chose fishing, which seems, at first sight, quite unlike their work. It was relaxing, it took them outdoors and let them "get away from it all." But, like their work, fishing did not demand much initiative or attention. Most of all, noted Blum, it permitted the psychological mechanisms of "busy-ness" to continue. Thus fishing actually required the same attitude, effort, and attention as the job from which it was superficially so different.[52]

[50]Irving Howe, "Notes on Mass Culture," *Politics* (Spring 1948).
[51]Parker, *The Future of Work and Leisure*, p. 73.
[52]Fred H. Blum, *Toward a Democratic Work Process* (New York: Harper & Row, 1953), pp. 109-110.

People whose work demands considerable involvement and responsibility are likely to blend their leisure with their work. A survey by J. E. Gerstl and S. P. Hutton indicated that 23 percent of professional engineers had hobbies related to engineering.[53] As many as 73 percent have work-connected reading as one of their hobbies. David Riesman observed that people often move from jobs where good performance requires them to cope with many interpersonal situations to leisure activities where interpersonal relations require them to give workmanlike performances.[54]

By contrast, people whose work involves only a few hours on the job, or whose work is unrewarding, tend to follow a leisure style like that of people with no jobs at all. Much of their leisure is spent watching television indiscriminately just to pass time. They seem to be trying to dispel their restlessness by habitual retreats into escapist entertainment.[55] (See Figure 13-1.)

For one segment of the work force, the leisure problem is an extraordinary lack of leisure time. People in the upper working strata may take longer holidays and retire earlier than others, but they usually find their work absorbing, and spend many extra hours at it. Such a pattern is typical of leaders in politics, business, the military, the academic disciplines, the arts, and entertainment, as well as millions of others at less exalted levels. This growing minority, who wish to work 55 hours or more a week, generally receive rewards that compensate for their limited leisure time.

Work-Leisure Fusion.   While off-time leisure is increasing, leisure also colors life on the job. In some companies, union shop stewards spend much of their energy—once directed entirely toward resisting the abuses and encroachment of management—maintaining a comfortable level of sociability and gossip. Moreover, management has had to design and furnish its plants and factories to accommodate employee tastes developed during their increased leisure-time activities. This is one reason why many factories have been moved to pleasant suburbs.

Leisure, in fact, now confers status on work, where once work alone conferred status. According to David Riesman and Warner Bloomberg, workers have their own symbols of glamour—color television sets, stereo systems, sleek cars, and similar consumer hard goods.[56] Similarly, they can bring their personal status to their workplace from the world outside by indulging in such exotic or exciting activities as boating or race-car driving, by traveling extensively, or by engaging in union or local politics. Instead of the slow climb up the in-plant hierarchy, younger workers can now outrank many "senior" employees through a more personal and visible kind of status.

Tilgher suggests, indeed, that the secular religion of work that flourished most richly in America seems now to be producing an exact opposite, a religion of recreation, pleasure, and amusement. Today our society allocates a significant part of its economic resources—6.6 percent of the national

[53]J. E. Gerstl and S. P. Hutton, *Engineers: The Anatomy of a Profession* (London: Tavistock, 1966), pp. 138-139.

[54]David Riesman, "Some Observations on Changes in Leisure Attitudes," *Antioch Review* 4 (1952), 417-436.

[55]Harold L. Wilensky, "Mass Society and Mass Culture: Interdependence or Independence?" *American Sociological Review* (April 1964), pp. 173-197.

[56]David Riesman and Warner Bloomberg, "Work and Leisure: Fusion or Polarity?" in Nosow and Form, *Man, Work, and Society*, pp. 35-41.

Figure 13-1

Characteristics of Persons
Reporting Television
Viewing as Favorite
Evening Pastime.

Source: U.S. Department of
Commerce, Bureau of the
Census, *Social Indicators*
(Washington, D.C.: U.S.
Government Printing Office,
1977).

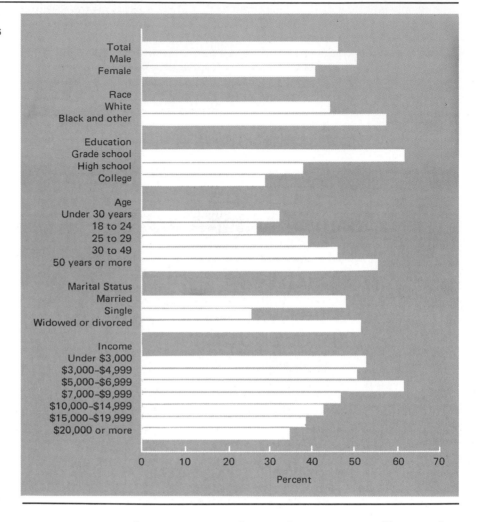

income—to personal consumption and expenditures.[57] It would seem that leisure, humor, and play will always absorb a great deal of human energy, whether they have to be "worked at" or not.

Occupational Health

People have been concerned about the physical toll exacted by work since Ancient Greece. Medical writings reveal that Roman physicians recognized an unusually high frequency of lung disease among metal workers, miners, and weavers of asbestos cloth. During the Renaissance, each craft was known to have it unique maladies. But it was the advent of the Industrial Revolution that created a new wave of deadly occupational hazards.[58]

[57]*Statistical Abstract of the United States, 1978*, p. 444.
[58]See Henry E. Sigerst, *Civilization and Disease* (Chicago: University of Chicago Press, 1962).

The American labor movement from its very beginning made safety one of its priorities, waging a constant battle for a better work environment. Despite this long history of concern and awareness, occupational health remains a serious problem. In 1971 alone, there were 14,000 fatal on-the-job accidents in the United States. More than two million persons were injured, and 100,000 were permanently disabled.[59]

As destructive as they are, industrial accidents are only part of the problem of occupational health. In the last decade, proponents of occupational health have widened their focus to include not just accidents but illnesses, and to concentrate on preventing work-related diseases rather than merely treating or compensating workers for them. The situation is grim: the Public Health Service estimates that not only do 100,000 Americans die of job-related diseases each year, but 390,000 new cases occur. In addition, 10 percent of all cancer deaths of American males have occupational origins.[60]

Although white-collar workers and professionals also face occupational illnesses, certain groups of workers, primarily blue-collar workers, seem to bear inordinate risks, since health hazards are most prevalent in the factory, on the farm, and in the mines and mills.

Statistically, the most dangerous workplaces are the mines and farms. Coal miners are exposed to a variety of dangers from floods, cave-ins and, explosions to a less dramatic kind of killer—respiratory disease. Unless a mine is properly ventilated, the atmosphere is thick with coal dust; years of breathing this air causes incurable lung ailments. The most common of these is silicosis, a disease that the World Health Organization (WHO) brands as "the major cause of disability and mortality" among occupational illnesses.[61] The most widely publicized miner's disease, however, is the fatal pneumoconiosis, or black lung; it is estimated that between 8 and 10 percent of America's miners have it. Technology is now available to clean the mine's atmosphere and permissible dust levels were set by the 1969 Coal Mine and Safety Act, but enforcement has not been strict.

Next to the risks of the miner stand those of the farmer. While farm laborers comprised only 4.4 percent of the American labor force in 1971, they accounted for 16 percent of the occupational injuries. Their biggest on-the-job danger comes from herbicides and pesticides, often overused or misused. Workers are frequently assigned to freshly treated fields or bombarded by sprayers as they work. Public health officials suspect that the poisoning problem is underestimated. One house-to-house California survey showed that many impoverished migrant workers who were ill from poisoning had not consulted a doctor; and those who did often received incorrect diagnoses and/or the doctors failed to report the cases to the authorities.[62]

In the 1970s, government concern with occupational illness resulted in two significant pieces of legislation—the Occupational Safety and Health Act and the Toxic Substances Control Act, passed in 1970 and 1976 respectively. The first established two new bodies: the Occupational Safety and Health Administration (OSHA), the part of the Department of Labor that establishes

[59]Joseph A. Califano, "Occupational Safety and Health: A Healthier Working Environment," *Vital Speeches of the Day*, vol. 44, no. 24 (October 1, 1978), 738.

[60]Erik Eckholm, "Unhealthy Jobs," *Environment*, vol. 19, no. 6 (August/September 1977), 29.

[61]Erik Eckholm, "Unhealthy Jobs," p. 34.

[62]Joel Schwartz, "Poisoning Farmworkers," *Environment*, vol. 17, no. 5 (June 1975), 26-33.

health standards for industry; and the National Institute for Occupational Safety and Health (NIOSH), the part of the Department of Health, Education and Welfare (HEW) that researches work hazards. The second act established guidelines and systems for screening and controlling dangerous substances.

These agencies face a formidable task—enforcement of safety standards. In order to meet these new standards, industry must spend sizable sums of money on new equipment and/or plant remodeling. In an era of spiraling inflation, expensive energy and threats from imports, they are extremely reluctant to assume this added burden. If pressed hard, business has the power to strike back at OSHA through sympathetic legislators who control the agency's budget appropriations. (See Chapter 12.)

The recent battle over cotton dust levels in the textile and cottonseed oil industries is a prime example of the problems of imposing health standards. Constant inhalation of the cotton dust that fills the air of mills causes a fatal and irreversible respiratory disease called byssinosis or brown lung. Out of 800,000 textile workers in this country, 150,000 have brown lung and 35,000 more are disabled from it.

Although byssinosis was first recognized in the eighteenth century (English workers have been compensated for the disease since 1941), the American textile industry attempted to deny its existence. Company doctors and physicians in one-industry, corporate-dominated mill towns diagnosed brown lung as emphysema. People who had the disease did not know what really was afflicting them or what had caused it. It was not until 1968 that brown lung was officially recognized as an occupational illness.[63] It took another eight years of pressure from the Amalgamated Clothing and Textile Workers Union and other labor groups to set standards for allowable levels of cotton dust. These were defined in 1976 as 200 micrograms of dust per cubic meter of air, but neither business nor labor was satisfied with this level. Labor insisted that a level of 100 was the maximum for safety; and industry, complaining that it would cost $2.7 billion to meet the new 200-microgram level, maintained that a level of 1,000 was sufficient. Nonetheless, the government gave industry seven years to comply with the 200-microgram standard and the debate continues, along with the spread of brown lung.

OSHA, in fact, has little control over business. The fines levied are relatively small and are often reduced by judicial appeals. Corporations would rather pay the fines than meet the standards. Pro-business congressmen are sympathetic to industry lobbyists, and, in the case of the cottonseed oil producers, used their budgetary power to persuade OSHA to cease plant inspections.[64]

Perhaps the greatest health hazard comes from the young and burgeoning chemical industry. Born out of the technological advances made during and just after World War II, the chemical industry has revolutionized American life with an array of synthetic products. Chemicals are involved in the manufacture of almost every product we use—from clothing to lawn food. Recently, statistics showed that chemicals could produce something else— cancer. Workers exposed to certain chemicals were discovered to have an unusually high rate of malignancies. They frequently suffered from other health problems as well, such as nervous disorders, sterility, and birth defects.

[63]Jerry DeMuth, "Brown Lung in the Cotton Mill," *America* (March 18, 1978), p. 108.
[64]DeMuth, Brown Lung," p. 108.

Some chemicals produce a disastrous impact in a very short time. Kepone, a pesticide once manufactured by the Life Sciences Company, is one example. Safety standards at the firm's Hopewell, Virginia, plant were extremely lax, and chemical dusts clogged the work area. Life Sciences employees were soon manifesting strange symptoms and feeling ill. Examinations revealed that Kepone had caused liver damage and made many of them sterile. Nor was the Kepone poisoning confined to the workers. Families of Life Sciences workers who had breathed the dust from their clothing or bodies were also stricken. Eventually, it was discovered that the entire environment of Hopewell was contaminated—Kepone was in the soil, air, and water. The plant was shut down, and sections of the nearby James River were closed to fishing, an important local industry. Despite all these tardy precautions, Kepone was found in fish as far away as the Chesapeake Bay.

By contrast, other substances may take years to demonstrate their deadly effects. It is these delayed reactions that pose the greatest threat. It is possible for generations of workers to have daily contact with a carcinogen, for example, without anyone suspecting the hazard. This is precisely what happened with acrylonitrile, one of the "miracle" compounds that spawned not only new products, but a new industry. It was not until 1977, after more than 25 years of production, that its effects appeared in tragically high cancer statistics among those who had produced and processed it. Although it is now on the Environmental Protection Agency's danger list, 10,000 workers are still exposed to it in concentrations that seem capable of causing cancer in humans.[65]

The most notorious case of delayed reaction to carcinogens is asbestos. A mineral, not a chemical, asbestos has multiple uses and was handled by workers in scores of industries—from construction to beer brewing. Over one million men and women who worked in America's shipyards during World War II had extensive contact with it. As a result, an estimated 400,000 of them will die of a rare type of lung cancer. Their families may also be in jeopardy. Wives who did their laundry, children whom they played with—all were exposed to clinging asbestos particles that could doom them to cancer. HEW has begun a massive educational program to alert persons who were exposed to asbestos to the dangers they may now face. It is hoped that some lives will be saved through early detection and treatment.

There is a strong possibility that the tragedy of these asbestos workers will be repeated in other industries. At present, there are 19,000 known toxic materials in use in factories; OSHA has issued guidelines on only 400 of them. There are 2,400 suspected carcinogens, but only 16 carcinogens have been so designated and regulated. In human terms, this means that 14 million workers may be exposed to toxic substances, and 16,000 to carcinogens every work day.[66]

Manufacturers often do not realize the contents of the substances used in their plants. The only ingredients that must be labeled are the 16 official carcinogens. To complicate matters even further, many products are sold under brand names that mask their true contents. Lists of ingredients may also contain brand names. NIOSH is attempting to analyze all these products, but at present only a little more than half of them have been screened.

[65]Peter Behr, "Controlling Chemical Hazards," *Environment*, vol. 20, no. 6 (July/August 1978), 26.

[66]Dorothy McGhee, "The Secret Killers," *The Progressive* (August, 1977), p. 26.

A shipyard worker wears protective clothing to guard against the carcinogenic effects of asbestos. Unfortunately, the known danger of unguarded asbestos handling is only a small problem when compared to the health hazard represented by contact with thousands of non-regulated substances.

UPI

NIOSH-regulated toxic chemicals were found in 45 percent of them, and regulated carcinogens in 2 percent.[67]

It has been suggested that all products be sold under both their generic and brand names, and that a complete list of ingredients appear on all packages. This has not yet become law. It is extremely difficult, as the controversy over saccharin has shown, to prove that a substance causes cancer and to ban its use. Even scientists disagree about how much proof is needed to establish a causal relationship.

Meanwhile, the chemical analysis program continues. Estimates claim that if work continues at the present rate, it will take one hundred years to set standards for all the chemicals currently in use—and new ones are introduced at the rate of one every twenty minutes.

Various interim procedures have been recommended, such as the regular screening of workers to determine the levels of toxic substances in their systems and the use of protective masks and clothing. Because of the harm that toxic substances can wreak on the fetus and on children still to be conceived, it has been suggested that all fertile women of childbearing age be excluded from certain jobs.

Occupational health is an issue loaded with moral, medical, and economic questions. Business cites the enormous impact the needed changes will have on our entire economy. Acrylonitrile manufacturers calculate that it will cost them $100 million for each life saved by adherence to health standards.[68] Industry representatives insist that their research shows the government's claims to be exaggerated, and they say their tests show there are safe levels of exposure to most substances. Others argue that compulsory adherence will put them out of business or force them to relocate to other countries. Many workers, more fearful of imminent unemployment than future illness, agree with their employers and take their chances in the workplace.

Proponents of occupational health, on the other hand, insist that their proposed standards will cut operating expenses and boost productivity. At least 25 million workdays are lost each year, they point out, because of occupational injuries and diseases. The resulting compensation cost industry $11 billion in 1976 alone.

The fundamental question is, of course, one of human life and the quality of that life. It is a question that cannot be answered in dollars and cents. Is it right for certain groups to serve as guinea pigs exposed to untested chemicals? Is it right for a disproportionately large number of people to risk their lives to provide a smaller, more elite group with goods and profits? Should we risk the well-being of entire communities that happen to be adjacent to factories? The subtle and complex issues that surround these questions continue to provoke debate and continue to grow.

Prospects

Despite the Full Employment Act of 1948, that made explicit the policy of government to work toward the reduction of unemployment, millions today are without jobs, many for sustained periods. As suggested in Chapters 7 and

---

[67]McGhee, "The Secret Killers," p. 26.
[68]Behr, "Controlling Chemical Hazards," p. 26.

8, government policies have, at best, resulted in only a minimal decline in the unemployment picture. Substantial new efforts must be made to reduce the discrimination that prevents women and minorities from achieving job equality and to increase the number of jobs available.

The government has been particularly reluctant to hold corporations partially accountable for the decline in available jobs. Corporations employ over 50 percent of the work force,[69] making it absurd to consider them "private" institutions with all the rights, autonomy, and freedom of action of individuals. As many critics are beginning to contend, corporations will have to reevaluate their interests and priorities and accept a much larger share of public responsibility. For example, instead of building more profit- and efficiency-enhancing automated factories that throw thousands out of work, corporations should be expected, and perhaps forced by government regulation, to try to create more jobs to help relieve part of the unemployment problem—or at least to help keep it from increasing.[70] The government might also subsidize companies to maintain their payrolls in time of economic recession, as many foreign governments do.

Another area that may require some major changes in public policy is the so-called education inflation. During the 1950s and 1960s, it was assumed that people would have to be educated for a longer time, and more intensely, for the highly demanding technological jobs that were certain to evolve; and at first the increase in white-collar and professional jobs made a college education seem necessary for many. This in turn bred "credentialism," an attitude among employers who valued the number of degrees a prospective employee had more than actual learning and/or experience. Indeed, economic studies during those years harped on the financial rewards that would accrue to those who held advanced degrees.[71]

In fact, over the last twenty years most jobs have not demanded an increase in education. As a result many workers tend to be "overeducated" and frustrated. Studies show that the more education workers have, the more likely they will be to seek better jobs, and be less productive and more dissatisfied with their present ones. In one survey, over 33 percent of the employees interviewed believed they had more education than their jobs required.[72]

Any prospective solution to the overeducation problem will have to consider individual needs and capabilities, and eventually the traditional patterns of education and work may have to be altered. There will always be some who want a university education—either for itself or as the prelude to a job. But perhaps most people would get more from college only after they have had some work experience; and still others might find themselves learning all the skills they need directly from their job.[73]

As leisure time has increased, there has been a proliferation of organizations and agencies, both commercial and nonprofit, devoted to recreational activities. In the future we can expect more and better

[69]H.E.W., *Work in America*, p. 21-22.

[70]Neil W. Chamberlain, *The Limits of Corporate Responsibility* (New York: Basic Books, 1973), pp. 204, 206.

[71]H.E.W., *Work in America*, p. 135.

[72]Sar A. Levitan and William Johnston, *Work Is Here to Stay, Alas* (Salt Lake City, Utah: Olympus, 1973), p. 74.

[73]Janice N. Hedges, "New Patterns for Working Time," *Monthly Labor Review* (February 1973), p. 7.

community planning for recreation and increased public recreation services from higher levels of government. Indeed, some researchers predict that recreation will take on the attributes and status of a profession in the near future.[74] Recreation professionals would have the task of developing and coordinating recreational activities to satisfy the needs of society and of the individual.

One requirement for the future is the development and implementation of educational changes that will prepare people for a "leisure age." Vocational preparation should not be the sole objective of education in a society in which the demands of work on time and energy are expected to decrease. Rather, another goal of the schools should be to provide people with the skills and capabilities required to achieve self-actualization in a non-work-oriented world.[75]

[74]Norman P. Miller and Duane Robinson, *The Leisure Age: Its Challenge to Recreation* (Belmont, Calif.: Wadsworth, 1963), p. 12.

[75]William Faunce, *Problems of Industrial Society* (New York: McGraw-Hill, 1968), pp. 173-174.

Summary

While work provides workers with the essentials of life, and society with the goods and services it needs, it also confers a sense of self-worth and determines one's place in the social structure. Although the Greeks and Romans considered work a curse, the Hebrews and Christians regarded it to be important to physical and spiritual well-being; Martin Luther endowed work with religious significance, and John Calvin transformed it into an end in itself.

Since 1900 the occupational structure of the United States has changed from a largely agricultural base to one dominated by white-collar employment and specialized into thousands of different occupations. Today, most people work in large bureaucratic organizations; relatively few are self-employed. Older men are gradually being eliminated from the labor force, and women of all ages are beginning to participate in greater numbers.

The lack of any deep satisfaction in much routine work today has produced social alienation, with its attendant psychological damage, among both blue- and white-collar employees. The economic recession of the 1970s and, to a lesser degree, automation have created another major social problem—large-scale unemployment. Automation, at present, seems to serve the needs of management more than workers; if adopted on a wide scale, it would involve a reduction of work skills for most workers and a realignment of authority for a few.

Job satisfaction and dissatisfaction seem to depend on separate factors. Satisfaction is related to achievement, recognition, responsibility, meaningful work, and, of course, income; dissatisfaction is caused by such factors as too close supervision, poor working conditions, low pay, isolation, and boring work.

Despite the economic slowdown, most working people have more leisure time than ever before. Leisure time, however, is often meaningful only in relation to work; and many leisure-time activities share common characteristics with work.

The health of thousands of workers is impaired each year by job-related accidents and pollution, particularly in mines, on farms, and in the chemical and textile industries. The Occupational Safety and Health Administration (OSHA), which sets health standards for industry, lacks adequate regulatory powers. Its standards are opposed both by business, which resents government interference, and by labor which considers them inadequate.

Many social critics are advocating that corporations take on a larger share of responsibility for solving many work-related problems, in view of the fact that they employ such a large part of the work force. Another shift in public policy will have to occur in order to make the educational criteria for most jobs more realistic.

Bibliography

Berman, Daniel M. *Death on the Job: Occupational Health and Safety Struggles in the U.S.* New York: Monthly Review Press, 1979.

Best, Fred, ed. *The Future of Work.* Englewood Cliffs, N.J.: Prentice-Hall, 1973.

Braverman, Harry. *Labor & Monopoly Capital: The Degradation of Work in the Twentieth Century.* New York: Monthly Review Press, 1974.

Chamberlain, Neil W. *The Limits of Corporate Responsibility.* New York: Basic Books, 1973.

Gooding, Judson. *The Job Revolution.* New York: Walker, 1972.

Jaques, Eliot. *Work, Creativity, and Social Justice.* New York: International Universities Press, 1970.

Levitan, Sar A., and Johnston, William B. *Work Is Here to Stay, Alas.* Salt Lake City, Utah: Olympus, 1973.

Marcson, Simon. *Automation, Alienation, and Anomie.* New York: Harper & Row, 1970.

Parker, Stanley. *The Future of Work and Leisure.* New York: Praeger, 1971.

Sexton, P., and Sexton, B. *Blue Collars and Hard Hats: The Working Class and the Future of American Politics.* New York: Random House, 1971.

Terkel, Studs. *Working.* New York: Avon, 1972.

Wolfbein, Seymour. *Work in American Society.* Glenview, Ill.: Scott, Foresman, 1971.

14

Urban Problems

Facts about Urbanism

- Almost 75 percent of the American population lives in an urban area, yet in a recent poll, only 13 percent considered cities the most desirable place to live.

- Since 1947, the central cities have lost more than 1,100,000 manufacturing jobs.

- Until the mid-1960s, only 0.5 percent of all federal expenditures was spent on urban renewal.

- In 1978, less than 10 percent of the federal budget was allocated for direct aid to cities.

- Since World War II, the suburbs have grown twice as fast as the central cities.

- Suburban shopping centers now account for more than half of all retail sales in the United States.

I view great American cities as pestilential to the morals, health, and the liberties of man.

—Thomas Jefferson, 1780

The city has become the central feature of modern civilization . . . rural civilization, whose making engaged mankind since the dawn of history, is passing away. The city has erased the landmarks of an earlier society. Man has entered an urban age.

—Frederick C. Howe, 1906

The American City

Americans have been flocking to the cities for more than 200 years. In 1780, 90 percent of the American population lived in rural areas; by 1900, only about 65 percent did; in 1920, the urban/rural ratio was approximately 50/50. By 1975, more than 150 million people—nearly 75 percent of the United States population—resided in urban areas, and an additional 20 percent lived within the labor-shed—the zone of reasonable commutation—of a central city.[1]

There is every indication that the urbanization of America will continue. Sociologists are unanimous in their prediction that an ever-increasing share of the country's population will live and work within metropolitan areas.[2] If, as Frederick Howe predicted, we have entered an urban age, what can we expect of life in the new metropolis? And what is life like there now?

Although cities have changed tremendously throughout history, there are some basic similarities between cities of today and those of ancient and medieval times. As in the past, cities are dependent upon an agricultural

[1]John Kasarda, "Urbanization, Community and the Metropolitan Problem," in *Handbook of Contemporary Urban Life*, ed. David Street (San Francisco: Jossey-Bass, 1978), p. 33.

[2]Benjamin Chinitz, "City and Suburb," in *The Economics of Metropolitan Growth*, ed. Benjamin Chinitz (Englewood Cliffs, N.J.: Prentice-Hall, 1964), p. 12.

hinterland able to produce enough extra food for both consumption and resale. An intricate transportation system is also required to facilitate the movement of goods, and an ever-increasing division of labor is necessary to manufacture these and other articles for trade. Strikes by farmers and dairymen, or truckers and transportation workers, can starve a city as easily as a mass exodus of skilled laborers to suburbia or an energy crisis can wreak havoc with its industrial base.

Cities and the Industrial Revolution

The history of the city in the United States begins after the Industrial Revolution. The United States remained essentially an agrarian country until the nineteenth century, and the few existing cities were scarcely more than market towns. It was efficient transportation and the effects of industrialization that caused the bulk of urban growth. Just as technological innovation, like the use of cast iron in building construction and the invention of the elevator, made it possible for a city to expand vertically in a veritable forest of "skyscrapers," more efficient modes of transportation, like horse-drawn buses and railroads, made it possible for the city to expand horizontally as well.[3] Railway lines and telegraph wires crossed the continent, tying cities closely to the middle-American agricultural heartland. In turn, these improved methods of communication promoted westward expansion and the development of new cities. Many towns were built around railroad lines. Such urban growth provided a larger market for agricultural products, which motivated farmers to invent new ways of growing and harvesting crops to increase efficiency and minimize expense. In a circle of prosperity, the resultant technological advancements aided the continued development of the city. As cities grew, the co-existence of large populations within limited amounts of space began to present special problems. Living within a concentrated community focuses attention on matters of mutual concern and need, concerns that even the individualistically inclined American populace was unable to ignore. Lighting, fire protection, the care of streets, crime prevention, sewage disposal, water, community health, and marketing facilities all became part of the community consciousness, and therefore the concern of municipal governments.

Urban Growth and Social Problems

It was not until the twentieth century that systems for proper disposal of waste and for furnishing an adequate water supply were finally developed. Previously, "the removal of garbage generally devolved on roving swine and goats, while drainage remained pretty much an unsolved problem, though in a few communities householders laid private sewers."[4] Cities were notorious for death rates that were substantially higher than rural areas, with larger cities suffering higher rates than smaller cities.[5] Writing in 1899, Arnold Weber attributed this "excessive urban mortality . . . to lack of pure air, water and sunlight, together with uncleanly habits of life induced thereby." He went on to say, however, that there was "no inherent external reason why men should die faster in larger communities than in small hamlets, provided

[3]Edgar Butler, *The Urban Crisis: Problems and Prospects in America* (Santa Monica, Calif.: Goodyear, 1977), p. 36.

[4]Arthur M. Schlesinger, "The City in American History," in *Reader in Urban Sociology*, ed. Paul H. Hatt and Albert J. Reiss, Jr. (Glencoe, Ill.: Free Press, 1951), p. 109.

[5]Butler, *The Urban Crisis*, p. 36.

they are not too ignorant, too stupid, or too individualistic to cooperate in the security of common benefits."[6] In fact, innovations in medicine and sanitation did reduce the unhealthy conditions of early urban life.

Management Problems Due to Congestion

In general, as cities have grown larger and more crowded, it has become more difficult to manage them. Early American cities were homogenous and relatively small in both area and population. So few Americans lived in them that urban problems could either be ignored or were manageable in the context of the times. As cities grew in size, however, so did their problems. Traffic and transportation facilities were often inadequate; people demanded a variety of municipal services, such as sewage disposal, fire and police protection, and a clean water supply, all of which increased governmental costs. In 1844, New York City was the first to incorporate police services within the municipal government. Prior to that, cities used a combination of private day policemen and part-time hired night watchmen. Gradually, other public services—fire protection, water, sewage, and the like—were incorporated into the city government.[7]

In the mid-1800s, as cities became more congested, slums began to emerge, inhabited mostly by the thousands of immigrants from Ireland, Germany, Italy, and Poland.

> In 1890, New York (including the still legally separate municipality of Brooklyn) contained more foreign-born residents than any city in the world. The city had half as many Italians as Naples, as many Germans as Hamburg, twice as many Irish as Dublin, and two and a half times the numbers of Jews in Warsaw. In 1893, Chicago contained the third largest Bohemian community in the world; by the time of the First World War, Chicago ranked only behind Warsaw and Loda as a city of Poles.[8]

With the emergence of slums came political "machines." These machines drew support from the slum dwellers, the criminal classes, and the fire companies, trafficking in franchises for the new municipal services and setting the stage for the wanton municipal corruption that followed the Civil War.[9] Andrew D. White, in 1890, noted: "With very few exceptions, the city governments of the United States are the worst in Christendom—the most expensive, the most inefficient, and the most corrupt."[10]

Anti-Urban Bias

Anti-urban sentiment appears to be a tradition in American life. Observers like Walt Whitman, who wrote that "the work of man . . . is great . . . in these ingenuities, streets, goods, houses, ships . . . these hurrying, feverish, electric crowds of men," were definitely in the minority.[11] Public sentiment

---

[6]Arnold R. Weber, "Labor Market Perspectives of the New City," in *Urbanism in World Perspective: A Reader*, ed. Sylvia Fleis Fava (New York: Thomas Y. Crowell Company, 1968), p. 348.

[7]Butler, *The Urban Crisis*, p. 37.

[8]Charles N. Glaab and A. Theodore Brown, *A History of Urban America* (New York: Macmillan, 1967), p. 139.

[9]Schlesinger, "The City in American History," p. 115.

[10]Andrew D. White, "The Government of American Cities," *Forum*, vol. 10 (1890-1891).

[11]Walt Whitman, *Democratic Vistas and Other Papers* (New York: Scholarly Press, 1970).

against cities generally echoed the anti-urban bias of Thomas Jefferson, who wrote that "the mobs of great cities add just so much to the support of pure government, as sores do to the strength of the human body."[12]

Obviously, the current conflict between the city and suburbia is nothing new. It has been a continuing theme in utopian literature for centuries. America was founded on the myth of the gentleman farmer. American literature, particularly in the nineteenth century, extolled the virtues of the self-sufficient farmer, enshrined in an agricultural paradise, evoking memories of simpler, happier, more innocent times.[13]

From the outset, the city has been perceived as contrary to the "natural" relationship between the person and the environment. Jacques Ellul asserts that the "city was, from the day of its creation, incapable, because of the motives behind its construction, of any other destiny than that of killing the country, where God put man to enable him to live his life as best he could. The City was built as protection for man."[14] Ellul perceives the city as a fortress where we may attempt to hide from the judgment of God. His assertions have no base in accepted sociological thought, but they are in an old anti-urban tradition that is by no means dead. Although the image of the sacred city does appear, for example, Jerusalem or Rome, it is the image of the sinful city—Sodom and Gomorrah, "Gay Paree"—that predominates. Heresy and vice are associated with the city: virtue and justice live in the country.[15]

In the 1970s the American public was asked: "If you could live anywhere in the United States that you wanted to, would you prefer a city, suburban area, small town or farm?" Only 13 percent of those queried opted for life in a city. Of those who were already living in cities of 500,000 or more, 80 percent claimed to prefer not to live there.[16] This is not surprising. Anti-urban bias has become so firmly embedded in the fabric of American consciousness that a profound conflict exists between the values of what is perceived to be the "real, genuine America" and the attraction of the city and its cluster of old and new technologies.[17]

Political figures from Andrew Jackson, Abraham Lincoln, and William Jennings Bryan to Lyndon Johnson and Jimmy Carter, have all stressed the virtues of their rural upbringings. Cities have consistently been associated with corruption, with the "shame" of political machines and the "danger" of immigrant hordes.[18] The dichotomy modern man experiences between rural life and city life has crystallized into what Claude Fischer calls the four rural-city polarities: 1. nature versus art; 2. familiarity versus strangeness; 3. community versus individualism; and 4. tradition versus change.[19] It is obvious and undeniable that big cities offer a different environment from that

---

[12]Thomas Jefferson, *Notes on the State of Virginia*, ed. Bernard Wishy and William C. Leuchtenburg (New York: Harper & Row, 1977), p. 118.

[13]Jeffrey K. Hadden and Josef J. Barton, "An Image That Will Not Die: Thoughts on the History of Anti-Urban Ideology," in *The Urbanization of the Suburbs*, ed. Louis H. Masoti and Jeffrey K. Hadden (Beverly Hills, Calif. and London: Sage Publications, 1973), p. 93.

[14]Jacques Ellul, *The Technological Society* (New York: Knopf, 1964), pp. 8, 58.

[15]Hadden and Barton, "An Image That Will Not Die," p. 15.

[16]*Gallup Opinion Index, 1973*, no. 94, p. 31.

[17]Leo Marx, *The Machine in the Garden: Technology and the Pastoral Ideal in America* (New York: Oxford University Press, 1964), pp. 22–23, 29–32.

[18]Schlesinger, "The City in American History," pp. 116-117.

[19]Claude S. Fischer, *The Urban Experience* (New York: Harcourt Brace Jovanovich, 1976), p. 18.

provided by small towns or rural places. The concept of urbanism seeks to explain this unique environment and its effects on urban populations. Individualism, inter-group conflict and accommodation, and the continued emergence of new groups and communities are all products of urban life. In our discussion of urbanism, we shall stress the special consequences for people and their communities of life in cities.

Urbanism: The Social Psychology of Cities

Determinism There are several theories of urbanism. Historically, the oldest and most influential is called determinism, or the *"Wirthian Theory,"* after Louis Wirth, its leading proponent in the United States. Wirth's basic argument is that cities increase both social and personality disorders. He categorizes the city as "a relatively large, dense, and permanent settlement of socially heterogeneous individuals."[20] Borrowing extensively from the teachings of another sociologist, Georg Simmel, Wirth argues that the urban environment literally assaults the city dweller with multiple and intense stimuli. The pressures of this over-abundance of stimulation forces Wirth's urbanities to adapt in order to maintain their mental equilibrium. It is Wirth's contention that the resultant adaptation adversely affects the city dweller. The mechanisms that permit the urbanite to withstand the shock of multiple stimuli also cause the city dweller to be insulated from other people. As a result, the typical city resident "becomes aloof, brusque, impersonal in his dealings with others, and emotionally buffered in his human relationships."[21] When such withdrawal fails to counter the effects of over-stimulation, people experience "psychic overload," resulting in irritation, anxiety, and nervous strain.

Wirth asserts that this interpersonal estrangement loosens the bonds that unite people. In some cases, these bonds are completely severed, resulting in anti-social and alienated behavior. When people are left without emotional support or societal restraint, they begin to act out their fantasies. According to Wirth, this explains both the intense creativity and technological advancement as well as the psychopathic and criminal behavior that is so prevalent in cities. Each extreme is a result of looser social mores and interpersonal relationships.

Another by-product of city life is the economic process of competition, comparative advantage, and specialization. One outgrowth of this is evidenced in community differentiation. In most cases, this differentiation is most plainly visible in the division of labor, although it exists in other forms as well, for example, in separate districts for business, residence, and entertainment. In an urban environment, people often assume many roles during an average day involving social interaction with co-workers, neighbors, close friends, and family. In Wirth's opinion, the very multiplicity of people and places that compete for an urbanite's time and attention weakens social bonds. As people continue to enter into primary relationships outside the family, the family becomes less important. Since many of these relationships are scattered across the city, neighbors also play a less significant role. It is Wirth's contention that such loosening of social ties produces an alienated condition that he terms

[20]Fischer, *The Urban Experience*, p. 29.
[21]Fischer, *The Urban Experience*, p. 31.

anomie, in essence, the weakening of those norms that govern acceptable social behavior. Once the personal approach to preserving societal norms becomes weakened, other attempts to control social behavior must be made. Most often, this takes the form of impersonal complaints to governmental authorities. Wirth asserts that such impersonal control can never fully replace the power and moral strength of small, primary groups. Therefore, he considers cities, with their inclination toward individualism, estrangement, stress and especially social disorganization, as societies in which social relationships are weak. Such weakness may indeed provide more freedom for individuals, but it also promotes a debilitated moral order, an affliction that permits social disruption and promotes personality disorders.

Although Wirth is recognized as the spokesman for the classic view of urbanism, his theories are by no means accepted by all urban sociologists. Herbert Gans, for example, has challenged Wirth's ideas with his own "compositional" theory of urbanism.[22] The difference between the two theories rests on an opposing view of how the city affects the existence of small groups. Compositionalists see the city as a mosaic of social worlds—intimate social circles with their roots in kinship, ethnicity, neighborhoods, occupations, and life-styles. Whereas Wirth believes that the pressures of the city disrupt these worlds, drawing people away from close association with family and neigh-

[22]Fischer, *The Urban Experience*, pp. 33-34.

Compositionalism

This neighborhood block party on New York's Upper West Side illustrates the Compositionalist Theory; cities create a mosaic of social and cultural groups.
Jan Lukas/Photo Researchers, Inc.

bors, compositionalists believe that these worlds persist undiminished in an urban setting. Gans contends, in fact, that the closeness of the social worlds envelops and protects individuals from the pressures of city life.

Compositionalists cite economic position, cultural characteristics, and marital and family status as the determinants of personal behavior. The strength of these attributes, rather than the size or density of the community at large, molds a person's social and psychological experience. To a compositionalist, the social-psychological effects of urbanism are meaningless, which, of course, directly contradicts the determinist theory, which views cities as having a direct impact on the coherence of such groups.

Subculturism   Claude S. Fischer has developed a theory of urbanism that agrees with the determinists in acknowledging that cities produce major social-psychological effects. Fischer, however, believes that these effects occur not because social groups break down, but because cities foster new ones.

Known as the "subcultural theory,"[23] Fischer's argument suggests that the most socially significant consequence of an urban community is the promotion of diverse subcultures—culturally distinctive groups such as college students, Chinese-Americans, artists, and homosexuals, for example. Contrary to Wirth, who believes that no significant primary social relationships can be achieved in an urban environment, Fischer believes that people in cities live within meaningful social worlds. More importantly, subculturalists contend that large communities attract immigrants precisely because of this distinctively urban phenomenon. In Fischer's view, urbanism intensifies subcultures. This is accomplished in part through critical mass: a large city is more apt to attract a sizable proportion of a given subculture than a smaller community. This same process operates for artists, academics, bohemians, corporate executives, criminals, and computer programmers as well as for ethnic, racial, or sexual minorities.

Subcultural intensification also occurs through multi-group contact. In a densely populated environment, subcultures are constantly bumping into one another. Sometimes these groups co-exist amicably, like police and gays in New York and San Francisco; in other instances, such as with blacks and Irish in Boston, tensions mount. Even when one subculture finds another annoying, threatening, or both, a common reaction is to embrace one's own social world all the more firmly, thereby contributing to subculture intensification.

Urban Unconventionality   One of the major and constant themes in Western culture is that cities are hotbeds of radicalism and social deviance. Research has shown that the larger the community, the greater the likelihood that its citizens will be unconventional and noncomformist.[24] This is true with every culture, every period of history, and within all walks of life. The cities are always first with the latest product—be it a style of fashion or a technological advance. From the city, new ideas spread outward to the hinterlands; rural residents are often the last to relinquish accepted attitudes and standards of behavior. As a result, small

[23]Fischer, *The Urban Experience*, p. 35.
[24]Claude S. Fischer, "Urbanism As A Way of Life," *Sociological Methods and Research*, vol. 1, no. 2 (November 1972), 2.

towns and rural areas tend to preserve the traditional virtues in the face of urban unconventionality, and perceive city dwellers as either criminal, immoral, scary, innovative, or any combination thereof. (In turn, of course, urbanites tend to consider the rest of the country backward and dull.)

One growing urban phenomenon that inspires intense mistrust outside of cities is the nontraditional family unit. In cities, people tend to remain single longer; marriages more frequently end in divorce; and families are apt to be smaller. One of the principal reasons for this is that urban dwellers, because of their exposure to a multitude of life-style choices, are often involved in less conventional family structures than their rural counterparts. City dwellers are frequently more amenable to and more capable of satisfying personal needs with people and activities outside the family. As a consequence, they depend less on relatives for personal interaction.

Nontraditional Family Units

All three theories of urbanism—determinism, compositionalism, and subculturalism—agree that the family serves fewer functions in the city than in the country. They disagree, however, on how this affects the intensity of family ties. Ethnographic reports from around the world indicate that familial bonds persist and even thrive in an urban situation. Survey studies conducted in several American cities disclosed that not only do city inhabitants enjoy frequent interaction with their families, but that they also tend to visit with and rely upon their relatives substantially more than they rely upon any other primary association.[25] Although the family is essential for fewer functions in an urban environment than in a rural one, family ties appear to be as close and as

[25]Fischer, *The Urban Experience*, p. 143.

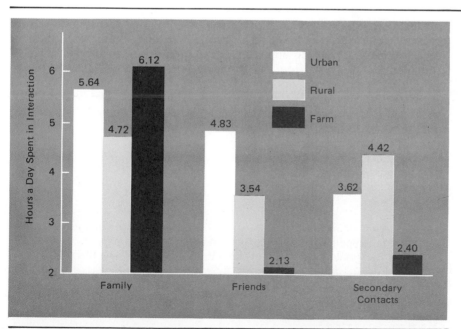

Figure 14-1

Average Time Spent Each Day with Family, by Urban, Rural and Farm Populations

Source: Claude S. Fischer, *The Urban Experience* (New York: Harcourt Brace Jovanovitch, 1976), p. 140.

psychologically important in the city as in the country. The life-style of a family may be changed by urbanizaton, but family units both persist and flourish in an urban setting. (See Figure 14-1.)

Metropolis and Megalopolis

Metropolis   In the nineteenth century, the mass migration from the farms to the cities was described as a rural-urban flow. But with 95 percent of the United States population living in or near urban areas, the pattern of flow has changed from rural-urban to inter-metropolitan.[26] In 1910, the Bureau of the Census identified 25 "metropolitan districts." This term was designed to assist in the measurement of urban populations, which, even then, could no longer be contained within the traditional urban political boundaries. These districts varied in size from the largest—New York, with its 616,927 acres of land and 6,474,568 people—to the smallest—Portland, Oregon, with a population of 215,048 and a land area of 43,538 acres. Through the metropolitan district approach, the unity of such urban areas as the Twin Cities of Minnesota, the cities on San Francisco Bay, and the two Kansas Cities along the Missouri-Kansas border were identified. The importance of the continuous clusters along the eastern seaboard around Philadelphia, New York, and Boston also became apparent. Since then, the continued growth of these several metropolitan regions has led many urban sociologists to predict what may well be the next stage in urban orbanization—the megalopolis.

Megalopolis   Jean Gottmann was the first to use the term "megalopolis," which is often applied to an urban region that contains several metropolitan areas, just as "con-urbation" identifies an urban region composed of several former cities. The term "megalopolis" is actually more functionally operative in Europe, where it ideally identifies the vast urban region along the Ruhr River in the Amsterdam-Haarlem-Leiden-The Hague-Rotterdam-Utrecht complex in the Netherlands.[27] But the dramatic urbanization along the east coast of the United States, stretching from Boston to Miami Beach, may soon require use of the term "megalopolis" in this country.

How do "metropolitan" and "urban" differ? An urban area usually contains a large population within a limited area. A metropolitan region contains several urban communities, all of which are located in close proximity to one another. For example, as an urban area, New York City contains 4,977 people per square mile. The Greater New York Metropolitan Area contains not only New York City, but also parts of New Jersey (including Newark), Connecticut, Long Island, and Westchester County.[28]

Urban Growth and the Transportation Boom   The dominant theme in the history of the American city in the twentieth century is metropolitanism. The growth of metropolitanism is often associated with the widespread availability of the automobile. Although the importance of the automobile in this process cannot be disputed, there were other factors

---

[26]Chinitz, "City and Suburb," p. 3.
[27]Glaab and Brown, "The Emergence of Metropolis," p. 12.
[28]Chinitz, "City and Suburb," p. 3.

that enabled large cities to develop into metropolitan areas. Modern merchandising, with its emphasis on widespread trade, innovations in printing that permitted newspapers to print more cheaply and therefore circulate more widely, and refinements in short-distance transportation and communication all brought the life of the inner city out to its suburban regions. In fact, one convenient method of estimating the range of metropolitan influence utilized by urban sociologists in the past was to measure the circulation of city newspapers.[29]

Relatively primitive communication and transportation facilities and the need for defensive fortifications forced ancient and medieval cities to be compact, and the movement of their inhabitants was restricted to a relatively small area. This was also true for cities in the United States throughout most of the nineteenth century, when walking was the chief mode of transportation. After 1870, however, several major advances, beginning with the horse-drawn streetcar, allowed urban residents the luxury of living up to five miles from their place of business. The day of the commuter had dawned. Electric trolley lines and streetcars were introduced in the 1880s and 1890s, extending the commuting distance to ten miles—nearly twice as far. When rapid-transit electric trains were implemented around the turn of the century, the distance doubled once again.[30]

Suburbanization

The trend toward suburbanization began in earnest with the introduction of commuter railways. As wealthy third- and fourth-generation urbanites retreated from the central city, putting increasing distances between their residences and their places of business, the separation between low income and high income neighborhoods increased markedly. Quick to follow the trend, commercial institutions began their own redistribution process. The first to vacate the central city were convenience goods and service establishments, those businesses most dependent upon the type of customer that was rapidly escaping to suburbia. While these businesses and various manufacturing concerns were leaving the central city, professional service organizations were moving in, creating a central business district composed of administrative, communications, financial, and other businesses that serviced the entire metropolitan region.

By the 1930s, the automobile had made suburban development a major factor in the economic, social, and political life of the United States.[31] Motor vehicle registration increased from 8,000 in 1900 to 26,352,000 in 1930, representing an increase from approximately one automobile for every 10,000 persons to one automobile per household.[32] The automobile altered the shape of urban expansion. Whereas previous suburban growth had developed along railroad lines and other public transport systems, the automobile permitted a much more dispersed growth. By 1930, urban sprawl was well on its way.

This rapid growth among the outlying rings of metropolitan areas occurred so dramatically that, by 1950, suburbs were growing two and a half times faster than central cities. In 1910, only 15.7 percent of the total United States

[29]Glaab and Brown, "The Emergence of Metropolis," p. 15.
[30]Butler, *The Urban Crisis*, p. 36.
[31]Kasarda, "The Metropolitan Problem," p. 30.
[32]Glaab and Brown, "Metropolis," pp. 16-17.

population lived in metropolitan rings; by 1950 48.6 percent did. And the trend has continued. The total population in 1965 had risen to 194 million; of that number, 130 million people lived in the 219 metropolitan areas recorded by the Census Bureau. Two-thirds of the populace lived in metropolitan districts. Between 1960 and 1965, the growth rate for the United States as a whole was 7.1 percent; the growth rate for non-metropolitan areas was only 5.7 percent, while the rate of increase among the metropolitan population was 9.3 percent. Within that same time period, the growth of metropolitan rings increased by 14.5 percent, markedly faster than the increase within the central cities, which was only 7.9 percent.[33]

This steady growth has posed many problems for the older cities, particularly for their internal structure and composition. As Benjamin Chinitz stated, there is nothing homogeneous about a metropolitan area.[34] With the increasing differentiation between central city and suburban ring, and the subsequent outflow of population and industry, America's cities are beset with social and economic problems of seemingly insurmountable proportions. As urban history shows, the steady flight to the suburbs by business, industry, and residents—all eager for less expensive and more comfortable quarters—has made renovation and rehabilitation of the central city both difficult and expensive. In many older metropolitan areas, particularly those in the Northeast, the abandonment of urban neighborhoods to the poor, who are ill-equip-ped to move, has led to the proliferation of slums, causing both the economic base and the actual population of the city to decline.[35] (See Chapter 7.)

Urban Problems

Deconcentration   The primary cause of central city decay is deconcentration: the flight to the suburbs of the middle and upper-middle class families; the tremendous influx into the central cities of poor minority groups, the chronically unemployed, the aged, and others who tend to be more of a fiscal liability than an asset to central city budgets; the retreat by commerce and industry from the taxing jurisdiction of the central cities; the disparity between available jobs within the central city and the resident labor force that is not equipped to fill those jobs; and the daily flow into the city of residents of the suburban rings, who utilize public facilities without paying for their upkeep. All of these circumstances, as John Kasarda enumerates, increase the debt service for the central cities at a time when their fiscal base contracts and their public service needs have increased substantially.[36]

The decade between 1920 and 1930 was a period of pronounced deconcentration, or suburbanization, in the United States. In every decade since 1930, the population within the suburban rings increased substantially more than the populations of the central cities. By the 1960s, suburbanization accounted for practically all growth within metropolitan areas. Although deconcentration started as early as 1900, it was only after World War II that suburbanization created problems, essentially because the redistribution of

[33]Glaab and Brown, "The Emergence of Metropolis," p. 13.
[34]Chinitz, "City and Suburb," pp. 22-23.
[35]Chinitz, "City and Suburb," p. 27.
[36]Kasarda, "The Metropolitan Problem," p. 44.

As consumers and then business and industry have moved away from the city, there has been a continuing growth in the number of suburban shopping malls, and the volume of commercial business they do.
UPI

the population slipped over city limits and because federal policies encouraged the flow of the population away from the cities.[37] Suburbanization of the middle and upper-middle classes is directly attributable to the emergence of the automobile, commuter railroads, rising real incomes, federally insured home mortgages, and state and federally-funded suburban highway systems, all of which reduced both the cost and the inconvenience of life outside the central city. As people left the city, business and industry quickly followed. The years from 1954 to 1977 saw the construction of more than 15,000 suburban shopping centers and regional shopping-malls which, by 1978, were responsible for more than one-half the annual retail sales in the United States.[38]

Manufacturing Relocation

Manufacturers saw the advantages of suburban relocation when they were able to minimize their transportation and freight costs by locating near suburban highway systems. The traditional advantages of central city location no longer applied. Between 1947 and 1972, metropolitan central cities lost a net total of 1,146,845 manufacturing jobs; suburban rings acquired 4,178,230.[39]

To a certain extent, the departure of manufacturing concerns from the central city has been balanced by an influx of new types of establishments, offering specialized goods and services. Legal, government, and professional complexes, service organizations such as airline ticket agencies, advertising firms, and brokerage houses all have increased substantially within recent years. And yet, although the percentage of white collar jobs has increased in the central cities, it has increased four times faster in the outlying suburban areas.[40]

One could argue that urban problems as arising basically from the redistribution of population and industry to the suburbs, a shift made possible by technological changes in manufacturing and transportation. After all, on

[37]Kasarda, "The Metropolitan Report," pp. 32-35.
[38]Kasarda, "The Metropolitan Problem," p. 35.
[39]Kasarda, "The Metropolitan Problem," pp. 47-48.
[40]Kasarda, "The Metropolitan Problem," pp. 36-38.

one level suburbanization is simply the result of the natural flow of the population to outlying areas of cheaper land; but there is more to it than that. Inherent in the suburban dream is the desire to combine the conveniences of modern technology with the eighteenth-century myth of the gentleman farmer, still a dominant theme in American culture.[41]

Suburban Living: The "American Dream."   Thomas Jefferson's pastoral America has evolved into the present-day domesticated rural ideal of the middle class—i.e., suburbia. The late nineteenth century saw the construction of garden suburbs, such as Grosse Pointe and Shaker Heights. The twentieth century suburb is a variation on the same theme. As Jeffrey Hadden and Josef Barton explain, suburbs provide urban dwellers with the opportunity "to obtain attractive homes at a modest cost, to get into the genuine unspoiled country, to take their own social life with them, to restore to the land its elemental charm."[42]

The suburban home became a sanctuary, a refuge for the middle class from the pressures of urban society. Moreover, the traditional American dream—the rural ideal and the pleasures of family life—encourages deconcentration. At first, for those who could afford it, the balance was achieved through a house in the country and a home in the city. Once transportation facilities became revolutionized, a single home somewhere in the bucolic middle became the American ideal. In droves, upper-income city families relinquished the inner city to the poor, immigrants, and blacks.

> The norm of middle class aspiration is suburbia, and as our middle class has expanded, the distance between the city and the consensus of the good life has grown. Look at the advertisements of happy families drinking beer, washing the car, or tinkering with hobbies. . . . Rarely is there a city in the background. In the pictorial representation of the American Dream the *mis en scene* is suburbia. Idealogically, as well as physically, no dialect jokes, no racial characteristics mar the picture. All that is behind us; it is *similarity* that is celebrated, often with deliberate moral overtones.[43]

Federal Encouragement   Public policy—particularly in regard to urban renewal and highway construction—encouraged suburbanization to the detriment, and/or destruction, of inner city neighborhoods. Inequities in financial opportunities—particularly Federal Housing Authority (FHA) or Veterans Administration (VA) mortgages—made it more attractive and easier to buy a house in the suburbs than in the aging residential areas of the city. Since the larger proportion of the full mortgage is interest and therefore tax-deductible, simple economics makes it more expedient for most American families to move to the suburbs where they at least stand a chance of buying adequate housing.[44]

As Bernard Weissbourd points out, federal financing for home ownership—primarily in the suburbs—is much more accessible than are

[41] Hadden and Barton, "An Image That Will Not Die," p. 79.
[42] Hadden and Barton, "An Image That Will Not Die," p. 79.
[43] William H. Whyte, "The Anti-City," in *Man and the Modern City*, ed. Elizabeth Geen, Jeanne R. Lowe, and Kenneth Walker (Pittsburgh: University of Pittsburgh Press, 1963), p. 50.
[44] Hadden and Barton, "An Image That Will Not Die," p. 108.

funds for rental housing in the city.[45] Most public housing programs in the central cities have had less than favorable results. Except in the very few cases where careful planning made it possible to achieve successfully integrated projects, these public housing policies have merely managed to keep lower-income people in the city, thereby strengthening patterns of segregation.[46]

Federal funds, distributed under the Federal Defense Highway Program, have continually subsidized the automobile, while federal aid to mass transportation projects has been almost impossible to acquire. By encouraging highway construction rather than strengthening commuter mass-transportation, government encourages industry to leave the city, thereby eliminating a major portion of the central city's tax base. As Weissbourd has determined,

> a lower tax base means less money for education and for the adjustment of rural migrants to urban life. Poor schools and changing neighborhoods encourage middle-class white families to move to the suburbs. Higher welfare costs increase the tax rate and thus encourage industry to relocate in outlying areas. All of these factors are interrelated.[47]

And all of these factors undermine the vibrancy of urban life.

Socioeconomic Composition of Urban Population

Minority Migration

Today's cities are largely populated by immigrants from rural America who came for better jobs, higher wages, improved schooling for their children, and a generally higher standard of living.[48] This migration began in Colonial times, but was accelerated in the 1920s when the drop in foreign immigration forced America's cities to look to the rural heartland for cheap labor. With the prospect of ready employment in the industrial cities of the Northeast, the Midwest, and the South, large numbers of rural blacks moved to urban areas. This migration considerably altered the social patterns of the larger urban communities. Unlike the foreign migrants, who had settled in mixed urban enclaves and began to intermarry and disperse, the blacks in Northern cities settled in neighborhoods that quickly became and remained all black. Whereas earlier foreign immigrants gradually increased their incomes and moved out of the immigrant neighborhoods, the black settlements remained more permanent, creating cities within cities. The trend toward suburbanization of the wealthy had already been established among the cities' white populations. The urban segregation of blacks increased this tendency. As a result, upward mobility of blacks was severely limited and the precedent was set for increased economic and cultural segregation in today's cities.[49] (See Chapter 8.)

[45]Bernard Weissbourd, "Segregation, Subsidies and Megalopolis," in Fava, *Urbanism in World Perspective*, p. 546.

[46]Harold Mayer and C. Stein, "Public Housing as Community," *Architectural Record* (April 1964), p. 169.

[47]Weissbourd, "Segregation, Subsidies and Megalopolis," p. 548.

[48]Fischer, *The Urban Experience*, p. 79.

[49]Glaab and Brown, "The Emergence of Metropolis," p. 19.

Voluntary and Involuntary Segregation

Residential segregation usually occurs for two reasons: 1) voluntary concentration pertains to those people who choose to live with others similar to themselves, such as in the ethnic, artistic, or homosexual neighborhoods of big cities; and 2) involuntary segregation occurs when various segments of the population—blacks, Jews, the aged—are socially and/or economically forced to live in specific areas of the city. Although most immigrant groups to America's cities chose at first to live together in urban enclaves, the predicament among today's urban black and other racial minorities is more one of involuntary segregation. Within black neighborhoods, there is further substantial segregation according to income.[50] Phoebe Cottinham found that segregation of black families by income within the black community resembles the segregation of whites within white communities.[51] An earlier study by Ozzie Edwards shows that as relative income and socioeconomic status increase, segregation of ethnic populations decreases.[52]

For most city dwellers this means a limited choice of life-styles. This is especially true for minority groups and poor whites—in particular the elderly—and is caused as much by negative self-image as by racial and economic segregation. It is difficult for the poor, the aged, and the personally deficient to escape from undesirable or dangerous urban areas. As a consequence, the extent to which these people can be described as *voluntary* residents of a particular urban neighborhood is negligible. As neighborhoods decline, all people whose daily activity takes them into those areas face the hardships brought about by loss of mortgage money and other types of capital, and the types of support facilities and community services necessary for health and well-being. In order to withstand the deterioration of neighborhoods, a minimal economic base must be maintained, a base that will in turn sustain and encourage community participation and organization. As blue collar jobs continue to decline in central cities, and basic municipal services such as adequate housing and transportation facilities deteriorate, faith in community restoration and development fades, causing the inner city to crumble. Although the urbanization of American society has erased many social inequities, it has increased the problems faced by most metropolitan areas. Kasarda suggested that

> city populations have become poorer and more dependent; the city tax bases erode as industry, commerce, and jobs move to suburbia; these movements create transportation problems for inner city residents; and the cities continue to bear the costs of providing both daytime cultural and commercial amenities and nighttime facilities for entertainment and vice versa for their suburban visitors.[53]

Cities Lack Opportunities for Unskilled Labor

As highly skilled personnel move to the cities to fill professional, white-collar jobs, most unskilled or semi-skilled blue-collar positions have been transferred to the suburbs. This has dramatically curtailed those jobs that black and

[50]Wilfred G. Marston, "Socioeconomic Differentials Within Negro Areas of American Cities," *Social Forces* 48 (December 1969), 665-676.

[51]Phoebe H. Cottingham, "Black Income and Metropolitan Residential Segregation," *Urban Affairs Quarterly* 10 (March 1975), 273-296.

[52]Ozzie L. Edwards, "Patterns of Residential Segregation within a Metropolitan Ghetto," *Demography* 7 (May 1970), 185-193.

[53]David Street, "Life in Urbanized American," in Street, *Handbook of Contemporary Urban Life*, p. 637.

other racial and ethnic minorities who have come to the cities of the Northeast are most suited to fill. Industry's flight to the suburbs has widened the distance between the prospective employee's residence and prospective place of employment. As a result, job potential and upward mobility are severely impaired, increasing unemployment and welfare roles, and thereby eroding the cities' tax base and increasing municipal costs.[54]

Black migration to large cities has taken on a different aspect in recent years since many black migrants come from other urban communities rather than from rural areas. As a result, they tend to be, on the average, more highly educated and of a higher occupational status than existing black populations within the cities to which they migrate. Since housing in most of America's larger cities is now determined socioeconomically rather than racially, these blacks seek housing that is in line with their income level so their place of residence will be widely dispersed throughout the entire city.

Studies show that blacks and whites respond similarly to the social and economic forces that produce general differentiation of residential neighborhoods.[55] Within racially mixed neighborhoods, both black and white residents will be of a comparable socioeconomic status. As upper-income whites vacate their central city homes for the suburbs, they are generally replaced by blacks of an equal income bracket. Low-status neighborhoods tend to retain their low-status makeup.

Finances

A recent study on urban conditions, conducted by Richard P. Nathan and James W. Fossett of the Brookings Institution, showed that the economic gap between healthy and distressed cities has worsened in recent years, despite some signs of improvement in certain troubled areas. Many urban specialists fear that cities experiencing financial difficulties will channel funds away from improving essential services, such as streets, water and sewage systems, and mass transportation facilities, in order to finance their debts and meet operating costs. If this happens, the cities will be damaging their ability to function in years ahead.[56] Unfortunately, given the current national reluctance to deal with the predicament of America's large urban centers, most cities have very little choice.

Between 1848 and 1956, the expenditures of city governments rose only by about 75 percent. Since 1960, however, they have risen by almost 500 percent.[57] Population shifts within the boundaries of the central cities—shifts caused by geographic, social, and economic considerations—have further increased the financial pressures on the central cities. Within the larger cities, the increased concentration of low-income groups demands larger financial investment in both welfare programs and projects for social development. For many cities, competition with the suburbs requires large-scale physical

[54]Arnold R. Weber, "Labor Market Perspectives of the New City," p. 72.

[55]Karl E. Taeuber and Alma F. Taeuber, "Negroes in Cities," in Fava, *Urbanism in World Perspective*, pp. 271-272.

[56]Robert Reinhold, "For the Present: Cleveland Is a Sad but Special Case," *New York Times*, December 17, 1979, Sec. 4, p. 1.

[57]U.S. Department of Commerce, Bureau of the Census, *Statistical Abstract of the United States, 1970* (Washington, D.C.: U.S. Government Printing Office, 1971), p. 300.

rehabilitation and redevelopment projects. Otherwise, they will lose residents and businesses, and private as well as public investment, to outlying suburban rings.

Heavy Taxes   With the heavy exodus of industry to the suburbs, the real estate tax base of most central cities has reached the limit of economic feasibility. Property assessments provide cities with their major source of tax revenue, yet cities have fallen behind in the percentage of each tax dollar they are able to utilize. Weissbourd has suggested that

> the wealth produced by the cities has been drained out by federal taxes and re-distributed first to agriculture, second to suburbia, and third to the cities. At the same time, the welfare costs of the cities have increased their tax bases, so that what the federal government has contributed in the form of urban renewal has been taken away by the costs of municipal services.[58]

Housing

The majority of America's poor live in substandard, deteriorated housing that has been rejected by those with incomes that allow them to move to better accommodations. (See Chapters 7 and 8.) America's minorities—blacks, Hispanics, the aged—inhabit this substandard housing for two reasons: 1) most cannot afford an alternative; and 2) discrimination, on both a personal and institutional level, conspire to keep minorities, even those whose incomes are sufficient to enable them to relocate, in the slums. As a result, central city housing is at a premium. Most new housing is being built in the suburbs for those with middle- and upper-incomes; the older, inner-city housing within the metropolitan complex is taken over by the poor.

Urban Renewal and   Some urban and housing experts argue that many sections of today's cities that
Slum Clearance   are severely run down and even economically devastated can be rehabilitated. But as Lyle Shannon stated several years ago: "Unfortunately, the contention that slum clearance is a solution to a multitude of social problems may detract from more basic arguments for providing adequate housing for the less fortunate and their families."[59] Other sociologists argue that urban renewal is neither a relevant nor an advantageous solution to social problems. James Wilson states that "urban renewal has bypassed the real problems, or, in some cases, made them worse."[60]

Standard procedure in most urban renewal or redevelopment programs involves the mass removal and clearance of the slum housing. To accomplish this, the residents of these areas are forced to relocate. Since most urban renewal projects result in more expensive housing than that which it replaced, original residents of the areas are, for the most part, unable to return to their former neighborhoods. Those who are economically able to return, however,

[58]Weissbourd, "Segregation, Subsidies and Megalopolis," p. 555.
[59]Lyle W. Shannon, *An Assessment of the Need for Public Housing in Des Moines* (Iowa City, Iowa: University of Iowa Press, 1966).
[60]James Q. Wilson, "Urban Renewal Does Not Always Renew," *Harvard Today* (January 1965), pp. 2-8.

find that the characteristics that made their neighborhood their own—churches, schools, family, and friends—are no longer in place. The majority of those dislocated as a result of renewal move to areas as nearby as possible. As Nathaniel Lichfield wrote: "Most people who move because of urban renewal, move into adjacent areas that probably will be cleared in subsequent projects, which once again will require them to move."[61]

Instead of providing adequate housing at a low cost, most urban renewal drives out the poor from rehabilitated areas since most of the redeveloped

[61]Nathaniel Lichfield, "Relocation: The Impact on Housing Welfare," *Journal of the American Institute of Planners* 27 (August 1961), 199-203.

Atlanta's modern downtown area contrasts with the substandard housing just blocks away. Either racism or poverty or both often deny a city's poor better housing opportunities.
Allen Green/Photo Researchers, Inc.

housing is for those with high incomes, in direct competition with the suburbs. The idea of providing low-cost housing for low-income residents has never been a financially feasible proposition since public housing, the alternative, has seldom been politically expedient.

Governmental policies and management practices are extremely effective in controlling both the use and occupancy of housing projects for the poor. By restricting public housing exclusively to the poorest, federal policy often insures the almost immediate development of what has been called the "federal slum." By keeping members of the working poor with slightly larger than poverty-level incomes from living in these housing projects, the government restricts the developments to the very poor, to those on welfare, to broken families, and to the disabled. Public housing projects quickly become economic ghettos with "large concentrations of people with the greatest number of problems and the least amount of success in overcoming them."[62]

Government

Loss of Urban Self-Determinism

A major cause of the fiscal crises affecting the cities today is the inequitable distribution of economic resources and service costs between the cities and their suburban rings. This is caused by the rapid growth of metropolitan regions without a reorganization of the regions' political structure.[63] Traditionally, counties, municipalities, and townships all functioned to help state governments carry out their obligations within the political and legal systems, such as conducting elections and providing services. Responsibility for local issues fell exclusively upon the local governments. As population increased, townships were incorporated into small cities, and small cities were joined to larger ones. The emergence of special districts added to the intricacies of metropolitan government. As Butler indicated:

> Special districts have proliferated in urban regions, and there appears to be no abatement of this process. While many special districts cover only a small portion of the urban complex, others cover the entire metropolitan area. And some extend beyond the metropolitan region—for example, mass transit districts, airport districts, and harbor districts. These larger special districts have some elements of metropolitan-wide government, and they may be indicative of the future as more and more consolidation and unification takes place.[64]

Dependence on State and Federal Aid

The last decade has seen the growing dependence of cities upon state and federal government aid, both financial and political. Between 1970 and 1978, federal grants to state and local governments have more than tripled—from $24 billion to $81 billion. In 1978, more than $25 billion went to cities. This money was utilized by most cities, particularly the declining ones, to finance basic services, even though that was never the intention of federal aid. The paychecks of municipal and county employees throughout the nation have

---

[62]Harvey M. Choldin, "Social Life and the Physical Environment," in Street, *Handbook of Contemporary Urban Life*, p. 372; see also Scott Greer, "Urban Renewal and American Cities: The Dilemma of Democratic Intervention," in *Studies in Urban Society*, ed. Frank L. Sweetser (New York: Thomas Y. Crowell Company, 1970), pp. 170-171.

[63]Street, *Handbook of Contemporary Life*, p. 41.

[64]Butler, *The Urban Crisis*, pp. 103-104.

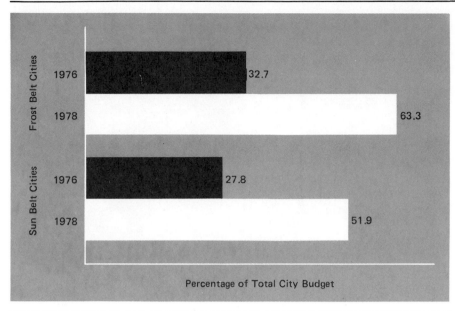

Figure 14-2

Cities' Increasing
Dependence on Federal
Aid

Source: The New York Times,
January 21, 1979, p. 33.

been underwritten with federal funds. Today, if the flow of funds to the cities were halted, all cities, especially those in decline, would be in danger of financial collapse.[65] (See Figure 14-2.) Needless to say, the federal funding of services that were previously considered under local domain is—however necessary—in direct contradiction to the American tradition of self-determination.

Jurisdictional Conflicts

In discussing which governmental agencies should be responsible for specific services and policies, it is obvious that such concerns as air and water pollution demand control over an entire area, rather than by strict municipal boundaries. This is also true for arterial waterways, mass transit, and water supplies. Less clear is the situation involving recreational facilities, public institutions such as libraries and museums, and public services such as police and fire protection. The benefits of all of these are not restricted to the borders of a single municipal jurisdiction. But, on the other hand, neither are they equally proportioned throughout the entire metropolitan community.[66] Who then is to pay how much for these necessary services?

David Street explains that city governments have been forced to bear the financial burden for municipal services, even though these services are extensively utilized by suburban residents. Thousands of visitors flock to city museums and parks every day, placing additional burdens on sanitation and public health facilities and transportation avenues, all of which must be paid

[65]John Herbers, "Probable Cut in U.S. Aid Termed Threat to Revitalization of Cities," *New York Times*, January 21, 1979.

[66]Harvey E. Brazer, "Some Fiscal Implications of Metropolitanism," in *Metropolitan Issues: Social, Governmental, Fiscal*, ed. Guthrie S. Birkhead (Syracuse, N.Y.: Maxwell Graduate School of Citizenship and Public Affairs, February 1962), pp. 61-82.

Garbage strikes and other city labor disputes have added to municipalities' need to seek federal aid for basic city services.
UPI

for by city taxes and municipal funds. In this way city residents assume the tax burden for their suburban neighbors.[67]

According to Thompson, whatever its actual political boundaries may be, a metropolitan area is in fact a single economic entity, with an integrated labor market, a unified transportation surface, and a closely interrelated set of housing submarkets.[68] To divide this single entity into several separate local, public economies results in wide-spread inefficiency. For example, there is the obvious problem of duplication of services. Thompson has shown that

> such duplication of local public facilities and services prevents the achievement of internal economies of scale, and autonomous municipalities complicate and inhibit the spatial coordination needed to lower the costs or raise the quality of public services in contiguous service units that share area-wide flows of vehicles, water and wastes that crisscross their common and largely arbitrary boundaries.[69]

Prospects

The emergence of the "sunbelt" as the urban area of the future has posed several problems for the older, large cities in northern industrial states. The employment base is shifting from these older cities to the emerging metropolitan areas of the South and West; as a result, their city tax bases are eroding, and inner-city unemployment, burgeoning welfare rolls, and

[67]Kasarda, "The Metropolitan Problem," p. 40.
[68]Wilbur R. Thompson, "The Economic Base of Urban Problems," in *Contemporary Economic Issues,* ed. Neil W. Chamberlain (Homewood, Ill.: Richard D. Irwin, 1969), p. 41.
[69]Thompson, "The Economic Base of Urban Problems," p. 41.

increased debt service are rising dramatically.[70] (See Table 14-1.) In short, the quality of life for many in these cities has suffered. To reverse this trend, several measures, both economic and social, need to be undertaken. As Weissbourd suggests, there is a tendency to assume that the flight to the

[70]Kasarda, "The Metropolitan Problem," p. 54.

Table 14-1
Cities Ranked by Population

1978 rank	1970 rank	Population	Change	Percent change
1	1	New York 7,422,831	−472,732	− 6.0%
2	2	Chicago 3,074,084	−295,273	− 8.8%
3	3	Los Angeles 2,743,994	− 65,819	− 2.0%
4	4	Philadelphia 1,797,403	− 199,395	− 6.6%
5	7	Houston 1,455,046	+222,244	+ 18.0%
6	5	Detroit 1,314,206	− 199,395	− 6.6%
7	8	Dallas 848,829	+ 4,428	+ 0.5%
8	6	Baltimore 827,439	− 78,348	− 8.6%
9	14	San Diego 789,059	+ 92,032	+ 13.0%
10	15	San Antonio 783,765	+ 129,612	+20.0%
11	11	Indianapolis 708,867	− 37,435	− 5.0%
12	9	Washington 700,130	− 56,380	− 7.4%
13	20	Phoenix 679,512	+ 97,950	+ 17.0%
14	17	Memphis 667,880	+ 44,350	+ 7.0%
15	13	San Francisco 663,478	− 52,196	− 7.0%
16	12	Milwaukee 661,082	− 56,290	− 7.8%
17	10	Cleveland 625,643	−125,236	−17.0%
18	16	Boston 618,250	− 22,821	− 3.6%
19	19	New Orleans 580,959	− 12,512	− 2.0%
20	31	San Jose, Calif. 573,806	+ 112,594	+24.0%

Note that all seven cities that gained population between 1970 and 1978 were in the sunbelt—Houston, Dallas, San Diego, San Antonio, Phoenix, Memphis and San Jose.
Source: © 1978 by *The New York Times* Company. Reprinted by Permission.

suburbs is an indication that people prefer a suburban home to a residence in the city.[71] Statistics prove, however, that across the nation residential land values in the cities are substantially higher than in the suburbs indicating that a central location is desirable to many. The fact that housing in the central city, particularly the expensive high-rise apartment complexes, is at a premium indicates that there is a growing market for city dwellings. According to Weissbourd, the fact that a central location still retains great economic value is the best evidence that the city can be restored. Vernon adds that the task of restoring the city also becomes easier since almost all American cities contain large areas of relatively inexpensive industrial land.[72]

Central-City Revitalization   Many urban sociologists view restoration projects in inner-city neighborhoods, such as Capitol Hill in Washington, D.C. and Park Slope and Cobble Hill in Brooklyn, N.Y., as indications of a revival of central-city life. Others are encouraged by the growth of luxury apartments and condominiums in and around business districts of most urban centers.[73] The majority of the new homesteaders are not middle- and upper-income families with school-age children, but rather are single adults, young professionals, recently-married couples, and older, wealthier couples whose children have left home.[74] Blake Fleetwood commented:

> It is becoming apparent that America's oldest cities, not only New York but Boston, Philadelphia, and Washington, are . . . beginning to be resettled. The signs are all around us. Young professional prople are flocking into New York City. Rents are higher than ever before, and vacant apartments are hard to come by.[75]

Industry's Return.   Besides the return of the middle class, if today's cities are to become fully revitalized they will also require the return of some of the industry that departed for the cheaper labor force and expanded facilities of the suburbs. Indeed, this seems to be occuring. In New York City, for example, private enterprise committed nearly a billion dollars in 1977 to construction in midtown Manhattan. Several new office towers and high-rise apartments were constructed on speculation. New York's renaissance is typical of what has been happening in other large cities. British urbanologist Peter Hall describes the process this way:

> At the very center of each world city there is found a small nucleus of highly-skilled professionals who live, in one way or another, by creating, processing, or exchanging ideas. The stockbroker, considering the fortunes of a hundred companies in a dozen countries; the company lawyer, pondering a difficult piece of patent law; the consultant; the university professor; the editor; the television producer; the advertising copywriter; the freelance photographer. All these people live only on their ideas, The central business district therefore can be seen as a specialized machine for producing, processing and trading

---

[71]Weissbourd, "Segregation, Subsidies and Megalopolis," p. 551.
[72]Vernon, *The Myth and Reality of Our Urban Problems,* pp. 45-46.
[73]Weissbourd, "Segregation, Subsidies and Megalopolis," pp. 551-554.
[74]Kasarda, "The Metropolitan Problem," p. 56.
[75]Blake Fleetwood, "The New Elite and an Urban Renaissance," *New York Times Magazine,* January 14, 1979, p. 16.

specialized intelligence. And the ideas industry is growing many times faster than industry as a whole.[76]

In other words, cities to a certain degree are helping to solve their problems by attracting new—and affluent—urban migrants.

Increased Revenues.   Ultimately, survival for America's cities depends upon increased revenues. To achieve this, both the states and the federal government must recognize and accept their fiscal obligations to the life of the city. Such services as welfare, public health, public housing, and urban renewal—all of which benefit populations well beyond the immediate residents of the central cities—deplete municipal tax revenues inordinately, and thereby create inequities that pose larger problems for the socioeconomic well-being of America's metropolitan communities. Financial responsibility for all areas in which local residents are being forced to pay for the conveniences of residents from neighboring regions—whether they be suburban rings, contiguous states, or other counties—must be taken over by a larger governmental body, either a metropolitan commission, the state government, or a federally-licensed program. Harvey Brazer suggests that "a federation of municipalities may assume responsibility for planning, water

[76]Peter Hall, *The World's Cities* (New York: McGraw-Hill, 1966).

Despite financial problems, racial tensions, and housing shortages, there can be a hopeful future for American cities. New York is drawing young and wealthy professionals who contribute to the city's vitality and prosperity.
UPI

supply, sewage disposal, arterial highways, and mass transit, all of which involve economies of scale as well as spillover effects."[77]

Such a redistribution of jurisdiction would compensate for the inequalities produced by residents of one community working in another. The implementation of non-property taxes and user-charge financing would also help to alleviate this problem. Although very little is currently known about the effects of property tax on land use in metropolitan areas, many sociologists believe that a tax that imposes substantial penalties upon improvement, a tax that rewards decay and dilapidation; and a tax that encourages land speculation that may possibly result in inordinately high social costs cannot be a healthy contributor to the economic and fiscal well-being of any urban area.[78]

Diverting federal funds into the development of mass transport systems, promoting well-planned policies that stabilize existing city neighborhoods and foster the construction of adequate urban housing for all income levels, and recognizing that the city plays an essential role in the socioeconomic growth of the nation as a whole are fundamental to reversing urban decay. Thomas Jefferson and the American myth to the contrary, the city has become the central feature of modern civilization. Programs that encourage rural or suburban development to the detriment of the cities are, as the research attests, shortsighted. The future of civilization rests with the world's cities. As it was put so prophetically, nearly a century ago: rural civilization is passing away; this is indeed an urban age.

[77]Brazer, "Some Fiscal Implications," p. 148.
[78]Brazer, "Some Fiscal Implications," p. 149.

Summary

The city has become a major feature of modern civilization. Despite Thomas Jefferson's belief that cities are "pestilential to the morals, health and the liberties of man," more than 75 percent of the population of the United States now resides in urban or metropolitan areas.

Advancements in communications and technology—especially the invention of the automobile—made possible the expansion of the city. This outward growth is known as suburbanization. The growth of the suburbs brought about the decline of the central city; the flight of industry and skilled labor to the suburbs and to the sunbelt is the primary cause of urban decay. This has placed severe burdens on the financial resources of the cities. Many urban specialists fear that the cities experiencing financial difficulties will channel funds away from essential services in order to finance other, more pressing municipal concerns.

Today's cities are primarily populated by people from rural areas who come to the city in search of better jobs, higher wages, and improved schooling for their children. Housing within the central city is at a premium. As slum neighborhoods are cleared in urban renewal projects, large segments of the urban population are displaced from their homes. Oftentimes, the so-called low-income housing built to replace the slums is too expensive for those displaced to return.

Cities are becoming increasingly dependent on state and federal governments for financial assistance. Because many consumers of central city services live and work in the suburbs, they do not share in the financial responsibility for maintaining such things as parks, zoos, libraries, and museums. The burden falls on the central city taxpayer to support services that are used by both city residents and residents of the greater metropolitan area.

There are three theories on the effects of urbanism on the population: a) Determinism, b) Compositionalism, and c) Subculturalism. *Determinists* argue that the pressures of the city force urbanites to become defensive and aloof, and inhibit them from forming meaningful personal relationships. *Compositionalists* believe that the pressures of the city have little effect on its population, since urbanites live within homogeneous social worlds of their own—either familial, economic, religious, ethnic, racial, or professional—that protect them from outside influences. *Subculturalists* believe that the pressures of the city cause these social worlds to exist and indeed to flourish.

There is evidence that the central city is experiencing a revitalization process. There has been a resurgence in the life of many central cities. Young professional people and older couples have been moving into the city. As industry has moved out of the central city, other types of businesses—investment banking, advertising, financial management, law firms, and the like—have moved in, establishing the central city as an area of idea- rather than product-oriented businesses.

If the city is to thrive, alternative ways must be found to finance services such as welfare, public health, public housing, and urban renewal—all of which benefit populations beyond the immediate boundaries of the central cities and deplete municipal tax revenues. Responsibility for maintaining metropolitan services must be borne by all area citizens, not just by those populations living within the immediate locale of the services.

Bibliography

Butler, Edgar W. *The Urban Crisis: Problems and Prospects in America*. Santa Monica, Calif.: Goodyear, 1977.

Fischer, Claude S. *The Urban Experience*. New York: Harcourt Brace Jovanovich, 1976.

Marx, Leo. *The Machine in the Garden: Technology and the Pastoral Ideal in America*. New York: Oxford University Press, 1964.

Masoti, Louis H., and Hadden, Jeffrey K., eds. *The Urbanization of the Suburbs*. Beverly Hills, Calif./London, England: Sage Publications.

Street, David, ed. *Handbook on Contemporary Urban Life: An Examination or Urbanization, Social Organization and Metropolitan Politics*. San Francisco, Calif.: Jossey-Bass, 1978.

Sweetser, Frank L., ed. *Studies in Urban Society*. New York: Thomas Y. Crowell Company, 1970.

15

The Population Crisis

Facts about the Population Crisis

- The world's population is increasing at the rate of 200,000 people a day.

- If the current rate of population growth continues, the population of the world will double in 35 years.

- Nine out of every ten people added to the world's population will be in the poorer, developing countries.

- By the year 2000, Asia alone will contain almost as many people as there are in the entire world today.

- Since 1965, world food-production has increased about 32 percent, but because of population growth, per capita food production has increased only 7 percent, and this is mostly in the developed countries. In the developing countries, per capita food production has dropped *below* 1965 levels, even though total food production has increased.

In recent years animal studies have provided clear evidence of some of the harmful effects of overpopulation. Laboratory animals that are subjected to serious overcrowding become nervous, irritable, and often abnormally aggressive; natural cleanliness gives way to soiled fur and littered cages; mating may not take place or females may abandon their newborn young; even cannibalism can occur, especially among rodents. Such behavior seems to result from physiological damage brought on by the stress of the crowded conditions; this damage will not be completely healed even if the animal is later returned to a normal environment.

Sometimes, too, a delicate equilibrium between population and environment can be catastrophically upset by what appears to be a minor change. For example, adding even one or two more fish to a fully populated aquarium may destroy the oxygen balance and kill off large numbers of fish. Likewise, a few extra sheep or goats on an overgrazed pasture may kill the grass and allow erosion and soil loss.

The harmful effects of human overpopulation are more difficult to prove, yet it is not hard to find similarities to the animal situation. Crowded living conditions in cities or neighborhoods seem to be associated with a rise in tensions, hostilities, violence, and outright crime; dirty streets, dirty air, and inadequate garbage collection are almost the rule.

Other, specifically human problems are also accentuated by overpopulation. How shall we provide jobs for all those who need to work? How shall we ensure adequate housing and recreation for everyone? How shall we maintain public services without which a complex society could not function—reliable transportation, adequate power supply, firefighting, medical care, food and product distribution?

These are problems of the industrialized and highly urbanized nations such as the United States. The so-called developing nations, still largely agrarian, face critical problems of a different type: how to bring basic education and health care to growing numbers of mostly rural poor; how to initiate and carry out major economic development projects when the gains are offset—often before they can even be felt—by having to be divided among an ever larger population.

But the problems of overpopulation transcend national boundaries. At the present rapidly expanding rate of demand, the world's available supplies of oil, coal, and natural gas may be consumed within a few generations; in addition, there is a limit to the amount of food our planet can be expected to produce. Rapid encroachments on the shrinking wilderness have threatened many species of wild animals with extinction. Chemical pollution appears to be endangering our largest lakes and possibly even the oceans; damage from this could be irreversible. (These and other environmental problems are examined in Chapter 16.) Finally, the contrast between the "haves" and the "have nots" among nations, together with the pressure exerted by rising populations against finite resources, exacerbates international tension.

For all these reasons, problems caused by overpopulation cannot be ignored. In the following sections, we shall consider some population statistics and their meaning, and discuss, in greater detail, the effects of rapid population growth in industrialized and in developing countries.

Scope of the Population Problem

In the 1600s, the start of what most historians call the modern era, the world's population was about 500 million. It had taken nearly 2.5 million years—the estimated time during which humanity and its humanlike ancestors have existed—to reach that level. By 1850, about two hundred years later, the population doubled, and by 1950, the count had reached 2.5 billion—a further increase of 1.5 billion in a hundred years.[1] In 1979, total world population was estimated at over 4 billion—an increase of 1.2 billion in 26 years.[2] By the year 2000, according to United Nations' estimates, the population of the world will probably total about 6.5 billion.[3] (See Figure 15-1.)

As we consider the dimensions of the population explosion, we should remember that the areas with the highest annual rates of population growth are also those that have the lowest per capita gross national product (GNP). (The GNP is a nation's income from the sale of all its products, goods, and raw materials.) (See Table 15-1.) An agrarian nation usually has a relatively small GNP, since it does not produce the refined or manufactured items that normally command the highest market prices. Moreover, the larger the population among whom a nation's per capita income is *theoretically* divided, the smaller each person's share becomes. (Note the emphasis on "theoretical" shares and divisions. In reality income is never divided equally among all residents of any nation.) In short, those countries where people's lives and living conditions most need improvement are precisely the countries whose population is increasing so rapidly that most people are scarcely better off than they were a generation ago, despite often gigantic efforts by their own and other governments and by the United Nations.[4]

[1]Philip M. Hauser, "World Population Growth" in *The Population Dilemma*, 2nd ed., ed. P. M. Hauser (Englewood Cliffs, N.J.: Prentice-Hall, 1970).

[2]Agency for International Development, *Annual Report* (Washington, D.C.: U.S. Government Printing Office, 1976).

[3]"The Grinding Arithmetic for the Year 2000," *UNESCO Courier* (May 1974), p. 9.

[4]Paul R. Ehrlich, *The Population Bomb*, rev. ed. (New York: Ballantine Books, 1971).

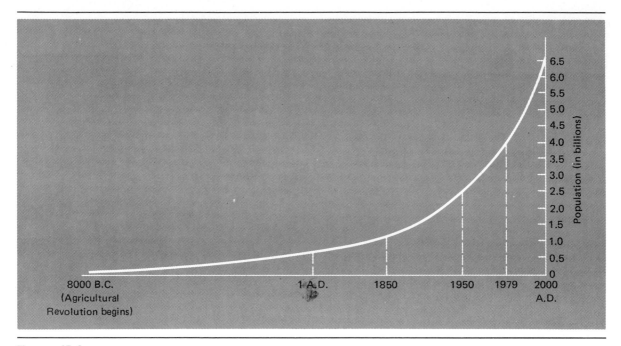

Figure 15-1
World Population Growth
(8000 B.C. to A.D. 2000)
Source: United Nations
estimates.

We shall not discuss the political implications of such a situation, but they are grave. Without fundamental changes in the social institutions of many underdeveloped nations, it is likely that the relentless pressures of expanding populations will contribute to an accumulation of tensions and hatreds and to the outbreak of revolutions and civil wars.[5]

[5]See Kingsley Davis, "Population Policy: Will Current Programs Succeed?" in *The American Population Debate,* ed., Daniel Callahan (Garden City, N.Y.: Doubleday, 1971), pp. 227–258.

Table 15-1
Probable Pattern of
Population Growth

Region	Present Population (in millions)	Estimated Population in the Year 2000 (in millions)	Percent Increase
Asia	2,500	3,757	63
Europe	674	540	13
Africa	436	834	111
Latin America	357	625	91
North America	228	296	22
Australia	14	33	57
World	*4,209*	*6,406*	*59*

Note: Over 80 percent of the world's population is in the poorer, developing regions. Over 90 percent of the population increase will take place in these regions.
Source: The World Almanac & Book of Facts, 1979 edition: © Newspaper Enterprise Association, New York, NY; 1978.

Rapid population growth is not a new phenomenon. For at least 50 years, the
rate of growth in the developing nations has been steadily rising, while at the
same time dropping in the industrialized countries.[6] Generally the population
boom is thought to be the result of a rising birthrate, but the problem is more
complicated and involves several factors.

Population Growth

Crude Birth and Deathrates.   A crude birthrate of 20, for example,
means that each year a given group of 1,000 persons will produce 20 babies.
This does not tell us what percentage of the population is of childbearing age,
nor how many people can afford children. Neither does it tell us how long
those 20 babies are likely to live—particularly, whether or not they
themselves will live long enough to produce children. Similarly, a crude
deathrate of 10, indicates only that among a group of 1,000 persons, 10 will die
every year. Again, this figure tells us nothing about the distribution of
deaths—whether they occurred among old people or people of childbearing
age.

Rate of Population Growth.   The differential between the (crude)
birthrate and the deathrate is called the rate of population growth or natural
increase. (It is also affected by migrations to and from the particular unit, a
factor that can be discounted for the purposes of this discussion.) In our
hypothetical 1,000-person group, in which 20 persons were added by birth
and 10 removed by death, the total population at the end of the year is
1,010—a rate of population growth of 1 percent. (*Zero population growth*, in
the sense the term is popularly used, is not directly related to birth- and deathrates. It is a condition that exists when a generation produces only enough
children to replace iteself—that is, when an average of two children are born
to each set of parents.)

Taken as a whole, the peoples of the world are not reproducing at a rate
higher than in the past, but more people are living to the age of fertility and
beyond. In effect, more babies are surviving to produce babies themselves.

This change is traceable to several causes: enormous advances in
sanitation, medicine, and public health; our increased ability to control
excessive cold, heat, and other dangers to life in our environment; and our
greater power to prevent or quickly counteract the effects of famine, drought,
flood, and similar natural disasters. Thus, the population crisis of our time
supports the thesis proposed in the opening chapter of this book: social
problems are problems that affect large masses of people and are the
unintended, unanticipated results of values and behavior that have previously
been regarded as useful and good.

The Effects of Population Growth

The social and ecological effects of overpopulation are serious wherever they
occur; however, since they are experienced differently by the highly
industrialized, relatively affluent nations and by the largely agrarian poorer
nations, one must consider the two areas separately.

[6]John D. Durand, "The Modern Expansion of World Population," *Proceedings of the
American Philosophical Society* 3 (June 1967), 137; and Hauser, "World Population Growth," p.
15.

Population Problems in Industrial Countries

Economic Growth.   The more prosperous nations of the world include those of Europe and North America, plus Japan, Israel, Australia, New Zealand, and South Africa. They are well developed industrially, their per capita GNP is high, and they may reasonably expect to eliminate poverty altogether.

It has been contended, particularly recently, that poverty is an inevitable by-product of Western capitalism. The implication is that socialism and communism, the other major economic systems of the modern world, tend naturally to eliminate poverty. Since neither pure capitalism nor pure communism is followed by any major industrialized nation, the proposition cannot be definitely tested. Most Western nations have found it necessary to introduce a considerable amount of government regulation of prices, profits, hours, and conditions of work, and much else that bears on the creation and distribution of wealth. At the same time, many socialist governments have had to make some concessions to the profit motive in order to stimulate production.

In any case, it seems increasingly evident that whatever the politicoeconomic system of a society, rapid population growth impedes the effort to distribute more equally even abundant material wealth. For one thing, population growth is usually more rapid among the poor. In the United States, for example, birthrates are consistently higher among the poor minority groups than among relatively well-to-do nonminorities. "Approximately 42 percent of American families with more than 5 children are poor, whereas only 10 percent with 1 or 2 children are poor."[7] Whatever may cause this pattern, the result is social and economic strain. For the United States, and for most other industrialized nations, a low or even zero rate of population growth appears to be economically desirable—a smaller population would mean a larger per capita income.[8]

Other important challenges in today's urban, industrialized nations—equalization of employment opportunities, better access to housing, more efficient dispensing of essential public services, and the like—are more difficult to achieve if population growth is not curbed. Indeed, some leading economists suggest that population control in a country such as the United States must accompany reevaluation of the traditional capitalist assumption that an ever-greater labor force consuming an ever-growing national product is essential or even desirable.

Kenneth E. Boulding, for example, argues that our country operates on a "cowboy economy," an exploitative system that appeared perfectly legitimate when it seemed that the wide frontier spaces of America could never be filled up. Now, however, we have begun to realize that the resources of even the richest nations are limited, and that we must learn how to live within those limits. We must develop, says Boulding, a "spaceman economy," geared to efficient use and reuse of the supplies we carry aboard this "spaceship earth."[9] In such an economy, the values of unlimited production and consumption would give way to a recognition of the interdependence of all aspects of life,

---

[7]Paul R. Ehrlich and Anne H. Ehrlich, *Population, Resources, Environment,* 2nd ed. (San Francisco: Freeman, 1972), p. 322.

[8]Stephen Enke, "Is a Stationery U.S. Population Desirable and Possible?" General Electric *Tempo,* mimeograph, 1969.

[9]Kenneth E. Boulding, "The Economics of the Coming Spaceship Earth," in *The Environmental Handbook,* ed. Garrett de Bell (New York: Ballantine Books, 1970), p. 96.

and to careful planning, so that all needs might be adequately met. Part of the program would necessarily involve limiting population.

Quality of Life.   Many of the problems associated with rapid population growth can be expressed in dollars and cents, or in figures on a table or a graph; but others—those concerned with what has come to be called the "quality of life"—are harder to define. One can measure the loss to commercial lumber interests when fire destroys a forest. But how can we measure the loss in recreation, in personal renewal and discovery of the world, when a wooded area rich with wildlife becomes a corporate subdivision or a shopping center? One can estimate the number of commuters delayed and the work hours lost in a traffic tie-up on a congested freeway. One can count the unemployed youths lined up outside a plant where an inadequate number of job openings have been announced. But what of the energy spent in rage that might have been turned to creative achievement; what of the hopelessness and resentment where there might have been joy and friendship? Such questions were once considered irrelevant, but unless we are prepared to believe that humanity's highest goal is mere physical survival, they now seem highly pertinent.

To the extent that rapid population growth is a factor in creating or aggravating these problems—which to varying degrees are faced by all industrialized societies today—it is a serious social problem. Indeed, some say it is the first problem to be reckoned with:

> The crux of the matter is not whether the world can adjust to the present high rates of population growth but rather how much better the prospects for development would be if these high rates could be reduced.[10]

Hunger.   As we shall see later in the chapter, experts strongly disagree about whether or not the world can produce enough food to feed its population. What is not debatable, however, is that many people do not have enough to eat. In fact, some 50 percent of the world's population is undernourished; many millions literally starve each year. An additional 16 percent of the world's population is malnourished, subsisting on a diet that is below the acceptable minimum for human beings.

Most of the world's hungry live in the nonindustrialized, agrarian countries of Asia and Africa. Ironically, many agrarian nations were once exporters of food and taken as a group, third-world countries are still not importers of foodstuffs. Their huge population growth during the last quarter-century, however, has turned many of these countries into food importers. They no longer produce enough food to feed their own populations. Even accelerating food-aid from other countries has not kept pace with the growth in population. At best, increasing numbers of people in the developing countries are being kept at the same inadequate level of nutrition. The worse—and more likely—prospect is that the number of people dying of starvation will increase, unless some way can be found to feed more people or reduce the rate of population growth.

The relationship between population and food supply is brought into

In some crowded, underdeveloped nations, the street is the home and starvation the lot of the poor. Here a drought victim in Niger is begging for food.

Chester Higgins/Photo Researchers, Inc.

Population Problems in Agrarian Countries

---

[10]George C. Zaida, "Population Growth and Economic Development," *Studies in Family Planning,* no. 42 (New York: Population Council, May 1969), 1.

focus when it is realized that a little over one acre of farmland is required to produce the minimal amount of food each person requires. Unfortunately, most of the world's available land is already being cultivated. Increasing the crop yield of each acre—the purpose of the so-called "green revolution"— requires expensive tools and methods beyond the reach of most poor countries. The most effective fertilizers, for example, are derived from petroleum, the cost of which has increased enormously. Agrarian nations simply cannot afford the agricultural equipment and technology they so desperately need, and as a result, most of their ever-increasing population must live with the pain of hunger on a daily basis, and suffer enormously high rates of disease and death caused by malnutrition.[11]

Effects of Economic Development.   To understand why the economics of underdeveloped, largely agrarian societies are affected by rapid population growth in a fashion different from that of industrialized countries, it is necessary to explore in depth the concept of per capita income.

Economists estimate that to raise the living standard of a nation with a stable population, an investment (whether in private or in public funds) between 3 and 5 percent of annual income in new income-producing development must be made. When a population is growing at the rate of 3 percent a year, not unusual for developing nations today, an investment of up to 20 percent of the national income is required to raise the nation's economic standards. Few poor nations can afford anything like this. Among those nations that are able to make the necessary investment, the continuing population growth spreads the resulting benefits so thinly that the sacrifice scarcely seems worth the struggle. It is important to realize that a population with an annual growth rate of only 3 percent *doubles* in 23 years, so it would require herculean efforts on the part of a nation for its economic development even to keep pace with such population growth.

Many South American nations are a dismal example. In the 1960s, the total investment of the Latin American countries in their own development amounted to 16.8 percent of their aggregate GNP.[12] With a stable population, this would have increased the per capita incomes of Latin Americans at least 4 percent per year. Instead, excessive population growth reduced the rise in per capita income to barely more than 1.5 percent per year—an increase of only $15 on every $1,000 earned.[13] In other words, the economic growth of these nations barely kept pace with their increased populations. As the Red Queen in *Alice in Wonderland* said: "Here, you see, it takes all the running you can do to keep in the same place."

Whereas industrialized nations are attempting to distribute their wealth more equitably and are limited to a substantial degree by population growth, the underdeveloped nations must struggle simply to achieve a bare subsistence level. In this effort, the higher rate of population growth is an enormous handicap. To be sure, agrarian societies in our time have to contend with other serious internal problems as well—problems of education, health, language, political instability, and often tribal or regional rivalries that prevent united action. But almost all authorities agree that little progress can

[11]Shirley F. Hartley, "Our Growing Problem: Population," *Social Problems* 21 (Fall 1973), 190–206.

[12]*Economic Bulletin for Latin America* 11 (April 1966), 8.

[13]Theodore Morgan and George W. Betz, *Economic Development: Readings in Theory and Practice* (Belmont, Calif.: Wadsworth, 1970), p. 19.

be anticipated for these countries while populations continue to grow at the present explosive rates.

Is there any prospect that the population increase in the agrarian societies will actually lessen? Some population experts, on the basis of a "theory of demographic transition,"[14] believe it will. According to this theory, in all societies the lowering of the deathrate is eventually followed by a voluntary drop in the birthrate. Ultimately this results in a slower rate of population growth. In Europe, for instance, the deathrate began to decline as early as 1650, because of commercial and agricultural changes, increased political stability, and the disappearance of the long-endemic Black Death. After 1850, with the effects of the Industrial Revolution and the rise of modern medicine, the decline became almost spectacular. For most of this period, the birthrate remained high, and Europe's population increased, from about 103 million in 1650 to more than 200 million in 1850, despite incessant wars and a large migration to America.[15]

But sometime in the nineteenth century, or slightly earlier in such countries as France, the birthrate began to fall, and continued to drop through the beginning of the twentieth century, until during the 1930s some European countries actually faced the possibility of an overall population decline. This trend was reversed to some extent after 1940, but the birthrate remained low enough so that European growth rates today average less than 1 percent per year, as compared with an average 2.1 percent for the world as a whole, and over 3 percent in some of the underdeveloped nations.

Proponents of the theory of demographic transition believe that the deathrates in developing countries will also eventually decline and lead to a drop in the birthrate. This would then eventually slow the population growth of poorer nations to a more desirable pace. Barry Commoner therefore advocates the massive export of funds, medical personnel, and food from the industrialized countries to the developing ones so that the death rates will be lowered. Only then, he suggests, will these countries be motivated to lower their birthrate.[16]

The theory, however, has not convinced many experts who point out that even at its height in the late nineteenth century, the population of the industrialized West expanded at a much lower rate than that of today's third-world nations. A voluntary drop in birthrate sufficient to significantly slow down the 2.4 to 3 percent annual growth rate of these poor nations is, admittedly, somewhat difficult to imagine, even if enormous food and medical supplies were forthcoming. Moreover, the populations of poor agrarian nations have an excessively high proportion of children and young adults that will probably push the birthrate to even higher levels. (See Figure 15-2.) And finally, emigration, which significantly helped reduce the populations of nineteenth-century Europe, is simply impossible today—there is nowhere to go. Neither North America nor Australia any longer welcomes large-scale emigrations.

In order to industrialize, a nation needs not only capital to invest in new income-producing developments, but also labor whereby a significant propor-

---

[14]For a fuller explanation of this theory, see Hauser, "World Population Growth," p. 13–15.

[15]Ehrlich and Ehrlich, *Population, Resources, Environment,* pp. 16–17.

[16]Barry Commoner, "How Poverty Breeds Population (and Not the Other Way Around)," *Ramparts* (August–September 1975), pp. 21ff.

tion of its work force is trained and available for productive work in the new industrial facilities. Not only do these people help to produce new wealth, but by spending their increased earnings, they help to consume the products created, thereby increasing profits and supplying new capital to continue the cycle of expansion. (This traditional concept of constant economic expansion is applied today primarily to the developing nations; it must be modified with regard to the heavily industrialized ones.) In Brazil, for example, the largest single group in the population is between the ages of 5 and 9, followed by those between 1 and 4 and between 10 and 14. In Sweden, by contrast, the largest group is between 20 and 24, followed by that between 25 and 29. Clearly, the labor force in Sweden is much larger, in proportion to the total population, than in Brazil. (Actually, in Brazil, children 14 and under do a great deal of work; in most developing nations child labor is a major factor in the work force; however, children tend to work in farm areas, not industries.)

It is not only the children in a society who are unavailable for income-producing work, but those who take care of them, whether parents, relatives, or neighbors, are, as a rule, economically unproductive. The recent movement to establish day-care centers is an effort to deal with this situation in our own society. In agrarian nations, the problems can be partially met by having the child accompany the parent to work in the fields, but such a solution is impracticable on a modern assembly line. Regardless of the child-care methods employed, a society with a high proportion of young children will have to spend more of its working hours than it can probably afford in looking after them. Furthermore, since poor nations tend to have higher fertility rates than industrialized ones, the Brazilian mother is probably bearing children more often and for more of her potential childbearing span

Figure 15-2
Population (in Millions) by Age and Sex, United States and Brazil

Source: United Nations *Statistics*
The United States population will increase through the 1980s. If the present falling birthrate continues, U.S. population growth will eventually decline. Brazil, by contrast, is already overpopulated and its population will continue to increase unless stringent programs are adopted. The lowest end of the age scale represents the largest proportion of population. The children of this group will rapidly increase the size of Brazil's population.

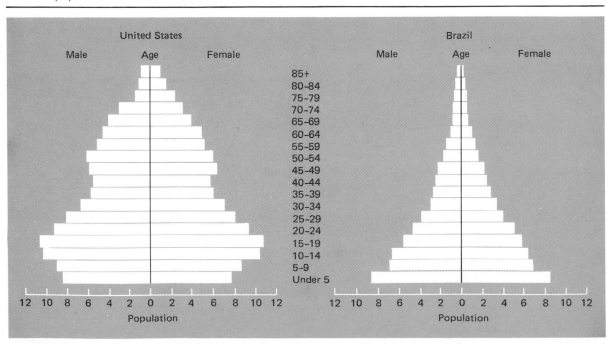

than the Swedish mother, and is therefore out of the labor market for a longer time.

Meanwhile, breadwinners are struggling to support expanding families. In an agrarian society, these breadwinners are likely to be unskilled laborers who work a dawn-to-dark schedule at low-paying jobs in order to provide a bare subsistence for themselves and their dependents. Even if training for skilled, higher-paying work were available, the chances are they would not have the time or energy to take advantage of it. And if, drawn by rumors of riches, they move their families to the city, they are likely to find that the pay there is no better, and the cost of living is far higher, than in the village they left. Either on the farm or in the city, they are likely to remain only marginally productive.

Moreover, the adverse consequences of this production of more children than the society needs or can use carries over into the next generation. Breaking the cycle of poverty requires, among other things, education; but a nation, most of whose people have barely enough food to live, can seldom build schools or pay teachers. Most children in these societies will be offered barely an elementary education; and many will enter the labor market before they have even learned to read and write. Those who do manage to acquire a decent education may find that with limited industrial development, their country has few jobs to offer them; so they, too, will remain unproductive and poor.

Finally, as already suggested, these children will bear more children, in ever-increasing numbers. What will be the population pressures and the poverty then? And is there any way to break the cycle? The picture, most authorities agree, is grim. It becomes more grim when one considers the political aspects. In the past, most human beings tended to accept poverty as their fate; now many people, in even the poorest nations, understand that economic betterment is possible, and they are demanding it as a right. Since explosive population growth prevents the improvement of living conditions, it contributes to the political unrest that breeds revolutions, topples governments, and sustains bloody civil and international wars.

Urbanization. In the process of expanding its industry, a nation inevitably also expands its cities. As agricultural improvements produce more crops with less labor, the surplus rural population migrates to the towns to find work in factories and mills. The more rapidly this population shift occurs, the more likely it is to cause substantial social problems. In the West, a rapid and explosive rural-to-urban population shift occurred in the nineteenth century, during the height of the Industrial Revolution. In the United States, for example, barely 6 percent of the population lived in urban centers in 1800. By 1900, 40 percent of the population lived in the increasingly dense urban-industrial complexes. Today about 75 percent are concentrated in and around urban centers.[17] The trend shows no sign of stopping.

The same thing is happening today in many of the developing nations and it is happening a great deal faster. The population of Nairobi, the capital of Kenya, is now growing at the rate of 7 percent per year. This is double the growth rate of Los Angeles in the boom decade of 1950–1960. Abidjan, the capital of the Ivory Coast, is growing by nearly 10 percent per year. Lusaka, the capital of Zambia, and Lagos, the capital of Nigeria, are each expanding at

[17]Ehrlich and Ehrlich, *Population, Resources, Environment,* pp. 43–45.

the unprecedented rate of 14 percent per year. If this rate of growth continues, Lagos, which in 1970 had a population of 1.4 million, will have 4 million by 1985—almost tripling its population in fifteen years.[18]

It is not generally realized that, of the twenty largest cities in the world—all of which have populations in excess of 3 million—more than half are in poor, developing nations (see Table 15-2): India (Bombay), Indonesia (Jakarta), Pakistan (Karachi), Brazil (São Paulo and Rio de Janeiro), Egypt (Cairo), Iran (Teheran), South Korea (Seoul), Thailand (Bangok), Mexico (Mexico City), the Philippines (Manila), and China (Shanghai, Peking, Tienstin, Shenyang). Only New York, London, Moscow, Leningrad, and Tokyo are in countries we generally consider urban and industrialized.[19]

If cities in urban, industrialized America are suffering today from overcrowding, inadequate housing and services, and all the other consequences of too-rapid population growth, it is not difficult to imagine what the situation must be like in the poor nations of Africa, South America, and Asia that have had far less time to cope with explosive industrialization. Also, their impoverished rural masses come to city life at a far lower level of education, vocational aptitude, and general readiness for the demands of the urban environment than do rural emigrants in the West.

The physical congestion and environmental deterioration of some of the giant cities of the underdeveloped nations make a horrifying impression on Westerners. "Shantytowns" spring up on city hillsides, in public parks, on malls, in vacant lots, along rivers, even on rooftops and in cemeteries. Like multiplying amoebae they spread, housing thousands upon thousands of people in flimsily built shelters. They have inadequate sanitation facilities, or none at all; personal hygiene and privacy are virtually unknown. Their inhabitants, illiterate and hungry, are easy prey for sickness, violence, and utter despair. The number of such squatters in the cities of Peru has been estimated to be 1 million, and growing. In Manila, the total is expected to pass 1 million in the 1980s. In Ankara, Turkey, nearly half of the city's total population is said to be

[18]"Exodus to the City," *UNESCO Courier* (July–August 1974), pp. 40–41.
[19]*The World Almanac, 1979* (New York: Newspaper Enterprises Association, 1979), p. 105.

Table 15-2
Largest Cities of the World

City and Country	Population	City and country	Population
1. Shanghai, China	10,820,000	11. Jakarta, Indonesia	6,178,000
2. Tokyo, Japan	8,643,000	12. Cairo, Egypt	6,133,000
3. Mexico City, Mexico	8,628,000	13. Bombay, India	5,970,575
4. Manila, Philippines	7,800,000	14. Rio de Janeiro, Brazil	4,857,500
5. Moscow, U.S.S.R.	7,632,000	15. Bangkok, Thailand	4,556,500
6. Peking, China	7,570,000	16. Karachi, Pakistan	4,465,000
7. New York, N.Y., U.S.A.	7,481,600	17. Leningrad, U.S.S.R.	4,311,000
8. São Paulo, Brazil	7,198,600	18. Tientsin, China	4,280,000
9. London, England	7,111,000	19. Teheran, Iran	4,000,000
10. Seoul, South Korea	6,884,000	20. Shenyang, China	3,750,000

Source: United Nations estimates.

The squalor of a congested Brazilian slum is juxtaposed to the clean lines of urban skyscrapers.
Carl Frank/Photo Researchers, Inc.

composed of shantytown squatters.[20] That the misery of the situation is everywhere compounded—and solutions further complicated—by too-rapid population growth in the country as a whole is only one more aspect of the painfully complex problems facing poor and underdeveloped nations today.

Attitudes Toward Population Control

Given all these facts, and the conclusions drawn from them, it might seem that no one could realistically doubt the existence of a serious worldwide population crisis. In fact, there are those who do, including reputable scholars who simply cannot be dismissed as fools or bigots.[21] The denials of the population crisis tend to fall into one of three main categories.

  "There is no population problem as such. The problem is only how to

[20]Charles Abrams, "The Uses of Land in Cities," *Scientific American* 213 (September 1965).
[21]See Michael Teitelbaum, "Population and Development: Is a Consensus Possible?", *Foreign Affairs* (July 1974).

support a growing population." The proponents of this view include some highly intelligent believers in the infinite power of science and technology to increase food supply indefinitely through the green revolution (the development of more nourishing and higher-yield varieties of grain and other staple food crops); tap as yet untouched reserves of water far below the earth's surface; develop previously undreamed-of materials to replace dwindling natural resources; harness new sources of power from beyond our planet; and find ways to halt or even reverse the damaging effects of population. As one of them has argued: "Natural resource scarcity and diminishing returns through time are not a curse that society must bear."[22]

To support this contention, they cite humanity's past records of discovery and invention, and point out that so far all those predicting the starvation or self-destruction of *Homo sapiens* have been wrong. It should be noted, however, that there have never been as many people on the earth as there are today, nor has there ever been such a global scarcity of natural resources. Furthermore, even if a growing population could somehow be supported, the quality of life on earth—in terms of pollution and crowding, for example— would almost certainly decline.

"The population problem is really a problem of population distribution of people." Resettle or relocate people so as to break up overly dense concentrations, and the economic, ecological, and social problems automatically become smaller, more manageable, ultimately more susceptible to solution. As Herman P. Miller says:

> We have serious population problems today and they are likely to intensify in the next 15 years. These problems relate to the geographic distribution and to the values of our people rather than to their numbers and rates of growth.[23]

The logical extreme of this argument, advocated by some of its adherents, is that the ultimate solution to overpopulation is enforced or encouraged migration to sparsely settled areas of the globe, or even to other planets and to artificial satellites. The feasibility of this solution, however, is questionable. Much of the remaining wilderness of the earth is desert, mountain, or arctic ice, incapable of supporting more than a tiny population at best; and of the rest, some areas are vitally needed as wilderness. The vast Amazon basin, for example, is the world's largest reservoir of oxygen-producing vegetation. Unless there is a considerable technological breakthrough, it seems extraterrestrial migration is likely to occur only in science fiction. The largest spacecraft yet launched have carried only three in their crew, on a short journey to our own nearby moon, and at a cost of billions of dollars. To maintain the earth's population at its present level, some 200,000 people per day would have to be transported into space.

"There is a population problem, but it is not our problem. Anyway, it is not all that urgent." Many Americans take this position, according to a Gallup Poll. Eighty-seven percent of those sampled conceded that population

---

[22]Harold J. Barnett, "The Myth of Our Vanishing Resources," *Trans-Action* (June 1967), p. 10. Also see Parker G. Morden and Dennis Hodgson, eds., *Population, Environment, and Quality of Life* (New York: Wiley, 1975).

[23]Herman P. Miller, "Is Overpopulation Really the Problem?" *National Industrial Conference Board Report*, vol. 7 (May 1970).

growth in America was a problem now "or would be by the year 2000."[24] Only 54 percent feared that it would affect the quality of their own lives, and only 41 percent considered it a major issue requiring immediate action. The majority of those who did view overpopulation as critical, urgent, and likely to affect them personally were people under 20, especially the college-educated.

Because of the complexity and historical importance of the views of various religions on population growth and its control, they merit special consideration. The official Roman Catholic doctrine on birth control is, of course, best known and most controversial in our society. Briefly, it states that sexual intercourse is intended by God as a means both to the growth of love between the partners and to the transmission of new life, and that if one part of this purpose is deliberately frustrated, God is flouted and everyone concerned is harmed. Therefore, the use of any artificial means of preventing conception is considered sinful—a violence done to the natural order of things as established by God.

Religious Attitudes

Despite the Church's official prohibition, studies show that a large majority of American Catholic couples use some sort of contraception.[25] Officially, the Church has sanctioned only the rhythm method, in an apparent effort to strike a middle course. In 1968, after the controversy over permissible methods of birth control had reached monumental proportions, Pope Paul VI issued his encyclical *Humanae Vitae* (On the Transmission of Human Life); to the disappointment of many Catholics, the pope reiterated the Church's ban on artificial contraception. While recognizing that "responsible parenthood" may sometimes entail the deliberate limiting of family size, he maintained that since the Church has no power to change the moral law established by God, it therefore cannot legitimize artificial methods of preventing birth. This decision has evidently been unacceptable in practice to many otherwise devout Roman Catholics, and has resulted in a good many conflicts of conscience among them. In fact, one 1976 study suggested that a massive decline in church attendance could be directly attributed to *Humanae Vitae*.[26]

Actually, the encyclical makes some thoughtful points about the possible harm to persons and society as a result of contraceptive practice, although it does not clearly establish the cause and effect of this harm. For instance, it is possible that the habit of intercourse for pleasure alone, without the responsibility implied by the possibility of conception, may ultimately encourage the participants to regard one another merely as instruments of rather selfish pleasure, thus preventing any deep personal relationship from developing. On a broader scale, a government might plausibly claim that if voluntary contraception is permissible for individuals, the state has the right to impose it "for the good of society," which in turn could easily degenerate into violations of basic human rights, tyranny, and even genocide.

[24]Gallup Organization, Inc. News release, Research Department, Planned Parenthood-World Population, April 1971. This was the most recent Gallup Poll on this subject.

[25]Charles F. Westhoff and Elise F. Jones, "The Secularization of U.S. Catholic Birth Control Practices," *Family Planning Perspectives*, vol. 9, no. 5 (1977), 203–207.

[26]Andrew Greeley, *Catholic Schools in a Declining Church* (New York: Sheed and Ward, 1976).

Certainly, it is hardly to be expected that widespread use of artificial contraceptives will affect *only* the birthrate. Unfortunately, *Humanae Vitae* failed to address itself seriously to the population question as a whole, and offered no real guidance to persons physically or psychologically unable to use the rhythm method. Consequently, it has seemed to most people merely to restate an outmoded position, and has largely been disregarded in practice.

Most of the other major religions have taken a less restrictive approach. Well before World War II, for example, many Protestant thinkers had taught that contraception was not an ecclesiastical concern but was a matter of conscience to be decided by the people directly affected. Some branches of Judaism have likewise held that contraception does not destroy the spiritual sanctity of marriage and may, in fact, enhance it by freeing the couple from the burden of unwanted children. The Eastern Orthodox Churches, while officially condemning contraception, defer in practice to the wishes of the couple involved. Two of the three major Eastern religions—Islam and Hinduism—have traditionally rejected any interference with fertility and birth. Yet the attitude and practices of their adherents have changed, and several Islamic governments have advocated family planning for Muslims.[27] Buddhism, the third large Oriental faith, regards procreation and family life as of secondary importance, so that, apparently, contraception is not an issue.[28]

Population Control Programs— Voluntary or Compulsory

It seems clear that only a large-scale program can effect a prompt and substantial drop in a nation's population growth rate. But what kind of program? Specifically, can voluntary birth control suffice, or is a compulsory program necessary?

The Voluntary Approach

Voluntary birth control is customarily thought of in terms of family planning; organized attempts to promote it began in England as early as 1820. From 1830 to about 1870, several books on the subject appeared both in England and in the United States. Religious, political and medical opposition mounted, and in 1873 the passage of the "Comstock law" outlawed the dissemination by mail of birth control information in the United States. Most of the states also passed suppressive legislation, and in 1890 the importation of birth control literature was banned. For practical purposes, any distribution of birth control information or equipment was illegal in this country until well into the twentieth century. After about 1916 physicians were permitted to prescribe birth control for health reasons, first in New York State and later elsewhere; but it was not until 1965 that the Supreme Court ruled unconstitutional a Connecticut statute forbidding the use of contraceptives. The following year the last of the "Comstock laws" was repealed (by Massachusetts).[29]

[27]W. Parker Maudin, *Muslim Attitudes toward Family Planning* (New York: Population Council, 1967).

[28]Arthur McCormack, *The Population Problem* (New York: Crowell, 1970), p. 157.

[29]Linda Gordon, *Woman's Body, Woman's Right* (New York: Penguin, 1974).

Similar situations existed in Europe; yet, the rate of population growth in the Western world dropped during this period. Today, improved methods of birth control and greatly relaxed restrictions on their use allow one to hope that voluntary family planning would be sufficient to keep the world's population within bounds. Is this in fact the case?

What Is Family Planning?   Essentially, a voluntary family planning program allows couples to have as many children as they want. While this usually means enabling them to limit childbearing, it can also involve helping couples who want children and have been unable to have them. The stress is usually placed on the good of the family—especially the health of mother and children, and the ability to provide education and other desired advantages.

Weaknesses of Family Planning.   Kingsley Davis points out some fundamental weaknesses of the family planning approach as a means for large-scale population control.[30] Chief among these is its basic assumption that the number of children a couple want is the number they ought to have. In a poor country with a growth rate of 3 percent per year, the family of five and six children, probably desired by most couples, will be anything but desirable for the economic health of the country—or for the family's own chances of economic betterment.

A second criticism of the family planning emphasis is that it neglects the whole field of pregnancy among unmarried women. Even in the United States, where contraceptives and contraceptive information are in general quite freely available, the number of pregnancies among unmarried women and young girls remains high. (See Chapter 10.) A successful population control program would have to deal with this aspect of the situation.

Finally, the strongly medical emphasis of the usual family planning program can also limit its large-scale effectiveness, particularly in developing countries where doctors and nurses are usually scarce.

Social Change and the Birthrate.   There is no doubt that certain changes in overall attitudes and social structures can affect how people plan their lives. The women's liberation movement has undoubtedly created (or reinforced) in many women of childbearing age a disinclination to be "just wives and mothers." As better job opportunities become available for women, as sexual relationships independent of marriage are increasingly taken for granted, as women begin to see themselves as creative and productive persons who may or may not choose to include marriage and childbearing in their personal lives, there is bound to be an effect on the birthrate. Recent surveys already suggest that the number of children desired by the average young married woman in the United States is less than it was a few years ago. (See Chapters 9 and 11.)

Davis, however, proposes much more drastic and deliberate social changes to discourage population growth. For instance, financial advantages, such as tax benefits, might be offered to the unmarried; financial disincentives, such as the loss of tax deductions or of insurance benefits, might be imposed upon any child above a certain number. Other changes would seek to weaken the institution of the family rather than merely limit its size: dropping the use of family names; giving the school more control than the parents over

[30]Davis, "Population Policy," pp. 229–238, 247–248.

the children; releasing grown children from any responsibility for the support of their parents. Such moves might indeed tend to reduce the birthrate; however they would also outrage so many people that it seems unlikely that they could be imposed by legislation, at least in the United States in the near future. Gradual changes in attitude might, in the long run, make some of them acceptable.

Compulsory Birth Control

A pro-abortionist rally protests a ban on federal funding of abortions. These women are concerned that the lack of government support will force many poorer women to have babies they do not want or to seek dangerous illegal abortions.

UPI

In some primitive societies, sexual taboos have, sometimes inadvertently, created a birth-control system fairly well adapted to the particular tribal situation. Among certain African tribes, for example, a women may not have intercourse while she is nursing a child—which usually means for about two years. Modern societies are not prepared to function on this basis, however, and various proposals have been made by experts who believe that some sort of compulsion is needed if population growth is not to entail global disaster.

One such possibility is the sterilization of parents who have had a specified number of children. India adopted this plan on a voluntary basis in 1976, with financial incentives to encourage volunteers. It is estimated that from April 1976 to March 1977, more than eight million sterilizations were performed. As might be expected, this birth control program met with considerable resistance. Although no one in India disputed the need to curb

the rate of population growth, the government was severely criticized for what was considered a compulsory, rather than a strictly voluntary, policy.

Another alternative, suggested by Kenneth B. Boulding, is a licensing system, whereby a woman at her marriage would be issued a license entitling her to a certain number of children. She could sell or give her rights, if she did not wish to use them, to another woman who might want more than her licensed share.

If researchers succeed in developing a long-term timed-release contraceptive for implantation under the skin, this could be used to sterilize temporarily all girls at puberty and all women after childbirth; government approval would be required to have it removed. Or perhaps an antifertility agent (of a type not yet developed) could be added to water supplies or staple foods.

The danger to freedom and the possibilities of abuse inherent in any program for compulsory birth control are obvious. It is hard to imagine how such a program could be enforced except under a strong totalitarian system not unlike the Indian one Prime Minister Indira Gandhi tried to form. Probably most people would accept it only if they were convinced that nothing less could save the world from catastrophe. As Frank Notestein, the well-known demographer, predicted six years before the Gandhi government was toppled, any attempt by a developing country to force its people to use birth control methods "would be more likely to bring down the government than the birth rate."[31] For the time being, voluntary birth control seems to be the most realistic—and most desirable.

Most proponents of family planning support a complementary program of abortion and contraception as the most effective means of reducing population growth. Jaroslav F. Hulka has determined that in societies in which two or three children constitute the ideal family size, the average couple that marries in its late 20s faces 12 to 15 years of potentially fertile marriage after the last desired conception. Of these couples, 80 out of 100 will experience an unwanted pregnancy if they consistently employ 95 percent effective contraceptive devices such as a condom or a diaphragm; 30 out of 100 will experience pregnancy if they use 99 percent effective devices such as the intra-uterine device (IUD) or the pill. It is therefore assumed that in societies where 2–3 births is the per-woman average, abortion—legal or otherwise—is necessary to keep the birthrate down. A study conducted in Taiwan in 1968 corroborates this theory. Without benefit of induced abortion, the lifetime fertility rate at which the women in the study were reproducing within that year would have been 12 to 19 percent higher than it actually was.[32]

Opposition to abortion from religious and community leaders has not prevented most world governments from easing their abortion laws. Even where abortion is a criminal offense, the practice continues. The case for more liberalized abortion laws is based on a need to insure the public health by reducing the number of deaths attributable to illegal abortions, to provide

[31]Lynn C. Landman, "Birth Control in India: The Carrot and the Rod?" *Family Planning Perspectives*, vol. 9, no. 3 (1977), 101.
[32]Jaroslav F. Hulka, "A Mathematical Model Study of Contraceptive Efficiency and Unplanned Pregnancies," *American Journal of Obstetrics and Gynecology*, vol. 104 (1969), 443–447; and Dorothy Nortman, "Changing Contraceptive Patterns: A Global Perspective," *Population Bulletin*, vol. 32, no. 3 (August 1977), 23–24.

access to safe abortion to women of all economic levels (not just the wealthy), to give women control over their own bodies, and to stem the growing birthrate that is approaching epidemic proportions. It has been estimated, however, that when effective contraception becomes available to all, the number of abortions should decline. Widespread adoption of sterilization, the most effective of all contraceptive methods, should diminish the necessity of abortion as a backstop to contraceptive failure.

Population Control Programs in the Advanced Nations

As has already been pointed out, the birthrate in the industrialized nations had begun to drop before the institution of organized family planning programs. The organized programs have probably accelerated the process, however, especially in the United States: they have made information and contraceptives more widely available; they have worked to repeal laws against the use of contraceptives; and they have influenced opinion in favor of birth control. In both the United States and Europe today, most couples use some form of contraceptive technique, though not always the most effective ones.

Nevertheless, even in the West the birthrate remains higher than is necessary for replacement. The population of the United States and Europe is growing at the rate of just under 0.6 percent per year—a figure that seems small until it is realized that if the population continues to grow at its present low rate, the United States and Europe will almost double their populations in about 90 years. (At present rates, the entire world will double its population in less than 35 years.)

Some encouragement is offered by statistics showing a decline in the fertility rate among poor women, traditionally a high fertility rate group.[33] Though the rate is much above that for women at higher income levels, it has nevertheless dropped substantially—by over 20 percent. That this decline has occurred when family planning programs, now federally assisted, and improved contraceptive methods are rapidly becoming available to poorer couples suggests that organized family planning may have been a significant factor.

It is still too early to assess fully the effect on population growth of the movement toward legalized abortion, though it is already clear that the availability of abortion has reduced the number of illegitimate births. (See Chapter 11.) No matter what method of voluntary contraception is used, however, some unwanted pregnancies are bound to occur, and it is safe to assume that many women who would not risk an illegal abortion will have a legitimate one. It is also safe to assume that some of these women would have preferred a perfectly reliable and convenient contraceptive that would have prevented pregnancy in the first place; so perhaps legalized abortion as a method of birth control will turn out to be only a stopgap measure, useful principally until unwanted pregnancies become uncommon.

All things considered, if present trends continue, it is reasonably likely that the advanced nations will be able to hold their population growth to desirable levels by voluntary means. But these countries at present contain less than a quarter of the total world population. What about the rest?

[33]Frederick S. Jaffe, "Low-Income Families: Fertility Changes in the 1960s," *Family Planning Perspectives* 4 (January 1971), 43–47.

Efforts to reduce the population growth rate in the developing countries face considerably greater obstacles than in the older industrialized nations. In an agrarian society, large families are both a source of pride and an economic asset. A man's virility may be judged by his ability to beget children; a woman's main purpose in life may be to bear and rear them. Very young children can work in the fields, grown children can support aging parents. Sometimes extra children can work and help put the eldest child through school. Later, the eldest can earn the extra income to put the next child through school, and so on down the line.[34] Such cultural patterns, in a tightly knit traditional society, are not easily changed.

Many people in parts of the world are still largely uninformed about even basic sanitation, personal hygiene, and such routine matters as keeping a schedule. There are still back-country clinics where a doctor dares not give an outpatient a week's supply of pills, because the patient is likely to go off and swallow them all at once. Medication has to be doled out one dose at a time, and taken on the spot while the attendant watches. The difficulties of using an oral contraceptive, or for that matter the rhythm method, under such conditions hardly need to be pointed out. Likewise, popularizing the use of diaphragms, condoms, and other such devices is difficult in a culture that has never even seen these forms of contraception.

The severe shortage of trained medical personnel in most underdeveloped countries also hampers the establishment of effective programs. Such contraceptive devices as the diaphragm must be individually fitted and prescribed, and the IUD, in some ways the most desirable for large-scale use, must be inserted by a doctor and should be periodically checked. As for sterilization, it requires a doctor and, for women, hospital facilities.

Despite these handicaps, a few of the poor nations have significantly curbed population growth with voluntary, government-supported programs. Most of these programs were begun in the 1960s, and by the mid-1970s over 20 countries had official family planning programs of some sort. The most successful so far have been in relatively small and comparatively developed areas such as Taiwan, Hong Kong, and Singapore. In the first two, the birthrate had started to drop slightly even before the official programs were begun, but the programs appear to have accelerated the process. By the end of the 1960s the birthrate in Taiwan was down about one-third from the rate ten years earlier. Hong Kong and Singapore showed similar drops.[35] No other poor nation has come close to matching these rates of decline. Yet every one of these countries still has an overall population growth rate of more than 2 percent—sufficient to double its population in less than 35 years.

At the opposite end of the scale from these small and, for Asia, relatively prosperous countries lies India, with one-third the area of the United States, two and one-half times its population, and a per capita GNP of $110 per year, as compared with over $6,000 for the United States. Birth control in India has gone through several stages. The voluntary, family planning programs of the 1950s and early 1960s were succeeded, as we have seen, by the authoritarian

---

[34]Mahmood Mamdani, *The Myth of Population Control* (New York: Monthly Review Press, 1972).

[35]Frank W. Notestein, Dudley Kirk, and Sheldon Segal, "The Problem of Population Control," in Hauser, *The Population Dilemma*, p. 150.

Gandhi regime's emphasis on sterilization—first encouraged, then compulsory. This program was enormously unpopular and provoked resentment that played a large part in the collapse of Mrs. Gandhi's administration. Her successors have reverted to a largely ineffectual voluntary campaign to limit population through education and encouragement. What the future will bring—besides more hungry Indians—is unclear.[36]

Part of the difficulty in India is the existence of several non-Western medical and religious traditions that have tended to oppose the program. But probably the greatest problem is the sheer size of the task—the attempt to inform and persuade more than 100 million couples of childbearing age, jammed into city slums or scattered in thousands of tiny rural villages, still so conditioned by centuries of abject poverty that they simply cannot imagine that any human effort could possibly make a difference. Moreover, as heirs of a proud and ancient culture, they revere, "the way it has always been," even if life is hard; and proposals for change seem much more dangerous to them than to the Westerner who is accustomed to reading about a new technological miracle every other Monday. Before the birthrate can be lowered significantly, India's government will have to find some way to overcome these psychological obstacles and the opposition of the native medical systems. In the meantime, the growth of industrialization and improved agricultural production seems to be making some small headway against ancient poverty, even in the face of rapid population growth. Whether they can continue to do so until the growth rate can be brought down, only time will tell.

The Peoples' Republic of China, the other Asian giant, is a special case, and precise demographic information about it is impossible to find. An initial family planning movement in the 1950s was relatively ineffective and was abandoned after two or three years. In the 1960s, after the upheavals of the Cultural Revolution subsided, the effort was renewed, and appears to have had considerably more success. Nonetheless, in the absence of hard data, estimates of the Chinese birthrate range from 14 to 37 per 1,000 of the population.[37]

Birth control education has been most effective in the cities—as many as 70 percent of the women of childbearing age in Peking use some method of birth control—but in recent years a vigorous campaign has been carried to the countryside as well. In this, the extensive political organization of Chinese Communism has provided a vast network of village-level workers who can urge family planning on the villagers as friends and fellow laborers. Stress on the personal advantages of a small family is combined with appeals for loyalty and self-abnegation on behalf of the state, and social pressure, rather than outright coercion, is applied. The recommended minimum age for marriage is 25 for women, 30 for men, and there is considerable pressure to adhere to it.

Oral contraceptives are most commonly used, followed by the IUD (a specially shaped IUD has been developed that is less likely than others to be expelled by women doing heavy, manual labor). A once-a-month pill is also being tried experimentally. All contraceptives are free or available at very low prices, and the village "barefoot doctors" provide instructions on their use. Abortions are likewise free or inexpensive, and are available on demand.

Since China's present population is more than 800 million, even a 1

The contrast of this woman's Muslim dress to the contraceptive device she is examining captures one difficulty in introducing family planning to developing nations: traditional cultures are often a barrier to technological innovation.

Paolo Koch/Photo Researchers, Inc.

[36]Landman, "Birth Control in India," pp. 101–110; Nortman, "Changing Contraceptive Patterns," pp. 29–30.

[37]Nortman, "Changing Contraceptive Patterns," pp. 27–29.

percent increase would add about 200 million more people by the end of the century. China's available cropland is already farmed as intensively as any on earth; therefore, this giant country must reduce its growth rate much more rapidly than any other nation has ever been able to do, while greatly modernizing and expanding its productive capacity. Apparently the sheer size and urgency of the task have forced the implementation of an unusually vigorous and effective program. It may be, therefore, that some of the Chinese techniques will eventually prove useful in other heavily populated areas as well, particularly those of Asian cultural tradition.[38]

Prospects

The social problems confronting the nations of the world in the wake of the global population explosion of the twentieth century are unprecedented in their complexity. The tangle of conflicting interests, of short-range benefits versus long-range risks, of clashing motivations and contradictory impulses is forbidding enough as to render the most cheerful optimist cautious, if not downright pessimistic, about the prospects for solutions to the problems of overpopulation.

Whatever other issues the world and its individual nations attempt to solve—hunger or plenty, war or peace, environmental disruption and pollution or conservation, economic growth or stagnation, political freedom or faceless regimentation, capitalism or socialism in its various forms—it seems safe to say that unless the problems of overpopulation that complicate and aggravate them all are confronted first, or at least simultaneously, there is likely to be no satisfactory solution to any of them.

In the United States the average number of births per family is now 1.8—below the number of zero population growth. Because the large number of people born during the "baby boom" of the late 1940s and early 1950s are now in their reproductive years, however, the population of the United States will actually increase through the 1980s. Only then, if present birthrates are maintained, will it begin to level off. Until then, the problems caused by an increasing population—overcrowding, loss of recreational areas, pollution— may be expected to multiply.

In other parts of the world, the picture is grim. Many developing countries with relatively successful birth control programs are experiencing a modest decline in their birthrates. But because their birthrates have been so high, their populations continue to increase. Some other countries with rapidly expanding populations have no birth control programs at all.

What will be the consequences of such population growth? In many of the developing countries, starvation and death on a massive scale already seem imminent. The growing political consciousness of these countries, however, makes it unlikely that they will willingly accept the wholesale decimation of their citizenry, particularly when people in other countries have an overabundance of food. Wars and uprisings are likely to increase as the developing nations demand their fair share of the world's resources.

Other consequences may be more subtle, but in the long run may be almost as harmful. To many thinkers, mandatory sterilization is an attractive

[38]*Population and Family Planning in the People's Republic of China* (Washington, D.C.: Victor-Bostrom Fund Committee and Population Crisis Committee, 1971).

solution. And many of those who undergo sterilization procedures are unaware of the purpose of these operations—they are merely offered some payment for submitting to them. The idea of freedom, as it is understood in Western nations, may become obsolete in the developing countries if a policy of forced sterilization is adopted. But if population growth in these countries is not curbed voluntarily, forced sterilization may become the only available alternative.

The United States and Western Europe will be able to feed their own populations for the foreseeable future. They too, however, will be affected by the population crisis and not just because their quality of life will deteriorate or because they may be forced by other nations to share their wealth. They will be affected because their entire moral or ethical foundations will be shaken as the number of those starving continues to grow. Already there are those who favor a "lifeboat ethic," which suggests that the poorer nations be permitted to starve. One who holds this point of view put it this way:

> So long as nations multiply at different rates, survival requires that we adopt the ethic of the lifeboat. A lifeboat can only hold so many people . . . . It is literally beyond our ability to save them all . . . . International granaries and lax immigration policies must be rejected if we are to save something for our grandchildren.[39]

Such a philosophy must be rejected if Western nations are to survive in their present form; for if life in other countries is considered meaningless, it will soon be considered so in our own. It is the responsibility of the developing countries to curb their burgeoning population growth; it is the responsibility of the wealthier, developed countries to help feed all the living. Whether these responsibilities will be met remains to be seen, but at present the prospects are not hopeful.

[39]Garrett Hardin, in Commoner, "How Poverty Breeds Population," p. 22.

Summary

The population of the world has been increasing at an enormous rate, largely because advances in medicine and technology have enabled more people to survive and reproduce.

In the industrialized nations, this population growth has hampered economic development and affected the quality of life. In the developing countries, population growth, coupled with a diminishing food supply, has caused outright starvation and death and stifled economic development. The nation's wealth, already inadequate, must be divided among greater numbers, and the large proportion of young children in these societies means that not enough labor is available for productive work. One added consequence of population growth has been a rapid increase in the urban population in the developing countries, as whole families leave marginal farm areas in the usually vain hope of finding work in the cities.

There are those who maintain that a population crisis does not exist—that a growing population can be supported or overly dense populations can be broken up. Others feel the problem is not serious, or that it has been exaggerated. These arguments ignore the fact that world resources are already strained, and that much of the world's available croplands are already being farmed. Yet most of the world's population already experiences hunger on a daily basis.

It seems clear that a large-scale birth control program is needed. Voluntary family planning programs already exist in many countries, though their effectiveness is limited by their medical emphasis and their concentration on married couples. In the developing nations, there are often cultural barriers to birth control programs. Although some experts advocate compulsory birth control programs, compulsion carries with it a great potential for abuse and a great threat to human freedom.

Bibliography

Ehrlich, Paul R., and Ehrlich, Anne H. *Population, Resources, Environment: Issues in Human Ecology,* 2nd ed. San Francisco: Freeman, 1972.

Goldscheider, Calvin. *Population, Modernization, and Social Structure.* Boston: Little, Brown, 1971.

Hartley, Shirley F. *Population: Quantity vs. Quality.* Englewood Cliffs, N.J.: Prentice-Hall, 1972.

Heer, David M. *Society and Population,* 2nd ed. Englewood Cliffs, N.J.: Prentice-Hall, 1975.

Lappe, Frances F., and Collins, Joseph. *Food First: Beyond the Myth of Scarcity.* Boston: Houghton Mifflin, 1977.

McCormack, Arthur. *The Population Problem.* New York: Crowell, 1970.

Meadows, D. H. *The Limits of Growth in a Finite World.* New York: Wiley, 1974.

Stanford, Quentin H. *The World's Population: Problems of Growth.* New York: Oxford University Press, 1972.

Westoff, Leslie A., and Westoff, Charles F. *From Now to Zero: Fertility, Contraception and Abortion in America.* Boston: Little, Brown, 1971.

16

The Environmental Crisis

Facts about the Environmental Crisis

- Since 1750, 799 species of plants and animals have become extinct in the United States.
- Air and water pollution cause $23.5 billion worth of damage annually to health, property, and crops in the United States.
- Some 197 million tons of human-made pollutants are added to the air every year.
- Every day each New York City resident inhales enough cancer-producing substances to equal two packs of cigarettes.
- At present rates of demand, world reserves of such vital materials as lead, silver, tungsten, and mercury will be exhausted within 40 years.

All animals need air, water, land, energy, and other organisms to exist, and human beings are no exception. Our urban, industrial society, however, has increasingly estranged us from an awareness of our day-to-day relationship to the physical environment. Most people feel that water is something that comes out of a tap, that the air is everywhere, and if the city seems crowded, they can always move to the suburbs. But the cumulative effect of what we are doing on and to the earth seems to be bringing us to the brink of an environmental crisis: by intervening in the many natural cycles that permit the life process to continue through renewal and replenishment, we are seriously compromising the capacity of our environment to support life. More people are making increasing demands on a world with fixed resources, and the world is beginning to reveal the limits of its ability to satisfy those demands.

The air is becoming filled with pollutants, some of which are highly toxic to human beings and other organisms. Many of our waterways have been reduced to open, running sewers, and the discharge of our effluents is "killing" bodies of water as vast as the Great Lakes and befouling the oceans, incidentally endangering an important part of our food supply. We are creating mountains of solid waste for which we are running out of disposal sites. Although we know that there is no biologically safe level of radioactivity, we are committing ourselves to the construction of numerous nuclear power plants. Finally, the noise levels in our cities are sufficiently high to affect our physical and emotional well-being.

Not only are we polluting what we may perhaps be unable to repair, but we are destroying what cannot be replaced. We have already exterminated several species of animals; and, in our eagerness to produce all the material goods we think we need, we are rapidly depleting the available stocks of gas, oil, coal, and other mineral resources. The question is whether we will become aware of what we are doing to the environment, and be willing to change, before we end by destroying ourselves.

There are two social ramifications to this question. First, the environmental crisis has been caused, fundamentally, by the socially organized activity of human beings. Social goals, values, norms and operations have disrupted the proper, balanced processes of nature. Second, the environmental crisis in turn can be expected to affect society. The pressures of increasing scarcity—of space, of raw materials, of food, of water and clean air, of quiet—are likely both to make people more dependent on one another and to tempt them into more bitter competition. Such competition, in turn, will aggravate many existing social problems—poverty and all its associated ills, the difference in living standards between rich and poor nations, international jealousy, violence at all levels of society—and could easily cause wars.

Because of society's role in causing the environmental crisis, we must reorganize and redirect our social organization if we are to have any hope of really solving the crisis. And the new organization will have to deal with the unpleasant fact that while the human population is vastly larger than ever before, the natural environment is not. This means that the changes will probably have to be very deep and basic: we will not be able to "go back" to any system that may have worked in the past.

To reach an understanding of why this is so, and what kinds of changes will be needed, we must examine some aspects of the environmental problem more closely.

Dimensions of the Problem

Four ecological concepts are basic to understanding the environmental crisis: interdependence, diversity, limits, and complexity. *Interdependence* literally means that everything is related to, and depends on, everything else; there is no beginning or end to the "web of life." *Diversity* refers to the existence of several different life and life-support forms. A basic principle of ecology is that the greater the diversity of species, the greater the probability for survival of any given species. *Limits* are of several kinds. First, there is a finite limit to the growth of any organism. Second, there is a limit to the numbers of a given species that an environment—including other organisms—can support. Finally, there is a finite limit to the amount of materials available in the earth's ecosystem. *Complexity* refers to the intricacy of the relationships that constitute the "web." Because of this complexity, interventions in the environment frequently lead to unanticipated and undesired consequences. Dichloro-diphenyl-trichloro-ethane (DDT), for example, was once repeatedly sprayed over large areas of land to eliminate various disease-carrying or crop-destroying insects. To an impressive degree it succeeded. But DDT is a long-lasting chemical, and its effects are not limited to insects. Much of it washed from the farmlands and forests into rivers and oceans, where it was taken up by small organisms at the bottom of the food chain. Eventually, as small creatures consumed tiny plants and larger creatures consumed smaller ones, several species of fish-eating birds accumulated so much of the poison that their eggs had thin shells that consistently broke before hatching. The species were in grave danger of extinction, although the users of DDT never intended such a result.[1] Only federal restrictions on the use of DDT prevented the wholesale elimination of these bird species.

One of the major difficulties in dealing with the environmental crisis, then, is the number of problems involved and the complexity of their relationships. A full discussion of the nature of our environmental problems

[1] Paul R. Ehrlich and Anne H. Ehrlich, *Population, Resources, Environment*, 2nd ed. (San Francisco: Freeman, 1972), pp. 208–209.

must include air and water pollution, land degradation, natural resource depletion, solid waste disposal, and a variety of other environmental hazards. We will consider each of these problems and their interrelationships and then will examine our technological and social systems to determine the origins of this complex problem.

Air Pollution   Let us take two hypothetical people and do terrible things to them. We shall put the first person into a sealed, airtight box. As the person breathes, the oxygen in the box will be replaced with carbon dioxide until eventually the person asphyxiates. The second person will also be placed in a sealed box, but one with an entry tube into which we can rapidly pump a large quantity of automobile exhaust. This person will succumb well before the oxygen-carbon dioxide balance is disturbed.

These examples demonstrate facts about air and our relationship to it. First, we have evolved over the millennia in an atmosphere of a given composition and quality, and our biological health depends on the atmosphere remaining in approximately that state. Second, just as the sealed box limited the amount of air available to the person trapped in it, so too is our atmosphere limited. Third, the air can carry substances that are harmful or lethal. An excess of any foreign substance in a given place is what is meant by pollution. If the atmosphere is not overburdened, natural processes will cleanse it and preserve its composition. Through photosynthesis, for example, green plants combine water with the carbon dioxide we (and other organisms) exhale, and produce oxygen and carbohydrates; this is one of the basic life cycles. But these natural processes, like other resources, have limits. They can remove only a limited quantity of harmful substances from the air; and if pollution exceeds their capacity to remove it, the air will become progressively more dangerous to humanity.

Yet we are overtaxing the atmosphere. Although the specific nature of air pollution varies from one locality to another (as a function of geography, climate, and type and concentration of industry), we can identify some of the common primary components. These include organic compounds (hydrocarbons); oxides of carbon, nitrogen, and sulfur; lead and other metals; and particulate matter (soot, fly ash). In urban areas, it is estimated that at least 80 percent of the air pollution is caused by motor vehicles.[2] The remainder comes from the burning of fossil fuels (oil and coal) in power-generating plants, airplanes, and homes; airborne "wastes" from manufacturing processes; and municipal trash burning. In all, almost 200 million tons of pollutants are poured into the atmosphere over the United States each year.[3] (See Table 16–1.) Furthermore, certain chemical processes frequently render these pollutants more dangerous after they reach the atmosphere. In the presence of sunlight, the emission of hydrocarbons and nitrogen oxides (primarily from cars) produces the photochemical soup called "smog" that envelops many of our cities; and various oxides combine with water vapor in the atmosphere to produce corrosive acids that eat away the surface of many buildings.

[2]Robert Rienow and Leona Train Rienow, *Moment in the Sun* (New York: Ballantine, 1967), p. 143; *Statistical Abstract of the United States, 1978*, United States Environmental Protection Agency (Washington, D.C.: U.S. Government Printing Office, 1978), p. 215.
[3]Ehrlich and Ehrlich, *Population, Resources, Environment*, p. 147.

Category	Carbon Monoxide	Sulfer Oxides	Hydro-carbons	Particles	Nitrogen Oxides	Total
Transportation	76.8	.9	11.9	1.3	11.1	102.0
Fuel combustion (Stationary)	1.3	24.1	1.5	5.1	13.0	45.0
Industrial processes	8.6	4.5	10.4	6.9	.8	31.2
Miscellaneous	6.3	.1	6.1	1.0	.9	13.8
Solid waste disposal	3.1	—	.9	.4	.1	4.5
Total	96.1	29.6	30.8	14.7	25.9	196.5

Source: Environmental Protection Agency.

Table   16-1
Major Sources of Air Pollution (in Millions of Tons Annually)

In recent years air pollution has increased to the point where it can only be classified as chronic and acute; we seem unable to conceive of there being "no" pollution. New York City had a particularly acute incident on Thanksgiving, 1966, when a thermal inversion (a mass of cool air flows over a hot air mass and prevents the hot air mass from rising, thus trapping the pollutants over an area) developed. The numbers of those hospitalized for respiratory ailments, particularly among the very young and very old, increased sharply.[4] But New Yorkers were more fortunate than the residents of Donora, Pennsylvania, in 1948, when a similar incident trapped all the fumes from a steel mill, a sulfuric acid plant, and a zinc plant. Over 40 percent of the town's population of 14,000 became ill, and 20 people died before the four-day crisis ended. And the "Black Fog" of London, in 1952, lasted four days and resulted in the deaths of approximately 4,000 people.[5]

The effects of chronic air pollution on human health are less dramatic and direct than those of the acute situations already described, but they are of greater long-run significance for human health. Continued exposure to air pollutants and their accumulation in the body—essentially a slow poisoning process—increase the incidence of such illnesses as bronchitis, emphysema, and lung cancer.[6] Air pollution also causes severe eye, nose, and throat irritations; it has been estimated that breathing New York City air is the equivalent of smoking two packs of cigarettes a day, with comparable consequences.[7] Poor visibility as a result of smog has also been cited as a major factor in both automobile and airplane accidents.

Air pollution has economic effects as well. Accelerated deterioration of property increases maintenance and cleaning costs; blighted crops mean lost income for farmers and higher food prices for the consumer; pollution-caused illnesses erode productivity, reduce workers' earnings, and raise the cost of medical care for everyone. The sulfur emitted each year from the smokestacks

[4]Gerald Leinwand, *Air and Water Pollution* (New York: Washington Square Press, 1969), p. 13.

[5]Donald E. Carr, "The Disasters," in *Society and Environment: The Coming Collision*, ed. Rex R. Campbell and Jerry L. Wade (Boston: Allyn and Bacon, 1972), pp. 131–132.

[6]Ehrlich and Ehrlich, *Population, Resources, Environment*, pp. 147–152.

[7]Rienow and Rienow, *Moment in the Sun*, p. 141.

of factories and power plants in the United States would be worth at least $300 million if it could be recovered.[8] In total, the dollar cost of air pollution has been estimated at $11 billion a year.[9]

Finally, air pollution may have a dangerous long-term effect on the earth's ecosystem. For example, some studies suggest that fluorocarbon gases, commonly used in spray cans and refrigerating systems, may be breaking down the earth's protective ozone layer.[10] (The ozone layer surrounds the earth from an altitude of 8 to 30 miles above sea level; it screens out many of the sun's harmful rays.) Fluorocarbon molecules, according to these studies, are not broken down in the earth's lower atmosphere, but continue to rise to a much higher altitude. Here they are broken up by high intensity radiation, and begin to chemically destroy ozone molecules. If this theory proves correct, the destruction of the ozone layer will lead to a much higher worldwide incidence of skin cancer and crop failure; there may also be changes in the world's climate. Preliminary tests that have been performed suggest that fluorocarbons may, indeed, be harmful to the earth's ozone layer.[11]

[8]Leinwand, *Air and Water Pollution*, pp. 24–26.

[9]C. W. Girffin, Jr., "America's Airborne Garbage," in Campbell and Wade, *Society and Environment*, p. 145.

[10]See Philip H. Howard and Arnold Hanchett, "Chlorofluorocarbon Sources of Environmental Contamination," *Science* (July 1975), pp. 217–219.

[11]"Spray Can Scare: The Latest Findings," *U.S. News & World Report* (September 29, 1975), p. 62.

Figure 16-1

The Increase in Artificially Produced Carbon Dioxide

Source: Figure 1-16 from *Fundamental Ecology* by Arthur S. Boughey, (Intext). Copyright © 1971 by Harper & Row, Publishers, Inc. Reprinted by permission of the publisher.

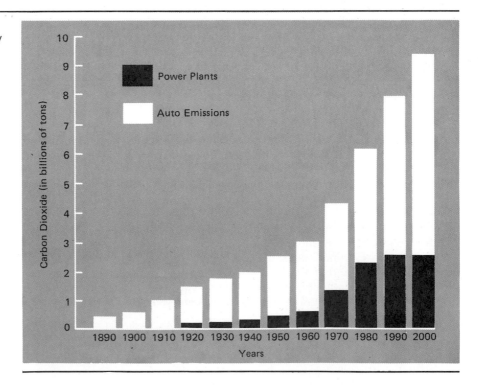

Other effects of air pollution may involve temperature changes. For example, the amount of carbon dioxide in the atmosphere is estimated to have increased about 25 percent during the past century and is expected—assuming we do nothing to prevent it—to increase by another 25 percent in the next 30 years (see Figure 16–1). Some scientists are concerned that such a buildup could produce a "greenhouse" effect in the atmosphere. That is, the carbon dioxide would trap heat near the earth's surface, raising the average temperature of the atmosphere. Such overheating, even by a few degrees, could melt the polar icecaps, with calamitous results. So far, however, the danger appears to be in the opposite direction: the average world temperature has actually declined slightly since 1940, giving rise to the fear that suspended particulates in the air may be preventing solar energy from reaching the earth. If so, this could eventually result in a cooling sufficient to usher in another ice age.[12]

Water Pollution

Water is constantly on the move, in what is known as the hydrologic cycle. It is found in the atmosphere as vapor; it condenses and falls to the earth as rain, snow, or dew; it percolates underground or runs off the surface into streams, rivers, and finally oceans; it evaporates into the atmosphere as vapor once again; and the cycle continues. While on the ground, it may be absorbed into the roots of plants, and through the leaves eventually be evaporated back into the atmosphere; or it may be drunk from streams by animals or people, and be evaporated or excreted back into the earth or air. Or it may sink into underground reservoirs and be stored up for millions of years, perhaps under enormous pressure, until it is released back into the cycle.

It is quite possible for water to be used more than once as it passes through a single round of the hydrologic cycle, if it is sufficiently purified between uses by natural or artificial means. But we have been accustomed to using "new" water rather than purifying the "old," and thus we remove fresh water from the continent faster than it is being replaced through the cycle. The nation's daily water requirement is expected to reach 1,300 billion gallons by the end of the century, but the best estimates indicate that only 700 billion gallons can be made available.[13] Intensive reuse is thus a necessity—but for water to be reused, its quality must be maintained, and we render much of our water unfit for reuse through various kinds of pollution: raw and inadequately treated sewage, oil, synthetic organic chemicals (detergents, pesticides), inorganic chemicals and mineral substances, plant nutrients, radioactivity, and heat. We, therefore, face a dual crisis with respect to water: the amount available to us will be insufficient for our demands, and what will be available will be of steadily deteriorating quality.

Just as air can cleanse itself if not overburdened, so too can rivers, lakes, and oceans purify themselves naturally. But we have been discharging wastes, directly and indirectly, into our waterways in amounts that prohibit such natural purification. Existing sewage treatment facilities discharge between 20

[12]Tom Alexander, "Some Burning Questions about Combustion," in Campbell and Wade, *Society and Environment*, pp. 137–138; and Ehrlich and Ehrlich, *Population, Resources, Environment*, pp. 237–242.

[13]John Hamer, "Drinking Water Safety," *Editorial Research Reports* (February 15, 1974), pp. 136–137.

and 30 percent of our raw sewage into whatever body of water is used for disposal.[14] The bacteria in such untreated sewage renders the water unfit for drinking, swimming, and many industrial uses. Finally, the use of oxygen to decompose the waste reduces the life-support capacity of the water, with a consequent decline in the number and variety of fish. As our population grows, the problem of waste disposal will become even more acute.

Current farming practices, such as the extensive use of nitrate and phosphate fertilizers, also seriously impair water quality. Rain and irrigation cause the runoff of large quantities of these materials into rivers and lakes. The fertilizers work in water much as they do on land, producing algae "blooms"—huge masses of algae that grow very quickly and then die. As with the decomposition of sewage, the decay of these "blooms" consumes oxygen, thereby killing off fish and other animals that have high oxygen requirements. As the algae decay, they settle to the bottom of the water, along with various compounds of nitrogen and phosphorus. The bottom of Lake Erie at one point had a layer of such muck ranging from 20 to 125 feet thick. Only intensive efforts by environmentalists to stop pollutants from being discharged into the lake and adjoining interways saved Lake Erie from total destruction. But as late as 1976, almost 16 million gallons of pollutants were dumped into the Great Lakes.[15]

The use of long-lasting pesticides, such as DDT, has widely contaminated water, as was already noted. Such compounds are especially dangerous because they accumulate in the tissues of animals who eat them. Not only did DDT almost exterminate several species of birds, but its accumulation in fish had rendered some of them inedible. Although the use of DDT has largely been banned, we and other organisms will continue to accumulate what has already been deposited; in fact, many humans begin ingesting the poison at birth because of particularly high concentrations in human milk. Our knowledge of the effects on human health and longevity of ingesting and storing such poisons is still sketchy, but we shall find out more as new generations of children mature. In effect, we are conducting a massive global experiment in which we and all other living things are the guinea pigs.

One reason why long-lasting poisons such as DDT and radioactive wastes pose such a serious problem is the process known as biological magnification, whereby the concentration of a given substance increases as it ascends in the food chain. A study of the Columbia River in the western United States revealed that while the radioactivity of the water was insignificant, "the radioactivity of the river plankton was 2,000 times greater; the radioactivity of the fish and ducks feeding on the plankton was 15,000 and 40,000 times greater, respectively; the radioactivity of young swallows fed on insects caught by their parents in the river was 500,000 times greater; the radioactivity of the egg yolks of water birds was more than a million times greater."[16] Presumably, the radioactive isotopes are released into the river by the nuclear power plant at Hanford, Washington. People who live downriver from such plants ingest and store radioactive isotopes with the water they drink and the fish and other

[14]Donald E. Carr, "The Politics of Pollution," in Campbell and Wade, *Society and Environment*, p. 84.

[15]*Statistical Abstract of the United States, 1978*, U.S. Coast Guard (Washington, D.C.: U.S. Government Printing Office, 1978), p. 217.

[16]Richard Curtis and Elizabeth Hogan, *Perils of the Peaceful Atom* (New York: Ballantine, 1969), p. 194.

Water pollution not only makes water unfit for human use but also destroys fish life. The discharge of industrial pollutants has killed all fish in this body of water.

Gilles Peress/Magnum

local foods they eat. Because most radioactive substances retain their potency for many years—even centuries—the presence of these isotopes adds significantly to the normal "background" radiation naturally present in the environment. This means an increased potential for damage to human health, in terms of a higher incidence of cancer and genetic defects.

Another form of water pollution comes from heat—the so-called thermal pollution. The effluents of many factories and generating plants—especially nuclear power plants—are warmer than the rivers and lakes into which they flow, and when discharged in quantity they may raise the water temperature by as much as 10 to 30 degrees Fahrenheit. Such thermal pollution can be ecologically devastating.[17] Because most aquatic animals are cold-blooded, they are at the mercy of the surrounding water temperature. If the temperature rises beyond the point of an organism's capacity for metabolic adjustment, the animal will die. Since larvae and young fish are far more susceptible to death through slight temperature variations than are mature organisms, and since rises in temperature also interfere with the spawning and migratory patterns of many organisms, thermal pollution may exterminate some aquatic populations through reproductive failure.

Other serious and widespread forms of water pollution include:

• the discharge of oil—both unintentional, through the "blowing" of offshore wells and leakage from storage facilities and ships, and intentional, through the practice of flushing out tankers at sea—with consequent destruction of marine and bird life and the despoiling of beaches;

• the discharge of various industrial chemicals, such as methyl mercury into rivers and oceans, where they accumulate to lethal levels in the bodies of fish through the process of biological magnification;[18]

• the discharge, from food processing, textile, paper, steel, and other plants, of wastes that are either toxic themselves or combine with so much dissolved oxygen in the water as to prove indirectly fatal to fish;[19]

• acid runoff from strip mining, which is destructive to life in streams and rivers.

Nonrenewable Resources and Solid Waste Disposal

Since both air and water can cleanse themselves if they are not overburdened, they are in a sense renewable resources. Once an oil field has been pumped out, however, it is not going to fill again, nor is the earth going to replace the iron ore of an exhausted mine—at least, not within the probable life span of the human race. Fossil fuels, metals, and other minerals are, therefore, nonrenewable resources: they exist only in finite quantity. Unfortunately, however, we behave as though the supply were infinite. We take resources that occur in limited, concentrated form in nature and, via our technology, disperse them into the environment in such a way that they are neither technologically nor economically recoverable. There is no way, for instance, to reclaim the lead that is added to automobile fuel and then released, along with other exhaust products, into the air, where it disperses throughout the

[17]John R. Clark, "Heat Pollution," in Campbell and Wade, *Society and Environment*, p. 94.

[18]Rienow and Rienow, *Moment in the Sun*, p. 250.

[19]Carr, "The Politics of Pollution," pp. 81–83.

Northern Hemisphere as far away as the Arctic icecap. Usage of this sort is doubly destructive. Not only are we running out of lead, but we are turning it into a pollutant that is ingested and stored in our bodies at a level approaching toxicity.

In order to satisfy the requirements of its standard of living, the United States, although it constitutes only 6 percent of the world's population, consumes approximately 30 percent of the annual world energy output and supply of industrial raw materials.[20] This has several important consequences. First, we now import many of those materials from the still developing areas of the world. As these areas increase the pace of their development, they are going to restrict the export of such resources, and the competition for what is exported will increase. How then will we insure a steady supply of needed raw materials without exacerbating world tensions? (See Chapter 15.)

Second, we do not really "consume" most products, despite our designation as a "consumer society." It is more accurate to say that we buy things, use them, and then throw them away, so that we have several hundred million tons of solid wastes to dispose of every year. These wastes include food, paper, glass, plastics, wood, abandoned cars, cans, metals, paints, dead animals, and a host of other things. Estimates of the cost of disposing of such wastes run as high as $3 billion annually.[21]

The two principal methods of solid waste disposal are landfill and incineration. Although landfills are supposed to meet certain sanitary standards, the Department of Health, Education, and Welfare (HEW) found that "less than half the cities and towns in the United States with populations of more than 2,500 dispose of community refuse by approved sanitary and nuisance-free methods."[22] "Sanitary landfills" are allowed to become breeding grounds for rats; improperly designed municipal incinerators are principal contributors to urban air pollution. Many cities on both coasts use the ocean as a dumping ground for waste disposal. New York City's practice of hauling tons of refuse out to sea each day and dumping it has made a "dead sea" out of a large area in the Atlantic Ocean.

The large-scale introduction of plastics and other synthetics has produced a new waste disposal problem, for whereas organic substances are eventually decomposed through bacterial action, plastics are generally totally immune to biological decomposition, and remain in their original state when they are buried or dumped. If burned, they become air pollutants in the form of hydrocarbons and nitrogen oxides.

Nuclear power plants pose a special problem. For various technical reasons, the fuel in a reactor's core must be periodically replaced. This requires careful planning and handling, because the radioactivity of nuclear fuels increases as they are used. David Lilienthal, the first chairman of the Atomic Energy Commission, describes the problem:

These huge quantities of radioactive wastes must somehow be removed from the reactors, must—without mishap—be put into containers that will never rupture; then these vast quantities of poisonous stuff must be moved either to a burial

[20]*Statistical Abstract of the United States, 1978,* p. 608.
[21]Rienow and Rienow, *Moment in the Sun,* p. 137.
[22]Sheldon A. Mix, "Solid Wastes: Every Day, Another 800 Million Pounds," in Campbell and Wade, *Society and Environment,* p. 184.

ground or to reprocessing plants, handled again, and disposed of, by burial or otherwise, with a risk of human error at every step.[23]

There are now 64 operable nuclear power plants in the United States. Current government policy envisions building 300 to 500 more reactors—six to ten per state. Each of these has a projected lifespan of 30 to 40 years, at which time the contents of the reactors must be removed and the contaminated structure itself must be destroyed. It is estimated that this will cost between $40–70 million.

The danger from processing such material is evident when we consider that absorption of less than one curie of strontium-90, a radioactive isotope, is lethal to a human being, and that by the year 2000, assuming present nuclear power plant construction plans are realized, radioactive wastes will contain 6 billion curies of strontium-90. These wastes will have to be safely stored for up to 1,000 years before they become harmless. During that time, any alteration in the seismological conditions of the burial site could disturb the radioactive material and contaminate the area. Even assuming that such burial sites are not disrupted by earthquakes or wars, we are saddling future generations with their perpetual custody. The recent near-disaster at the Three Mile Island nuclear reactor in Pennsylvania reminds us of how potentially dangerous nuclear plants can be.

[23]Curtis and Hogan, *Perils of the Peaceful Atom*, p. 175.

After a court injunction forbidding trespassing, antinuclear demonstrators are dragged away from a reactor construction site. Opponents of nuclear power are concerned with the disposal of radioactive wastes and the possibility of human error causing accidents at any step in the process.
UPI

A forest is full of life: trees, grass, moss, and other plants; deer, squirrels, birds, and other animals; worms, beetles, bacteria, and other inhabitants of the soil. All of these draw their sustenance from the soil, eventually die, and are decomposed to provide sustenance for succeeding generations. The forest depends upon water for its survival and also serves as a giant storage facility for it, trapping rainfall in its spongy soil and releasing it gradually to streams and springs. Other water is absorbed by plants and released into the surrounding atmosphere. Meanwhile, by photosynthesis, the foliage takes up carbon dioxide from the air and releases oxygen, thus helping to maintain the natural atmospheric balance.

Any ecosystem, such as a forest, swamp, or prairie, is a complex matrix of interrelated and interacting organisms and processes, both supporting its own patterns of life and contributing to those of the larger regional, continental, and planetary ecosystems. Serious alteration of a local ecosystem, therefore, can affect the balance of life in a larger area. Yet, through greed and/or ignorance of ecological principles, humanity has diminished or destroyed the capacity of large land areas to support life. We are only beginning to recognize the possible consequences.

When Europeans first appeared in what is now the continental United States, over 40 percent of the land was forested; today, after several centuries of logging, agriculture, and urbanization, that figure is about 30 percent.[24] Paul R. Ehrlich and Anne H. Ehrlich have described what follows the wholesale logging of a forest:

> Numerous animals that depend on the trees for food and shelter disappear. Many of the smaller forest plants depend on the trees for shade; they and the animals they support also disappear. With the removal of trees and plants, the soil is directly exposed to the elements, and it tends to erode faster. Loss of topsoil reduces the water-retaining capacity of an area, diminishes the supply of fresh water, causes silting of dams, and . . . flooding . . . . Deforestation . . . reduces the amount of water transferred from ground to air by the trees in the process as "transpiration." This modifies the weather downwind of the area, usually making it more arid and subject to greater extremes of temperature.[25]

Even huge deserts can be created by humanity's misuse of the environment. The Sahara was created partly by overgrazing, deforestation, and poor irrigation of land that was once capable of supporting at least some plant and animal life. The Sahara continues to grow: today it is advancing southward at a rate of several miles a year. The same process can be seen in many parts of Asia, India, and Europe. In 1882, 9.4 percent of the earth's total land area was classified as desert or wasteland; by 1952, 23.3 percent was so classified. In America a 1934 "vast transcontinental windstorm" blotted out the sun from the Rocky Mountains to the Atlantic Coast, announcing that large, once-fertile areas of Kansas, Texas, Oklahoma, Colorado, and New Mexico had become a desolate dust bowl.[26] Such irreparable losses are particularly intolerable in view of the rapidly increasing need for food to sustain a burgeoning world population.

It takes anywhere from 300 to 1,000 years to produce one inch of topsoil, under the most favorable conditions. Yet many areas of the earth are losing

[24]United States Forest Service statistic.
[25]Ehrlich and Ehrlich, *Population, Resources, Environment*, p. 202.
[26]Fairfield Osborn, *Our Plundered Planet* (New York: Pyramid, 1968), pp. 51–52.

topsoil at the rate of several inches per year because of poor management that exposes the soil to wind and water erosion. In addition, the fertility of the land is destroyed as a result of increasing mechanization and urbanization. Unlike horses, mules, and other beasts of burden, tractors do not help to fertilize the land they plow; when food is shipped from farm to city, the organic wastes, instead of being returned to the land, are flushed away to pollute the rivers, lakes, and oceans. Massive amounts of artificial fertilizers—phosphates and nitrates—have been used to supplement declining natural fertility, and to improve the productivity of land that is naturally deficient. But, as we have seen, a large quantity of these artificial fertilizers is washed into rivers and lakes, where it too contributes to pollution.

Other Hazards   Besides widely acknowledged environmental problems, other threats to our well-being arise from the indiscriminate use of our incomplete technological knowledge. These include noise pollution, chemical hazards, and a variety of undesirable consequences associated with certain large-scale engineering projects.

Noise Pollution.   Noise is a purely dysfunctional consequence of our technology. It is produced by airplanes, cars, buses, trucks, motorcycles, motorboats, factory machinery, dishwashers, garbage disposals, vacuum cleaners, television, radio, phonographs, air conditioners, jack-hammers, bulldozers, and a hundred other tools of our social existence. Noise, which above a certain level can be harmful even when it is not consciously being heard, directly affects our physical and emotional well-being (see Figure 16-2). Studies have shown that we suffer from greater hearing losses with increasing age than in the past, and that noise significantly contributes to the tension level of daily life, sometimes even precipitating stress-related illnesses such as peptic ulcer and hypertension.[27]

Chemicals.   Pressure at all levels to get new products on the market has permitted the widespread use of various poisons (pesticides and herbicides) without adequate prior testing of their long-run cumulative effects—the massive introduction of such synthetics as plastics, which create serious problems of disposal; the use of untested industrial chemicals such as vinyl chloride gas, which has been implicated in at least 20 deaths from cancer of the liver and in a higher incidence of miscarriages among the wives of men who work with it;[28] and an incredible proliferation in the variety and amount of what are called food "additives." There are over 2,500 food additives in current use in the United States; each individual has an average intake of over three pounds per year. Additives are used to grow and process food. Yet we know little about the long-term effects of continuous ingestion of each such substance, and almost nothing about the possible synergistic effects on the body of the millions of possible combinations of substances.[29]

Large-Scale Engineering Projects.   Perhaps because it gives them a sense of mastery over fate, people have always taken immense pride in their

[27]Ehrlich and Ehrlich, *Population, Resources, Environment,* p. 177; Rienow and Rienow, *Moment in the Sun,* pp. 179–194.

[28]*New York Times,* February 4, 1976, p. 23.

[29]Rienow and Rienow, *Moment in the Sun,* pp. 197–198.

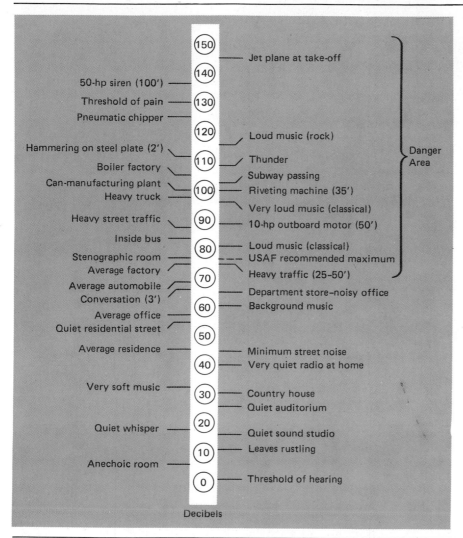

Figure 16-2
Decibel Values of Common Environmental Sounds
Source: Richard H. Wagner, *Environment and Man.* 2nd ed. (New York: Norton, 1974).

ability to change the face of the earth in ways they have deemed beneficial. They have frequently failed, however, to anticipate and assess the possible costs associated with such benefits. Thus a new dam is hailed, both as an engineering masterpiece in its own right and because it opens up new lands for agriculture, settlement, and recreation (although sometimes there is a net loss of wilderness and recreational land). Less often recognized is that while a dam may permit the controlled distribution of water to desired locations, it also "costs" water through evaporation. Furthermore, large dams have caused significant earthquakes, even in geologically inactive areas, because of the tremendous pressures exerted by the billions of gallons of water they store. The giant Aswan Dam in Egypt epitomizes the potential of such large projects for producing other unwanted and unpredicted consequences. Although relatively new, the dam is already being blamed by ecologists for diminishing

This area of land in Tennessee was left completely barren by strip mining.

Kenneth Murray/Nancy Palmer

the once rich sardine fishing in the Nile delta through the silting up of nutrients behind the dam.

Another hazard to the environment is strip mining. Most coal in the United States lies deep within the earth; in order to obtain it, underground mining is necessary. A significant percentage of coal, however, lies close enough to the surface for strip mining, in which the top layers of soil are removed and the coal is excavated. While strip mining is cheaper (and safer) than underground mining, it causes much greater harm to the environment. Vast areas of land are left scarred by huge, ugly trenches and denuded of all life. And because the topsoil is removed from the earth's surface during the strip-mining process, healthy plant life can never return. Finally, because the delicate soil balance is disturbed, water supplies in the area are often irreversibly damaged; increased erosion at the mining site can cause both local and distant water sources to be contaminated by sediment, dissolved acids, and other pollutants.

Though some states strictly regulate strip mining in theory—requiring, for example, that the topsoil be replaced when mining is completed—such regulations are not uniformly enforced. With oil supplies becoming depleted and the nation's energy needs growing, strip mining will probably become more widespread in the near future. Unless reclamation laws—requiring that a strip-mining site be returned to premining condition—are passed and vigorously enforced, much land will be destroyed.

Origins of the Problem

An investigation of winter fish kills in Wisconsin lakes led to the unlikely conclusion that they were caused by snowmobiles. Heavy snowmobile use on a lake during the winter compacts the snow and makes the ice opaque. This reduces the amount of sunlight reaching the underwater plants that need it for photosynthesis. The plants' oxygen production declines, causing them to die, and their decomposition consumes considerable amounts of what oxygen is left in the water. The fish are then asphyxiated.

As this example suggests, we can best understand our environmental crisis as the interaction of three systems; the "natural" environment, our technological system, and our social system. The fish, ice, water, oxygen, plants, and the photosynthesis process are all elements of the natural system. The snowmobile is an element of our technological system. That it is produced, marketed, bought, and used, and that there is no one to hold responsible for the fish kills is a product of our social system. That the fish are indirectly and unintentionally killed by the snowmobiles illustrates the all too frequent dysfunctional consequences of the effects of our social and technological systems on the natural system.

Taking a broader perspective, we can define the natural system as containing these elements and their interrelationships; air, water, earth, solar energy, plants, animals, and mineral resources. Our technological system includes electricity-generating facilities, manufacturing processes and plants, various methods for extracting mineral resources, transportation, farming, and the actual consumption and residue disposal of the products of those processes. Our social system includes our attitudes, beliefs and values, and institutional structures. And as with the fish and the snowmobiles, so in larger matters we must look to our social and technological systems for the origins of the present crisis in our natural system.

One element that transcends these systems' boundaries is that of population size. (See Chapter 15.) Quantitative increases often produce qualitative changes. Thus, as the population of a given society increases, societal relationships also tend to increase and to become more complex. To satisfy needs and desires, the technological system likewise becomes more elaborate and complex. Finally, the needs of the swelling numbers become an intolerable burden on the natural system and threaten its very survival. As a system becomes more complex, it may become more fragile: small, tolerable changes in one element may be transformed through system dynamics into large, destructive changes in other elements.

Technology requires energy, and our basic source of energy is the sun. Through photosynthesis, plants produce not only oxygen, but the carbohydrates that are the basis of our organic food supply and the fossil fuel deposits (coal and oil) from which we derive most of our electricity and heat. The electrical energy requirements of our society are enormous, and they are expected to double every ten years or less if the future repeats the past. One consequence of this projection has been government encouragement of nuclear power to complement rather than replace fossil-fuel generating plants. Both nuclear and fossil-fuel plants, however, are major polluters, contributing massive amounts of sulfur oxides, hydrocarbons, and particulate matter to the air and heat to the water. With nuclear power plants, there is always the possibility of contamination from enormous amounts of radioactivity released in an accident at the plant or in the transportation, storage, or disposal of nuclear fuels. Also, in their daily operations these plants require enormous amounts of water that is polluted with both heat and radioactive waste.

Since the known sources of fossil fuels are rapidly being depleted, new sources must be discovered in order to maintain and increase our level of energy production. Despite many leaks, offshore oil drilling continues, and its importance is growing. The quest for cheap coal has already led to the devastation of vast areas of West Virginia, Ohio, and Pennsylvania through strip mining.

Many of the dysfunctional aspects of the manufacturing and farming elements of our technological system were detailed earlier in this chapter. One element deserving further attention is transportation. There are more than 200 million motor vehicles in the world, and half are in the United States. Automobiles consume almost half of the crude petroleum production in the United States, and do so very inefficiently. Automobiles, a prime producer of air and noise pollution, consume about 4 gallons per 100 passenger miles, while a bus consumes around 0.8 gallons and a train 0.36. Furthermore, we have lost millions of acres of land to build the highways for automobile travel and seriously exacerbated the problem of insufficient space in and around American cities.[30] (See Chapter 14.)

So deep is our society's faith in the value of technology that although every technological "advance" is accompanied by unwanted, unintended, and unhappy consequences, we have failed to establish any comprehensive social control over technological development or use. In reaction to those consequences, many people have now become blindly "antitechnology." It must be emphasized that our environmental crisis is a function, not of technology *per se*, but of the failure of our social system to develop a technology compatible with the requirements of environmental health. To correct that failure, we must first identify the values and beliefs that have led us to befoul our environment and strain its resources.

One such is the belief, expressed in the Old Testament, that in creating the universe, God placed humanity at the apex of all living things, giving us dominion over all other species. This anthropocentric view of the physical universe led to a belief that humanity did not belong to the natural world; rather, the world belonged to it, to be exploited for humanity's purposes.[31] The companion belief, that they were reponsible for the way in which they used it, was too easily overlooked.

When the first European settlers came to America, the land and its resources seemed limitless. No matter how rapidly colonization occurred, there always seemed to be new land on which to settle. The coupling of the concepts of an ever-expanding frontier and of the supremacy of people over

[30]Kenneth P. Cantor, "Warning: The Automobile Is Dangerous to Earth, Air, Fire, Water, Mind, and Body," in *The Environmental Handbook*, ed. Garrett de Bell (New York: Ballantine, 1970), pp. 206–207.

[31]Lynn White, Jr., "The Historical Roots of Our Ecological Crisis," in de Bell, *Environmental Handbook*, pp. 12–26.

nature sent nineteenth-century America out to "conquer the continent," much as today we speak of "conquering space." In the process, we devastated our wildlife, and came near to exterminating the Indian population.

We produce an incredible number and variety of goods in this country, ample evidence of the high value placed on material objects. Our materialism would appear to derive from three sources. One is the Calvinist doctrine of predestination, which asserted that each person was predestined before birth to go either to heaven or to hell. Although one's ultimate destination was never certain, it seemed reasonable to assume that those of whom God approved would be blessed with success in this world also, while those destined to be condemned would be similarly unsuccessful here. It thus became important to demonstrate one's salvation by visibly achieving success; and what better way to do this than through the personal possession of material objects?

A second possible source of our materialism is the fact that all societies establish status systems for differentiating their members; in our society the acquisition of goods is an important factor in determining a person's status.[32]

Finally, there is our concept of life as progress. We take for granted that our standard of living should be constantly improved, and that this means growth in material wealth. This concept seems so natural to us that we tend to regard as primitive or backward those cultures, past and present, that advise people to be contented with what they have.

Given our belief that there are limitless resources available for our exploitation, and the value we place on the possession of material objects, it is no surprise that we have come to worship growth for growth's sake. Thus, a government that was formed to promote the general welfare and ensure that each individual could enjoy "life, liberty, and the pursuit of happiness" has come to measure general welfare by gross national product and "the pursuit of happiness" by per capita income.

The primacy of economics over environment became a guiding principle in our legal system. Until recently, there was no basis for an action in law in which one could act as an advocate for the state of the environment itself; in order to sue a despoiler, plaintiffs had to establish that they or their property had suffered economic injury. And now that we do have some laws specifically designed to protect the environment, the penalties for breaking them are also economic—larger or smaller fines. In most cases the fines have been relatively small, and the laws have not always been very energetically enforced.

Modern technology developed largely because of our economic structure, for the entrepreneurs of our "free-enterprise" system favored labor-saving machinery. Capital came to replace property as the primary source of power and entrepreneurs were able to raise capital by demonstrating that they could make a profit on its investment. That meant minimizing costs, and since the rivers and the air charged nothing for their services as waste disposal agents, they were used. The process of making free (ab)use of the environment has now come to be recognized as in fact the "externalization" of costs that should properly be reflected in the price of a given product; when a steel plant, for example, discharges waste into a river at no cost to itself, it has artificially lowered the price of steel. When environmentalists and economists today say that we are going to have to spend tens of billions of dollars to

[32]Campbell and Wade, *Society and Environment*, p. 339.

restore (if we can) the quality of our environment, what they are really doing is presenting us with a bill long overdue.

Having delineated some of the attitudes and values that have led to our environmental crisis, we must now examine the behavior of some of our social institutions—government, corporations, and schools—to assess their role in creating the problem.

Before the recent creation of the Environmental Protection Agency (EPA), governmental responsibility for the state of the environment was divided among several departments. Air pollution control was the concern of HEW, which was also responsible for food and drug regulation. Water pollution control was assigned to the Department of the Interior, which also had responsibility for conservation of wildlife and natural resources and for administering the national parks, seashores, and forests. Responsibility for pesticides, which we have seen to be a significant source of air and water pollution and a danger to wildlife, was vested in the Department of Agriculture's Pesticide Regulation Division. Energy production, with the exception of nuclear power generation, which is licensed by the Nuclear Regulatory Commission, is still regulated by the Federal Power Commission. The independent National Academy of Science and Technology is an important governmental advisory body on science policy, and the Department of Commerce has an Undersecretary for Science and Technology. Finally, Congress has various committees responsible for conducting hearings and developing legislation on different aspects of the environment, and the president has a Science Advisory Council and a Council on Environmental Quality.

With such a thicket of federal agencies, one might wonder naively why there should be an environmental crisis at all. Unfortunately, conflicts of interest developed in the federal regulatory process. Too often, agencies that were set up to protect the public interest became advocates for the industries they were intended to regulate. (See Chapter 12.) Thus, as part of the Agriculture Department, the Pesticide Regulation Division performed more as a lobbyist for the pesticide industry than as protector of the environment. The Nuclear Regulatory Commission is supposed to promote as well as to regulate the nuclear power industry. It has generally tended to stress promotion and has given too little thought to the dangers inherent in the processing, handling, usage, transportation, and storage of nuclear fuels. The Department of the Interior is responsible for managing public lands to make maximum use of their recreational and natural resource potentials. Too frequently this has led to their exploitation for grazing, mining, and logging, and to their conversion from wilderness areas into what might be termed "nature-consumption packages." Finally, the administrative procedures specified by the major federal laws for the development and application of air- and water-quality standards are often cumbersome, time-consuming, and not sufficiently stringent. (More recent federal environmental legislation will be discussed later in this chapter.)

The federal government itself has also often helped to degrade the environment. Several projects of the Army Corps of Engineers can properly be called "eco-catastrophes." These include the series of canals in Florida that have lowered the water table in the Everglades and destroyed much of the area's wildlife. The Corps of Engineers has also constructed several dams.

Through its decision to invest heavily in highway construction while giving little support to mass transit, the federal government has contributed to air pollution and other dysfunctions associated with our transportation system.

Until recently, the primary concern shown by state governments for the environment was in conservation and recreation. The past few years have seen a marked increase in concern and action by the states in air and water pollution control, but the record of achievement has generally been poor. There are several important reasons for this failure. First, state programs have been hampered by a lack of funds to build pollution-control facilities and to staff their regulatory agencies. Second, they have been cautious about prosecuting companies doing business in their states, lest business move elsewhere, giving the state a reputation for "toughness" that would deter companies from opening new facilities. Finally, water and air transcend political boundaries: the sources of pollution are often beyond a state's jurisdiction.

Municipalities and counties are the governmental bodies usually responsible for sewage and solid waste disposal. This record has also been poor. Most sewage passes, untreated, into convenient waterways. Garbage is generally disposed of either by burning or by landfill; the burning procedure causes air pollution and landfill—even when billed as "sanitary"— frequently produces stinking morasses. Coastal cities are particularly bad offenders. New York City has managed to destroy a portion of the Atlantic Ocean by its garbage dumping; San Francisco is filling in its bay with garbage, with potentially drastic consequences for its climate; Galveston pours millions of gallons of raw sewage into the Gulf of Mexico each day.

It would be easy to attribute the environmental failures of government to citizen apathy, as evidenced by an unwillingness to provide sufficient funds for control facilities and personnel, but the roots go much deeper. We have evolved an economy based on overconsumption, coupled with a vast array of objects designed to be used once or briefly and then discarded. This brings us to a consideration of the role of the major corporations in the creation of our environmental problems.

The rapid growth of many companies after World War II, when the demand for consumer goods was particularly heavy, led to a number of significant changes in the nature of the American economy. The old virtue of corporate stability was replaced by a drive for growth for its own sake, both in the economy as a whole and for each company. It was, therefore, no longer enough to satisfy customer needs; companies, through the use of advertising, began to create demand.[33] People were no longer customers; they became consumers, to be manipulated into desiring products for which they had no real need—products that contributed to their standard of living but not always to the quality of their lives. (See Chapter 12.)

Creation of consumer demand still did not satisfy the passion for growth. Corporations began to manufacture products designed to be replaced within a short time ("planned obsolescence"), or to be used once and then discarded. Automobiles are now designed to last about three years (just long enough to finish the payments), paper diapers replace washable cotton, foods are

[33]See Vance Packard, *The Hidden Persuaders* (New York: McKay, 1957); and John Kenneth Galbraith, *The Affluent Society* (Boston: Houghton Mifflin, 1971).

double- and triple-packaged, bottles and cans are to be discarded after a single use (some companies have printed on the backs on their bottles "No deposit, no return—not to be refilled" and on the front, ever mindful of their image, "Please help fight litter—dispose of properly"). Annually, over $25 billion alone is spent on packaging in the United States, and most of these packaging materials are discarded, amounting to at least 13 percent of municipal solid wastes.[34] It is in this way that we drain our natural resources, befoul our air and water, and create mountains of solid waste.

It would be wrong to assume, however, that our environmental crisis is primarily a function of capitalist greed. Communist countries have also been preeminently concerned with economic growth. The goals have been the same in both systems—only the means of organization have differed—and both are suffering the same unwanted consequences. If the Communists' environmental problems seem less severe, it is only because their industrial production is less efficient. What should be understood, then, is that any materialist society lacking proper control is bound to produce an environmental crisis, and that our corporations have a vested interest in keeping our society on its present course. Automobile and petroleum companies traditionally head the *Fortune 500* list that ranks American corporations according to largest sales. These companies make their money from the products that cause much of our pollution. Thus corporations will probably continue to oppose stringent environmental legislation, while seeking to represent themselves as nonpolluters.

One argument corporations have used to try to block environmental legislation is that the costs of pollution-control efforts are too high—that the money spent on these efforts increases the costs of goods to consumers, reduces sales and ultimately causes unemployment. This argument of "jobs versus the environment" was used with particular effectiveness during the economic recession of the mid-1970s, when many deadlines for meeting air- and water-quality standards were postponed as a result of industry pressure. In fact, studies have found that federal environmental controls cost each citizen only about $47 annually, and that environmental programs—particularly the building of new sewage facilities—have already resulted in several hundred thousand new jobs.[35] The rehabilitation of waterways and the building of new, nonpolluting mass transit systems—to cite just two examples—would create many additional new jobs.

Social Action The nature and extent of our ecological crisis has led many to conclude that if we continue on our present course, we are going to have a catastrophe. Scientists' projections based on current trends point to a future in which life would be like that of our forebears: "nasty, brutish and short."[36] The task before us, then, is to plan an alternative future. If we conceive of that alternative, however, merely as present society without present problems— no hunger, no pollution—we are unlikely to achieve it. Present problems, as we have seen, are largely outgrowths of past and present society. We must be

[34]United States Department of Commerce, *Containers and Packaging* (January 1974), pp. 3–4; see William E. Small, *Third Pollution* (New York: Praeger, 1971), p. 21.

[35]"Attacks on Environmental Rules Blunted," *New York Times* (March 15, 1976), pp. 1 ff.

[36]See Paul Ehrlich, "Eco-catastrophe," in Campbell and Wade, *Society and Environment*, pp. 269–280.

prepared to make basic changes in our attitudes toward nature and the material world, and this is likely to entail changes in the organization of our social and economic life.

Educating the Public

Despite the attention focused on environmental problems in recent years, there is still a need for massive public education that will make known facts about the state of the environment, how it got that way, and what can be expected to happen if we continue on our present course. People must be persuaded to change their attitudes and learn that the resources of the earth are not limitless. This entails a dual attack on our materialist and growth-valuing attitudes. If there are limits to the amount of goods we can produce, then we must jettison the concept that "more is better," because at some point there can be no "more." We must also manage some kind of relatively fair and equal distribution of our limited supply of life-supporting and life-enhancing goods among all the inhabitants of the earth. Such a redistribution is implicit in the concept of a finite environment, for all inhabitants depend on one another and must be able to live in cooperation and reasonable harmony in order to survive.[37]

In the schools, education would be based on a philosophy that views people as belonging to the world rather than it belonging to them. It would encourage students to concern themselves less with material acquisition and more with the quality of life as reflected in the ability to live harmoniously with the environment. Children would be taught the value of cooperative, rather than competitive, behavior.

At the college level, science and engineering students would be required to study the social impact of science, and the relation of their own disciplines to environmental health. Specialization and fragmentation of knowledge are probably unavoidable in an advanced, technological society; but such training in "social accountability," coupled with the primary educational experience described above, should produce scientists and engineers who would regard the exercise of their knowledge in a framework of ecological awareness as a fundamental part of their jobs.

Recycling

One of the great lessons to be learned from studying the natural world is the concept of cyclical processing; every natural process, as we have seen, forms one part of a cycle of constant removal. Once we recognize that our environment is finite, we must increasingly recycle what we use. There should be no problem of solid waste disposal, because there should be no solid waste. The recycling of all materials should be "programmed" in advance—what is output for a given system should be recycled as input, after usage, for the same or another system. There would be no "final use" for a product; it would always be in process. This would probably require legislation on the national level, regulating the distribution of goods in our society. Before manufacturers would be permitted to market a product, they would be required to demonstrate that it could be recycled and needed. Similarly, municipalities would not be permitted to discharge their solid wastes into

[37]Kenneth E. Boulding, "The Economics of the Coming Spaceship Earth," in de Bell, *Environmental Handbook,* pp. 96–101.

waterways, but would be required to have effective recycling programs. Such programs could be developed on an industry-wide basis. They might rely on large deposits that would encourage the customer to return the used product (automobiles, bottles, cans); contracts with waste-collection agencies, municipal or private, that would directly return the product (paper, for example); or separation at centrally located trash reclamation sites.

In some areas of the country—and in some industries—successful recycling programs are already under way. For example, there are now 1,300 aluminum reclamation centers throughout the nation that recycle over 17 percent of the country's aluminum cans. More than 100 cities have paper-collection programs; as a result, about 22 percent of all paper manufactured in the United States is recycled. In St. Louis, recycling has advanced to the point where a new plant has been built to recycle almost all of the city's refuse—almost 8,000 tons a day.

Such recycling not only helps save the environment, but it is also profitable. It has been estimated that ordinary disposal of wastes costs this nation some $3.5 billion annually. Recycling wastes would enable companies and municipalities to save the energy needed to produce new materials and to use or even sell the materials derived from the waste. As one observer pointed out:

> For every ton of steel produced from recycled municipal solid waste instead of ore, the following things happen:
>
> Enough electricity is saved to power the average American home for eight months—a 74 percent saving in the amount of energy consumed to produce that one ton of steel.
>
> Two hundred pounds of air pollutants, of the kind produced in making steel from ore, are not produced—an 86 percent decline in air pollution.
>
> About 6,700 gallons of fresh water are not used—a 40 percent saving.
>
> As the water that is used is returned to streams and sewers, 102 pounds of water pollutants are not discharged—a 76 percent reduction.
>
> And 2.7 tons of mining wastes are not heaped on the landscape around the mine.[38]

Increasingly, it is becoming expensive *not* to recycle.

The concept of recycling also applies to industrial effluents; just as the final product must be recycled, so must the by-products of the manufacturing process. Much of what is effluent in one process can be used as input in other processes. A company should be required by law to return water at the same temperature and quality at which it was withdrawn and either to remove potential pollutants at some early stage in the manufacturing process or to trap them later. Again, the relevant legislation would probably have to be at the national level; otherwise, "havens" of pollution would be created in states or municipalities that failed to pass the necessary laws. Penalties for violation might range from fines and/or plant shutdown to criminal charges against managements.

The recycling concept is directly applicable to another important cluster

[38]Boyce Rensberger, "Coining Trash," *New York Times Magazine* (December 7, 1975), pp. 31 ff.

of environmental problems: urban sewage disposal, the stripping of nutrients from farm soil, and the run-off of artificial fertilizers from farms into waterways. Treated sewage makes excellent fertilizer, and if this were shipped from city to farm we would solve the disposal problem and considerably lessen the need for artificial fertilizers.

An important ramification of the recycling process is that it would require what are currently construed as "external" costs to be included, along with the current internal costs of production, in determining the price of the product. Thus the cost of environmental cleanliness would be borne by manufacturers (or their customers) rather than by the public as a whole. Presumably the burden of these costs would goad the corporations into making the fullest possible use of waste products and effluents.

One of many recycling centers organized in response to public recognition of the finite nature of our resources.
Katrina Thomas/Photo Researchers, Inc.

**Technology
Assessment**

The "invisible hand" that Adam Smith, the eighteenth-century economist, said was guiding the free-enterprise system pulled out of the American economy in the early 1930s, and the federal government stepped in and announced that henceforth it would accept primary responsibility for the economy. We have engaged in a "free technology" system which closely parallels the free-enterprise system, and the quality of our environment is "crashing" today in a fashion not unlike that of the stock market in 1929. That is, a system that was generally believed to be stable has proved to be unstable. Once again the government is having to intervene to restore balance and to regulate future activities. This time it will probably be necessary to devise ways of continually assessing the state of our technology and determining what present and new technologies we shall utilize. Such assessment procedures will require a technological sophistication that we do not yet possess: the ability to accurately predict the probable indirect effects of a given technological innovation.[39] Only then could we be sure that any particular technological "advance" would be of greater benefit than cost to society, and assessment must be coupled with regulation. For the government merely to publish assessment reports would accomplish little; the assessing body must also have the authority to enforce its recommendations upon industry.

The three technological areas that especially require the attention of an assessing/regulating authority are energy production, transportation, and chemicals.

Energy Production.   Our requirements for electric power are expected to double over the next decade—and to double again in the decade after that. This raises two important questions: How much of that demand should we satisfy (or allow to come into being, since much of it is created by the utility companies)? And how shall we generate the electricity? We currently employ three technologies for the generation of electrical power: fossil-fuel combustion, water power, and nuclear power. Each of them generates its own problems along with electricity. We need to support research and experimentation with other forms of power generation—particularly solar energy—and decide, first on an ecological basis and second on a cost/benefit basis, which is the most beneficial balance of generating capability. To do this, we must consider *all* the costs—the expense of eliminating pollution from fossil-fuel generation, the risks of nuclear power, and whatever else is involved.

If we are to avoid "blackouts" and "brownouts" and the waste of scarce resources, we need to develop a national energy policy that will assign priorities and/or a system of allocation for electricity consumption. Thus we might decide to limit automation and rely on human power, or to ration the amount of electricity each household and company may consume over a given period of time, or to restrict the production of household and office "labor-saving" devices, or to set general priorities on the types of products that can be made.

Transportation.   The automobile is generally conceded to be a technological horror. It produces 60 percent of our urban air pollution; it is inefficient compared with other forms of transport; it is dangerous—about 50,000 people are killed each year in auto accidents; and it requires

[39]See *Technology Assessment: Hearings Before the Subcommittee on Science, Research and Development,* (Washington, D.C.: U.S. Government Printing Office, 1970).

ever-increasing amounts of public money and land for highway construction. Putting improved anti-pollution devices on cars will not begin to solve our transportation problems. We must also rebuild our declining railroad systems, probably by diverting highway funds. Public transport systems in cities—buses and subways—must be updated and run for the convenience of their passengers. Many cities are already considering, and others are, banning private automobile traffic from some of their streets during certain hours of the day. (See Chapter 14.) Bikeways should be provided for the growing number of cyclists. We need to develop technologies that can deal with the needs of individual and mass transportation in ways that are in harmony with the capacities and resources of the environment.

Chemicals. Over 500 new chemicals are introduced into our environment each year, yet we ordinarily have little or no knowledge about their biological consequences. Several classes of chemicals have proved to be seriously dysfunctional. These include the pesticides such as DDT and the other chlorinated hydrocarbons; herbicides such as 2,4-D and 2,4,5-T, which were widely used in Vietnam; and plastics and unnecessary food additives. We need alternatives to the use of poisons for insect control, such as applied natural biological controls, and new criteria for regulating the use of additives on the basis of biological and not marketing considerations.

The widespread concern about the earth's ecological balance that developed during the 1960s resulted in the passage of a number of laws designed to control or reduce the harm being done to our environment. The National Environmental Police Act (NEPA) of 1970 required, for the first time, that before federal projects (or projects requiring federal approval) are undertaken, public hearings on possible environmental effects must be held and environmental impact studies must be filed. A major achievement of NEPA was to delay the construction of the Alaskan oil pipeline until safeguards were established to ensure that the pipeline's environmental impact would be minimized. The Clean Air Act of 1970 established the federal EPA and empowered it to set and enforce standards of air quality. The EPA has since been given authority over most matters involving environmental quality. For example, the Federal Water Pollution Control Act Amendments of 1972 made it illegal to discharge pollutants into a water supply without a permit. The stated goal of the law, enforced by the EPA, is to eliminate all water pollution by the mid-1980s.

Unfortunately, despite such legislation, the battle against ecological disaster is still far from being won. The National Wildlife Federation publishes an annual environmental-quality index that measures the environmental status of seven major categories: wildlife, living space, soil, timber, minerals, water, and air. According to the federation's 1976 seventh annual index, the quality of all these categories has declined since 1969, despite the environmental legislation of the intervening years.[40] Much of the blame for this situation lies with industry, which has strongly resisted compliance with environmental laws. Enforcement of automobile emission standards, for

Legislation

[40]"Seventh Environmental Quality Index," *National Wildlife Magazine* (February–March 1976).

example, was delayed for many years because automobile company lobbyists claimed that the standards were unrealistic. The economic recession of the mid-1970s also retarded environmental efforts: industry was able to convince Congress to postpone deadlines for meeting air- and water-quality standards because pollution-control devices were too expensive in a depressed economy. Finally, the EPA itself, either because of its inadequate staff, its sensitivity to pressures from industry, or both, has been unable or unwilling in some instances to stringently enforce environmental laws.

Clearly, we need a renewed commitment to the environmental legislation that already exists. As we have seen, the idea that pollution-control efforts cost too much money is a myth. In fact, quite the contrary: it is pollution and waste that cost too much by depleting our resources, ravaging our environment, and ruining our health. A firm determination by government, industry, and the individual citizen to insure that environmental laws are obeyed and enforced would do much to begin to reduce the deterioration of our environment.

Additional legislation is required, however, in order to achieve the cleanest, healthiest environment possible. Prohibiting industrial land use in scenic or ecologically important areas; setting rigid controls on off shore drilling; limiting automobile size and weight to use less fuel and produce less pollution; providing additional funds for mass transit, to reduce the reliance on automobiles; making recycling mandatory; and setting new standards of air and water quality that will ultimately eliminate pollution almost completely—these are some of the additional steps that need to be taken before the environmental crisis can be solved.

Population Control

A viable alternative future involves stabilizing population size—sometimes known as "zero population growth." We must seek to achieve this by social regulation, as opposed to the "natural" or unsocial forms of regulation, such as famine, disease, and war, that kept population growth relatively stable until the last few centuries. (This was discussed more fully in Chapter 15.)

Creating the Future

The alternative future we have been describing—an alternative to a septic world characterized by environmental crises—can only exist if people want it strongly enough. This requires organization and knowledge. There is already a loose confederation of groups of concerned citizens, ranging from traditional conservationists to radical activists. They need to coordinate their activities and to develop positive programs for change—programs that concentrate on education and regulation. We have already considered the former; environmental groups must continue to disseminate information and press for the necessary new emphases in school curricula.

As for regulation, in our society law is the primary regulator of behavior, and environmentalists must learn how to use it to gain their ends. Besides direct lobbying for legislation to require recycling, population and pollution control, and technology assessment, environmental groups should apply pressure through the courts to ensure that public officials enforce laws already on the books.

They should also urge the Federal Trade Commission and the Federal Communications Commission to adopt more stringent regulations for radio and television advertisements. Such rules might provide that advertisements be limited to one minute of each broadcast hour, and that equal time be accorded free to recognized, environmental groups; and they might prohibit the advertising of products that directly impair the environment or that are demonstrably hazardous to human health, much in the way that cigarette advertising has been banned from television.

Prospects

Given the proposition that the survival of any given species depends on a diversity of other life forms, we must seriously consider whether humanity will survive; for we have, within the past century and at an increasing rate during this century, caused the near- or total-extinction of many organisms and endangered the lives of many others. Several species of birds and fish have ceased to reproduce, as a consequence of high-level DDT concentrations in their bodies, and as such are as good as extinct. Some scientists fear that similar, persistent poisons are also killing phytoplankton, the plants that provide oxygen in the oceans and are eaten by the animals at the bottom of the ocean food chains. One study found that 85 percent of the nation's larger lakes are already being choked by the proliferation of algae.[41]

As a test for air quality, miners used to carry a canary in a cage down into pits with them; when the canary sickened, the miners knew it was time to leave the mine. We cannot leave the earth. According to some experts, the question is only whether we will take corrective action before we succumb. The recommendations for such corrective action usually envision limiting both economic and population growth.

Other environmental scientists, along with researchers in related disciplines, are less apocalyptic in their views. Their arguments tend to center on two beliefs: first, that added economic growth is needed not only to satisfy present world demand for food and the artifacts of a high standard of living, but also to clean up the environmental mess we have already made; second, that the technology of the future will provide us with the means for restoring the environment while maintaining present life styles and improving the quality of life in poorer countries. Adherents of these views acknowledge that their predictions assume that a means will be found to limit world population growth. One study concluded that the costs of environmental cleanup for 14 major industries would not be severe either for the industries involved or for the economy as a whole, and might, in fact, be more than balanced by the long-term savings that would accrue from the cessation of the damage caused by present pollution.[42]

The overall outlook is not encouraging; our problems are numerous, varied, and complex. Educating the public is a lengthy, time-consuming process. Social changes generally occur slowly. Most of the power in any society is inevitably committed to maintaining the *status quo,* and we are running out of lead time. It will be difficult for a people intensely concerned with the acquisition of material objects voluntarily to limit such acquisitions and renounce the goal of ever-increasing material wealth.

[41]"A Turn in the Tide—Pollution Battle Being Won?" *U.S. News & World Report* (August 4, 1975), p. 57.
[42]"The Modest Price of Purging Pollution," *Business Week* (March 18, 1972), pp. 18–19.

Beyond the question of change is the problem of incomplete knowledge. Our understanding of the natural system and how it functions is still elementary, and we cannot always be sure what will rescue the environment.

Of course, we need not be entirely pessimistic. Many people around the world are becoming aware of, and concerned about, the environment. The levels of some air pollutants (such as sulfur dioxide) in the United States have started to decline as a result of air pollution standards, although the levels of many other pollutants remain unchanged or are rising. There are some expectations that the nation's waters will be comparatively clean by the end of the twentieth century, and a potential mass movement against nuclear power reactors has been stirring in the United States for several years. One such group, a coalition of anti-nuclear organizations called the Clamshell Alliance, has formed in New England to demonstrate against the construction of nuclear power plants at several area sites. Utilizing non-violent tactics learned from the American Friends Service Committee (Quakers) and approaching the problem at a community level, the Alliance has successfully organized thousands of area citizens in several peaceful demonstrations, and has thus far postponed nuclear power plant construction. The essential question that remains to be resolved is: Can we change our living habits and our social institutions before the harm we are doing to the environment—and to ourselves—becomes irreversible?

Summary

Though all of us depend on the environment for our existence, we have been abusing it to the point where the quality of life has been reduced, and our ability to survive is being threatened. The pollutants we pour into the air cause illness and even death and result in increased economic costs, due to deterioration of property and wasted resources, and may cause harm to the earth's entire ecosystem. The pollutants we pour into our waters render them useless for humans or for industry and kill essential fish and plant life. Many of these harmful pollutants accumulate in living species and ascend through the food chain, ultimately being ingested by people. Even the way we dispose of our solid and nuclear wastes is inefficient and potentially harmful. Add to this the wholesale degradation of land that is occurring, the growing amount of noise pollution, the proliferation of untested chemicals in our industries and in our food, and our fondness for large-scale engineering projects that cause damage, and it is clear that we are faced with an environmental crisis.

The origins of the crisis lie in our faith in the value of technology, our traditional belief that we should dominate the earth, and our emphasis on materialism and progress. Though many laws exist to maintain standards of environmental quality, they have not been stringently enforced. Clearly, our style of life and our attitudes will have to change before the damage to the environment can be halted and reversed.

Such a change will have to be effected in several ways: through public education programs to make people more ecologically aware; through implementation of recycling programs; through the development of less wasteful technologies; and through the passage and enforcement of environmental legislation. Only renewed dedication to saving the environment can save us from disaster and move us toward an ecologically sound alternative future.

Bibliography

Campbell, Rex R. and Wade, Jerry L. *Society and Environment: The Coming Collision.* Boston: Allyn and Bacon, 1972.

de Bell, Garrett. *The Environmental Handbook.* New York: Ballantine, 1970.

Falk, Richard A. *This Endangered Planet.* New York: Random House, 1971.

Goldman, Marshall I., ed. *Critical Issues in Controlling Pollution.* Englewood Cliffs, N.J.: Prentice-Hall, 1972.

Hefrich, Harold W., Jr. *The Environmental Crisis: Man's Struggle to Live with Himself.* New Haven, Conn.: Yale University Press, 1970.

Meadows, Dennis, *et al. Dynamics of Growth in a Future World.* New York: Wiley, 1974.

Murdoch, William W., ed. *Environment: Resources, Pollution and Society.* Stamford, Conn.: Sinauer Associates, 1971.

Odum, Howard T. *Environment, Power and Society.* New York: Wiley-Interscience, 1971.

Wagner, Richard H. *Environment and Man,* 2nd ed. New York: Norton, 1974.

Name Index

Subject Index